Natural Legal Language Processing Workshop (NLLP 2021)

Punta Cana, Dominican Republic
10 November 2021

ISBN: 978-1-7138-9167-3

Printed from e-media with permission by:

Curran Associates, Inc.
57 Morehouse Lane
Red Hook, NY 12571

CURRAN ASSOCIATES INC. proceedings.com

Some format issues inherent in the e-media version may also appear in this print version.

Printed with permission by Curran Associates, Inc. (2024)

Association for Computational Linguistics
209 N. Eighth Street
Stroudsburg, Pennsylvania 18360

Phone: 1-570-476-8006
Fax: 1-570-476-0860

acl@aclweb.org

Additional copies of this publication are available from:

Curran Associates, Inc.
57 Morehouse Lane
Red Hook, NY 12571 USA
Phone: 845-758-0400
Fax: 845-758-2633
Email: curran@proceedings.com
Web: www.proceedings.com

EMNLP 2021

Natural Legal Language Processing (NLLP)

Proceedings of the 2021 Workshop

November 10, 2021
Punta Cana, Dominican Republic

Introduction

Welcome to the third edition of the NLLP (Natural Legal Language Processing) Workshop, co-located with the 2021 Conference on Empirical Methods in Natural Language Processing.

Different industrial sectors have embraced natural language processing (NLP) technologies, which have altered services and products in healthcare, finance, education among others. The legal domain provides enormous potential for generating interesting research problems. Electronic tools are increasingly used for all types of legal tasks and that use is predicted to grow sharply. By its very nature, the practice of law necessarily involves the analysis and interpretation of language. The potential for NLP applications to provide benefit to practitioners of law and consumers of legal services around the world is enormous.

We organized this workshop to bring together researchers and practitioners from around the world who develop NLP techniques for legal data. This is an exciting opportunity to expand the boundaries of our field by identifying new problems and exploring new data as it interacts with the full inventory of NLP and machine learning approaches. In this spirit, the Organizing and Program Committee was assembled to include researchers from both academia and industry, from NLP and legal backgrounds.

We were interested in the following types of papers: (1) applications of NLP methods to legal tasks; (2) experimental results using and adapting NLP methods in legal documents; (3) descriptions of new legal tasks for NLP; (4) creation of curated and/or annotated resources; (5) descriptions of systems which use NLP technologies for legal text; (6) industrial research in this area and (7) interdisciplinary position papers. We offered the option of submitting original unpublished research as non-archival in order to accommodate publication of the work at a later date in a conference or journal. These papers were reviewed following the same procedure as archival submissions. We also offered a venue for presentation for papers accepted to the Findings of EMNLP 2021 on the above topics.

We received a record number of 48 submissions and accepted 28 papers for an overall acceptance rate of 58.3% percent, all being presented orally. Out of the 28 accepted papers, 17 are long papers, 7 are short papers and 4 are original work submitted as non-archival. Each paper was reviewed by 3 or 4 members of the Program Committee. The papers cover a wide range of topics from new data sets for legal NLP and Transformer models pre-trained on legal corpora to information retrieval, extraction, question answering, classification, parsing, and summarization for legal documents to legal judgment prediction, legal dialogue, legal reasoning, and ethics.

We thank our two invited speakers for accepting our invitation: John Armour Professor of Law and Finance at Oxford University and Sylvie Delacroix, Professor in Law and Ethics at the University of Birmingham. In the tradition of past NLLP workshops, the invited speakers are legal scholars with an interest in empirical methods for legal analysis including artificial intelligence and NLP methods. We hope their talks offer a fresh perspective for the attendees.

We thank everyone who expressed interest in the workshop, all authors of submitted papers, members of the Program Committee who did an excellent job at reviewing papers given a short turnaround time, everyone attending the workshop, the EMNLP 2021 conference for hosting us and the workshop and publication chairs for their support. We thank our sponsors – Bloomberg and Bloomberg Law – for their contributions.

The NLLP Workshop organizers.

`http://nllpw.org`

Organizers:

Nikolaos Aletras, University of Sheffield (UK)
Ion Androutsopoulos, Athens University of Economics and Business (Greece)
Leslie Barrett, Bloomberg Law (USA)
Cătălina Goanţă, Maastricht University (The Netherlands)
Daniel Preoţiuc-Pietro, Bloomberg (USA)

Program Committee:

Tomaso Agnoloni, Institute of Legal Information Theory and Technologies (Italy)
Elliott Ash, ETH Zürich (Switzerland)
Breck Baldwin, Columbia University (US)
Andrew Blair-Stanek, Johns Hopkins University (US)
Lukasz Borchmann, Applica.ai (Poland)
Ilias Chalkidis, University of Copenhagen (Denmark)
Rajarathnam Chandramouli, Stevens Institute of Technology (US)
Daniel Chen, Toulouse School of Economics(France)
Marina Danilevsky, IBM Research (US)
Tony Davis, Southern Oregon University (US)
Stefania Degaetano-Ortlieb, Saarland University (Germany)
Luigi Di Caro, Turin University (Italy)
Fabiana Di Porto, University of Salento (Italy)
Kasper Drazewski, The European Consumer Organization (Italy)
Arthur Dyevre, Katholieke Universiteit Leuven (Belgium)
Emmanouil Fergadiotis, NCSR "Demokritos" & AUEB (Greece)
Frank Giaoui, Optimalex Legal Analytics & Columbia University (US)
Matthias Grabmair, Technical University of Münich (Germany)
Nils Holzenberger, Johns Hopkins University (US)
Dan Katz, Illinois Tech - Chicago Kent College of Law (US)
Ilan Kernerman, K Dictionaries (Israel)
Manolis Koubarakis, University of Athens (Greece)
Vasileios Lampos, University College London (UK)
Jochen Leidner, Coburg University (Germany)
Monika Leszczynska, Maastricht University (The Netherlands)
Junyi Jessy Li, University of Texas at Austin (US)
Ruta Liepina, Maastricht University (The Netherlands)
How Khang Lim, Singapore Management University (Singapore)
Prodromos Malakasiotis, NCSR "Demokritos" & AUEB (Greece)
Adam Meyers, New York University (US)
Jelena Mitrovic, University of Passau (Germany)
Paulo Quaresma, Universidade de Évora (Portugalia)
Georg Rehm, DFKI (Germany)
George Sanchez, Thomson Reuters (US)
Thibault Schrepel, Vrije Universiteit (The Netherlands)
Mathias Siems, European University Institute (Italy)
Dan Simonson, BlackBoiler LLC (US)
Jerrold Soh, Singapore Management University (Singapore)

Gerasimos Spanakis, Maastricht University (The Netherlands)
Andrea Tagarelli, University of Calabria (Italy)
Amelia Taylor, Malawi Polytechnic (Malawi)
Dimitrios Tsarapatsanis, University of York (UK)
Gijs Van Dijck, Maastricht University (The Netherlands)
Mihaela Vela, Saarland University (Germany)
Adam Wyner, Swansea University (UK)
Marcos Zampieri , Rochester Institute of Technology (US)

Invited Speakers:

John Armour, Oxford University (UK)
Sylvie Delacroix, University of Birmingham (UK)

The Power of Legislatures in Hungary - A Text Reuse Analysis

Authors: Miklós Sebők (Centre for Social Sciences, Budapest), Anna Szekély (Centre for Social Sciences, Budapest) and István Járay (Centre for Social Sciences, Budapest)

Abstract

In this paper we shed fresh light on parliaments' "viscosity": their ability to withstand government pressure when it comes to passing laws, choosing Hungary as a case of our study. We use state-of-the-art NLP methods (in the subfield of text reuse analysis) to gauge the changes of bill texts. We expect the bill's institutional and intrinsic features and partisan and coalition politics to largely influence the likelihood of bill change. Our results show that international treaties and bills submitted during electoral years are amended less likely. Furthermore, certain policy areas also decrease the likelihood of bill change, especially those which are connected to the core functions of the state: Law and order, defense, international affairs, and government operation.

LexGLUE: A Benchmark Dataset for Legal Language Understanding in English

Authors: Ilias Chalkidis (University of Copenhagen); Abhik Jana (UniversitÃ¤t Hamburg); Dirk Hartung (Bucerius Law School); Michael Bommarito (Stanford Law School); Ion Androutsopoulos (Athens University of Economics and Business); Daniel Martin Katz (Illinois Tech - Chicago Kent College of Law); Nikolaos Aletras (University of Sheffield)

Abstract

Law, interpretations of law, legal arguments, agreements, etc. are typically expressed in writing, leading to the production of vast corpora of legal text. Their analysis, which is at the center of legal practice, becomes increasingly elaborate as these collections grow in size. Natural language understanding (NLU) technologies can be a valuable tool to support legal practitioners in these endeavors. Their usefulness, however, largely depends on whether current state-of-the-art models can generalize across various tasks in the legal domain. To answer this currently open question, we introduce the Legal General Language Understanding Evaluation (LexGLUE) benchmark, a collection of datasets for evaluating model performance across a diverse set of legal NLU tasks in a standardized way. We also provide an evaluation and analysis of several generic and legal-oriented models demonstrating that the latter consistently offer performance improvements across multiple tasks.

AutoLAW: Augmented Legal Reasoning through Legal Precedent Prediction

Authors: Robert Zev Mahari (Human Dynamics Group, MIT Media Lab, Massachusetts Institute of Technology; Harvard Law School)

Abstract

This paper demonstrate how NLP can be used to address an unmet need of the legal community and increase access to justice. The paper introduces Legal Precedent Prediction (LPP), the task of predicting relevant passages from precedential court decisions given the context of a legal argument. To this end, the paper showcases a BERT model, trained on 530,000 examples of legal arguments made by U.S. federal judges, to predict relevant passages from precedential court decisions given the context of a legal argument. In 96% of unseen test examples the correct target passage is among the top-10 predicted passages. The same model is able to predict relevant precedent given a short summary of a complex and unseen legal brief, predicting the precedent that was actually cited by the brief's co-author, former U.S. Solicitor General and current U.S. Supreme Court Justice Elena Kagan.

Privacy Policy Question Answering Assistant A Query-Guided Extractive Summarization Approach

Authors: Moniba Keymanesh (The Ohio State University); Micha Elsner (The Ohio State University); Srinivasan Parthasarathy (The Ohio State University)

Abstract

Existing work on making privacy policies accessible has explored new presentation forms such as color-coding based on the risk factors or summarization to assist users with conscious agreement. To facilitate a more personalized interaction with the policies, in this work, we propose an automated privacy policy question answering assistant that extracts a summary in response to the input user query. This is a challenging task because users articulate their privacy-related questions in a very different language than the legal language of the policy, making it difficult for the system to understand their inquiry. Moreover, existing annotated data in this domain are limited. We address these problems by paraphrasing to bring the style and language of the user's question closer to the language of privacy policies. Our content scoring module uses the existing in-domain data to find relevant information in the policy and incorporates it in a summary. Our pipeline is able to find an answer for 89% of the user queries in the privacyQA dataset.

Table of Contents

Conference Program

08:00–08:10 *Workshop Opening*

08:10–09:00 *Invited Talk*
John Armour

09:00–09:15 *A Corpus for Multilingual Analysis of Online Terms of Service*
Kasper Drawzeski, Andrea Galassi, Agnieszka Jablonowska, Francesca Lagioia, Marco Lippi, Hans Wolfgang Micklitz, Giovanni Sartor, Giacomo Tagiuri and Paolo Torroni

09:15–09:30 *Named Entity Recognition in the Romanian Legal Domain*
Vasile Pais, Maria Mitrofan, Carol Luca Gasan, Vlad Coneschi and Alexandru Ianov

09:30–09:45 *The Power of Legislatures in Hungary - A Text Reuse Analysis*
Miklós Sebők, Anna Szekély and István Járay

09:45–10:00 *Swiss-Judgment-Prediction: A Multilingual Legal Judgment Prediction Benchmark*
Joel Niklaus, Ilias Chalkidis and Matthias Stürmer

10:00–10:15 *LexGLUE: A Benchmark Dataset for Legal Language Understanding in English*
Ilias Chalkidis, Abhik Jana, Dirk Hartung, Michael Bommarito, Ion Androutsopoulos, Daniel Martin Katz and Nikolaos Aletras

10:15–10:30 *'Just What do You Think You're Doing, Dave?' A Checklist for Responsible Data Use in NLP*
Anna Rogers, Tim Baldwin and Kobi Leins

10:30–10:45 *Break*

10:45–11:00 *Automated Extraction of Sentencing Decisions from Court Cases in the Hebrew Language*
Mohr Wenger, Tom Kalir, Noga Berger, Carmit Klar Chalamish, Renana Keydar and Gabriel Stanovsky

11:00–11:15 *A Multilingual Approach to Identify and Classify Exceptional Measures against COVID-19*
Georgios Tziafas, Eugenie de Saint-Phalle, Wietse de Vries, Clara Egger and Tommaso Caselli

11:15–11:30 *Multi-granular Legal Topic Classification on Greek Legislation*
Christos Papaloukas, Ilias Chalkidis, Konstantinos Athinaios, Despina Pantazi and Manolis Koubarakis

11:30–11:40 *Machine Extraction of Tax Laws from Legislative Texts*
Elliott Ash, Malka Guillot and Luyang Han

10 November 2021

11:40–11:50	*jurBERT: A Romanian BERT Model for Legal Judgement Prediction* Mihai Masala, Radu Cristian Alexandru Iacob, Ana Sabina Uban, Marina Cidota, Horia Velicu, Traian Rebedea and Marius Popescu
11:50–12:00	*JuriBERT: A Masked-Language Model Adaptation for French Legal Text* Stella Douka, Hadi Abdine, Michalis Vazirgiannis, Rajaa El Hamdani and David Restrepo Amariles
12:00–12:10	*Few-shot and Zero-shot Approaches to Legal Text Classification: A Case Study in the Financial Sector* Rajdeep Sarkar, Atul Kr. Ojha, Jay Megaro, John Mariano, Vall Herard and John P. McCrae
12:10–13:00	*Lunch Break & Virtual Town Hall*
13:00–13:45	*Invited talk: Data Trusts as a Bottom-up Empowerment Tool* Sylvie Delacroix
13:45–14:00	*AutoLAW: Augmented Legal Reasoning through Legal Precedent Prediction* Robert Zev Mahari
14:00–14:10	*A Free Format Legal Question Answering System* Soha Khazaeli, Janardhana Punuru, Chad Morris, Sanjay Sharma, Bert Staub, Michael Cole, Sunny Chiu-Webster and Dhruv Sakalley
14:10–14:20	*Searching for Legal Documents at Paragraph Level: Automating Label Generation and Use of an Extended Attention Mask for Boosting Neural Models of Semantic Similarity* Li Tang and Simon Clematide
14:20–14:30	*GerDaLIR: A German Dataset for Legal Information Retrieval* Marco Wrzalik and Dirk Krechel
14:30–14:45	*Break*
14:45–15:00	*SPaR.txt, a Cheap Shallow Parsing Approach for Regulatory Texts* Ruben Kruiper, Ioannis Konstas, Alasdair J.G. Gray, Farhad Sadeghineko, Richard Watson and Bimal Kumar
15:00–15:15	*Capturing Logical Structure of Visually Structured Documents with Multimodal Transition Parser* Yuta Koreeda and Christopher Manning
15:15–15:30	*Legal Terminology Extraction with the Termolator* Nhi Pham, Lachlan Pham and Adam L. Meyers

10 November 2021

15:30–15:45 *Supervised Identification of Participant Slots in Contracts*
Dan Simonson

15:45–16:00 *ContractNLI: A Dataset for Document-level Natural Language Inference for Contracts*
Yuta Koreeda and Christopher Manning

16:00–16:10 *Named Entity Recognition in Historic Legal Text: A Transformer and State Machine Ensemble Method*
Fernando Trias, Hongming Wang, Sylvain Jaume and Stratos Idreos

16:10–16:25 *Break*

16:25–16:40 *Summarization of German Court Rulings*
Ingo Glaser, Sebastian Moser and Florian Matthes

16:40–16:55 *Privacy Policy Question Answering Assistant A Query-Guided Extractive Summarization Approach*
Moniba Keymanesh, Micha Elsner and Srinivasan Parthasarathy

16:55–17:10 *Learning from Limited Labels for Long Legal Dialogue*
Jenny Hong, Derek Chong and Christopher Manning

17:10–17:20 *Automating Claim Construction in Patent Applications: The CMUmine Dataset*
Ozan Tonguz, Yiwei Qin, Yimeng Gu and Hyun Hannah Moon

17:20–17:30 *Effectively Leveraging BERT for Legal Document Classification*
Nut Limsopatham

17:30–17:45 *Semi-automatic Triage of Requests for Free Legal Assistance*
Meladel Mistica, Jey Han Lau, Brayden Merrifield, Kate Fazio and Timothy Baldwin

17:45–18:00 *Automatic Resolution of Domain Name Disputes*
Wayan Oger Vihikan, Meladel Mistica, Inbar Levy, Andrew Christie and Timothy Baldwin

A Corpus for Multilingual Analysis of Online Terms of Service

Kasper Drazewski[1] and **Andrea Galassi**[2] and **Agnieszka Jablonowska**[3]

Francesca Lagioia[3] and **Marco Lippi**[4] and **Hans Wolfgang Micklitz**[3]

Giovanni Sartor[3] and **Giacomo Tagiuri**[3] and **Paolo Torroni**[2]

[1]Bureau Européen des Unions de Consommateurs, Brussels, Belgium
[2]DISI, University of Bologna, Italy
[3]European University Institute, Florence, Italy
[4]DISMI, University of Modena and Reggio Emilia, Italy
[1,3]{name.surname}@eui.eu
[2]a.galassi@unibo.it, paolo.torroni@unibo.it
[4]marco.lippi@unimore.it

Abstract

We present the first annotated corpus for multilingual analysis of potentially unfair clauses in online Terms of Service. The data set comprises a total of 100 contracts, obtained from 25 documents annotated in four different languages: English, German, Italian, and Polish. For each contract, potentially unfair clauses for the consumer are annotated, for nine different unfairness categories. We show how a simple yet efficient annotation projection technique based on sentence embeddings could be used to automatically transfer annotations across languages.

1 Introduction

Cultural and linguistic diversity is a guiding principle of the European Union. Within the context of an ever expanding EU, the concept of multilingualism stands out as one of the most prominent symbols of European historical, political, social and cultural diversity.[1] From a legal perspective, the EU commitment to multilingualism is significant not only as a guarantee of legal certainty, clarity, and transparency, but also democratic accountability. Accordingly, for example, the EU legislation is generally published in all official languages.[2]

While multilingualism certainly has important benefits, it also comes with costs and challenges. To illustrate, the existence of 24 official versions of every legal act, all of which are equally authentic,[3] may inevitably create interpretative difficulties. In this regard, the Court of Justice has repeatedly found that the wording used in one language version of a Union provision cannot serve as the only basis for its reading, and has pointed to the role of cross-language comparisons as well as teleological and systematic methods of interpretation.[4] Ethnic languages, and related requirements, are also an important issue in the EU internal market and consumer protection policies. The EU has so far mostly left this matter to national authorities, recognizing the associated tensions and cultural contexts.[5] For example, the EU has refrained, so far, from regulating languages in which standard terms in consumer contracts should be drafted, allowing for differing approaches to emerge in various jurisdictions (Loos, 2017).[6] In view of the above, and considering that consumer protection authorities and non-governmental organisations in Europe tend to operate in their respective languages, ef-

[1]A recent indication of the importance of multilingualism for the EU is found in the European Commission Communication of 22 November 2005 "A New Framework Strategy for Multilingualism" (COM(2005) 596 final).

[2]Regulation No 1 determining the languages to be used by the European Economic Community [1958] OJ 17/385 with subsequent amendments. Consider also the right to good administration, as expressed in Article 41(4) of the Charter of Fundamental Rights of the European Union [2012] OJ C 326/391.

[3]Judgment of the Court of 6 October 1982, C-283/81 - CILFIT, ECLI:EU:C:1982:335, para. 18.

[4]See, e.g., judgment of the Court of 19 December 2013, C-281/12 - Trento Sviluppo, ECLI:EU:C:2013:859, para. 25 and the case law cited.

[5]On the one hand, language requirements give rise to additional costs for the traders who wish to engage in cross-border transactions. On the other hand, they might be justified for consumer protection reasons.

[6]In the context of pre-contractual information see also: Article 6(7) of Directive 2011/83/EU of the European Parliament and of the Council of 25 October 2011 on consumer rights, amending Council Directive 93/13/EEC and Directive 1999/44/EC of the European Parliament and of the Council and repealing Council Directive 85/577/EEC and Directive 97/7/EC of the European Parliament and of the Council [2011] OJ L 304/64.

Natural Legal Language Processing Workshop 2021, pages 1–8

fective consumer protection technologies must be capable of dealing with multilingual landscapes.

In this work, we focus on the automated detection of unfair clauses in Terms of Service (ToS), which are usually available in multiple languages. In particular, we investigate methods for automatically transferring the annotations made on ToS in the context of the Claudette project [7] onto the corresponding versions of the same documents in a target language, where such resources and expertise may be lacking.

Our ultimate goal is to use automatically generated annotations for training linguistic tools, usually available only in English, like Claudette, for the target language without resorting to expert annotators in that language. This would leverage the creation of classifiers that can leverage the linguistic resources available in the target language, to analyze documents in that language.

From a machine learning point of view, the question is whether we shall necessarily train independent models for each and every language. This paper only partially answers the question, by extending previous work (Galassi et al., 2020) towards three different languages and by making a novel multilingual corpus available to the community. Future research will consider training and comparing the classifiers.

2 Corpus

We built a multilingual parallel corpus consisting of 25 Terms of Service annotated in English, Italian, German and Polish. These languages are spoken in large EU countries as well as in different regions, and they have been selected based on the availability of mother tongue legal experts for the annotation task.

The analysed ToS were retrieved from the Claudette pre-existing corpus, covering 100 English ToS (Lippi et al., 2019; Ruggeri et al., 2021). Such terms mainly concern popular digital services provided to consumers, including leading online platforms (such as search engines and social media). The predominant language of drafting of these ToS is English, with differing availability of corresponding ToS in other languages.

To carry out the present study, the ultimate 25 ToS[8] were selected on the basis of three main criteria: a) their availability in the four selected languages; b) the possibility of identifying a correspondence between the different versions, given their publication date; and c) the similarity of their structure (e.g. number of clauses, sections, etc.). To illustrate, while ToS in both German and Italian were identified for 63 out of the 100 ToS contained in the pre-existing Claudette training corpus, Polish versions were found for only 42 of these 63 ToS. Out of the 42 ToS available in the four languages, we selected those with the more closely corresponding versions based on criteria b) and c) above. Perfect correspondence across the 4 languages, however, could not be achieved for all 25 ToS. As further discussed in Section 3, some discrepancies may persist.

We hypothesise that a particularly strong similarity between the English ToS and other language versions exists where the latter are translations of the former. Although we could not assess this comprehensively in the present study, we infer from the wording of the ToS that at least in 9 out of 25 cases, German, Italian and Polish documents were indeed translations of the English originals. More specifically, in the ToS of 9 companies[9] we identified explicit references to the language of the terms. Consider, for example, the following clause taken from Mozilla ToS (updated June 23, 2016) and its corresponding German version:

> *In the event of a conflict between a translated version of these Terms and the English language version, the English language version shall control.* (line 71).

> *Im Falle eines Konflikts zwischen der übersetzten Version dieser Bedingungen und der englischen Fassung gilt die englische Fassung.* (line 71).

A more comprehensive verification whether different language versions of the ToS were translated from the English original was not possible at this stage of research.

The analysed corpus contains, in its English version, 6,831 sentences and 678 labelled clauses, divided in nine categories of clause unfairness, i.e., arbitration (<*a*>), unilateral change (<*ch*>), content removal (<*cr*>), jurisdiction (<*j*>), choice of law

[7] `http://claudette.eui.eu`

[8] In particular, we selected the ToS offered by: Booking.com, Dropbox, Electronic Arts, Evernote, Facebook, Garmin, Google, Grindr, Linkedin, Mozilla, Pinterest, Quora, Ryanair, Skype, Skyscanner, Snapchat, Spotify, Terravision, Tinder, Tripadvisor, Tumblr, Uber, Weebly, Yelp and Zynga.

[9] Booking.com, Dropbox, Evernote, Grindr, Mozilla, Skype, Tumblr, Yelp, Zynga.

(<*law*>), limitation of liability (<*ltd*>), unilateral termination (<*ter*>), contract by using (<*use*>), and privacy included (<*pinc*>). While the first eight categories have been described by Lippi et al. (2019), the latter, i.e., the privacy included category, has been recently introduced to identify clauses stating that consumers consent to the privacy policy simply by using the service. Such clauses have been always considered potentially unfair.[10]

In the annotations, to indicate the degree of unfairness a numeric value has been appended to each XML tag, with a value 1 meaning clearly fair, 2 potentially unfair, and 3 clearly unfair. For instance, the <*j3*> label indicates that a certain clause concerns jurisdiction and it has been marked as clearly unfair.

Table 1 shows some statistics on the corpus, by reporting the number of annotated clauses for each tag, across the four different languages. The whole annotated corpus is made freely available for research purposes and can be downloaded at `http://claudette.eui.eu/corpus_multilingual_NLLP2021.zip`.

	DE	EN	IT	PL
a1	3	3	4	4
a2	22	29	29	35
a3	3	4	4	4
ch2	98	100	103	103
ch3	1	1	0	0
cr2	25	27	28	26
cr3	23	24	24	26
j1	14	15	15	15
j3	46	49	48	50
law1	18	16	16	19
law2	33	39	36	36
ltd1	19	27	16	17
ltd2	212	229	216	229
ltd3	1	1	1	1
pinc2	17	21	20	21
ter2	69	71	71	75
ter3	49	49	50	49
use2	54	58	58	61
total	707	753	739	771

Table 1: Corpus statistics: we report the number of annotated clauses for each tag, across the four different languages. Suffices 1, 2, and 3 represent levels of fairness: 1 means clearly fair, 2 stays for potentially unfair, and finally 3 for clearly unfair.

3 Discrepancies

Our analysis revealed some discrepancies across the different language versions of the selected documents. This makes the projection task particularly challenging, also affecting the performance evaluation whenever a perfect match between documents is missing.

A general observation concerns the asymmetric length of documents across the different language versions. In some cases, this is the product of missing/extra clauses, for example because of country-specific terms. This is the case, among others, for the Terravision and Spotify ToS (see discussion infra in this section). In other cases, asymmetric length is a feature of linguistic differences. Take for example Evernote ToS that, while showing a remarkable similarity of structure across the 4 languages (no extra/missing clauses), shows a different word and sentence count across the 4 languages: 6,798 words for the Polish version (283 sentences), 7,580 for the German (291 sentences), 7,902 for the Italian (270 sentences) and 7,795 for the English version (279 sentences).

Moving from the structure of documents to the analysis of sentences, we identified four types of discrepancy across languages.

The first one concerns sentence structure. This type of discrepancy is mostly illustrated by situations in which the same information, contained in a single clause in the English version, is split into more than one clause in the target languages (or vice versa). In some cases such situations do not appear very problematic as the same tag of the original English sentence is identically reproduced across the two sentences in the target language.[11]

In other cases the implications for annotation are more problematic, as nested tags may need to be manually split. Consider for instance the following sentence from the Tripadvisor ToS (updated October 1, 2018) in its English and Italian version.

> *<ch2><use2>We may change or otherwise modify the Agreement in the future*

[10] As an example consider the following clause taken from the Evernote ToS: *<pinc2>By using the Service, you acknowledge, accept and agree with all provisions of the Privacy Policy, including, without limitation, the use and treatment of the text, images, and other data you choose to input, upload, or store in Evernote (collectively, "Content") and your personal information in accordance with such Privacy Policy.</pinc2>*.

[11] See, e.g., the clause on contract termination in English and Italian versions of the Dropbox ToS (updated April 17, 2018), line 58.

in accordance with the Terms and Conditions herein, and you understand and agree that your continued access or use of this Website after such change signifies your acceptance of the updated or modified Agreement.</use2></ch2> (line 7).

<ch2>*TripAdvisor si riserva il diritto di cambiare o altrimenti modificare l'Accordo in futuro, in conformità ai termini e alle condizioni ivi espresse.*</ch2> <use2>*L'Utente accetta pertanto che l'accesso a o l'utilizzo continuato del portale successivamente alle modifiche implica l'accettazione dell'Accordo così come aggiornato o modificato.*</use2> (line 7).

Other problematic cases may be those in which only one of the two sentences in the target language is relevant and should be marked as unfair. Consider the following clause from the Google ToS (updated April 30, 2014) and their Polish version:

<cr2>*We may review content to determine whether it is illegal or violates our policies, and we may remove or refuse to display content that we reasonably believe violates our policies or the law.*</cr2> (line 21)

Możemy sprawdzać treści w celu określenia, czy są one nielegalne lub czy naruszają nasze zasady. <cr2>*Jeśli stwierdzimy, że dany materiał jest niezgodny z tymi zasadami lub obowiązującym prawem, możemy go usunąć lub odmówić jego wyświetlenia.*</cr2> (line 21)

In this case, the different segmentation results in only one of the sentences in the target language being annotated as a potentially unfair content removal clause. The preceding part, related to the reviewing of the content, remains irrelevant for the envisaged task.

A second type of discrepancy consists in errors or inaccuracies in translation from the source English ToS into the target languages.

Consider the following example from the English and Polish versions of the Yelp ToS (updated November 27, 2012).

<ch2><ter3><ltd2>*We reserve the right to modify, update, or discontinue the Site at our sole discretion, at any time, for any or no reason, and without notice or liability.*</ltd2></ter3></ch2> (line 141)

<ch2><ter3>*Zastrzegamy sobie prawo do modyfikowania, aktualizowania i wyłączania Witryny wedle własnego uznania, w dowolnym momencie, z dowolnego powodu i bez wcześniejszego powiadomienia.* </ter3></ch2> (line 141)

While the first clause was correctly marked under three categories, the Polish version only relates to termination and unilateral change, without any reference to liability. Such a discrepancy does not exist in either German or Italian, which suggests a translation inaccuracy.

Similarly, consider the following clause taken from the Evernote ToS and their Italian version (updated August 28, 2017):

<use2>*If you do register for or otherwise use our Service you shall be deemed to confirm your acceptance of the Terms and your agreement to be a party to this binding contract.*</use2> (line 4).

La registrazione al Servizio o il suo uso richiedono di confermare la propria accettazione dei Termini, cosa che rende di conseguenza l'utente un soggetto vincolato al presente contratto. (line 4).

Here the English sentence is a clear example of a contract by using clause, thus potentially unfair (by registering, the consumer consents to the ToS). By contrast, the Italian translation simply states that in order to register for the service, the consumer needs to accept the terms. Thus, the Italian version has not been annotated. A similar discrepancy is not observed in the German and Polish versions of this sentence, which again suggests a translation error.

The third type of discrepancy we identify is missing/extra clauses, meaning the absence of certain clauses in the different versions of the ToS. Consider, for instance, the following clause taken from the Terravision ToS (date of update not provided; ToS accessed on 31 January 2021), which is completely missing in the Italian ToS:

<ltd2>Terravision is not liable for any lost or stolen items or baggage.</ltd2> (line 101).

The same is true for arbitration and jurisdiction clauses in the English version of the Spotify ToS, which are absent in the German version (effective as of 9 September 2015).[12]
Terms of service in target languages may further include extra (potentially) unfair clauses. Consider, for example, the Polish version of the Garmin ToS (updated April 3, 2014) containing an extra clause marked under the category of privacy included.[13]

Missing/extra clauses may be the product of an omission or error, but they also may be product of deliberate choices to draft contracts differently for different national markets. Such different choices may be made necessary by country-specific services offered only at certain locations, by the need to comply with country-specific regulation, or, more generally, as product of the company's intention to regulate the contractual relationship differently in different countries. For example, the need to comply with country specific regulation may result in substantive differences in clauses providing for age requirements to use certain services.[14]
In a few cases, especially in the German versions of some ToS, an entirely different approach is adopted to the drafting of clauses related to certain matters, like provider's liability. Among others such discrepancies were found in the Electronic Arts ToS.[15]

The fourth type of discrepancy derives from the choice of legal terminology, which may be more or less deliberate. Indeed, legal languages remain profoundly culture-bound and terminological nuances in different languages may be difficult to capture regardless of the applied translation process.
In our corpus this type of discrepancy emerges in relation to the use of particular terms, for instance terms related to responsibility and liability. Unlike in English, in the other languages of our corpus such a distinction is hard to capture.
Consider, for instance, the following clause taken from the Pinterest ToS (updated May 1, 2018) and its Polish and Italian counterparts that employ the expressions "odpowiedzialność" and "responsabilità", without differentiation between responsibility and liability:

<ltd2>Pinterest takes no responsibility and assumes no liability for any User Content that you or any other person or third party posts or sends using our Service.</ltd2> (line 88)

<ltd2>Pinterest nie ponosi odpowiedzialności za jakiekolwiek Treści użytkownika, które Ty lub inni użytkownicy albo osoby trzecie umieszczacie lub wysyłacie przy użyciu naszych usług.</ltd2> (line 88)

<ltd2>Pinterest non si assume alcuna responsabilità per i Contenuti dell'utente che tu o qualsiasi altra persona o terza parte pubblicate o inviate utilizzando il nostro Servizio.</ltd2> (line 88)

While linguistic variations related to responsibility (obligations) and liability do not always entail differing annotations, they sometimes may. Consider, for example, the following situation from the Terravision ToS (as accessed on 31 January 2021):

<ltd2>Terravision is not liable to passengers who did not reserve their trip.</ltd2>

Terravision non ha alcun obbligo nei confronti dei passeggeri che non hanno prenotato la corsa.

Here, a translation of the English term "to be liable" into the more generic Italian "avere obbligo" results in different annotation choices in the different languages.

Finally, as a general remark, it is important to note that deviations from the English source ToS are uneven across languages, being largest in German ToS. This may suggest that the drafting of such ToS is done by human agents, who may pay more attention to the national legal context and specific terminologies than automated translators. For example, note the markedly different take on the matter of privacy and data protection in these clauses of Spotify, where the German drafters refrained from packaging data protection consent with the agreement to the ToS:

[12]More specifically, a sizeable proportion of ToS concerning dispute resolution was removed from the German version and replaced with a single clause (line 175).

[13]Cf. the Polish version of Garmin ToS, line 74.

[14]Cf. the English and German versions of Electronic Arts ToS (updated May 17, 2018) at line 33.

[15]See the English version of Electronic Arts ToS at line 164, and the German version of corresponding ToS at lines 164-166.

<pinc2>Your agreement with us includes these Terms and Conditions of Use ("Terms") and our Privacy Policy.</pinc2> <pinc2>(The Terms, Privacy Policy, and any additional terms that you agree to, as discussed in the Entire Agreement section, are referred to together as the "Agreements".)</pinc2> (line 37)

Ihre Vereinbarung mit uns schließt diese Geschäfts- und Nutzungsbedingungen („Bedingungen") ein sowie jegliche weitere Vereinbarung, der Sie zustimmen, wie im Abschnitt Vollständiger Vertrag beschrieben (gemeinsam als die „Vereinbarungen" bezeichnet). (line 37)

The hypothesis of a more careful drafting being applied in the drafting of German language documents seems confirmed by the fact that retrieving identical corresponding versions of ToS was most hard for German. Conversely, we observed a lower mismatch in both Polish and Italian ToS, where significant structural differences can be retrieved only in limited cases.

4 Experiments

We employ the same methodology proposed in Galassi et al. (2020), by extending the study to two additional languages, namely Italian and Polish. The general idea of the methodology is to transfer the annotations of a given English document onto the same document, given in a different language. As a first step, we exploit an automatic translation system to obtain English sentences from the target language (i.e., German, Polish, or Italian). Then, we find correspondences between the original (tagged) English sentences and the ones (untagged) obtained via translation. In this way, the annotations of the first document can be associated to the sentences in the second document. For this step, any distance or metric that measures the (dis-)similarity between sentences can be exploited. In this work, we use the distance between ELMo (Peters et al., 2018) sentence embeddings coupled with Dynamic Time Warping (Berndt and Clifford, 1994), which was the approach achieving the best performance in Galassi et al. (2020). Finally, the projected annotations are then easily associated back to the original sentences in the target language.

	DE	IT	PL
Precision	0.87	0.94	0.90
Recall	0.95	0.98	0.97
F1-macro	0.91	0.94	0.91
F1-micro	0.91	0.96	0.93
F1-weighted	0.91	0.96	0.93

Table 2: Projection results for the three languages.

To segment our documents into sentences we exploit the `Spacy` python package,[16] whereas for translation into English we use the `deep_translator` python library, in particular the Google translator.[17] We measure the performance of our system by considering the result of the projection as a multi-label classification task on the sentences of the target documents. We report precision as the percentage of projected tags that are correct and recall as the percentage of original tags that have been correctly matched to the target document, in both cases macro-averaged over the documents. F1-macro is the harmonic mean between the first two metrics. We also report the F1-micro, which sums up all the true positives, false positives, and false negatives, without distinguishing among the classes, i.e., tags. Finally, the F1-weighted is the weighted sum of the F1 scores computed per each class (tag), where the weight is given by the support (i.e., number of tagged sentences) of each tag.

As shown in Table 2, the projection works very well for all three languages, with an F1-macro larger that 0.90 for all the languages. The approach performs particularly well for Italian, where a 0.97 recall is obtained, with a 0.94 precision. Polish is the second-best performing language, with German only slightly worse in terms of precision, which is still very high, though.

5 Discussion

Discrepancies across language versions may significantly affect the performance of the projection task. In particular, we found that the system produces some erroneous results where a) there is no correspondence between clauses (e.g., some of them are missing in one or more language versions); b) sentences are split differently; c) there is a mismatch in the ToS structure; d) incorrect translations or

[16] `https://spacy.io/`

[17] `https://deep-translator.readthedocs.io/`

specific linguistic choices can be identified.

As an example of no correspondence between clauses, consider the Electronic Arts ToS (updated May 17, 2018), in which liability clauses are built in an entirely different manner between English and German. In this case the projection missed the two following clauses, which have no equivalent in the English version:

> *<ltd2>Bei kostenpflichtigen EA-Services ist die Haftung von EA außer in Fällen der Verletzung von Leib, Leben oder Gesundheit auf Vorsatz und grobe Fahrlässigkeit beschränkt.</ltd2> [...] <ltd2>In Fällen leichter Fahrlässigkeit haftet EA jedoch nur für die schuldhafte Verletzung von wesentlichen Vertragspflichten, wie z.B. Verzug oder Unmöglichkeit der Leistung Die Haftung im Falle der Verletzung einer solchen wesentlichen Vertragspflicht ist beschränkt auf den typischen Schaden, der bei Abschluss dieses Vertrages für EA aufgrund der Umstände vorhersehbar war.</ltd2>* (line 162).

As for the different segmentation of sentences, consider the following example taken from the Evernote ToS (updated August 28, 2017), where two consecutive <ch2> clauses in the English version were split by a third innocuous clause in the German version.

> *<ch2>These Terms may be amended as new features, technology, or legal requirements arise, so please check back from time to time.</ch2><ch2>If we make a significant change, we'll notify you and, where required, seek your consent.</ch2>*

> *<ch2>Diese Bedingungen können sich ändern, wenn neue Funktionen, Technologien oder rechtliche Anforderungen vorliegen.</ch2>* [misidentified as <ch2>] *Werfen Sie also immer mal wieder einen Blick auf diese Seite, um stets auf dem neuesten Stand zu sein. <ch2>Bei wesentlichen Änderung werden wir Sie darüber informieren und gegebenenfalls Ihre Einwilligung einholen.</ch2>*

Division of longer passages into shorter sentences as well as discrepancies in the documents' structure have been identified as recurrent causes of false positives and false negatives also in relation to examples reported in Section 3. This is the case, among others, for the previously described term on content removal in the Polish version of the Google ToS, where only one of the resulting sentences in the target language merited annotation. Erroneous projection outcomes could also be identified when a longer English sentence, marked under two categories using a nested tag, was divided into two shorter sentences in the target language, each annotated under one category. The previously mentioned clause in the Tripadvisor ToS on unilateral change and contract by using illustrates such a case. Moreover, a comparably high number of false positives and negatives was observed in relation to Terravision, where the document structure varied in different language versions, among others due to country-specific terms.

Finally, as an example of incorrect projection due to translation errors and linguistic choices, consider the case of a clause in Grindr ToS (updated 13 March 2020), where the phrase "bez zobowiązań" (without commitments) was used instead of a reference to liability. While this clause was not marked in the target language, the system nonetheless incorrectly recognized it as a potentially unfair limitation of liability.

The same was true for the previously mentioned clause in the Italian Terravision ToS, referring to a generic term "obbligo". Erroneous projection results were further identified in relation to the previously mentioned clause in the Yelp ToS, which in the Polish version lacked reference to liability. Similarly, a clause on contract by using, which was marked in the English ToS of Evernote, but not in their Italian version, was found among false positives.

6 Conclusions

This paper presents an extension of the annotation projection technique presented in Galassi et al. (2020) for the automated detection of potentially unfair clauses in online ToS by applying it to multiple languages. The presented approach directly addresses the call for automatically transferring the annotations made on legal documents in a language with significant linguistic resources and domain experts, such as English, onto the corresponding versions of the same documents in a target language, where such resources and expertise may be lacking. This approach does not apply to online ToS only, but to a wide category of legal documents, and in particular within the European Union, with a great variety of different languages.

For these reasons, we presented the first multilingual corpus for the detection of potentially unfair clauses for the consumers in online ToS. The data set consists of 25 contracts tagged in four different languages (English, German, Italian, and Polish) for a total of 100 documents. We illustrated the discrepancies across the different versions of the same contract, and we analyzed the major causes of errors in the projection process.

In the future, we will further study correspondence between the English and other language versions, and consider whether computational methods can be deployed to confirm existence of translations. Our final aim is to compare machine learning predictors trained on original and projected annotations, to assess whether the projection procedure can substitute the time-consuming task of document annotation performed by experts.

References

Donald J Berndt and James Clifford. 1994. Using dynamic time warping to find patterns in time series. In *KDD workshop*, pages 359–370. AAAI Press.

Andrea Galassi, Kasper Drazewski, Marco Lippi, and Paolo Torroni. 2020. Cross-lingual annotation projection in legal texts. In *Proceedings of the 28th International Conference on Computational Linguistics*, pages 915–926.

Marco Lippi, Przemysław Pałka, Giuseppe Contissa, Francesca Lagioia, Hans-Wolfgang Micklitz, Giovanni Sartor, and Paolo Torroni. 2019. Claudette: an automated detector of potentially unfair clauses in online terms of service. *Artificial Intelligence and Law*, 27(2):117–139.

Marco B.M. Loos. 2017. Double dutch-on the role of the transparency requirement with regard to the language in which standard contract terms for b2c-contracts must be drafted. *Journal of European Consumer and Market Law*, 6(2).

Matthew E. Peters, Mark Neumann, Mohit Iyyer, Matt Gardner, Christopher Clark, Kenton Lee, and Luke Zettlemoyer. 2018. Deep contextualized word representations. In *NAACL-HLT*, pages 2227–2237, New Orleans, Louisiana. Association for Computational Linguistics.

Federico Ruggeri, Francesca Lagioia, Marco Lippi, and Paolo Torroni. 2021. Detecting and explaining unfairness in consumer contracts through memory networks. *Artificial Intelligence and Law*, pages 1–34.

Named entity recognition in the Romanian legal domain

Vasile Păiș, Maria Mitrofan, Carol Luca Gasan, Vlad Coneschi, Alexandru Ianov
Research Institute for Artificial Intelligence "Mihai Drăgănescu", Romanian Academy
vasile,maria@racai.ro

Abstract

Recognition of named entities present in text is an important step towards information extraction and natural language understanding. This work presents a named entity recognition system for the Romanian legal domain. The system makes use of the gold annotated LegalNERo corpus. Furthermore, the system combines multiple distributional representations of words, including word embeddings trained on a large legal domain corpus. All the resources, including the corpus, model and word embeddings are open sourced. Finally, the best system is available for direct usage in the RELATE platform.

1 Introduction

Natural language processing for the legal domain has its own unique challenges. This is due to the way legal documents are structured as well as to the domain-specific language being used. Technology dealing with legal documents has received increased attention in recent years. This can be seen from the number of recent scientific papers being published, the existence of the Natural Legal Language Processing (NLLP) workshop (Aletras et al., 2019, 2020) and different international projects dealing with natural language processing for the legal domain.

Named entity recognition (NER) is the process of identifying text spans that refer to real-world objects, such as organizations or persons, etc. One of the annotation schemes being used in a large number of works was introduced by the CoNLL-2003 shared task on language independent NER (Tjong Kim Sang and De Meulder, 2003) and refers to names of persons, organizations and locations. This annotation scheme can be applied in the legal domain as well, thus allowing existing systems to try to annotate legal documents (with or without being adapted to legal text). However, domain-specific entities are usually added to enhance the information extraction capabilities of text processing algorithms specifically designed for the legal domain. Dozier et al. (2010), while dealing with depositions, pleadings and trial-specific documents, propose including entities for attorneys, judges, courts and jurisdictions. Glaser et al. (2018) proposed adding the entities date, money value, reference and "other" for analyzing legal contracts. Leitner et al. (2019, 2020) proposed using 7 coarse-grained entity classes which can be further expanded into 19 fine-grained classes.

In the context of the "Multilingual Resources for CEF.AT in the legal domain" (MARCELL) project [1] a large, clean, validated domain-specific corpus was created. It contains monolingual corpora extracted from national legislation (laws, decrees, regulations, etc.) of the seven involved countries, including Romania (Tufiș et al., 2020). All seven corpora are aligned at topic level domains. The Romanian corpus was preprocessed (split at sentence level, tokenized, lemmatized and annotated with POS tags) using tools developed in the Research Institute for Artificial Intelligence "Mihai Drăgănescu", Romanian Academy (RACAI). Named entities were identified using a general-purpose tool (Păiș, 2019). This tool was designed for general Romanian language and allowed only four entity types: organizations, locations, persons and time expressions. The tool was not trained on any legal texts.

For the purposes of this work, we created a manually annotated corpus, comprising legal documents extracted from the larger MARCELL-RO corpus. We choose an annotation scheme covering 5 entity classes: person (PER), location (LOC), organization (ORG), time expressions (TIME) and legal document references (LEGAL). References are introduced similar to the work of Landthaler et al. (2016) and the coarse-grained class proposed by Leitner et al. (2019), without additional sub-classes.

[1] https://marcell-project.eu/

Natural Legal Language Processing Workshop 2021, pages 9–18
November 10, 2021.

Thus, they are references to legal documents such as laws, ordinances, government decisions, etc. For the purposes of this work, in the Romanian legal domain, we decided to explore only these coarse-grained classes, without any fine-grained entities. This has the advantage of allowing the corpus to be used together with other general-purpose NER corpora. Furthermore, it allows us to judge the quality of the resulting NER system against existing systems. In order to train domain-specific NER systems, we constructed distributional representations of words (also known as word embeddings) based on the entire MARCELL corpus. Finally, we explored several neural architectures and adapted them as needed to the legal domain.

This paper is organized as follows: in Section 2 we present related work, in Section 3 is described the LegalNERo corpus, Section 4 presents the legal domain word embeddings, Section 5 describes the NER system architecture, while Section 6 gives the results and finally conclusions are presented in Section 7.

2 Related work

Legal NER is an important task in extracting key information from legal documents, such as dates, references to different types of legal documents, locations, organizations and persons. As Zhong and Tang (2020) stated, once the NEs are identified and classified they can be used in workflows to perform different functionalities such as document anonymization or case summarization.

One of the pioneering work in this research area was made by Dozier et al. (2010). The authors examined legal NEs in US depositions, pleadings, case law and other legal documents using statistical models, context rules, and a lookup list of NEs. They also developed different taggers for NEs such as document type of jurisdiction, obtaining an F1 score of 0.92 for the NEs belonging to jurisdiction class. This work formed the basis for Cardellino et al. (2017) to develop a tool for identifying, classifying and linking legal NEs. They trained and evaluated different systems (Stanford NER [2], a Support Vector Machine, and a neural network (NN)) on Wikipedia and on decisions coming from the European Court of Human Rights, obtaining an F1 score of 0.86 using NN and an F1 score of 0.56 using Stanford NER.

Glaser et al. (2018) studied and evaluated on German legal data three NER systems. GermaNER, a generic German NER tagger, has been adapted to identify and classify NEs such as persons, organizations, locations, and dates and money values. The second NER system used was DBpedia Spotlight pipeline, an interlinking hub, a tool that can be used to perform annotation tasks on a text provided by a user (Mendes et al., 2011). The third NER system employed in this task was based on contract templates to identify NEs (Minakov et al., 2007). For GermaNER pipeline and DBpedia Spotlight pipeline the evaluation was performed on a corpus of 500 judgements, and achieved an F1 score of 0.8 and 0.87 respectively. The template NER system was evaluated on a corpus of contract templates and obtained an F1 score of 0.92.

Leitner et al. (2019) also evaluated two systems, based on Conditional Random Fields (CRFs) and bidirectional Long-Short Term Memory Networks (BiLSTMs), on NER for German language documents from the legal domain. The evaluation was performed on a German court decisions corpus annotated with 19 fine-grained classes, and also with 7 generalised coarse-grained classes. The best performance achieved by the CRFs was 93.23 on fined-grained classes and 93.22 on coarse-grained classes, and the BiLSTMs models reach a maximum of 95.46 for the fined-grained classes and 95.95 for coarse-grained ones. In the Lynx project[3] (Moreno-Schneider et al., 2020) a set of services, including NER, were developed in order to help with the creation of a legal domain knowledge graph (Legal Knowledge Graph – LKG) and its use for the semantic analysis of documents in the legal domain.

Barriere and Fouret (2019) described a method to generate contextual dictionaries for NER. The system was evaluated on a French legal corpus of 94 court decisions (276,705 tokens), which was annotated with 4 classes of entities. The best performance of this system was 96.52.

Even though there are several NER systems trained for Romanian language both for general language (Păiș, 2019) and specialised domains (Mitrofan, 2019), regarding the legal domain, the experiments are very few and the performances are low (for example Tufiș et al. (2020) note an average precision of 64.1% on a random sample extracted from the MARCELL-RO corpus, using the system devel-

[2] https://nlp.stanford.edu/software/CRF-NER.html

[3] https://www.lynx-project.eu/

oped in (Păiș, 2019)). Apart from the new LegalNERo corpus (see Section 3), existing Romanian NER corpora do not focus on the legal domain. Romanian TimeBank (Forăscu and Tufiş, 2012) is an annotated parallel corpus for temporal information. The RONEC (Dumitrescu and Avram, 2020) news corpus contains 26,377 named entities, belonging to 16 different classes. SiMoNERo (Barbu Mititelu and Mitrofan, 2020) is a gold standard corpus for biomedical domain, manually annotated with four types of domain-specific named entities.

3 The LegalNERo corpus

Annotation of the LegalNERo corpus was performed by 5 human annotators, supervised by two senior researchers at the Institute for Artificial Intelligence "Mihai Drăgănescu" of the Romanian Academy (RACAI). For annotation purposes we used the BRAT tool[4] (Stenetorp et al., 2012), integrated in the RELATE platform (Păiș et al., 2020). Inside the legal reference class, we considered subentities of type organization and time. This allows for using the LegalNERo corpus in two scenarios: using all the 5 entity classes or using only the remaining general-purpose classes.

The LegalNERo corpus contains a total of 370 documents from the larger MARCELL-RO corpus. These documents were split amongst the 5 annotators, with certain documents being annotated by multiple annotators. Each annotator manually annotated 100 documents. The annotators were unaware of the overlap, which allowed us to compute an inter-annotator agreement. We used the Cohen's Kappa measure and obtained a value of 0.89, which we consider to be a good result.

The raw annotations were obtained in the BRAT specific format, consisting of text spans, characterized by start and end positions with the associated entities. However, since many NER systems make use of token-based annotations, we further employed the Romanian pipelines integrated in the RELATE platform (Păiș, 2020) and annotated the corpus at token level. For tokenization, lemmatization, part-of-speech tagging and dependency parsing we used UDPipe. Finally, the named entity annotations were mapped to tokens and exported in CoNLL-U Plus format[5], similar to the original format being used in the MARCELL-RO corpus.

Statistic	Value
Documents	370
Sentences	8,284
Tokens	265,335
Unique lemmas	12,887
RDF Triples	5,761,781

Table 1: LegalNERo corpus statistics

Entity	Number
Person	914
Location	2,276
Organization	4,824
Time	2,213
Legal Ref	3,387
Total	*13,614*

Table 2: Number of entities, considering all the entity types

Additionally, location entities were mapped to the GeoNames[6] ontology, but this information was not used for the purposes of this work. Nevertheless, the information is available in the LegalNERo corpus for future use. Finally, since we have multiple annotation levels available, we converted all the data into RDF format, specific to Linguistic Linked Open Data (LLOD) and made this available in the Linked Open Data Cloud[7].

Key statistics computed on the LegalNERo corpus are presented in Table 1. The number of entities, considering all the entity types, are given in Table 2, while considering only persons, locations, organization and time expressions are given in Table 3. These numbers are obtained at entity level (not at token level). We further computed in Table 4 the average number of tokens associated with each entity type.

Results presented in Table 4 clearly indicate that the legal reference entity type has the largest number of tokens (7.29 in average). A typical example is "ORDIN nr. 625 din 25 aprilie 2019" ("Order no. 625 from 25 April 2019"). Nevertheless, longer entities are also present, such as "Ordinul președintelui Casei Naționale de Asigurări de Sănătate nr. 141 / 2017" ("Order of the president of the National Health Insurance House no. 141 / 2017"). This example has 12 tokens and contains an orga-

[4]https://brat.nlplab.org/

[5]https://universaldependencies.org/ext-format.html

[6]https://www.geonames.org/

[7]https://lod-cloud.net/dataset/racai-legalnero

Entity	Number
Person	914
Location	2,276
Organization	6,209
Time	4,643
Total	*14,042*

Table 3: Number of entities, without the legal reference entity type

Entity	# Tokens
Person	2.30
Location	1.38
Organization	4.04
Time	2.31
Legal Ref	7.29

Table 4: Average number of tokens for each entity type

nization sub-entity ("Casei Naționale de Asigurări de Sănătate" / "National Health Insurance House") as well as a time expression ("2017").

4 Romanian legal-domain word embeddings

Previously computed Romanian word embeddings (Păiș and Tufiș, 2018) made use of the Representative Corpus of Contemporary Romanian Language (CoRoLa) (Tufiș et al., 2019). This large corpus contains texts from multiple domains, including the legal domain. However, in addition to the legal domain, the CoRoLa corpus contains texts from completely different areas, such as news, literature and mathematics. This makes the CoRoLa-based embeddings suitable for general tasks, but also allows for creation of legal-domain specific representations.

For the purposes of this work, in addition to the already available CoRoLa embeddings, we constructed word representations based on the entire MARCELL-RO corpus. We used the same approach which obtained the best performing CoRoLa embeddings. Thus, we used the FastText[8] toolkit (Joulin et al., 2017) and produced vector representations of dimension 300, while considering only words appearing a minimum of 20 times. Furthermore, the model made use of n-gram windows of dimension 5. The resulting embeddings are available for download within the RELATE platform[9].

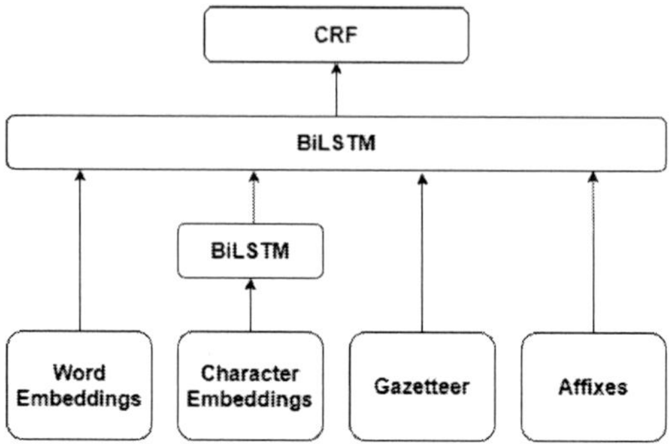

Figure 1: System architecture

For Romanian language there are currently no legal domain contextual embeddings, like the Legal-BERT (Chalkidis et al., 2020) model for English. Furthermore, existing Romanian BERT models, like (Masala et al., 2020; Ștefan Daniel Dumitrescu et al., 2020), were not trained on corpora containing legal documents.

5 System architecture

Our proposed NER model makes use of recurrent neural networks, based on BiLSTM cells, with a final CRF layer. For features we considered word representations, character embeddings, gazetteer resources and known affixes. The word embeddings are initialized from a pre-trained model and are fine-tuned during training. The character embeddings are computed during training and the embedding layer is followed by a BiLSTM layer helping with the representation generation. For implementation we used a modified version (Armengol-Estapé et al., 2019) of the NeuroNER (Dernoncourt et al., 2017) software package. This implementation was further adapted to our needs in order to allow online model serving. The overall system diagram is presented in Figure 1.

To construct the gazetteer resources we employed the GeoNames database for the country Romania and the JRC-Names[10] (Steinberger et al., 2011) multilingual named entity collection. These two collections cover a large number of entity names like locations, organizations and persons.

We trained multiple models using different features. This includes different word embeddings

[8]`https://fasttext.cc/`

[9]`https://relate.racai.ro/index.php?path=ner/demo`

[10]`https://ec.europa.eu/jrc/en/language-technologies/jrc-names`

(CoRoLa and MARCELL embeddings) and also combinations of the two embeddings. Previous work (Păiș and Mitrofan, 2021), (Casillas et al., 2019) has shown that using different word embeddings and combinations can improve NER performance. For each word representation we adapted the main BiLSTM layer size to match the embedding size. For example, in the case of CoRoLa embeddings we used a layer with size 300 and in the case of CoRoLa + MARCELL embeddings we used a layer with size 600. This was done to accommodate the increased vector size associated with the word representation.

In addition to the main BiLSTM layer size, we used a character BiLSTM of size 25. Furthermore, to prevent overfitting, a dropout of probability 50% was introduced. A gradient clipping (Pascanu et al., 2013) with a value of 5 is used to deal with exploding gradients. Finally, we use a stochastic gradient descent (SGD) algorithm with a learning rate of 0.005.

Besides experimenting with the aforementioned NER models, we also made tests with an ensemble method that combines the results from the different models. The idea was to see what combination provides better results and in what conditions. We've used four types of operations for combining the results. The first one is the union of two or more models. The second one is the full intersection of two or more models. In this case, if for the same set of tokens the annotations are different then none of them are represented in the final set. The third type is the implementation of a majority voting system, meaning that if an entity span has the same annotation in $(n/2) + 1$ cases, where n is the total number of models used, it is the winner. For example, given at least three models it takes at least two of the candidates with the same annotation to allow it to be represented in the final set. The fourth one is a merge between two or more models where for a given set of tokens the longest annotation between all of them is represented in the final set.

Afterwards, for each of the resulting final sets, the precision, recall and F1 scores are computed against the gold corpus for each entity types in the corpus. The macro average score is finally calculated. Each of these pairs of combinations and scores are then recorded and a best that has the highest F1 score is calculated. The final step of measuring the precision, recall and F1 scores was done using NeuroNER evaluation script, in order to have a consistency with the initial models scores.

6 Results

Experiments were performed on the two perspectives associated with the corpus: the complete set of 5 classes (person, organization, location, time expressions and legal reference) and the reduced set (person, organization, location, time expression). In the second case, we took into consideration the additional annotations associated with the 4 remaining classes present inside the legal reference entities. Furthermore, in order to explore the impact of different features, we conducted multiple experiments on each perspective. Each experiment was allowed to train for at most 100 epochs. However, we used early stopping in case no improvement was perceived on the validation set for 10 epochs. As a result, neither of the experiments actually trained for the maximum of 100 epochs.

The LegalNERo corpus was split into three sub-corpora for training, validation during training and testing on data unseen during training. We used a 80% split for training and 10% for each of the validation and testing sub-corpora. The split was realized at file level, thus the training split contains 290 files, while the validation and test splits contain 40 files each. For reproducibility of the reported results as well as for comparison with future models, we offer the splits for download from the RELATE platform[11,12].

Using the same splits, we also trained baseline models using well-known libraries such as spaCy [13]. The spaCy library provides a variety of tools for fast text processing and is developed as a modular pipeline. For implementation of our models we focused onto two critical components of the spaCy pipeline, namely the components which are responsible for converting string tokens to vectors and the named entity recognition component. During training, besides word embeddings, we used spaCy's class Lexeme [14], as an entry in the vocabulary. A Lexeme has no string context, it is a word type, as opposed to a word token. It therefore has no part-of-speech tag, dependency parse, or lemma (if lemmatization depends on the part-of-speech tag). After exhaustive tests, the representative model for each

[11]https://relate.racai.ro/resources/legalnero/legalnero_split_5classes.zip

[12]https://relate.racai.ro/resources/legalnero/legalnero_split_4classes.zip

[13]https://spacy.io/

[14]https://spacy.io/api/lexeme

word embedding source also had its own optimal selection of the parameters that can be found at [15]. All of them made use of at least one of the affixes and some of them also used the shape. The spaCy's training process, which is stopped automatically when the F1 score doesn't vary very much for a couple of epochs, guarantees saving the best model from all checkpoints. Although it doesn't save any information during training, we used wandb [16] in order to retrieve the aforementioned data. Using spaCy, the best F1 score was 83.77, for all the five entity classes and using ro_core_news_lg[17] embeddings with a layer of size 300. When the LEGAL class was excluded and with the same embeddings configuration, the F1 score obtained by spaCy is 86.21.

In Table 5 are presented different experiments using the system architecture described in Section 5, for all the entities. Similarly, in Table 6 are given results from experiments without the legal reference entity class. The usage of gazetteer resources helps to increase the F1 score associated with persons, locations and organizations. Therefore the best models associated with the two scenarios make use of gazetteers.

Table 7 presents the results of the four types of ensemble operations. It can be seen that the best F1 score (90.36) was achieved by reunion of three models, two containing all types of entities and one obtained without legal entity type (CoRoLa+MARCELL Y N). The model, CoRoLa+MARCELL Y N presented in Table 3 has significantly contributed to increasing the F1 score. Another important observation presented in Table 7 is that an ensemble of models can, in principle, perform better than any individual model, because the various errors of the models were averaged out. It can also be seen that the F1 score for each operation is greater than the ones obtained by individual models.

The resulting best performing models are available for direct online usage through the RELATE platform[18]. This integration allows the user to enter a Romanian legal document inside the platform's web interface, select the desired model, by using a dropdown menu, and then execute the model. The selected model together with the raw text are sent to the server process, which produces a list of recognized entities. These are returned to the user and displayed in the web interface. The interface is presented in Figure 2 and example results are presented in Figure 3. Furthermore, pre-trained models can be downloaded from the same interface.

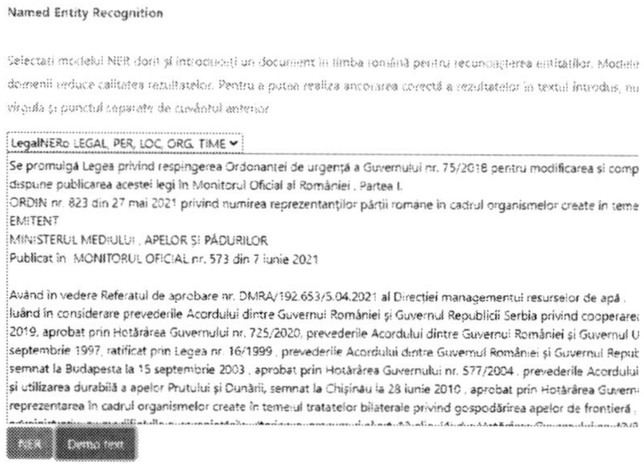

Figure 2: Web interface for interacting with the Romanian Legal NER models

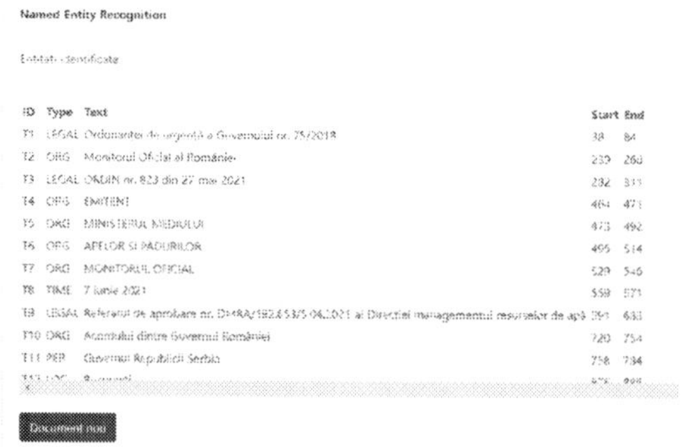

Figure 3: Romanian Legal NER results presented in RELATE

7 Conclusions

This paper introduced a neural named entity recognition system designed specifically for the Romanian legal domain. It employed the LegalNERo corpus for training and evaluation. The system is available for querying inside the RELATE platform and pre-trained models are available for download. As indicated in Section 6, the best performing models made use of word embeddings trained on the legal-domain MARCELL corpus. When considering all the entity types available, CoRoLa and

[15] https://spacy.io/api/lexeme#attributes

[16] https://wandb.ai/site

[17] https://spacy.io/models/ro#ro_core_news_lg

[18] https://relate.racai.ro/index.php?path=ner/demo

Embeddings	Gaz.	Affixes	LEGAL	PER	LOC	ORG	TIME	Macro AVG
			Validation set					
CoRoLa	N	N	84.58	81.75	76.11	80.07	84.12	81.37
CoRoLa	Y	N	84.88	80.67	76.73	80.11	83.72	81.26
CoRoLa	Y	Y	83.72	**83.00**	74.10	80.15	84.21	81.09
MARCELL	N	N	85.79	82.87	75.15	82.56	79.91	81.29
MARCELL	Y	N	82.75	78.88	77.44	**82.95**	**85.65**	**81.56**
MARCELL	Y	Y	**86.12**	81.30	73.58	81.10	82.48	80.97
CoRoLa+MARCELL	N	N	84.51	77.42	74.78	80.54	84.30	80.32
CoRoLa+MARCELL	Y	N	85.61	79.52	71.78	80.86	83.76	80.33
CoRoLa+MARCELL	Y	Y	83.84	77.11	**77.58**	80.78	81.78	80.24
			Test set					
CoRoLa	N	N	**90.50**	95.56	70.59	76.26	**85.93**	83.90
CoRoLa	Y	N	90.06	98.08	75.37	78.38	82.42	85.03
CoRoLa	Y	Y	89.80	95.56	73.33	75.80	84.53	83.94
MARCELL	N	N	90.41	97.38	70.30	76.70	81.64	83.49
MARCELL	Y	N	86.98	98.48	**75.94**	**80.60**	84.09	**85.34**
MARCELL	Y	Y	90.12	96.65	69.77	74.23	85.55	83.39
CoRoLa+MARCELL	N	N	88.18	**98.50**	75.62	76.65	84.39	84.74
CoRoLa+MARCELL	Y	N	89.68	97.04	75.21	78.69	83.08	84.83
CoRoLa+MARCELL	Y	Y	89.42	96.99	70.03	79.10	80.54	83.40

Table 5: F1 scores for different models, considering all entities

Embeddings	Gaz.	Affixes	PER	LOC	ORG	TIME	Macro AVG
			Validation set				
CoRoLa	N	N	80.50	73.65	**87.17**	82.68	81.17
CoRoLa	Y	N	80.63	**78.92**	85.96	83.07	**82.21**
CoRoLa	Y	Y	79.01	75.00	85.81	84.15	81.18
MARCELL	N	N	**81.75**	73.58	86.17	83.51	81.57
MARCELL	Y	N	79.35	75.53	85.47	**85.45**	81.78
MARCELL	Y	Y	80.65	71.97	86.40	83.94	81.10
CoRoLa+MARCELL	N	N	77.05	75.76	85.89	84.59	81.04
CoRoLa+MARCELL	Y	N	81.12	73.23	85.48	83.69	81.13
CoRoLa+MARCELL	Y	Y	76.54	75.29	85.99	85.12	81.05
			Test set				
CoRoLa	N	N	96.27	66.86	80.34	89.81	83.35
CoRoLa	Y	N	96.65	72.13	81.36	88.31	84.64
CoRoLa	Y	Y	97.69	69.54	80.09	89.06	84.10
MARCELL	N	N	96.68	74.01	81.24	91.65	85.94
MARCELL	Y	N	**98.86**	69.83	79.85	91.93	85.14
MARCELL	Y	Y	96.68	74.49	78.87	**92.18**	85.66
CoRoLa+MARCELL	N	N	**98.86**	69.59	**82.13**	90.51	85.29
CoRoLa+MARCELL	Y	N	97.40	72.88	80.89	90.28	85.39
CoRoLa+MARCELL	Y	Y	**98.86**	**76.01**	80.89	91.39	**86.84**

Table 6: F1 scores for different models, considering only person, location, organization and time expression

Operation	LEGAL	PER	LOC	ORG	TIME	Macro AVG
Reunion	90.42	98.17	78.96	91.61	92.44	**90.36**
Intersection	90.12	98.66	65.45	87.67	86.64	86.14
Voting algorithm	90.41	99.33	75.05	91.18	90.57	89.37
Longest span	89.35	98.66	70.59	89.95	86.22	87.29

Table 7: F1 scores for different ensembles for test set, considering all entities

MARCELL embeddings seem to provide similar performance (Table 5, F1 difference on the test set is less than 1%). However, when considering only persons, organizations, locations and time expressions (Table 6), MARCELL embeddings provide over 1% F1 improvement compared to CoRoLa, while a combination of CoRoLa and MARCELL embeddings provide the best results with an improvement of over 2% over simple CoRoLa based embeddings. Even more, an ensemble model combining models with all the entity types with a model without the legal reference entity type achieves the best performance on the test set with almost 5% improvement, considering overall macro F1. As future work we foresee expanding the LegalNERo corpus with additional annotations including fine-grained classes of entities and to make more experiments with different NER architectures.

References

Nikolaos Aletras, Elliott Ash, Leslie Barrett, Daniel Chen, Adam Meyers, Daniel Preotiuc-Pietro, David Rosenberg, and Amanda Stent, editors. 2019. *Proceedings of the Natural Legal Language Processing Workshop 2019*. Association for Computational Linguistics, Minneapolis, Minnesota.

Nikolaos Aletras, Androutsopoulos Ion, Leslie Barrett, Adam Meyers, and Daniel Preotiuc-Pietro, editors. 2020. *Proceedings of the Natural Legal Language Processing Workshop 2020*.

Jordi Armengol-Estapé, Felipe Soares, Montserrat Marimon, and Martin Krallinger. 2019. Pharmaconer tagger: a deep learning-based tool for automatically finding chemicals and drugs in spanish medical texts. *Genomics Inform*, 17(2):e15–.

Verginica Barbu Mititelu and Maria Mitrofan. 2020. The Romanian medical treebank-SiMoNERo. In *Proceedings of the The 15th Edition of the International Conference on Linguistic Resources and Tools for Natural Language Processing – ConsILR-2020*, pages 7–16.

Valentin Barriere and Amaury Fouret. 2019. May i check again?–a simple but efficient way to generate and use contextual dictionaries for named entity recognition. application to french legal texts. *arXiv preprint arXiv:1909.03453*.

Cristian Cardellino, Milagro Teruel, Laura Alonso Alemany, and Serena Villata. 2017. A low-cost, high-coverage legal named entity recognizer, classifier and linker. In *Proceedings of the 16th edition of the International Conference on Articial Intelligence and Law*, pages 9–18.

Arantza Casillas, Nerea Ezeiza, Iakes Goenaga, Alicia Pérez, and Xabier Soto. 2019. Measuring the effect of different types of unsupervised word representations on medical named entity recognition. *International Journal of Medical Informatics*, 129:100–106.

Ștefan Daniel Dumitrescu, Andrei-Marius Avram, and Sampo Pyysalo. 2020. The birth of romanian BERT. In *Proceedings of the 2020 Conference on Empirical Methods in Natural Language Processing: Findings, EMNLP 2020, Online Event, 16-20 November 2020*, volume EMNLP 2020 of *Findings of ACL*, pages 4324–4328. Association for Computational Linguistics.

Ilias Chalkidis, Manos Fergadiotis, Prodromos Malakasiotis, Nikolaos Aletras, and Ion Androutsopoulos. 2020. LEGAL-BERT: the muppets straight out of law school. *CoRR*, abs/2010.02559.

Franck Dernoncourt, Ji Young Lee, and Peter Szolovits. 2017. NeuroNER: an easy-to-use program for named-entity recognition based on neural networks. *Conference on Empirical Methods on Natural Language Processing (EMNLP)*.

Christopher Dozier, Ravikumar Kondadadi, Marc Light, Arun Vachher, Sriharsha Veeramachaneni, and Ramdev Wudali. 2010. *Named Entity Recognition and Resolution in Legal Text*, pages 27–43. Springer Berlin Heidelberg, Berlin, Heidelberg.

Ștefan Daniel Dumitrescu and Andrei-Marius Avram. 2020. Introducing RONEC - the Romanian named entity corpus. In *Proceedings of the 12th Language Resources and Evaluation Conference*, pages 4436–4443, Marseille, France. European Language Resources Association.

Corina Forăscu and Dan Tufiş. 2012. Romanian timebank: An annotated parallel corpus for temporal information. In *Proceedings of the Eighth International Conference on Language Resources and Evaluation (LREC'12)*, pages 3762–3766.

Ingo Glaser, Bernhard Waltl, and Florian Matthes. 2018. Named entity recognition, extraction, and linking in german legal contracts. In *IRIS: Internationales Rechtsinformatik Symposium*, pages 325–334.

Armand Joulin, Edouard Grave, Piotr Bojanowski, and Tomas Mikolov. 2017. Bag of tricks for efficient text classification. In *Proceedings of the 15th Conference of the European Chapter of the Association for Computational Linguistics: Volume 2, Short Papers*, pages 427–431, Valencia, Spain. Association for Computational Linguistics.

Jörg Landthaler, Bernhard Waltl, and Florian Matthes. 2016. Unveiling references in legal texts-implicit versus explicit network structures. In *IRIS: Internationales Rechtsinformatik Symposium*, volume 8, pages 71–8.

Elena Leitner, Georg Rehm, and Julian Moreno-Schneider. 2019. Fine-grained named entity recognition in legal documents. In *Semantic Systems. The Power of AI and Knowledge Graphs*, pages 272–287, Cham. Springer International Publishing.

Elena Leitner, Georg Rehm, and Julian Moreno-Schneider. 2020. A dataset of German legal documents for named entity recognition. In *Proceedings of the 12th Language Resources and Evaluation Conference*, pages 4478–4485, Marseille, France. European Language Resources Association.

Mihai Masala, Ştefan Ruseti, and Mihai Dascalu. 2020. RoBERT – a Romanian BERT model. In *Proceedings of the 28th International Conference on Computational Linguistics*, pages 6626–6637, Barcelona, Spain (Online). International Committee on Computational Linguistics.

Pablo N Mendes, Max Jakob, Andrés García-Silva, and Christian Bizer. 2011. Dbpedia spotlight: shedding light on the web of documents. In *Proceedings of the 7th international conference on semantic systems*, pages 1–8.

Igor Minakov, George Rzevski, Petr Skobelev, and Simon Volman. 2007. Creating contract templates for car insurance using multi-agent based text understanding and clustering. In *International Conference on Industrial Applications of Holonic and Multi-Agent Systems*, pages 361–370. Springer.

Maria Mitrofan. 2019. *Extragere de cunostinte din texte în limba româna si date structurate cu aplicatii în domeniul medical*. Ph.D. thesis, Romanian Academy.

Julian Moreno-Schneider, Georg Rehm, Elena Montiel-Ponsoda, Víctor Rodriguez-Doncel, Artem Revenko, Sotirios Karampatakis, Maria Khvalchik, Christian Sageder, Jorge Gracia, and Filippo Maganza. 2020. Orchestrating NLP services for the legal domain. In *Proceedings of the 12th Language Resources and Evaluation Conference*, pages 2332–2340, Marseille, France. European Language Resources Association.

Razvan Pascanu, Tomas Mikolov, and Yoshua Bengio. 2013. On the difficulty of training recurrent neural networks. In *Proceedings of the 30th International Conference on International Conference on Machine Learning - Volume 28*, ICML'13, pages 1310–1318. JMLR.org.

Vasile Păiş. 2019. *Contributions to semantic processing of texts; Identification of entities and relations between textual units; Case study on Romanian language*. Ph.D. thesis, Romanian Academy.

Vasile Păiş. 2020. Multiple annotation pipelines inside the relate platform. In *The 15th International Conference on Linguistic Resources and Tools for Natural Language Processing*, pages 65–75.

Vasile Păiş and Maria Mitrofan. 2021. Assessing multiple word embeddings for named entity recognition of professions and occupations in health-related social media. In *Proceedings of the Sixth Social Media Mining for Health (#SMM4H) Workshop and Shared Task*, pages 128–130, Mexico City, Mexico. Association for Computational Linguistics.

Vasile Păiş and Dan Tufiş. 2018. Computing distributed representations of words using the CoRoLa corpus. *Proceedings of the Romanian Academy Series A - Mathematics Physics Technical Sciences Information Science*, 19(2):185–191.

Vasile Păiş, Dan Tufiş, and Radu Ion. 2020. A processing platform relating data and tools for romanian language. In *Proceedings of The 12th Language Resources and Evaluation Conference*, pages 81–88, Marseille, France. European Language Resources Association.

Ralf Steinberger, Bruno Pouliquen, Mijail Kabadjov, Jenya Belyaeva, and Erik van der Goot. 2011. JRC-NAMES: A freely available, highly multilingual named entity resource. In *Proceedings of the International Conference Recent Advances in Natural Language Processing 2011*, pages 104–110, Hissar, Bulgaria. Association for Computational Linguistics.

Pontus Stenetorp, Sampo Pyysalo, Goran Topić, Tomoko Ohta, Sophia Ananiadou, and Jun'ichi Tsujii. 2012. brat: a web-based tool for NLP-assisted text annotation. In *Proceedings of the Demonstrations at the 13th Conference of the European Chapter of the Association for Computational Linguistics*, pages 102–107, Avignon, France. Association for Computational Linguistics.

Erik F. Tjong Kim Sang and Fien De Meulder. 2003. Introduction to the CoNLL-2003 shared task: Language-independent named entity recognition. In *Proceedings of the Seventh Conference on Natural Language Learning at HLT-NAACL 2003*, pages 142–147.

Dan Tufiș, Maria Mitrofan, Vasile Păiș, Radu Ion, and Andrei Coman. 2020. Collection and annotation of the Romanian legal corpus. In *Proceedings of the 12th Language Resources and Evaluation Conference*, pages 2773–2777, Marseille, France. European Language Resources Association.

Dan Tufiș, Verginica Barbu Mititelu, Elena Irimia, Vasile Păiș, Radu Ion, Nils Diewald, Maria Mitrofan, and Onofrei Mihaela. 2019. Little strokes fell great oaks. creating CoRoLa, the reference corpus of contemporary romanian. *Revue Roumaine de Linguistique*, 64(3):227–240.

Qing Zhong and Yan Tang. 2020. An attention-based bilstm-crf for chinese named entity recognition. In *2020 IEEE 5th International Conference on Cloud Computing and Big Data Analytics (ICCCBDA)*, pages 550–555. IEEE.

Swiss-Judgment-Prediction: A Multilingual Legal Judgment Prediction Benchmark

Joel Niklaus
Research Center for Digital Sustainability
Institute of Computer Science
University of Bern
Bern, Switzerland
joel.niklaus@inf.unibe.ch

Ilias Chalkidis
Coastal NLP Group
Department of Computer Science
University of Copenhagen
Copenhagen, Denmark
ilias.chalkidis@di.ku.dk

Matthias Stürmer
Research Center for Digital Sustainability
Institute of Computer Science
University of Bern
Bern, Switzerland
matthias.stuermer@inf.unibe.ch

Abstract

In many jurisdictions, the excessive workload of courts leads to high delays. Suitable predictive AI models can assist legal professionals in their work, and thus enhance and speed up the process. So far, Legal Judgment Prediction (LJP) datasets have been released in English, French, and Chinese. We publicly release a multilingual (German, French, and Italian), diachronic (2000-2020) corpus of 85K cases from the Federal Supreme Court of Switzerland (FSCS). We evaluate state-of-the-art BERT-based methods including two variants of BERT that overcome the BERT input (text) length limitation (up to 512 tokens). Hierarchical BERT has the best performance (approx. 68-70% Macro-F1-Score in German and French). Furthermore, we study how several factors (canton of origin, year of publication, text length, legal area) affect performance. We release both the benchmark dataset and our code to accelerate future research and ensure reproducibility.

1 Introduction

Frequently, legal information is available in textual form (e.g. court decisions, laws, legal articles or commentaries, contracts). With the abundance of legal texts comes the possibility of applying Natural Language Processing (NLP) techniques to tackle challenging tasks (Chalkidis and Kampas, 2018; Zhong et al., 2020; Chalkidis et al., 2021b). In this work, we study the task of Legal Judgment Prediction (LJP) where the goal is to predict the outcome (verdict) of a decision given its facts (Aletras et al., 2016; Şulea et al., 2017; Luo et al., 2017; Zhong et al., 2018; Hu et al., 2018; Chalkidis et al., 2019). Many relevant applications and tasks, such as court opinion generation (Ye et al., 2018) and analysis (Wang et al., 2012) have been also studied, while there is also work aiming to interpret (explain) the decisions of particular courts (Ye et al., 2018; Chalkidis et al., 2021a).

Models developed for LJP and relevant supportive tasks may assist both lawyers, e.g., help them prepare their arguments by identifying their strengths and weaknesses, and judges and clerks, e.g., review or prioritize cases, thus speeding up judicial processes and improving their quality. Especially in areas with many pending cases such as Indian[1] and Brazilian[2] jurisdictions or US immigration cases[3] the deployment of such models may drastically shorten the backlog. Such models can also help legal scholars to study case law (Katz, 2012) and help sociologists and research ethicists to expose irresponsible use of AI in the justice system (Angwin et al., 2016; Dressel and Farid, 2018). So far, LJP datasets have been released for English (Katz et al., 2017; Medvedeva et al., 2018; Chalkidis et al., 2019), French (Şulea et al., 2017) and Chinese (Xiao et al., 2018; Long et al., 2019).

[1] https://tinyurl.com/mjy2uf9a
[2] https://tinyurl.com/2uttucmn
[3] https://tinyurl.com/4ybhhff8

Natural Legal Language Processing Workshop 2021, pages 19–35
November 10, 2021. ©2021 Association for Computational Linguistics

We introduce a new multilingual, diachronic LJP dataset of FSCS cases, which spans 21 years (from 2000 to 2020) containing over 85K (50K German, 31K French and 4K Italian) cases. To the best of our knowledge, it is the only publicly available multilingual LJP dataset to date. Additionally, it is annotated with publication years, legal areas and cantons of origin; thus it can be used also as test-bed for fairness and robustness in the critical application of NLP to law (Wang et al., 2021).

Rogers (2021) argues that the NLP community is investing many more resources in the development of models rather than data. As a result, there are not enough challenging, high-quality and well curated benchmarks available. Rogers assumes that the main reason for this imbalance is that the "data work" is considered less prestigious and top conferences are more likely to reject resource (dataset) papers. With our work (and the associated code and data) we hope to make a valuable contribution to the legal NLP field, where there are not many ready-to-use benchmarks available.

Contributions

The contributions of this paper are threefold:

- We publicly release a large, high quality, curated, multilingual, diachronic dataset of 85K Swiss Federal Supreme Court (FSCS) cases annotated with the respective binarized judgment outcome (*approval/dismissal*), posing a challenging text classification task. We also provide additional metadata, i.e., the publication year, the legal area and the canton of origin per case, to promote robustness and fairness studies on the critical area of legal NLP (Wang et al., 2021).

- We provide experimental results with strong baselines representing the current state-of-the-art in NLP. Since the average length of the facts (850 tokens in the French part) is longer than the 512 tokens limit by BERT (Devlin et al., 2019), special methods are needed to cope with that. We show results comparing standard BERT models (up to 512 tokens) with two variants (hierarchical and prolonged BERT) that use up to 2048 tokens.

- We analyze the results of the German dataset in terms of diachronicity (publication year), legal area and input (text) length and the French dataset by canton of origin. We find that performance deteriorates as cases are getting more complex (longer facts), while also performance varies across legal areas. There is no sign of performance fluctuation across years.

2 Related Work

European Court of Human Rights (ECtHR)

Aletras et al. (2016) introduced a dataset of 584 ECtHR cases concerning the violation or not of three articles of the European Convention of Human Rights (ECHR). They used a Support Vector Machine (SVM) (Cortes and Vapnik, 1995) with Bag-of-Words (BoW) (n-grams) and topical features on a simplified binarized LJP. In contrast to our work, they evaluated with random 10-fold cross-validation instead of the more realistic temporal split based on the date (Søgaard et al., 2021). Medvedeva et al. (2018) extended the ECtHR dataset to include 9 instead of 3 Articles resulting in a total of approx. 11.5K cases. They also experimented with an SVM operating on n-grams on the LJP task. Chalkidis et al. (2019) experimented on a similarly sized dataset using neural methods. On the binary LJP task, they improve the state-of-the-art using a hierarchical version of BERT. Additionally, they experimented with a multi-label LJP task predicting for each of the 66 ECHR Articles whether it is violated or not.

Supreme Court of the United States (SCOTUS)

Katz et al. (2017) experimented on LJP with 28K cases from the SCOTUS spanning almost two centuries. They trained a Random Forest (Breiman, 2001) classifier using extensive feature engineering with many non textual features. Kaufman et al. (2019) improved results using an ADABoost (Freund and Schapire, 1997) classifier, while also incorporating more textual information (i.e., statements made by the court judges during oral arguments).

French Supreme Court (Court of Cassation)

Şulea et al. (2017) studied the LJP task on a dataset of approx. 127K French Supreme Court cases. They experimented on a 6-class and a 8-class setting using an SVM with BoW features. They reported very high scores, which they claim are justified by the high predictability of the French Supreme Court. Although they used as input the entire case description and not only the facts, thus there is a strong possibility of label information leak. They also used 10-fold stratified cross-validation selecting the test part at random.

German Courts

Urchs et al. (2021) present a corpus of over 32K German court decisions from 131 Bavarian courts. The corpus is annotated with rich metadata including, among others, facts and judgment outcome needed for the LJP task. They present sample experiments predicting the type of the decision (judgment, resolution or other) and detecting conclusion, definition and subsumption in a subset of 200 randomly chosen and manually annotated decisions. They used traditional Machine Learning (ML) methods such as Logistic Regression (LR) on unigrams (BoW features) and SVM on Term Frequency - Inverse Document Frequency (TF-IDF) features.

Supreme People's Court of China (SPC)

Luo et al. (2017) experimented with the Hierarchical Attention Network (Yang et al., 2016) on Chinese criminal cases. They trained a model jointly on charge prediction, a form of LJP, and the relevant criminal law article extraction task using the relevant articles as support for the charge prediction. Xiao et al. (2018) introduced a large-scale LJP dataset of more than 2.6M Chinese criminal cases from the SPC. Their dataset is annotated with extensive metadata such as applicable law articles, charges, and prison terms. Zhong et al. (2018) viewed the dependencies between the different subtasks of LJP as a Directed Acyclic Graph (DAG) and apply a topological multitask learning framework. They work on three different datasets each containing Chinese criminal cases. Long et al. (2019) studied the LJP task on 100K Chinese divorce proceedings considering three types of information as input: applicable law articles, fact description, and plaintiffs' pleas. Li et al. (2019) use a multichannel attentive neural network on four datasets containing Chinese criminal cases. They considered all three subtasks of the Chinese LJP datasets: charges, law articles and prison term. Yang et al. (2019) apply a recurrent attention network on three Chinese LJP datasets.

3 Data Description

3.1 Dataset Construction

The decisions were downloaded from the platform entscheidsuche.ch and have been pre-processed by the means of HTML parsers and Regular Expressions (RegExps). The dataset contains more than 85K decisions from the FSCS written in three languages (50K German, 31K French, 4K Italian) from the years 2000 to 2020.[4] The FSCS is the last level of appeal in Switzerland and hears only the most controversial cases which could not have been sufficiently well solved by (up to two) lower courts. In their decisions, they often focus only on small parts of previous decision, where they discuss possible wrong reasoning by the lower court. This makes these cases particularly challenging.

In order to fight the reproducibility crisis (Britz, 2020), we release the Swiss-Judgment-Prediction dataset on Zenodo[5] and on Hugging Face[6], while also open-sourcing the complete code used for constructing the dataset[7] as well as for running the experiments[8] on GitHub.

3.2 Structure of Court Decisions

A typical Swiss court decision is made up of the following four main sections: *rubrum*, *facts*, *considerations* and *rulings*.[9] The *rubrum* (introduction) contains the date and chamber, mentions the involved judge(s) and parties and finally states the topic of the decision. The *facts* describe what happened in the case and form the basis for the considerations of the court. The higher the level of appeal, the more general and summarized the facts. The *considerations* reflect the formal legal reasoning which form the basis for the final ruling. Here the court cites laws and other influential rulings. The *rulings*, constituting the final section, are an enumeration of the binding decisions made by the court. This section is normally rather short and summarizes the considerations.

3.2.1 Use of Facts instead of Considerations

We deliberately did not consider the considerations as input to the model, unlike Aletras et al. (2016) for the following reasons.The facts are the section which is most similar to a general description of the case, which may be more widely available, while

[4]The dataset is not parallel, all cases are unique and decision are written only in a single language.

[5]https://zenodo.org/record/5529712

[6]https://huggingface.co/datasets/swiss_judgment_prediction

[7]https://github.com/JoelNiklaus/SwissCourtRulingCorpus

[8]https://github.com/JoelNiklaus/SwissJudgementPrediction

[9]See examples in Figures 5 and 6 of Appendix B

Split	de			fr			it		
	approval	dismissal	total	approval	dismissal	total	approval	dismissal	total
train	8369 (24%)	27003 (76%)	35452	5197 (25%)	15982 (75%)	21179	625 (20%)	2447 (80%)	3072
val	959 (20%)	3746 (80%)	4705	649 (21%)	2446 (79%)	3095	65 (16%)	343 (84%)	408
test	1915 (20%)	7810 (80%)	9725	1264 (19%)	5556 (81%)	6820	152 (19%)	660 (81%)	812
all	11243 (23%)	38639 (77%)	49882	7110 (23%)	23984 (77%)	31094	842 (20%)	3450 (80%)	4292

Table 1: The number of cases per label (*approval*, *dismissal*) in each language subset.

being less biased.[10] Additionally, the facts do not change that much from one to the next level of appeal (apart from being more concise and summarized in the higher levels of appeal). According to estimations from several court clerks we consulted, the facts take approximately 10% of the time for drafting a decision while the considerations take 85% and the outcome 5% (45%, 50% and 5% in penal law respectively). So, most of the work being done by the judges and clerks results in the legal considerations. Therefore, we would expect the model to perform better if it had access to the considerations. But on the other hand, the value of the model would be far smaller, since most of the work is already done, once the considerations are written. Thus, to create a more realistic and challenging scenario, we consider only the facts as input for the predictive models.

3.3 The Binarized LJP Task - Verdict Labeling Simplification

The cases have been originally labeled with 6 labels: *approval, partial approval, dismissal, partial dismissal, inadmissible* and *write off*. The first four are judged on the basis of the facts (merits) and the last two for formal reasons. A case is considered *inadmissible*, if there are formal deficiencies with the appeal or if the court is not responsible to rule the case. A court rules *write off* if the case has become redundant so there is no reason for the proceeding anymore. This can be for several reasons, such as an out-of-court settlement or procedural association (two proceedings are unified). *Approval* and *partial approval* mean that the request is deemed valid or partially valid respectively. *Dismissal* and *partial dismissal* mean that the request is denied or partially denied respectively. A *partial* decision is usually ruled in parallel with a decision of the opposite kind or with *inadmissible*.

In practice, court decisions may have multiple requests (questions), where each can be judged individually. Since the structure of the outcomes in the decisions is non-standard, parsing them automatically is very challenging. Therefore, we decided to focus on the main request only and discard all side (secondary) requests. Even the main request sometimes contains multiple judgments referring to different parts of the main request, with some more important than others (it is very hard to automatically detect their criticality). So, to simplify the task and make it more concise, we transform the document labeling from a list of partial judgments into a single judgment, as follows:

1. We excluded all cases that have been ruled with both an approval and a dismissal in the main request, since that could be rather confusing.
2. We excluded cases ruled with *write off* outcomes since these cases are rejected for formal reasons that are not written (described) in the facts. Therefore, a model has no chance of inferring it correctly. We also excluded cases with *inadmissible* outcomes for similar reasons.
3. Since *partial* approvals/dismissals are very hard to distinguish from *full* approvals/dismissals respectively, we converted all the partial ones to full ones. Thus, the final labeling includes two possible outcomes, approvals and dismissals (i.e., the court "leans" positive or negative to the request).

By implementing these simplifications, we made the dataset more feasible (solvable) and semantically coherent targeting the core ruling process (see Section 5). Table 2 shows the numbers of decisions after each processing step. Note that we reduced the dataset with these preprocessing steps significantly (from over 141K to close to 85K decisions) to achieve higher quality. We also made the task structurally simpler by converting it from a multi-label to a binary classification task.[11]

The dataset is highly imbalanced containing more than $\frac{3}{4}$ dismissed cases (see Table 1 for de-

[10]Note however, that the facts are drafted together with the considerations and are often formulated in a way to support the reasoning in the considerations.

[11]Although, we look forward to recover at least part of the complexity in the future, if we have the appropriate resources to manually extract per-request judgments, introducing a new multi-task (multi-question) LJP dataset.

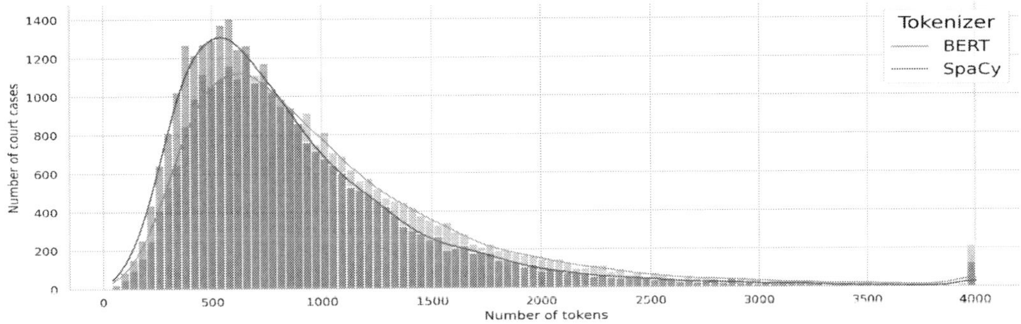

Figure 1: The distribution of the document (the facts of a case) length for French decisions. The blue histogram shows the document (case) length distribution in regular words (using the spacy tokenizer (Honnibal et al., 2020)). It is useful for a human estimation of the length and for methods building upon word embeddings (Mikolov et al., 2013; Pennington et al., 2014). The orange histogram shows the distribution in sub-word units (generated by the SentencePiece tokenizer (Kudo and Richardson, 2018) used in BERT). It is useful e.g. for estimating the maximum sequence length of a BERT-like model. Decisions with length over 4000 tokens have been grouped in the last bin.

tails). The label skewness makes the classification task quite hard and beating dummy baselines, e.g., predicting always the majority class, on micro-averaged measures (e.g., Micro-F1) is challenging. In our opinion, macro-averaged measures (e.g., Macro-F1) are more suitable in this setting, since they consider both outcomes (classes); they can also better discriminate better methods. In other words, they favor models that can actually learn the task (discriminate the two classes) and they do not always predict the majority class, i.e., *dismissal*, regardless of the facts.

Language	Total	2000-2020	Rulings	Judgments	Binarized
de	96337	95449	95273	84083	49882
fr	52278	51748	49132	49083	31094
it	8784	8643	8457	8441	4292
all	157399	155840	152862	141607	85268

Table 2: *Rulings* is the number of cases where rulings could be extracted. *Judgments* is the number of cases where we could extract any judgment types described in Section 3.3. *Binarized* is the number of cases considered in the final dataset after removing decisions containing labels other than *approval* or *dismissal*.

3.4 Case Distribution

This Section presents statistics about the distribution of cases according to different metadata like input (text) length, legal area and origin cantons.

3.4.1 The Curse of Long Documents

Figure 1 shows the distribution of the document (facts of the case) length of French cases.[12] We see that there are very few decisions with more than 2K tokens in German (very similar for Italian). The French decisions are more evenly distributed, including a large portion of decisions with more than 4K tokens. For all languages, there is a considerable portion of decisions (50%+) containing more than 512 sub-word units (BERTs maximum sequence length) posing a fundamental challenge for standard BERT models.

3.4.2 Legal Areas

Table 3 presents the distribution of legal areas across languages. The legal areas are derived from the chambers where the decisions were heard. The website of the FSCS[13] describes in detail what kinds of cases the different chambers hear.

Legal Area	de	fr	it
public law	12182 (24%)	8514 (27%)	1583 (37%)
penal law	10942 (22%)	8039 (26%)	692 (16%)
social law	10742 (22%)	4048 (13%)	673 (16%)
civil law	8208 (16%)	7348 (24%)	763 (18%)
insurance law	7625 (15%)	2950 (9%)	561 (13%)
other	183 (0.4%)	195 (0.6%)	20 (0.5%)

Table 3: The distribution of legal areas in each language subset.

3.4.3 Origin Cantons

To study robustness and fairness in terms of geographical (regional) groups, we extracted the canton of origin from the decisions. As we observe in Table 4, most of the cantons (e.g., Zürich, Ticino) are monolingual and the distribution of the cases across cantons is very skewed with 1-2 cantons per language covering a large portion of the total cases.

[12]See Figures 7 and 8 in Appendix C for the German and Italian cases, respectively.

[13]`https://tinyurl.com/52a4x8yz` (in German)

Canton of Origin	de	fr	it
Zürich (ZH)	**12749 (25%)**	-	-
Berne (BE)	4705 (9%)	469 (2%)	-
Lucerne (LU)	3124 (6%)	-	-
Uri (UR)	248 (0.5%)	-	-
Schwyz (SZ)	1408 (3%)	-	-
Obwalden (OW)	190 (0.4%)	-	-
Nidwalden (NW)	364 (0.7%)	-	-
Glarus (GL)	363 (0.7%)	-	-
Zug (ZG)	1321 (3%)	-	-
Fribourg (FR)	487 (1%)	1826 (6%)	-
Soleure (SO)	2022 (4%)	-	-
Basel-City (BS)	1651 (3%)	-	-
Basel-Country (BL)	1578 (3%)	-	-
Schaffhausen (SH)	591 (1%)	-	-
Appenzell Outer-Rhodes (AR)	73 (0.2%)	-	-
Appenzell Inner-Rhodes (AI)	103 (0.2%)	-	-
St. Gall (SG)	3188 (6%)	-	-
Grisons (GR)	1300 (3%)	-	85 (2%)
Argovia (AG)	5494 (11%)	-	-
Thurgovia (TG)	2066 (4%)	-	-
Ticino (TI)	-	-	**3302 (77%)**
Vaud (VD)	-	**8926 (29%)**	-
Valais (VS)	502 (1%)	2095 (7%)	-
Neuchâtel (NE)	-	1732 (6%)	-
Genève (GE)	-	**9320 (30%)**	-
Jura (JU)	-	630 (2%)	-
Swiss Confederation (CH)	1854 (4%)	348 (1%)	83 (2%)
uncategorized	4488 (9%)	5742 (18%)	818 (19%)

Table 4: The distribution of cantons of origin in each language subset. No entry means that this language is not spoken in that canton. The cantons are ordered in the official order determined by the Swiss Confederation (mostly based on the date of entry into the confederation). High-resource cantons (> 20% of decisions per language) are marked in bold. Low-resource cantons (< 5% of decisions per language) are underlined.

4 Methods

4.1 Baselines

We first experiment with three baselines. The first one is a *majority* baseline that selects the majority (*dismissal*) class always across cases. The *stratified* baseline predicts labels randomly, respecting the training distribution. The last baseline is a *linear* classifier relying on TF-IDF features for the 35K most frequent n-grams in the training set.

4.2 BERT-based methods

BERT (Devlin et al., 2019) and its variants (Yang et al., 2020; Liu et al., 2019; Lan et al., 2020), inter alia, dominate NLP as state-of-the-art in many tasks (Wang et al., 2018, 2019). Hence, we examine an arsenal of BERT-based methods.

Standard BERT We experimented with monolingual BERT models for German (Chan et al., 2019), French (Martin et al., 2020) and Italian (Parisi et al., 2020) and also the multilingual BERT of (Devlin et al., 2019). Since the facts are often longer than 512 tokens (see Section 3 for details), there is a need to adapt the models to long textual input.

Long BERT is an extension of the standard BERT models, where we extend the maximum sequence length by introducing additional positional embeddings. In our case, the additional positional encodings have been initialized by replicating the original pre-trained 512 ones 4 times (2048 in total). While Long BERT can process the full text in the majority of the cases, its extension leads to longer processing time and higher memory requirements.

Hierarchical BERT, similar to the one presented in Chalkidis et al. (2019), uses a shared standard BERT encoder processing segments up to 512 tokens to encode each segment independently. To aggregate all (in our case 4) segment encodings, we pass them through an additional Bidirectional Long Short-Term Memory (BiLSTM) encoder and concatenate the final LSTM output states to form a single document representation for classification.

5 Experiments

In this Section, we describe the conducted experiments alongside the presentation of the results and an analysis of the results of the German dataset in terms of diachronicity (judgment year), legal area, input (text) length and canton of origin.

5.1 Experimental SetUp

During training, we over-sample the cases representing the minority class (*approval*).[14] Across BERT-based methods, we use Early Stopping on development data, an initial learning rate of 3e-5 and batch size 64 across experiments. The standard BERT models have been trained and evaluated with maximum sequence length 512 and the two variants of BERT with maximum sequence length 2048. The 2048 input length has been chosen based on a balance between memory and compute restrictions and the statistics of the length of facts (see Section 3.4.1), where we see that the vast majority of cases contains less than 2K tokens. Additionally, this gives us the possibility to investigate differences by input (text) length (see Section 5.3.2). We report both micro- and macro-averaged F1-score on the test set. Micro-F1 is averaged across samples whereas Macro-F1 is averaged across samples inside each class and then across the classes. Therefore, a test example in

[14] In preliminary experiments, we find that this sampling methodology outperforms both the standard Empirical Risk Minimization (ERM) and the class-wise weighting of the loss penalty, i.e., considering each class loss 50-50.

Model	de		fr		it	
	Micro-F1↑	Macro-F1↑	Micro-F1↑	Macro-F1↑	Micro-F1↑	Macro-F1↑
baselines						
Majority	**80.3**	44.5	**81.5**	44.9	**81.3**	44.8
Stratified	66.7 ± 0.3	50.0 ± 0.4	66.3 ± 0.2	50.0 ± 0.4	69.9 ± 1.8	48.8 ± 2.4
Linear (BoW)	65.4 ± 0.2	52.6 ± 0.1	71.2 ± 0.1	56.6 ± 0.2	67.4 ± 0.5	53.9 ± 0.6
standard (up to 512 tokens)						
Native BERT	74.0 ± 4.0	63.7 ± 1.7	74.7 ± 1.8	58.6 ± 0.9	76.1 ± 3.7	55.2 ± 3.7
Multilingual BERT	68.4 ± 5.1	58.2 ± 4.8	71.3 ± 4.3	55.0 ± 0.8	77.6 ± 2.4	53.0 ± 1.1
long (up to 2048 tokens)						
Native BERT	76.5 ± 3.7	67.9 ± 1.8	77.2 ± 3.4	68.0 ± 1.8	77.1 ± 3.9	**59.8 ± 4.6**
Multilingual BERT	75.9 ± 1.6	66.5 ± 0.8	73.3 ± 1.9	64.3 ± 1.5	76.0 ± 2.6	58.4 ± 3.5
hierarchical (two-tier 4× 512 tokens)						
Native BERT	77.1 ± 3.7	**68.5 ± 1.6**	80.2 ± 2.0	**70.2 ± 1.1**	75.8 ± 3.5	57.1 ± 6.1
Multilingual BERT	76.8 ± 3.2	57.1 ± 0.8	76.3 ± 4.1	67.2 ± 2.9	72.4 ± 16.6	55.5 ± 9.5

Table 5: All the models have been trained and evaluated in the same language. With *Native BERT* we mean the BERT model pre-trained in the respective language. The best scores for each language are in bold. Given the high class imbalance, BERT-based methods under-perform in Micro-F1 compared to the *Majority* baseline, while being substantially better in Macro-F1.

a minority class has a higher weight in Macro-F1 than an example from the majority class. In classification problems with imbalanced class distributions (such as the one we examine), Macro-F1 is more realistic than Micro-F1 given that we are equally interested in both classes. Each experiment has been run with 5 different random seeds. We report the average score and standard deviation across experiments. The experiments have been performed on a single GeForce RTX 3090 GPU with mixed precision and gradient accumulation. We used the Hugging Face Transformers library (Wolf et al., 2020) and the BERT models available from `https://huggingface.co/models`.

5.2 Main Results

Table 5 shows the results across methods for all language subsets. We observe that the native BERT models outperform their multi-lingual counterpart; while not being domain-specific, these models can still better model the case facts. Given the high class imbalance, all BERT-based methods under-perform in Micro-F1, being biased towards *dismissal* performance compared to the naive Majority baseline, while doing substantially better in Macro-F1. Hierarchical and Long BERT-based methods consistently out-perform the linear classifiers across languages (+10% in Macro-F1), while standard BERT is comparable or better than linear models, although it considers only up to 512 tokens. While performance of BERT-based methods is quite comparable between the German and French subsets with 35K and 21K training samples respectively, it is far worse in the Italian subset, where there are only 3K training samples. In two out of three languages (German and French with 20K+ training samples) hierarchical BERT has borderline better performance compared to long BERT (+1.6-2.2% in Macro-F1), but in both cases the difference is very close to the error margin (standard deviation). We would like to remark that the results of Hierarchical BERT could possibly be improved considering a finer segmentation of the text into sentences or paragraphs.[15] We leave the investigation for alternative segmentation schemes for future work.

5.3 Discussion - Bivariate Analysis

In this section, we analyze the results in relation to specific attributes (publication year, input (text) length, legal area and canton of origin) in order to evaluate the model robustness and identify how specific aspects affect the model performance.

[15] Currently, we segment the text into chunks of 512 tokens to avoid excessive padding that will further increase the needed number of segments and will lead to even higher time and memory demands.

Legal Area			standard		long		hierarchical	
Legal Area	# cases	approval rate	Micro-F1↑	Macro-F1↑	Micro-F1↑	Macro-F1↑	Micro-F1↑	Macro-F1↑
<u>public law</u>	2587	20.6%	66.6 ± 6.2	53.1 ± 1.8	64.6 ± 6.7	53.8 ± 2.1	64.8 ± 8.1	53.7 ± 3.0
penal law	2900	21.0%	83.6 ± 1.8	74.8 ± 1.5	87.6 ± 1.6	81.1 ± 2.3	88.4 ± 1.0	82.6 ± 2.5
social law	661	19.3%	71.1 ± 4.3	65.2 ± 2.6	74.8 ± 4.0	69.1 ± 2.8	75.4 ± 3.9	69.4 ± 2.5
civil law	1574	16.5%	73.6 ± 4.8	55.5 ± 1.0	79.0 ± 3.4	65.1 ± 2.4	78.9 ± 3.8	65.9 ± 2.8

Table 6: We used the German native BERT model pre-trained and evaluated on the German data. In the German test set there are no insurance law cases and only 3 cases with other legal areas. The area where models perform best is in bold and the area where they perform worst is underlined.

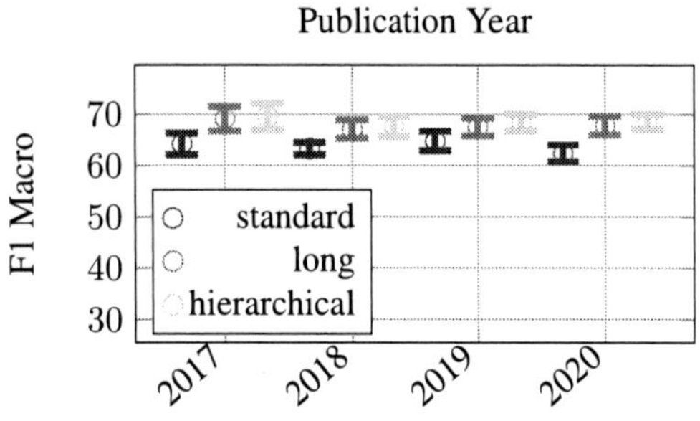

Figure 2: This table compares the different BERT types on cases from different years. We used the native German BERT model.

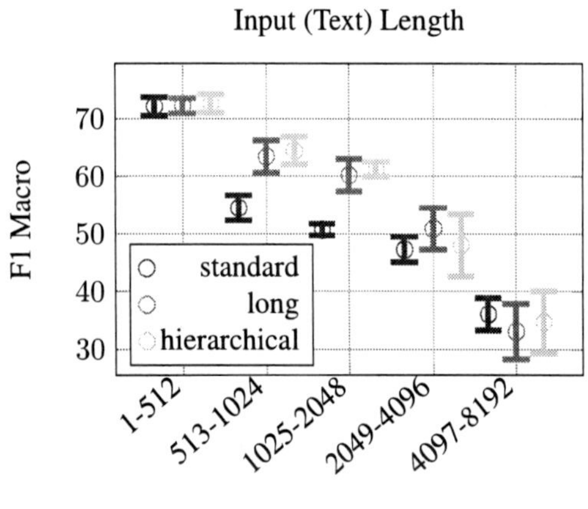

Figure 3: This table compares the different long BERT types on different input (text) lengths. We used the native German BERT model.

5.3.1 Diachronicity

In Figure 2, we present the results grouped by years in the test set (2017-2020). We cannot identify a notable fluctuation in performance across years as there is a very small decrease in performance (approx. -2% in Macro-F1); most probably because the testing time-frame is really short (4 years). Comparing the performance between the validation (2015-2016) and the test (2017-2020) set (approx. 70% vs. 68.5%), again we do not observe an exceptional fluctuation time-wise.

5.3.2 Input (Text) Length

In Figure 3, we observe that model performance deteriorates as input (text) length increases, i.e., there is an absolute negative correlation between performance and input (text) length. The two variants of BERT improve results, especially in cases with 512 to 2048 tokens. Since the two variants of BERT have a maximum length of 2048 they perform similar to the standard BERT type in cases longer than 2048 tokens.

5.3.3 Legal Area

In Table 6, we observe that the models do not equally perform across legal areas. All models seem to be much more accurate in penal law cases, while the performance is much worse (approx. 30%) in public law cases. According to the experts, the jurisprudence in penal law is more united and aligned in Switzerland and outlier judgments are rarer making the task more predictable. Additionally, in the case of not enough evidence the principle of *"in dubio pro reo"* (reasonable doubt) is applied. [16] Another possible reason for the higher performance in penal law could be the increased work performed by the legal clerks in drafting the facts of the case (see Section 3.2.1), thus including more useful information relevant to the task.

5.3.4 Canton of Origin

In Figure 4, we observe a performance disparity across cantons, although this is neither correlated with the number of cases per canton, nor with the dismissal/approval rate per canton. Thus, the disparity is either purely coincidental and has to do with the difficulty of particular cases in some cantons or there are other factors (e.g., societal, economics) worth considering in future work.

[16] The principle of *"in dubio pro reo"*, i.e., "When in doubt, in favor of the defendant.", is only applicable in penal law cases.

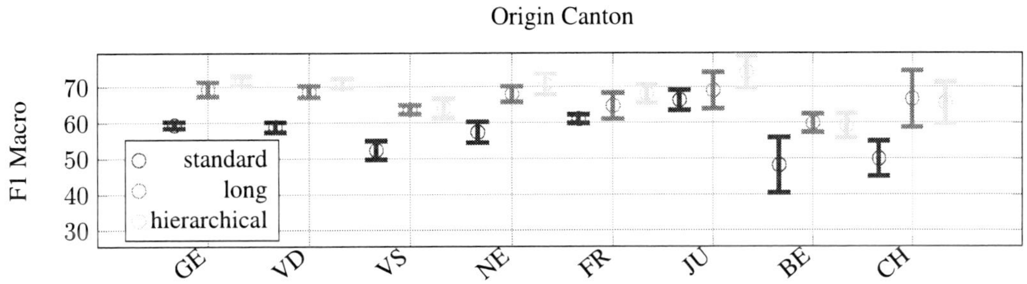

Figure 4: This table compares the different long BERT types on different origin cantons. We used the native French BERT model. The cantons are sorted by the number of cases in the training set descending.

6 Conclusions & Future Work

We introduced a new multilingual, diachronic dataset of 85K Swiss Federal Supreme Court (FSCS) cases, including cases in German, French, and Italian. We presented results considering three alternative BERT-based methods, including methods that can process up to 2048 tokens and thus can read the entirety of the facts in most cases. We found that these methods outperform the standard BERT models and have the best results in Macro-F1, while the naive majority classifier has the best overall results in Micro-F1 due to the high class imbalance of the dataset (more than $\frac{3}{4}$ of the cases are dismissed). Further on, we presented a bivariate analysis between performance and multiple factors (diachronicity, input (text) length, legal area, and canton of origin). The analysis showed that performance deteriorates as input (text) length increases, while the results in cases from different legal areas or cantons vary raising questions on models' robustness under different attributes.

In future work, we would like to investigate the application of cross-lingual transfer learning techniques, for example the use of Adapters (Houlsby et al., 2019; Pfeiffer et al., 2020). In this case, we could possibly improve the poor performance in the Italian subset, where approx. 3K cases exists, by training a multilingual model across all languages, thus exploiting all available resources, ignoring the traditional language barrier. In the same direction, we could also exploit and transfer knowledge from other annotated datasets that aim at the LJP task (e.g., ECtHR and SCOTUS).

More in depth analysis on robustness is also an interesting future avenue. In this direction, we would like to explore distributional robust optimization (DRO) techniques (Koh et al., 2021; Wang et al., 2021) that aim to mitigate disparities across groups of interest, i.e., labels, cantons and/or legal areas could be both considered in this framework.

Another interesting direction is a deeper analysis with models handling long textual input (Beltagy et al., 2020; Zaheer et al., 2020) using alternative attention schemes (window-based, dilated, etc.). Furthermore, none of the examined pre-trained models is legal-oriented, thus pre-training and evaluating such specialized models is also needed, similarly to the English Legal-BERT of Chalkidis et al. (2020).

Ethics Statement

The scope of this work is not to produce a robot lawyer, but rather to study LJP in order to broaden the discussion and help practitioners to build assisting technology for legal professionals. We believe that this is an important application field, where research should be conducted (Tsarapatsanis and Aletras, 2021) to improve legal services and democratize law, while also highlight (inform the audience on) the various multi-aspect shortcomings seeking a responsible and ethical (fair) deployment of technology. In this direction, we provide a well-documented public resource for three languages (German, French, and Italian) that are underrepresented in legal NLP literature. We also provide annotations for several attributes (year of publication, legal area, canton/region) and provide a bivariate analysis discussing the shortcomings to further promote new studies in terms of fairness and robustness (Wang et al., 2021), a critical part of NLP application in law. All decisions (original material) are publicly available on the entscheidsuche.ch platform and the names of the parties have been redacted (See Figures 5 and 6) by the court according to its official guidelines[17].

[17] https://tinyurl.com/mtu23szy (In German)

Acknowledgements

This work has been supported by the Swiss National Research Programme "Digital Transformation" (NRP-77)[18] grant number 187477. This work is also partly funded by the Innovation Fund Denmark (IFD)[19] under File No. 0175-00011A. We would like to thank: Daniel Kettiger, Magda Chodup, and Thomas Lüthi for their legal advice, Adrian Jörg for help in coding, and Entscheidsuche.ch for providing the data.

References

Nikolaos Aletras, Dimitrios Tsarapatsanis, Daniel Preoţiuc-Pietro, and Vasileios Lampos. 2016. Predicting judicial decisions of the European Court of Human Rights: a Natural Language Processing perspective. *PeerJ Computer Science*, 2:e93. Publisher: PeerJ Inc.

Julia Angwin, Jeff Larson, Surya Mattu, and Lauren Kirchner. 2016. Machine bias: There's software used across the country to predict future criminals. and it's biased against blacks. *ProPublica*.

Iz Beltagy, Matthew E. Peters, and Arman Cohan. 2020. Longformer: The Long-Document Transformer. *arXiv:2004.05150 [cs]*. ArXiv: 2004.05150.

Leo Breiman. 2001. Random forests. *Machine Learning*, 45(1):5–32.

Denny Britz. 2020. AI Research, Replicability and Incentives.

Ilias Chalkidis, Ion Androutsopoulos, and Nikolaos Aletras. 2019. Neural Legal Judgment Prediction in English. In *Proceedings of the 57th Annual Meeting of the Association for Computational Linguistics*, pages 4317–4323, Florence, Italy. Association for Computational Linguistics.

Ilias Chalkidis, Manos Fergadiotis, Prodromos Malakasiotis, Nikolaos Aletras, and Ion Androutsopoulos. 2020. LEGAL-BERT: The muppets straight out of law school. In *Findings of the Association for Computational Linguistics: EMNLP 2020*, pages 2898–2904, Online. Association for Computational Linguistics.

Ilias Chalkidis, Manos Fergadiotis, Dimitrios Tsarapatsanis, Nikolaos Aletras, Ion Androutsopoulos, and Prodromos Malakasiotis. 2021a. Paragraph-level rationale extraction through regularization: A case study on european court of human rights cases. In *Proceedings of the Annual Conference of the North American Chapter of the Association for Computational Linguistics*, online.

[18]https://www.nfp77.ch/en/

[19]https://innovationsfonden.dk/en

Ilias Chalkidis, Abhik Jana, Dirk Hartung, Michael Bommarito, Ion Androutsopoulos, Daniel Martin Katz, and Nikolaos Aletras. 2021b. LexGLUE: A Benchmark Dataset for Legal Language Understanding in English.

Ilias Chalkidis and Dimitrios Kampas. 2018. Deep learning in law: early adaptation and legal word embeddings trained on large corpora. *Artificial Intelligence and Law*, 27:171–198.

Branden Chan, Timo Möller, Malte Pietsch, Tanay Soni, and Chin Man Yeung. 2019. deepset - Open Sourcing German BERT.

C. Cortes and V. Vapnik. 1995. Support vector networks. *Machine Learning*, 20:273–297.

Jacob Devlin, Ming-Wei Chang, Kenton Lee, and Kristina Toutanova. 2019. BERT: Pre-training of Deep Bidirectional Transformers for Language Understanding. *arXiv:1810.04805 [cs]*. ArXiv: 1810.04805.

Julia Dressel and Hany Farid. 2018. The accuracy, fairness, and limits of predicting recidivism. *Science Advances*, 4(10).

Yoav Freund and Robert E Schapire. 1997. A decision-theoretic generalization of on-line learning and an application to boosting. *Journal of Computer and System Sciences*, 55(1):119–139.

Matthew Honnibal, Ines Montani, Sofie Van Landeghem, and Adriane Boyd. 2020. spaCy: Industrial-strength Natural Language Processing in Python.

Neil Houlsby, Andrei Giurgiu, Stanislaw Jastrzebski, Bruna Morrone, Quentin de Laroussilhe, Andrea Gesmundo, Mona Attariyan, and Sylvain Gelly. 2019. Parameter-efficient transfer learning for nlp. In *Proceedings of the 36th International Conference on Machine Learning (ICML)*, Long Beach, CA, USA.

Zikun Hu, Xiang Li, Cunchao Tu, Zhiyuan Liu, and Maosong Sun. 2018. Few-Shot Charge Prediction with Discriminative Legal Attributes. In *Proceedings of the 27th International Conference on Computational Linguistics*, pages 487–498, Santa Fe, New Mexico, USA. Association for Computational Linguistics.

Daniel Martin Katz. 2012. Quantitative legal prediction-or-how I learned to stop worrying and start preparing for the data-driven future of the legal services industry. *Emory Law Journal*, 62:909.

Daniel Martin Katz, Michael J. Bommarito Ii, and Josh Blackman. 2017. A general approach for predicting the behavior of the Supreme Court of the United States. *PLOS ONE*, 12(4):e0174698. Publisher: Public Library of Science.

Aaron Russell Kaufman, Peter Kraft, and Maya Sen. 2019. Improving supreme court forecasting using boosted decision trees. *Political Analysis*, 27(3):381–387.

Pang Wei Koh, Shiori Sagawa, Henrik Marklund, Sang Michael Xie, Marvin Zhang, Akshay Balsubramani, Weihua Hu, Michihiro Yasunaga, Richard Lanas Phillips, Irena Gao, Tony Lee, Etienne David, Ian Stavness, Wei Guo, Berton A. Earnshaw, Imran S. Haque, Sara Beery, Jure Leskovec, Anshul Kundaje, Emma Pierson, Sergey Levine, Chelsea Finn, and Percy Liang. 2021. WILDS: A benchmark of in-the-wild distribution shifts. In *International Conference on Machine Learning (ICML)*.

Taku Kudo and John Richardson. 2018. SentencePiece: A simple and language independent subword tokenizer and detokenizer for Neural Text Processing. *arXiv:1808.06226 [cs]*. ArXiv: 1808.06226.

Zhenzhong Lan, Mingda Chen, Sebastian Goodman, Kevin Gimpel, Piyush Sharma, and Radu Soricut. 2020. ALBERT: A Lite BERT for Self-supervised Learning of Language Representations. *arXiv:1909.11942 [cs]*. ArXiv: 1909.11942.

Shang Li, Hongli Zhang, Lin Ye, Xiaoding Guo, and Binxing Fang. 2019. MANN: A Multichannel Attentive Neural Network for Legal Judgment Prediction. *IEEE Access*, 7:151144–151155. Conference Name: IEEE Access.

Yinhan Liu, Myle Ott, Naman Goyal, Jingfei Du, Mandar Joshi, Danqi Chen, Omer Levy, Mike Lewis, Luke Zettlemoyer, and Veselin Stoyanov. 2019. RoBERTa: A Robustly Optimized BERT Pretraining Approach. *arXiv:1907.11692 [cs]*. ArXiv: 1907.11692.

Shangbang Long, Cunchao Tu, Zhiyuan Liu, and Maosong Sun. 2019. Automatic Judgment Prediction via Legal Reading Comprehension. In *Chinese Computational Linguistics*, Lecture Notes in Computer Science, pages 558–572, Cham. Springer International Publishing.

Bingfeng Luo, Yansong Feng, Jianbo Xu, Xiang Zhang, and Dongyan Zhao. 2017. Learning to Predict Charges for Criminal Cases with Legal Basis. In *Proceedings of the 2017 Conference on Empirical Methods in Natural Language Processing*, pages 2727–2736, Copenhagen, Denmark. Association for Computational Linguistics.

Louis Martin, Benjamin Muller, Pedro Javier Ortiz Suárez, Yoann Dupont, Laurent Romary, Éric Villemonte De La Clergerie, Djamé Seddah, and Benoît Sagot. 2020. CamemBERT: a Tasty French Language Model. pages 7203–7219.

Masha Medvedeva, Michel Vols, and Martijn Wieling. 2018. Judicial decisions of the European Court of Human Rights: Looking into the crystal ball. In *Proceedings of the Conference on Empirical Legal Studies*, page 24.

Tomas Mikolov, Kai Chen, Greg Corrado, and Jeffrey Dean. 2013. Efficient Estimation of Word Representations in Vector Space. *arXiv:1301.3781 [cs]*. ArXiv: 1301.3781.

Loreto Parisi, Simone Francia, and Paolo Magnani. 2020. UmBERTo: an Italian Language Model trained with Whole Word Masking. Original-date: 2020-01-10T09:55:31Z.

Jeffrey Pennington, Richard Socher, and Christopher Manning. 2014. Glove: Global Vectors for Word Representation. In *Proceedings of the 2014 Conference on Empirical Methods in Natural Language Processing (EMNLP)*, pages 1532–1543, Doha, Qatar. Association for Computational Linguistics.

Jonas Pfeiffer, Ivan Vulić, Iryna Gurevych, and Sebastian Ruder. 2020. MAD-X: An Adapter-Based Framework for Multi-Task Cross-Lingual Transfer. In *Proceedings of the 2020 Conference on Empirical Methods in Natural Language Processing (EMNLP)*, pages 7654–7673, Online.

Anna Rogers. 2021. Changing the World by Changing the Data. In *Proceedings of the 59th Annual Meeting of the Association for Computational Linguistics and the 11th International Joint Conference on Natural Language Processing (Volume 1: Long Papers)*, pages 2182–2194, Online. Association for Computational Linguistics.

Anders Søgaard, Sebastian Ebert, Jasmijn Bastings, and Katja Filippova. 2021. We need to talk about random splits. In *Proceedings of the 2021 Conference of the European Chapter of the Association for Computational Linguistics (EACL)*, Online.

Dimitrios Tsarapatsanis and Nikolaos Aletras. 2021. On the ethical limits of natural language processing on legal text. In *Findings of the Association for Computational Linguistics: ACL-IJCNLP 2021*, pages 3590–3599, Online. Association for Computational Linguistics.

Stefanie Urchs, Jelena Mitrović, and Michael Granitzer. 2021. Design and Implementation of German Legal Decision Corpora:. In *Proceedings of the 13th International Conference on Agents and Artificial Intelligence*, pages 515–521, Online Streaming, — Select a Country —. SCITEPRESS - Science and Technology Publications.

Alex Wang, Yada Pruksachatkun, Nikita Nangia, Amanpreet Singh, Julian Michael, Felix Hill, Omer Levy, and Samuel R Bowman. 2019. SuperGLUE: A Stickier Benchmark for General-Purpose Language Understanding Systems. page 30.

Alex Wang, Amanpreet Singh, Julian Michael, Felix Hill, Omer Levy, and Samuel Bowman. 2018. GLUE: A Multi-Task Benchmark and Analysis Platform for Natural Language Understanding. In

Proceedings of the 2018 EMNLP Workshop BlackboxNLP: Analyzing and Interpreting Neural Networks for NLP, pages 353–355, Brussels, Belgium. Association for Computational Linguistics.

William Yang Wang, Elijah Mayfield, Suresh Naidu, and Jeremiah Dittmar. 2012. Historical Analysis of Legal Opinions with a Sparse Mixed-Effects Latent Variable Model. In *Proceedings of the 50th Annual Meeting of the Association for Computational Linguistics (Volume 1: Long Papers)*, pages 740–749, Jeju Island, Korea. Association for Computational Linguistics.

Yuzhong Wang, Chaojun Xiao, Shirong Ma, Haoxi Zhong, Cunchao Tu, Tianyang Zhang, Zhiyuan Liu, and Maosong Sun. 2021. Equality before the law: Legal judgment consistency analysis for fairness. *Science China - Information Sciences*, abs/2103.13868.

Thomas Wolf, Lysandre Debut, Victor Sanh, Julien Chaumond, Clement Delangue, Anthony Moi, Pierric Cistac, Tim Rault, Remi Louf, Morgan Funtowicz, Joe Davison, Sam Shleifer, Patrick von Platen, Clara Ma, Yacine Jernite, Julien Plu, Canwen Xu, Teven Le Scao, Sylvain Gugger, Mariama Drame, Quentin Lhoest, and Alexander Rush. 2020. Transformers: State-of-the-Art Natural Language Processing. In *Proceedings of the 2020 Conference on Empirical Methods in Natural Language Processing: System Demonstrations*, pages 38–45, Online. Association for Computational Linguistics.

Chaojun Xiao, Haoxi Zhong, Zhipeng Guo, Cunchao Tu, Zhiyuan Liu, Maosong Sun, Yansong Feng, Xianpei Han, Zhen Hu, Heng Wang, and Jianfeng Xu. 2018. CAIL2018: A Large-Scale Legal Dataset for Judgment Prediction. *arXiv:1807.02478 [cs]*. ArXiv: 1807.02478.

Ze Yang, Pengfei Wang, Lei Zhang, Linjun Shou, and Wenwen Xu. 2019. A Recurrent Attention Network for Judgment Prediction. In *Artificial Neural Networks and Machine Learning – ICANN 2019: Text and Time Series*, Lecture Notes in Computer Science, pages 253–266, Cham. Springer International Publishing.

Zhilin Yang, Zihang Dai, Yiming Yang, Jaime Carbonell, Ruslan Salakhutdinov, and Quoc V. Le. 2020. XLNet: Generalized Autoregressive Pretraining for Language Understanding. *arXiv:1906.08237 [cs]*. ArXiv: 1906.08237.

Zichao Yang, Diyi Yang, Chris Dyer, Xiaodong He, Alex Smola, and Eduard Hovy. 2016. Hierarchical attention networks for document classification. In *Proceedings of the 2016 Conference of the North American Chapter of the Association for Computational Linguistics: Human Language Technologies*, pages 1480–1489, San Diego, California. Association for Computational Linguistics.

Hai Ye, Xin Jiang, Zhunchen Luo, and Wenhan Chao. 2018. Interpretable Charge Predictions for Criminal Cases: Learning to Generate Court Views from Fact Descriptions. In *Proceedings of the 2018 Conference of the North American Chapter of the Association for Computational Linguistics: Human Language Technologies, Volume 1 (Long Papers)*, pages 1854–1864, New Orleans, Louisiana. Association for Computational Linguistics.

Manzil Zaheer, Guru Guruganesh, Kumar Avinava Dubey, Joshua Ainslie, Chris Alberti, Santiago Ontanon, Philip Pham, Anirudh Ravula, Qifan Wang, Li Yang, et al. 2020. Big bird: Transformers for longer sequences. *Advances in Neural Information Processing Systems*, 33.

Haoxi Zhong, Zhipeng Guo, Cunchao Tu, Chaojun Xiao, Zhiyuan Liu, and Maosong Sun. 2018. Legal Judgment Prediction via Topological Learning. In *Proceedings of the 2018 Conference on Empirical Methods in Natural Language Processing*, pages 3540–3549, Brussels, Belgium. Association for Computational Linguistics.

Haoxi Zhong, Chaojun Xiao, Cunchao Tu, Tianyang Zhang, Zhiyuan Liu, and Maosong Sun. 2020. How does NLP benefit legal system: A summary of legal artificial intelligence. In *Proceedings of the 58th Annual Meeting of the Association for Computational Linguistics*, pages 5218–5230, Online. Association for Computational Linguistics.

Octavia-Maria Şulea, Marcos Zampieri, Mihaela Vela, and Josef van Genabith. 2017. Predicting the Law Area and Decisions of French Supreme Court Cases. In *Proceedings of the International Conference Recent Advances in Natural Language Processing, RANLP 2017*, pages 716–722, Varna, Bulgaria. INCOMA Ltd.

A Training Effort

Type	BERT	RoBERTa
standard	3.377E+11	3.398E+11
long	1.365E+12	1.374E+12
hierarchical	1.476E+12	1.477E+12

Table 7: This table shows the total floating point operations per epoch per training example used for training each type. Each model has been trained for 2 to 4 epochs (variable because of early stopping). This table can be used to choose a suitable model with limited resources. Additionally, it can be used to measure the environmental impact.

Table 7 shows the training effort required for finetuning each type. Training one of the types capable of handling long input results in 4 to 5 times more training operations compared to the standard model. This seems justifiable since the gain from the longer models in terms of F1 score is considerable. Also, the entire cost of finetuning is relatively small.

B Examples

In this appendix we show some examples of court decisions with their respective labels. Figure 5 shows an example of a dismissed decision and Figure 6 an example of an approved decision. Both decisions are relatively short, but still contain all sections (rubrum, facts, considerations and judgments). They are both very recent, dating from 2019 and 2017 respectively.

C Input Length Distribution

In this appendix we show the input length distributions for the German (Figure 7) and Italian (Figure 8) datasets. We observe that the average Italian decision is longer than the average German decision. Additionally, there is also a higher density in moderately long decisions (over 1000 tokens) and there are many more decisions over 4000 tokens. Apart from the availability of more training data in the German dataset, the shorter decisions may also be an important factor in the better performance we see in most models trained on the German dataset in comparison to the Italian case and to some extent the French case (see Table 5).

D Tables to Plots

In this appendix, we show tables belonging to plots in the main paper to show the exact numbers. Table 8 shows the results regarding the different input lengths. Table 9 shows the results regarding different years in the test set. Table 10 shows the model performance across different cantons.

E Training with Class Weights

In this appendix we show the results of training the models with class weights instead of oversampling. Table 11 shows the training results. We notice, that for many configurations (especially with XLM-R), the model only learns the majority classifier. This leads to a very low Macro-F1 score. We also experimented with undersampling as an alternative to oversampling, but saw similar results to the training with class weights.

F Classifier Confidence

In this appendix, we discuss the reliability of the confidence scores of the classifier output alongside the predictions. The confidence scores are computed by taking the softmax on the classifier outputs, so that we get a probability (confidence) score of a given class between 0 and 100. The hierarchical and long BERT types show an increase in both the confidence in the correct predictions and the incorrect predictions compared to the standard BERT type (with the increase in the correct predictions being more pronounced). This finding holds across all three languages.

Model	standard		long		hierarchical	
	Micro-F1↑	Macro-F1↑	Micro-F1↑	Macro-F1↑	Micro-F1↑	Macro-F1↑
1-512 (5479 decisions)	81.1 ± 2.7	72.1 ± 1.6	80.8 ± 2.5	72.2 ± 1.3	39.3 ± 37.2	25.1 ± 17.4
513-1024 (3364 decisions)	65.3 ± 6.2	65.3 ± 6.2	71.8 ± 5.4	63.4 ± 2.8	43.3 ± 30.8	30.5 ± 13.2
1025-2048 (788 decisions)	63.8 ± 4.9	50.7 ± 1.0	69.1 ± 5.4	60.2 ± 2.8	54.9 ± 26.7	37.2 ± 15.3
2049-4096 (82 decisions)	64.9 ± 6.7	47.3 ± 2.2	65.1 ± 9.2	50.9 ± 3.6	60.2 ± 13.3	48.0 ± 5.4
4097-8192 (12 decisions)	56.7 ± 7.0	36.1 ± 2.8	50.0 ± 10.2	33.1 ± 4.8	50.0 ± 11.8	34.7 ± 5.4

Table 8: Results on the German data grouped by text length. Performance deteriorates as text length is increased.

Model	standard		long		hierarchical	
	Micro-F1↑	Macro-F1↑	Micro-F1↑	Macro-F1↑	Micro-F1↑	Macro-F1↑
2017	73.9 ± 4.2	64.2 ± 2.1	77.1 ± 3.9	69.1 ± 2.4	77.4 ± 3.9	69.5 ± 2.6
2018	74.2 ± 3.8	63.3 ± 1.2	76.6 ± 3.7	67.1 ± 1.8	76.7 ± 4.0	67.6 ± 1.9
2019	74.5 ± 4.0	64.8 ± 1.9	76.0 ± 3.7	67.5 ± 1.7	76.9 ± 3.8	68.3 ± 1.6
2020	73.5 ± 4.2	62.4 ± 1.6	76.6 ± 3.4	67.8 ± 1.8	77.4 ± 3.1	68.5 ± 1.5

Table 9: We used the German native BERT model pretrained and evaluated on the German data.

Canton			standard		long		hierarchical	
Canton	# cases	approval rate	Micro-F1↑	Macro-F1↑	Micro-F1↑	Macro-F1↑	Micro-F1↑	Macro-F1↑
Berne (BE)	332	9.5%	79.4 ± 4.6	48.2 ± 7.7	78.7 ± 4.7	59.9 ± 2.6	78.5 ± 2.7	59.2 ± 3.4
Fribourg (FR)	1121	14.7%	76.7 ± 3.1	61.1 ± 1.2	75.8 ± 5.2	64.7 ± 3.6	79.5 ± 3.4	68.1 ± 2.6
Vaud (VD)	5684	17.0%	76.0 ± 1.8	58.8 ± 1.4	78.9 ± 3.0	68.7 ± 1.6	82.5 ± 1.7	71.1 ± 1.4
Valais (VS)	1399	20.6%	75.1 ± 1.0	52.4 ± 2.6	75.0 ± 2.6	63.7 ± 1.2	76.1 ± 3.3	64.0 ± 2.6
Neuchâtel (NE)	1226	14.9%	76.2 ± 3.6	57.4 ± 2.9	79.0 ± 3.9	68.0 ± 2.2	82.3 ± 2.7	70.8 ± 2.9
Genève (GE)	6017	21.8%	72.0 ± 3.1	59.4 ± 0.9	76.0 ± 3.3	69.4 ± 2.0	79.4 ± 2.3	71.8 ± 1.7
Jura (JU)	425	15.7%	80.1 ± 3.2	66.3 ± 2.8	78.9 ± 5.8	69.0 ± 5.1	83.8 ± 4.3	74.2 ± 4.5
Swiss Confederation (CH)	227	26.7%	70.0 ± 2.7	50.0 ± 4.9	72.0 ± 8.7	66.6 ± 7.9	73.3 ± 4.4	65.5 ± 5.8

Table 10: We used the French native BERT model pretrained and evaluated on the French data. The number of cases is counted on the training set per canton. The approval rate is calculated on the test set.

Model	de		fr		it	
	Micro-F1↑	Macro-F1↑	Micro-F1↑	Macro-F1↑	Micro-F1↑	Macro-F1↑
baselines						
Most Frequent	80.3	44.5	81.5	44.9	81.3	44.8
Stratified	66.7 ± 0.3	50 ± 0.4	66.3 ± 0.2	50 ± 0.4	69.9 ± 1.8	48.8 ± 2.4
Uniform	50 ± 0.3	44.8 ± 0.4	50 ± 0.6	44.5 ± 0.5	49.7 ± 2.4	44 ± 2.3
standard						
Native BERT	71.1 ± 3.3	62.6 ± 1.6	72.8 ± 5.5	58.2 ± 1.2	67 ± 13.1	49.4 ± 5.1
XLM-RoBERTa	77.8 ± 6.3	47.3 ± 6.3	76.1 ± 7.4	48.4 ± 4.9	80.4 ± 1.9	44.7 ± 0.4
long						
Native BERT	81.9 ± 1.2	**69.5 ± 0.9**	**81.8 ± 1.5**	69.4 ± 1.7	80.2 ± 1.4	46.1 ± 2.2
XLM-RoBERTa	**81.5 ± 0.7**	59.4 ± 9.6	81.5 ± 0.5	51.3 ± 8.8	81.3	44.8
hierarchical						
Native BERT	78.6 ± 2.1	69.2 ± 0.6	79.3 ± 0.8	**70 ± 0.7**	80.6 ± 1.1	**50.5 ± 6.5**
XLM-RoBERTa	80.3	44.5	80.3 ± 1.8	49.6 ± 9.8	81.3	44.8

Table 11: All the models have been trained and evaluated in the same language. With *Native BERT* we mean the BERT model pretrained in the respective language. The *Most Frequent* baseline just selects the majority class always. The *Stratified* baseline predicts randomly, respecting the training distribution. The best scores for each language are in bold. To combat label imbalance, we weighted the minority class samples more in the loss function.

Model	de		fr		it	
	Correct↑	Incorrect↓	Correct↑	Incorrect↓	Correct↑	Incorrect↓
standard	75.8 ± 13.6	64.7 ± 10.6	71.9 ± 12.2	64.4 ± 9.8	77.6 ± 12.2	68.3 ± 11.3
long	78.9 ± 12.2	65.8 ± 10.9	78.3 ± 11.6	67.8 ± 11.0	81.2 ± 11.2	68.4 ± 10.5
hierarchical	86.6 ± 15.9	69.3 ± 13.6	85.9 ± 15.2	70.8 ± 13.9	88.7 ± 14.7	71.4 ± 13.4

Table 12: This table shows the average confidence scores (0-100) of the different types of multilingual BERT models on the test set for correct and incorrect predictions respectively. Both the mean and standard deviation are averaged over 5 random seeds. The model has been finetuned on the entire dataset (all languages) and evaluated on the respective language.

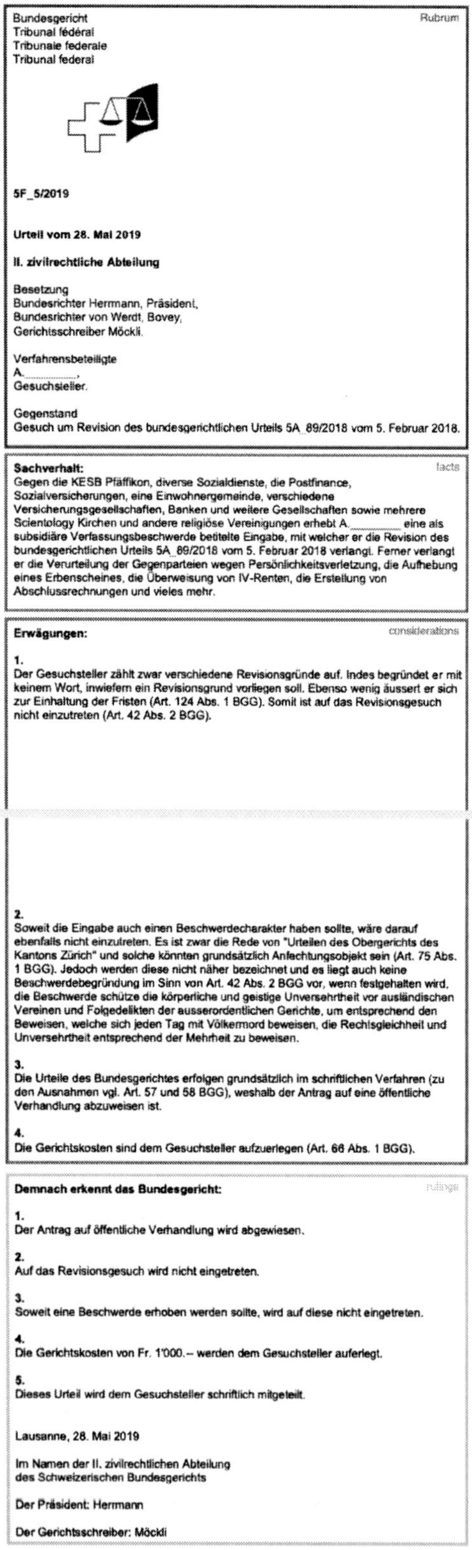

Bundesgericht
Tribunal fédéral
Tribunale federale
Tribunal federal

Rubrum

5F_5/2019

Urteil vom 28. Mai 2019

II. zivilrechtliche Abteilung

Besetzung
Bundesrichter Herrmann, Präsident,
Bundesrichter von Werdt, Bovey,
Gerichtsschreiber Möckli.

Verfahrensbeteiligte
A.________,
Gesuchsteller.

Gegenstand
Gesuch um Revision des bundesgerichtlichen Urteils 5A_89/2018 vom 5. Februar 2018.

Sachverhalt:

facts

Gegen die KESB Pfäffikon, diverse Sozialdienste, die Postfinance, Sozialversicherungen, eine Einwohnergemeinde, verschiedene Versicherungsgesellschaften, Banken und weitere Gesellschaften sowie mehrere Scientology Kirchen und andere religiöse Vereinigungen erhebt A.________ eine als subsidiäre Verfassungsbeschwerde betitelte Eingabe, mit welcher er die Revision des bundesgerichtlichen Urteils 5A_89/2018 vom 5. Februar 2018 verlangt. Ferner verlangt er die Verurteilung der Gegenparteien wegen Persönlichkeitsverletzung, die Aufhebung eines Erbenscheines, die Überweisung von IV-Renten, die Erstellung von Abschlussrechnungen und vieles mehr.

Erwägungen:

considerations

1.
Der Gesuchsteller zählt zwar verschiedene Revisionsgründe auf. Indes begründet er mit keinem Wort, inwiefern ein Revisionsgrund vorliegen soll. Ebenso wenig äussert er sich zur Einhaltung der Fristen (Art. 124 Abs. 1 BGG). Somit ist auf das Revisionsgesuch nicht einzutreten (Art. 42 Abs. 2 BGG).

2.
Soweit die Eingabe auch einen Beschwerdecharakter haben sollte, wäre darauf ebenfalls nicht einzutreten. Es ist zwar die Rede von "Urteilen des Obergerichts des Kantons Zürich" und solche könnten grundsätzlich Anfechtungsobjekt sein (Art. 75 Abs. 1 BGG). Jedoch werden diese nicht näher bezeichnet und es liegt auch keine Beschwerdebegründung im Sinn von Art. 42 Abs. 2 BGG vor, wenn festgehalten wird, die Beschwerde schütze die körperliche und geistige Unversehrtheit vor ausländischen Vereinen und Folgedelikten der ausserordentlichen Gerichte, um entsprechend den Beweisen, welche sich jeden Tag mit Völkermord beweisen, die Rechtsgleichheit und Unversehrtheit entsprechend der Mehrheit zu beweisen.

3.
Die Urteile des Bundesgerichtes erfolgen grundsätzlich im schriftlichen Verfahren (zu den Ausnahmen vgl. Art. 57 und 58 BGG), weshalb der Antrag auf eine öffentliche Verhandlung abzuweisen ist.

4.
Die Gerichtskosten sind dem Gesuchsteller aufzuerlegen (Art. 66 Abs. 1 BGG).

Demnach erkennt das Bundesgericht:

rulings

1.
Der Antrag auf öffentliche Verhandlung wird abgewiesen.

2.
Auf das Revisionsgesuch wird nicht eingetreten.

3.
Soweit eine Beschwerde erhoben werden sollte, wird auf diese nicht eingetreten.

4.
Die Gerichtskosten von Fr. 1'000.– werden dem Gesuchsteller auferlegt.

5.
Dieses Urteil wird dem Gesuchsteller schriftlich mitgeteilt.

Lausanne, 28. Mai 2019

Im Namen der II. zivilrechtlichen Abteilung
des Schweizerischen Bundesgerichts

Der Präsident: Herrmann

Der Gerichtsschreiber: Möckli

Figure 5: This is an example of a dismissed decision: `https://tinyurl.com/n44hathc`

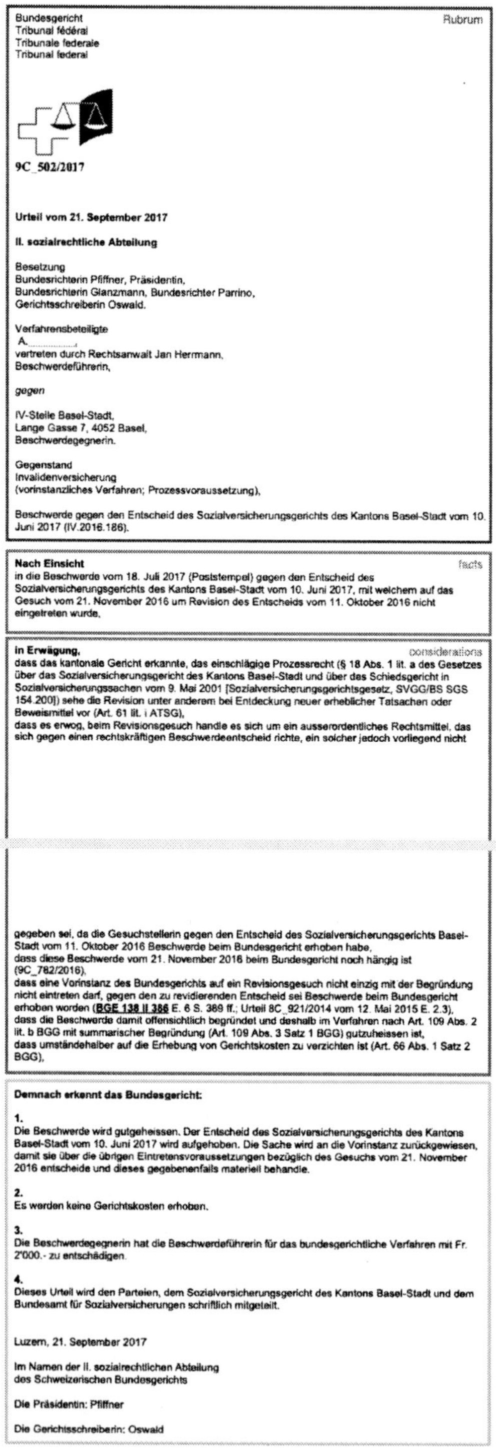

Bundesgericht
Tribunal fédéral
Tribunale federale
Tribunal federal

Rubrum

9C_502/2017

Urteil vom 21. September 2017

II. sozialrechtliche Abteilung

Besetzung
Bundesrichterin Pfiffner, Präsidentin,
Bundesrichterin Glanzmann, Bundesrichter Parrino,
Gerichtsschreiberin Oswald.

Verfahrensbeteiligte
A.________,
vertreten durch Rechtsanwalt Jan Herrmann,
Beschwerdeführerin,

gegen

IV-Stelle Basel-Stadt,
Lange Gasse 7, 4052 Basel,
Beschwerdegegnerin.

Gegenstand
Invalidenversicherung
(vorinstanzliches Verfahren; Prozessvoraussetzung),

Beschwerde gegen den Entscheid des Sozialversicherungsgerichts des Kantons Basel-Stadt vom 10. Juni 2017 (IV.2016.186).

Nach Einsicht

facts

in die Beschwerde vom 18. Juli 2017 (Poststempel) gegen den Entscheid des Sozialversicherungsgerichts des Kantons Basel-Stadt vom 10. Juni 2017, mit welchem auf das Gesuch vom 21. November 2016 um Revision des Entscheids vom 11. Oktober 2016 nicht eingetreten wurde,

in Erwägung,

considerations

dass das kantonale Gericht erkannte, das einschlägige Prozessrecht (§ 18 Abs. 1 lit. a des Gesetzes über das Sozialversicherungsgericht des Kantons Basel-Stadt und über das Schiedsgericht in Sozialversicherungssachen vom 9. Mai 2001 [Sozialversicherungsgerichtsgesetz, SVGG/BS SGS 154.200]) sehe die Revision unter anderem bei Entdeckung neuer erheblicher Tatsachen oder Beweismittel vor (Art. 61 lit. i ATSG),
dass es erwog, beim Revisionsgesuch handle es sich um ein ausserordentliches Rechtsmittel, das sich gegen einen rechtskräftigen Beschwerdeentscheid richte, ein solcher jedoch vorliegend nicht

gegeben sei, da die Gesuchstellerin gegen den Entscheid des Sozialversicherungsgerichts Basel-Stadt vom 11. Oktober 2016 Beschwerde beim Bundesgericht erhoben habe,
dass diese Beschwerde vom 21. November 2016 beim Bundesgericht noch hängig ist (9C_782/2016),
dass eine Vorinstanz des Bundesgerichts auf ein Revisionsgesuch nicht einzig mit der Begründung nicht eintreten darf, gegen den zu revidierenden Entscheid sei Beschwerde beim Bundesgericht erhoben worden (**BGE 138 II 386** E. 6 S. 389 ff.; Urteil 8C_921/2014 vom 12. Mai 2015 E. 2.3),
dass die Beschwerde damit offensichtlich begründet und deshalb im Verfahren nach Art. 109 Abs. 2 lit. b BGG mit summarischer Begründung (Art. 109 Abs. 3 Satz 1 BGG) gutzuheissen ist,
dass umständehalber auf die Erhebung von Gerichtskosten zu verzichten ist (Art. 66 Abs. 1 Satz 2 BGG),

Demnach erkennt das Bundesgericht:

1.
Die Beschwerde wird gutgeheissen. Der Entscheid des Sozialversicherungsgerichts des Kantons Basel-Stadt vom 10. Juni 2017 wird aufgehoben. Die Sache wird an die Vorinstanz zurückgewiesen, damit sie über die übrigen Eintretensvoraussetzungen bezüglich des Gesuchs vom 21. November 2016 entscheide und dieses gegebenenfalls materiell behandle.

2.
Es werden keine Gerichtskosten erhoben.

3.
Die Beschwerdegegnerin hat die Beschwerdeführerin für das bundesgerichtliche Verfahren mit Fr. 2'000.- zu entschädigen.

4.
Dieses Urteil wird den Parteien, dem Sozialversicherungsgericht des Kantons Basel-Stadt und dem Bundesamt für Sozialversicherungen schriftlich mitgeteilt.

Luzern, 21. September 2017

Im Namen der II. sozialrechtlichen Abteilung
des Schweizerischen Bundesgerichts

Die Präsidentin: Pfiffner

Die Gerichtsschreiberin: Oswald

Figure 6: This is an example of an approved decision: `https://tinyurl.com/mjxfjn65`

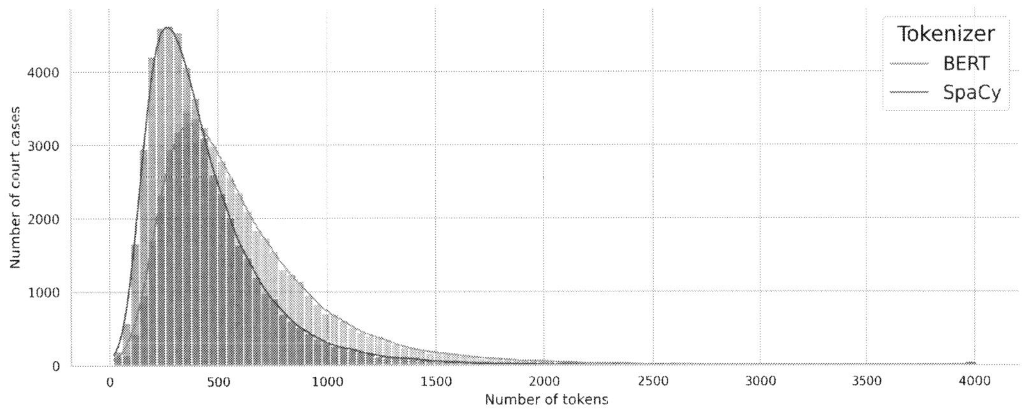

Figure 7: This histogram shows the distribution of the input length for German decisions. The blue histogram is generated from tokens generated by the spacy tokenizer (regular words). The orange histogram is generated from tokens generated by the SentencePiece tokenizer used in BERT (subword units). Decisions with length over 4000 tokens are grouped in the last bin (before 4000).

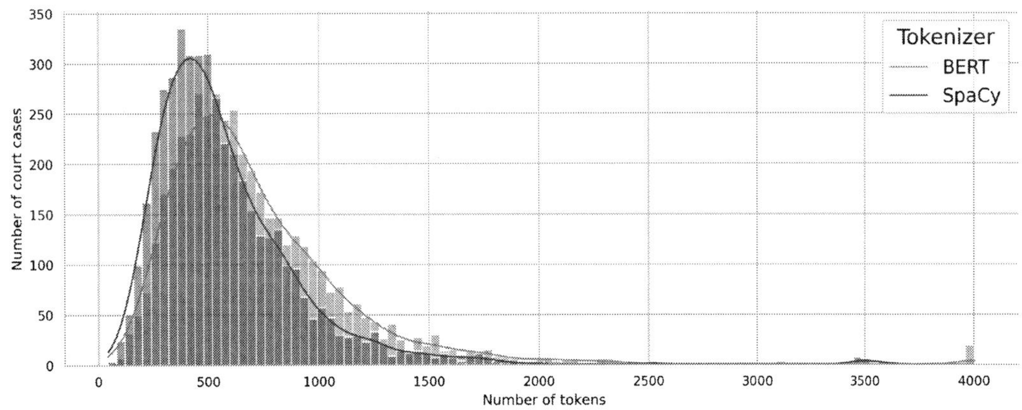

Figure 8: This histogram shows the distribution of the input length for Italian decisions. The blue histogram is generated from tokens generated by the spacy tokenizer (regular words). The orange histogram is generated from tokens generated by the SentencePiece tokenizer used in BERT (subword units). Decisions with length over 4000 tokens are grouped in the last bin (before 4000).

Automated Extraction of Sentencing Decisions from Court Cases in the Hebrew Language

Mohr Wenger[◇*] **Tom Kalir**[◇*] **Noga Berger**[♠]
[♠†]**Carmit Klar Chalamish** **Renana Keydar**[♣♡] **Gabriel Stanovsky**[◇]
[◇]School of Computer Science and Engineering [♣]Faculty of Law [♡]Digital Humanities
The Hebrew University of Jerusalem, Jerusalem, Israel
[♠] The Association of Rape Crisis Centers in Israel
[†] Department of Criminology, Conflict Resolution, Management
Negotiation Graduate Program, Bar-Ilan University, Israel
{mohr.wenger, renana.keydar, gabriel.stanovsky}@mail.huji.ac.il

Abstract

We present the task of Automated Punishment Extraction (APE) in sentencing decisions from criminal court cases in Hebrew. Addressing APE will enable the identification of sentencing patterns and constitute an important stepping stone for many follow up legal NLP applications in Hebrew, including the prediction of sentencing decisions. We curate a dataset of sexual assault sentencing decisions and a manually-annotated evaluation dataset, and implement rule-based and supervised models. We find that while supervised models can identify the sentence containing the punishment with good accuracy, rule-based approaches outperform them on the full APE task. We conclude by presenting a first analysis of sentencing patterns in our dataset and analyze common models' errors, indicating avenues for future work, such as distinguishing between probation and actual imprisonment punishment. We will make all our resources available upon request, including data, annotation, and first benchmark models.

1 Introduction

The legal world is rife with data, from constitutions and national legislation to legal cases and court decisions. Much of the legal data, however, comes in unstructured formats that pose critical challenges for extracting and analyzing it in systematic ways. In addition, different countries vary in their legal systems, norms and conventions, further compounding the challenges in developing multilingual approaches (Peruginelli, 2009).

While legal NLP is gaining traction in recent years (Van Gog and Van Engers, 2001; Dale, 2019; Zhong et al., 2020), relatively little attention has been given to low-resource settings outside of the English language, where the availability of tools such as large pretrained language models, syntactic parsers, or named entity recognizers is limited.

In this work, conducted as part of an on-going collaboration with The Association of Rape Crisis Centers in Israel (**ARCCI**), we focus specifically on the task of Automated Punishment Extraction (**APE**) in sexual assault cases in Hebrew within Israeli court sentencing decisions (see formal task definition in Section 2). Punishment decisions are of special importance as they constitute a prerequisite for many other downstream tasks in legal NLP and digital humanities, such as legal prediction of judicial decisions (Aletras et al., 2016; Branting et al., 2021) and detecting biases in court decisions (Pinto et al., 2020). APE is difficult in the Israeli court system. This is due to the fact that sentencing decisions for criminal offences are reported, in natural language idiomatic to the legal field, in the written sentencing decision. We focus on sexual assault cases due to the legal and public debate around claims of lenient punishments (Phillips and Chagnon, 2020), that in the absence of systematic rigorous data collection cannot be empirically examined and assessed. This worldwide debate requires legal NLP methods in multiple languages and legal systems.[1]

To address this challenge, we begin by curating a dataset of sexual assault sentencing decisions from the years 1990-2021 and manually annotate punishment in a subset of 100 cases with the use of legal experts in our team and in collaboration with ARCCI (Section 3). Following, in Section 4, we use this data to build several models for the APE task, including rule-based and supervised methods, based on linguistically and semantically in-

[*] Equal contribution.

[1] https://www.haaretz.com/israel-news/.premium-women-decry-lenient-rape-sentence-1.5383195, https://balkaninsight.com/2021/04/05/victims-discouraged-by-lenient-sentences-for-sex-crimes-in-serbia/.

Natural Legal Language Processing Workshop 2021, pages 36–45
November 10, 2021. ©2021 Association for Computational Linguistics

formed features, setting first benchmark results on the APE task in Hebrew. We thoroughly analyze our models' performance in Section 5, finding that they are capable of extracting the correct punishment in 68% of the cases,while the best model's average error is roughly 5 months, attesting to the difficulty of the task. Based on our models, we find that in our data the median predicted punishment is 3 years, while more than a third of the punishments are below 15 months. Although these figures are obtained on a medium-size corpus, using automatic measures which do not account for the type of offense, we note that they are well below the maximum punishments for sexual offenses as determined by the Israeli legislator, which range between 2-7 years for indecent acts and sodomy and up to 20 years for aggravated rape.

We conclude by analyzing common error patterns in our models. For example, we find that models often tend to erroneously extract a probation imprisonment punishment instead of the actual imprisonment punishment. Distinguishing between the two is left as an interesting avenue for future work. To the best of our knowledge, this is the first examination of automatic punishment extraction in the Hebrew language. It includes data collection, annotation, and benchmark models. We hope it will spur further research into this important task.

2 Task Definition

We define the task of **APE** as the process of automatically extracting the punishment from the sentencing decision. In the Israeli legal system, the punishment is given in a separate sentencing decision, following a plea bargain or a guilty verdict. In the sentencing decision, the court can impose different types of punishment: imprisonment, probation, or community service. In addition, the court can also impose fines and order the defendant to pay restitution to the victim. We consider all of the punitive elements mentioned as part of the APE process. However, in this work, we focus on the extraction of the *actual* imprisonment (i.e. jail time). Given the text of a sentencing decision, we first need to distinguish between the different types of punishment (imprisonment, probation, community work, fines, etc.); then, we need to extract only the sentence that relates the duration of the *actual* imprisonment penalty, i.e. the number of months or years in prison imposed on the defendant. This is particularly challenging since the court decision often includes both the duration of the actual imprisonment, as well as the duration of the conditional imprisonment (i.e. probation). Both are referred to in Hebrew using the same term ``Ma'asar" (lit. imprisonment), and indicated by the same units of months and years. For example (translation and emphasis by the authors):

> ``We impose on the defendant the following punishment: 48 months *imprisonment*, of which the defendant will serve 30 months actual *imprisonment* and the rest, 18 months, will be conditional *imprisonment*...(CrimC 1124/04)".

In this case, the APE task is to extract ``30 months" as the the actual imprisonment punishment. This also exemplifies the typical linguistic difficulty of the task --- The noun ``imprisonment" repeats three times, referring first to the total punishment imposed, then to the actual imprisonment, and then to the probation.

3 A Corpus of Annotated Sentencing Decisions in Israeli Law

This section describes the construction of our corpus, which to the best of our knowledge is the first annotated legal corpus of sentencing decisions in sexual assault cases in Hebrew. In Section 3.1 we discuss the cases comprising the corpus, consisting of 30 years of sentencing decisions in sexual offense cases, and in Section 3.2 we present the manual annotation schema of the different types of punishment and the duration (in months and years) of the actual or conditional imprisonment which the courts imposed in these cases.

3.1 Data Collection

We compiled a corpus containing sentencing decisions from Israel Magistrate and District Courts, from the years 1990 - 2021, as collected by Nevo legal database.[2] All the cases in the corpus deal with sexual offenses under sections 345-351 of the Israel Penal Law, 5737-1977, including offenses of rape, sodomy, indecent acts and sex offenses within the family.

[2] https://www.nevo.co.il. The data does not represent all the cases that were held in court but only those that were documented in the Nevo database.

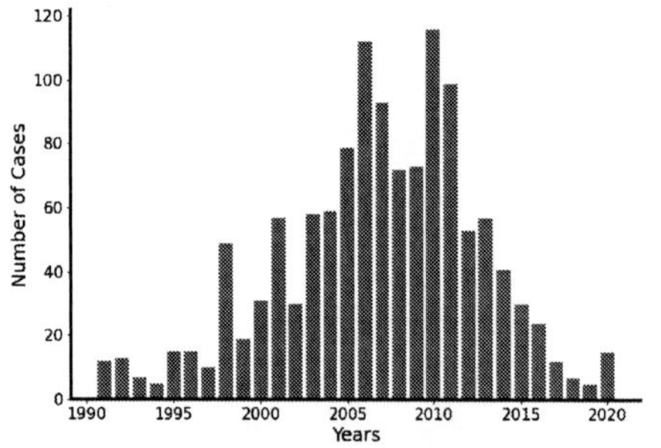

Figure 1: Distribution of legal cases in our corpus by year. The small number of cases before year 2000 is probably due to changes in digitization of legal documents.

The characteristics of our corpus are presented in Table 1 and Figure 1. This corpus, which is available upon request, directly lends itself for the quantitative exploration of sentencing and punishment patterns in sexual assault cases in the Israeli legal system, as well as for other areas of criminal law. In total this includes 1043 cases, 181k sentences and 3M words, of which we annotated a subset of 100 cases that include 13k sentences and 210k words. The sentences vary much in length with an average length of 16.5+-15.4 words in all files and 25+-16.5 words in the annotated subset.[3]

3.2 Annotation

We set out to annotate the punishment as defined in Section 2 in a sample of 100 sentencing decisions. We achieve this in two semi-automatic annotation steps as exemplified in Table 2 and elaborated below. This setup was found to be useful both in terms of the annotation quality, as well as in providing direct supervision signal for the intermediate tasks. All annotations were done by legal scholars and practitioners or under their guidance and supervision.

Imprisonment Sentence Identification. This is a sentence level, binary annotation task, as exemplified in the third column in Table 2 (labelled ``Prison [Y/N]"). We identified that the actual imprisonment is often contained within a single sentence in the decision. Sometimes this sentence also contains the conditioned punishment, for example, see Table 2, where the third row shows the verdict of 48 months imprisonment, of which 30 months are actual imprisonment and the remaining 18 are conditioned. In other cases where the actual and conditional imprisonment are in separated sentences, we were interested in the actual imprisonment. In Table 2 we see four different sentences that contain the word ``imprisonment", however only the third sentence contains the actual imprisonment imposed on the defendant. In this case it contains also the conditioned imprisonment but this is not always the case, in section 5 we will see how this affects our models' performance.

Naturally, the vast majority of sentences should be labelled negatively, as most of the sentences do not convey the punishment. To ease the annotation process, we automatically labelled as negative all sentences which did not contain a phrase from a predefined list of words indicating sentencing decisions and which were found to convey the punishment in our data. Each sentence was linked to its document, so that in cases of ambiguity we could evaluate the single sentence against the full judicial decision to reach a conclusive annotation. This resulted in negative annotation for 11.2K sentences in our dataset (85%). The remaining sentences (15%) were manually annotated with the guidance and supervision of legal scholars.

A major challenge in annotating these remaining sentences was differentiating between the punishment imposed on the defendant in this particular case and the discussion of previous punishments. For example, reference to punishments that were imposed on the defendant in previous cases or punishments that were given in similar cases which then serve to establish the punishment standard. These often use similar terminology to that of the current punishment, for example see the second row of Table 2. In other cases, a sentence containing the imprisonment in the current case is followed by a sentence which activates a previous probation. In such cases, we annotate both sentences as conveying an imprisonment.

This annotation step resulted in 132 sentences annotated positively with either actual imprisonment or probation, while the remaining 13K sentences were marked negatively, either automatically or by human experts. This annotation averaged 1.26 sentence marked positive for conveying the punishment per case, thus matching our intuition that the punishment in each decision tends to

[3]The high variance in decisions' length in the legal domain is due in part to the difficulty in segmenting legal texts, as noted by Sanchez (2019).

	Cases	Sentences	Words	Sentence Length (words)		
				Average length	Min	Max
All	1043	181K	3M	16.5[±15.4]	0	433
Annotated	100	13K	210K	25[±16.5]	3	321

Table 1: Statistics of our annotated data, referring to the full corpus as well as to the annotated subset. In both cases, each legal decision contains many sentences and the length of the decisions varies considerably.

Hebrew example	English translation	Comments	Punishment
אשר על כן, עתרה התובעת להטלת עונש מאסר בפועל על הנאשם לתקופה ממושכת, למאסר על תנאי ולפיצוי משמעותי למתלוננת.	*Therefore, the prosecution requested to impose a punishment of lengthy actual imprisonment, conditional imprisonment, and significant compensation to the victim.*	The prosecution's position on the desired punishment for the defendant. We attempt to rule it out based on the verb "request" and based on the fact that there are no numbers in this sentence.	0
כך, לדוגמא, בע"פ 1049/12, פלוני נ' מדינת ישראל, הורשע המערער בביצוע מעשה מגונה בנכדתו בת ה-9 (...) ובגין זאת הוטל עליו עונש מאסר למשך 12 חודשים, מאסר על תנאי ופיצוי בסך 40,000 ₪.	*Thus for example in CrimA 1049/12 Anon v The State of Israel the appellant was convicted of committing an indecent act on his 9-year-old granddaughter (...) and for that, he was sentenced to 12 months actual imprisonment, probation, and a fine of 40,000 NIS.*	A reference in the decision to punishments that were imposed in prior cases, usually as example for standard of punishment. We attempt to rule it out based on the past tense of the verb "was sentenced" and characters such as "/" that mark the docket number of a prior court case.	0
48 חודשי מאסר, מהם ירצה הנאשם 30 חודשי מאסר בפועל, והיתרה, 18 חודשים, תהיה על תנאי.	*48 months imprisonment, of which the defendant will serve 30 months of actual imprisonment and the rest, 18 months, in conditional imprisonment.*	Combined punishment statement consisting of an actual imprisonment and probation. We attempt to extract only the number of months of actual imprisonment [30], while ruling out the total months [48] and the probation months [18]. In cases of combined punishment, we do not rule out the sentence. One way is to check if it contains the term "and the rest", which indicates the actual imprisonment, preceding the term "and the rest"	30
עונש המאסר בפועל, יחל ביום 31.	*Actual imprisonment will start on 31.*	Procedural orders regarding the execution of the imprisonment. These are normally short sentences that include the word for imprisonment and a number (normally either date or hour), which render them very confusing for our models. In addition, in many cases they appear not as a full sentence but in fact truncated immediately after the first period due to limitations of sentence extraction. We attempt to rule them out by the fact that they do not contain a time unit.	0
תשלום קנס בשיעור 5,000 ש"ח או 30 ימי מאסר תחתיו.	*A fine of 5,000 NIS or 30 days imprisonment instead.*	A fine that is given in addition to the actual imprisonment. The fine can be substituted by a 30-day imprisonment alternative. We attempt to rule it out based on the word "fine" that does not appear in a sentence reflecting the actual imprisonment.	0

Table 2: APE annotation example, including all the sentences in which the Hebrew word for imprisonment appears. We provide an example from our data for some of the challenges of this task. We refer to some of these examples once more in the models' error analyses in Section 5. For brevity's sake we condense the two annotation phases into a single "prison time" column, which is marked zero if the sentence does not convey a punishment.

be conveyed in a single sentence.

Imprisonment Time Annotation. In the second stage, we manually annotate an integer denoting the duration (in months) of imprisonment, as exemplified in the last column in Table 2 (denoted ``Prison time"). We presented our annotators with the sentences found in the previous stage to contain an imprisonment punishment, and ask them to label the number of actual imprisonment time in months. For example, the third sentence in Table 2 is annotated with 30 months of imprisonment. Overall, punishments vary between 0 months (no actual imprisonment) to 168 months (14 years actual imprisonment). The average punishment was 32 months, and the median was 15 months.

4 Models

We present several models for predicting the imprisonment incurred in free text sentencing decisions. The high-level approach, depicted in Figure 2, is composed of two steps, following the human annotation process, described in the previous section. First, we identify sentences containing the imprisonment punishment (Section 4.1), from which we extract the term itself, and normalize to number of imprisonment months (Section 4.2).

4.1 Imprisonment Sentence Detection

First, we try to find the sentences conveying the imprisonment. We start with a keyword based approach to filter a subset of relevant sentences (e.g., the Hebrew word for imprisonment). This allows us to reduce the number of sentences per case from hundreds or even thousands to approximately 14 sentences per case on average.

Following, we aim to extract one sentence predicted to contain the imprisonment. We experiment with a rule-based approach, and several machine learning models, including SVM and random forest. In all models we use linguistic as well as structural document-level features, such as the position of the sentence within the document.

Rule-based approach. This approach consists of a scoring system for several keywords, compiled based on the authors' legal expertise. Specifically, we created four lists: two lists with strong and moderate words that indicate this is the target sentence, hence ``positive words", and two lists including strong and moderate words that indicate the sentence probably does **not** include the imprisonment decision in the case, hence ``negative words", Each of these were heuristically scored based on an held-out development set. A sentence was deemed positive if and only if its score surpasses a threshold, determined as well based on the development set. See the full details in our codebase, to be made available upon publication.

- Strong positive words: verbs that indicate the judicial decision on the punishment, such as ``sentencing", ``deciding", ``imposing" etc., all in present tense.
- Moderate positive words: include the infinitive form of the strong positive words. In Hebrew, these can be used both as past and present tense, which is why we decided to score these moderately, in case these were used to refer to past decisions, which the judge uses to establish the punishment standard.
- Moderate negative words: characters such as brackets and backslash that indicate a reference to a docket number, usually of a previous legal case.
- Strong negative words: Hebrew words relating a request or petition brought before the court regarding the desired punishment, usually by one of the sides, as opposed to the final judicial decision which is an order of the court.

Supervised modeling. This approach consists of using features similar to the rule-based approach, and experimenting with different machine learning techniques for determining their weights. This is divided to two stages: *Stage 1* - identifying punishment sentences by assigning probabilities and choosing all sentences above a threshold. *Stage 2* - extracting a single sentence in each document, which includes the actual imprisonment, since our final goal is extracting the number of imprisonment months. For this we perform an argmax over the probabilities assigned by the model:

$$M(D) = \arg\max_{s \in D} P_{\theta_M}(s)(1)$$

Where D is a legal case, composed of a list of sentences s, M denotes different models whose weights are denoted with θ_M, and $M(D)$ is the predicted sentence from case D according to model

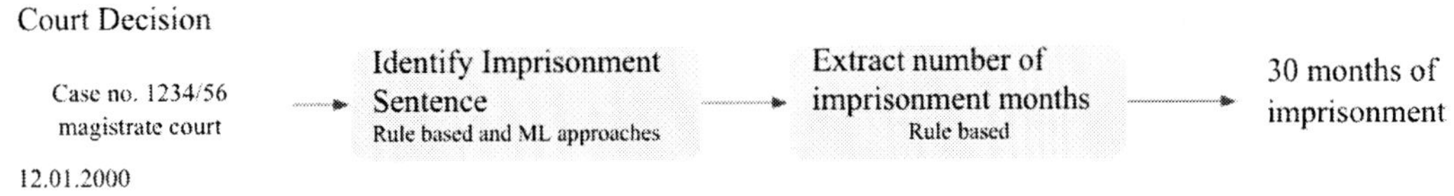

Figure 2: High-level diagram of our models for extracting duration of imprisonment from court decisions (left) to imposed punishment (right). We begin by identifying candidate sentences for containing the imprisonment (Section 4.1), followed by an extraction of the imprisonment term, in months (Section 4.2).

M. Within this framework, we compare two models: support vector machine (**SVM**; Cortes and Vapnik 1995) and random forest (**RF**; Ho 1995), both trained and tested using cross-validation on the annotated subset.

4.2 Extracting the number of months of imprisonment

After identifying a candidate sentence for imprisonment, we implement the following pipeline to extract the number of months of imprisonment incurred.

Identifying numbers in Hebrew. First, we identify all candidate numbers in the sentence. To achieve this we use a regular expression for each digit, as well as rules for converting multiple-digit numbers.

The Hebrew number, similar to English, has a basic form that appears if it is between 0 - 10, an indicator for if it is between 10-20 and a slightly different form for if it is a multiplication of ten (i.e., twenty, thirty). However, there are also several differences that pose challenges unique to Hebrew:

- *Suffixes that are range dependant* - we introduced different rules to account for Hebrew morphology in different number ranges.
- *One year/ One month punishment can be deduced only by elimination* - Hebrew does not have a non-specific determiner, so a punishment of one year for example can be phrased as ``year of imprisonment", without a time unit (``one") or a determiner. Similarly, for any number above twenty, it is accepted in Hebrew to mention the time unit in single form rather than plural form (``20 year"). We overcome this challenge by using elimination for determining the found time unit was an indicator for 1 year / 1 month.

Model	Sent F1	APE F1	Avg Err (Months)
Rule-based	**0.68**	**0.65**	**5**
RF	0.61	0.58	11.6
SVM	0.54	0.5	10

Table 3: Full task evaluation using the sentences extracted by the different models. It shows that in the overall task the rule based models achieved the highest accuracy and also the lowest average distance from the ground truth of actual imprisonment (manually tagged).

- *Spelling variation* - Spelling in Hebrew often varies due to its treatment of vowels, which are sometimes indicated with diacritics (Niqqud), or omitted altogether (Ravid and Haimowitz, 2006). To address this, we account for all the possible vowels and syllable combination for all digits.

Identifying the imprisonment duration. Following, we aim to find the number that indicates the length of actual imprisonment. First, we checked the following heuristic - is this sentence of the form ``The total sentence of Z units of time, which consists of X actual imprisonment time and Y conditioned imprisonment" (see row 3 of table 2), if so, we return the value X. This was done by checking if there are exactly three numbers mentioned, and if Z=X+Y. If that is in fact the case, then we return X as the actual imprisonment. Otherwise, we created a scoring method, which looks for certain features, such as the distance between the number and some time unit indicator such as ``years" or ``months", or the distance between the number and the end of the document. This was also locally assessed, i.e. there was no absolute threshold and the number with the best score within each sentence was chosen.

5 Evaluation

In this section we analyze the performance of the models described in section 4 in the different

Model	Recall	Precision	F1
SVM	0.9	0.86	0.88
RF	1	0.8	0.89

Table 4: A comparison between the first stage of the supervised approaches in their ability to identify the sentence that includes the punishment. Note this is the ability to extract 2 - 5 sentences of which only one is correct, for the full APE task we need to choose the correct one.

stages of the task. The main results are presented in Table 3. In addition, we examine supervised model performance on sentence identification in Table 4, perform manual error analysis in Table 5, and plot punishment trends on the entire corpus in Figure 1. We draw several conclusions based on these results.

The supervised models present high accuracy in the sentence identification task. Both supervised models in Table 4 show high recall in tagging the sentences which convey the imprisonment. However, they also tag some additional false positive sentences, hence decreasing the precision rate. In total, this results in between 2 and 5 sentences tagged as positive in each document.

The supervised models' probability is not well-calibrated. The APE task requires choosing one sentence from which the number of months of actual imprisonment is extracted in the next stage. This means that for each false positive sentence there is exactly one equivalent false negative. Hence, in our case precision equals recall. In the rule-based approach we noticed that a different threshold applies for each legal case, hence we scored them separately. Our assumption was that the supervised models would score similar features to those used in the rule-based in a more accurate way. Thus we attempted a similar local threshold approach, by performing argmax on the learner probability of all sentences from the same legal case, as defined in Equation 1. However this was not the case, as observed in Table 3, the rule-based approach achieves better results in extracting a single sentence and also in extracting the actual imprisonment time. This points to the supervised models' probability not being calibrated, perhaps due to the low resrouce domain and small number of samples.

All models tend to confuse probation with actual imprisonment. Error analysis in Table 5 shows that the most common error was extracting a sentence with the probation rather than the actual imprisonment. We remind that ``probation" in Hebrew is phrased ``conditional imprisonment", which may lead to this confusion. In many cases, probation and actual imprisonment are pronounced in one sentence. In other cases, the probation directly follows the pronouncement of the actual imprisonment, and has similar syntactic and semantic cues.

Other error patterns. Rule-based and RF errors are similar, containing mostly references from past cases. This type of error includes sentencing decisions either of similar crimes or past cases of the defendant (see Table 2, row 2). These sentences are similar in structure to those reflecting the actual imprisonment, and also confused legal expert annotators. In contrast, SVM errs on extracting sentences describing fines (accompanied by an alternative of imprisonment) or procedures regarding the execution of the incurred imprisonment rather than sentences reflecting actual imprisonment duration. While those cases include a number and the Hebrew word for imprisonment, they are easily ruled out by human annotators. Both learners use this word as a feature, however SVM still makes mistakes classifying fines.

Inter-annotator agreement reveals the limitations of the sentence-level approach. We asked legal experts to evaluate the rule-based performance by rating each sentence that the rule-based model predicted as whether it reflects the actual imprisonment or not. This is the same task the models were required to perform. We used Cohen's kappa to measure the inter annotators agreement for each pair, presented at table 6 and Fleiss' kappa (Fleiss, 1971) for measuring the level of agreement between five different annotators and three different classes (sentence is indicative of punishment/is not indicative of punishment/cannot decide). The annotators achieved a score of 0.341 which is considered a fair agreement (Viera et al., 2005). On average the taggers managed to correctly find the actual imprisonment in 79% of the sentences. In many cases the annotators expressed doubt regarding their ability to tag the sentence as the actual imprisonment solely based on the single sentence extracted by the algo-

Error Type	% of examined cases RB	SVM	RF	Example (English Translation)
Probation	36%	37.5%	**65%**	*In addition, 18 months probation.*
Ref to prev. case	**46%**	-	18%	*Sentenced to 12 months actual imprisonment.*
Fines	-	**27.5%**	-	*A fine of 5,000 NIS or 30 days imprisonment instead.*
Procedural	-	**17.5%**	-	*Imprisonment starts at 31.*

Table 5: Error analysis for all three models (Rule-Based, Support-Vector Machine, and Random Forest). We used for imprisonment sentence detection. Sentences that contain probation are the only common cause for errors in all models. In both supervised approaches they are also responsible for the highest percent of errors. For the rule based we observe that references to past cases were more confusing, this was also confusing for the manual tagging task. In total the RF and rule based were more similar in their error analysis than the SVM. The remaining errors for each classifier did not fall under a common category and could be generally defined as miscellaneous.

	ann1	ann2	ann3	ann4	ann5
ann1	-	0.13	0.46	0.36	0.34
ann2	0.13	-	0.14	0.31	0.42
ann3	0.46	0.14	-	0.48	0.34
ann4	0.36	0.31	0.48	-	0.63
ann5	0.34	0.42	0.34	0.63	-

Table 6: Agreement between each pair of annotators in terms of Cohen's Kappa. The 5-way agreement between all annotators is 0.341 Fleiss' kappa.

rithm, without the context of the full judicial decision. This suggests a limit to the ability to determine whether a sentence from a legal document contains an actual imprisonment time, without the larger document context.

There is room for improvement in extracting the actual imprisonment sentence. Table 3 demonstrates the different models' performances in the full APE task. In this case, the rule-based approach performs best with an average error of 5 months, while supervised models reach an average error of 10-11.6 months. This table also shows how sentence extraction accuracy alone does not predict the ability to succeed in APE task. This is also affected by the type of mistakes, i.e. when the wrong sentence is predicted, the number of months extracted is not directly related to the actual imprisonment. However, given the correct sentence, extracting the duration of imprisonment was accurate in 89.7% of the cases. Therefore improvements could be achieved by better extraction of the actual imprisonment sentence. Future work may consider separately tagging the probation sentence, as its structure might be easier for the model to learn. Once learned, it could be used as an anchor. This problem could also benefit from employing contextualized representations such as adapting a Hebrew language model, such as Alephbert (Seker et al., 2021) to the legal domain, an approach recently shown effective in English (Chalkidis et al., 2020).

A post-hoc summary of the legal decision improves performance. Nevo, the legal database we use, provides a ``mini ratio", a post-hoc summary of each decision in a few sentences, written by Nevo's editorial team. When we add this mini ratio to the annotation, it increases the supervised models' ability to extract the target sentence by about 50%, showing that shorter inputs lead to better generalization on small-scale datasets.

Identifying sentencing patterns in sexual assault cases in Israel. Using our best performing model, we present rough statistics regarding the punishments given in the past thirty years in Figure 3. The median sentenced punishment throughout all legal decisions of our data is 36 months, however we observe most commonly punishments are under a year. While the sentencing decisions are generally available in legal search engines, annotating them is an expensive process. For this reason many statistical observations are hard to obtain. This demonstrates the potential contribution of our task from a socio-legal point of view.

6 Related Work

Most related to our work are those that bring together domain expertise with ML models to extract information from specialized texts. This is the case for Soh et al. (2019) who showed that conditional random fields perform better than DNN for sentence border detection for the legal domain. While this is considered a closed problem in NLP they showed that this is not the case for legal texts.

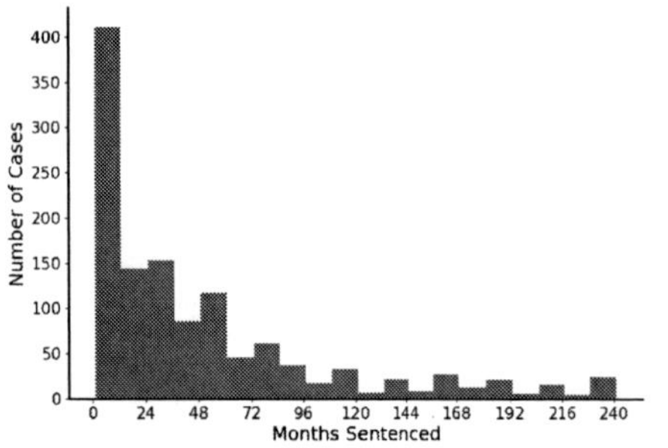

Figure 3: The distribution of predicted punishments in our corpus. These were extracted using our rule-based model which performed best on this task. Median predicted punishment is 3 years, while more than a third of the punishments are below 15 months.

Similar paradigms can be found in the medical field, where domain knowledge also plays a crucial role. Malmasi et al. (2019) show that in some cases a rule-based approach achieves better performances than SVM. Chalkidis et al. (2020) recently introduced a language model fine-tuned superficially for the English legal domain. Taking a similar approach for the APE task is an interesting avenue for future work.

7 Conclusions

In this work we created the first annotated corpus of Hebrew language sentencing decisions, focusing on sexual assaults. We compared a rule-based approach with supervised learners using the unique attributes of the legal language for representing sentences. We found that the rule-based approach achieved best results with an average error rate of 5 months and accuracy of 68% in extracting the punishment sentence. Our analysis shows that such research could focus on fine tuning of the supervised models. While supervised learning models help us narrow down a full legal document to 2 - 5 sentences that include the punishment, further research can contribute in reaching a single target sentence, which could also benefit from our error analysis, especially regarding the probation sentences, perhaps targeting them separately in a prior task and using them as features.

Acknowledgments

We thank the anonymous reviewers for their helpful comments and feedback. This work was supported in part by a research gift from the Allen Institute for AI and by a research grant from the Center for Interdisciplinary Data Science Research (CIDR) at the Hebrew University of Jerusalem.

References

Nikolaos Aletras, Dimitrios Tsarapatsanis, Daniel Preoţiuc-Pietro, and Vasileios Lampos. 2016. Predicting judicial decisions of the european court of human rights: A natural language processing perspective. *PeerJ Computer Science*, 2:e93.

L Karl Branting, Craig Pfeifer, Bradford Brown, Lisa Ferro, John Aberdeen, Brandy Weiss, Mark Pfaff, and Bill Liao. 2021. Scalable and explainable legal prediction. *Artificial Intelligence and Law*, 29(2):213--238.

Ilias Chalkidis, Manos Fergadiotis, Prodromos Malakasiotis, Nikolaos Aletras, and Ion Androutsopoulos. 2020. Legal-bert: The muppets straight out of law school. *arXiv preprint arXiv:2010.02559*.

Corinna Cortes and Vladimir Vapnik. 1995. Support-vector networks. *Machine learning*, 20(3):273--297.

Robert Dale. 2019. Law and word order: Nlp in legal tech. *Natural Language Engineering*, 25(1):211--217.

Joseph L Fleiss. 1971. Measuring nominal scale agreement among many raters. *Psychological bulletin*, 76(5):378.

Tin Kam Ho. 1995. Random decision forests. In *Proceedings of 3rd international conference on document analysis and recognition*, volume 1, pages 278--282. IEEE.

Shervin Malmasi, Wendong Ge, Naoshi Hosomura, and Alexander Turchin. 2019. Comparison of natural language processing techniques in analysis of sparse clinical data: insulin decline by patients. *AMIA Summits on Translational Science Proceedings*, 2019:610.

Ginevra Peruginelli. 2009. Accessing legal information across boundaries: a new challenge. *International Journal of Legal Information*, 37(3):276--305.

Nickie D Phillips and Nicholas Chagnon. 2020. "six months is a joke": Carceral feminism and penal populism in the wake of the stanford sexual assault case. *Feminist criminology*, 15(1):47--69.

Alexandra Guedes Pinto, Henrique Lopes Cardoso, Isabel Margarida Duarte, Catarina Vaz Warrot, and Rui Sousa-Silva. 2020. Biased language detection in court decisions. In *Intelligent Data Engineering and Automated Learning -- IDEAL 2020*, pages 402--410, Cham. Springer International Publishing.

Dorit Ravid and Sarit Haimowitz. 2006. The vowel path: Learning about vowel representation in written hebrew. *Written Language & Literacy*, 9(1):67--93.

George Sanchez. 2019. Sentence boundary detection in legal text. In *Proceedings of the Natural Legal Language Processing Workshop 2019*, pages 31--38, Minneapolis, Minnesota. Association for Computational Linguistics.

Amit Seker, Elron Bandel, Dan Bareket, Idan Brusilovsky, Refael Shaked Greenfeld, and Reut Tsarfaty. 2021. Alephbert:a hebrew large pre-trained language model to start-off your hebrew nlp application with.

Jerrold Soh, How Khang Lim, and Ian Ernst Chai. 2019. Legal area classification: A comparative study of text classifiers on Singapore Supreme Court judgments. In *Proceedings of the Natural Legal Language Processing Workshop 2019*, pages 67--77, Minneapolis, Minnesota. Association for Computational Linguistics.

R. Van Gog and T.M. Van Engers. 2001. Modeling legislation using natural language processing. In *2001 IEEE International Conference on Systems, Man and Cybernetics. e-Systems and e-Man for Cybernetics in Cyberspace (Cat.No.01CH37236)*, volume 1, pages 561--566 vol.1.

Anthony J Viera, Joanne M Garrett, et al. 2005. Understanding interobserver agreement: the kappa statistic. *Fam med*, 37(5):360--363.

Haoxi Zhong, Chaojun Xiao, Cunchao Tu, Tianyang Zhang, Zhiyuan Liu, and Maosong Sun. 2020. How does nlp benefit legal system: A summary of legal artificial intelligence. *arXiv preprint arXiv:2004.12158*.

A Multilingual Approach to Identify and Classify Exceptional Measures Against COVID-19

Georgios Tziafas[1], **Eugenie de Saint-Phalle**[2], **Wietse de Vries**[3],
Clara Egger[2] and **Tommaso Caselli**[3]
1. Artificial Intelligence 2. IRIO 3. CLGC
University of Groningen
g.tziafas@student.rug.nl,
{e.de.saint-phalle|wietse.de.vries}@rug.nl
{c.m.egger|t.caselli}@rug.nl

Abstract

The COVID-19 pandemic has witnessed the implementations of exceptional measures by governments across the world to counteract its impact. This work presents the initial results of an on-going project, EXCEPTIUS, aiming to automatically identify, classify and compare exceptional measures against COVID-19 across 32 countries in Europe. To this goal, we created a corpus of legal documents with sentence-level annotations of eight different classes of exceptional measures that are implemented across these countries. We evaluated multiple multi-label classifiers on a manually annotated corpus at sentence level. The XLM-RoBERTa model achieves highest performance on this multilingual multi-label classification task, with a macro-average F1 score of 59.8%.

1 Introduction

The increasing availability of digitized and publicly available legal documents has boosted political scientists, legal scholars, lawyers and policy-makers to apply Human Language Technologies (HLT) to discover, analyze, digest, and use automatically extracted information. All of these operations fall under the larger area of study that can be labeled as Legal Artificial Intelligence, or LegalAI (Zhong et al., 2020). Similarly to any domain that wants to apply HLT to process written documents, LegalAI requires the development of both domain-specific languages resources (e.g., annotated corpora or embedding representations (Chalkidis et al., 2019c; Kornilova and Eidelman, 2019; Holzenberger et al., 2020; Luz de Araujo et al., 2020; Samy et al., 2020)) and tools (e.g., language specific natural language processing pipelines (Koeva et al., 2020; Moreno-Schneider et al., 2020) or pretrained language models (Chalkidis et al., 2020)). At the same time, LegalAI presents an additional challenge when it comes to the development of multilingual systems. With very few exceptions (e.g., EU-level legislation), in the domain of LegalAI, natural languages are strictly connected to countries, meaning that different legislative systems and practices may be in place. For instance, although French-speaking countries share a common language, their legal traditions widely differ making comparisons across legal systems uneasy. Nevertheless, the adoption of a multilingual approach may prove valuable especially to legal practitioners and scholars as well as political scientists and policy-makers who are increasingly interested in comparing legal systems and examining how legal concepts "travel" across time and spaces. Commonly used data collection and analysis techniques - largely relying on manual or rule-based coding of legal documents - have so far prevented the development of meaningful and systematic analyses allowing the comparison of fine-grained classes.

In this paper we investigate the potential of multilingual pretrained language models in order to facilitate the analysis, exploration, and comparison of legal texts on COVID-19 exceptional measures. Our major contributions can be summarised as follows:

- the creation of a **new corpus** of legislative documents from 21 European countries manually annotated for exceptional measures against COVID-19 (Sections 2 and 3);
- the development of a **rich taxonomy** (eight classes and 83 subclasses) to identify and compare exceptional measures in a consistent way (Sections 4);
- the development of a **multi-label classifier** based on XLM-RoBERTa (Conneau et al., 2019) to identify exceptional measures at sentence level (Section 5).

2 The Exceptional Measures Against COVID-19 in Europe

The COVID-19 pandemic has led governments around the world to take exceptional measures

Natural Legal Language Processing Workshop 2021, pages 46–62
November 10, 2021. ©2021 Association for Computational Linguistics

in order to contain the spread of the virus. Such exceptional decision-making has seen executives challenge the scope and legality of their powers, as well as impose restrictions on democratic processes, the rule of law, fundamental rights and civil liberties. These exceptional measures considerably vary from one country to another, even in cases where some forms of coordination are claimed to be in place, like in the European Union. Countries sharing close political culture and institutions reacted in contrasting ways, as attested by the sharp difference between the Belgian and Dutch responses to the crisis between March and June 2020. While the Dutch government implemented one of the softest approaches in Europe relying on people's compliance with governmental recommendations, Belgium introduced very early a strict lockdown. This diversity is not only practical but also semantic. While many countries relied on a "lockdown" to contain the spread of the virus, restrictions vary in scope while enforcement modalities are unequally coercive (Engler et al., 2021; Egger et al., 2021). This fragmented political response sparked interest from researchers in political science, economics, and law that started to trace exceptional decision-making in times of COVID-19 (Porcher, 2020; Hale et al., 2021). To the best of our knowledge, all current data collection efforts are based on manual or rule-based methods applied to press releases (Hopkins and King, 2007; Grimmer and Stewart, 2013; Wiedemann, 2013; Wettstein, 2014) or on experts survey. Yet, in the specific case of the COVID-19, such methods suffer from three core limitations:

Decisions were taken on different legal bases There is a variety of legislative tools that have been put in action across countries to counteract the spreading of the virus. Some governments activated crisis-management instruments and legal frameworks, including, but not limited to, the activation of state of emergency provisions (Bjørnskov and Voigt, 2021) that predate the crisis. Others took decisions in an *ad hoc* manner on the basis of executive, legal or administrative acts taken not only at the national but also at the subnational level.

Measures evolved quickly At least for the first wave of the COVID-19 (late January - June 2020), measures evolved on a weekly, and sometimes, on a daily basis, requiring researchers to handle a very large amount of constantly evolving textual data. Since the application of close reading methods (i.e., extensive manual annotation) to such a large amount of documents is a daunting task to perform over a reasonable period of time, most of the competing research teams opted for collecting data on broad classes of events (lockdown, border closure, state of emergencies) based on press releases, conferences or experts opinions. The lack of fine grained classes derived from legal texts provides a false impression of homogeneity between various governmental responses, especially in a context of semantic ambiguity about the measures used.

Different countries, multiple languages Being a pandemic, the COVID-19 emergency affected the entire world. This global condition is accompanied by a rich and diverse language composition of any corpus created to investigate and compare the legislative measures of different countries. The intrinsic multi-lingual nature of this corpus has raised additional challenges for coding methods traditionally used in social sciences. Only a few legal texts are translated in English and some national languages are spoken by a fairly limited number of people.

Against such a background, we have initiated a research project, EXCEPTIUS (Exceptional measures in times of COVID-19) [1] to collect and document metrics of exceptionalism in 30 countries of the European Economic Area (EEA), plus UK and Switzerland, starting from late January 2020. EXCEPTIUS intends to address the abovementioned challenges in the analysis of COVID-19 measures in three ways. First, measures are automatically captured from a homogeneous corpus of legal sources uniquely allowing researchers to analyse the diversity of the legal instruments used to contain the COVID-19 pandemic. Press releases or expert surveys commonly used in competing projects only capture such dimensions indirectly and imperfectly. Second, our project defines the most comprehensive taxonomy of exceptional measures in the field of democratic governance, the rule of law and fundamental rights and liberties. The automatic application of such taxonomy to a comprehensive legal corpus allows to conciliate the need to rely on fine-grained categories with the constraints deriving from the analysis of a large and constantly evolving corpus. Last, we adopt a

[1] For a description of the research project and initial results, see https://exceptius.com/

multi-lingual approach to automatically analyse the sources of COVID-19 legislation, limiting the bias associated with the translations of the original texts in English.

The reliance on multi-lingual methods adopts a philosophical perspective of Artificial Intelligence (AI) as a problem-solving tool rather than as an adaptive mechanism mimicking human abilities (Winograd, 1997; Auernhammer, 2020; Caselli et al., 2021). The "intelligent" systems developed in this project (see Section 5) do not aim at substituting humans but are designed to account for different development cycles *with* humans in the loop. The use of automatic methods based on HLT allows us to overcome in a smart and fast way the three challenges previously described.

3 Corpus Collection

The corpus collection process has been overseen by four political science experts working in partnership with national legal experts. All documents were retrieved from official governmental websites that publish legal acts. The identification of the relevant documents has been done by means of 4 keywords (i.e., "COVID", "COVID-19", "Coronavirus" and "Health emergency"). For each language, the corresponding language specific keywords were used. In this initial phase, we focus on a sample of 19 EEA countries on measures adopted at the national level. To do so, we identify publicly available links to relevant documents [2] plus UK and Switzerland. We could not find corresponding documents for two countries of the EEA (i.e., Bulgaria and Greece). All documents have been collected either by manually downloading them or by automatic scraping.[3] For countries with more than one official language (e.g., Switzerland), legal acts were collected in all available languages.[4]

A total of 6,449 documents has been collected and stored in text format so far. Documents form a homogeneous set of existing COVID-19 legislation. Such legislation however includes a variety of texts adopting by political authorities acting at different levels. Beside legal acts - adopted by national parliaments - the corpus also includes executive acts - adopted by governmental authorities which were granted exceptional powers during the COVID-19 crisis - and administrative acts which mainly specifies how the implementation modalities of measures adopted by parliaments and governments. The distribution of the documents per country varies greatly: from 9 on the federal level in Germany to 969 in Slovenia, with 212.5 being the median. These differences are mainly due to a variability across the countries concerning the institutional levels responsible for taking actions against the spread of COVID-19: for example, the low number of German documents reflects the fact that the *Länder* were responsible for enacting COVID-related measures. We further process all documents using the SpaCy UDPipe 2 NLP pipeline[5] (Straka and Straková, 2017) using models trained on the Universal Dependencies project (Nivre et al., 2016, 2020). Although the UDPipe models may be sub-optimal for processing legal documents, the availability of models and unified representations (i.e., same sets of labels for parts-of-speech tagging and dependency relations) for all the languages of the corpus is an advantage. The SpaCy UDPipe 2 pipeline successfully processed 6,049 documents, providing sentence splitting, tokenization, part-of-speech tagging, and dependency relations. Not processed documents are due to issues in the text format due to the conversion process from pdf or other formats. An full overview of the processed data is reported in Table A.1 in Appendix A.

The corpus covers 17 languages, 16 belonging to the Indo-european family and one to the Uralic family (i.e., Hungarian). The length of the documents is a dimension of variation among the countries, dependent mostly on different archival practices across the countries. Some countries include only the changes to legal acts, while others combine the original text and the changes. A further peculiarity concerns the levels of detail that accompany the modalities of the measures taken, with some countries being very precise and others addressing the issue in a much broader manner. These dissimilarities can be observed by looking at the average number of sentences per country / per language. Countries such as Switzerland, Latvia, Slovenia, and Czechia appear to have the longest documents

[2] The EEA countries are: Austria, Belgium, Croatia, Cyprus, Czechia, Denmark, France, Germany, Hungary, Ireland, Italy, Latvia, Lithuania, Netherlands, Poland, Sweden, and Spain.

[3] All scripts, corpus, annotated data, and system(s) are available at `https://github.com/tommasoc80/COVID19_emergency_event`

[4] Belgium is an exception: we could collect only documents in French.

[5] `https://spacy.io/universe/project/spacy-udpipe`

Class Id	Class Label	# Subclasses	Example
E1	State of Emergency	18	*A restriction or requirement imposed under paragraph (1)— (a)by the Secretary of State may be varied (orally or in writing) by the Secretary of State;*
E2	Restrictions of fundamental rights and civil liberties	5	*The conditions or measures which may be specified under paragraph (2)(d) include (b)a restriction on P's activities;*
E3	Restrictions of daily liberties	10	*Where paragraph (2) applies, the Secretary of State or, as the case may be, registered public health consultant may impose on or in relation to P one or more screening requirements.*
E4	Closures / lockdown	15	*During the emergency period, no person may participate in a gathering which— (b)takes place indoors,*
E5	Suspension of international cooperation and commitments	6	*We are also working urgently to ensure international governments have sensible plans to enable the return of British and other travelers and, crucially, that they keep borders open for enough time to allow people to return home on commercial flights.*
E6	Police mobilization	14	*∗Controls will be carried out by police and municipal police.*
E7	Army mobilization	9	*∗Operation Resilience mobilizes the military and civilian personnel of all the armies, [...] who contribute to the fight against the spread of the COVID-19 epidemic in three main areas*
E8	Government oversight	6	*[The Scottish Ministers must] (a) take account of any information about the nature and number of incidents of domestic abuse occurring during the reporting period to which the review relates given to them*

Table 1: Overview of the exceptional measures' classes, including the associated number of subclasses. Examples 1–5 and 8 are extracted from UK legislative documents; examples 7 and 6, marked with an ∗, are translations from a French legislative document.

(with an average number of sentences per document ranging between 803.26 for Swiss documents in French to 525.13 for Czechia). On the other hand, Croatia, France, Italy, Norway, Hungary, Belgium, Denmark, Germany, Austria, and Sweden have the shortest documents with an average of 36.95 sentences per document, with Croatia being the shortest (3.98 sentences per document) and Ireland the longest (72.35 sentences per document). All remaining countries have lengths ranging between 129.75 sentences (Spain) and 397.16 (Cyprus).

The current corpus consists of 18,714,750 tokens. Variation in the number of tokens is quite spread, with Slovenia having more than 4 millions tokens and Norway only 6,037, followed by Germany with 12,011 tokens. Aggregating per language [6] changes the distribution of the data, leaving Norwegian as the least represented language, followed by Lithuanian with 42,761 tokens. In this setting, seven languages have more than 1 million tokens (French, Slovene, Latvian, Greek, English, Dutch, and Spanish). At this point, two remarks deserve to be made about our corpus. First, although comprehensive, our corpus is relatively small and its limited size may negatively impact the quality of subsequent analyses. We are aware of this limitation and intend to address it in future work. Second, and while the size of the documents varies per country, our corpus includes relatively short documents when compared to other types of legislation. This may be due to the specific nature of the issue at stake as COVID-19 containment measures were taken in an ad hoc, fragmented nature and were often not based on pre-existing crisis-management legislation.

4 Annotating Exceptional Measures

The identification of the exceptional measures has been conducted by applying a taxonomy of 8 classes. Note that, although the overall project focuses on a large range of subclasses, the size of the corpus and the dispersion of the subclasses in the initial phase of project presented in this paper did not allow to annotate documents at the subclass level.

Defining the taxonomy A multidisciplinary Scientific Board of 8 experts in comparative politics,

[6] Besides some inherent differences, the varieties of German used in Switzerland, Austria and Germany have been lumped together; the same has been done for French in Switzerland, France, and Belgium, English in Ireland and United Kingdom, and Italian for Italy and Switzerland.

Country	# Docs.	# Sent.	Exceptional Classes								No Class
			E1	E2	E3	E4	E5	E6	E7	E8	
Belgium	41	1,307	97	59	108	124	4	7	0	15	10,042
France	43	465	81	118	129	197	17	2	26	4	3,146
Hungary	6	95	0	1	2	3	0	1	0	0	753
Italy	72	928	66	94	126	211	1	7	1	31	6,887
Netherlands	11	171	0	0	12	58	0	0	0	0	2,153
Norway	18	277	13	6	40	58	31	0	23	5	2,040
Poland	20	95	22	6	17	34	0	1	4	5	671
UK	70	807	205	50	110	100	9	0	0	126	5,880
total	281	4,145	484	334	541	785	62	18	54	186	31,573

Table 2: Manual annotation: overview of the number of documents, sentences, and exceptional classes per country. *No Class* indicates the overall number of cases when a class is assigned the label 0.

crisis-management policies, public health, comparative law and human right law from five EU countries identified the eight classes and 83 subclasses that compose the taxonomy. The classes and their subclasses have been identified by applying both top-down and bottom-up methods. In particular, this was done by reviewing similar annotation initiatives (Cheng et al., 2020; Porcher, 2020; Hale et al., 2021) and by manually analyzing a random sample of 50 documents from the corpus. The sample contains at least one document per country. Table 1 illustrates the eight classes, the associated number of subclasses, and one example.[7] The classes cover key measures and variations in the level of coercion used in their implementation. Gathering data on implementation modalities is crucial to capture differences in policy styles that may be hidden between the use of the same term to refer to COVID-19 policy responses.

Annotating the measures A subset of 281 documents in eight languages has been selected for manual annotation. The annotation of the exceptional measures applies at sentence-level. The sample is based on the French, Polish, Dutch, English, Hungarian, Belgian, Italian, and Norwegian subcorpora. Annotators were allowed to assign as many subclasses as they consider relevant to each sentence, but with a total of eight main classes of exceptional measures. Sentences can potentially entail multiple exceptional classes, making this a multi-label annotation task. The annotation process results in eight binary annotations per sentence, with 0 if the specific class is not identified within the sentence and 1 if it is.The annotation has been conducted by three experts in political science working under the supervision of the project's Scientific Board. Since the annotators are not fluent in all languages and due to the impossibility of recruiting expert native speakers, some documents need to be translated[8] into English to be manually annotated. No inter-annotator agreement study has been conducted in this initial phase. We intend to remedy this limitation in the project's next development cycle. However, during the annotation phase, annotators met on a weekly basis to discuss ambiguous cases and the guidelines. Annotators are encouraged to propose new classes or subclasses. For a new (sub)class to be accepted, the measure should have been independently identified by the majority of the annotators. In this phase, no new classes were proposed.

Table 2 summarizes the results of the manual annotation. Differences across countries affects the distribution of the exceptional classes. Most sentences are mapped to one class only, making the absence of any measure (i.e., the 0 label) by far the most frequent. This is expected given the peculiar structure and style of legal texts. The variation in the distribution of the exceptional classes affects both the presence of specific classes in some countries and their frequency. For instance, France is the only country where all exceptional classes are present (although with varying frequencies); the Netherlands is the country with the fewest classes (only two, namely E3, indicating restrictions of daily liberties, and E4, regulating closures/lockdown); finally, Hungary is the country with the least amount of mentions of measures,

[7]The full list of the subclasses is presented in Appendix C.

[8]We used the Google Translate API.

Split	# Sent.	Exceptional Classes							
		E1	E2	E3	E4	E5	E6	E7	E8
Train	3,312	383	253	412	617	52	15	45	146
Dev	418	54	39	71	74	4	2	4	21
Test	418	47	42	62	93	6	1	5	19

Table 3: Data distributions for the train, dev and test splits.

with only seven annotations. In general, the most frequent classes are E3 and E4, while E6 and E7, involving police and army involvement respectively, are the least frequent. Although partial, the manual annotation already provides an indication of the difference and similarities of how different countries and political systems reacted to COVID-19.

5 Experiments

We have run a set of experiments to develop a tool to support the work of political scientists and other scholars to analyse the large amount of documents in the corpus. In this paper, we present the first development cycle of this tool that targets the automatic identification of the exceptional measures at class level. We opted for this setting mainly due to the low amount of positive instances and the sparseness of the subclass annotation. In particular, we investigate an array of machine learning algorithms distinguishing between feature-based (Section 5.1) and model-based (Section 5.2). The goal is to identify which approach works best for this task. Following the annotation method, the task is framed as a multi-label sentence classification task. Given the distribution of the manually annotated data per language and country, we opted to experiment directly using a multi-lingual setting. We report in Table 3 the split of the data into training, development, and test that we used for our experiments. Full details of the data distribution per country and per language is presented in Table A.2 in Appendix B

5.1 Feature-based Methods

We adopt a standard method for sentence representation, akin to the *Bag of Embeddings (BoE)* paradigm (Jin et al., 2016). In particular, we extract features from the input text to embed each sentence and use a shallow learning architecture for classifying it to (possibly more than one) related exceptional class. Representations include:

N-grams We extract *Term Frequency — Inverse Document Frequency (TF-IDF)* features based on both word and character n-grams, with $n \in \{2, ..., 5\}$ for words and $\{3, 7\}$ for characters. We deal with the sparsity of the resulting features by applying *Latent Semantic Analysis (LSA)*, by decomposing the n-gram feature matrix into its truncated singular value components (Halko et al., 2010). The overall feature extraction - decomposition pipeline transforms each sentence of our input text to a single dense vector.

Word Embeddings We utilize a multilingual version of the pretrained GloVe word vectors (Pennington et al., 2014; Ferreira et al., 2016). Word vectors from each sentence are aggregated using average pooling in order to provide a single vector representation for the sentence.

Feature vectors from both methods are concatenated and used as input to a classifier, which is trained on our supervised corpus using the sum of eight parallel binary cross-entropy losses, one per exceptional class, as to accommodate the potential existence of all classes within the same sentence. We experiment with three classifiers, namely: i) a *Support Vector Machine (SVM)* with a linear kernel, ii) a *Multi-Layered Perceptron* (MLP) with a single hidden layer and iii) a bi-directional *Gated Recurrent Unit (GRU)* neural network encoder (Chung et al., 2014) that contextualizes the input sentence before concatenating with the LSA-based feature vector and passing to the classifier. This latter method operates directly on GloVe embeddings, serving as a trainable alternative to the simple average pooling strategy used in the first two bagging approaches. For training the neural methods we use the `AdamW` optimizer (Kingma and Ba, 2017; Loshchilov and Hutter, 2017), and select hyperparameters after performing grid-search. Resulting values are: learning rate of 10^{-3}, dropout probability 0.25, weight decay of 10^{-2}, MLP hidden size of 128, GRU hidden size of 150, 100 LSA components and an early stop patience of 3 epochs. We perform model selection based on the performance in the development set, using averaged F1-score as the target metric for early stopping and report results on the test set.

5.2 Model-based Methods

In this second experiment setting, we initially followed the standard approach of fine-tuning a Transformer-based Language Model (TLM) on the annotated data. After experimenting with a range of multilingual models, we report the results of the best model, namely XLM-RoBERTa (Conneau et al., 2019). We fine-tuned XLM-RoBERTa using the `AdamW` optimizer with a learning rate of 3×10^{-5} and weight decay of 10^{-2}. Similar to the word-embedding setting, we train using a binary-cross entropy per output objective, and report results on the test set after selecting models according to their F1-score performance in the development set.

Besides obtaining state-of-the-art performances, it is known that generic TLMs suffer when applied to domains different from the one(s) used to train them. Different solutions have been proposed to address this issue, including creating new TLMs from scratch (Lee et al., 2020; Beltagy et al., 2019), using domain- or task-adaptive pretraining (Gururangan et al., 2020a; Chalkidis et al., 2020; Rietzler et al., 2020), and, more recently, developing modular domain experts (Gururangan et al., 2021). Given the peculiarity of the task and the domain of the texts, we explore the potential effectiveness of adding an intermediate training step in the performance of the language model in the downstream classification task, aiming at first adapting the pretrained language model to the domain before fine-tuning. We thus further pre-train XML-RoBERTa using the entire collection of document composing the corpus (i.e, 6,649; Section 3). We replicate the XLM-RoBERTa pretraining process, applying the same random chances for masking and making sure that continuous spans of part-word tokens are mutually masked. We split our dataset into train-dev-test splits using $80 - 10 - 10\%$ of the documents per country (with a minimum of 2 documents for each split) and train with a masked language modeling *(MLM)* objective. The dev split has been used to select the best further trained model. We use a batch size of 16, and train for a maximum of 36 epochs, where the MLM loss saturates. Once the newly adapted model has been generated, we repeat the fine-tuning and evaluation step that we applied for the generic XLM-RoBERTa model.

6 Results

Comparative results for the supervised multi-label classification task for all methods are presented in Table 4. We evaluate against several sentence and word-level multi-label metrics and include results from a dummy baseline that always predicts negative existence of exceptional classes for all samples. We followed an evaluation approach similar to *Named Entity Recognition (NER)*, where only the positive classes are evaluated. The high accuracy metrics in the dummy case showcase the under-representation of positive classes, further highlighting the challenge of the task. However, it is apparent that all learning methods greatly aid in modeling the task, with the best performing method being the XLM-RoBERTa language model. Although marginal, the better performance of the further trained model (row *XLM(pre@36)* in Table 4) suggests the potential effectiveness of this technique.

We further evaluate the best system, *XLM(pre@36)*, for its language adaptation capacity by performing a series of zero-shot experiments. In particular, we fine-tune the XLM-RoBERTa models using the manually annotated training data from all countries/languages except one that is used for testing. With this experiment we want to identify whether our multilingual model is capable of learning cross-lingual concepts that are general enough to successfully detect the measures in new languages. This is also a strategy to check the expected performance of the trained models on the not-annotated documents of the corpus. The results of this experiment (presented in Table 5) highlight the intrinsic challenge of multilingual knowledge transfer across legal domains: even though sharing linguistic information, each country is very much bound to the specifics of their legal system. This is mostly evident in the results for Belgium and France, where even though both datasets are in French and comparable in size (see Table 2), individual scores are higher than 60% only when country specific training material is added. However, we observe that on average the zero-shot performance is on par with the feature-based baselines, hinting towards the benefits of incorporating such a multilingual zero-shot system

Model	Accuracy		Hamming Loss		F1-Score	Precision	Recall
	all(%)	events(%)	all(%)	events(%)	(%)	(%)	(%)
dummy	51.4	0.0	92.2	84.0	–	–	0.0
SVM	68.1	39.5	95.0	90.3	37.2	29.5	50.8
MLP	60.6	24.7	94.0	88.4	25.7	18.5	50.4
Bi-GRU	62.2	40.0	93.8	89.7	46.6	42.1	51.1
XLM(no-pre)	69.2	54.6	95.5	**93.5**	59.2	**62.6**	60.0
XLM(pre@36)	**71.3**	**57.7**	**95.6**	93.4	**59.8**	55.9	**62.8**

Table 4: Comparative performance of all baselines for the supervised multi-label document classification task. We report sentence and event-level (hamming) accuracy (%), as well as F1-score, precision and recall, averaged across all classes after computed independently for each of the eight binary classification tasks.

Country	F1-Score		Precision		Recall	
	zero(%)	train(%)	zero(%)	train(%)	zero(%)	train(%)
Belgium	43.7	**72.0**	55.9	**84.9**	36.6	**64.5**
Poland	58.3	**58.3**	53.3	**53.3**	66.7	**66.7**
France	31.8	**81.8**	27.0	**82.9**	39.3	**84.7**
Italy	33.5	**58.0**	43.1	**64.6**	36.9	**56.7**
Netherlands	20.6	**55.0**	37.5	**62.5**	23.6	**50.0**
Norway	15.5	**41.4**	13.5	**40.5**	18.9	**47.7**
UK	38.4	**69.0**	42.3	**69.5**	37.0	**70.4**
average	34.5	**62.2**	38.9	**65.6**	37.0	**62.9**

Table 5: F1-score, Precision, and Recall for the zero-shot (*zero*) and full fine-tuning (*train*) of the domain adapted XLM-RoBERTa model for each individual country in the manually annotated data. Hungarian documents are excluded due to their very limited size and number of positive class examples. Exceptional classes that are absent from the test split of some countries are disregarded from the calculation of the average.

in a human-in-the-loop co-annotation scenario, serving as a draft analysis that human experts can iterate over in future development cycles of the system.

7 Related Work

LegalAI has a longstanding tradition with early works dating back from the 1960s (Kort, 1957; Ulmer, 1963) and has seen the development of a variety of tasks ranging from the development of domain specific ontologies and lexica (Breukers and Hoekstra, 2004; Lame, 2005; Peters et al., 2007; Bonin et al., 2010; Francesconi et al., 2010), to automatic classification of legislative documents (Bartolini et al., 2004; Moens et al., 2007; Gonçalves and Quaresma, 2005; de Maat et al., 2010; Chalkidis et al., 2019b; Soh et al., 2019), automatic summarization (Farzindar and Lapalme, 2004; Galgani et al., 2012; Polsley et al., 2016; Feijo and Moreira, 2019), court judgment predictions (Zhong et al., 2018; Ye et al., 2018; Chalkidis et al., 2019a; Medvedeva et al., 2020), legal entities detection and classification (Cardellino et al., 2017; Leitner et al., 2020), and question answering systems (Taniguchi and Kano, 2016; Delfino et al., 2018; Kien et al., 2020).

Most of current work is embedded in the paradigm of Deep Learning, using embedding representations, neural networks or large pre-trained language models. The emergence of Deep Learning has been accompanied by a growth in specialized embedding representations for the legal domain. Similarly to other areas of applications of HLT, the legal domain has seen two waves of embedding methods. The first is has seen the application of static methods (e.g., `Word2Vec`, `GloVe`, `FastText`, `Doc2Vec`, a.o.) based on characters, words, or even documents (Ash and Chen, 2017;

Chen and Ash, 2019; Chalkidis and Kampas, 2019; Kayalvizhi et al., 2019; Noguti et al., 2020) and their integration in neural network architectures. The second wave has seen the development of contextualized representations and the generation of domain-specific transformer based language models (Chalkidis et al., 2020). Our work is related to this second wave of embedding representations, in particular, by using a generic multilingual pre-trained model such as XLM-RoBERTa. On the contrary, rather than creating domain specific and multilingual language models from scratch, we applied Task Adaptive Pretraining (TAP) on the line of Gururangan et al. (2020b) to the generic XLM-RoBERTa as a strategy to boost early domain adaptation.

Similarly to previous work, we perform an Information Extraction task framed as classification problem at sentence level. Neill et al. (2017) introduces a sentence classification task aiming at extracting different modalities from financial legislative document in English. Modality plays a pivotal role in order to distinguish between what is permitted, prohibited, obliged. They are able to achieve an F1 score of .79 using a BiLSTM model and combining an ensemble of domain specific and generic word embedding representations based on `Word2Vec`. Chalkidis et al. (2018) improves along different dimensions including a more powerful Bi-LSTM system, a larger dataset, and the use of more fine-grained classes. Other works have applied the same task to sentences in German tenancy law (Waltl et al., 2017), and US and Italian regulations (Kiyavitskaya et al., 2008).

Other works have focused on the extraction of contract elements (Chalkidis et al., 2017) or text classification (Sulea et al., 2017; Wei et al., 2018; Chalkidis et al., 2019b). To the best of our knowledge, we have identified limited previous work on multilingual or cross-lingual applications to the legal domain (Galassi et al., 2020; Chalkidis et al., 2021). In this respect, in our work the multilingual dimension plays a pivotal role in the development of our approach. Given the homogeneity of the topic of the legislative documents taken into account (i.e., COVID-19 legislation), the multilingual dimension has been exploited to account for the limited amount of manually annotated documents in each language and country.

8 Conclusion and Future Work

In this paper, we have presented a new corpus and a taxonomy to identify exceptional measures implemented to counteract the COVID-19 emergency across 21 countries. A subset of the corpus (281 documents, 4,145 sentences) has been manually annotated. The data have been successfully applied to develop a fist version of a classifier based on a domain-adapted multi-lingual language model (XLM-RoBERTa) to support experts in investigation of the measures and their impact in the society. Besides the relatively small size of the training data, the final score of the system (F1 score 59.8) indicates promising applicability at the final stage of the project.

In the future, we plan to develop the project in two directions. First, we will extend the corpus to include additional countries/languages and extend the data to the regional/municipal levels. This will allow us to further adapt XLM-RoBERTa. Active learning methods can be adopted to boost the annotation process, leveraging on the fine-tuned models to auto-tag and manually review documents in batches to accelerate the annotation process. Second, we plan to develop a fine-grained version of the classifier to include the taxonomy's subclasses. Finally, we wish to further study the predictions of the classification system in the unsupervised data and identify potential cross-lingual keywords and/or topics that relate to each exceptional class separately.

Acknowledgments

This work is part of the EXCEPTIUS project, financed by Dutch Organization for Health Development and Research (ZonMw, project number: 10430032010026).

References

Elliott Ash and Daniel L Chen. 2017. Judge embeddings: Toward vector representations of legal belief. Technical report, Technical report.

Jan Auernhammer. 2020. Human-centered ai: The role of human-centered design research in the development of ai. In *Synergy - DRS International Conference 2020*, Online. Design Research Society.

Roberto Bartolini, Alessandro Lenci, Simonetta Montemagni, Vito Pirrelli, and Claudia Soria. 2004. Automatic classification and analysis of provisions in italian legal texts: a case study. In *OTM Confederated*

International Conferences" On the Move to Meaningful Internet Systems", pages 593–604. Springer.

Iz Beltagy, Kyle Lo, and Arman Cohan. 2019. SciBERT: A pretrained language model for scientific text. In *Proceedings of the 2019 Conference on Empirical Methods in Natural Language Processing and the 9th International Joint Conference on Natural Language Processing (EMNLP-IJCNLP)*, pages 3615–3620, Hong Kong, China. Association for Computational Linguistics.

Christian Bjørnskov and Stefan Voigt. 2021. This time is different?—on the use of emergency measures during the corona pandemic. *European Journal of Law and Economics*, pages 1–19.

Francesca Bonin, Felice Dell'Orletta, Giulia Venturi, and Simonetta Montemagni. 2010. Singling out legal knowledge from world knowledge. an nlp–based approach. In *Proceedings of the 4th Workshop on Legal Ontologies and Artificial Intelligence Techniques*, pages 39–50.

Joost Breukers and Rinke Hoekstra. 2004. Epistemology and ontology in core ontologies: Folaw and lricore, two core ontologies for law. In *Proceedings of the Workshop on Core Ontologies in Ontology Engineering (EKAW04)*.

Cristian Cardellino, Milagro Teruel, Laura Alonso Alemany, and Serena Villata. 2017. Legal NERC with ontologies, Wikipedia and curriculum learning. In *Proceedings of the 15th Conference of the European Chapter of the Association for Computational Linguistics: Volume 2, Short Papers*, pages 254–259, Valencia, Spain. Association for Computational Linguistics.

Tommaso Caselli, Roberto Cibin, Costanza Conforti, Enrique Encinas, and Maurizio Teli. 2021. Guiding principles for participatory design-inspired natural language processing. In *Proceedings of the 1st Workshop on NLP for Positive Impact*, pages 27–35, Online. Association for Computational Linguistics.

Ilias Chalkidis, Ion Androutsopoulos, and Nikolaos Aletras. 2019a. Neural legal judgment prediction in English. In *Proceedings of the 57th Annual Meeting of the Association for Computational Linguistics*, pages 4317–4323, Florence, Italy. Association for Computational Linguistics.

Ilias Chalkidis, Ion Androutsopoulos, and Achilleas Michos. 2017. Extracting contract elements. In *Proceedings of the 16th edition of the International Conference on Articial Intelligence and Law*, pages 19–28.

Ilias Chalkidis, Ion Androutsopoulos, and Achilleas Michos. 2018. Obligation and prohibition extraction using hierarchical RNNs. In *Proceedings of the 56th Annual Meeting of the Association for Computational Linguistics (Volume 2: Short Papers)*, pages 254–259, Melbourne, Australia. Association for Computational Linguistics.

Ilias Chalkidis, Emmanouil Fergadiotis, Prodromos Malakasiotis, Nikolaos Aletras, and Ion Androutsopoulos. 2019b. Extreme multi-label legal text classification: A case study in EU legislation. In *Proceedings of the Natural Legal Language Processing Workshop 2019*, pages 78–87, Minneapolis, Minnesota. Association for Computational Linguistics.

Ilias Chalkidis, Emmanouil Fergadiotis, Prodromos Malakasiotis, and Ion Androutsopoulos. 2019c. Large-scale multi-label text classification on EU legislation. In *Proceedings of the 57th Annual Meeting of the Association for Computational Linguistics*, pages 6314–6322, Florence, Italy. Association for Computational Linguistics.

Ilias Chalkidis, Manos Fergadiotis, and Ion Androutsopoulos. 2021. Multieurlex – a multi-lingual and multi-label legal document classification dataset for zero-shot cross-lingual transfer.

Ilias Chalkidis, Manos Fergadiotis, Prodromos Malakasiotis, Nikolaos Aletras, and Ion Androutsopoulos. 2020. LEGAL-BERT: The muppets straight out of law school. In *Findings of the Association for Computational Linguistics: EMNLP 2020*, pages 2898–2904, Online. Association for Computational Linguistics.

Ilias Chalkidis and Dimitrios Kampas. 2019. Deep learning in law: early adaptation and legal word embeddings trained on large corpora. *Artificial Intelligence and Law*, 27(2):171–198.

Daniel L Chen and Elliott Ash. 2019. Case vectors: spatial representations of the law using document embeddings. *Law as Data*, 11.

Cindy Cheng, Joan Barceló, Allison Spencer Hartnett, Robert Kubinec, and Luca Messerschmidt. 2020. Covid-19 government response event dataset (coronanet v. 1.0). *Nature human behaviour*, 4(7):756–768.

Junyoung Chung, Çaglar Gülçehre, KyungHyun Cho, and Yoshua Bengio. 2014. Empirical evaluation of gated recurrent neural networks on sequence modeling. *CoRR*, abs/1412.3555.

Alexis Conneau, Kartikay Khandelwal, Naman Goyal, Vishrav Chaudhary, Guillaume Wenzek, Francisco Guzmán, Edouard Grave, Myle Ott, Luke Zettlemoyer, and Veselin Stoyanov. 2019. Unsupervised cross-lingual representation learning at scale. *CoRR*, abs/1911.02116.

Emile de Maat, Kai Krabben, and Radboud Winkels. 2010. Machine learning versus knowledge based classification of legal texts. In *Legal Knowledge and Information Systems*, pages 87–96. IOS Press.

Pedro Delfino, Bruno Cuconato, Guilherme Paulino Passos, Gerson Zaverucha, and Alexandre Rademaker. 2018. Using openwordnet-pt for question answering on legal domain. In *Proceedings of the 9th Global Wordnet Conference*, pages 105–112.

Clara Marie Egger, Raul Magni-Berton, Sebastian Roché, and Kees Aarts. 2021. I do it my way: Understanding policy variation in pandemic response across europe. *Frontiers in Political Science*, 3:17.

Sarah Engler, Palmo Brunner, Romane Loviat, Tarik Abou-Chadi, Lucas Leemann, Andreas Glaser, and Daniel Kübler. 2021. Democracy in times of the pandemic: explaining the variation of covid-19 policies across european democracies. *West European Politics*, pages 1–22.

Atefeh Farzindar and Guy Lapalme. 2004. Legal text summarization by exploration of the thematic structure and argumentative roles. In *Text Summarization Branches Out*, pages 27–34.

Diego Feijo and Viviane Moreira. 2019. Summarizing legal rulings: Comparative experiments. In *Proceedings of the International Conference on Recent Advances in Natural Language Processing (RANLP 2019)*, pages 313–322, Varna, Bulgaria. INCOMA Ltd.

Daniel C. Ferreira, André F. T. Martins, and Mariana S. C. Almeida. 2016. Jointly learning to embed and predict with multiple languages. In *Proceedings of the 54th Annual Meeting of the Association for Computational Linguistics (Volume 1: Long Papers)*, pages 2019–2028, Berlin, Germany. Association for Computational Linguistics.

Enrico Francesconi, Simonetta Montemagni, Wim Peters, and Daniela Tiscornia. 2010. Integrating a bottom–up and top–down methodology for building semantic resources for the multilingual legal domain. In *Semantic processing of legal texts*, pages 95–121. Springer.

Andrea Galassi, Kasper Drazewski, Marco Lippi, and Paolo Torroni. 2020. Cross-lingual annotation projection in legal texts. In *Proceedings of the 28th International Conference on Computational Linguistics*, pages 915–926.

Filippo Galgani, Paul Compton, and Achim Hoffmann. 2012. Combining different summarization techniques for legal text. In *Proceedings of the workshop on innovative hybrid approaches to the processing of textual data*, pages 115–123.

Teresa Gonçalves and Paulo Quaresma. 2005. Is linguistic information relevant for the classification of legal texts? In *Proceedings of the 10th international conference on Artificial intelligence and law*, pages 168–176.

Justin Grimmer and Brandon M Stewart. 2013. Text as data: The promise and pitfalls of automatic content analysis methods for political texts. *Political analysis*, 21(3):267–297.

Suchin Gururangan, Mike Lewis, Ari Holtzman, Noah A Smith, and Luke Zettlemoyer. 2021. Demix layers: Disentangling domains for modular language modeling. *arXiv preprint arXiv:2108.05036*.

Suchin Gururangan, Ana Marasovic, Swabha Swayamdipta, Kyle Lo, Iz Beltagy, Doug Downey, and Noah A. Smith. 2020a. Don't stop pretraining: Adapt language models to domains and tasks. *CoRR*, abs/2004.10964.

Suchin Gururangan, Ana Marasović, Swabha Swayamdipta, Kyle Lo, Iz Beltagy, Doug Downey, and Noah A. Smith. 2020b. Don't stop pretraining: Adapt language models to domains and tasks. In *Proceedings of the 58th Annual Meeting of the Association for Computational Linguistics*, pages 8342–8360, Online. Association for Computational Linguistics.

Thomas Hale, Noam Angrist, Rafael Goldszmidt, Beatriz Kira, Anna Petherick, Toby Phillips, Samuel Webster, Emily Cameron-Blake, Laura Hallas, Saptarshi Majumdar, et al. 2021. A global panel database of pandemic policies (oxford covid-19 government response tracker). *Nature Human Behaviour*, 5(4):529–538.

Nathan Halko, Per-Gunnar Martinsson, and Joel A. Tropp. 2010. Finding structure with randomness: Probabilistic algorithms for constructing approximate matrix decompositions.

Nils Holzenberger, Andrew Blair-Stanek, and Benjamin Van Durme. 2020. A dataset for statutory reasoning in tax law entailment and question answering. In *Proceedings of the 2020 Natural Legal Language Processing (NLLP) Workshop,*, San Diego, US. CEUR Workshop Proceedings.

Daniel Hopkins and Gary King. 2007. Extracting systematic social science meaning from text. *Manuscript available at http://gking. harvard. edu/files/words. pdf*, 20(07).

Peng Jin, Yue Zhang, Xingyuan Chen, and Yunqing Xia. 2016. Bag-of-embeddings for text classification. In *IJCAI*, volume 16, pages 2824–2830.

S Kayalvizhi, D Thenmozhi, and Chandrabose Aravindan. 2019. Legal assistance using word embeddings. In *FIRE (Working Notes)*, pages 36–39.

Phi Manh Kien, Ha-Thanh Nguyen, Ngo Xuan Bach, Vu Tran, Minh Le Nguyen, and Tu Minh Phuong. 2020. Answering legal questions by learning neural attentive text representation. In *Proceedings of the 28th International Conference on Computational Linguistics*, pages 988–998, Barcelona, Spain (Online). International Committee on Computational Linguistics.

Diederik P. Kingma and Jimmy Ba. 2017. Adam: A method for stochastic optimization.

Nadzeya Kiyavitskaya, Nicola Zeni, Travis D Breaux, Annie I Antón, James R Cordy, Luisa Mich, and John Mylopoulos. 2008. Automating the extraction of rights and obligations for regulatory compliance. In *International Conference on Conceptual Modeling*, pages 154–168. Springer.

Svetla Koeva, Nikola Obreshkov, and Martin Yalamov. 2020. Natural language processing pipeline to annotate Bulgarian legislative documents. In *Proceedings of the 12th Language Resources and Evaluation Conference*, pages 6988–6994, Marseille, France. European Language Resources Association.

Anastassia Kornilova and Vladimir Eidelman. 2019. BillSum: A corpus for automatic summarization of US legislation. In *Proceedings of the 2nd Workshop on New Frontiers in Summarization*, pages 48–56, Hong Kong, China. Association for Computational Linguistics.

Fred Kort. 1957. Predicting supreme court decisions mathematically: A quantitative analysis of the "right to counsel" cases. *American Political Science Review*, 51(1):1–12.

Guiraude Lame. 2005. Using nlp techniques to identify legal ontology components: concepts and relations. In *Law and the Semantic Web*, pages 169–184. Springer.

Jinhyuk Lee, Wonjin Yoon, Sungdong Kim, Donghyeon Kim, Sunkyu Kim, Chan Ho So, and Jaewoo Kang. 2020. Biobert: a pre-trained biomedical language representation model for biomedical text mining. *Bioinformatics*, 36(4):1234–1240.

Elena Leitner, Georg Rehm, and Julian Moreno-Schneider. 2020. A dataset of German legal documents for named entity recognition. In *Proceedings of the 12th Language Resources and Evaluation Conference*, pages 4478–4485, Marseille, France. European Language Resources Association.

Ilya Loshchilov and Frank Hutter. 2017. Fixing weight decay regularization in adam. *CoRR*, abs/1711.05101.

Pedro Henrique Luz de Araujo, Teófilo Emídio de Campos, Fabricio Ataides Braz, and Nilton Correia da Silva. 2020. VICTOR: a dataset for Brazilian legal documents classification. In *Proceedings of the 12th Language Resources and Evaluation Conference*, pages 1449–1458, Marseille, France. European Language Resources Association.

Masha Medvedeva, Michel Vols, and Martijn Wieling. 2020. Using machine learning to predict decisions of the european court of human rights. *Artificial Intelligence and Law*, 28(2):237–266.

Marie-Francine Moens, Erik Boiy, Raquel Mochales Palau, and Chris Reed. 2007. Automatic detection of arguments in legal texts. In *Proceedings of the 11th international conference on Artificial intelligence and law*, pages 225–230.

Julian Moreno-Schneider, Georg Rehm, Elena Montiel-Ponsoda, Víctor Rodriguez-Doncel, Artem Revenko, Sotirios Karampatakis, Maria Khvalchik, Christian Sageder, Jorge Gracia, and Filippo Maganza. 2020. Orchestrating NLP services for the legal domain. In *Proceedings of the 12th Language Resources and Evaluation Conference*, pages 2332–2340, Marseille, France. European Language Resources Association.

James O' Neill, Paul Buitelaar, Cecile Robin, and Leona O' Brien. 2017. Classifying sentential modality in legal language: a use case in financial regulations, acts and directives. In *Proceedings of the 16th edition of the International Conference on Articial Intelligence and Law*, pages 159–168.

Joakim Nivre, Marie-Catherine de Marneffe, Filip Ginter, Yoav Goldberg, Jan Hajič, Christopher D. Manning, Ryan McDonald, Slav Petrov, Sampo Pyysalo, Natalia Silveira, Reut Tsarfaty, and Daniel Zeman. 2016. Universal Dependencies v1: A multilingual treebank collection. In *Proceedings of the Tenth International Conference on Language Resources and Evaluation (LREC'16)*, pages 1659–1666, Portorož, Slovenia. European Language Resources Association (ELRA).

Joakim Nivre, Marie-Catherine de Marneffe, Filip Ginter, Jan Hajič, Christopher D. Manning, Sampo Pyysalo, Sebastian Schuster, Francis Tyers, and Daniel Zeman. 2020. Universal Dependencies v2: An evergrowing multilingual treebank collection. In *Proceedings of the 12th Language Resources and Evaluation Conference*, pages 4034–4043, Marseille, France. European Language Resources Association.

Mariana Y Noguti, Eduardo Vellasques, and Luiz S Oliveira. 2020. Legal document classification: An application to law area prediction of petitions to public prosecution service. In *2020 International Joint Conference on Neural Networks (IJCNN)*, pages 1–8. IEEE.

Jeffrey Pennington, Richard Socher, and Christopher D. Manning. 2014. Glove: Global vectors for word representation. In *Empirical Methods in Natural Language Processing (EMNLP)*, pages 1532–1543.

Wim Peters, Maria-Teresa Sagri, and Daniela Tiscornia. 2007. The structuring of legal knowledge in LOIS. *Artificial Intelligence and Law*, 15(2):117–135.

Seth Polsley, Pooja Jhunjhunwala, and Ruihong Huang. 2016. CaseSummarizer: A system for automated summarization of legal texts. In *Proceedings of COLING 2016, the 26th International Conference on Computational Linguistics: System Demonstrations*, pages 258–262, Osaka, Japan. The COLING 2016 Organizing Committee.

Simon Porcher. 2020. Response2covid19, a dataset of governments' responses to covid-19 all around the world. *Scientific data*, 7(1):1–9.

Alexander Rietzler, Sebastian Stabinger, Paul Opitz, and Stefan Engl. 2020. Adapt or get left behind: Domain adaptation through BERT language model finetuning for aspect-target sentiment classification. In *Proceedings of the 12th Language Resources and Evaluation Conference*, pages 4933–4941, Marseille, France. European Language Resources Association.

Doaa Samy, Jerónimo Arenas-García, and David Pérez-Fernández. 2020. Legal-ES: A set of large scale resources for Spanish legal text processing. In *Proceedings of the 1st Workshop on Language Technologies for Government and Public Administration (LT4Gov)*, pages 32–36, Marseille, France. European Language Resources Association.

Jerrold Soh, How Khang Lim, and Ian Ernst Chai. 2019. Legal area classification: A comparative study of text classifiers on Singapore Supreme Court judgments. In *Proceedings of the Natural Legal Language Processing Workshop 2019*, pages 67–77, Minneapolis, Minnesota. Association for Computational Linguistics.

Milan Straka and Jana Straková. 2017. Tokenizing, POS tagging, lemmatizing and parsing UD 2.0 with UDPipe. In *Proceedings of the CoNLL 2017 Shared Task: Multilingual Parsing from Raw Text to Universal Dependencies*, pages 88–99, Vancouver, Canada. Association for Computational Linguistics.

Octavia-Maria Sulea, Marcos Zampieri, Shervin Malmasi, Mihaela Vela, Liviu P Dinu, and Josef Van Genabith. 2017. Exploring the use of text classification in the legal domain. *arXiv preprint arXiv:1710.09306*.

Ryosuke Taniguchi and Yoshinobu Kano. 2016. Legal yes/no question answering system using case-role analysis. In *JSAI International Symposium on Artificial Intelligence*, pages 284–298. Springer.

S Sidney Ulmer. 1963. Quantitative analysis of judicial processes: Some practical and theoretical applications. *Law and Contemporary Problems*, 28(1):164–184.

Bernhard Waltl, Johannes Muhr, Ingo Glaser, Georg Bonczek, Elena Scepankova, and Florian Matthes. 2017. Classifying legal norms with active machine learning. In *JURIX*, pages 11–20.

Fusheng Wei, Han Qin, Shi Ye, and Haozhen Zhao. 2018. Empirical study of deep learning for text classification in legal document review. In *2018 IEEE International Conference on Big Data (Big Data)*, pages 3317–3320. IEEE.

Martin Wettstein. 2014. Content analysis of mediated public debates: Methodological framework for a computer-assisted quantitative content analysis. *Zurich, Switzerland: University of Zürich Institute of Mass Communication and Media Research (IPMZ)*.

Gregor Wiedemann. 2013. Opening up to big data: Computer-assisted analysis of textual data in social sciences. *Historical Social Research/Historische Sozialforschung*, pages 332–357.

Terry Winograd. 1997. From Computing Machinery to Interaction Design. In Peter Denning and Robert Metcalfe, editors, *Beyond Calculation: The Next Fifty Years of Computing*, pages 149–162. Springer-Verlag.

Hai Ye, Xin Jiang, Zhunchen Luo, and Wenhan Chao. 2018. Interpretable charge predictions for criminal cases: Learning to generate court views from fact descriptions. In *Proceedings of the 2018 Conference of the North American Chapter of the Association for Computational Linguistics: Human Language Technologies, Volume 1 (Long Papers)*, pages 1854–1864, New Orleans, Louisiana. Association for Computational Linguistics.

Haoxi Zhong, Zhipeng Guo, Cunchao Tu, Chaojun Xiao, Zhiyuan Liu, and Maosong Sun. 2018. Legal judgment prediction via topological learning. In *Proceedings of the 2018 Conference on Empirical Methods in Natural Language Processing*, pages 3540–3549.

Haoxi Zhong, Chaojun Xiao, Cunchao Tu, Tianyang Zhang, Zhiyuan Liu, and Maosong Sun. 2020. How does NLP benefit legal system: A summary of legal artificial intelligence. In *Proceedings of the 58th Annual Meeting of the Association for Computational Linguistics*, pages 5218–5230, Online. Association for Computational Linguistics.

A Data Overview

Table 1 illustrates the basic statistics per country and per language of the processed documents in the corpus.

Country	Language	# Docs.	# Sent.	# Tokens	Vocab. Size	Avg. Sent. Length
Austria	German	240	13,041	331,924	13,577	25.45
Belgium	French	640	33,296	1,133,309	15,459	34.03
Croatia	Croatian	218	868	636,457	61,774	733.24*
Cyprus	Greek	276	109,617	1,218,917	38,022	11.11
Czechia	Czech	43	22,581	213,113	12,303	9.43
Denmark	Danish	207	6,927	160,692	6,201	23.19
France	French	493	7,449	637,800	13,240	85.62
Germany	German	9	515	12,011	1,549	23.32
Hungary	Hungarian	150	3,430	134,906	6,965	39.33
Ireland	English	137	9,913	219,848	4,860	22.17
Italy	Italian	72	1,107	46,337	3,972	41.85
Latvia	Latvian	400	238,034	1,800,733	67,905	7.56
Lithuania	Lithuanian	30	4,579	42,761	4.187	9.33
Netherlands	Dutch	499	135,464	1,662,255	47,834	12.27
Norway	Norwegian Bokmål	18	307	6,037	1,837	19.72
Poland	Polish	274	78,274	888,000	23,150	11.34
Slovenia	Slovene	952	530,892	4,340,178	32,091	8.17
Spain	Spanish	669	86,807	1,790,097	38,168	20.62
Sweden	Swedish	220	13,801	130,014	4,920	9.42
	French	112	89,966	1,013,258	9,569	11.26
Switzerland	German	110	62,192	581,009	11,473	9.34
	Italian	112	62,397	713,278	9,660	11.43
UK	English	168	50,470	1,054,190	12,567	20.88
total	–	6,049	1561,927	18,767,124	441,283	–
average	–	263	67,909.87	815,961.91	19,186.22	52.18
median	–	207	22,581	636,457	12,303	19.72

A.1: Basic statistics of the corpus.

The average sentence length for Croatia is due to the SpaCy UDPipeline failing to correctly split sentences when end of the sentence punctuation marks are missing.

B Manual Annotation: Train, Dev, and Test Data Distribution

Country	Split	# Sent.	Exceptional Classes							
			E1	E2	E3	E4	E5	E6	E7	E8
	Train	1,045	81	43	78	94	4	6	0	10
Belgium	Dev	131	8	8	17	16	0	1	0	3
	Test	131	8	8	13	14	0	0	0	2
	Train	371	65	97	108	156	14	2	21	3
France	Dev	47	9	12	10	18	1	0	3	0
	Test	47	7	9	11	23	2	0	2	1
	Train	75	0	1	2	1	0	1	0	0
Hungary	Dev	10	0	0	1	0	0	0	0	0
	Test	10	0	0	0	1	0	0	0	0
	Train	742	54	68	88	164	1	5	0	21
Italy	Dev	93	8	12	23	17	0	1	1	5
	Test	93	4	14	15	30	0	1	0	5
	Train	135	0	0	7	47	0	0	0	0
Netherlands	Dev	18	0	0	1	7	0	0	0	0
	Test	18	0	0	4	4	0	0	0	0
	Train	221	8	5	32	43	25	0	20	4
Norway	Dev	28	2	0	2	8	2	0	0	1
	Test	28	3	1	6	7	4	0	3	0
	Train	75	18	5	11	26	0	1	4	4
Poland	Dev	10	3	1	3	3	0	0	0	1
	Test	10	1	0	3	5	0	0	0	0
	Train	648	157	34	86	86	8	0	0	104
UK	Dev	81	24	6	14	5	1	0	0	11
	Test	81	24	10	10	9	0	0	0	11
	Train	3,312	383	253	412	617	52	15	45	146
total	Dev	418	54	39	71	74	4	2	4	21
	Test	418	47	42	62	93	6	1	5	19

A.2: Overview of the manually annotated data.

C Full taxonomy of the classes and subclasses

Class ID	Class label	# of subclasses	Subclass labels
E1	State of Emergency	18	1. State of emergency. 2. Executive decision-making 3. Suspension of parliamentary debates 4. Suspension of elections 5. Suspension of initiatives & referendums 6. Suspension of constitutional courts 7. Suspension of legal advisory bodies 8. Suspension of ordinary courts 9. Suspension of subnational competence 10. Set up of a dedicated crisis accountability mechanism 11. Limitations to political opposition parties 12. Limitations to civil society organizations / intermediary associations 13. Extension of military powers/duties 14. Extension of police powers / duties 15. To check presence on street at any time or place 16. Powers to listen to conversations, access data of phones by police 17. Powers to enter homes to check lockdown at discretion of police 18. To check purchases in authorized shops / supermarkets
E2	Restrictions of fundamental rights and civil liberties	5	1. Restrictions of freedom of movement 2. Neighborhood lockdown 3. Restrictions of freedom of speech (including social media, excluding media) 4. Restrictions of freedom of press 5. Restrictions of freedom of association
E3	Restrictions of daily liberties	10	1. Wearing of masks 2. COVID19 tracking app 3. Self-isolation / quarantine 4. Stay at home requirements 5. Use of the self-filled form 6. Ban on private gatherings 7. Authorized radius outside home 8. Ban on visiting vulnerable groups 9. Restrictions on funerals 10. Restrictions on sport activities
E4	Closures / lockdown	15	1. Closure of venues of entertainment and culture 2. Ban on public gatherings 3. Daycare closure 4. Primary school closure 5. Secondary school closure 6. University / tertiary school closure 7. Closure of non-essential shops 8. Workspace closure 9. Restrictions on international travel 10. Restrictions on internal travel 11. Closure of bus network 12. Closure of metro / subway system 13. Closure of railway network 14. Closure of airports / international flights 15.Curfew implementation
E5	Suspension of international cooperation and commitments	6	1. Changes of asylum-seeking procedures evaluation 2. Suspension of trade agreements 3. Suspension of visa/permits delivery 4. Closure of embassies/ consulates 5. Repatriation of national citizens abroad 6. Recall of foreign troops abroad

Class ID	Class label	# of subclasses	Subclass labels
E6	Police mobilization	14	1. Federal / national force 2. Size of forces mobilized 3. Local forces 4. Size of forces mobilized 5. Transportation police 6. Size of forces deployed 7. Other additional public agents 8. Size of forces mobilized 9. Private forces 10. Size of forces deployed 11. Extension of powers, type of agents 12. Extension of power, if type 1 13. Extension of power, if type 2 14. Extension of power, if type 3
E7	Army mobilization	9	1. Support to health authority 2. Public order 3. Enforcing lockdown / curfew 4. Border protection 5. Enforcement of executive orders in civilian environment 6. Military on the street 7. Deployment of the military in public buildings 8. Deployment of the military in private buildings 9. Prison sentences for non-compliance
E8	Government oversight	6	1. Press conferences of the Executive 2. Publicity of executive measures 3. Creation of specific (ad hoc) accountability mechanism 4. Parliamentary investigation committee 5. Other investigation committee 6. Creation of certification of information by gov. system

Multi-granular Legal Topic Classification on Greek Legislation

Christos Papaloukas † **Ilias Chalkidis**‡
Konstantinos Athinaios † **Despina-Athanasia Pantazi** † **Manolis Koubarakis** †
† National and Kapodistrian University of Athens, Greece
[christospap, dpantazi, koubarak]@di.uoa.gr
‡ University of Copenhagen, Denmark
ilias.chalkidis@di.ku.dk

Abstract

In this work, we study the task of classifying legal texts written in the Greek language. We introduce and make publicly available a novel dataset based on Greek legislation, consisting of more than 47 thousand official, categorized Greek legislation resources. We experiment with this dataset and evaluate a battery of advanced methods and classifiers, ranging from traditional machine learning and RNN-based methods to state-of-the-art Transformer-based methods. We show that recurrent architectures with domain-specific word embeddings offer improved overall performance while being competitive even to transformer-based models. Finally, we show that cutting-edge multilingual and monolingual transformer-based models brawl on the top of the classifiers' ranking, making us question the necessity of training monolingual transfer learning models as a rule of thumb. To the best of our knowledge, this is the first time the task of Greek legal text classification is considered in an open research project, while also Greek is a language with very limited NLP resources in general.

1 Introduction

In recent years, there has been intensified activity in the adaptation of Artificial Intelligence technologies to the legal domain (Chalkidis and Kampas, 2018; Zhong et al., 2020; Chalkidis et al., 2021), in which legal practitioners are required to analyze and review an overwhelming amount of legal data, mostly being plain text documents. This process requires dedication and an extraordinary level of resources, both concerning human resources along with the use of automated techniques to sift rationally through data. However, more sophisticated automated techniques are able to assist legal experts in making obsolete many labour-intensive manual tasks. These techniques are mostly contained in the area of machine learning and natural language processing (NLP).

With legal text processing being an emerging subarea of NLP, many relevant applications have been derived such as legal topic classification (Nallapati and Manning, 2008; Chalkidis et al., 2020a) legal information extraction (O'Neill et al., 2017; Chalkidis et al., 2018), legal entity recognition (Chalkidis et al., 2017a; Angelidis et al., 2018; Leitner et al., 2019), court opinion generation and analysis (Wang et al., 2012; Ye et al., 2018), legal judgement prediction (Aletras et al., 2016; Xiao et al., 2018; Chalkidis et al., 2019a) and many more. However, current legal NLP studies are mainly focused in English and Chinese, with very limited resources being available in other languages.

Our work focuses on the task of *multi-class legal topic classification*, where the goal is to identify the relevant thematic topic that represents a document. In our case, thematic topics (categories) are available in a multi-level hierarchy from broader to more specialized ones. The main contributions of our work are listed below:

- We introduce Greek Legal Code (*GLC*), a dataset consisting of approx. 47k legal resources from Greek legislation. The origin of *GLC* is "Permanent Greek Legislation Code - Raptarchis", a collection of Greek legislative documents classified into multi-level (from broader to more specialized) categories.
- We study the task of multi-class legal topic classification for Greek legislation by examining a battery of advanced methods, ranging from traditional machine learning techniques and RNN-based methods, to state-of-the-art Transformer-based methods. We discuss the results and lay the groundwork for further research.

Considering that Greek is a language with few NLP resources, we anticipate that our study will be a significant contribution for the Greek NLP community. To enhance the available NLP resources and foster reproducible results, we make both our code and dataset publicly available.

Natural Legal Language Processing Workshop 2021, pages 63–75
November 10, 2021.

2 Related Work

Mencia and Fürnkranzand (2007) introduced a legal topic classification task using a dataset obtained from the EUR-LEX[1] database, which includes EU laws that have been tagged with EUROVOC concepts. They used multiple binary Perceptrons, one for each label, and multi-label pairwise Perceptrons on top of Bag-of-Words (BoW) representations. While the methods seem primal and inefficient by today's standards, the EURLEX dataset is widely adopted as a notable benchmark in Large-scale Multi-label Text Classification (LMTC) literature.

Nallapati and Manning (2008) were also among the first who investigated the task of text classification in the legal domain where machine learning classifiers such as SVMs were insufficient. They experimented with a dataset of 5.5k US docket entries of court cases. The authors stress the importance of feature selection in such specialized domains and expose the limitations of classifiers relying on BoW featues to capture the intricacies of natural language, widespread in specialized domains such as the legal one.

Undavia et al. (2018) applied neural networks on legal document classification in a similar task, classification of legal court opinions. They used a dataset of 8k US Supreme Court (SCOTUS) opinions, where they targeted two sub-tasks, depending on the total output categories: 15 broad and 279 finer-grained categories. They experimented with shallow neural networks using different word embeddings, where their best model (word2vec + CNN) scored 72.4% accuracy in the 15-classes task and 31.9% accuracy in the 279-classes task. They concluded claiming that an RNN-based network together with domain-specific word embeddings could possibly tackle the task with higher accuracy.

Chalkidis et al. (2019c) experimented with several classifiers on a novel dataset of 57k legislative documents (EURLEX57k) from EUR-LEX in English. They demonstrated that that BiGRUs with self attention outperform CNN-based methods that employ the label-wise attention mechanism. Using domain-specific word embeddings and context-sensitive ELMO (Peters et al., 2018) embeddings improves the overall performance. Furthermore, the authors experimented with BERT (Devlin et al., 2019) obtaining the best results

In a more recent and extended version of this study, Chalkidis et al. (2020b) evaluated a battery of LMTC methods ranging from RNN-based Label-Wise Attention Networks (LWANs) to Probabilistic Label Trees (PLTs) (Prabhu et al., 2018; Khandagale et al., 2019; You et al., 2019) and Transformer-based models (BERT, ROBERTA) (Devlin et al., 2019; Liu et al., 2019) on three English datasets: EURLEX57k (Chalkidis et al., 2019c), MIMIC-III (Johnson et al., 2016) and AMAZON13k (Lewis et al., 2004). The experimental results show that PLT-based methods outperform LWANs, while Transformer-based approaches surpass state-of-the-art in two out of three datasets. Furthermore, a new state-of-the-art method is introduced which combines BERT and LWAN, giving the best results overall. Furthermore, the case of few and zero-shot learning is studied with new models that leverage the label hierarchy and yield better results.

Following literature, we examine traditional machine learning methods and the RNN-based methods used in Chalkidis et al. (2019c) and Chalkidis et al. (2020b) and investigate whether these methods can perform equally well in multi-class text classification as they do in the multi-label setting. Furthermore, we examine several BERT-based methods, including multi-lingual models (Devlin et al., 2019; Conneau et al., 2020) that have not been studied to date in the context of legal NLP.

Most of the preceding efforts focus on the English language and limited studies and resources exist considering languages other than English and Chinese. While recently there is a new wave of studies on NLP tasks focused on the Greek language (Athanasiou and Maragoudakis, 2017; Papantoniou and Tzitzikas, 2020; Pitenis et al., 2020; Koutsikakis et al., 2020), there is limited work for legal NLP in Greek (Angelidis et al., 2018). To the best of our knowledge, this is the first study on the task of Greek legal text classification, where experiments range from traditional machine learning to transfer learning models.

3 GLC Dataset

3.1 Original Data

The "Permanent Greek Legislation Code - Raptarchis[2]" is a thorough catalogue of Greek legislation since the creation of the Greek state in 1834 until 2015. It includes Laws, Royal and Presidential Decrees, Regulations and Decisions, retrieved from the Official Government Gazette,

[1]See https://eur-lex.europa.eu/.

[2]Mr. P. Raptarchis is the original curator of this collection.

where Greek legislation is published. This collection is one of the official, publicly available sources of classified Greek legislation suitable for our classification task.[3]

Currently, the original catalogue is publicly offered in MS Word (.doc) format through the portal e-Themis[4], the legal database and management service of it, under the administration of the Ministry of the Interior (Affairs)[5]. E-Themis is primarily focused on providing legislation on a multitude of predefined thematic categories, as described in the catalogue. The main goal is to help users find legislation of interest using the thematic index.

The original collection follows a bibliographic structure (Figure 1).[6] It consists of 47 legislative *volumes* and each volume corresponds to a main thematic topic. Inside each volume, the main thematic topic is divided into thematic subcategories which are called *chapters* and subsequently, each chapter breaks down to *subjects* which contain the legal resources. The total number of chapters is 389 while the total number of subjects is 2285, creating an interlinked thematic hierarchy. Thus the task is defined as a *multi-level text classification task*, where the goal is to predict the thematic category at each level (volume, chapter, subject).

An example of this thematic hierarchy is the volume of "Criminal Law", which is divided into 9 chapters. "International Criminal Law" and "Military Criminal Law" are two out of the nine chapters. Subsequently, "International Criminal Law" is subdivided into 8 subjects (e.g., "Genocide", "Counterfeiting" etc.) and "Military Criminal Law" is subdivided into 4 subjects (e.g., "Military Criminal Code", "Legal Remedies" etc.). Another example is the volume of "Labour Law", divided into 17 chapters. Two of those are "Collective Employment Contracts" and "Hygiene and Safety of Employees". "Collective Employment Contracts" is subdivided into 7 subjects (e.g., "Limits of Salaries", "Holiday Allowance" etc.) and "Hygiene and Safety of Employees" is subdivided into 3 subjects (e.g., "Hygiene And Safety Of Workplaces And Employees", "Work Health Books" etc.).

For the study presented in this paper, we curated

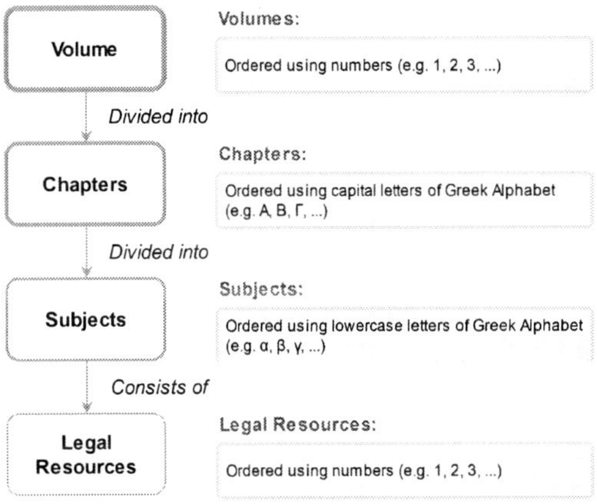

Figure 1: Original GLC thematic hierarchy

and publicly release a new dataset named Greek Legal Code (*GLC*), containing all the available legislation from the original catalogue in JSON format. Each JSON file contains a legal resource (law) along with its metadata, i.e., thematic topics, publication year, document type, etc., as they were extracted from the original documents.[7]

3.2 Dataset Statistics

In this section, we present a detailed quantitative analysis of the final dataset, consisting of 47,563 documents (i.e., categorized legal resources).

Data Split *GLC* is split into three subsets: training (60%), development (20%) and test (20%), as shown in Table 1. The documents are distributed uniformly for all levels of the class hierarchy in order to achieve the same level of partitioning from bottom to top (i.e., from each subject to the whole dataset).

Subset	Docs	Mean # of tokens / doc	(<100 tokens)
Train (60%)	28536	600	15412 (54%)
Dev. (20%)	9511	574	5175 (54.4%)
Test. (20%)	9516	595	5075 (53.3%)
Total:	47563	594	25662 (54%)

Table 1: Dataset split and statistics.

Document Size In Figure 2, we observe that more than half of the documents in our dataset have less than 100 tokens. We see that most of the documents are not that long, with their total number of tokens being below the mean number of tokens across all documents. Many records (documents) in GLC, especially the older ones have only

[3]Another official source is that of European Legislation written in modern Greek, available at: https://eur-lex.europa.eu/browse/directories/legislation.html.

[4]The portal is hosted at https://www.secdigital.gov.gr/e-themis/, where you can find the thematic index (hierarchy).

[5]https://www.ypes.gr

[6]In fact, it originated through a proper printed thesaurus.

[7]In Appendix A, we present in great detail the preprocessing procedure.

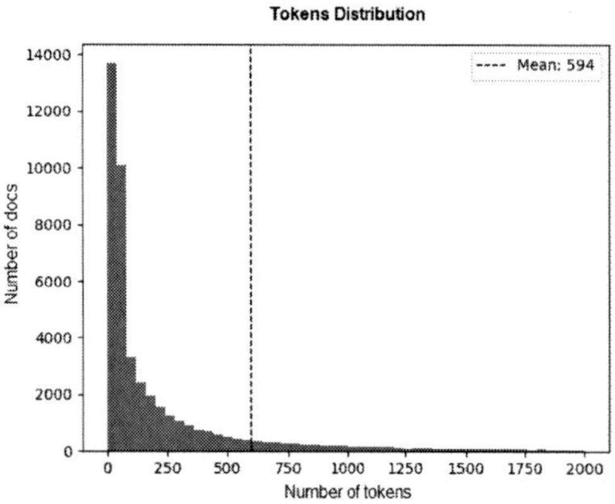

Figure 2: Tokens' distribution over docs in GLC

the descriptive title of the legal resource or a small part of it and not the full text.

	Total	Frequent	Few-shot (<10)	Zero-shot
Volume	47	47 (100%)	0	0
Chapter	389	333 (85.6%)	53 (13.6%)	3 (00.7%)
Subject	2285	712 (31.2 %)	1431 (62.6%)	142 (06.2%)

Table 2: Number of classes per thematic level and their distribution to frequent-few-zero categories

Label Frequency *GLC* classes are divided into three categories for each thematic level: *frequent classes*, which occur in more than 10 training documents and can be found in all three subsets (training, development and test); *few-shot classes*[8] which appear in 1 to 10 training documents and also appear in the documents of the development and test sets, and *zero-shot classes* which appear in the development and/or test, but not in the training documents. As demonstrated in Table 2, many classes are under-represented, especially in the thematic level of subjects, causing the appearance of few- and zero-shot categories. The appearance of underrepresented classes increases as we move towards more specific thematic levels. Table 3 shows the total number of documents per category and thematic level.

	Total	Frequent	Few-shot (<10)	Zero-shot
Volume	47563	47563 (100%)	0	0
Chapter	47563	47108 (99.0%)	445 (00.9%)	10 (<00.1%)
Subject	47563	38475 (80.9%)	8870 (18.6%)	218 (00.5%)

Table 3: Number of documents as labeled per thematic level and their distribution to frequent-few-zero categories

[8]The terms few-shot and zero-shot are used to express the underrepresentation of classes in *GLC* rather than transfer learning approaches as in other deep learning literature.

In the volume level, all the classes belong to the frequent category and are sufficiently represented, as more than 10 documents per class exist in the training data. In the chapter level, few-shot classes appear and are rather underrepresented as most documents are classified among frequent classes, leaving less than 1% of the total documents to be associated with ~14% of the total classes. In the subject level, data are even more unequally distributed over classes. The majority of documents are classified into frequent classes, leaving more than half of the total classes (~63%) to be associated with less than 20% of the total documents, along with 142 classes having zero representation at the training subset.

4 Task and Methods

4.1 Multi-class Legal Topic Classification for Greek Legislation

We study multi-class legal topic classification for Greek legislation using the *GLC* dataset[9]. *GLC* offers 3 hierarchical levels of thematic categorization, forming a tree structure that follows the original GLC organization as explained in Section 3.1. We divide the classification task for *GLC* into three separate classification tasks. Each task deals with a different level of the thematic hierarchy (i.e., volume, chapter or subject) and the classifier's objective is to predict the correct class out of all the classes in this specific thematic level.

4.2 Methods

In our study, we consider an arsenal of nine methods ranging from traditional machine learning techniques (2) and RNN-based methods (3), to state-of-the-art Transformer-based methods (4).

SVM-BOW: Support Vector Machines (SVMs) is a strong baseline for the multi-class classification problem as it is one of the highest performing traditional ML methods. We represent the legal documents using Bag-of-Words (BoW) features, getting the most frequent n-grams across all training data, weighted by TF-IDF.

XGBOOST-BOW: XGBoost (Chen and Guestrin, 2016) is a scalable, fast and robust open-source implementation[10] of the Gradient Boosting decision tree algorithm. In XGBoost, the model is fitted on the gradient of loss generated from the previous

[9]Available at: https://huggingface.co/datasets/greek_legal_code

[10]Available at: https://github.com/dmlc/xgboost/

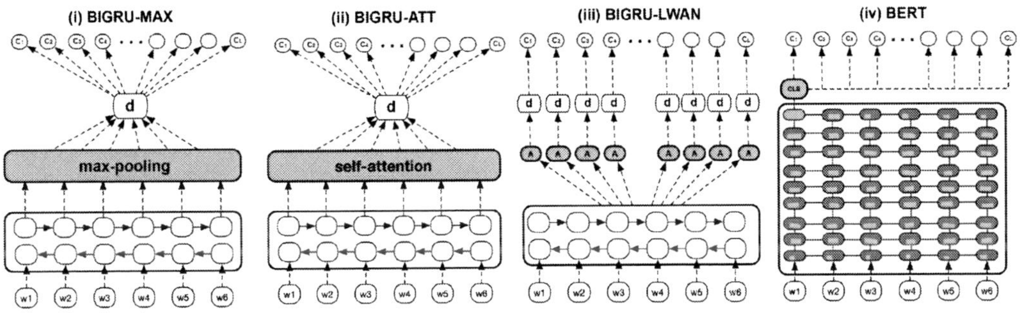

Figure 3: Illustration of (i) BIGRU-MAX, (ii) BIGRU-ATT, (iii) BIGRU-LWAN and (iv) BERT

step and the gradient boosting algorithm is modified so that it works with any differentiable loss function. In our case, the documents are represented using BoW features weighted by TF-IDF (similarly to SVM-BOW).

BIGRU-MAX: The first RNN-based method that we examine is BiGRU with max-pooling, employing pre-trained, domain-specific word embeddings (Angelidis et al., 2018).[11] The stacked BiGRU encoder converts the pre-trained word embeddings $\mathbf{w}_i$ into context-aware embeddings $\mathbf{h}_i$. Context-aware token embeddings pass through a max-pooling layer to produce the final document representation $\mathbf{d}$ by reducing the initial matrix (token-wise vectors) into a single vector but hopefully, keep the most salient information. Finally, a dense layer with L output units and the *softmax()* activation is deployed, to transform the document representation $\mathbf{d}$ into a probability distribution over L classes. L is defined according to the examined task, i.e., L=47 for the volume-level task, L=389 for the chapter-level task and L=2285 for the subject-level task.

BIGRU-ATT: The second RNN-based method is a BiGRU network with self-attention (Xu et al., 2015; Chalkidis et al., 2019c). This methods uses the very same word embedding and BiGRU encoder, similarly to the previously described method (BIGRU-MAX). Instead of max-pooling, it uses the self-attention mechanism to produce a final document representation $\mathbf{d}$. This representation is computed as the weighted sum of the BiGRU context-aware embeddings $\mathbf{h}_i$, weighted by the self-attention scores a_i produced as:

$$a_i = \frac{\exp\left(\mathbf{h}_i^\top \mathbf{u}\right)}{\sum_j \exp\left(\mathbf{h}_j^\top \mathbf{u}\right)} \tag{1}$$

$$\mathbf{d} = \frac{1}{T}\sum_{i=1}^{T} a_i \mathbf{h}_i \tag{2}$$

T represents the document's length in words while $\mathbf{u}$ is a trainable vector used to compute the attention scores a_i over $\mathbf{h}_i$. Similarly to BIGRU-MAX, a final dense layer with L output units and *softmax()* activation is deployed to predict the correct output class using a probability distribution over all the classes.

BIGRU-LWAN: The third RNN-based method replaces the self-attention mechanism of BIGRU-ATT with the label-wise attention mechanism. The original Label-Wise Attention Network (LWAN) was introduced in Mullenbach et al. (2018) using a CNN-based encoder. Later on, (Chalkidis et al., 2019c,b) replaced it with a BiGRU encoder. In contrast with BIGRU-ATT, this label-wise attention technique uses L independent attention heads, one per class, generating L label-wise document representations $\mathbf{d}_l$ from the sequence of $\mathbf{h}_i$ vectors produced by the BiGRU encoder. The intuition is that each label-wise document embedding is dedicated in predicting the corresponding class, focusing on possibly different aspects of each representation $\mathbf{h}_i$. In effect, different parts of the representation may be more relevant for different classes.

$$a_{li} = \frac{\exp\left(\mathbf{h}_i^\top \mathbf{u}_l\right)}{\sum_{i'} \exp\left(\mathbf{h}_{i'}^\top \mathbf{u}_l\right)} \tag{3}$$

$$\mathbf{d}_l = \frac{1}{T}\sum_{i=1}^{T} a_{li} \mathbf{h}_i \tag{4}$$

Again, T represents the document's length in words while $\mathbf{u}_l$ ($l = 1, 2, ..., L$) is a trainable vector

[11] Angelidis et al. (2018) released a Word2Vec model trained on Greek legal corpora, including Greek national and EU legislation.

used to compute the attention scores a_{li} of the l-th attention head. Then, each attention head $\mathbf{d}_l$ goes through an independent dense layer for each class and similarly to the previous methods, *softmax()* activation is deployed to transform the document representation **d** into a probability distribution over L classes.

M-BERT: BERT (Devlin et al., 2019) is a Transformer-based (Vaswani et al., 2017) language model initially developed by Google. In BERT, deep bidirectional representations are pre-trained from unlabeled text by jointly conditioning on both left and right context. As a result, for any new task, the pre-trained BERT model can be fine-tuned with just one additional task-specific output layer trained with task-specific data. We employ the multilingual version of the 12-layer BERT-BASE-CASED model, which supports modern Greek, alongside 99 languages, out-of-the-box. We add linear layer on top of M-BERT encoder followed by a *softmax()* activation. This extra dense layer is fed with the so-called "classification token" ([cls]) of the BERT encoder as described in (Devlin et al., 2019), serving as the final document representation.

XLM-ROBERTA: The next BERT-based model we examine is XLM-RoBERTa (Conneau et al., 2020), a multilingual adaptation of RoBERTa (Liu et al., 2019). RoBERTa is built following BERT's architecture, while removed the next-sentence pre-training objective and trained with much larger batches and higher learning rate. Based on this study, Conneau et al. (2020) proposed the XLM-RoBERTa model, which supports 100 different languages (Greek included) and is trained on 2.5TB of filtered Common Crawl data.

GREEK-BERT: We also experiment with GREEK-BERT (Koutsikakis et al., 2020), a native monolingual version of BERT, trained solely on modern Greek, achieving state-of-the-art results in several NLP tasks. GREEK-BERT was pre-trained on 29GB of text from a corpus consisting of the Greek part of Wikipedia, the Greek part of the European Parliament Proceedings Parallel Corpus (Europarl) (Koehn, 2005) and OSCAR (Ortiz Suárez et al., 2019), a clean version of Common Crawl. Even though multilingual models like the previous two offer exceptional performance, monolingual models usually surpass them in most downstream tasks. Again, GREEK-BERT follows the previous BERT models configuration.

GREEK-LEGAL-BERT: Finally, we experiment with GREEK-LEGAL-BERT (Athinaios, 2020), another BERT-flavored model for modern Greek. Its pre-training corpus is based entirely on Greek legal documents and consists of around 5GB of Greek and EU legislation documents retrieved by Nomothesia[12] (Chalkidis et al., 2017b), a Greek legislative Knowledge Base. It also follows the previously described configuration.

Method	Hyperparameters
SVM-BOW	Kernel: [linear, rbf] C: [0.25, 0.50, 0.75, 1] N-Grams: [(1,3), (1,5)] Max-Features: [200k, 400k]
XGBOOST-BOW	Booster: gbtree with softmax N-Estimators: 800 Max-Depth: [4, 5, 7, 10] Min-Child-Weight: [2, 5, 10]
BIGRU-*	HYPEROPT[13]on: Layers: [1, 2] Units: [200, 300, 400] Dropout: [0.1, 0.2, 0.3, 0.4] Word Dropout: [0, 0.01, 0.02] Batch Size: [8, 16]
BERT	Dropout: 0.1 Learning Rate: [1e-5, 2e-5, 3e-5, 5e-5] Batch Size: 8

Table 4: Hyper parameters search space for all models

5 Experiments

5.1 Experimental SetUp

We tune all methods by grid-searching over the core hyper-parameters (per method) presented in Table 4, except the RNN-based methods where we used HyperOpt due to the large search space. We select the models with the best performance on the development set. We use early stopping on the development loss using the Adam (Kingma and Ba, 2015) optimizer. All BERT models follow the base configuration, i.e., 12 layers with 786 units and 12 attention heads each.[14] We report micro-averaged Precision (P), Recall (R), and F1-score (F1) on the test set. For each method, we perform 5 runs with different seeds and report the average. We report results for the frequent and few-shot classes (when available), omitting results for zero-shot classes since our methods are incapable of zero-shot learning. We release our code for reproducibility:[15]

[12]http://legislation.di.uoa.gr.

[13]See: https://hyperopt.github.io/hyperopt/

[14]All models are available at https://huggingface.co/models.

[15]See: https://github.com/christospi/glc-nllp-21.

MODEL	*Volume (47 classes)*						*Chapter (389 classes)*								
	ALL LABELS			FREQUENT			ALL LABELS			FREQUENT			FEW-SHOT		
	P	R	F1	P	R	F1	P	R	F1	P	R	F1	P	R	F1
SVM-BOW	85.3	85.3	85.3	85.3	85.3	85.3	77.9	77.9	77.9	77.9	78.6	78.2	**90.0**	09.3	16.8
XGBOOST-BOW	77.2	77.2	77.2	77.2	77.2	77.2	67.5	67.5	67.5	67.8	68.1	67.9	19.2	10.3	13.4
BIGRU-MAX	84.3	84.3	84.3	84.3	84.3	84.3	77.5	77.5	77.5	77.9	77.9	77.9	44.9	45.4	45.1
BIGRU-ATT	86.4	86.4	86.4	86.4	86.4	86.4	81.1	81.1	81.1	81.1	81.6	81.3	86.7	40.2	54.9
BIGRU-LWAN	84.1	84.1	84.1	84.1	84.1	84.1	76.8	76.8	76.8	76.9	77.3	77.1	63.8	30.9	41.7
M-BERT	85.8	85.8	85.8	85.8	85.8	85.8	80.2	80.2	80.2	80.1	80.6	80.4	81.0	43.9	56.6
XLM-ROBERTA	85.0	85.0	85.0	85.0	85.0	85.0	80.6	80.6	80.6	80.6	81.0	80.8	80.3	37.9	51.3
GREEK-BERT	87.5	87.5	87.5	87.5	87.5	87.5	82.4	82.4	82.4	82.4	82.8	82.6	81.0	45.2	**57.8**
GREEK-LEGAL-BERT	**89.4**	**89.4**	**89.4**	**89.4**	**89.4**	**89.4**	**84.3**	**84.3**	**84.3**	**84.4**	**84.8**	**84.6**	79.0	**45.8**	**57.8**

Table 5: Experimental results for *Volume* and *Chapter* levels.

5.2 Volume-level Classification Evaluation

In volume-level classification, all the 47 possible classes are sufficiently represented and belong to the frequent category, while the mean number of documents per class is approximately 1k. However, we acknowledge class imbalance (label skewness) as a challenge in our dataset, though not so evident here. Table 5 (first zone) demonstrates the results for this task. SVM-BOW proves to be a strong competitor in the first classification task (85.3 in F1). Interestingly, it outperforms two of our neural methods with domain-specific word embeddings, namely BIGRU-MAX and BIGRU-LWAN with 84.3 and 84.1 F1 scores, respectively. As for XGBoost, although it seemed quite promising and very fast at training, its inadequate F1 score of 77.2 places it at the bottom of the list for this task.

Among the RNN-based neural methods, BIGRU-ATT achieves an F1 score of 86.4 outperforming the rest of the RNN-based methods. Its results indicate the significance of two of its fundamental features: (i) the domain-specific word2vec embeddings and (ii) the cumulative self-attention head that provides an advantageous final document representation. Compared to BIGRU-MAX, we believe that its max-pooling layer hinders some of the document's particularities and thus, it yields a lower score. Likewise, the BIGRU-LWAN method with L different attention heads seems to be more tailor-made for multi-label classification tasks, as it does not offer any performance improvement compared to BIGRU-ATT.

GREEK-LEGAL-BERT proves to be the best method we experimented with, achieving a score of 89.4 in F1, followed by the generic GREEK-BERT with a score of 87.5 in F1. The two multilingual models (M-BERT and XLM-ROBERTA) also achieve satisfying F1 scores (85.8 and 85.0), confirming their claim to offer top-notch results in most downstream NLP tasks. The results demonstrate that monolingual models are able to surpass other advanced multilingual transformer-based models. We hypothesize that the fact that GREEK-LEGAL-BERT is pre-trained entirely on Greek legal corpora is the main reason of its superiority, while the specialization in the Greek language, alongside GREEK-BERT, seems even more critical.

5.3 Chapter-level Classification Evaluation

In Table 5 (second zone) we observe again that XGBOOST-BOW has the lowest performance with 67.5 in overall F1 score with SVM-BOW being the second worst overall (77.9) alongside BIGRU-MAX. The ranking of BERT-based models is similar to the previous task (Volume-level classification), i.e., monolingual models outperform their multilingual counterparts, while GREEK-LEGAL-BERT is better by 2% compared to the generic GREEK-BERT model. These results further supporting our intuition on the importance of native language support and domain knowledge.

Inspecting the few-shot label results, we observe that BIGRU-ATT and BERT models outperform BIGRU-MAX by 10%, while the traditional machine learning approaches have terrible performance (approx. 15 F1). These results highlight the importance of the attention mechanism and its capability to focus in specific parts of the text that are more prominent in relation to the downstream task and the specific labels.

5.4 Subject-level Classification Evaluation

In the last sub-task, where there are many more classes (2285 in total), we observe a similar ranking in the methods (Table 6). However, the absolute difference in few-shot labels' scores is higher this time, when comparing either the attention-based method with BIGRU-MAX (approx. +20% F1) or monolingual with multilingual BERT models (approx. +9% F1).

MODEL	*Subject (2285 classes)*								
	ALL LABELS			FREQUENT			FEW-SHOT		
	P	R	F1	P	R	F1	P	R	F1
SVM-BOW	37.9	37.9	37.9	37.9	47.8	42.3	00.0	00.0	00.0
XGBOOST-BOW	55.3	55.3	55.3	56.1	64.8	60.1	46.9	19.1	27.2
BIGRU-MAX	62.9	62.9	62.9	66.0	70.5	68.1	47.1	37.8	42.0
BIGRU-ATT	74.8	74.8	74.8	75.3	79.6	77.4	72.6	61.1	66.3
BIGRU-LWAN	65.2	65.2	65.2	68.1	72.8	70.4	50.7	40.4	45.0
M-BERT	76.8	76.8	76.8	79.8	82.5	81.1	64.4	59.7	62.0
XLM-ROBERTA	78.0	78.0	78.0	80.3	83.4	81.8	68.2	62.1	65.0
GREEK-BERT	79.4	79.4	79.4	80.5	83.9	82.2	**74.6**	67.0	70.6
GREEK-LEGAL-BERT	**81.2**	**81.2**	**81.2**	**83.0**	**85.5**	**84.2**	73.6	**69.4**	**71.4**

Table 6: Experimental results for *Subject* level.

5.5 General Observations

There are two main observations:

- Pre-trained Transformer-based models perform exceptionally and the performance gains compared to traditional machine learning methods and RNN-based methods are increasing in relation to the number of labels. We can only speculate the following: (a) sub-word units used by Transformer-based models potentially play an important role in morphological rich languages like Greek, compared to full words processed by the rest of the examined models; and (b) the multi-head attention mechanism can better distill important detailed (specialized) information to distinguish categories (labels).
- The Label-wise Attention Network (LWAN) under-performs in the newly introduced multi-class text classification task. Again, we can only speculate that the produced label-wise document representations that improve results over the standard universal attention mechanism in the multi-label setting (Chalkidis et al., 2020a) lead to a "greedy" over-scoring (produced logits) followed by an aggressive label competition (softmax over logits) in the examined multi-task setting leading to negative (poor) results.

We aim to further review and validate these observations, while also study the reasons behind those thoroughly in the future, possibly using more datasets and ablation studies (e.g., train RNN-based methods with pretrained sub-word embeddings).

6 Conclusions and Future Work

We introduced Greek Legal Code (*GLC*), a new publicly available dataset consisting of 47k Greek legislation resources. Relying on this dataset, we experimented with several classifiers, ranging from traditional machine learning and recurrent models to state-of-the-art transfer learning models. Through their performance evaluation, we realized that although traditional machine learning classifiers (e.g., SVM-BOW) set strong baselines for some of the considered tasks, they fall short against more sophisticated methods. In contrast, RNN-based methods relying on BiGRUs provide improved overall performance and were competitive to multilingual transformer-based architectures (M-BERT, XLM-ROBERTA). Beyond doubt, monolingual transformer-based models (GREEK-BERT and GREEK-LEGAL-BERT) lead to state-of-the-art results, especially when they are pre-trained on in-domain corpora.

Nonetheless, more emphasis should be given to the qualitative and quantitative characteristics of the examined datasets. Intricacies like class imbalance, data scarcity and diversity apparently need special handling. Regarding our study, we noticed that few-shot and especially zero-shot classes need to be properly handled with appropriate methods, as standard classifiers are insufficient. As for the recent trend to develop novel monolingual BERT-based models, results show that already established multilingual models are incredibly powerful even in monolingual tasks. While research is on-going and these models are continuously being improved, also taking into consideration the computational costs, it is quite challenging to motivate researchers into making an effort to train monolingual models for medium or small-sized languages; especially when multilingual models can perform equally well or occasionally, even better.

In future work, we plan to investigate specialized methods with improved few-shot and zero-shot performance (Hu et al., 2018; Rios and Kavuluru, 2018; Chalkidis et al., 2019c) that leverage various data properties (e.g., label descriptors and label hierarchy). Also, we intend to apply deep learning techniques that take into account the hierarchy of classes in datasets like *GLC*, where there is an underlying taxonomy (Kowsari et al., 2017; Chalkidis et al., 2020b; Manginas et al., 2020). Furthermore, experimenting with similar datasets like that of EU Legislation written in Greek will allow us to confirm our current conclusions. For example in the future, we could consider Cypriot legislation[16] to evaluate the out-of-domain generalization of models trained on Greek legislation. Finally, our long term goal is to support and encourage further research in NLP for the Greek language by publishing novel datasets, introducing and experimenting with state-of-the-art methods.

[16]http://www.cylaw.org/nomoi/

Acknowledgements

This work has received funding from the European Union's Horizon 2020 research and innovation programme under grant agreement No 825258. This work is also partly funded by the Innovation Fund Denmark (IFD)[17] under File No. 0175-00011A.

References

N. Aletras, D. Tsarapatsanis, D. Preotiuc-Pietro, and V. Lampos. 2016. Predicting judicial decisions of the european court of human rights: a natural language processing perspective. *PeerJ Comput. Sci.*, 2.

Iosif Angelidis, Ilias Chalkidis, and Manolis Koubarakis. 2018. Named entity recognition, linking and generation for greek legislation. In *JURIX*.

V. Athanasiou and M. Maragoudakis. 2017. A novel, gradient boosting framework for sentiment analysis in languages where nlp resources are not plentiful: A case study for modern greek. *Algorithms*, 10:34.

Konstantinos Athinaios. 2020. Named Entity Recognition using a Novel Linguistic Model for Greek Legal Corpora based on BERT model. *BS Thesis, School of Science, Department of Informatics and Telecommunications*.

Ilias Chalkidis, Ion Androutsopoulos, and Nikolaos Aletras. 2019a. Neural legal judgment prediction in English. In *Proceedings of the 57th Annual Meeting of the Association for Computational Linguistics*, pages 4317–4323, Florence, Italy. Association for Computational Linguistics.

Ilias Chalkidis, Ion Androutsopoulos, and Achilleas Michos. 2017a. Extracting contract elements. In *Proceedings of the 16th Edition of the International Conference on Articial Intelligence and Law*, ICAIL '17, page 19–28, New York, NY, USA. Association for Computing Machinery.

Ilias Chalkidis, Ion Androutsopoulos, and Achilleas Michos. 2018. Obligation and prohibition extraction using hierarchical RNNs. In *Proceedings of the 56th Annual Meeting of the Association for Computational Linguistics (Volume 2: Short Papers)*, pages 254–259, Melbourne, Australia. Association for Computational Linguistics.

Ilias Chalkidis, Emmanouil Fergadiotis, Prodromos Malakasiotis, Nikolaos Aletras, and Ion Androutsopoulos. 2019b. Extreme multi-label legal text classification: A case study in EU legislation. In *Proceedings of the Natural Legal Language Processing Workshop 2019*, pages 78–87, Minneapolis, Minnesota. Association for Computational Linguistics.

[17]https://innovationsfonden.dk/en

Ilias Chalkidis, Emmanouil Fergadiotis, Prodromos Malakasiotis, and Ion Androutsopoulos. 2019c. Large-scale multi-label text classification on EU legislation. In *Proceedings of the 57th Annual Meeting of the Association for Computational Linguistics*, pages 6314–6322, Florence, Italy. Association for Computational Linguistics.

Ilias Chalkidis, Manos Fergadiotis, Sotiris Kotitsas, Prodromos Malakasiotis, Nikolaos Aletras, and Ion Androutsopoulos. 2020a. An empirical study on large-scale multi-label text classification including few and zero-shot labels. In *Proceedings of the 2020 Conference on Empirical Methods in Natural Language Processing (EMNLP)*, pages 7503–7515, Online. Association for Computational Linguistics.

Ilias Chalkidis, Manos Fergadiotis, Sotiris Kotitsas, Prodromos Malakasiotis, Nikolaos Aletras, and Ion Androutsopoulos. 2020b. An empirical study on large-scale multi-label text classification including few and zero-shot labels. In *Proceedings of the 2020 Conference on Empirical Methods in Natural Language Processing (EMNLP)*, pages 7503–7515, Online. Association for Computational Linguistics.

Ilias Chalkidis, Abhik Jana, Dirk Hartung, Michael Bommarito, Ion Androutsopoulos, Daniel Martin Katz, and Nikolaos Aletras. 2021. LexGLUE: A Benchmark Dataset for Legal Language Understanding in English.

Ilias Chalkidis and Dimitrios Kampas. 2018. Deep learning in law: early adaptation and legal word embeddings trained on large corpora. *Artificial Intelligence and Law*, 27:171–198.

Ilias Chalkidis, Charalampos Nikolaou, Panagiotis Soursos, and Manolis Koubarakis. 2017b. Modeling and querying greek legislation using semantic web technologies. In *The Semantic Web*, pages 591–606, Cham. Springer International Publishing.

T. Chen and C. Guestrin. 2016. Xgboost: A scalable tree boosting system. *ACM-SIGKDD*.

A. Conneau, K. Khandelwal, N. Goyal, V. Chaudhary, G. Wenzek, F. Guzmán, E. Grave, M. Ott, L. Zettlemoyer, and V. Stoyanov. 2020. Unsupervised cross-lingual representation learning at scale. *ArXiv*, abs/1911.02116.

J. Devlin, M. Chang, K. Lee, and K. Toutanova. 2019. Bert: Pre-training of deep bidirectional transformers for language understanding. In *NAACL-HLT*.

Z. Hu, X. Li, C. Tu, Z. Liu, and M. Sun. 2018. Few-shot charge prediction with discriminative legal attributes. In *COLING*.

A. Johnson, T. J. Pollard, L. Shen, L. H. Lehman, M. Feng, M. Ghassemi, B. Moody, P. Szolovits, L. Celi, and R. G. Mark. 2016. Mimic-iii, a freely accessible critical care database. *Scientific data*, 3(1):1–9.

Sujay Khandagale, Han Xiao, and Rohit Babbar. 2019. Bonsai - Diverse and Shallow Trees for Extreme Multi-label Classification. *CoRR*, abs/1904.08249.

D. P. Kingma and J. Ba. 2015. Adam: A method for stochastic optimization. *CoRR*, abs/1412.6980.

Philipp Koehn. 2005. Europarl: A parallel corpus for statistical machine translation. In *MTSUMMIT*.

John Koutsikakis, Ilias Chalkidis, Prodromos Malakasiotis, and Ion Androutsopoulos. 2020. Greek-bert: The greeks visiting sesame street. In *11th Hellenic Conference on Artificial Intelligence*, SETN 2020, page 110–117, New York, NY, USA. Association for Computing Machinery.

K. Kowsari, D. Brown, M. Heidarysafa, K. Meimandi, M. Gerber, and L. Barnes. 2017. Hdltex: Hierarchical deep learning for text classification. *ICMLA*.

Elena Leitner, Georg Rehm, and Julian Moreno-Schneider. 2019. Fine-grained Named Entity Recognition in Legal Documents. In *Semantic Systems. The Power of AI and Knowledge Graphs. Proceedings of the 15th International Conference (SEMANTiCS 2019)*, number 11702 in Lecture Notes in Computer Science, pages 272–287, Karlsruhe, Germany. Springer. 10/11 September 2019.

D. D. Lewis, T. G. Rose Y. Yang, and F. Li. 2004. Rcv1: A new benchmark collection for text categorization research. *J. Mach. Learn. Res.*, 5:361–397.

Y. Liu, M. Ott, N. Goyal, J. Du, M. Joshi, D. Chen, O. Levy, M. Lewis, L. Zettlemoyer, and V. Stoyanov. 2019. Roberta: A robustly optimized bert pretraining approach. *ArXiv*, abs/1907.11692.

Nikolaos Manginas, Ilias Chalkidis, and Prodromos Malakasiotis. 2020. Layer-wise guided training for BERT: Learning incrementally refined document representations. In *Proceedings of the Fourth Workshop on Structured Prediction for NLP*, pages 53–61, Online. Association for Computational Linguistics.

Eneldo Loza Mencia and Johannes Fürnkranzand. 2007. An Evaluation of Efficient Multilabel Classification Algorithms for Large-Scale Problems in the Legal Domain. In *Proceedings of the 1st Linguistic Annotation Workshop*, pages 126–132, Halle, Germany.

J. Mullenbach, S. Wiegreffe, J. Duke, J. Sun, and J. Eisenstein. 2018. Explainable prediction of medical codes from clinical text. *ArXiv*, abs/1802.05695.

R. Nallapati and C. D. Manning. 2008. Legal docket classification: Where machine learning stumbles. *EMNLP*.

J. O'Neill, P. Buitelaar, C. Robin, and L. O' Brien. 2017. Classifying Sentential Modality in Legal Language: A Use Case in Financial Regulations, Acts and Directives. In *Proceedings of the 16th International Conference on Artificial Intelligence and Law (ICAIL)*, pages 159–168, London, UK.

Pedro Javier Ortiz Suárez, Benoît Sagot, and Laurent Romary. 2019. Asynchronous pipelines for processing huge corpora on medium to low resource infrastructures. Proceedings of the Workshop on Challenges in the Management of Large Corpora (CMLC-7) 2019. Cardiff, 22nd July 2019, pages 9 – 16, Mannheim. Leibniz-Institut für Deutsche Sprache.

K. Papantoniou and Y. Tzitzikas. 2020. Nlp for the greek language: A brief survey. *11th Hellenic Conference on Artificial Intelligence*.

Matthew E. Peters, Mark Neumann, Mohit Iyyer, Matt Gardner, Christopher Clark, Kenton Lee, and Luke Zettlemoyer. 2018. Deep contextualized word representations. In *Proceedings of the 2018 Conference of the North American Chapter of the Association for Computational Linguistics: Human Language Technologies, Volume 1 (Long Papers)*, pages 2227–2237, New Orleans, Louisiana. Association for Computational Linguistics.

Z. Pitenis, M. Zampieri, and T. Ranasinghe. 2020. Offensive language identification in greek. In *LREC*.

Yashoteja Prabhu, Anil Kag, Shrutendra Harsola, Rahul Agrawal, and Manik Varma. 2018. Parabel: Partitioned Label Trees for Extreme Classification with Application to Dynamic Search Advertising. In *Proceedings of the 2018 World Wide Web Conference*, WWW '18, pages 993–1002, Republic and Canton of Geneva, Switzerland.

A. Rios and R. Kavuluru. 2018. Few-shot and zero-shot multi-label learning for structured label spaces. *EMNLP*.

S. Undavia, A. Meyers, and J. Ortega. 2018. A comparative study of classifying legal documents with neural networks. *FedCSIS*.

A. Vaswani, N. Shazeer, N. Parmar, J. Uszkoreit, L. Jones, A. N. Gomez, L. Kaiser, and I. Polosukhin. 2017. Attention is all you need. In *NIPS*.

W. Yang Wang, E. Mayfield, S. Naidu, and J. Dittmar. 2012. Historical analysis of legal opinions with a sparse mixed-effects latent variable model. In *ACL*.

Chaojun Xiao, Haoxi Zhong, Zhipeng Guo, Cunchao Tu, Zhiyuan Liu, Maosong Sun, Yansong Feng, Xianpei Han, Zhen Hu, Heng Wang, and Jianfeng Xu. 2018. CAIL2018: A Large-Scale Legal Dataset for Judgment Prediction. *arXiv:1807.02478 [cs]*. ArXiv: 1807.02478.

K. Xu, J. Ba, R. Kiros, K. Cho, A. C. Courville, R. Salakhutdinov, R. Zemel, and Y. Bengio. 2015. Show, attend and tell: Neural image caption generation with visual attention. In *ICML*.

H. Ye, X. Jiang, Z. Luo, and W. Chao. 2018. Interpretable charge predictions for criminal cases: Learning to generate court views from fact descriptions. *ArXiv*, abs/1802.08504.

Ronghui You, Zihan Zhang, Ziye Wang, Suyang Dai, Hiroshi Mamitsuka, and Shanfeng Zhu. 2019. AttentionXML: Label Tree-based Attention-Aware Deep Model for High-Performance Extreme Multi-Label Text Classification. In *Advances in Neural Information Processing Systems 32*, pages 5812–5822. Curran Associates, Inc.

Haoxi Zhong, Chaojun Xiao, Cunchao Tu, Tianyang Zhang, Zhiyuan Liu, and Maosong Sun. 2020. How does NLP benefit legal system: A summary of legal artificial intelligence. In *Proceedings of the 58th Annual Meeting of the Association for Computational Linguistics*, pages 5218–5230, Online. Association for Computational Linguistics.

A Dataset Curation

We describe in-detail the processing method we followed to generate *GLC* and describe the data structure of the final JSON documents.

A.1 Parsing the Original Documents

The original legislative volumes are encoded in MS Word (.doc) format. While most of them follow the double-column format, there are cases where they also include text in single-column format or even include scanned documents or images as legal resources, making the initial data quite noisy. Considering our objective, these abnormalities should be revised, and all the additional metadata contained in the .doc file (e.g., font style, size, page margins) should be removed. Thus, converting these documents into plain text files was of significant importance. To achieve that, we used docx2txt[18], a python utility that detects and extracts text from .doc files.

Examining the output text files, we encountered problematic samples that needed special handling. For example, we found significant keywords (e.g., "ΘΕΜΑ" which means subject) missing from text or even having typos, subject IDs found inline with subject titles etc., mostly due to minor inaccuracies in the text conversion. Furthermore, multiple white spaces, multiple new lines and special or corrupted characters occurred in the text. To overcome these complications, we performed data cleaning using heuristics and regular expressions to produce neat text files that follow the same normalized structural pattern.

Next, we built a rule-based parser in Python which receives these text files as input and produces JSON files that will be the inputs to our classifiers. The goal here is to separate legal resources into single documents, along with all their related metadata such as ID, publication year, title etc. and their classification hierarchy (i.e., in which volume, chapter and subject they belong to). Each final JSON file represents a unique legal resource, ready to be fed into the machine-learning models we built. The parser builds in memory a tree of depth 4 that represents the whole GLC hierarchy. The first level consists of the thematic volumes while the second level contains all the thematic chapters for each volume. The third level includes the thematic subjects of the individual chapters, and finally, the leaf nodes represent the legal resources. An overview of the tree can be found in Figure 4.

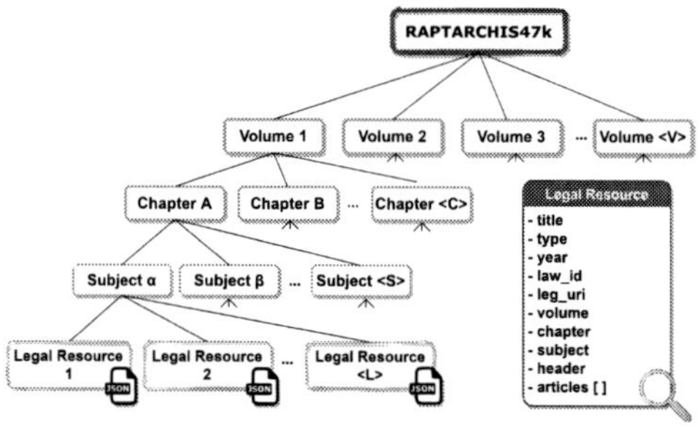

Figure 4: Tree representation of GLC thematic hierarchy

With the use of regular expressions, the parser organizes the content to its thematic hierarchy. Each legal resource may contain the whole original legislative document, some articles of it or even a short sentence (usually its original title or a short description). Hence, the parser attempts to identify and separate any existing articles. However, if this is not feasible, it just keeps the whole body as a text chunk. No deeper parsing is performed (i.e., in paragraphs, sentences) as this is out of scope. The final step is to populate the leaf nodes (i.e., the legal resources) with the appropriate metadata and enhance the available text samples. To accomplish this, the parser uses the metadata fragment of each legal resource to extract the necessary information. Specifically, the words of interest are shown in Figure 5, depicting an example of a metadata fragment.

23. LAW no. 2104 of 2/2 Dec. 1992
(Government Gazette A΄195)

Ratification of the European Convention for the recognition and enforcement of decisions concerning the custody of children and for the restoration of their custody. [...]

Order ID: **Type:** **Law ID:** **Year:**

Figure 5: Legal resource's metadata (translated)

Again, with proper regular expressions, the parser manages to retrieve the requested information. Also, having available the type, the year of publication and the ID of each legal resource, the parser is able to uniquely identify each one of them by using the following pattern: ***{type}/{year}/{id}***. Exploiting that, it searches for duplicate legal resources that may exist in the dataset. For example,

[18]Available at: https://github.com/ankushshah89/python-docx2txt/.

one law may be present in more than one subject due to the thematic variety of its articles. To avoid any complexities and because our task is multi-class and not multi-label classification, the parser removes these resources entirely from the dataset.

Moreover, the parser manages to enhance the content of some legal resources (depending on their type[19]) by utilizing the platform Nomothesia[20] (Chalkidis et al., 2017b). Nomothesia makes Greek legislation available as open linked data using semantic web technologies. Through its RESTful API and by adopting the following URI template: *http://www.legislation.di.uoa.gr/eli/* ***{type}/{year}/{id}***/*data/json* the parser manages to retrieve the text of any legal resource in JSON format, as offered through Nomothesia. Then, it compares the number of tokens of the original and the fetched text fragments and eventually keeps the more extensive. In that way, the parser succeeds in enhancing the size and quality of the dataset.

For each final document, the text content consists of the header along with the body. In case of successful parsing the body consists of multiple articles. Otherwise, it only contains a single text passage. Evaluating the final data, we noticed that many legal resources have limited tokens count (as shown in charts of Section 3.2). However, we consider this not to be a crucial problem since meaningful information (e.g., highly representative words) is quite dense in most of these samples as shown in Figure 6.

VOLUME (18) PRESS AND TOURISM
CHAPTER (B) TOURISM
SUBJECT (A) SCHOOL OF TOURISM PROFESSIONS
14. ROYAL DECREE **of 21 May / 26 June 1959** On the imposition of penalties and the characterization of conduct of the students of the Higher Education of the School of Tourism Professions and graduation, etc.

Figure 6: Small-sized sample of GLC indicating highly representative words (translated)

Finally, the complete dataset, consisting of JSON files following the format of Figure 7 is distributed to train, development and test subsets as described in Section 3.2.

[19]See the supported legislation types at: http://legislation.di.uoa.gr/search/.

[20]See: http://legislation.di.uoa.gr/.


```
{
  "title": "17. ΠΡΟΕΔΡΙΚΟ ΔΙΑΤΑΓΜΑ υπ'αριθ. 234",
  "type": "ΠΡΟΕΔΡΙΚΟ ΔΙΑΤΑΓΜΑ",
  "year": "1996",
  "law_id": "234",
  "leg_uri": "http://legislation.di.uoa.gr/eli/pd/1996/234",
  "volume": "ΒΙΟΜΗΧΑΝΙΚΗ ΝΟΜΟΘΕΣΙΑ",
  "chapter": "ΔΙΑΦΟΡΕΣ ΒΙΟΜΗΧΑΝΙΕΣ",
  "subject": "ΔΗΜΟΣΙΑ ΕΠΙΧΕΙΡΗΣΗ ΠΕΤΡΕΛΑΙΟΥ",
  "header": "Αύξηση κατά δεκαπέντε [...] Α.Ε.».",
  "articles": [
    "\nΕγκρίνεται η από 22 [...] δραχμών η κάθε μία.",
    "\nΤο Διάταγμα αυτό ισχύει από την [...] διατάγματος."
  ]
}
```


Figure 7: Final legal resource as JSON. The legal resource has been parsed and enhanced with two articles, as fetched from Nomothesia web platform

Machine Extraction of Tax Laws from Legislative Texts

Elliott Ash
ETH Zurich
ashe@ethz.ch

Malka Guillot
HEC Liège
guillotm@uliege.be

Luyang Han
ETH Zurich
hanluyang0521@gmail.com

Abstract

Using a corpus of compiled codes from U.S. states containing labeled tax law sections, we train text classifiers to automatically tag tax-law documents and, further, to identify the associated revenue source (e.g. income, property, or sales). After evaluating classifier performance in held-out test data, we apply them to an historical corpus of U.S. state legislation to extract the flow of relevant laws over the years 1910 through 2010. We document that the classifiers are effective in the historical corpus, for example by automatically detecting establishments of state personal income taxes. The trained models with replication code are published at https://github.com/luyang521/tax-classification.

1 Introduction

A foundational task in legal document analysis is to determine a document's area of legal practice – for example, tax law. In a law firm or court administrative office, distinguishing tax-related matters from others is necessary for assigning work to lawyers or judges who have the right expertise. In the scope of income reporting and payments, having the relevant statutes and cases to hand is necessary for complying with the law without overpaying. In empirical legal studies, measurement of the volume, complexity, or other features of tax laws is predicated on extracting those laws in the first place.

This essential task – of distinguishing different legal topics, such as which laws are about tax – has traditionally been done by hand. Tax law materials are assembled in books and databases by trained experts. Building and maintaining these materials is costly, especially in updating corpora to accommodate new material, such as newly enacted statutes. A cheaper and quicker approach would have broad benefits in private legal practice, in the courts, and in academic research.

This paper provides a method and tools for automatically tagging plain-text documents with their relevance to tax law. We use machine learning applied to the law texts to distinguish tax legislation from non-tax legislation in the jurisdictional context of U.S. states. Further, within the set of tax laws, we train a second model to classify the associated source – e.g. personal income, sales, property.

The approach works as follows. We start with a corpus of tax code sections, with class labels generated from section headers. The plain texts of the code sections are transformed to frequency distributions over a vocabulary of tens of thousands of phrases. Using those phrase frequencies as inputs, we train a binary text classifier to all statutes to predict the label of tax-related or not. We train a second multinomial classifier on the subset of tax law statutes to predict the tax source label – individual income tax, corporate income tax, property tax, etc. For the first binary classifier, we get the best performance with a regularized logistic regression (95% accuracy). For the multinomial source classifier, we get the best performance with a random forest classifier (73% accuracy).[1]

We then apply these classifiers to assign labels in an historical corpus of state session laws, issued biennially over the century starting in 1910 and ending in 2010. We validate that the model attends to tax-related language in the target corpus and is 90% accurate in a sample of sentences classified as tax-related or not. As an empirical validation, we show that the volume of legal texts related to personal income tax jumps up sharply in the bienniums when a state income tax is introduced, but there is no such jump for tax laws from other sources besides personal income.

Our classifier and this paper add to the growing

[1]The open-source package, with the trained models and sample code, is available at https://github.com/luyang521/tax-classification.

Natural Legal Language Processing Workshop 2021, pages 76–85

literature in applied legal NLP (Palau and Moens, 2009; Kim et al., 2019; Alberts et al., 2020). More specifically, we add to the work on automated classification of relevant legal topics (e.g. Howe et al., 2019). Substantively, the paper is related to others focusing on tax law (Waltl et al., 2017; Sengupta and Dave, 2021). Besides their applications in industry, these text-based legal tools will be useful for empirical legal studies on taxation, such as Alarie et al. (2016) and Choi (2020).

2 Corpus Data

Our training corpus for learning to classify texts is a collection of compiled codes from U.S. states, obtained from LexisNexis in 2017. A document is a statute section. Each section is labelled for whether it is related to taxes or not. Within those related to taxes, we have additional labels for the category of taxation.

These labels were produced through a partly automated iterative process, overseen by a lawyer with U.S. legal training. First, we applied automated pattern matching on the legislative section headings to identify sections related to taxes.[2] The lawyer annotator inspected the associated statutes, and we refined the pattern matches until obtaining high precision and recall. Second, within the tax-related statutes, we produced another set of patterns to match different tax sources. These were also iteratively checked in conjunction with the lawyer annotator. Tax-related statutes that did not get assigned to a source are assigned to an Other category.

Table 1 shows the distribution of labels in the annotated dataset. Taxes are a substantial component of state codes at 6.9%, but the classification task is still quite unbalanced. Similarly, the tax sources are unbalanced, with the largest category (other) at 28.2% and the smallest category (license taxes) at 2.0%.

The application data set for analyzing flows of legislation is the State Session Laws for 1900-2010, obtained from HeinOnline. These are 2,506,513 statutes coming from the annual or biennial session laws enacted by U.S. states in any given year.

[2]Note that the pattern matching is applied to the full hierarchy of section headings, going from title to chapter to section. So for example, if the chapter is called "Taxation" and the section is called "Relief", that section would be coded as tax-related based on the higher-level chapter heading. Similarly, in the chapter on "Education", the section on "Education Tax" would be coded as tax-related but the section on "Teacher Training" would not.

Table 1: Label Distribution in Source Data

A. Tax-Related or Not

	Number of Sections	Percentage
Tax related	45468	6.87%
Not tax-related	616449	93.13%

B. Tax Source

Tax source	Number of Sections	Percent
Corporate tax	2727	6.00%
Energy tax	3665	8.06%
Excise tax	7494	16.48%
Income tax	4768	10.49%
Inheritance tax	1259	2.77%
License tax	898	1.98%
Property tax	8591	18.90%
Sales tax	3229	7.10%
Other	12837	28.23%

The data come as raw OCR from document scans, with a sample shown in Appendix Table A.1. The data are segmented into statutes through an automated process. The resulting statute sections are not annotated as being related to taxes or not. In addition, they do not contain section headers, so using the header-based pattern matching approach is not feasible.

Before getting to the modeling, we build a joint vocabulary from the historical session laws and modern codes. In both corpora, we break down the plain text into countable features. Each statute section is represented as a frequency distribution over a vocabulary of words, bigrams (two-word phrases), and trigrams (three-word phrases). The vocabulary is filtered to the 50,000 most frequent words and phrases used in both corpora, after dropping any phrases appearing in more than 75% of documents.

3 Machine Extraction of Tax Laws

This section describes how we train a model to predict whether a statute section is tax related. We start with the annotated modern codes sections, and the n-gram features described above. The task is to train a text classifier to reproduce the annotated labels, extracted from the statute section headers, based on the statute body text. For evaluation, we split the set of codes into 80% training set and 20% test set.

For the machine classification, we experimented with two models: logistic regression and a random forest classifier (e.g. Friedman et al., 2001).[3]

[3]We also experimented with a convolutional neural net

For each of these models, we performed grid search to select hyperparameters with five-fold cross-validation in the training set. The selected settings are reported in Appendix Table A.2. One of the hyperparameters was the degree of additional feature selection within the training set using a chi-squared test. For example, for logistic regression, the model uses only the 2000 most predictive features, uses balanced class weights, and adds weak L2 regularization (penalty = .01).

Table 2: Performance of Tax-Law Classifiers

Model	Test Accuracy	Test AUCROC	Test F1	Test Precision	Test Recall
Logistic	0.952	0.901	0.552	0.783	0.427
Random Forest	0.950	0.889	0.503	0.790	0.368

Figure 1: Calibration Plot for Tax-Law Classifier

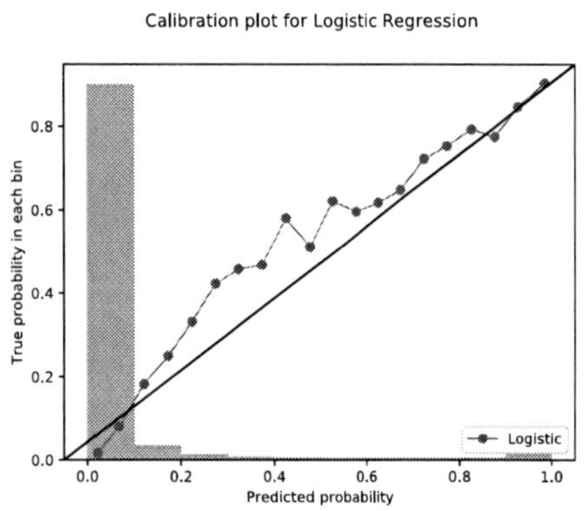

Table 2 reports the test-set evaluation results for the tax-law classifier. Performance is quite good for both classifiers, with logistic regression doing slightly better with test-set accuracy = .952, and AUC = .901. The model is somewhat conservative in identifying tax statutes (recall = .427), but with good precision (.783). In addition, the logistic regression model is well-calibrated (Figure 1), properly ranking statute sections by their probability of being about taxes, and faithfully replicating the test-set distribution. Finally, we assessed the qualitative validity of the classifier by analyzing the phrases that are most predictive of the label (Appendix Table A.3). They are quite intuitive, including "tax", "taxpayer", "tax imposed", "revenue", "department of revenue", and "assessor".

applied to word embeddings. This approach performed significantly worse than the logistic regression and random forest, so we do not report the results. Exploring the gains from neural nets in this task is an important area for future work.

Thus, we are confident with the performance of the tuned logistic regression model, for the purposes of classifying documents as tax-related or not.

4 Classifying Tax Laws by Tax Source

The next task is to classify the source of taxed value. The corpus used is the set of annotated statute sections that were labeled as tax-related. Each statute is labeled according to one of the nine classes listed in Table 1 Panel B. We do stratified sampling to preserve the class distribution across train (80%) and test (20%) set.

Logistic regression performed poorly on this task, so we focus on the random forest classifier.[4] Again, hyperparameters were selected through five-fold cross-validated grid search (Appendix Table A.4). We have a feature set of 10K n-grams, balanced class weights, and 500 decision trees in the ensemble.

Table 3: Performance of Tax-Source Classifier

A. Overall Performance

Model	Test Acc.	Test F1	Test Prec.	Test Recall
Random Forest	0.728	0.728	0.745	0.728

B. Performance by Class

	Precision	Recall	F1-score
Corporate tax	0.71	0.47	0.56
Energy tax	0.87	0.71	0.78
Excise tax	0.82	0.71	0.76
Income tax	0.79	0.73	0.76
Inheritance tax	0.82	0.74	0.78
License tax	0.96	0.76	0.85
Property tax	0.76	0.7	0.73
Sales tax	0.78	0.67	0.72
Other	0.61	0.83	0.71

Table 3 Panel A reports the aggregate metrics for classifying tax source labels. The accuracy is 73%, with a weighted average precision of .75. Unsurprisingly, the source classifier is less accurate than the earlier binary classifier. It has to decide between nine classes with significant overlap in language.

Looking at the metrics separately by class, Panel B shows that precision is quite high across all classes, but recall varies significantly. For example, income tax has a precision of .79 and recall of .73, while sales tax has a precision of .78 and recall of

[4]As mentioned in the footnote above, we also tried a convolutional neural net model, which performed even worse than logistic regression.

.67. The highest-recall category "Other", is also the lowest-precision. This means that the classifier is somewhat conservative in identifying particular tax sources and often errs by putting documents in the "other" bin.

For a qualitative assessment, Appendix Table A.5 shows the set of words and n-grams that the model most associates with each tax-source class. They are quite intuitive – for example, "gasoline" and "fuel" are associated with energy, "cigarettes" with excise, "decedent" with inheritance, and "property" with property. Overall, these phrases suggest that the classifier is capturing legally relevant features, rather than correlated features.

5 Application to State Session Laws

We now have two trained text classifiers. One can distinguish legislative documents related to tax law from legislative documents on other legal areas. The second one can take documents related to tax law and tell use the value source from which the tax is derived. Now we show the usefulness of these classifiers by applying them to an historical corpus of 2.5M state session laws.

Table 4: Distribution of Labels in State Session Laws

A. Tax Related

	Number of statutes	Percent
Tax related	108109	4.31%
Not tax-related	2398404	95.69%

B. Source Proportions

Tax source	Tax-related	Not tax-related
Corporate tax	2.48%	0.43%
Energy tax	5.94%	1.03%
Excise tax	9.30%	5.90%
Income tax	10.92%	0.72%
Inheritance tax	1.87%	0.76%
License tax	0.57%	0.11%
Property tax	28.57%	7.01%
Sales tax	9.83%	0.75%
Other	30.52%	83.29%

For each statute, we form a predicted probability that it is about taxes using the first tax detection model, trained on the modern codes. We take as tax laws the set of statutes that have a greater than 50% chance of being part of the tax code. The resulting labels are tabulated in Table 4 Panel A. We find that about 4.3% of statutes are about taxes, not too far from the 6.9% of sections observed in the modern codes. The proportion of statutes about taxes has not greatly changed over time, which is reassuring that even though we use modern statutes to train the model, the resulting predictions should be valid even for the early historical years of the statutes.

To obtain some qualitative confidence in the classifier, we applied it at the sentence level for a large sample of statute sections. We then ranked the sentences by predicted probability of being tax related. Appendix Table A.6 shows the top-20 sentences in the sample by predicted class probability on tax-related; Appendix Table A.7 shows an equivalent list but filtering out sentences containing the string "tax". The retrieved sentences are clearly and definitively related to tax law, and the assignment does not depend on the presence of the word "tax". For comparison, Appendix Table A.8 shows the 20 sentences with the lowest class probability (so least likely to be tax-related). On an inspection, these don't mention anything related to taxes, and tend to have more of a focus on courts and judicial issues.

For a more comprehensive evaluation about the cross-domain accuracy, we sampled 100 sentences from the historical corpus, 50 from each predicted class (tax-related or not). The lawyer annotator performed a blind tagging of the sentences as tax-related or not-tax-related.[5] The manual annotations matched the model predictions in 90% of the observations, quite close to the accuracy from the original domain.

Next, the tax-source classifier is applied to the documents in the historical state session laws and class predictions are formed. Table 4 Panel B shows the distribution across classes. In the Tax-Related column, the relative frequencies roughly match up to the distribution in the 2017 codes, with for example 29% about property tax and 11% about income tax. For comparison, the third column shows the predicted tax-source probabilities for the statutes classified as not tax related. A full 83% of these documents are put into the "Other" category, reflecting that these statutes tend not to contain tax-related content that would allow the tax-source model to classify them.[6]

[5]The annotator's task was to answer the question: "Is this sentence making a rule related to taxation, or is it part of the state tax law?" Note that it is often unclear from a single sentence how to answer this question, so the annotator made a best guess. Performance metrics based on reading longer documents, such as sections or chapters, may be different. We have not evaluated performance longer documents given the significant annotation resources required.

[6]We attempted to evaluate the performance of the tax-source classifier at the sentence level, as done with the tax-related classifier. However, we found that the source classifier does not work well on the sentence level. There is not enough

As a final validation step, we check that the introduction of a new tax system – the state personal income tax – is reflected in the measurements generated by our classifiers. We have records of the years where each U.S. state first collected a state income tax. We assess the dynamic impact of the introduction of the tax on the legislative output across tax sources. If our classifier is working well, we would expect a sharp and substantial jump in income-tax legislation at the time of these reforms. We would expect no significant change in tax legislation on other sources besides personal income.

To test these expectations, we estimate a panel event study model with distributed lags and leads by biennium (Schmidheiny and Siegloch, 2019), with state and biennium fixed effects and standard errors clustered by state. Because we would expect that legislation could be passed in the biennium before the tax was first collected, the coefficients are estimated relative to two bienniums before the introduction of the tax. We look at two outcomes. First, we use the log number of words in statutes classified as tax-related and related to income tax. Second, we use the log number of words in statutes classified as tax-related but related to any tax source besides income tax.

Figure 2 Panel A shows the coefficients and 95% confidence intervals from the first panel event study regression. We can see that there is a clear jump in income-tax legislation text in the biennium before the tax introduction, which increases even more drastically in the biennium where income taxes are first collected (a six log points increase). The effect on flow of legislation gradually decreases but remains consistently positive and statistically significant, reflecting that additional legislation is needed to maintain and clarify the policy – for example, to update rates, to add exemptions, and to close statutory loopholes.

Meanwhile, Figure 2 Panel B shows the equivalent event study effect on tax-related legislation for *other* tax sources besides income tax. There is no effect at all on this outcome, as expected for a placebo test. Together, the event study regressions indicate that the tax classifier is precisely capturing

Figure 2: Effect of State Income Tax on Income Tax Legislation

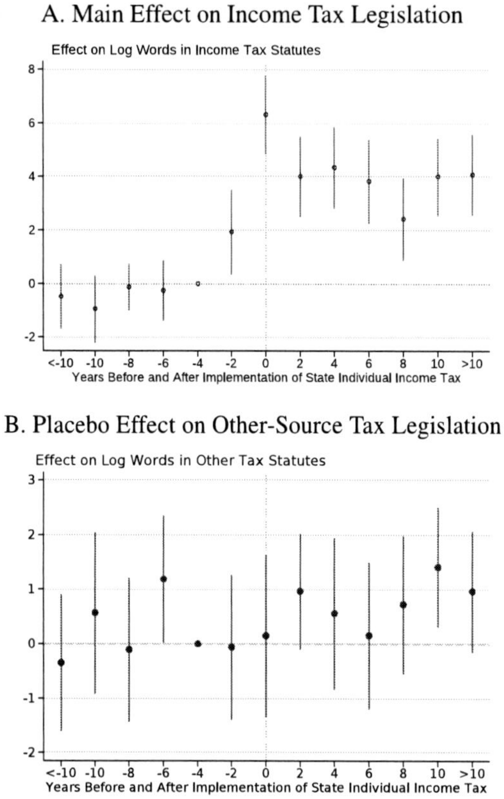

the income-tax components of historical statutes, and not other potentially correlated components.

6 Conclusion

In this paper, we have introduced a classifier for identifying tax laws in legislative corpora, and a second classifier for identifying the source within the set of tax laws. The approach uses a ground-truth corpus of U.S. state codes labelled based on the statute section headers and a random forest classifier applied to n-gram representations of the documents. The trained classifiers perform well in the original domain according to the standard test-set performance metrics.

We provide trained models and code as an open-source package for the research community. In an application, we illustrate how to use the trained model in a new domain – a century of historical statutes from U.S. states. A number of validation steps provide confidence in the usefulness of the classifier for this application and others, whether in the legal tech industry or in empirical legal scholar-

information in a single sentence to make a confident determination, and the resulting top-ranked classes are noisy and mostly incorrect. The source classifier requires longer documents, such as full statute sections. We did not have sufficient annotation resources for a trained lawyer to read lengthy statute documents and determine a single tax source. Further evaluation in application domains could be considered in future work.

ship.

Notwithstanding the promising results from these validations, our approach for classifying tax laws has a number of limitations which could be addressed in future work. First, the model is trained and validated only for U.S. state legislation. It is unclear whether it would work for federal or local legislation in the United States, and it is unlikely the model would work well in other countries. Extending the approach to other jurisdictions would present a clear and straightforward benefit. It could also be fruitful to experiment with models that work across jurisdictions, perhaps including metadata on the jurisdiction.

Second, the approach has been limited to classical machine learning models and has not used deep learning. While our initial experimentation with convolutional neural nets have been unsuccessful, there is clearly additional room for performance gains using state-of-the-art models, especially transformers (e.g. Liu et al., 2019; Wolf et al., 2020). A difficulty with the standard transformer models is the maximum context length, which is shorter than many statute documents. That difficulty might be addressed by creative document segmenting, or by adopting the newer generation of long-document transformers that use sparse attention (e.g. Zaheer et al., 2020).

References

Benjamin Alarie, Anthony Niblett, and Albert H Yoon. 2016. Using machine learning to predict outcomes in tax law. *Can. Bus. LJ*, 58:231.

Houda Alberts, Akin Ipek, Roderick Lucas, and Phillip Wozny. 2020. Coliee 2020: Legal information retrieval and entailment with legal embeddings and boosting. In *JSAI International Symposium on Artificial Intelligence*, pages 211–225. Springer.

Jonathan H Choi. 2020. An empirical study of statutory interpretation in tax law. *NYUL Rev.*, 95:363.

Jerome Friedman, Trevor Hastie, Robert Tibshirani, et al. 2001. *The elements of statistical learning*, volume 1. Springer series in statistics New York.

Jerrold Soh Tsin Howe, Lim How Khang, and Ian Ernst Chai. 2019. Legal area classification: A comparative study of text classifiers on singapore supreme court judgments. *arXiv preprint arXiv:1904.06470*.

Mi-Young Kim, Juliano Rabelo, and Randy Goebel. 2019. Statute law information retrieval and entailment. In *Proceedings of the Seventeenth International Conference on Artificial Intelligence and Law*, pages 283–289.

Yinhan Liu, Myle Ott, Naman Goyal, Jingfei Du, Mandar Joshi, Danqi Chen, Omer Levy, Mike Lewis, Luke Zettlemoyer, and Veselin Stoyanov. 2019. Roberta: A robustly optimized bert pretraining approach. *arXiv preprint arXiv:1907.11692*.

Raquel Mochales Palau and Marie-Francine Moens. 2009. Argumentation mining: the detection, classification and structure of arguments in text. In *Proceedings of the 12th international conference on artificial intelligence and law*, pages 98–107.

Kurt Schmidheiny and Sebastian Siegloch. 2019. On event study designs and distributed-lag models: Equivalence, generalization and practical implications.

Souvik Sengupta and Vishwang Dave. 2021. Predicting applicable law sections from judicial case reports using legislative text analysis with machine learning. *Journal of Computational Social Science*, pages 1–14.

Bernhard Waltl, Georg Bonczek, Elena Scepankova, Jörg Landthaler, and Florian Matthes. 2017. Predicting the outcome of appeal decisions in germany's tax law. In *International Conference on Electronic Participation*, pages 89–99. Springer.

Thomas Wolf, Julien Chaumond, Lysandre Debut, Victor Sanh, Clement Delangue, Anthony Moi, Pierric Cistac, Morgan Funtowicz, Joe Davison, Sam Shleifer, et al. 2020. Transformers: State-of-the-art natural language processing. In *Proceedings of the 2020 Conference on Empirical Methods in Natural Language Processing: System Demonstrations*, pages 38–45.

Manzil Zaheer, Guru Guruganesh, Kumar Avinava Dubey, Joshua Ainslie, Chris Alberti, Santiago Ontanon, Philip Pham, Anirudh Ravula, Qifan Wang, Li Yang, et al. 2020. Big bird: Transformers for longer sequences. In *NeurIPS*.

A Appendix

Table A.1: Example of Text: Statute 761 from the 767 Volume of California's State Law (1990)

SEC. 3.5. +} Section 23603 of the Revenue and Taxation Code is amended to read: 23603. (a) For income years beginning on or after January 1, 1991, and before January 1, 1996, there shall be allowed as a credit against the "tax" (as defined by Section 23036) an amount equal to 55 percent of the qualified cost paid or incurred by the taxpayer for low-emission vehicles or low-emission conversion devices. The credit allowed by this section shall be claimed in the income year the device is installed or, in the case of a new low-emission motor vehicle, the income year the low-emission vehicle is placed in service, and shall not exceed one thousand dollars ($1, 000) per automobile, motorcycle, or two person passenger vehicle, or three thousand five hundred dollars ($3, 500) for a vehicle whose weight is in excess of 5, 750 pounds.

Table A.2: Hyperparameters selected: Tax-Law Classifiers

Model	Features Selected by Chi Square Selector	Hyperparameters Selected
Logistic Regression	2000	class weight : 'balanced' penalty : 'l2' inverse of regularization strength C : 100
Random Forest	30,000	class weight : 'balanced' max features: 35 max depth: 50 number of estimators: 800

Table A.3: Text Features Associated with Tax-Related Classifier

tax, taxpay, tax_impos, depart_of_revenu, exempt, assess, taxabl, taxabl_year, collect, privileg_tax, tax_credit, tax_levi, such_tax, tax_year, taxat, sale, for_the_taxabl_year, tax_liabil, amount_of_tax, taxpay_shall, revenu

Table A.4: Hyperparameters selected in Tax-Source Classifier

Model	**Features Selected by Chi Square Selector**	**Hyperparameters Selected**
Random Forest	10,000	class weight : 'balanced' max features: 50 max depth: 100 number of estimators: 500

Table A.5: Text Features Associated with Tax-Source Class Predictions

Tax Sources							
Corporate	**Energy**	**Excise**	**Income**	**Inheritance**	**License**	**Property**	**Sales**
incom_year	gasolin	ani	taxpay	deced	licens_tax	ani	tangibl_person_properti
section	ani	cigarett	ani	inherit_tax	privileg_tax	assessor	ani
taxpay	motor_fuel	tax	section	estat	ani	section	sale
ani	fuel	section	of_the_intern_revenu	ani	act_to	tax	sale_and_use_tax
franchis_tax	special_fuel	stamp	taxabl_year	estat_tax	gross_receipt	properti	section
of_the_intern_revenu	distributor	tax_impos	incom	tax	virginia	year	retail
corpor	section	state	code	feder_estat_tax	privileg_licens	counti	tax
state	state	provis	adjust_gross_incom	section	busi	assess	sale_tax
net_incom	sever_tax	act_to	gross_incom	death_tax	privileg	act_to	state
tax	tax	nineteen_hundr	incom_tax	death	code	taxat	use_tax

Table A.6: Sentences in State Session Laws with High Class Probability on Tax-Related

State	Year	Sentence
HI	1987	If the taxpayer is married at the close of the taxable year, the credit shall be allowed under subsection (a) only if the taxpayer and the taxpayers spouse file a joint return for the taxable year.
CA	1979	(d) For purposes of this section, except in the case of a husband and wife who live apart at all times during the taxable year, if the taxpayer is married at the close of the taxable year, the credit provided by this section shall be allowed only if the taxpayer and his spouse file a joint return for the taxable year.
FL	1977	The term "estimated tax" shall mean the amount the taxpayer estimates to be his tax under this part for the taxable year.
NM	1977	The credit provided by this section may be deducted from the taxpayers New Mexico income tax liability for the taxable year.
FL	1984	The amount of emergency excise tax paid or accrued as a liability to this state under chapter 221 which tax is deductible from gross income in the computation of taxable income for the taxable year.incurred for the taxable year which is equal to the amount of the credit allowable for the taxable year.
MN	2011	For individuals, the term "estimated tax" means the amount the taxpayer estimates is the sum of the taxes imposed by chapter 290 for the taxable year.
OK	1989	The Tax Commission shall deduct from any income tax refund due to a taxpayer the amount of delinquent state tax, and penalty and interest thereon.
GA	1977	If the taxpayer is married at the close of the taxable year, the credit shall be allowed under subsection (a) only if the taxpayer and his s5pose file a joint return for the taxable year."
KY	1974	(a) T]the amount of federal income tax actually paid or accrued for the taxable year on taxable income as defined in Section 63 of the Internal Revenue Code, and taxed under the provisions of this chapter.
CA	1939	Income Tax Act in the gross income of such person for the taxable year in which or with which the taxable year of the taxpayer ends; and.
NC	2005	The Secretary of Revenue shall determine from all available evidence the taxpayers correct tax liability for the taxable year.
AZ	2005	If the taxpayer has attained the age of sixty-five before the close of the taxable year filing a separate or joint return and the taxpayer is not claimed as a dependent by another taxpayer.2.
FL	1985	(2) The tax imposed by this section shall be an amount equal to 5 1/2 percent of the taxpayers net income for the taxable year.
CA	1979	(2) If the taxpayer is married at the close of the taxable year, the credit shall be allowed under subdivision (a) only if the taxpayer and his spouse file a joint return for the taxable year.
CA	1979	(5) (A) Except in the case of a husband and wife who live apart at all times during the taxable year, if the taxpayer is married at the close of the taxable year, the exclusion provided by this subdivision shall be allowed only if the taxpayer and his spouse file a joint return for the taxable year.
NM	1977	(4) the credit provided by this section may be deducted from the taxpayers New Mexico income tax liability for a taxable year ending in 1976.
NM	1977	(4) the credit provided by this section may be deducted from the taxpayers New Mexico income tax liability for a taxable year ending in 1977.
IN	2007	A taxpayer is entitled to a credit against the taxpayers state tax liability for a taxable year in an amount equal to fifty percent (50%) of the costs incurred by the taxpayer during the taxable year for providing a qualified wellness program for the taxpayers employees during the taxable year.
OR	2009	(A) For [himself or herself] the taxpayer if [he or she] the taxpayer is blind at the close of the taxable year; and.
NM	1977	The credit provided by this section may only be deducted from the taxpayers New Mexico income tax liability for the taxable year in which the equipment was installed on the taxpayers property.

Table A.7: Sentences in State Session Laws with High Class Probability on Tax-Related, Not Mentioning "Tax"

State	Year	Sentence
UT	2000	(3) The county auditor shall record the assessment upon the assessment books in the same manner provided under Section 59-2-1011 in the case of a correction made by the county board of equalization, and no county board of equalization or assessor may change any assessment so fixed by the commission.
AZ	1989	Upon preparation of he rolls, the assessor shall apply the appropriate percentage to the full cash value and limited property value of all property so that the assessel valuation will be shown.
UT	2008	(4) (a) Before the county board of equalization grants any application for exemption or reduction, the county board of equalization may examine under oath the person or agent making the application.
UT	2008	(b) The value fixed by the assessor may not be reduced by the county board of equalization or by the commission.
UT	1992	The value fixed by the assessor may not be reduced by the county board of equalization or by the commission.
CA	1992	All real property not already assessed up to the 1975-76 full cash value may be reassessed to reflect that valuation.
CA	1979	STrATUTES OF 1979. ownership of real property occurs, the assessor shall reappraise such real property at its full cash value.
AZ	1985	Upon preparation of the rolls, the assessor shall apply the appropriate percentage to the full cash value and limited property value of all property so that the assessed valuation will be shown.
FL	1998	(a) Review and approve all budgets and recommended budget amendments in the Florida state community college system.
CA	1941	In determining the actual value" of intangible personal property, the assessor shall not take into account the existence of ally custom or common method, if any, in arriving at the full cash value of any class or classes of property.SEC.
UT	2000	(21) "Use," as used in Part 3, Special Fuel, means the consumption of special fuel for the operation or propulsion of a motor vehicle upon the public highways of the state and includes the reception of special fuel into the fuel supply tank of a motor vehicle.
HI	1956	(e) In the determination of the basis or adjusted basis of any stock, securities or other property.
NE	2004	(4) In any year, the county assessor or the county board of equalization may cause a review of any exemption to determine whether the exemption is proper.
CA	1939	of any county determine that, in order to equalize the assessment of property within the county, an appraisal of all or any class of property is required, the clerk of the board of supervisors and the assessor shall certify this determination to the State Board of Equalization.
MT	1989	The department may request additiinal federal authority for work training programs through the budget amendment process.
MT	1989	the outbreak is an emergency for budget amendment purpnses under 17-7.401 through If the department dies not have sufficient resources to perform the 10-year brand rerecord as required by 81-3-104. the lak if resources is an emergency for budget amendment purposes under 17.7-401 through 17.7-405.
AZ	1989	A person who owns, controls or possesses property valued by the county assessor may each year designate an agent to act on his behalf on any matter relating to the review of the valuation of the property before the assessor and the county board of equalization.
UT	2008	(2) The county board of equalization shall notify an owner of exempt property that has previously received an exemption but failed to file an annual statement in accordance with Subsection (9)(c), of the county board of equalizations intent to revoke the exemption on or before April 1.
UT	1992	(7) "Use," as used in Part 3, means the consumption of special fuel for the operation or propulsion of a motor vehicle upon the public highways of the state and includes the reception of special fuel into the fuel supply tank of a motor vehicle.
NE	2007	Only the county assessor may appeal the grant of such an exemption by a county board of equalization.

Table A.8: Sentences in State Session Laws with Low Class Probability on Tax-Related

State	Year	Sentence
UT	2000	(i the registered agent of the corporation, if the notice or certificate is required to be mailed to the registered agent; or.
HI	2009	[(a)] A registered agent of a domestic or foreign limited liability company may resign from the registered agents appointment by [signing and delivering to the directe for filing the signed statement Of resignation.
CA	1992	(c) If the child is the subject of a guardianship petition, the adoption petition shall so state and shall include the caption and docket number or have attached a copy of the letters of the guardianship or temporary guardianship.
ID	1979	(f) That the address of its registered office and the address of the business office of its registered agent, as changed, will be identical.
CO	1967	The provisions of this subsection (4) shall in no way affect the right of a corporation to file a statement of change of registered office or registered agent as provided in subsection (1) of this section.
AZ	2005	(a) IF THE DISCLAIMANT IS AN INDIVIDUAL, THE DISCLAIMED INTEREST PASSES AS IF THE DISCLAIMANT HAD DIED IMMEDIATELY BEFORE THE TIME OF DISTRIBUTION.
HI	2009	(d) A commercial registered agent shall promptly furnish each entity represented by it with notice in a record of the filing of a statement of change relating to the name or address of the agent and the changes made by the filing.
GA	1955	Whenever a general court-martial is reduced below five members, the trial shall not proceed unless the convening authority appoints new members sufficient in number to provide not less than five members.
UT	2000	Mi the registered agent of the limited liability company Lat Rh; addres -at forth in the limited Umitedmembers.
AZ	1985	THE COURT THAT ISSUED THE SUPPORT ORDER LACKED PERSONAL JURISDICTION OVER THE OBLIGOR.3.
HI	2011	failure to file[-] ar record[- -registef] the disclaimer does not affect its validity as between the disclaimant and persons to whom the property interest or power passes by reason of the disclaimer."
KY	1974	(I) The registered agent so appointed by a corporation shall be agent of such corporation upon whom any process, notice or demand required or permitted by law to be served upon the corporation may be served.
ME	1915	Special courts-martial may consist of any number of officers from three to five, inclusive.-summary.
IL	2003	The court shall condition the appointment of the confidential intermediary on the petitioners payment of the intermediarys fees and expenses in advance of the commencement of the work of the confidential intermediary.
VA	2000	(d) The warranty under this section is not subject to the preclusion in SS 59.1-501.13(a) (1) on disclaiming diligence, reasonableness, or care.
CA	1992	(b) A support order made in this state may also be registered pursuant to Sections 4849 to 4853, inclusive, in any county in which either the obligor or the child who is the subject of the order resides.
CO	1993	(1) AS LONG AS THIS STATE REMAINS THE RESIDENCE OF THE OBLIGOR, THE INDIVIDUAL OBLIGEE, OR THE CHILD FOR WHOSE BENEFIT THE SUPPORT ORDER IS ISSUED; OR.
CA	1992	(1) If the support order was issued by a court of this state, perfect an appeal to the proper appellate court.
AZ	2008	The court may establish a permanent guardianship between a child and the guardian if the prospective guardianship is in the childs best interests and all of the following apply.1.
MI	2002	(p) Disclaiming or limiting the implied warranty of merchantability and fitness for use, unless a disclaimer is clearly and conspicuously disclosed.

jurBERT: A Romanian BERT Model for Legal Judgement Prediction

Mihai Masala, Radu Iacob
University Politehnica of Bucharest,
313 Splaiul Independentei, 060042,
Bucharest, Romania
{mihai_dan.masala, radu.iacob}@upb.ro

Ana Sabina Uban, Marina Cidota
University of Bucharest,
14 Academiei, 010014
Bucharest, Romania
{ana.uban, marina.cidota}@gmail.com

Horia Velicu
BRD Groupe Societe Generale
1-7 Ion Mihalache, 0111171
Bucharest, Romania
horia.velicu@brd.ro

Traian Rebedea
University Politehnica of Bucharest,
313 Splaiul Independentei, 060042,
Bucharest, Romania
train.rebedea@upb.ro

Marius Popescu
University of Bucharest,
14 Academiei, 010014
Bucharest, Romania
marius.popescu@fmi.unibuc.ro

Abstract

Transformer-based models have become the de facto standard in the field of Natural Language Processing (NLP). By leveraging large unlabeled text corpora, they enable efficient transfer learning leading to state-of-the-art results on numerous NLP tasks. Nevertheless, for low resource languages and highly specialized tasks, transformer models tend to lag behind more classical approaches (e.g. SVM, LSTM) due to the lack of aforementioned corpora. In this paper we focus on the legal domain and we introduce a Romanian BERT model pre-trained on a large specialized corpus. Our model outperforms several strong baselines for legal judgement prediction on two different corpora consisting of cases from trials involving banks in Romania.

1 Introduction

In recent years, a paradigm shift stormed the entire NLP field. Transformer (Vaswani et al., 2017) blocks allowed the development of large models that efficiently exploit the power of transfer learning. Pre-training transformers on large unlabeled text data, followed by a fast fine-tuning step has become the de facto approach across the field. Moreover, transformer based architectures (Devlin et al., 2019; Liu et al., 2020; Yang et al., 2019; Radford et al., 2018, 2019; Brown et al., 2020; Zhang et al., 2019) have achieved state-of-the-art results on several generic NLP tasks ranging from natural language understanding (Wang et al., 2018, 2019; Lai et al., 2017), question answering (Rajpurkar et al., 2018; Reddy et al., 2019) to Text-to-SQL (Yu et al., 2018, 2019b,a). Nevertheless, for low resource languages or highly specialized domains, pre-trained language models tend to underperform in part due to the lack of pre-training data or due to the generic nature of these large corpora. For this reason, specific BERT models have been trained and developed for numerous lan-

Natural Legal Language Processing Workshop 2021, pages 86–94
November 10, 2021.

guages such as French (Martin et al., 2020; Le et al., 2020), Dutch (de Vries et al., 2019; Delobelle et al., 2020), Romanian (Masala et al., 2020; Dumitrescu et al., 2020), Finish (Virtanen et al., 2019), Spanish (Cañete et al., 2020) and for highly specialized domains such as Science (Beltagy et al., 2019), Legal (Chalkidis et al., 2020) or Biomedical (Lee et al., 2019).

In this work we set out to investigate the possibility of adapting and applying BERT models for legal judgement prediction on a small, noisy dataset, in a low resource language (Romanian). The corpus we use is a realistic representation of the kind of machine-readable data that is available to practitioners in this specialized field. The data, provided by a Romanian bank, is composed of original lawsuit documents, and features the most frequent types of cases pertinent to the banking domain.

Our contributions can be summarized as follows:

- We publicly release the first, to the best of our knowledge, pre-trained BERT models[1] specialized for the Romanian juridical domain.
- We propose and extensively analyze a general methodology for applying BERT models on real world juridical cases.
- We obtain state-of-the-art results on a small, noisy, highly specialized industry-provided corpus.

2 Related Work

The legal domain provides a wide range of different tasks in which NLP techniques can and have been used. Such tasks include detection of argumentative sentences (Moens et al., 2007; Palau and Moens, 2009), report summarization (Hachey and Grover, 2006; Galgani et al., 2012) or identification of the law areas that are relevant to a case (Boella et al., 2011; Şulea et al., 2017; Sulea et al., 2017).

Sulea et al. (2017) propose the usage of an ensemble of Support Vector Machines (SVMs) on word unigram and bigrams to solve three tasks related to French Supreme Court cases: predicting the law area of a case, predicting case ruling and estimating the time span of a given case or ruling. Similarly, Medvedeva et al. (2018) use SVMs on textual features (mainly word n-grams) to analyze and predict cases from the European Court of Human Rights. Katz et al. (2017) use random forest classifiers over handcrafted features (based rather on the context of the case than on the textual arguments) to predict the ruling of the Supreme Court of the United States. Chalkidis et al. (2020) investigate the usage of BERT models on multiple legal corpora. Their experiments show that further fine-tuning a general BERT model or training one from scratch on juridical data produces state-of-the-art results for legal text classification tasks. While both strategies are valid and the best one might depend on the given task, in our work we decide to pre-train a BERT model from scratch as we employ a significantly larger pre-training corpus (with a raw size of 160GB compared to only 12GB collected by Chalkidis et al. (2020)).

For small and noisy data, such as the real world BRDCases dataset we use in our work, large models may underperform compared to simpler models (Ezen-Can, 2020; Lai et al., 2021). Lately, string kernels (Lodhi et al., 2000, 2002), an efficient character-level comparison technique, have been used with promising results in low resource settings such as native language identification (Ionescu et al., 2016), dialect identification (Butnaru and Ionescu, 2018, 2019), chat understanding (Masala et al., 2018) or automated essay scoring (Cozma et al., 2018).

Dataset	Scope	Entries	Size
RoJur	pre-training	11M	-
RoBanking	downstream	108K	2,212 / 1,309
BRDCases	downstream	149	12,119 / 12,090

Table 1: Dataset statistics. Size is presented in terms of jurBERT tokens with mean and median values separated by /.

3 Datasets

The first dataset we employ, RoJur, comprises all the final rulings, containing both civil and criminal cases, published by any Romanian civil court between 2010 and 2018. Each sample contains: a description of the involved parties, a summary of the critical arguments made by the plaintiffs and the defendants, the legal reasoning behind the verdict and the final verdict itself. The names of the entities involved, as well as other identification details are anonymized throughout the document. Notably, the document is written by a human expert (i.e. the judge presiding over the case) who may have

[1]https://huggingface.co/readerbench

Model	MLM Acc	NSP Acc
jurBERT-base	89.36	99.23
jurBERT-large	90.05	99.29

Table 2: jurBERT NSP and MLM performance on the evaluation corpus

restructured or rephrased the original arguments made by the involved parties. We note that RoJur is a private corpus that can be rented for a significant fee.

We devise a second dataset, RoBanking, from rulings encountered in RoJur. Specifically, we extract common types of cases pertinent to the banking domain (e.g. administration fee litigations, enforcement appeals). From each ruling we only keep the summary of the arguments provided by the plaintiffs and the defendants, and a boolean value denoting which party was favoured in the final verdict.

Finally, we use BRDCases, representing a collection of cases in which a particular Romanian bank (BRD Groupe Société Générale Romania) was directly involved. Each sample contains a section with the arguments provided by the plaintiff and a section for those provided by the defendant. The content of each section is extracted from the original lawsuit files. The plaintiff section is obtained through an OCR process and by employing heuristics to remove content that may be irrelevant to the case. Consequently, the text is likely to contain typographical errors and other artifacts. Moreover, there may be significant differences in writing style, stemming from the possible gap in juridical knowledge between the involved parties. However, this type of input is a realistic representation of the machine readable data that is available to the attorneys handling a specific case in a Romanian bank.

Statistics pertaining to each dataset are presented in Table 1. The size of RoJur (160 GB as stored on disk) enabled us to pretrain a BERT model from scratch for the Romanian juridical domain. The remaining datasets, RoBanking and BRDCases, were used for downstream applications.

4 Model - jurBERT

For all intents and purposes we stick to the same model architecture and training procedure proposed by Devlin et al. (2019). We opt to train two variants of jurBERT, namely jurBERT-base and jurBERT-large, with Whole Word Masking (WWM), each with the same vocabulary of 33k tokens, for 40 epochs on a v3-8 TPU (kindly provided by Tensorflow Research Cloud[2]). For efficiency reasons we train with sequence lengths of 128 for 90% of the training steps, while for the last 10% of steps we use sequence lengths of 512. Evaluation results on the pre-training corpus, RoJur, are depicted in Table 2.

5 Evaluation

We evaluate our pre-trained model on the task of predicting whether the final verdict in a legal case is favourable to the plaintiff or the defendant. To this end, we leverage RoBanking and BRDCases. Despite the similarity in structure, there are significant differences between the two datasets, as presented in Section 3.

We extensively explore different fine-tuning strategies, to enable efficient transfer learning and to prevent catastrophic forgetting. Inspired by previous approaches (Araci, 2019; Howard and Ruder, 2018; Sun et al., 2019) we investigate several strategies for dealing with long texts (e.g. using the first, middle or last part of the text), pooling type (i.e. <CLS>, mean or max), layer unfreezing (e.g. optimize all weights all throughout the training process, gradual unfreezing of layers), learning rate (i.e. constant, discriminative or slanted triangular learning rate), dropout value, final fully connected layers (sizes and numbers) and different combinations of mentioned strategies. We note that the setup for finding the best training strategy is iterative: we test all aspects of a given strategy, select the best and only then moving to the next step while retaining previous strategies. Henceforth, we refer to the best strategy[3] as the *optimized* strategy.

Both downstream tasks are framed as binary classification tasks (i.e. given the arguments, who wins the case). The results are reported using k-fold cross validation, with 5 folds for RoBanking and 10 folds for BRDCases. Cross-entropy loss is minimized using the Adam optimizer (Kingma and Ba, 2015) as each model is trained 3 times. Finally we report the mean AUC and the standard deviation for each model.

6 Results

The results on RoBanking, using only the plaintiff's plea, are presented in Table 3. The upper

[2]https://www.tensorflow.org/tfrc

[3]More details about the process of finding the best and final training configuration can be found in Appendix A

Model	Strategy	Mean AUC	Std AUC
CNN	-	79.60	*
BI-LSTM	-	80.99	0.26
RoBERT-small	classic	68.81	0.13
RoBERT-base	classic	78.52	0.09
RoBERT-large	classic	79.43	0.28
jurBERT-base	classic	81.01	0.19
jurBERT-large	classic	80.38	0.32
RoBERT-small	optimized	70.54	0.28
RoBERT-base	optimized	79.74	0.21
+ handcrafted	-	79.82	0.11
RoBERT-large	optimized	76.53	5.43
jurBERT-base	optimized	**81.47**	0.18
+ handcrafted	-	81.40	0.18
jurBERT-large	optimized	78.38	1.77

Table 3: Results on RoBanking using only the plea of the plaintiff.

Model	Strategy	Mean AUC	Std AUC
BI-LSTM	-	84.60	0.59
RoBERT-base	optimized	84.40	0.26
+ handcrafted	-	84.43	0.15
jurBERT-base	optimized	86.63	0.23
+ handcrafted	-	**86.73**	0.22
jurBERT-large	classic	82.04	0.64

Table 4: Results on RoBanking using pleas from both the plaintiff and defendant.

half of Table 3 introduces the considered baselines, namely two standard CNN and BI-LSTM models with an attention mechanism, followed by three variants of a state-of-the-art Romanian BERT model, RoBERT (Masala et al., 2020). More details regarding the baselines can be found in Appendix B. Lastly, we introduce our proposed model with its two variants. Note that for the upper half of Table 3 we use a classic finetuning strategy as proposed by Devlin et al. (2019). In the lower half of Table 3 we present results using the best finetuning strategy. First, we notice jurBERT consistently outperforms the considered baselines in any setting. One interesting observation is that while jurBERT large outperforms its *base* counterpart on the NSP and MLM tasks, it lags behind on downstream task performance irrespective of training strategy. Finally, incorporating the defendant's plea, leads to significant improvements for all considered models, as can be seen in Table 4.

In Table 5 we present the results on BRDCases. As this dataset is rather small and contains a significant amount of noisy data and very long texts, the challenge posed is significantly harder than in the case of RoBanking. Therefore, we notice the lower overall AUC score compared to the results for RoBanking. As this dataset is extremely small

Model	Mean AUC	Std AUC
SVM with SK	57.72	2.15
jurBERT-base†*	53.65	*
RoBERT-base	52.24	0.33
jurBERT-base	55.35	0.37
RoBERT-base†	53.24	1.76
+ handcrafted†	55.40	0.96
jurBERT-base†	59.65	1.16
+ handcrafted†	**61.46**	1.76

Table 5: Results on BRDCases. † denotes models that were first finetuned on RoBanking.* marks models with no further training on BRDCases, inference-only.

(only 149 entries) we introduce a simple Support Vector Machine (SVM) with string kernels as baseline. More details about the configuration used for the baseline can be found in Appendix B. In the first part of Table 5 we also present the model fine-tuned on RoBanking without further training on BRDCases. In the second half of Table 5 we present the results obtained by fine-tuning two different models on BRDCases, one only pre-trained and one pre-trained and further fine-tuned on RoBanking. While the two corpora differ in essence, fine-tuning on RoBanking greatly improves the downstream performance on BRDCases. Finally, we note the importance of the pre-training step (on RoJur corpus) as jurBERT consistently and significantly outperforms RoBERT for all considered models and experiments, but especially for the real-word use case (Table 5).

Lastly, we investigate the effectiveness of simple handcrafted features for the legal judgement prediction task. Handcrafted features include the county and the year for each case and, while already present in text, they were also added in the final decision layer in categorical form (one-hot encoding). Experiments with said features are marked accordingly (+ *handcrafted*) in Tables 3,4 and 5. In the case of RoBanking, the added features are not especially relevant, yielding mixed results: same or worse mean AUC when using only the plaintiff's plea; see Table 3), and slightly better results overall when using both the plaintiff's and the defendant's pleas (see Table 4). However, for BRDCases, handcrafted features provide a consistent improvement of around 2% absolute value for both RoBERT and jurBERT models (see Table 5). Our best model, jurBERT with added handcrafted features significantly outperforms the considered baseline with an almost 4% absolute value mean AUC increase.

7 Conclusions

In this work, to the best of our knowledge, we employed the first study on applicability of state-of-the-art NLP methods for Romanian legal judgement prediction. We pre-trained, released and evaluated our models with promising results on two highly practical datasets, RoBanking and BRD-Cases. On the first dataset, that contains a human-generated summary of key arguments, our model, jurBERT, outperforms the considered baselines. Turning to the second dataset, that contains all the original arguments of the involved parties, jurBERT is just slighty better than much simpler models, as it struggles to handle such long texts. Especially in this case, the limitations of BERT-like models with regards to the maximum input size are a significant factor that hampers their performance.

Our proposed methodology for legal judgment prediction on real world cases involves three steps. The first step is pre-training a BERT model on a general purpose collection of cases (in our case RoJur). The second step includes further training on a subset of the previous corpus (in our case RoBanking), in which the model learns to predict the verdict having access only to the summarized arguments of the involved parties. The final and the most important step in our work is training and evaluating on the industry-provided cases. One of our key findings is that the second step in this methodology is crucial for obtaining good results for legal judgment prediction. We emphasize that this methodology is language independent and can easily be applied to similar tasks.

Major improvement areas for our approach are the development and integration of more refined handcrafted features (e.g. the type of court or the identity of the judge) and tackling the problem of long texts that greatly exceed the maximum input size of our model. For the latter, lines of research include summarization of long texts or employing methods of increasing the inherent sequence length limit of transformer models (Zaheer et al., 2020; Beltagy et al., 2020).

References

Dogu Araci. 2019. Finbert: Financial sentiment analysis with pre-trained language models. *arXiv preprint arXiv:1908.10063*.

Iz Beltagy, Kyle Lo, and Arman Cohan. 2019. SciBERT: A pretrained language model for scientific text. In *Proceedings of the 2019 Conference on Empirical Methods in Natural Language Processing and the 9th International Joint Conference on Natural Language Processing (EMNLP-IJCNLP)*, pages 3615–3620, Hong Kong, China. Association for Computational Linguistics.

Iz Beltagy, Matthew E. Peters, and Arman Cohan. 2020. Longformer: The long-document transformer. *arXiv:2004.05150*.

Guido Boella, Luigi Di Caro, and Llio Humphreys. 2011. Using classification to support legal knowledge engineers in the eunomos legal document management system. In *Fifth international workshop on Juris-informatics (JURISIN)*.

Tom Brown, Benjamin Mann, Nick Ryder, Melanie Subbiah, Jared D Kaplan, Prafulla Dhariwal, Arvind Neelakantan, Pranav Shyam, Girish Sastry, Amanda Askell, Sandhini Agarwal, Ariel Herbert-Voss, Gretchen Krueger, Tom Henighan, Rewon Child, Aditya Ramesh, Daniel Ziegler, Jeffrey Wu, Clemens Winter, Chris Hesse, Mark Chen, Eric Sigler, Mateusz Litwin, Scott Gray, Benjamin Chess, Jack Clark, Christopher Berner, Sam McCandlish, Alec Radford, Ilya Sutskever, and Dario Amodei. 2020. Language models are few-shot learners. In *Advances in Neural Information Processing Systems*, volume 33, pages 1877–1901. Curran Associates, Inc.

Andrei Butnaru and Radu Tudor Ionescu. 2019. MOROCO: The Moldavian and Romanian dialectal corpus. In *Proceedings of the 57th Annual Meeting of the Association for Computational Linguistics*, pages 688–698, Florence, Italy. Association for Computational Linguistics.

Andrei M. Butnaru and Radu Tudor Ionescu. 2018. Unibuckernel reloaded: First place in arabic dialect identification for the second year in a row. *CoRR*, abs/1805.04876.

José Cañete, Gabriel Chaperon, Rodrigo Fuentes, Jou-Hui Ho, Hojin Kang, and Jorge Pérez. 2020. Spanish pre-trained bert model and evaluation data. In *PML4DC at ICLR 2020*.

Ilias Chalkidis, Manos Fergadiotis, Prodromos Malakasiotis, Nikolaos Aletras, and Ion Androutsopoulos. 2020. LEGAL-BERT: The muppets straight out of law school. In *Findings of the Association for Computational Linguistics: EMNLP 2020*, pages 2898–2904, Online. Association for Computational Linguistics.

Mădălina Cozma, Andrei Butnaru, and Radu Tudor Ionescu. 2018. Automated essay scoring with string kernels and word embeddings. In *Proceedings of the 56th Annual Meeting of the Association for Computational Linguistics (Volume 2: Short Papers)*, pages 503–509, Melbourne, Australia. Association for Computational Linguistics.

Wietse de Vries, Andreas van Cranenburgh, Arianna Bisazza, Tommaso Caselli, Gertjan van Noord, and Malvina Nissim. 2019. Bertje: A dutch bert model. *arXiv preprint arXiv:1912.09582*.

Pieter Delobelle, Thomas Winters, and Bettina Berendt. 2020. Robbert: a dutch roberta-based language model. *arXiv preprint arXiv:2001.06286*.

Jacob Devlin, Ming-Wei Chang, Kenton Lee, and Kristina Toutanova. 2019. BERT: Pre-training of deep bidirectional transformers for language understanding. In *Proceedings of the 2019 Conference of the North American Chapter of the Association for Computational Linguistics: Human Language Technologies, Volume 1 (Long and Short Papers)*, pages 4171–4186, Minneapolis, Minnesota. Association for Computational Linguistics.

Stefan Dumitrescu, Andrei-Marius Avram, and Sampo Pyysalo. 2020. The birth of Romanian BERT. In *Findings of the Association for Computational Linguistics: EMNLP 2020*, pages 4324–4328, Online. Association for Computational Linguistics.

Aysu Ezen-Can. 2020. A comparison of lstm and bert for small corpus. *arXiv preprint arXiv:2009.05451*.

Filippo Galgani, Paul Compton, and Achim Hoffmann. 2012. Combining different summarization techniques for legal text. In *Proceedings of the workshop on innovative hybrid approaches to the processing of textual data*, pages 115–123.

Ben Hachey and Claire Grover. 2006. Extractive summarisation of legal texts. *Artificial Intelligence and Law*, 14(4):305–345.

Jeremy Howard and Sebastian Ruder. 2018. Universal language model fine-tuning for text classification. In *Proceedings of the 56th Annual Meeting of the Association for Computational Linguistics (Volume 1: Long Papers)*, pages 328–339, Melbourne, Australia. Association for Computational Linguistics.

Radu Tudor Ionescu, Marius Popescu, and Aoife Cahill. 2016. String kernels for native language identification: Insights from behind the curtains. *Computational Linguistics*, 42(3):491–525.

Daniel Martin Katz, Michael J. Bommarito, II, and Josh Blackman. 2017. A general approach for predicting the behavior of the supreme court of the united states. *PLOS ONE*, 12(4):1–18.

Diederik P. Kingma and Jimmy Ba. 2015. Adam: A method for stochastic optimization. In *3rd International Conference on Learning Representations, ICLR 2015, San Diego, CA, USA, May 7-9, 2015, Conference Track Proceedings*.

Guokun Lai, Qizhe Xie, Hanxiao Liu, Yiming Yang, and Eduard Hovy. 2017. RACE: Large-scale ReAding comprehension dataset from examinations. In *Proceedings of the 2017 Conference on Empirical Methods in Natural Language Processing*, pages 785–794, Copenhagen, Denmark. Association for Computational Linguistics.

Tuan Lai, Heng Ji, and ChengXiang Zhai. 2021. BERT might be overkill: A tiny but effective biomedical entity linker based on residual convolutional neural networks. *CoRR*, abs/2109.02237.

Hang Le, Loïc Vial, Jibril Frej, Vincent Segonne, Maximin Coavoux, Benjamin Lecouteux, Alexandre Allauzen, Benoit Crabbé, Laurent Besacier, and Didier Schwab. 2020. FlauBERT: Unsupervised language model pre-training for French. In *Proceedings of the 12th Language Resources and Evaluation Conference*, pages 2479–2490, Marseille, France. European Language Resources Association.

Jinhyuk Lee, Wonjin Yoon, Sungdong Kim, Donghyeon Kim, Sunkyu Kim, Chan Ho So, and Jaewoo Kang. 2019. BioBERT: a pre-trained biomedical language representation model for biomedical text mining. *Bioinformatics*, 36(4):1234–1240.

Yinhan Liu, Myle Ott, Naman Goyal, Jingfei Du, Mandar Joshi, Danqi Chen, Omer Levy, Mike Lewis, Luke Zettlemoyer, and Veselin Stoyanov. 2020. RoBERTa: A robustly optimized BERT pretraining approach.

Huma Lodhi, Craig Saunders, John Shawe-Taylor, Nello Cristianini, and Chris Watkins. 2002. Text classification using string kernels. *J. Mach. Learn. Res.*, 2:419–444.

Huma Lodhi, John Shawe-Taylor, Nello Cristianini, and Christopher J. C. H. Watkins. 2000. Text classification using string kernels. In *Advances in Neural Information Processing Systems 13, Papers from Neural Information Processing Systems (NIPS) 2000, Denver, CO, USA*, pages 563–569. MIT Press.

Louis Martin, Benjamin Muller, Pedro Javier Ortiz Suárez, Yoann Dupont, Laurent Romary, Éric de la Clergerie, Djamé Seddah, and Benoît Sagot. 2020. CamemBERT: a tasty French language model. In *Proceedings of the 58th Annual Meeting of the Association for Computational Linguistics*, pages 7203–7219, Online. Association for Computational Linguistics.

Mihai Masala, Stefan Ruseti, and Mihai Dascalu. 2020. RoBERT – a Romanian BERT model. In *Proceedings of the 28th International Conference on Computational Linguistics*, pages 6626–6637, Barcelona, Spain (Online). International Committee on Computational Linguistics.

Mihai Masala, Stefan Ruseti, Gabriel Gutu-Robu, Traian Rebedea, Mihai Dascalu, and Stefan Trausan-Matu. 2018. Help me understand this conversation: Methods of identifying implicit links between cscl contributions. In *Lifelong Technology-Enhanced Learning*, pages 482–496, Cham. Springer International Publishing.

Masha Medvedeva, Michel Vols, and Martijn Wieling. 2018. Judicial decisions of the european court of human rights: Looking into the crystal ball. In *Proceedings of the Conference on Empirical Legal Studies*.

Marie-Francine Moens, Erik Boiy, Raquel Mochales Palau, and Chris Reed. 2007. Automatic detection of arguments in legal texts. In *Proceedings of the 11th International Conference on Artificial Intelligence and Law*, ICAIL '07, page 225–230, New York, NY, USA. Association for Computing Machinery.

Raquel Mochales Palau and Marie-Francine Moens. 2009. Argumentation mining: The detection, classification and structure of arguments in text. In *Proceedings of the 12th International Conference on Artificial Intelligence and Law*, ICAIL '09, page 98–107, New York, NY, USA. Association for Computing Machinery.

Alec Radford, Karthik Narasimhan, Tim Salimans, and Ilya Sutskever. 2018. Improving language understanding by generative pre-training.

Alec Radford, Jeffrey Wu, Rewon Child, David Luan, Dario Amodei, and Ilya Sutskever. 2019. Language models are unsupervised multitask learners. *OpenAI blog*, 1(8):9.

Pranav Rajpurkar, Robin Jia, and Percy Liang. 2018. Know what you don't know: Unanswerable questions for SQuAD. In *Proceedings of the 56th Annual Meeting of the Association for Computational Linguistics (Volume 2: Short Papers)*, pages 784–789, Melbourne, Australia. Association for Computational Linguistics.

Siva Reddy, Danqi Chen, and Christopher D. Manning. 2019. CoQA: A conversational question answering challenge. *Transactions of the Association for Computational Linguistics*, 7:249–266.

Octavia-Maria Sulea, Marcos Zampieri, Shervin Malmasi, Mihaela Vela, Liviu P Dinu, and Josef Van Genabith. 2017. Exploring the use of text classification in the legal domain. *arXiv preprint arXiv:1710.09306*.

Octavia-Maria Şulea, Marcos Zampieri, Mihaela Vela, and Josef van Genabith. 2017. Predicting the law area and decisions of French Supreme Court cases. In *Proceedings of the International Conference Recent Advances in Natural Language Processing, RANLP 2017*, pages 716–722, Varna, Bulgaria. INCOMA Ltd.

Chi Sun, Xipeng Qiu, Yige Xu, and Xuanjing Huang. 2019. How to fine-tune bert for text classification? In *Chinese Computational Linguistics*, pages 194–206, Cham. Springer International Publishing.

Ashish Vaswani, Noam Shazeer, Niki Parmar, Jakob Uszkoreit, Llion Jones, Aidan N Gomez, Ł ukasz Kaiser, and Illia Polosukhin. 2017. Attention is all you need. In *Advances in Neural Information Processing Systems*, volume 30. Curran Associates, Inc.

Antti Virtanen, Jenna Kanerva, Rami Ilo, Jouni Luoma, Juhani Luotolahti, Tapio Salakoski, Filip Ginter, and Sampo Pyysalo. 2019. Multilingual is not enough: Bert for finnish. *arXiv preprint arXiv:1912.07076*.

Alex Wang, Yada Pruksachatkun, Nikita Nangia, Amanpreet Singh, Julian Michael, Felix Hill, Omer Levy, and Samuel Bowman. 2019. Superglue: A stickier benchmark for general-purpose language understanding systems. In *Advances in Neural Information Processing Systems*, volume 32. Curran Associates, Inc.

Alex Wang, Amanpreet Singh, Julian Michael, Felix Hill, Omer Levy, and Samuel Bowman. 2018. GLUE: A multi-task benchmark and analysis platform for natural language understanding. In *Proceedings of the 2018 EMNLP Workshop BlackboxNLP: Analyzing and Interpreting Neural Networks for NLP*, pages 353–355, Brussels, Belgium. Association for Computational Linguistics.

Zhilin Yang, Zihang Dai, Yiming Yang, Jaime Carbonell, Russ R Salakhutdinov, and Quoc V Le. 2019. Xlnet: Generalized autoregressive pretraining for language understanding. In *Advances in Neural Information Processing Systems*, volume 32. Curran Associates, Inc.

Tao Yu, Rui Zhang, Heyang Er, Suyi Li, Eric Xue, Bo Pang, Xi Victoria Lin, Yi Chern Tan, Tianze Shi, Zihan Li, Youxuan Jiang, Michihiro Yasunaga, Sungrok Shim, Tao Chen, Alexander Fabbri, Zifan Li, Luyao Chen, Yuwen Zhang, Shreya Dixit, Vincent Zhang, Caiming Xiong, Richard Socher, Walter Lasecki, and Dragomir Radev. 2019a. CoSQL: A conversational text-to-SQL challenge towards cross-domain natural language interfaces to databases. In *Proceedings of the 2019 Conference on Empirical Methods in Natural Language Processing and the 9th International Joint Conference on Natural Language Processing (EMNLP-IJCNLP)*, pages 1962–1979, Hong Kong, China. Association for Computational Linguistics.

Tao Yu, Rui Zhang, Kai Yang, Michihiro Yasunaga, Dongxu Wang, Zifan Li, James Ma, Irene Li, Qingning Yao, Shanelle Roman, Zilin Zhang, and Dragomir Radev. 2018. Spider: A large-scale human-labeled dataset for complex and cross-domain semantic parsing and text-to-SQL task. In *Proceedings of the 2018 Conference on Empirical Methods in Natural Language Processing*, pages 3911–3921, Brussels, Belgium. Association for Computational Linguistics.

Tao Yu, Rui Zhang, Michihiro Yasunaga, Yi Chern Tan, Xi Victoria Lin, Suyi Li, Heyang Er, Irene Li, Bo Pang, Tao Chen, Emily Ji, Shreya Dixit, David Proctor, Sungrok Shim, Jonathan Kraft, Vincent Zhang, Caiming Xiong, Richard Socher, and

Dragomir Radev. 2019b. SParC: Cross-domain semantic parsing in context. In *Proceedings of the 57th Annual Meeting of the Association for Computational Linguistics*, pages 4511–4523, Florence, Italy. Association for Computational Linguistics.

Manzil Zaheer, Guru Guruganesh, Kumar Avinava Dubey, Joshua Ainslie, Chris Alberti, Santiago Ontanon, Philip Pham, Anirudh Ravula, Qifan Wang, Li Yang, et al. 2020. Big bird: Transformers for longer sequences. *Advances in Neural Information Processing Systems*, 33.

Zhengyan Zhang, Xu Han, Zhiyuan Liu, Xin Jiang, Maosong Sun, and Qun Liu. 2019. ERNIE: Enhanced language representation with informative entities. In *Proceedings of the 57th Annual Meeting of the Association for Computational Linguistics*, pages 1441–1451, Florence, Italy. Association for Computational Linguistics.

A Strategy search

Below are the details regarding the process of searching for the best strategy:

- Dealing with long texts, how to trim sequences longer than 512 tokens: first tokens, last tokens, first 128 tokens with the last 382 tokens, first 512 tokens aggregated with last 512 tokens, or first 512 tokens aggregated with middle 512 tokens and last 512 tokens. Best strategy for this step was: first 512 tokens concatenated with the last 512 tokens. This leads to a final representation (after BERT layer) of size 1,536 for *base* model and 2,048 for *large* model. Aggregation methods include concatenation, mean and max pooling.

- Pooling type: <CLS> token, mean or max pooling. Best strategy for this step: <CLS> token.

- BERT-layer unfreezing: training the full model from the first step, training only the classification layers for a number of epochs followed by training the whole model for another number of epochs, gradually unfreezing a number of layers per epochs.

- Learning rate: constant learning rate of 1e-5, 2e-5 or 5e-5, discriminative learning rate with decay factor of 0.95 or 0.90, slanted triangular learning rate with maximum learning rate of 1e-4, 2.5e-5 or 5e-5, cutout fraction of 0.1 and ratio of 32. The best strategy for this step: slanted triangular learning rate with maximum learning rate of 2e-5, cutout 0.1 and ratio of 32.

Parameter	Extra	Mean AUC	Std AUC
	Trimming		
first (f)	*	81.01	0.19
last (l)	*	80.31	0.22
middle (m)	*	80.29	0.05
first128 & last382	concat	80.79	0.23
first & last	mean	81.25	0.12
first & last	max	81.05	0.25
first & last	**concat**	**81.36**	**0.13**
first & middle & last	mean	81.18	0.22
first & middle & last	max	81.21	0.17
first & middle & last	concat	81.23	0.13
	Pooling type		
<CLS>	*	**81.36**	**0.13**
Mean	*	80.80	0.31
Max	*	80.90	0.28
	Layer unfreezing		
full model	*	**81.36**	**0.13**
classification + full	5,5	77.14	0.28
classification + full	3,7	79.98	0.55
gradually unfreezing	2	80.26	0.28
gradually unfreezing	3	80.73	0.33
	Learning Rate		
constant	1e-5	81.36	0.13
constant	2e-5	81.31	0.16
constant	5e-5	79.89	1.54
discriminative	1e-5, 0.95	80.70	0.09
discriminative	1e-5, 0.90	79.66	0.17
discriminative	2e-5, 0.95	81.28	0.20
discriminative	2e-5, 0.90	81.23	0.11
discriminative	5e-5, 0.95	80.34	1.68
discriminative	5e-5, 0.90	81.36	0.20
slanted triangular	0.1,1e-4,32	72.91	6.42
slanted triangular	0.1,5e-5,32	79.75	3.31
slanted triangular	**0.1,2.5e-5,32**	**81.45**	**0.21**
	Dropout value		
0.1	*	**81.45**	**0.21**
0.25	*	81.33	0.22
0.5	*	81.19	0.25
	Fully connected layers		
128	*	81.45	0.21
256,128	*	81.39	0.13
128,64	*	**81.47**	**0.18**
256,128,64	*	81.32	0.14
128,64,32	*	81.43	0.13

Table 6: Detailed results on RoBanking using only the plea of the plaintiff.

- Dropout value applied after BERT-layer: dropout values of 0.1, 0.25 or 0.5. The best value was obtained using a dropout value of 0.1.

- Configuration of fully connected layers after BERT-layer: (256,128) or (128,64) or (256,128,64) or (128,64,32). Best configuration is (128,64).

For more details and results for each individual component, refer to Table 6.

B Baselines Hyperparameters

- SVM with string kernels uses the combination of intersection, presence and spectrum string kernels on 5-7 character n-grams
- CNN with 300 feature maps of length 6, sequence lengths of 800 words, Adam Optimizer, learning rate = 0.001, dropout = 0.3
- BI-LSTM model comprises a BI-LSTM encoder with a global attention mechanism and a fully connected layer with 64 neurons. For the BI-LSTM encoder we used a dropout layer with 0.2 probability, and for the fully connected layer 0.1 dropout probability. The maximum sequence length is set to 800 and the input consists of Word2Vec embeddings of size 100, pretrained on the data reserved for training. We used Adam optimizer with default parameters (0.01 learning rate).

JuriBERT: A Masked-Language Model Adaptation for French Legal Text

Stella Douka
École Polytechnique
AUEB

Hadi Abdine
École Polytechnique

Michalis Vazirgiannis
École Polytechnique
AUEB

Rajaa El Hamdani
HEC Paris

David Restrepo Amariles
HEC Paris

Abstract

Language models have proven to be very useful when adapted to specific domains. Nonetheless, little research has been done on the adaptation of domain-specific BERT models in the French language. In this paper, we focus on creating a language model adapted to French legal text with the goal of helping law professionals. We conclude that some specific tasks do not benefit from generic language models pre-trained on large amounts of data. We explore the use of smaller architectures in domain-specific sub-languages and their benefits for French legal text. We prove that domain-specific pre-trained models can perform better than their equivalent generalised ones in the legal domain. Finally, we release JuriBERT, a new set of BERT models adapted to the French legal domain.

1 Introduction

Domain-specific language models have evolved the way we learn and use text representations in natural language processing. Instead of using general purpose pre-trained models that are highly skewed towards generic language, we can now pre-train models that better meet our needs and are highly adapted to specific domains, like medicine and law. In order to achieve that, models are trained on large scale raw text data, which is a computationally expensive step, and then are used in many downstream evaluation tasks, achieving state-of-the-art results in multiple explored domains.

The majority of domain-specific language models so far are applied to the English language. Abdine et al. (2021) published French word vectors from large scale generic web content that surpassed previous non pre-trained word embeddings. Furthermore, Martin et al. (2020) introduced CamemBERT, a monolingual language model for French, that is used for generic everyday text, and proved its superiority in comparison with other multilingual models. In the meantime, domain-specific language models for French are in lack. There is an even greater shortage when it comes to the legal field. Sulea et al. (2017) mentioned the importance of using state-of-the-art technologies to support law professionals and provide them with guidance and orientation. Given this need, we introduce JuriBERT, a new set of BERT models pre-trained on French legal text. We explore the use of smaller models architecturally when we are dealing with very specific sub-languages, like French legal text. Thus, we publicly release JuriBERT[1] in 4 different sizes online.

2 Related Work

Previous work on domain-specific text data has indicated the importance of creating domain-specific language models. These models are either adaptations of existing generalised models, for example Bert Base by Devlin et al. (2019) trained on general purpose English corpora, or pre-trained from scratch on new data. In both cases, domain-specific text corpora are used to adjust the model to the peculiarities of each domain.

A remarkable example of adapting language models is the research done by Lee et al. (2019) who introduced BioBERT, a domain-specific language representation model pre-trained on large scale biomedical corpora. BioBERT outperformed BERT and other previous models on many biomedical text mining tasks and showed that pre-training on specific biomedical corpora improves performance in the field. Similar results were presented by Beltagy et al. (2019) that introduced SciBERT and showed that pre-training on scientific-related corpus improves performance in multiple domains, and by Yang et al. (2020) who showed that FinBERT, pre-trained on financial communication cor-

[1]You can find the models in `http://master2-bigdata.polytechnique.fr/FrenchLinguisticResources/resources#juribert`

Natural Legal Language Processing Workshop 2021, pages 95–101
November 10, 2021.

pora, can outperform BERT on three financial sentiment classification tasks.

Moving on to the legal domain, Bambroo and Awasthi (2021) worked on LegalDB, a DistilBERT model (Sanh et al., 2019) pre-trained on English legal-domain specific corpora. LegalDB outperformed BERT at legal document classification. Elwany et al. (2019) also proved that pre-training BERT can improve classification tasks in the legal domain and showed that acquiring large scale English legal corpora can provide a major advantage in legal-related tasks such as contract classification. Furthermore, Chalkidis et al. (2020) introduced LegalBERT, a family of English BERT models, that outperformed BERT on a variety of datasets in text classification and sequence tagging. Their work also showed that an architecturally large model may not be necessary when dealing with domain-specific sub-languages. A representative example is Legal-BERT-Small that is highly competitive with larger versions of LegalBert. We intent to further explore this theory with even smaller models.

Despite the increasing use of domain-specific models, we have mainly been limited to the English language. On the contrary, in the French language, little work has been done on the application of text classification methods to support law professionals, with the exception of Sulea et al. (2017) that managed to achieve state-of-the-art results in three legal-domain classification tasks. It is also worth mentioning Garneau et al. (2021) who introduced CriminelBART, a fine-tuned version of BARThez (Eddine et al., 2020). CriminelBART is specialised in criminal law by using French Canadian legal judgments. All in all, no previous work has adapted a BERT model in the legal domain using French legal text.

3 Downstream Evaluation Tasks

In order to evaluate our models we will be using two legal text classification tasks provided by the Court of Cassation, the highest court of the French judicial order.

The subject of the first task is assigning the Court's Claimant's pleadings, "mèmoires ampliatifs" in French, to a chamber and a section of the Court. This leads to a multi-class classification task with 8 different imbalanced classes. In Table 1 we can see the eight classes that correspond to the different chambers and sections of the Court, as well as their support in the data. The classes represent

Class	Support
CO	28 198
C1_Section1	14 650
C1_Section2	16 730
C2_Section1	11 525
C2_Section2	9 975
C2_Section3	13 736
C3_Section1	16 176
C3_Section2	12 282

Table 1: Chambers and Sections of the Court of Cassation and data support

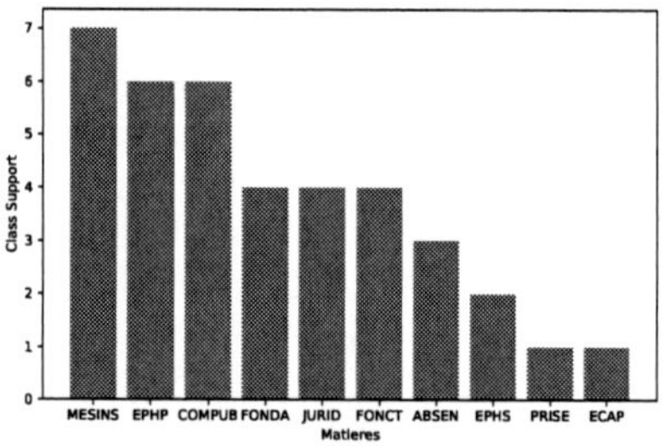

Figure 1: 10 Recessive Matieres

4 chambers: the first civil chamber (C1) that deals with topics like Civil Contract Law and Consumer Law, the second civil chamber (C2) with topics like Insurance Law and Traffic accidents, the third civil chamber (C3) dealing with Real property and Construction Law among other topics and the Commercial, Economic and Financial Chamber (CO) for Commercial Law, Banking and Credit Law and others. Each chamber has two or more sections dealing with different topics.

The second task is to classify the Claiment's pleadings to a set of 151 subjects, "matières" as stated in French. Figure 5 in appendix shows the support of the matières in the data. As we can see in Figure 1 the 10 recessive matières have between 7 to 1 examples in our dataset. We decided to remove the last 3 matières as they have less than 3 examples and therefore it is not possible to split them in train, test and development sets.

4 JuriBERT

We introduce a new set of BERT models pre-trained from scratch in legal-domain specific corpora. We train our models on the Masked Language Modeling (MLM) task. This means that given an input text sequence we mask tokens with 15% probability and the model is then trained to predict these masked tokens. We follow the example of Chalkidis et al. (2020) and choose to train significantly even smaller models, including Bert-Tiny and Bert-Mini. The architectural details of the models we pre-trained are presented in Table 2. We also choose to further pre-train CamemBERT Base on French legal text in order to better explore the impact of using domain-specific corpora in pre-training.

Training Data

For the pre-training we used two different French legal text datasets. The first dataset contains data crawled[2] from the Légifrance[3] website and consists of raw French Legal text. The Légifrance text is then cleaned from non French characters. We also use the Court's decisions and the Claimant's pleadings from the Court of Cassation that consists of 123361 long documents from different court cases. All personal and private information, including names and organizations, has been removed from the documents for the privacy of the stakeholders. The combined datasets provide us with a collection of raw French legal text of size 6.3 GB that we will use to pre-train our models.

Legal Tokenizer

In order to pre-train a new BERT model from scratch we need a new Tokenizer. We trained a ByteLevelBPE Tokenizer with newly created vocabulary from the training corpus. The vocabulary is restricted to 32,000 tokens in order to be comparable to the CamemBERT model from Martin et al. (2020) and minimum token frequency of 2. We used a RobertaTokenizer as a template to include all the necessary special tokens for a Masked Language Model. Our new Legal Tokenizer encodes the data using 512-sized embeddings.

JuriBERT

For the pre-training of the JuriBERT Model we used both the crawled Légifrance data and the Pleadings Dataset, thus creating a 6.3GB collection of legal texts. The encoded corpus was then used to pre-train a BERT model from scratch. Our model was pre-trained in 4 different architectures. As a result we have JuriBERT Tiny with 2 layers, 128 hidden units and 2 attention heads (6M parameters), JuriBERT Mini with 4 layers, 256 hidden units and 4 attention heads (15M parameters), JuriBERT Small with 6 layers, 512 hidden units and 8 attention heads (42M parameters) and JuriBERT Base with 12 layers, 768 hidden units and 12 attention heads (110M parameters). JuriBERT Base uses the exact same architecture as CamemBERT Base.

[2]We used Heritrix, a crawler that respects the robots.txt exclusion directives and META nofollow tags. See `https://github.com/internetarchive/heritrix3`

[3]`https://www.legifrance.gouv.fr/`

Model	Architecture	Params
JuriBERT Tiny	L=2, H=128, A=2	6M
JuriBERT Mini	L=4, H=256, A=4	15M
JuriBERT Small	L=6, H=512, A=8	42M
JuriBERT Base	L=12, H=768, A=12	110M
JuriBERT-FP	L=12, H=768, A=12	110M

Table 2: Architectural comparison of JuriBERT models

Task Specific JuriBERT

We also pre-trained a task-specific model that is expected to perform better in the classification of the Claiment's pleadings. For that we used only the Pleadings Dataset for the pre-training that is a 4GB collection of legal documents. The task-specific JuriBERT model for the Cour de Cassation task was pre-trained in 2 architectures, JuriBERT Tiny (L=2, H=128, A=2) and JuriBERT Mini (L=4, H=256, A=4).

JuriBERT-FP

Apart from pre-training from scratch we decided to also further pre-train CamemBERT Base on the training data. Our goal is to compare its performance with the original JuriBERT model to further explore the impact of using specific-domain corpora during pre-training. JuriBERT-FP uses the same architecture as CamemBERT Base and JuriBERT Base.

5 Methods

Pre-training Details All the models were pre-trained for 1M steps. A learning rate of $1e-4$ was used along with an Adam optimizer (β_1=0.9, β_2=0.999) with weight decay of 0.1 and a linear scheduler with 10,000 warm-up steps. All the models were pre-trained with batch size of 8 expect for JuriBERT Base and JuriBERT-FP that used batches of size 4. For the pre-training we used an Nvidia GTX 1080Ti GPU.

Model	Pre-training Corpora
CamemBERT	138GB
BARThez	66GB
JuriBERT	6.3GB
JuriBERT-FP	6.3GB
Task JuriBERT	4GB

Table 3: Size of pre-training corpora used by different models

Fine-tuning Details Our models were fine-tuned on the downstream evaluation task using the same classification head as Devlin et al. (2019) that consists of a Dense layer with tanh function followed by a Dense layer with softmax activation function and Dropout layers with fixed dropout rate of 0.1. We applied grid-search to the learning rate on a range of $\{2e-5, 3e-5, 4e-5, 5e-5\}$. We used an Adam optimizer along with a linear scheduler that provided the training with 100k warm-up steps. We train for a maximum of 30 epochs with patience of 2 epochs on the early stopping callback and checkpoints for the best model. For the classification we use only the paragraphs starting with 'ALORS QUE' from the Pleadings Dataset, as they include all the important information for the correct chamber and section. This was suggested by a lawyer from the Court of Cassation as the average size of a mèmoire ampliatif is extremely big, from 10 to 30 pages long. By using the 'ALORS QUE' paragraphs we have text sequences with average size of 800 tokens. For the chambers and sections classification task we split the data in 14% development and 16% test data. For the matières classification we split the data in 17% development and 14% test data and stratify in order to have all classes represented in each subset. Both tasks use a fixed batch size of 4. For the fine-tuning we used an Nvidia GTX 1080Ti GPU.

6 Results

The results on the downstream evaluation tasks are presented in Tables 4 and 5. We compare our models with two CamemBERT versions, Base and Large, and with BARThez, a sequence-to-sequence model dedicated to the French language. CamemBERT has been pre-trained on 138GB of French raw text from the OSCAR corpus. Despite the difference in pre-training corpora size, with our model using only 6.3GB of legal text, JuriBERT Small managed to outperform both CamemBERT Base and CamemBERT Large. This further proves the importance of domain-specific language models in natural language processing and transfer learning. Despite our expectations, the performance of JuriBERT Base does not exceed the performance of its smaller equivalent models. We attribute this peculiarity in the usage of smaller batch sizes when pre-training JuriBERT Base and also the fact that larger models usually need more computational resources and more time and data in order to converge.

JuriBERT Small also outperforms BARThez on the chambers and sections evaluation task, which is pre-trained on 66GB of French raw text and usually used for generative tasks. On the matières classification task BARThez is the dominant model with JuriBERT Small being second. We infer that the complexity of the second task benefits more from the robustness and size of BARThez than from the specific-domain nature of JuriBERT.

Comparing our models with the same architectures, it becomes apparent that all task-specific JuriBERT models perform better than their equivalent domain-specific JuriBERT models besides using only 4GB of pre-training data. The results confirm that a BERT model pre-trained from scratch only on the corpus that is then used for fine-tuning can perform better than a domain-specific one on the same task as we expected.

JuriBERT-FP outperforms JuriBERT Base and achieves similar results with CamemBERT Base on the chambers and sections classification task. This shows that further pre-training a general purpose language model can have better results than training from scratch. However, it did not manage to outperform JuriBERT Small in both tasks, which can be attributed to the smaller batch size used during pre-training and to the size of the model as mentioned before for JuriBERT Base. Unfortunately, there are no smaller versions of CamemBERT available to further test this theory. On the matières classification task, JuriBERT-FP still outperforms JuriBERT Base. On the contrary, it performs worse than CamemBERT Base. Along with the state-of-the-art results of BARThez, this leads us to believe that in order to achieve better results in more complex tasks JuriBERT models require more pre-training corpora.

All in all, JuriBERT Small achieves equivalent results with previous larger generic language models with an accuracy of 83.95% on the first task

Model	Lrate	Dev	Test
CamemBERT Base	$2e-5$	82.75	83.22
CamemBERT Large	$2e-5$	79.69	79.91
BARThez	$3e-5$	83.70	83.49
JuriBERT Tiny	$3e-5$	82.00	81.58
JuriBERT Mini	$3e-5$	83.08	82.62
JuriBERT Small	$3e-5$	83.86	**83.95**
JuriBERT Base	$3e-5$	82.26	82.51
Task JuriBERT Tiny	$4e-5$	81.91	81.59
Task JuriBERT Mini	$4e-5$	82.75	**82.66**
JuriBERT-FP	$2e-5$	83.07	**83.28**

Table 4: Accuracy of models on the chambers and sections classification task

Model	Lrate	Dev	Test
CamemBERT Base	$3e-5$	71.64	71.66
BARThez	$2e-5$	72.17	**72.09**
JuriBERT Small	$2e-5$	71.67	**71.80**
JuriBERT Base	$3e-5$	70.28	70.38
JuriBERT-FP	$2e-5$	70.99	**71.21**

Table 5: Accuracy of models on the matieres classification task

and 71.80% on the second task on the test data. JuriBERT Small, JuriBERT Mini and even JuriBERT Tiny all outperform JuriBERT Base, proving that smaller models architecturally can achieve comparable, if not better, results when we are training on very domain-specific data. A larger model, not only requires more resources to be trained, but is also not as efficient as its smaller equivalents. This is of major importance for researchers with limited resources available. Furthermore, JuriBERT-FP achieves better results than JuriBERT Base in both tasks. This leads us to infer that pre-training from an existing language model can be a major advantage, as opposed to randomly initialising our weights.

7 Limitations

As we mentioned before both JuriBERT Base and JuriBERT-FP have been pre-trained using smaller batch sizes than the other models due to limited resources. We acknowledge that this may have affected their performance compared to the other models. However, we believe that their lower performance can also be attributed to their size as larger models are computationally heavier and thus require more resources to converge.

Acquiring large scale legal corpora, especially for a language other than English, has proven to be challenging due to their confidential nature. For this reason, JuriBERT models were fine-tuned on two downstream evaluation tasks that contain data from the pre-training dataset collection. Further testing shall be required in order to validate the performance of our models on different tasks.

The differences in performance between the generic language models and the newly created JuriBERT models are very small. More specifically, only JuriBERT Small manages to outperform CamemBERT Base and Barthez with a difference in accuracy of 0.73%. We attribute this limitation in the use of much less pre-training data. However we emphasize that JuriBERT manages to achieve similar results despite the difference in pre-training corpora size. Thus, we expect JuriBERT to achieve better results in the future provided that we further pre-train with more data.

8 Conclusions and Future Work

We introduce a new set of domain-specific Bert Models pre-trained from scratch on French legal text. We conclude that our task is very specific and as a result it does not benefit from general purpose models like CamemBERT. We also show the superiority of much smaller models when training on very specific sub-languages like legal text. It becomes apparent that large architectures may in fact not be necessary when the targeted sub-language is very specific. This is important for researchers with lower resources available, as smaller models are fine-tuned a lot faster on the downstream tasks. Furthermore, we show that a BERT model pre-trained from scratch on task-specific data and then fine-tuned on this very task can perform better than a domain-specific model that has been pre-trained on a lot more data. We point out of course that a domain-specific model can outperform a task-specific one on other tasks and is generally preferred when we need a multi-purpose BERT model with many applications in the French legal domain. In future work, we plan to further explore the potential of JuriBERT in other tasks and as a result prove its superiority over the task-specific one.

References

Hadi Abdine, Christos Xypolopoulos, Moussa Kamal Eddine, and Michalis Vazirgiannis. 2021. Evaluation of word embeddings from large-scale french web content. *CoRR*, abs/2105.01990.

Purbid Bambroo and Aditi Awasthi. 2021. LegalDB: Long DistilBERT for legal document classification. In *2021 International Conference on Advances in Electrical, Computing, Communication and Sustainable Technologies (ICAECT)*, pages 1–4.

Iz Beltagy, Kyle Lo, and Arman Cohan. 2019. SciBERT: A pretrained language model for scientific text. In *Proceedings of the 2019 Conference on Empirical Methods in Natural Language Processing and the 9th International Joint Conference on Natural Language Processing (EMNLP-IJCNLP)*, pages 3615–3620, Hong Kong, China. Association for Computational Linguistics.

Ilias Chalkidis, Manos Fergadiotis, Prodromos Malakasiotis, Nikolaos Aletras, and Ion Androutsopoulos. 2020. LEGAL-BERT: The muppets straight out of law school. In *Findings of the Association for Computational Linguistics: EMNLP 2020*, pages 2898–2904, Online. Association for Computational Linguistics.

Jacob Devlin, Ming-Wei Chang, Kenton Lee, and Kristina Toutanova. 2019. BERT: Pre-training of deep bidirectional transformers for language understanding. In *Proceedings of the 2019 Conference of the North American Chapter of the Association for Computational Linguistics: Human Language Technologies, Volume 1 (Long and Short Papers)*, pages 4171–4186, Minneapolis, Minnesota. Association for Computational Linguistics.

Moussa Kamal Eddine, Antoine J.-P. Tixier, and Michalis Vazirgiannis. 2020. BARThez: a skilled pretrained French sequence-to-sequence model. *CoRR*, abs/2010.12321.

Emad Elwany, Dave Moore, and Gaurav Oberoi. 2019. BERT goes to law school: Quantifying the competitive advantage of access to large legal corpora in contract understanding. *CoRR*, abs/1911.00473.

Nicolas Garneau, Eve Gaumond, Luc Lamontagne, and Pierre-Luc Déziel. 2021. CriminelBart: A French Canadian legal language model specialized in criminal law. In *Proceedings of the Eighteenth International Conference on Artificial Intelligence and Law*, ICAIL '21, page 256–257, New York, NY, USA. Association for Computing Machinery.

Jinhyuk Lee, Wonjin Yoon, Sungdong Kim, Donghyeon Kim, Sunkyu Kim, Chan Ho So, and Jaewoo Kang. 2019. Biobert: a pre-trained biomedical language representation model for biomedical text mining. *CoRR*, abs/1901.08746.

Louis Martin, Benjamin Muller, Pedro Javier Ortiz Suárez, Yoann Dupont, Laurent Romary, Éric de la Clergerie, Djamé Seddah, and Benoît Sagot. 2020. CamemBERT: a tasty French language model. In *Proceedings of the 58th Annual Meeting of the Association for Computational Linguistics*, pages 7203–7219, Online. Association for Computational Linguistics.

Victor Sanh, Lysandre Debut, Julien Chaumond, and Thomas Wolf. 2019. DistilBERT, a distilled version of BERT: smaller, faster, cheaper and lighter. *CoRR*, abs/1910.01108.

Octavia-Maria Sulea, Marcos Zampieri, Shervin Malmasi, Mihaela Vela, Liviu P. Dinu, and Josef van Genabith. 2017. Exploring the use of text classification in the legal domain. *CoRR*, abs/1710.09306.

Yi Yang, Mark Christopher Siy Uy, and Allen Huang. 2020. Finbert: A pretrained language model for financial communications. *CoRR*, abs/2006.08097.

A Appendix

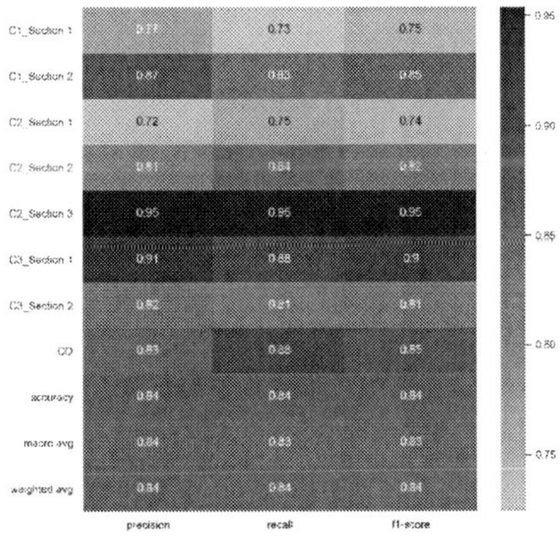

Figure 2: Accuracy, Precision, Recall and F1-Score of JuriBERT Small on the chambers and sections classification task on the test dataset. The graph contains all 8 classes.

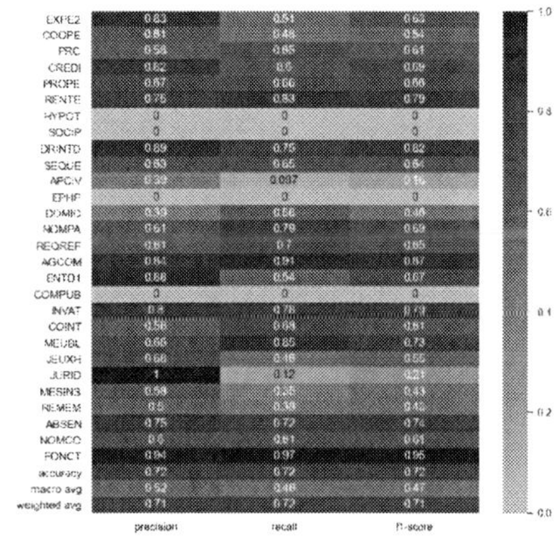

Figure 4: Sample of Accuracy, Precision, Recall and F1-Score of JuriBERT Small on the matieres classification task on the test dataset. The graph contains 28 classes and the overall accuracy of all 148 classes.

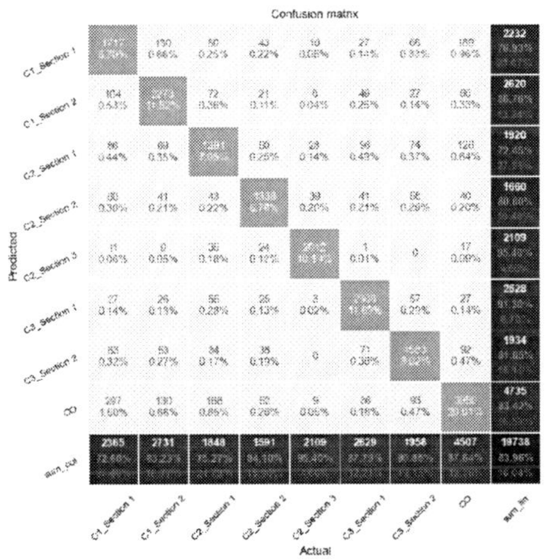

Figure 3: Confusion Matrix of JuriBERT Small on the chambers and sections classification task on the test dataset. The graph includes accuracy and error rate for each class.

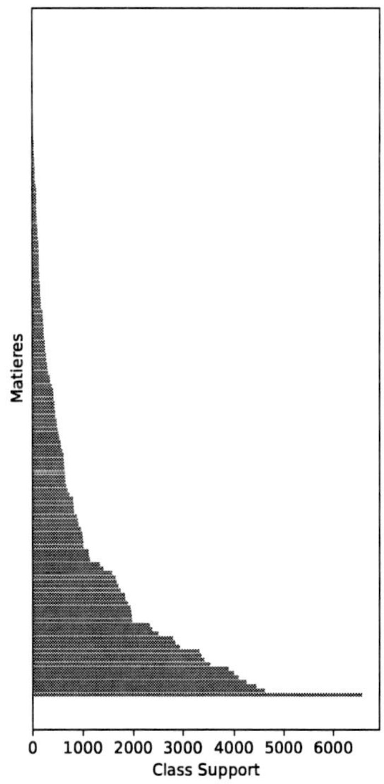

Figure 5: Support of the 151 Matieres in the Court of Cassation data.

Few-shot and Zero-shot Approaches to Legal Text Classification: A Case Study in the Financial Sector

Rajdeep Sarkar[1], **Atul Kr. Ojha**[1], **Jay Megaro**[2], **John Mariano** [2], **Vall Herard**[2] and **John P. McCrae**[1]

[1] Data Science Institute, National University of Ireland Galway, Ireland
[2] FMR LLC, Boston, USA

{rajdeep.sarkar, atulkumar.ojha, john.mccrae}@insight-centre.org
{jay.megaro, john.mariano, vall.herard}@fmr.com

Abstract

The application of predictive coding techniques to legal texts has the potential to greatly reduce the cost of legal review of documents, however, there is such a wide array of legal tasks and continuously evolving legislation that it is hard to construct sufficient training data to cover all cases. In this paper, we investigate few-shot and zero-shot approaches that require substantially less training data and introduce a triplet architecture, which for promissory statements produces performance close to that of a supervised system. This method allows predictive coding methods to be rapidly developed for new regulations and markets.

1 Introduction

Organizations that are governed by legal and regulatory statues concerning communications with the public are required to comply with principles-based content standards. As such, this involves a significant expense due to having to use highly qualified staff to review, iterate on communications internally and file content with regulators, externally. There is thus a substantial expense in terms of iteration time and specialized staff associated with this process. With recent advances in Natural Language Processing (NLP) technologies, it is increasingly becoming possible to automatically flag high-risk statements by *predictive coding* and thus reduce the cost of these manual reviews. However, each industry has specific regulatory requirements and modern NLP systems need large training sets to be effective, and as such it is challenging to develop such systems. In this paper, we focus on a single example of such a regulatory compliance in the financial domain under the US regulation FINRA 2210[1], which states that "no member may make any false, exaggerated, unwarranted, promissory or misleading statement or claim in any communication." We examine how we can train a system in the following settings: firstly in a traditional data-heavy supervised setting, where a large number of existing examples have been classified. Secondly, we investigate a zero-shot training situation, where we have asked a legal expert to provide only rough guidelines for what is not compliant with the legal code. Finally, we combine this in a few-shot setting and show that with comparatively little training data, we can achieve performance that is equivalent with the data-heavy supervised setting and thus enables text classification systems for regulatory compliance to be constructed quickly and with little effort allowing them to cover a wide range of industries and national regulatory frameworks.

[1] https://www.finra.org/rules-guidance/rulebooks/finra-rules/2210

2 Related Work

There has been some work in the area of legal text classification and the application of text classification techniques to legal texts has mostly been successful so far. Methods based on counting the words in the text and then classifying using machine learning approaches such as support vector machines (Cortes and Vapnik, 1995) for example by Sulea et al. (2017), where they applied this method to the classification of texts according to the legal area, ruling and time span of the text. Deep learning methods such as Convolutional Neural Networks (CNNs) have been shown to further improve the performance of such systems (Wei et al., 2018). More recently, the emergence of large pre-trained language models such as BERT (Devlin et al., 2019) has further increased the performance and Shaheen et al. (2020) showed that these models could be used to classify legal texts according to thousands of labels and even on multiple languages if sufficient training data exists.

A criticism of such NLP-based approaches to predictive coding, especially with the emergence of more sophisticated deep learning methods, is

Natural Legal Language Processing Workshop 2021, pages 102–106
November 10, 2021.

that they can appear to be 'black boxes', and thus there has been work in providing explainable systems (Mahoney et al., 2019) that can identify snippets and provides explanations for why they make certain predictions. Similarly, some work has gone into the investigation of specific complexities of legal texts, such as in Nallapati and Manning (2008), who showed that for some legal texts the complex combination of negative and positive statements can confused machine learning approaches. They showed that by combining these machine learning approaches with propositional logic, text classification systems could handle intricate legal wording.

3 Methodology

To solve the problem of legal text classification, we approach this with a triplet architecture (Wei et al., 2021) where an input sentence, s, is compared with a positive example s_+ and a negative example s_- as depicted in Figure 1. We begin by describing the model architecture. Then we discuss the triplet loss used for training the network. Finally, we describe the classification model used for the final classification.

3.1 Model Architecture

Most existing methods of text classification only consider the local features of the samples, and their experimental results show better performance than traditional non-deep learning methods. However, in these methods, the global features of the sample are usually ignored, and these ignored global features will affect the classification accuracy. These global features are key to the use-case presented. To solve this problem, a triplet capsule network framework is proposed for text classification, to optimize results.

A triplet network consist of three instances of the same neural network with shared parameters. The network takes as input three examples in each sample. The three samples consists of the anchor, positive and negative examples. The anchor and positive examples belong to the same class, while the negative example belongs to a different class. The network outputs two values, the distance between the anchor and the positive example and the distance between the anchor and the negative example.

We design a triplet network for the sentence classification task. The network encodes each incoming sentence using Sentence-BERT (Reimers and Gurevych, 2019) encoder. Sentence-BERT captures the contextual information in a sentence in a fixed-size vector representation. The contextual sentence representation is then fed to a two-layer perceptron. The hidden layer of the perceptron has ReLU (Nair and Hinton, 2010) activation for introducing non-linearity in the perceptron.

$$\mathbf{e}_s^1 = \text{S-BERT(s)} \tag{1}$$
$$\mathbf{e}_s^2 = RELU(W_{\theta,1}\mathbf{e}_s^1) \tag{2}$$
$$\mathbf{e}_s^3 = W_{\theta,2}\mathbf{e}_s^2 \tag{3}$$

where $W_{\theta,1} \in R^{d_{e^2} \times d_{e^1 h}}$ and $W_{\theta,2} \in R^{d_{e^3} \times d_{e^2}}$ and the parameter matrices to be learned during training. The Sentence-BERT model is also fine-tuned during the training procedure.

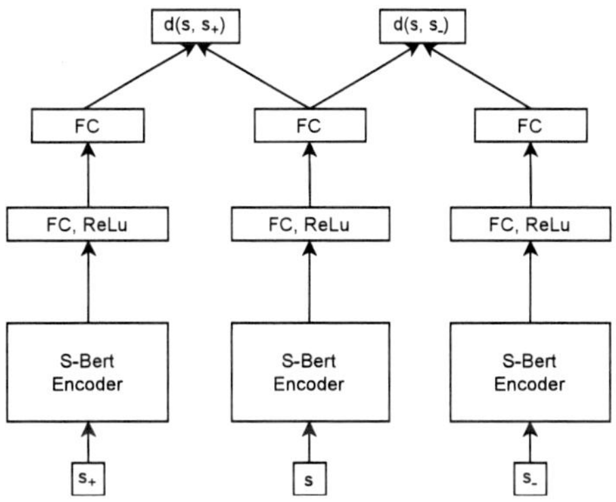

Figure 1: Overall architecture of our approach.

3.2 Triplet Loss

Triplet loss (Hoffer and Ailon, 2015) has been used in few-shot classification methods. Although introduced for images, it has been successfully adapted in natural language processing (Wei et al., 2021; Lauriola and Moschitti, 2021). Triplet loss enables the network to distinguish been positive and negative examples of a class. It is defined in Equation 4.

$$\mathcal{L}(D_+, D_-) = \|D_+, D_- - 1\|_2^2 \tag{4}$$

where D_+ and D_- are defined in Equation 7 and 8 respectively.

$$d_+(s, s_+) = \left\|\mathbf{e}_s^3 - \mathbf{e}_{s_+}^3\right\|_2 \tag{5}$$
$$d_-(s, s_-) = \left\|\mathbf{e}_s^3 - \mathbf{e}_{s_-}^3\right\|_2 \tag{6}$$
$$D_+ = \frac{e^{d_+(s,s_+)}}{e^{d_+(s,s_+)} + e^{d_-(s,s_-)}} \tag{7}$$
$$D_- = \frac{e^{d_-(s,s_-)}}{e^{d_+(s,s_+)} + e^{d_-(s,s_-)}} \tag{8}$$

Table 1: Performance of our few-shot learning model in comparison with other supervised and zero-shot learning methods.

Model	Precision	Recall	F1	Accuracy
Naive Bayes	0.78	0.48	0.60	0.75
MLP	0.66	0.70	0.68	0.75
SVM	0.76	0.67	0.71	0.79
S-BERT	0.72	0.69	0.70	0.78
Laser	0.75	0.68	0.71	0.79
Zero-Shot	0.48	0.75	0.59	0.60
Few-Shot(ours)	0.61	0.74	0.67	0.72

where $\|\cdot\|_2$ denotes the l_2 norm. The embeddings $\mathbf{e}_s$, $\mathbf{e}_{s_+}$ and $\mathbf{e}_{s_-}$ denote the representation of the anchor, positive and negative sentences from Equation 3 and e is Euler's number. The loss objective ensures that when $\frac{d_+(s,s_+)}{d_-(s,s_-)} \to 0$, then $\mathcal{L} \to 0$. We minimize $\mathcal{L}$ to learn the parameters of our model.

3.3 Classification

The network learns sentence representations where examples of the same class are close together. The closeness of two sentences is measured by calculating the euclidean distance between their representations from Equation 3. For the final classification, we use a Support Vector Machine (SVM) with Radial Basis Function (RBF) kernel. We use SVM for classification as it learns by minimizing the hinge loss which is similar to the loss used for training the triplet network. Given the sentence representation from Equation 3, the SVM outputs a probability p of a sentence being a promissory sentence. The sentence is classified being promissory using Equation 9.

$$\text{class}(s) = \begin{cases} \text{promissory} & p \geq \alpha \\ \text{not promissory} & p < \alpha \end{cases} \quad (9)$$

where α is a hyperparameter to be set.

4 Experimental Setup

4.1 Dataset

We retrieved data from internal and external data sources in the financial services industry to create the initial data sets for the approach. After data setup, we cleaned the data to remove duplicate and irrelevant content to ensure data quality before review. Each data point was reviewed and labelled by both in-house licensed staff and contractors to confirm the interpretation of regulatory content standards.

We split the dataset into training, development and test set. The training set contains 2,016 promissory sentences and 3,260 non-promissory sentence. The test set contains 860 and 1,402 promissory and non-promissory examples, respectively. For our few-shot learning model, we sample 40 promissory and 190 non-promissory examples sentences from the training set and learn our model on this subset.

4.2 Baselines and Evaluation Metrics

We compare the performance of our approach with the following supervised learning methods.

- Naive Bayes: We learn a Naive Bayes classification model using TF-IDF scores of the tokens in the sentence.
- Multi-Layer Perceptron (MLP): We learn a two-layer perceptron with ReLu activation in the hidden layer using the TF-IDF scores of the sentence tokens as input features to the model.
- SVM: Similar to the MLP model, we learn an SVM model for the classification task. We set the regularization parameter C and $gamma$ to 1.0 and 0.1 respectively.
- Sentence-BERT (Reimers and Gurevych, 2019): This setting is similar to our proposed approach. We encode each sentence into a fixed-sized vector using its Sentence-BERT embedding. The sentence embedding is then fed into a 3 layer fully connected neural network with ReLu activation in the first two layers. The model is learned by minimizing the cross-entropy loss of classification using the Adam optimizer.
- Laser (Artetxe and Schwenk, 2019): In this setting, we encode each sentence using its Laser embeddings. The remaining architecture remains the same as that used in the Sentence-BERT model.

In addition to the supervised approaches, we compare our few-shot learning approach against a zero-shot learning approach. Yin et al. (2019) suggested method for using pre-trained natural language inference models as sequence classifiers. Towards this end, we use BART model (Lewis et al., 2020) as our zero-shot learning model. We consider the sentences tagged as 'promissory' as the hypothesis. The probability of a sentence being the premise

	Sentence	Model Result	Gold Label
1	Stocks are an income source which main street is ignoring	non-promissory	promissory
2	It is going up in all currencies	non-promissory	promissory
3	Joe Smith picks the best stock in each sector for the fund	non-promissory	promissory
4	All rights reserved.	promissory	non-promissory
5	Save more now.	promissory	non-promissory
6	There is no action required on your part.	promissory	non-promissory

Table 2: Error Analysis: Examples where our few-shot model produces classification labels different from the gold labels.

for these tagged sentence is calculated using the BART model. We then consider the maximum of those scores, and if the maximum score is greater than 0.7, we classify the sentence as a promissory sentence.

4.3 Implementation Details

For the task, we use the Sentence-BERT base model. It encodes a sentence into a fixed-size vector of length 768. We set d_{e1}, d_{e2} and d_{e3} to 768, 300 and 10 respectively. For every positive sentence belonging to the promissory class, we sample three sentences from the non-promissory class as negative sentences. We use grid-search on the development set to set the values of hyperparameters. The batch size is set to 16 for the triplet network and the model trained using Adam optimizer (Kingma and Ba, 2015) with a learning rate of 1e-5 for 10 epochs. We set the cost parameter C of SVM to 0.03 and α in Equation 9 to 0.005.

5 Results

In section, we first perform a quantitative analysis of models. We then study a few examples where our approach produces results different from the gold standard dataset.

5.1 Quantitative Analysis

In this work, we propose a few-shot learning method for legal text classification. Table 1 shows the performance of different model. Even when training with a limited number of examples, the few-shot learning model achieves better recall performance as compared to different supervised models. We find that the precision of our model is better than the zero-shot learning model but lower than the supervised models. Overall the F-Measure shows that similar results can be obtained with a few-shot approach and this enables the goal of rapid training of systems for different legal tasks. In the situation where the classifier is applied as a first filter, a high recall is preferable as we would rather create more work for a second manual annotation than miss some important texts.

5.2 Qualitative Analysis

In Table 2, we see some examples of misclassifications made by our algorithm. It is obvious that this is a very challenging task, with subtle changes in meaning being important for the classification. Examples 3 and 6 both appear to make factual statements, however, Example 3 is classed as promissory due to the context that 'Joe Smith' is likely an agent of the company. Similarly, Example 2 is difficult to classify without context and this shows that the introduction of further context is most likely to improve the effectiveness of the approach.

6 Conclusion

We have investigated the use of few-shot and zero-shot text classification methods for the quick development of predictive coding systems for legal texts. We found that zero-shot systems have a substantial decrease in performance relative to a supervised approach. We then developed a few-shot approach based on a triplet architecture and showed that this model is within a few percentage points of the supervised system in performance but requires much less manual annotation in order to develop the system.

Acknowledgements

This work has been funded by FMR LLC. Researchers at the Data Science Institute are supported by Science Foundation Ireland as part of Grant Number SFI/12/RC/2289_P2, Insight SFI Centre for Data Analytics.

References

Mikel Artetxe and Holger Schwenk. 2019. Massively multilingual sentence embeddings for zero-shot cross-lingual transfer and beyond. *Trans. Assoc. Comput. Linguistics*, 7:597–610.

Corinna Cortes and Vladimir Vapnik. 1995. Support-vector networks. *Machine learning*, 20(3):273–297.

Jacob Devlin, Ming-Wei Chang, Kenton Lee, and Kristina Toutanova. 2019. BERT: Pre-training of deep bidirectional transformers for language understanding. In *Proceedings of the 2019 Conference of the North American Chapter of the Association for Computational Linguistics: Human Language Technologies, Volume 1 (Long and Short Papers)*, pages 4171–4186, Minneapolis, Minnesota. Association for Computational Linguistics.

Elad Hoffer and Nir Ailon. 2015. Deep metric learning using triplet network. In *Similarity-Based Pattern Recognition - Third International Workshop, SIMBAD 2015, Copenhagen, Denmark, October 12-14, 2015, Proceedings*, volume 9370 of *Lecture Notes in Computer Science*, pages 84–92. Springer.

Diederik P. Kingma and Jimmy Ba. 2015. Adam: A method for stochastic optimization. In *3rd International Conference on Learning Representations, ICLR 2015, San Diego, CA, USA, May 7-9, 2015, Conference Track Proceedings*.

Ivano Lauriola and Alessandro Moschitti. 2021. Answer sentence selection using local and global context in transformer models. In *Advances in Information Retrieval - 43rd European Conference on IR Research, ECIR 2021, Virtual Event, March 28 - April 1, 2021, Proceedings, Part I*, volume 12656 of *Lecture Notes in Computer Science*, pages 298–312. Springer.

Mike Lewis, Yinhan Liu, Naman Goyal, Marjan Ghazvininejad, Abdelrahman Mohamed, Omer Levy, Veselin Stoyanov, and Luke Zettlemoyer. 2020. BART: denoising sequence-to-sequence pre-training for natural language generation, translation, and comprehension. In *Proceedings of the 58th Annual Meeting of the Association for Computational Linguistics, ACL 2020, Online, July 5-10, 2020*, pages 7871–7880. Association for Computational Linguistics.

Christian J. Mahoney, Jianping Zhang, Nathaniel Huber-Fliflet, Peter Gronvall, and Haozhen Zhao. 2019. A framework for explainable text classification in legal document review. In *2019 IEEE International Conference on Big Data (Big Data), Los Angeles, CA, USA, December 9-12, 2019*, pages 1858–1867. IEEE.

Vinod Nair and Geoffrey E. Hinton. 2010. Rectified linear units improve restricted Boltzmann machines. In *Proceedings of the 27th International Conference on Machine Learning (ICML-10), June 21-24, 2010, Haifa, Israel*, pages 807–814. Omnipress.

Ramesh Nallapati and Christopher D. Manning. 2008. Legal docket classification: Where machine learning stumbles. In *Proceedings of the 2008 Conference on Empirical Methods in Natural Language Processing*, pages 438–446, Honolulu, Hawaii. Association for Computational Linguistics.

Nils Reimers and Iryna Gurevych. 2019. Sentence-BERT: Sentence embeddings using Siamese BERT-networks. In *Proceedings of the 2019 Conference on Empirical Methods in Natural Language Processing and the 9th International Joint Conference on Natural Language Processing, EMNLP-IJCNLP 2019, Hong Kong, China, November 3-7, 2019*, pages 3980–3990. Association for Computational Linguistics.

Zein Shaheen, Gerhard Wohlgenannt, and Erwin Filtz. 2020. Large scale legal text classification using transformer models. *CoRR*, abs/2010.12871.

Octavia-Maria Sulea, Marcos Zampieri, Shervin Malmasi, Mihaela Vela, Liviu P. Dinu, and Josef van Genabith. 2017. Exploring the use of text classification in the legal domain. In *Proceedings of the Second Workshop on Automated Semantic Analysis of Information in Legal Texts co-located with the 16th International Conference on Artificial Intelligence and Law (ICAIL 2017), London, UK, June 16, 2017*, volume 2143 of *CEUR Workshop Proceedings*. CEUR-WS.org.

Fusheng Wei, Han Qin, Shi Ye, and Haozhen Zhao. 2018. Empirical study of deep learning for text classification in legal document review. In *IEEE International Conference on Big Data, Big Data 2018, Seattle, WA, USA, December 10-13, 2018*, pages 3317–3320. IEEE.

Jason Wei, Chengyu Huang, Soroush Vosoughi, Yu Cheng, and Shiqi Xu. 2021. Few-shot text classification with triplet networks, data augmentation, and curriculum learning. In *Proceedings of the 2021 Conference of the North American Chapter of the Association for Computational Linguistics: Human Language Technologies, NAACL-HLT 2021, Online, June 6-11, 2021*, pages 5493–5500. Association for Computational Linguistics.

Wenpeng Yin, Jamaal Hay, and Dan Roth. 2019. Benchmarking zero-shot text classification: Datasets, evaluation and entailment approach. In *Proceedings of the 2019 Conference on Empirical Methods in Natural Language Processing and the 9th International Joint Conference on Natural Language Processing, EMNLP-IJCNLP 2019, Hong Kong, China, November 3-7, 2019*, pages 3912–3921. Association for Computational Linguistics.

A Free Format Legal Question Answering System

Soha Khazaeli
Janardhana Punuru
Chad Morris
Sanjay Sharma
Bert Staub
Michael Cole
LexisNexis | Legal & Professional, NC, USA
firstname.lastname@lexisnexis.com

Sunny Chiu-Webster
Facebook / WA, USA
sunnycw1@gmail.com

Dhruv Sakalley
Sensibill / Ontario, CANADA
dhruv.sakalley@gmail.com

Abstract

We present an information retrieval-based question answer system to answer legal questions. The system is not limited to a predefined set of questions or patterns and uses both sparse vector search and embeddings for input to a BERT-based answer re-ranking system. A combination of general domain and legal domain data is used for training. This natural question answering system is in production and is used commercially.

1 Introduction

Question answering (QA) applications range from simple yes/no systems to complex questions where answers might be synthesized from several sources (Voorhees and Tice, 2000). This work concerns a QA system for legal research. The system is designed to answer both factoid (Agichtein et al., 2005) and non-factoid questions. A short answer can satisfy factoid questions, e.g., "What is the burden of proof for breach of contract?". In contrast, non-factoid questions are open-ended and an adequate answer needs opinions or explanations (Hashemi et al., 2020), e.g., "Why does child support increase with income?".

A typical system user is a litigator seeking answers to case-specific legal questions. Those answers inform the creation of litigation documents, such as pleadings, briefs, and motions. A system should provide complete multiple-sentence answers with context that can be cited. A legal QA system must also handle questions where no single answer exists. For example, the useful answer may be jurisdiction specific, or be time frame dependent because the law evolves. Importantly, the best answers can depend on the lawyer's perspective because application of the law can make fine distinctions per the case facts, or recognizes competing principles or mitigating factors. Legal practice areas can have distinctive concerns. For example, the scope of legal principles and practice affecting family law legal matters is distinguishable from those applied in bankruptcy law. Developing an effective and useful question answering system in this setting faces state of the art challenges, including creation of training collections and performance metrics.

We present a retrieval-based legal domain QA system designed to provide useful answers for all legal practice areas. It is designed for customers with real-world tasks while meeting cost, response time, and scalability constraints. This system is in production and serving customers. We also describe an experiment methodology found to have pragmatic value in system development. The methodology can be useful in domains with similar context-laden QA characteristics.

2 Related Work

Recent deep learning open domain QA research successfully applied a retrieve and read paradigm. The retrieval step selects candidate documents, then a reading component finds answers (Chen et al., 2017; Das et al., 2019; Yang et al., 2019). We adopted a similar approach.

Often, the systems employ standard retrieval methods based on sparse vector space approaches like TF-IDF (Jones, 1972) and BM25 (Robertson and Spärck Jones, 1994). Dense vector representations with distributional semantic properties based on LSA (Landauer et al., 1998), GLoVe (Pennington et al., 2014), and sentence embedding (Reimers and Gurevych, 2019) are also used. Custom domain embedding methods such as Legal-bert have been studied (Chalkidis et al., 2020). The QA retrieval target is usually at the passage level rather than complete documents (Luan et al., 2021). Paragraph-based legal domain search has been studied (Zhang and Steiner, 2018). Answer extraction techniques have used Machine Reading Comprehension (MRC) (Seo et al., 2016) and DrQA (Chen et al., 2017). Several ranking models have been ap-

Natural Legal Language Processing Workshop 2021, pages 107–113
November 10, 2021. ©2021 Association for Computational Linguistics

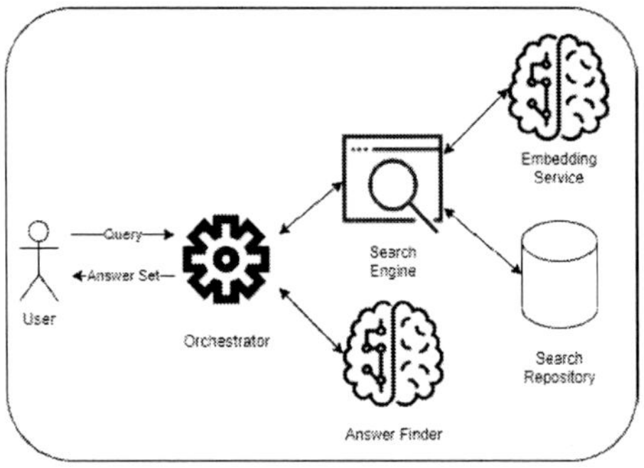

Figure 1: Two stage architecture for QA systems

plied in QA systems (Yang et al., 2019; Nogueira and Cho, 2019). One COLIEE[1] task is to answer yes/no legal questions and retrieve germane legal documents. Competitors have used TF-IDF and BM25, and also contextual embedding vectors such as BERT and ELMo, to score passages against the question (Rabelo et al., 2019). LexisNexis legacy answer cards address knowledge-based QA by detecting the user query intent and then serving a previously mined answer if appropriate (Kumar and Politi, 2019; Shankar and Buddarapu, 2018). The WestSearch QA system categorizes non-factoid questions to different frames. To answer a frame-specific question, a trained frame-specific question-answer pair classifier is used to recognize a retrieved passage as an answer (McElvain et al., 2019). Both of these commercial legal QA system can only handle a limited range of questions.

In contrast to the previous work, the system presented here is designed to answer almost all legal content questions without legal practice area restrictions. In particular, the question coverage is not limited by pattern or frame.

3 Methodology

The system selects answers by re-ranking search results obtained using both sparse vector techniques (BM25) and a dense vector approach (semantic embedding). Figure 1 shows a simplified system architecture. The *search repository* contains the passage text and passage embeddings. The *search engine* retrieves passages by text and embedding similarity. The *answer finder* re-ranks the retrieved passages.

3.1 Retrieving Passages

The search collection is a pool of passages that highlight key aspects of each legal document. It consists of case-law Headnotes [2] and RFCs [3]. The collection contains over 100 million passages. Our experiments were conducted with a 10% sample of the collection. The search engine has the usual goal of retrieving relevant passages. Beyond topical germaneness, the retrieval engine must also detect sufficient context in the passage. To that end, the retrieval answer set coverage is enriched using both sparse vector and semantic embedding passage representations. The system used a Query By Document method (QBD) (Yang et al., 2018), *more like this*, implemented with BM25 for sparse vector passage representation retrieval. The dense embedding enrichment used Legal GloVe and Legal Siamese BERT embeddings. The GloVe embeddings are built using 64GB of legal text with a 300K word vocabulary and 200 dimensions. Passages and questions are encoded using the average of the word embeddings.

The Siamese Legal BERT system is trained to retrieve similar passages in a contextual vector space (Reimers and Gurevych, 2019). The training data is a sample of 100,000 headnotes. Given a headnote, the most similar headnote using BM25 is identified as a positive similar passage. Five random headnotes are added as negative instances. We ensured discriminative challenge amongst the negative instances using a procedure described below. The system was trained using a regression objective function with cosine loss. The input sentence embedding uses the Legal BERT base model with mean pooling of the tokens embedding. The Legal BERT model was trained in-house from scratch with a custom legal vocabulary on the last 20 years of US case-law documents. The model is trained with $train\_batch\_size = 16$. We used Spearman and Pearson correlation upward trends as convergence indicators.

3.2 Answer Finder

The *answer finder* accepts a question passage pair and computes the probability the passage answers

[1] Competition on Legal Information Extraction/Entailment

[2] A LexisNexis headnote is a point of law expressed in a case written by a judge which is picked and edited by editors as a general point of law.

[3] An RFC (Reason For Citing) is an automatically extracted passage of a case which contains sentences near a document citation, such as a court case citation, that suggest the Reason(s) For Citing (RFC) (Humphrey et al., 2005).

the question. A BERT sequence binary classifier (Devlin et al., 2019) is trained on question-answer pairs. The *answer finder* input is the concatenation of question(Q) and passage(P) as "[CLS]<Q>[SEP]<P>[SEP]". *answer finder* is trained by fine tuning Legal BERT. The BERT classifier uses [CLS] representation with two fully connected layers with a final softmax layer.

The nature of legal language and the high-stakes nature of lawyer tasks require subject matter experts (SMEs) to judge legal QA system performance. The legal training data was created in-house by certified lawyers. The training dataset had over 10,000 annotated legal question answer pairs covering legal practice areas. Questions with long paragraph answers (107,089) are selected from Natural Questions (NQ) (Kwiatkowski et al., 2019) and added to training data to improve generalization.

The system was fine-tuned in two stages. First, question-answer pairs were created by selecting a random negative passage for each question. The tuned *answer finder* then predicts the probability on all negative samples. In the second stage, for each question the negative answer with the highest probability of being a good answer is selected. The goal is to increase the challenge of good answer discrimination. The validation set is real-world questions extracted from user-logs. The training hyper-parameters are: $learning\_rate : 2e-5$, $max\_seq\_length : 512$, $num\_train\_epochs : 3$, $do\_lower\_case : True$, $batch\_size = 8$. We found that examination of the first 128 word-pieces ($max\_seq\_length : 128$) doesn't significantly lower validation set accuracy, so that was used in large batch experiments. Reduced max_seq_length also improves latency performance in production.

4 Results

Table 1 shows the answer evaluation scale used by the subject matter experts (SMEs). Simple "yes/no" judgments are clearly inadequate for complex domain QA systems.

Score	Criteria
-1	so unrelated that a user will lose patience with the system ('silly')
0	off point and is not reasonably related
1	right topic but not an answer
2	partial answer
3	good answer

Table 1: Answer evaluation scale

Two test sets were used: 100 and 1000 questions. The small set proved valuable for rapid development cycles. Both sets consist of 50% actual user questions with additional questions from SMEs to ensure coverage of legal research goals including content, entity, and analytic questions. The QA system presented here focuses on answering content questions and may not provide good answers for entity and analytic questions. This limitation affects the performance for the smaller test set reported in Table 3. The performance of the system using the large test set are reported in Appendix A. The search corpus was bulk embedded and queried using BM25, Siamese Legal BERT, and Legal GloVe. Similarity calculations use the Euclidean metric. The input to *answer finder* is the top 30 retrieved passages for each retrieval method. *answer finder* re-ranks the list by answer probability and selects the top 3 passages. The top 3 passages for each method were evaluated. SMEs evaluated these answer sets in a random order.

Table 2 shows retrieved passages, system answers, and the SME evaluation for "Is an airline liable for its pilot's negligence?" BM25_MLT picked a long passage with multiple occurrences of 'airline', 'pilot', 'liable' and 'negligence'. It was judged as off point, despite some topical overlap. Legal GloVe and Legal Siamese BERT picked a semantically-similar short passage even though 'pilot' does not appear. It was judged as topical but not an answer. *answer finder* on BM25_MLT picked a good answer passage with all the question elements and actors, and also discusses the conditions in which the carrier is liable for a pilot's negligence. This passage was promoted from rank 27 of the 30 BM25_MLT passages.

The answer evaluation scale has five levels and the SMEs agreed that an acceptable answer will score a '2' or '3'. SME evaluator interrater agreement (IRR) is excellent, given the complexity of legal question answering task, with an agreement level of 84% for acceptable answers and 91% for unacceptable answers. Setting a threshold of '2' in the test set, the system performance was: F1 0.766, precision 0.827, recall: 0.713, and accuracy 0.759.

F1 and accuracy provide classifier performance metrics. The production legal research system presents the top three answers to users, so we also use ranked search results evaluation metrics

Table 2: Example question and passages (BM25_MLT: BM25 more-like-this, SL_BERT: Siamese Legal BERT, L_GloVe: Legal GloVe, AF: Answer Finder)

Is an airline liable for its pilot's negligence?	**SME label**	**Method**
A carrier would not be liable for an error of judgment of the pilot, not constituting positive negligence on his part in exercising such judgment; but liability is incurred if the pilot, by his negligent and careless conduct, has created a situation requiring the formation of a judgment and then errs in the exercise thereof.	3	AF on BM25_MLT
An airline corporation is not an insurer of the safety of its passengers. The liability of an airline corporation must be based on negligence.	1	L_GloVe, SL_BERT
Airline pilot who was accused of raping flight attendant has no tort claim against airline based upon its alleged negligent investigation of accusation, even if airline's policy of investigating sexual harassment complaints creates duty to use due care in conducting investigation,...	0	BM25_MLT

to assess the system performance with DCG (Discounted Cumulative Gain) and MRR (Mean Reciprocal Rank). In this system *answer finder* is employed as a re-ranker, but it could also be used as a threshold filter on the answers. Table 3 compares alternative combinations of system components. Promising system combinations are bolded. Production systems have practical constraints and cannot simply optimize performance without considering factors like user experience, cost, and scalability. Re-ranking retrieved passages by each retrieval method increased the average DCG, confirming the value of adding *answer finder* to the system. Another advantage of the re-ranker is the ability to combine multiple retrieval methods to improve DCG performance. Combining dense and sparse retrieved passages both increases system cost and creates scaling challenges. However, the richer representation can improve user experience because users are able to ask their question using a greater variety of words. Another advantage of using a re-ranker is the capacity to apply a threshold to help filter unrelated passages.

5 Error Analysis

Case-specific error-analysis helps to identify shortcomings in the training data coverage. Categorized DCG analysis indicates the QA system provides good answers for well-defined legal questions such as *standard of review*[4] question (e.g. What is standard of review for marital property allocation decision in Florida?) . *Single topic questions* are free format questions about specific legal issue, e.g "Can an executor compromise a claim without beneficiary consent?". The QA system performs significantly better than previous systems on single topic questions, although there remains room for improvement. Optimizing the real world performance of a legal QA system needs to consider the frequency of each question category, the space for improvement, and the question category importance judged by SMEs. We identified 16 categories to prioritize for high return on development investment. Single topic question is at the top of the list. Training data for this category will be created to improve system accuracy. Table 4 reports the average DCG@3 for seven high priority question categories.

6 Discussion and Future Work

This paper presents a new legal domain QA system that is deployed and serving customers. Legal QA systems must address a specialized domain language and provide contextualized answers in a high-stakes setting. We were able to develop a performant product using a 10% content sample and 100 questions drawn from previously seen real-world queries supplemented with expert-generated questions. This proved effective to evaluate alternative embedding methods and performance trade-offs for combination of fast retrieval system on all corpus and relatively slow re-ranking system on limited retrieved passages. The sampled collection and smaller question set enabled rapid design and test cycles. Later evaluation using the full collection and a much larger question set confirmed the

[4]The deference an appeals court will apply to a decision of a lower court `http://cdn.ca9.uscourts.gov/datastore/uploads/guides/stand_of_review/I_Definitions.html`

Table 3: QA metrics for methods (100 questions)(BM25_MLT: BM25 more-like-this, SL_BERT: Siamese Legal BERT, L_GloVe: Legal GloVe, AF: Answer Finder, AF 0.2: Answer Finder as an answer filter with threshold 0.2)

Method	DCG@3[a]	95% C.I.[b]	N silly[c]	Answered[d]	MRR@3[a]
BM25_MLT	4.052	-	7	100	0.411
SL_BERT	3.386	1.26	2	100	0.326
L_GloVe	2.855	1.25	7	100	0.285
AF BM25	**5.464**	1.43	7	100	**0.493**
AF SL_BERT	4.862	1.43	0	100	0.416
AF L_GloVe	4.281	1.40	7	100	0.397
AF (BM25, SL_BERT)	**5.605**	1.47	5	100	**0.483**
AF (BM25, L_GloVe)	5.502	1.47	8	100	0.481
AF (BM25, SL_BERT, L_GloVe)	5.533	1.45	6	100	0.492
AF 0.2 (BM25, SL_BERT)	**6.269**	1.52	**2**	89	**0.543**

[a] Avg for answered questions.
[b] confidence interval.
[c] Number of answers that are bad enough to impact user trust in the system.
[d] Number of questions answered.

Table 4: Seven high priority question categories on 1000 questions

Category	DCG@3[a]	Priority
Single topic questions	6.99	1
Questions about rules or statutes	5.46	2
Relationship questions[5]	7.58	3
Definitions	7.11	4
Statute of limitations[6]	9.23	5
Standard of review	11.52	6
Elements [7]	9.76	7

[a] Avg for answered questions in the category.

findings. The system is oriented to answering content questions and performs lower on entity and analytic questions. We intend to address this limitation by developing alternative approaches to handle other question types that can be combined with this content-oriented system.

Various development directions are being explored. Direct extensions of this work include use of a smaller Siamese BERT, vocabulary improvements for the models, training set enhancements targeting low performing legal areas, and training the *answer finder* component on augmented training data and smaller Legal-BERT models.

Acknowledgements

The complete production QA system includes important components not described here. It was developed by the authors and Shyjee Mathai, Aaron Pohl, Kishore Ethiraj, Randall Fee, Urvi Luhana, Jonathan Mitchall, Harris Joseph, David Borchers, Megan Bramhall, Serena Wellen, Rick McFarland, Eric Weiss, Sachin Kumar, Shashi Penumarthy, and Nagaraju Buddarapu. The evaluation team of in-house lawyers included Megan Bramhall, Elizabeth Hickey, Donna McMurry, and Brian Rouse.

References

Eugene Agichtein, Silviu Cucerzan, and Eric Brill. 2005. Analysis of factoid questions for effective relation extraction. In *Proceedings of the 28th annual international ACM SIGIR conference*, pages 567–568.

Ilias Chalkidis, Manos Fergadiotis, Prodromos Malakasiotis, Nikolaos Aletras, and Ion Androutsopoulos. 2020. Legal-bert: The muppets straight out of law school. *arXiv preprint arXiv:2010.02559.*

Danqi Chen, Adam Fisch, Jason Weston, and Antoine Bordes. 2017. Reading wikipedia to answer open-domain questions. In *Proceedings of the 55th Annual Meeting of the ACL (Volume 1: Long Papers)*, pages 1870–1879.

Rajarshi Das, Shehzaad Dhuliawala, Manzil Zaheer, and Andrew McCallum. 2019. Multi-step retriever-

[5]Asks about applicability of a legal concept on another one e.g. Is the continuous treatment doctrine applicable to negligence claims in Ohio?

[6]The time limit for plaintiff to file a complaint `https://www.nolo.com/dictionary/statute-of-limitations-term.html`

[7]Essential requirements to make a claim `https://www.law.cornell.edu/wex/element` e.g. What are the elements of constructive eviction?

reader interaction for scalable open-domain question answering. In *International Conference on Learning Representations*.

Jacob Devlin, Ming-Wei Chang, Kenton Lee, and Kristina Toutanova. 2019. Bert: Pre-training of deep bidirectional transformers for language understanding. In *Proceedings of the 2019 Conference of the NAACL: Human Language Technologies, Volume 1 (Long and Short Papers)*, pages 4171–4186.

Helia Hashemi, Mohammad Aliannejadi, Hamed Zamani, and W Bruce Croft. 2020. Antique: A non-factoid question answering benchmark. In *European Conference on Information Retrieval*, pages 166–173. Springer.

Timothy L Humphrey, Xin Allan Lu, Afsar Parhizgar, Salahuddin Ahmed, James S Wiltshire Jr, John T Morelock, Joseph P Harmon, Spiro G Collias, and Paul Zhang. 2005. Automated system and method for generating reasons that a court case is cited. US Patent 6,856,988.

Karen Sparck Jones. 1972. A statistical interpretation of term specificity and its application in retrieval. *Journal of documentation*.

Sachin Kumar and Regina Politi. 2019. Understanding user query intent and target terms in legal domain. In *International Conference on Applications of Natural Language to Information Systems*, pages 41–53. Springer.

Tom Kwiatkowski, Jennimaria Palomaki, Olivia Redfield, Michael Collins, Ankur Parikh, Chris Alberti, Danielle Epstein, Illia Polosukhin, Jacob Devlin, Kenton Lee, et al. 2019. Natural questions: a benchmark for question answering research. *Transactions of the ACL*, 7:453–466.

Thomas K Landauer, Peter W Foltz, and Darrell Laham. 1998. An introduction to latent semantic analysis. *Discourse processes*, 25(2-3):259–284.

Yi Luan, Jacob Eisenstein, Kristina Toutanova, and Michael Collins. 2021. Sparse, dense, and attentional representations for text retrieval. *Transactions of the ACL*, 9:329–345.

Gayle McElvain, George Sanchez, Sean Matthews, Don Teo, Filippo Pompili, and Tonya Custis. 2019. Westsearch plus: A non-factoid question-answering system for the legal domain. In *Proceedings of the 42nd International ACM SIGIR Conference*, pages 1361–1364.

Rodrigo Nogueira and Kyunghyun Cho. 2019. Passage re-ranking with bert. *arXiv preprint arXiv:1901.04085*.

Jeffrey Pennington, Richard Socher, and Christopher D Manning. 2014. Glove: Global vectors for word representation. In *Proceedings of the 2014 conference on empirical methods in natural language processing (EMNLP)*, pages 1532–1543.

Juliano Rabelo, Mi-Young Kim, Randy Goebel, Masaharu Yoshioka, Yoshinobu Kano, and Ken Satoh. 2019. A summary of the coliee 2019 competition. In *JSAI International Symposium on Artificial Intelligence*, pages 34–49. Springer.

Nils Reimers and Iryna Gurevych. 2019. Sentence-bert: Sentence embeddings using siamese bert-networks. In *Proceedings of the 2019 Conference on Empirical Methods in Natural Language Processing and the 9th International Joint Conference on Natural Language Processing (EMNLP-IJCNLP)*, pages 3973–3983.

Stephen E Robertson and Karen Spärck Jones. 1994. Simple, proven approaches to text retrieval. Technical report, University of Cambridge, Computer Laboratory.

Minjoon Seo, Aniruddha Kembhavi, Ali Farhadi, and Hannaneh Hajishirzi. 2016. Bidirectional attention flow for machine comprehension. In *International Conference on Learning Representations*.

Arunprasath Shankar and Venkata Nagaraju Buddarapu. 2018. Deep ensemble learning for legal query understanding. In *Proceedings of CIKM 2018 Workshop on Legal Data Analytics and Mining (LeDAM 2018), CEUR-WS. org*.

Ellen M Voorhees and Dawn M Tice. 2000. Building a question answering test collection. In *Proceedings of the 23rd annual international ACM SIGIR conference*, pages 200–207.

Eugene Yang, David D Lewis, Ophir Frieder, David A Grossman, and Roman Yurchak. 2018. Retrieval and richness when querying by document. In *DESIRES*, pages 68–75.

Wei Yang, Yuqing Xie, Aileen Lin, Xingyu Li, Luchen Tan, Kun Xiong, Ming Li, and Jimmy Lin. 2019. End-to-end open-domain question answering with bertserini. In *Proceedings of the 2019 Conference of the NAACL (Demonstrations)*, pages 72–77.

Paul Zhang and David Steiner. 2018. Systems and methods for paragraph-based document searching. US Patent 10,002,196.

A Some Analysis on the Production System

The production QA system is evaluated periodically on the larger 1000 question set. These question collections were created by legal domain experts to be representative of various practice areas and different question types. Each experiment requires evaluation of tens of thousands of question-answer pairs. Table 5 shows higher DCG compared to the internal evaluation because the production system is based on the complete content set. Some

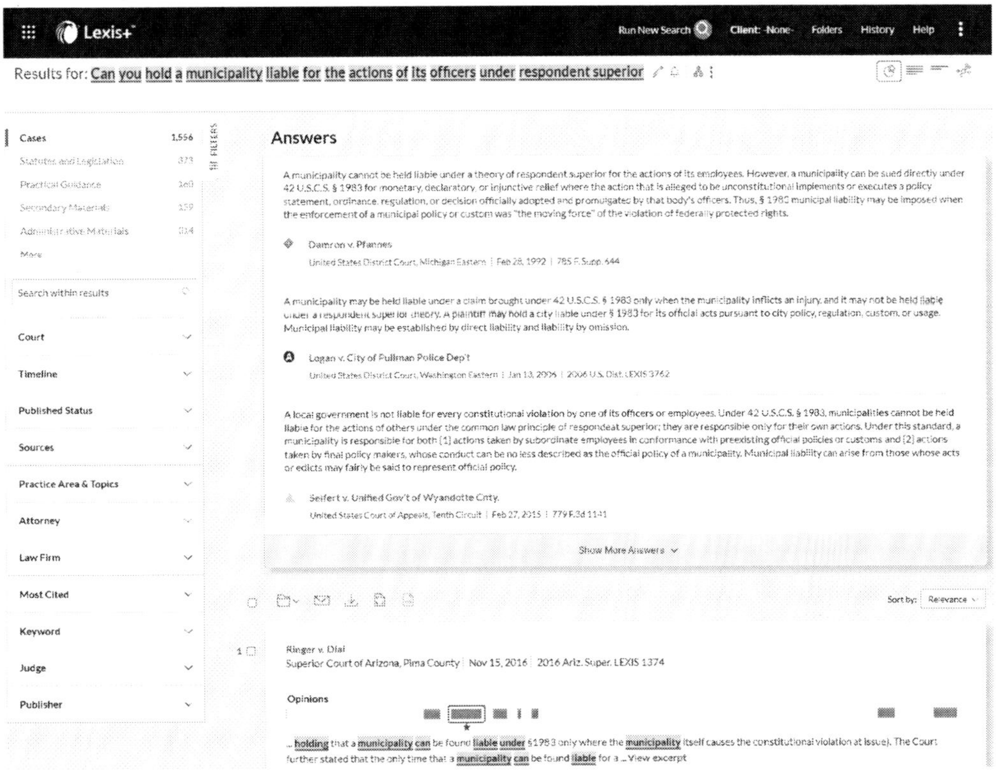

Figure 2: Customer facing application using the discussed components

additional filters are also implemented. Nonetheless, the method performance ranking is unchanged as compared to that using the smaller test collection and question sets. This confirms the usefulness of work with the smaller sets for development and tuning.

We also investigated answer variations for retrieval methods. Table 6 shows the distribution of surfaced answers, i.e. presented in the product UI, and customer-engaged answers by retrieval query method. Both retrieval methods provide passages recognized by the system as worthy answers. If an answer was retrieved by both retrieval methods there is a higher probability of user engagement.

B QA System in Production

Figure 2 shows a screen-shot of a product UI for the production QA system.

Table 5: Production system evaluation (1000 questions) (April 2020)

Method	Avg DCG@3
BM25_MLT	4.82
SL_BERT	3.62
AF on BM25	6.27
AF on SL_BERT	5.18
AF on BM25 + SL_BERT	6.28
AF on BM25 + L_GloVe	6.18
AF 0.3 on BM25 + SL_BERT	7.75

Table 6: Answer distribution by retrieval methods (May 2021)

Answers	BM25_MLT	Si_L_Bert	Both
surfaced	58.85%	31.53%	9.62%
engaged	56.48%	29.02%	14.50%

Searching for legal documents at paragraph level: Automating label generation and use of an Extended Attention Mask for boosting neural models of semantic similarity

Li Tang
Institute of Computational Linguistics
University of Zurich
li.tang@uzh.ch

Simon Clematide
Institute of Computational Linguistics
University of Zurich
simon.clematide@uzh.ch

Abstract

Searching for legal documents is a specialized Information Retrieval task that is relevant for expert users (lawyers and their assistants) and for non-expert users. By searching previous court decisions (cases), a user can better prepare the legal reasoning of a new case. Being able to search using a natural language text snippet instead of a more artificial query could help to prevent query formulation issues. Also, if semantic similarity could be modeled beyond exact lexical matches, more relevant results can be found even if the query terms don't match exactly. For this domain, we formulated a task to compare different ways of modeling semantic similarity at paragraph level, using neural and non-neural systems. We compared systems that encode the query and the search collection paragraphs as vectors, enabling the use of cosine similarity for results ranking. After building a German dataset for cases and statutes from Switzerland, and extracting citations from cases to statutes, we developed an algorithm for estimating semantic similarity at paragraph level, using a link-based similarity method. When evaluating different systems in this way, we find that semantic similarity modeling by neural systems can be boosted with an extended attention mask that quenches noise in the inputs.

1 Introduction

Retrieving and understanding legal documents can take a considerable amount of time, even for legal professionals. Searching a large database of previous cases (court decisions) that apply to a particular situation is an important part of legal work, as performed by lawyers and their legal assistants (Bhattacharya et al. 2019, Bhattacharya et al. 2020, Draijer 2019, Hafner 1980, Xiao et al. 2019, Zhong et al. 2020). Such a retrieval system may not only help expert users with deep expertise in the domain but can also benefit non-expert users. The latter can, for example, try to develop a preliminary understanding of a situation, when selecting or approaching a lawyer, to better navigate the justice system (Bhattacharya et al. 2019, Boniol et al. 2020, Chen et al. 2013, Tran et al. 2020). Both expert and non-expert users may then be interested in a) identifying where the legal problem fits in regarding legal concepts, b) what legal actions are potentially relevant, and c) what were the outcomes of similar cases (Bhattacharya et al. 2019, Hafner 1980, Zhong et al. 2020).

The above problem can therefore be formulated as a specialized Information Retrieval task that involves searching through a corpus of legal documents, before ranking them according to their relevance. While the concept of relevance in this context is conceptually and practically complex, we will focus our attention on a key aspect, the semantic similarity between a query and a candidate hit (Shao et al. 2020). Early attempts at developing such systems often involved the use of Boolean expressions as queries, where a document

Natural Legal Language Processing Workshop 2021, pages 114–122
November 10, 2021. ©2021 Association for Computational Linguistics

either matches or does not match a query, in accordance with the Boolean logic of a statement being either *True* or *False* (Manning et al. 2009). In the case of large document collections, the resulting number of matching documents can then easily exceed the number a human user could possibly sift through, resulting in the need to offer a rank ordering of results (Manning et al. 2009). The Boolean approach also suffers problems related to human error and cognitive load in query formulation, as the user must translate a meaningful query formulated in natural language into a Boolean expression such as *'theft AND (repeated OR sustained) AND employee'*, by guessing the exact terms used in the database in the documents of interest (Hafner 1980, Ter et al. 1996). Such guesswork about the terms likely to be used in relevant documents, through the resulting errors, can prevent the discovery of the most relevant documents in the database, for example if those documents used slightly different terms that those that were selected by the user.

As efforts to remedy such issues using linguistics and / or ontology-based approaches that explicitly model domain knowledge and language are rather expensive and difficult to keep up-to-date (Silveira et al. 2004), the research community is actively searching for new approaches to those problems, in particular the semantic similarity aspect of document relevance, as it enables improved document ranking.

Recently, data-driven neural approaches have emerged as promising components of a new generation of increasingly automatic systems that may require less human interference, curation or updating effort (Tran et al. 2020, Zhong et al. 2020). While this trend is in its early stages, its maturation could help to deal with some of the above-mentioned limitations. However, it was observed by many authors (Alberts et al. 2020, Bhattacharya et al. 2020, Chalkidis et al., 2020, Draijer 2019, Raghav et al. 2016, Shao et al. 2020, Van Opijnen & Santos 2017, Xiao et al. 2019, Wang et al. 2019, Zhong et al. 2020) that current neural systems for natural language understanding that perform very well in non-legal domains do not transfer easily to tasks in the legal domain, for a variety of reasons that make this domain especially challenging (see Table 1).

Challenge	Description
Length	Documents are often long and complex, with a large number of legal concepts that need to be modeled
Relevance	Domain-specific notions of relevance go beyond general concepts of document similarity
Language	A language that differs from regular language in terms of syntax, semantics, vocabulary and morphology
Accessibility	Accessibility of legal datasets is rather restricted, hindering research
Labels	Expert judgements of relevance or similarity is difficult and expensive to obtain
Models	Most current semantic similarity models (above the word level) struggle with out-of-domain data

Table 1: Domain adaptation challenges

Such research efforts can then be further complicated by the need to adjust such systems to legal documents written in non-English languages, as much of the research in the public domain has been performed on English language texts.

By performing the legal Information Retrieval task at the level of paragraphs rather than whole case documents, the modeling of semantic similarity is then focused on a more limited number of important legal concepts contained in such a paragraph, or query. For a user it can be helpful to first find the most semantically similar paragraphs with a few relevant legal concepts in a lengthy and complex case document, before reading the whole document. This way of defining the task also has another practical advantage, in the sense that many state-of-the-art (neural) models would struggle to encode the semantics of a very long text with hundreds of sentences in a useful way, while text at the level of one or a few sentences will be a more realistic input text to such models (Alberts et al. 2020, Shao et al. 2020). In the best case, such semantic similarity models at paragraph level should be invariant to differences in the input that do not matter for approximating relevance in this task, while they will be more selective to differences that do matter (Neculoiu et al. 2016).

The ability for a user to express a query in natural language rather than more artificial queries such as Boolean expressions could carry many advantages, if implemented successfully. By omitting the step of asking the user to translate their natural language query into such a query language, human errors linked with query formulation can be avoided. The potential ability of neural systems to enable a flexible data-driven modeling of semantic similarity, beyond the ranking of exact lexical matches between a candidate hit and a query, is highly relevant for enabling a wider variety of searches using natural language for expert and non-expert users with different degrees of domain knowledge. For the non-expert users, this aspect is likely to be even more important, due to their lack of familiarity with legal language and topics. In other words, progress in this area could help to further increase the accessibility of the legal system itself.

We have therefore identified the following three fundamental challenges for enabling German natural language queries in a collection of Swiss federal court decisions, namely a) how to best encode paragraph text as vectors that enable a good ranking of search hits (semantic modeling), so that the most relevant paragraphs would be scored highly, b) how to assess the semantic similarity between a query and a candidate hit in the absence of expensive expert judgements of relevance, using an automated mechanism that approximates such human judgement, c) the generation of relevant datasets for enabling such work, in particular Swiss cases and statutes that will be relevant for different tasks, including the extraction of relationships between cases and statutes. We also investigate the possibility of combining neural systems with some well-established components of non-neural systems in a way that would enhance the ability of the combined system to focus on the most important parts of the input, while modeling semantic similarity.

2 Related Work

Understanding the central concept of relevance in Information Retrieval tasks can depend on the particular user, task and other contextual factors (van Opijnen & Santos 2017), hindering the emergence of a clear consensus on this topic. Also, the construction of datasets that capture relevance as determined by human experts is challenging and expensive, leading to a paucity of such datasets in the public domain (Shao et al. 2020). Therefore, algorithms that could help to estimate important aspects of relevance could therefore help to enable more research on the challenges outlined above. With semantic similarity as a key aspect of relevance, and the paucity of human expert annotations in the field, the question of the automated generation of labels that can approximate such human judgement poses itself.

On a conceptual level, the computation of similarity between objects can not only be based on their context, but also on the link structure of a graph that describes relationships between those objects (Lu et al. 2006). Such link-based similarity can often complement content-based similarity measures. The application of this principle can be found in an area that is related to our task, namely a field called *context-aware citation recommendation*, which builds on link-based similarities between scientific publications using citations between them (He et al. 2020, Jeong et al. 2019). In the legal domain, citation networks can be described as linking case documents with relevant statutes, thereby generating a directed graph with two types of nodes (cases and statutes). The number of common out-citations can then be defined as *bibliographic coupling* (Kessler 1963), indicating link-based similarity between two case documents (Bhattacharya et al. 2020, Kumar et al. 2013, Raghav et al. 2015, Raghav et al. 2016). Bhattachyarya et al. (2020) have noted that the notion of semantic similarity is domain-specific, and not completely defined, as they developed a framework for the comparison of content-based with link-based similarity methods. Again, bibliographic coupling is used by calculating the number of common out-citations as a way of estimating semantic similarity between case documents.

As semantic similarity modeling of text at paragraph level (beyond a ranking of hits that is solely based on exact lexical matches with terms in the query), is a key challenge in this domain, lessons learned from the comparison of systems that model semantic similarity at sentence level (in various domains) may be relevant. For example, SentEval is an effort to evaluate sentence-to-vector encoders on a variety of tasks, including sentence similarity (Conneau et al. 2018). Bhattacharya et al. (2020) describe a dataset of 47 pairs of Indian Supreme Court case documents where similarity between each pair of documents is annotated on a scale from 0-10 by law experts, which the authors use to compare methods for modeling legal document similarity. However, it is important to keep in mind the many known domain-specific challenges (see Table 1), in addition to language-specific and legal system-specific challenges. In other words, we cannot assume that systems that did well in those benchmarking efforts will also do well in our task, even if such systems have shown great potential across languages, in other domains.

The most widely used classic non-neural model is often referred to as a *bag-of-words* model, with every word in the modeled vocabulary represented as a separate dimension in a vector space. Note that while such vector space models can enable a user to use natural language as a query, it will be unable to model an important aspect of semantic similarity, namely contributions based on word order (Mitchell & Lapata 2010). As semantically similar words are represented as distinct dimensions in that vector space, such similarities are not captured in bag-of-word models. These non-neural systems can provide useful baseline systems for comparisons with (neural) systems that aim to model these aspects of semantic similarity.

Neural systems for Natural Language Understanding published in recent years have demonstrated promising abilities in this regard, in terms of their ability to model both word order aspects as well as other aspects of semantic similarities in natural language text (Zhang et al. 2020, Bhattacharya et al. 2019).

3 Materials and Methods

3.1 Datasets

German language case documents published after the year 2000 that contain citations of Swiss law articles (statutes) were obtained from the website of the Swiss Federal Court ('Bundesgericht')[1]. Using the Python library *urllib* we developed a dedicated Web crawler to download the HTML of 2168 case documents for paragraph and citation extraction. Paragraph extraction was then performed on those HTML files, filtering for case paragraphs that contain citations, resulting in a set of 7562 case paragraphs for further processing. Swiss federal statutes cited by those case paragraphs were obtained from the official Swiss government website ('Systematische Rechtssammlung')[2], also in HTML format. Again, paragraphs were extracted, creating a hierarchy of documents containing many articles, and those articles containing one or more paragraphs ('Absatz'). In total, 38994 statute paragraphs were extracted from 109 statute documents.

3.2 Triples

Here, triples are directed relations that link a single case paragraph (the source) to specific statute articles (the target). To qualify, a citation needs to match one of two citation styles that unambiguously identify at least a specific article of that law: style 1 (e.g. 'Art. 1 Abs. 3 StGB') or style 2 (e.g. 'Art. 3 StGB'). Note that style 1 is more specific, as it points to a single paragraph ('Abs.' = 'Absatz') in that article, which will then consist of a single sentence or multiple sentences. Citations expressed in the case paragraphs were identified using regular expressions, in an automated way. Each of the resulting 14299 triples then contained a citation in the form of either style 1 (10998 triples) or style 2 (3301 triples), the full text of the statute paragraph the citation refers to, the case paragraph in which the citation was found, and the relevant case document ID ('caseName').

3.3 Baseline models

A random baseline was implemented as a minimal performance reference, to estimate the performance achieved by a random ranking of paragraphs in the search collection. This system omits the actual similarity model by generating random numbers for use in ranking the search results. To estimate the distribution of results from this random baseline, ten independent runs were performed.

Idf scores (Manning et al. 2009), that represent the number of documents in which a particular token occurs in the search collection, were calculated for all tokens in the vocabulary. Here, a document corresponds to a concatenation of all texts from all case paragraphs in the triples collection that originated from the same HTML-formatted case document.

[1] https://www.bger.ch

[2] https://www.fedlex.admin.ch

Using the above idf values, a non-neural baseline (NNB) that performs exact lexical matching at paragraph level was implemented. As in other bag-of-words models, the vectorization of an individual paragraph creates a separate dimension for each token in the vocabulary, with the final tf-idf score calculated by multiplying the frequency of that token in the paragraph with its idf value (Manning et al. 2009). A boosted version of that non-neural baseline (Boosted NNB) uses an additional token filter that reduces the final vocabulary, by accepting only tokens that start with a sequence of three alphabetical (non-numeric) characters and have a minimal length of 5 characters. This filter was motivated by the observation that many semantically non-informative tokens started with various non-alphabetical characters. The alternative of using each paragraph in the search collection as a document for tf-idf calculation using the standard Python module *'sklearn'* was also tested. In that case, idf values were not based on all case paragraphs in the triples collection, but on a smaller search collection of 69 case paragraphs used in the model evaluation.

3.4 Neural models

We tested different neural approaches for the semantic modeling of paragraphs. If not mentioned otherwise, default parameters were applied.

Two different implementations of the Universal Sentence Encoder (USE, Cer et al. 2018) were tested, a) the model 'xx use md' from the 'spacy' Python library, and b) the huggingface (*huFace*) implementation 'distilUSE'. Note that the huFace variant is a knowledge-distilled, smaller version of the original 15-language USE model.

The doc2vec model (Le & Mikolov 2014) was applied after training the model on our case paragraphs using a vector size of 100, a window size of 5 tokens, 12 epochs for training, and a maximal vocabulary size of 500, after an effort to optimize its hyper-parameters for maximal performance in the task outlined below.

Pre-trained BERT-based transformers that were tested include DistilBERT (German model) and GermanBERT (trained on German text including 20% legal documents), including standard *WordPiece* word segmentation on the input. As a vector that aggregates information from all input tokens, the hidden state of the 'CLS' token of the final BERT layer was used, without further fine-tuning of the pre-trained model. Such transformers offer the use of an *attention mask* for padding, to

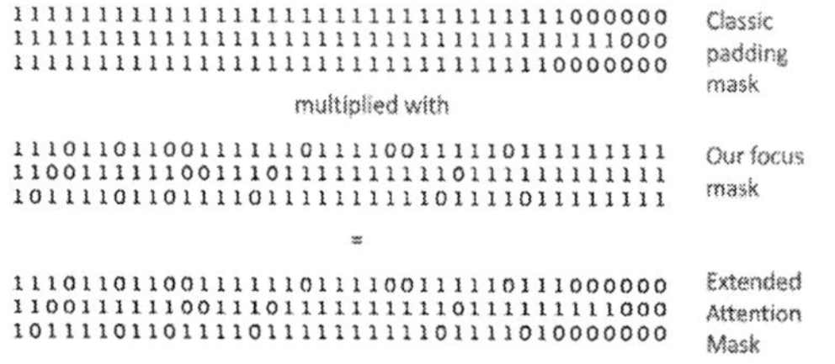

Fig. 1: Generation of the Extended Attention Mask, by multiplying a classic BERT attention mask for padding batch inputs with a focus mask we developed.

mask empty token positions after the last token in the input, when a batch of input sequences has varying length of sequences (Fig. 1). This attention mask represents a vector of binary 'hard gates' that cancel positions that should not get any attention calculated on them.

To combine the idf score aspect of the non-neural baseline systems with the neural models, tokens with low idf values were also assigned a zero value in that attention mask, resulting in what we call an *Extended Attention Mask.* This mask can suppress less informative tokens (with low idf values) in the input, changing the encoding of the paragraph as a result. At a more granular level, this Extended Attention Mask is generated as follows: before tokenization by *WordPiece*, tokens are screened against the idf threshold for masking. Tokens that do not pass are replaced by an underscore character, which in a second step, after using WordPiece for tokenization and subword segmentation, is replaced by a zero value instead of the original value of 1, in the focus mask. This means that transformer self-attention cannot be calculated on that token, even if the surrounding tokens receive self-attention. With the use of the underscore, subword segmentation is also avoided for the masked token.

3.5 Automated labels and model evaluation

An evaluation approach was designed using a set of queries that represent information needs and a set of case paragraphs as a search collection to match with those queries. To approximate the judgement of a human expert on the relevance of a search hit based on semantic similarity, an automatically generated, link-based similarity definition was developed. This link-based similarity definition uses *case pairs* that are deemed to be sufficiently similar as proxies for true hits, when calculating precision values for each

Fig. 2: A projection of the 69 query vectors used for model evaluation, using t-SNE to reduce 100-dimensional doc2vec-generated vectors to a position on this 2D map. Each vector is identified by an integer that represents its position in this list of query texts. Some case pairs are illustrated using red ellipses.

query. Such case pairs are defined as a pair of case paragraphs that share at least two different outgoing citations to the same statute articles in the triple collection. With the employed citations filter used in the generation of those triples, a sufficient level of specificity in terms of the statute target is ensured, thereby selecting a limited number of legal concepts as the semantic scope. To qualify, these two citations need to point to two different laws, or to two different law articles in the same law. A single shared citations was found insufficient in our exploratory work, to guarantee that most case pairs would indeed share a similar meaning that enables an approximation of relevance in this task, for non-experts. With those at least two shared citations as outlined above, we observed that the desired level of semantic similarity between case paragraphs was well approximated. Note that this definition of semantic modeling includes semantics encoded by word order, which cannot be modeled by (the baseline) bag-of-words models.

As a diversity of information needs is represented by a set of 69 queries (Fig. 2) with a large number of case pairs we selected for model evaluation, the

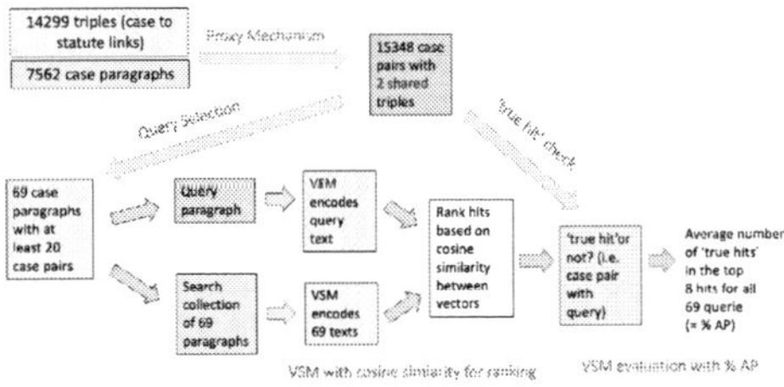

Fig. 3: Schematic overview of our method for model evaluation. From 7562 case paragraphs and 14299 triples, 15348 case pairs were identified (automated label generation). Those case pairs are then used to a) estimate 'true hits' for each query, as a basis for calculating an average precision over all 69 queries, b) as a filter for defining queries based on the triples.

average of the precision calculated for each query is then informative of a model's performance across this set of diverse queries. For calculating precision, the number of case pairs for a query is then used as an approximation of the number of true hits. As case paragraphs that are semantically similar may not always fulfil the selection criteria we defined for generating case pairs, the obtained average precision values may constitute an under-estimation of the number of true hits.

When comparing different models, each of the 69 queries selected from the 7562 case paragraphs was then encoded as a single vector by the tested model and compared with the vectors of the other 68 queries using cosine similarity. In other words, for each query, the other 68 queries were used as the search collection, representing paragraph texts in a database of legal documents.

4 Results and Discussion

For ten independent runs of the random baseline, the mean average precision (AP) was 13.15%, with a standard deviation of 1.06. The non-neural baselines performed considerably better, with a performance of 24.09% achieved by the simple sklearn baseline, and 41.30% by the basic non-neural baseline (NNB v1). The performance of the basic NNB can be further enhanced by applying a token filter using idf values calculated at case document level, up to a maximal level of 42.75% at an idf threshold of 2.12 (NNB v2). The curve in Fig. 4 shows a fine-grained analysis of the optimal idf threshold values, while Table 2 offers an overview of results obtained for different neural and non-neural models tested. The optimal threshold value of 2.12 for the idf score fits a human inspection of the relative importance of different words in case pairs (Fig. 5).

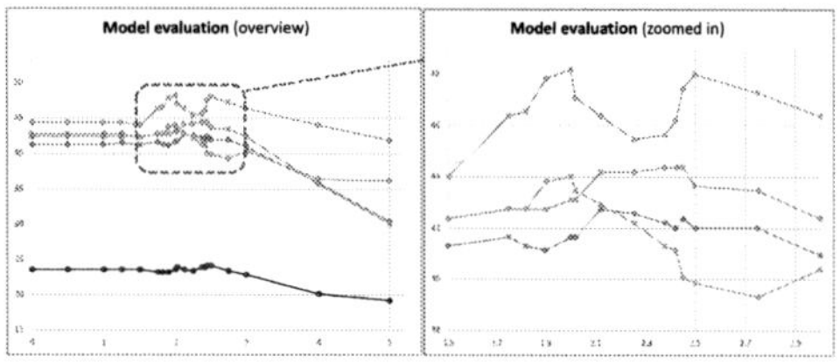

Fig. 4: Determination of the optimal idf threshold for non-neural and neural models. The performance at the optimal idf value corresponds to the v2 variant of the model shown in Table 2. idf threshold values are shown on the X axis, while the achieved %AP is shown on the Y axis. In dark grey, the *sklearn* model (left panel only). Non-neural baseline in light grey, and its boosted version (the best-performing non-neural model) in gold. DistilBERT in green, and GermanBERT (the best-performing neural model) in orange. The right panel shows a zoomed-in view, for the models that achieved a %AP of at least 38.

The ability of the neural models to outperform the best non-neural baseline (Boosted NNB) was then tested. The USE implementation *huFace* reached a performance of only 39.13%, so did not show a clear benefit over the Boosted NNB baseline. The *spacy* implementation, however, achieved 42.41 %, a gain of more than 3 percentage points. This difference between the two USE implementations may be explained by the fact that the *huFace* variant is not the full USE model, but a smaller, distilled version.

A clearly improved performance over the Boosted NNB was observed with GermanBERT, the model that was trained on 20% legal documents (cases and statutes in German language). This BERT-based model achieved a performance of 44.38%. With the use of the Extended Attention Mask, a maximal performance of 48.19% was reached at an optimal idf threshold of 2.0. For all tested BERT-based transformers, the use of the Extended Attention Mask resulted in clear improvements, at idf threshold values around 2 (compare Fig. 5), while distilled, smaller models (of USE and DistilBERT) did not perform well. In comparison, doc2vec achieved a performance of 45.47%, above NNB, but nowhere near the performance we saw with the Extended Attention Mask-boosted GermanBERT. While both DistilBERT and GermanBERT were trained solely using German data, only GermanBERT had legal documents in the training data. Note that this performance of GermanBERT was observed on a pre-trained model without any finetuning to the task.

Model	%AP (v1)	%AP (v2)	Opt. idf
sklearn	23.55	24.09	2.5
NNB	41.30	42.75	2.12
Boosted NNB	42.39	**44.38**	2.45
doc2vec	45.47	-	-
USE (huFace)	39.13	-	-
USE (spacy)	42.21	-	-
DistilBERT	42.75	44.02	2
GermanBERT	44.38	**48.19**	2

Table 2: Summary of model evaluation results. Some models are listed as two variants, one (v1) using a threshold of zero for idf scores (resulting in no filtering), and another (v2) that uses the optimal idf threshold. The performance of the best neural and non-neural models is shown in bold. A double line separates the non-neural (top) from the neural models (bottom). For BERT-like transformers that allowed the use of our Extended Attention Mask, the optimal idf value (see Fig. 4) is shown in the column 'Opt. idf' for the v2 variant of the model.

5 Conclusions

In the described semantic similarity modeling task, we found that the best neural model that was trained not only in the relevant language, but also in-domain data, offered a clear added value over the best non-neural model. This top performance was obtained by extending the use of the transformer attention mask to quench signals from less informative tokens (using idf scores), so they would not be considered in the model. The generated datasets of paragraphs extracted from Swiss cases and statutes, as well as citations in cases that point to statutes, when published can facilitate further research in this domain and task, which currently lacks such datasets. With the link-based automated labeling method we developed, the challenge of obtaining costly human expert annotations in this domain becomes less of an obstacle, aiding research into improved models (and their finetuning) that could help to reveal semantically similar paragraphs that may have been missed with the models we tested. Therefore, with this new framework, a new generation of

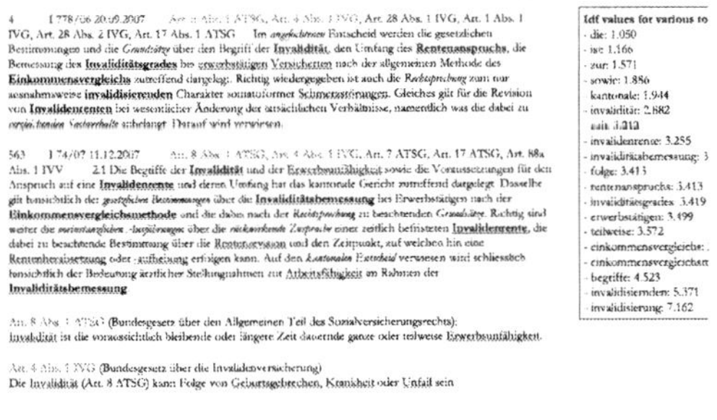

Fig. 5: Example for a case pair (case paragraphs No. 4 and No. 563, with their caseNames and full list of citations) with two shared citations (in blue) pointing to different statutes (ATSG and IVG). Note that semantic similarity of both case paragraphs, as defined using this link-based similarity method using shared citations, goes beyond exact lexical matching for many of the key terms, except the term denoting the main topic, 'Invalidität'. For comparison, the idf values of terms denoting key legal concepts in this case pair that contribute substantially to semantic similarity are shown below. Additional terms and expressions that are specific to legal language and not likely to occur in other domains are shown in italics. Also note how the statute texts are very concise and broadly understandable, which the case paragraph language is more about legal reasoning.

improved models can now be developed, for the task of searching Swiss court decisions using a wide range of natural language queries that represent information needs from expert and even non-expert users. The ability to model semantic similarity beyond exact lexical matching could then help a larger audience of non-expert users who may struggle with query formulation, to better access, understand and navigate the legal system.

Supplementary Material

The created datasets and Python code will be published on GitHub at https://github.com/lilytang2017

Acknowledgments

Martin Volk for his guidance on natural language processing and artificial intelligence in the legal domain.

References

Houda Alberts, Akin Ipek, Roderick Lucas, and Phillip Wozny. 2020. COLIEE 2020: Legal information retrieval & entailment with legal embeddings and boosting. In: Okazaki N., Yada K., Satoh K., Mineshima K. (eds) New Frontiers in Artificial Intelligence. JSAI-isAI 2020. Lecture Notes in Computer Science, vol 12758. Springer, Cham.

Paheli Bhattacharya, Kripabandhu Ghosh, Saptarshi Ghosh, Arindam Pal, Parth Mehta, Arnab Bhattacharya, and Prasenjit Majumber. 2019. FIRE 2019 AILA Track: artificial intelligence for legal assistance. Proc 11th Forum for Information Retrieval Evaluation.

Paheli Bhattacharya, Kripabandhu Ghosh, Arindam Pal, and Saptarshi Ghosh. 2020. Methods for computing legal document similarity: a comparative study. arXiv:2004.12307v1.

Paul Boniol, George Panagopoulos, Christos Xypolopoulos, Rajaa El Hamdani, David Restrepo Amariles, Michalis Vazirgiannis. 2020. Performance in the courtroom: automated processing and visualization of appeal court decisions in France. arXiv:2006.06251v2.

Daniel Cer, Yinfei Yang, Sheng-yi Kong, Nan Hua, Nicole Limtiaco, et al. 2018. Universal Sentence Encoder. arXiv:1803.11175

Ilias Chalkidis, Manos Fergadiotis, Prodomos Malakasiotis, Nikolaos Aletras, Ion Androutsopoulos. 2020. LEGAL-BERT: The Muppets straight out of Law School. EMNLP 2020 Findings, ACL: 2898-2904.

Yen-Liang Chen, Yi-Hung Liu, and Wu-Liang Ho. 2013. A text mining approach to assist the general public in the retrieval of legal documents. Journal of ASIS&T 64(2):280–290.

Alexis Conneau, and Douwe Kiela. 2018. SentEval: an evaluation toolkit for universal sentence representations. arXiv:1803.05449

Wilco Draijer. 2019. The creation and integration of a legal information retrieval system without manual query construction. Master thesis, Leiden University. Supervisor: Suzan Verbene.

Carole D. Hafner. 1980. Representation of knowledge in a legal information retrieval system. SIGIR '80: Proc 3rd Annual ACM Conf Res Dev Inf Retrieval. P 139-153

Qi He, Jian Pei, Daniel Kifer, Prasenjit Mitra, and Lee Giles. 2010. Context-aware citation recommendation. Proc 19th Int Conf WWW, pages 421-30. ACM.

Arthur Ter, Henderik Alex Proper, and Theo P. van der Weide. 1996. Query formulation as an information retrieval problem. The Computer Journal 39.

Chanwoo Jeong, Sion Jang, Hyuna Shin, Eunjeong Park, Sungchul Choi. A context-aware citation recommendation model with BERT and Graph Convolutional Networks. arXiv:1903.06464v1.

M.M. Kessler. 1963. Bibliographic coupling between scientific papers. American Documentation, 14: 10-25.

Sushanta Kumar, Polepalli Krishna Reddy, V. Balakista Reddy, and Malti Suri. 2013. Finding similar legal judgements under common law system. In DNIS, pages 103-116. Springer.

Quoc V. Le, and Tomas Mikolov. 2014. Distributed representations of sentences and documents. In Proceedings of the 31st International Conference on Machine Learning (ICML-14), pages 1188–1196

Wangzhong Lu, Jeannette Janssen, Evangelos Milios, and Nathalie Japkowicz. 2006. Node similarity in the citation graph. Knowl Inf Syst 11:105-29.

Christopher D. Manning, Prabhakar Raghavan, and Hinrich Schütze. 2009. An introduction to Information Retrieval. Online edition. Cambridge University Press, Cambridge, UK.

Jeff Mitchell, and Mirella Lapata. 2010. Composition in distributional models of semantics. Cognitive Science 34: 1388-1429.

Paul Neculoiu, Maarten Versteegh, and Mihai Rotaru. 2016. Learning text similarity with Siamese recurrent networks. Proc 1st workshop representation learning for NLP, pages 148-157.

K. Raghav, Pailla Balakrishna Reddy, V. Balakista Reddy, and Polepalli Krishna Reddy. 2015. Text and citations-based cluster analysis of legal judgments', in MIKE, pp. 449–459. Springer.

K. Raghav, Pailla Balakrishna Reddy, and V. Balakista Reddy. 2016) Analyzing the extraction of relevant legal judgments using paragraph-level and citation information. AI4JCArtificial Intelligence for Justice, page 30.

Yunqiu Shao, Jiaxin Mao, Yiqun Liu, Weizhi Ma, Ken Satoh, Min Zhang, and Shaoping Ma. 2020. BERT-PLI: Modeling paragraph-level interactions for legal case retrieval. Proc 29th Int Joint Conf AI (IJCAI-20).

Da Silveira, and Berthier A. Ribeiro-Neto. 2004. Concept-based ranking: a case study in the juridical domain. Inf. Process. Manage. 40 pages 791–805.

Vu Tran, Minh Le Nguyen, and Ken Satoh. 2020. Building legal case retrieval systems with lexical matching and summarization using a pre-trained phrase scoring model. ICAIL '19: Proc 17th Int Conf AI Law. p275-82.

Marc van Opijnen, and Cristiana Santos. 2017. On the concept of relevance in legal information retrieval. AI & Law 25:65-87.

Alex Wang, Amanpreet Singh, Julian Michael, Felix Hill, Omer Levy, and Samuel R. Bowman. 2019. GLUE: a multi-task benchmark and analysis platform for natural language understanding. ICLR 2019.

Chaojun Xiao, Haoxi Zhong, Zhipeng Guo, Cunchao Tu, Zhiyuan Liu et al. 2019. CAIL2019-SCM: a dataset of similar case matching in legal domain. arXiv:1911.08962v3

Haoxi Zhong, Chaojun Xiao, Cunchao Tu, Tianyang Zhang, Zhiyuan Liu, and Maosong Sun. 2020. How does NLP benefit legal system: A summary of legal artificial intelligence. arXiv:2004.12158v5

GerDaLIR: A German Dataset for Legal Information Retrieval

Marco Wrzalik and **Dirk Krechel**
RheinMain University of Applied Sciences, Germany
{firstname.lastname}@hs-rm.de

Abstract

We present GerDaLIR, a **German Dataset** for **Legal Information Retrieval** based on case documents from the open legal information platform *Open Legal Data*. The dataset consists of 123K queries, each labelled with at least one relevant document in a collection of 131K case documents. We conduct several baseline experiments including BM25 and a state-of-the-art neural re-ranker. With our dataset, we aim to provide a standardized benchmark for German LIR and promote open research in this area. Beyond that, our dataset comprises sufficient training data to be used as a downstream task for German or multilingual language models.

1 Introduction

There are few non-English datasets dedicated to Natural Legal Language Processing (NLLP) or Legal Information Retrieval (LIR). To our knowledge, not a single dataset exists that provides a standardized benchmark for LIR models on the German language. To this end we contribute GerDaLIR, a legal document retrieval dataset comprising a large document collection and corresponding queries forming a document ranking task. We provide a large amount of training data such that both unsupervised and supervised methods can be benchmarked. This also enables GerDaLIR to be used as a downstream task for German or multilingual language models. The task provided is a precedent retrieval task. As illustrated in Figure 1, we build GerDaLIR by extracting passages that reference other cases. For that we utilize 201,825 cases from the open legal information platform *Open Legal Data* (Ostendorff et al., 2020). We present baseline experiments on classic term-based retrieval methods, a semantic search approach based on word embeddings and a transformer-based re-ranker giving an orientation to other researchers using our dataset. In contrast to other LIR datasets based on precedent case retrieval, GerDaLIR offers the following unique characteristics:

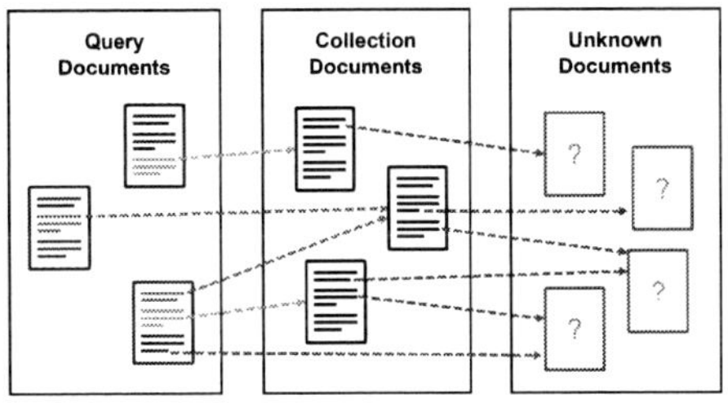

Figure 1: GerDaLIR comprises query-document pairs from passages that cite known collection documents.

Large Corpus Size. With a total of 144K relevance labels for 123K query passages and a collection of 131K documents comprising over 3M passages, GerDaLIR is – to our knowledge – bigger than any other LIR dataset. Its size enables GerDaLIR to be used for full-ranking evaluation.
German Language. The German language is GerDaLIR's most prominent feature and fills a gap in the community. Furthermore, in combination with the large training set, GerDaLIR can be used as a downstream task for German or multilingual language models, of which there are quite few.
Query Passages. Most other LIR datasets based on precedent retrieval provide entire case documents to be used as queries. It may be unclear to which part of a given case relevant cases should be retrieved. As GerDaLIR provides query *passages* rather than whole documents, it better reflects a practical use case.

The download links and descriptions to the format of GerDaLIR can be accessed via GitHub[1].

2 Other Datasets

There are several sources of LIR datasets and tasks. In the following, we outline those based on precedent retrieval.

[1]https://github.com/lavis-nlp/GerDaLIR

Natural Legal Language Processing Workshop 2021, pages 123–128

COLIEE 2020 Task 1. The *Competition on Legal Information Extraction/Entailment* (COLIEE) is a workshop that annually provides a number of tasks in the areas of legal document retrieval, question answering and entailment. COLIEE 2020 Task 1 (Rabelo et al., 2020) is a re-ranking task that provides for training: "520 base cases, each with 200 candidate cases from which the participants must identify those that should be noticed with respect to the base case". From the total of 104,000 candidates, 2,680 are labelled as positive. For testing they provide 130 base cases, a total of 26,000 candidates and 646 positive labels. The case documents are written in English and originate from the Federal Court of Canada. The workshop also provides tasks derived from the Japanese jurisdiction including original Japanese texts as well as English translations.

SigmaLaw. This dataset originates from the paper *Legal Document Retrieval using Document Vector Embeddings and Deep Learning* (Sugathadasa et al., 2018). It comprises 2,500 case documents and a citation graph indicating for each case which of the other cases are considered relevant.

FIRE 2017 IRLED. The *FIRE 2017 IRLED Track* presents a precedence retrieval task comprising 200 query cases, 2000 collection cases and 1000 positive relevance labels. The provided case documents originate from the Indian Supreme Court, which uses the English language in their proceedings.

3 Dataset Generation

GerDaLIR is based on parsed references in German case documents taken from *Open Legal Data*. Although precedent cases have no binding effect in the German law system, references to prior cases are very common and arguably play a big role in supporting a line of argument. By definition, such referenced cases are relevant to the case at hand. With this in mind, the idea behind GerDaLIR's task is simple: Passages containing one or more references to known cases become queries while the referenced cases are labelled as relevant. However, if a passage is used as a query, the document the passage originates from should not be used as an retrievable collection document. To achieve that, we classify case documents – as depicted in Figure 1 – into the following classes: Unknown documents belong to cases that we have seen references to, but are not part of *Open Legal Data*. Collection documents comprise the cases that will be indexed for the retrieval task, which mainly consist of those that only refer to unknown documents. Query documents are the documents from which queries are sampled. Assigned to these are cases that contain references to collection documents. If a case document refers to other query cases, but not to collection cases, it is also classified as a collection document. The case documents are divided into passages along margin numbers. It regularly happens that the references to a passage follow with a margin number. Those passages typically start with *Vgl.* ("compare") or *Siehe* ("see"). We use these and more indicator words in the beginning of a passage to detect such referential passages and assign their references to the previous passage, which is assumed to contain the corresponding statement or line of argument. The text describing the references, however, is not added to the passage, since we want models to rely on natural language rather than exploiting references or parts of them. For this reason, we attempt to replace any reference including those to statutes with a `[REF]` token. However, a small portion of references that we were unable to parse remain in the text. From the final text, we also remove any braced content, since they mostly contain comprehensively described references that are difficult to sanitize otherwise. After that we collect all passages from the query documents that are marked with references to one or more collection documents. These form a set of multi-sentence queries, each with at least one label to a relevant collection document. Finally, we perform a 0.8/0.1/0.1 split on the queries for training, development and testing respectively. The resulting size of GerDaLIR's collection, the queries and the labels are summarized in Table 1.

Table 1: GerDaLIR's dataset size

	Documents	Passages
Collection	131,446	3,095,383

	Train	Dev	Test
Queries	98,380	12,297	12,298
Pos. Labels	115,360	14,570	14,394

4 Baseline Methods

We conduct a series of baseline experiments demonstrating that GerDaLIR can be used to benchmark retrieval methods or to evaluate the language models used by them. The resulting measures also serve as an orientation to other researchers using the dataset. The methods considered are described below.

4.1 BM25 and TF-IDF

TF-IDF and BM25 are known as term-based or sparse retrieval methods. They are efficiently realized using inverted indexing. With that, they rely on exact term matches resulting in the tendency of missing relevant items. This tendency is often mitigated by employing a *stemmer* or *lemmatizer* normalizing each word to its base form. More detailed information can be found in *Introduction to Information Retrieval* by Manning et al. (2008).

4.2 Word Centroid Similarity

We introduce the *Word Centroid Similarity* (WCS), an unsupervised semantic textual similarity measure based on word embeddings (Mikolov et al., 2013). Retrieval with WCS can be described as a dense retrieval method, since a dense representation is assigned to each query, document or passage. This vector is the *centroid* or mean vector of the embeddings of the words that occur in the given text. Based on the centroids, we calculate the relevance score using the cosine similarity measure. Aggregating word embeddings for the measurement of textual similarity has been studied in the past with various aggregation methods, word embedding models and vector similarity or distance measures (Kusner et al., 2015; Glasgow et al., 2016; Rücklé et al., 2018; Landthaler et al., 2018). We include WCS as a semantic search counterpart to the term-based retrieval methods. With that we also demonstrate how GerDaLIR can be used to evaluate word embeddings in terms of their utility to information retrieval.

4.3 Neural Re-ranking

We conduct neural re-ranking experiments with a simple binary relevance classifier based on *Transformer Encoders* (Vaswani et al., 2017) that follows BERT's cross-encoding design for *sentence pair classification* (Devlin et al., 2019). Rankings result from the order of confidence with which given query-passage pairs are classified as relevant. Nogueira and Cho (2019) provide a more detailed description on the implementation of this model.

5 Experiments

In this section, we outline the experimental setup, describe the implementation of the methods described above, and briefly discuss the results.

5.1 Metrics

We measure standard information retrieval metrics for the evaluation of our baseline models. With the *mean reciprocal rank* cut off at the tenth position (MRR@10) and the *normalized discounted cumulative gain* cut off at the twentieth position (nDCG@20), we measure the ranking quality on the top positions. MRR@10 only considers the first hit and penalizes strongly for each rank below rank one while nDCG@20 takes all positively labeled documents into account and penalizes softer. Complementary to the ranking quality measures, we measure recall cut off at positions 100 and 1000 to coarsely illustrate the distribution of positive documents and the portion of documents that were missed completely.

5.2 With Passages to Document Rankings

There are various good reasons to perform passage retrieval although the actual targets are documents. In our work the reason behind this is two-fold: First, depending on the model, it could result in better rankings. Second, the model at hand might not be able to process whole documents. The neural re-ranker we use is limited to input sequences of 512 tokens. To cast passage rankings to document rankings, we map passages back to the documents they originate from and perform max-pooling on the scores along documents. However, many documents are represented by multiple passages and after pooling the lengths of the resulting document rankings are smaller than the initial passage ranking. For this reason we retrieve 2000 passages although we only analyze top-1000 document rankings. For the re-ranking, however, we utilize only the first 1000 passages as candidates (including multiple document occurrences) and cast to document ranking afterwards.

5.3 TF-IDF and BM25

We use *Elasticsearch*[2] to perform TF-IDF and BM25 retrieval. Its German analyzer includes a pre-processing pipeline that removes stop-words and performs stemming in accordance to the German language. BM25's parameters k1 and b are

[2] https://www.elastic.co/

Table 2: Baseline measures. Mode P and D denote passage-wise and document-wise retrieval (Section 5.2).

Method	Mode	MRR@10	nDCG@20	Recall@100	Recall@1000
TF-IDF	P	0.333	0.375	0.651	0.768
	D	0.336	0.386	0.701	0.809
BM25 ($k1 = 1.20, b = 0.75$)	P	0.365	0.409	0.693	0.800
	D	0.386	0.434	0.734	0.827
BM25_{tuned} ($k1 = 0.51, b = 0.72$)	P	0.372	0.417	0.703	0.803
BM25_{tuned} ($k1 = 0.90, b = 0.98$)	D	0.391	0.439	0.737	**0.829**
WCS – GloVe	P	0.242	0.278	0.539	0.695
	D	0.134	0.166	0.420	0.625
WCS – fastText	P	0.257	0.295	0.582	0.726
	D	0.153	0.188	0.468	0.668
Neural Re-ranking – BERT	P	0.416	0.465	**0.745**	0.789
Neural Re-ranking – ELECTRA	P	**0.436**	**0.481**	**0.743**	0.789

tuned based on the development set in the ranges of $[0.5, 2.0]$ and $[0.3, 1]$ respectively. For that we employ the Bayesian optimization algorithm provided by *Optuna*[3], with 100 trials and nDCG@20 as the metric being optimized. The default parameters and those resulted from the tuning are listed in Table 2. It is worth noting that for term-based retrieval methods, the document-wise retrieval (D) outperforms the passage-wise retrieval (P) as shown in Table 2. We hypothesize that in relevant documents, the important keywords occur more frequently throughout the entire document while in other, non-relevant documents, they occur only marginally in a few passages. This can be exploited through the term frequency in document-wise retrieval.

5.4 Word Centroid Similarity

We employ *GloVe* (Pennington et al., 2014) and *fastText* (Bojanowski et al., 2017) word embeddings in our WCS retrieval experiments. For that we train the embeddings based on the entire lowercased text from the cases in *Open Legal Data*, which comprises more than 465 million words. The training is performed using the original implementations for *GloVe*[4] and *fastText*[5]. For inference, we filter stopwords and normalize each word centroid to L2-norm before indexing in an *faiss*[6] inner product index with which a cosine similarity search index is realized. As shown in Table 2, fastText slightly outperforms GloVe. We hypothesize fastText is favorable for the German language, since it virtually realizes a compound splitter: FastText expands each word by character n-grams and calculates an aggregated representation using the n-grams and a representation for the entire word. Furthermore, if a word is out of vocabulary, there is a good chance of generating a meaningful representation using the character n-grams. The minimum and maximum size of those character n-gram are hyperparameters. We found that 5 for both minimum and maximum n-gram size perform best among various tested settings.

5.5 Neural Re-ranking

In recent years many modifications to the BERT model and its training procedure have been proposed such as ALBERT (Lan et al., 2020) or RoBERTa (Liu et al., 2019). The effectiveness gains of those modifications are often demonstrated on downstream tasks. In our neural re-ranking experiment, we compare a pretrained BERT model with a pretrained ELECTRA discriminator (Clark et al., 2020). We use the "base" variants of BERT and ELECTRA trained by Chan et al. (2020), which can be accessed via *Hugging Face*[7] with the identifiers `deepset/gbert-base` and `deepset/gelectra-base`. During fine-tuning we use top-100 BM25 rankings from which we randomly sample one negative candidate for each positive example. The pre-trained models are trained for 100 epochs on GerDaLIR's training

[3] https://optuna.org/

[4] https://github.com/stanfordnlp/GloVe

[5] https://fasttext.cc/

[6] https://faiss.ai/

[7] https://huggingface.co/deepset/

data with a learning rate of 1e-4 and an effective batch size of 768 samples (e.g. batches of 16 samples and 48 gradient accumulation steps for each update step). The final models are tested based on top-1000 passage rankings from BM25 as candidates. To those, the score max-pooling is not applied, but on the final re-ranked rankings. Therefore, many documents are represented by multiple passages and the final rankings are much shorter than 1000 documents, which negatively affects recall@1000. Due to the sequence length limitation, document-wise retrieval can not directly be performed with BERT or ELECTRA. Passages that exceed this limitation are divided along sentence boundaries, and the maximum score is applied to the passage. As shown in Table 1, the use of the ELECTRA model results in higher re-ranking quality in terms of MRR@10 and nDCG@20 compared to the BERT model, which is consistent with external experiments on other downstream tasks (Clark et al., 2020; Chan et al., 2020).

6 Conclusion & Future Work

We present GerDaLIR, a dataset filling the gap of a standardized IR benchmark for the German legal domain. We provide several baselines with which other researchers can compare their results. Our experiments demonstrate the use of GerDaLIR as a downstream task for German or multilingual language models. In future work, we plan to investigate the importance of in-domain pre-training to neural LIR models. We also intend to explore unsupervised methods that effectively leverage language models for domain-specific information retrieval, as well as approaches combining these with traditional term-based retrieval methods.

References

Piotr Bojanowski, Edouard Grave, Armand Joulin, and Tomás Mikolov. 2017. Enriching word vectors with subword information. *Trans. Assoc. Comput. Linguistics*, 5:135–146.

Branden Chan, Stefan Schweter, and Timo Möller. 2020. German's next language model. In *Proceedings of the 28th International Conference on Computational Linguistics, COLING 2020, Barcelona, Spain (Online), December 8-13, 2020*, pages 6788–6796. International Committee on Computational Linguistics.

Kevin Clark, Minh-Thang Luong, Quoc V. Le, and Christopher D. Manning. 2020. ELECTRA: pre-training text encoders as discriminators rather than generators. In *8th International Conference on Learning Representations, ICLR 2020, Addis Ababa, Ethiopia, April 26-30, 2020*. OpenReview.net.

Jacob Devlin, Ming-Wei Chang, Kenton Lee, and Kristina Toutanova. 2019. BERT: Pre-training of deep bidirectional transformers for language understanding. In *Proceedings of the 2019 Conference of the North American Chapter of the Association for Computational Linguistics: Human Language Technologies, Volume 1 (Long and Short Papers)*, pages 4171–4186, Minneapolis, Minnesota. Association for Computational Linguistics.

Kimberly Glasgow, Matthew J. Roos, Amy J. Haufler, Mark A. Chevillet, and Michael Wolmetz. 2016. Evaluating semantic models with word-sentence relatedness. *CoRR*, abs/1603.07253.

Matt J. Kusner, Yu Sun, Nicholas I. Kolkin, and Kilian Q. Weinberger. 2015. From word embeddings to document distances. In *Proceedings of the 32nd International Conference on Machine Learning, ICML 2015, Lille, France, 6-11 July 2015*, volume 37 of *JMLR Workshop and Conference Proceedings*, pages 957–966. JMLR.org.

Zhenzhong Lan, Mingda Chen, Sebastian Goodman, Kevin Gimpel, Piyush Sharma, and Radu Soricut. 2020. ALBERT: A lite BERT for self-supervised learning of language representations. In *8th International Conference on Learning Representations, ICLR 2020, Addis Ababa, Ethiopia, April 26-30, 2020*. OpenReview.net.

Jörg Landthaler, I Glaser, E Scepankova, and F Matthes. 2018. Semantic text matching of contract clauses and legal comments in tenancy law. In *Tagunsband IRIS: Internationales Rechtsinformatik Symposium*.

Yinhan Liu, Myle Ott, Naman Goyal, Jingfei Du, Mandar Joshi, Danqi Chen, Omer Levy, Mike Lewis, Luke Zettlemoyer, and Veselin Stoyanov. 2019. Roberta: A robustly optimized BERT pretraining approach. *CoRR*, abs/1907.11692.

Christopher D. Manning, Prabhakar Raghavan, and Hinrich Schütze. 2008. *Introduction to information retrieval*. Cambridge University Press.

Tomás Mikolov, Wen-tau Yih, and Geoffrey Zweig. 2013. Linguistic regularities in continuous space word representations. In *Human Language Technologies: Conference of the North American Chapter of the Association of Computational Linguistics, Proceedings, June 9-14, 2013, Atlanta, Georgia, USA*, pages 746–751. The Association for Computational Linguistics.

Rodrigo Nogueira and Kyunghyun Cho. 2019. Passage re-ranking with BERT. *CoRR*, abs/1901.04085.

Malte Ostendorff, Till Blume, and Saskia Ostendorff. 2020. Towards an open platform for legal information. In *Proceedings of the ACM/IEEE Joint Conference on Digital Libraries in 2020*, JCDL '20, page 385–388, New York, NY, USA. Association for Computing Machinery.

Jeffrey Pennington, Richard Socher, and Christopher D. Manning. 2014. Glove: Global vectors for word representation. In *Proceedings of the 2014 Conference on Empirical Methods in Natural Language Processing, EMNLP 2014, October 25-29, 2014, Doha, Qatar, A meeting of SIGDAT, a Special Interest Group of the ACL*, pages 1532–1543. ACL.

Juliano Rabelo, Mi-Young Kim, Randy Goebel, Masaharu Yoshioka, Yoshinobu Kano, and Ken Satoh. 2020. COLIEE 2020: Methods for legal document retrieval and entailment. In *New Frontiers in Artificial Intelligence - JSAI-isAI 2020 Workshops, JURISIN, LENLS 2020 Workshops, Virtual Event, November 15-17, 2020, Revised Selected Papers*, volume 12758 of *Lecture Notes in Computer Science*, pages 196–210. Springer.

Andreas Rücklé, Steffen Eger, Maxime Peyrard, and Iryna Gurevych. 2018. Concatenated p-mean word embeddings as universal cross-lingual sentence representations. *CoRR*, abs/1803.01400.

Keet Sugathadasa, Buddhi Ayesha, Nisansa de Silva, Amal Shehan Perera, Vindula Jayawardana, Dimuthu Lakmal, and Madhavi Perera. 2018. Legal document retrieval using document vector embeddings and deep learning. In *Science and information conference*, pages 160–175. Springer.

Ashish Vaswani, Noam Shazeer, Niki Parmar, Jakob Uszkoreit, Llion Jones, Aidan N. Gomez, Lukasz Kaiser, and Illia Polosukhin. 2017. Attention is all you need. In *Advances in Neural Information Processing Systems 30: Annual Conference on Neural Information Processing Systems 2017, December 4-9, 2017, Long Beach, CA, USA*, pages 5998–6008.

SPAR.txt, a cheap Shallow Parsing approach for Regulatory texts

Ruben Kruiper* and **Ioannis Konstas** and **Alasdair Gray**
School of Mathematics and Computer Sciences
Heriot-Watt University, Edinburgh, United Kingdom
*ruben.kruiper@hw.ac.uk

Farhad Sadeghineko and **Richard Watson** and **Bimal Kumar**
Department of Architecture and Built Environment
Northumbria University, Newcastle, United Kingdom

Abstract

Automated Compliance Checking (ACC) systems aim to semantically parse building regulations to a set of rules. However, semantic parsing is known to be hard and requires large amounts of training data. The complexity of creating such training data has led to research that focuses on small sub-tasks, such as shallow parsing or the extraction of a limited subset of rules. This study introduces a shallow parsing task for which training data is relatively cheap to create, with the aim of learning a lexicon for ACC. We annotate a small domain-specific dataset of 200 sentences, SPAR.txt[1], and train a sequence tagger that achieves 79,93 F1-score on the test set. We then show through manual evaluation that the model identifies most (89,84%) defined terms in a set of building regulation documents, and that both contiguous and discontiguous Multi-Word Expressions (MWE) are discovered with reasonable accuracy (70,3%).

1 Introduction

Non-compliance with building regulations has been linked to fatal incidents (Cook, 2017). However, ensuring that a building complies with regulations is complicated and time-consuming because:

- Regulations contain ambiguous and sometimes conflicting criteria (Cook, 2017; Hywel et al., 2020).
- Regulations change and are distributed over many documents (Fuchs, 2021), e.g., over 800 documents in the U.K. with many of them behind a paywall.
- Criteria often refer to entire sections in other documents, e.g., "*The emergency lighting should be installed in accordance with BS 5266: Part 1: 2016 as read in association with BS 5266: Part 7: 1999 (BS EN: 1838: 2013).*" (Scottish Government, 2020).
- Regulations differ per country, and some criteria borrowed from international regulations are not suited to the specific environment (Moon et al., 2019).

Automated Compliance Checking (ACC) could reduce the difficulty, time, costs and number of human errors made during compliance checking (Dimyadi and Amor, 2013; Preidel and Borrmann, 2018), as well as ease customisation and innovation in the building sector (Niemeijer et al., 2014). There exist two branches of ACC research. One focuses on tools that reason over a rule-base – often consisting of hard-coded rules (Pauwels et al., 2017; Solihin et al., 2019). The other branch attempts semantically parse the Natural Language regulations into rules that enable reasoning – a complex task that is of interest to the wider legal domain (Wyner et al., 2012).

This study presents a novel *shallow parsing* task, for which the creation of training data is cheap, and an accompanying small dataset of 200 sentences. The aim is to learn a semantic lexicon for ACC, which is often an important first step for semantic parsing because it enables the grounding of information units identified in a text – such as objects, interactions and constraints (Zettlemoyer and Michael, 2005; Kollar et al., 2010; Chen, 2012). Section 2 motivates our task and describes related work with a focus on parsing building regulations. 3 describes the task, as well as the collection of a small annotated dataset – SPAR.txt – for the task of discovering and identifying domain-specific terms, including Multi-Word Expressionss (MWE). In 4 we describe and train a sequence tagging model, which generalises well to unseen text within the same domain. 5 describes the evaluation of outputs, specifically with regards to the objects identified in a corpus of 13K sentences derived from the Scot-

[1] For the SCOTREG corpus, SPAR.txt dataset and code see: `https://github.com/rubenkruiper/SPaR.txt`

Natural Legal Language Processing Workshop 2021, pages 129–143
November 10, 2021.

tish Building Regulations (Scottish Government, 2020). Our model finds 89,84% of the terms explicitly defined in these documents. Furthermore, a significant proportion (70,3%) of these predictions matches exactly what a human annotator would consider to be an object in a given sentence context. We argue that our new task can provide a cheap approach to lexicon learning that could benefit (1) Information Extraction (IE) in support of ACC, (2) Information Retrieval (IR) in support of manual compliance checking, and (3) the mapping of unstructured text to a structured representation.

2 Related work

2.1 Semantic parsing for ACC

Semantic parsing revolves around learning the meaning of Natural Language and converting it to an executable logical form, which is a hard and unsolved task (Mooney, 2007; Artzi and Zettlemoyer, 2013). The fragmented structure of legal texts further complicates semantic parsing in legal domains (Lawsky, 2017), e.g., a clause may state that some object must comply with all of the regulations in some other section or document. Therefore, statutory reasoning requires defeasible logic representations that allow conclusions to be defeated on the basis of subsequent information (Pertierra et al., 2017). Due to the complexity of the task, existing approaches to semantic parsing in the ACC domain often limit their scope to parsing quantitative requirements in some small sub-domain (Fuchs, 2021; Moon et al., 2021).

In the ACC domain, studies on semantic parsing rely on traditional Rule-Based Systems to extract concepts and construct logical statements, e.g., (Zhang and El-Gohary, 2016b,a; Zhou and El-Gohary, 2019; Xu and Cai, 2019). Empirical approaches may be able to handle the combinatorial explosion caused by ambiguity in Natural Language (Wyner et al., 2012). But training data for such systems is difficult and costly to collect (Chen, 2012; Herzig and Berant, 2017). Unsurprisingly, Machine Learning studies in the ACC domain focus on simpler sub-tasks of semantic parsing for which training data is relatively easy to collect, such as Named Entity Recognition (Liu and El-Gohary, 2017; Moon et al., 2021) and Relation Classification (Zhong et al., 2020). This study follows a similar strategy to limit the complexity of annotation, see 3.2 and 3.3.

2.2 Shallow parsing for ACC

Orthogonal research on shallow parsing in the ACC domain includes (1) the decomposition of complex sentences into parts that are easier to process (Zhang and El-Gohary, 2019), and (2) more-or-less idiosyncratic semantic markup schemes that help identify requirements and their components in text, e.g., (Hjelseth and Nisbet, 2011) and (Zhang and El-Gohary, 2016b). Efforts to automate such shallow parsing approaches encountered performance issues when handling MWEs (Zhang and El-Gohary, 2019; Zhang and Nora, 2020).

Although the proper handling of MWEs is a key issue in Natural Language Processing (Siskind, 1996; Sag et al., 2002; Ramisch et al., 2018), extracting MWEs is especially relevant to IE in domains rich in technical terms (Baldwin and Kim, 2010) – such as the building regulations. Processing MWEs is a general requirement for ACC, because both single and multi-word concepts mentioned in regulations have to be aligned with components and values found in Building Information Model (BIM) models. Such BIM models rely on standards, such as the Industry Foundation Classes (IFC) data model, to facilitate amongst others compliance checking and information exchange between applications and potentially international stake-holders (Plume and Mitchell, 2007; Beetz et al., 2009; Pauwels et al., 2017). This study aims to automatically learn a vocabulary for ACC, which entails MWE processing.

2.3 Processing MWEs

Processing MWE can be divided into two sub-tasks: MWE discovery and MWE identification (Constant et al., 2017).

MWE discovery aims to find new types of MWEs in text corpora and storing them in a lexicon. Unsupervised approaches are used that rely on properties of MWEs that set them apart from random combinations of words, such as word collocation frequency (Manning et al., 2002; Pecina and Schlesinger, 2006), non-substitutability of component words (Lapata and Lascarides, 2003; Constant et al., 2017), and non-compositionality (Frege, 1996; Riedl and Biemann, 2015). The latter applies mostly to idiomatic expressions(Villavicencio and Idiart, 2019), such as '*cloud nine*'.

MWE identification revolves around annotating MWEs in a corpus, based on a lexicon or on results from MWE discovery (Constant et al., 2017).

	Domestic	Non-Domestic	Total
Terms defined in definitions section	128	127	128
Defined terms in text after lemmatisation and lower-casing	233	247	292
Number of terms linking to definitions section	4.687	5.368	10.055
Number of tokens	131.666	151.499	283.165
Vocabulary	8.285	8.925	9.837
Number of sentences	6.313	7.293	13.606
Mean sentence (word-level token) length, excluding punctuation	20,86	20,77	20,81
Standard deviation	11,96	12,32	12,16

Table 1: Statistics for the SCOTREG corpus – the number of defined terms, word-level tokens and sentences found in the domestic and non-domestic Scottish Building regulations.

This enables representing MWEs as single tokens, which has been shown to improve accuracy of NLP tasks (Green et al., 2011), such as dependency parsing (Nivre and Nilsson, 2004). Supervised approaches are used, amongst which sequence tagging has been found to work well (Constant et al., 2017), e.g., (Blunsom and Baldwin, 2006; Constant et al., 2012). Sequence tagging has also been used for joint MWE identification and Part-of-Speech (POS) tagging (Constant and Sigogne, 2011) and may be amended to handle discontiguous MWEs (Schneider et al., 2014).

This study explores sequence tagging for joint MWE processing. However, this study does not aim to handle idiomatic expressions or proverbs. Beyond research on MWE processing, a related task that focuses on identifying technical terms and Named Entities is concept mining, e.g., (Rajagopal et al., 2013; Poria et al., 2014). In contrast to these concept mining studies, we do not rely on dependency parses or external resources, such as ConceptNet (Speer et al., 2013).

3 MWE tagging for ACC

3.1 A building regulations corpus

Many building regulations are captured in formats that are not easily processed by computers, such as PDF (Fuchs, 2021). The Scottish Building Regulations (Scottish Government, 2020) are an exception and are openly available online. We scrape the domestic and non-domestic regulations, including text found in lists, side-notes, tables and captions.

We use TextBlob [2] for word-level tokenization (Penn Treebank Tokenizer) and sentence splitting (PunktSentenceTokenizer (Kiss and Strunk, 2006)). We will refer to the resulting corpus as SCOTREG. An overview of the size of SCOTREG in terms of sentences and tokens can be found in Table 1, as well as the number the terms defined in the '*Terms and definitions*' sections. Throughout SCOTREG defined terms provide a hyperlink to the definitions section. This enables us to count how often defined terms occur. Note these defined terms represent *classes*, they are expressed in various ways throughout the texts and some of the variations do not match any of the terms verbatim – even after lower-casing and lemmatizing.

3.2 Problem statement

The IFC schema does not comprehensively cover the terminology used in the building regulations. In "*A roof covering or roof light which forms part of an internal ceiling lining should* [...]"[3] the term '*roof light*' would fall under the more generic IFC class '*window*'. The problem is compounded as building regulations cover a wide range topics (and thus concepts) – from design and construction, including fire regulations and accessibility, to facility management, renovation and demolition (Pauwels et al., 2017). Despite the more fine-grained terminology used in the SCOTREG corpus, only 128 terms are defined – neither '*roof light*', '*roof covering*' nor '*internal ceiling lining*' are defined.

3.3 Task description

The task in this study is to identify low-level constituent parts of a sentence, which we will refer to as *spans*. We assume that contextual interdependencies between single-word and multi-word spans help tackle lexical sparsity of MWEs. Therefore, we tag both single words and groups of words in a sentence and we tag all tokens exhaustively, including punctuation. Whether spans comprise a single punctuation mark or a group of possibly discontiguous tokens, they should represent a coherent unit of grammatical meaning.

[2] `https://textblob.readthedocs.io/en/dev/`

[3] For an overview of used examples, the full sentences, and origin of these examples see Table 7 in Appendix B.

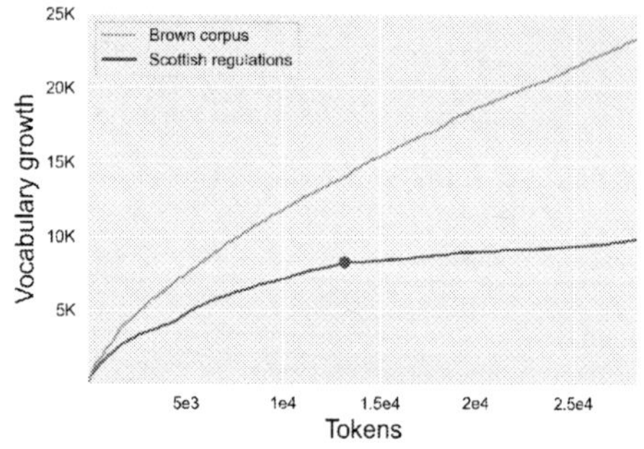

Figure 1: Vocabulary growth for the SCOTREG corpus in comparison to the heterogeneous BROWN corpus. The dot indicates the division between domestic and non-domestic building regulations.

- "*The Building (Scotland) Act 2003 gives Scottish Ministers* [...]"

'*The Building (Scotland) Act 2003*' is a Named Entity that should be treated as a single span. But a regular noun-chunking approach would break on the parentheses and the cardinal number – it may even treat every capitalised word as a proper noun.

- "*A roof covering or roof light which forms part of an internal ceiling lining should* [...]"

A constituency parser may break the term '*roof covering*' into separate words, because a POS tagger would typically assign '*covering*' the tag VBG.

- "[...], *a paved (or equivalent) footpath at least 900mm wide* [...]"

In this case, while we would like to split '*a paved (or equivalent) footpath*' into the spans: '*a paved footpath*', '*(*', '*)*', '*or*' and '*equivalent*'. In a downstream task this would allow us to define a class for '*paved footpath*', and reason over the equivalent types of footpaths. However, to extract '*a paved footpath*' from the sentence above, a discontiguous span representation is required.

3.4 Simplifying assumptions

For our task we rely on a simplified definition of MWEs: "*possibly discontiguous combinations of at least two tokens, where tokens are separated by white-spaces or punctuation in text*" – similar to (Villavicencio and Idiart, 2019). We also make two assumptions on the types of MWEs that we expect to find in the building regulation texts. First, we assume that the building regulations contain few to no idiomatic expressions, because these may introduce ambiguity. We justify this assumption as the building regulations use a slightly more formal syntax, albeit not as strict as other types of legal text (Chalkidis et al., 2020).

Second, we expect a relatively low variability in surface forms. Both for verbal expressions found in clauses, e.g., '*X should conform to Y*, and for the surface forms of MWEs that indicate technical terms, e.g., '*insulation envelope*' and '*self-contained emergency luminaries*'. A low variability in surface forms would be reflected by a relatively small vocabulary – which is thought to ease the complexity of various NLP tasks (Church, 2013). As can be seen in Figure 1, SCOTREG has in the order of 10K unique tokens for a total of 283K. In comparison to the more heterogeneous Brown corpus (Francis and Kucera, 1964), which has more than 23K unique tokens for the first 283K tokens, SCOTREG indeed has a small vocabulary.

3.5 Annotating SPAR.txt

A domain expert annotated a random selection of 200 sentences in BRAT (Stenetorp et al., 2012). Our assumption is that such a small dataset should suffice for achieving reasonable results on the proposed parsing task. Figure 2 exemplifies how annotations can span single words, multiple words and also indicate that two groups of words belong to a single, discontiguous span. To distinguish between verb-based and noun-based spans, as well as spans that belong to neither of these classes, we annotate the following span types:

- OBJECT spans indicate either real-world objects or distinguishable concepts. They include proper nouns, compounds, multi-word terms, and multi-word Named Entities, such as '*the Target Emissions Rating*', '*offensive fire-fighting*' and '*BS 8000-15: 1990*'. We include determiners as part of the OBJECT span during annotation, see Figure 2.

- ACTION spans may help identify whether a sentence expresses a requirement, similar to (Hjelseth and Nisbet, 2011). We include verbs, support verbs, prepositional verbs and verb-particle constructions, e.g., '*should be maintained*' and '*takes account of*', but we expect to split light-verb constructions, such as '*to take a shower*' (Constant et al., 2017) into '*to take*' and the OBJECT span '*a shower*'.

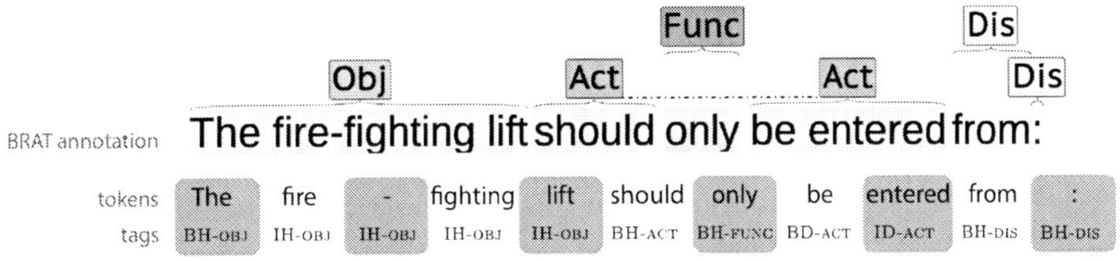

Figure 2: Example of an annotated sentence. The determiner at the start of the OBJECT span is taken to be part of the span. A discontiguous ACTION span is interjected by a FUNCTIONAL span that modifies the Verb-Phrase. During training the sentence is tokenized and the aim is to predict the correct tags for each token, see the tagging scheme described in Section 4.1. The identifier for this sentence in the dataset is '*d_2.14.4_i3_s_0*'.

- FUNCTIONAL spans are modifiers that are not inherently part of an OBJECT or ACTION span. They include adverbs and adjectives, e.g., '*main*' and '*principal*' in '*the main or principal bedroom*', as well as complex function words, e.g., '*up to*'.
- DISCOURSE spans include punctuation, coreference anaphora, conjunctions and disjunctions, e.g., ',', '*or*' and '*this*'.

MWEs can blur the lines between syntax and semantics (Green et al., 2011), with ambiguous cases leading to annotation inconsistencies (Hollenstein et al., 2016). Because the task involves annotating both the words that make up an MWE and those surrounding it, the annotator is forced to come up with more-or-less consistent decisions. As a tool to determine which words belong together, annotators are asked to rely on standard constituency tests:

- Substitution test – if you can substitute a part of a sentence with another word or group of words that belong to the same type, the part is a constituent.
- Pronoun test – if you can replace a part of a sentence with 'it', the part is a constituent.
- Question by repetition test – if you can repeat a part of a sentence, within a valid question, then it is a constituent.

Nevertheless, annotating MWEs often requires domain-specific knowledge and remains ambiguous. Using Figure 2 as an example, one might argue that the preposition '*from*' could be part of the ACTION span '*should be entered*' – considering that '*from*' converts '*to enter*' from an intransitive to a transitive verb. We define several loose guidelines to warrant further consistency in annotation:

1. **Punctuation** Unless punctuation should be part of an OBJECT span, such as the colon in the document name '*BS 800-15:1990*', then punctuation should be marked as DISCOURSE.
2. **Negation** Wherever negation is separable from other spans, e.g., '[...] *is not level* [...]', it should be annotated separately as a FUNCTIONAL span. In cases where negation is not separable, e.g., in '[...] *cannot gain* [...]', the current approach is to tag the word containing the negation as FUNCTIONAL.
3. **Granularity** Annotators should rely on domain knowledge to determine whether a Noun-Phrase should be split, e.g., '[...] *the effect of smoke travelling along a ceiling* [...]' should be broken up while "[...] *fire and rescue service personnel* [...]' should form a single span.
4. **Coordination** Coordinating conjunctions and disjunctions should be split. Coordinated MWEs may share a span, e.g., Figure 3 shows how a list of '*Standards*' share a word that is crucial to the semantics of the individual items. Similarly, conjunctions and disjunctions sometimes share a determiner, e.g., '*the size and orientation of the windows*' would include the spans '*the size*' and '*the orientation*'. The motivation is to help downstream tasks determine that both '*size*' and '*orientation*', here, are properties of '*the window*'.
5. **Overlap** We currently limit the annotation of discontiguous spans to a maximum of two parts. Therefore, overlapping spans should only occur this cannot be avoided, e.g., '*the Silver level*' and '*the Gold level*' in '*the Silver and Gold level*' would need to exist of three single-word spans to avoid overlap.

6. **Adverbs** typically express a manner, place, time, frequency, degree, and so on. The expectation is that such expressions will usually be labelled as FUNCTIONAL, e.g., '*only*' in Figure 2.

7. **Adjectives** typically modify nouns and may or may not be part of an OBJECT span. This decision would be based on whether the modified noun is likely to constitute a separate category or not. As an example, '*structural*' would be part of the OBJECT span '*the structural properties*' but a separate FUNCTIONAL span in '*matters of structural concern*'.

8. **Quantities and units** are treated as a single OBJECT span. If such a span modifies a noun, e.g., '*900mm wide*', then these would usually form two separate spans '*900mm*' and '*wide*'.

A second domain expert annotated 140 out of 200 sentences. The inter-annotator agreement was found to be Cohen k=0,79. We randomly divide the gold annotations into a 60/20/20 (%) split for train, development and test respectively – see Table 6 in Appendix A.

4 Training

4.1 Representing discontiguous spans

Regular tagging schemes, such as BIO and BIOUL, are unable to represent discontiguous spans (Schneider et al., 2014). We adopt a tagging approach that can handle discontiguous pairs of spans, similar to (Muis and Lu, 2016). Specifically, we use BH to indicate the beginning (head) of a span and IH to indicate subsequent tokens that belong to this span. If a second span exists that is part of a discontiguous MWE, then the beginning (discontiguous) of this second span is tagged BD, and subsequent tokens of that span are tagged ID. Tags are provided with a type to distinguish between OBJECT and ACTION spans etc. Figure 2 provides example tags for an annotated sentence. Notably, we assume that between the head and discontiguous spans of a given type, there exist no head-spans of the same type.

4.2 Model

We adopt a sequence tagging approach that has been shown to work well (Huang et al., 2015), where an embedded text sequence is encoded by a bidirectional Long Short-Term Memory network

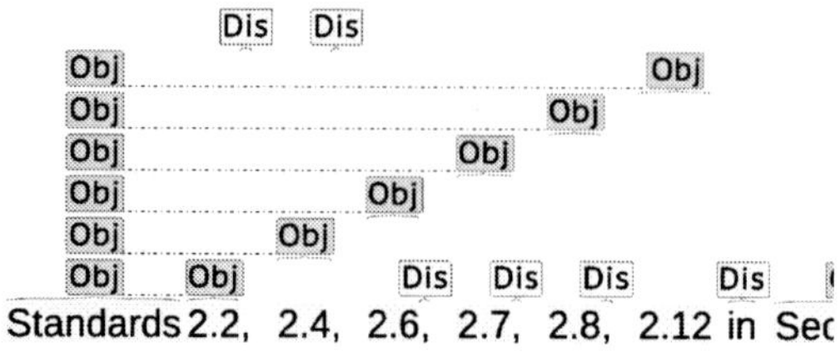

Figure 3: Example of an annotated coordination, where each of the items shares the word '*Standards*'. Note that only part of the sentence is shown here, the identifier for this sentence in the dataset is '*d_0.12.2_i3_#1_s_0*'.

(Hochreiter and Schmidhuber, 1997) and a Conditional Random Field (Lafferty et al., 1999) model is used to predict a tag for each token in the sequence. We modify the implementation found in AllenNLP[4] (Gardner et al., 2018). We embed text using pre-trained BERT embeddings (*bert-base-cased*) (Devlin et al., 2018) and rely on a single bi-LSTM layer (hidden dim. 384). We add a self-attention layer that captures relative positional information (Shaw et al., 2018), following (Huang et al., 2019). The encoded and attended representations are concatenated and projected through two linear layers (hidden dim. 60) before being passed to the CRF model. Table 2 provides an overview of results.

We compare the use of BERT (Devlin et al., 2018) and SPANBERT (*SpanBERT/spanbert-base-cased*) (Joshi et al., 2020) for tokenization and embedding. Our intuition is that the masked span Language Modelling task may help capture MWE properties used for MWE discovery, see 2.3. But in our experiments SPANBERT embeddings consistently perform worse, see Table 2. This may be due to a mismatch between the span types and sizes that SPANBERT was originally trained on – in SPANBERT all masked spans are contiguous – and the ones found in our training dataset. A more general issue is the imbalance of tag-types, see Table 3 for results on the test set per tag type.

5 Evaluation

Evaluating discovered lexical entries can be tricky (Constant et al., 2017). We limit our evaluation to the processing of OBJECT spans. First, we perform an extrinsic evaluation by comparing our model output against the defined terms in the SCOTREG

[4]`https://github.com/allenai/allennlp-models`

		P	R	F1
development	BERT	**80,18**	**81,76**	**80,96**
	SpanBERT	75,54	79,33	77,39
test	BERT	**79,93**	**80,89**	**79,93**
	SpanBERT	75,37	78,10	76,48

Table 2: Precision (P), recall (R), and F1-score (F1) on the development and test sets.

	P	R	F1	support
BH-obj	80,68	86,53	83,50	193
IH-obj	86,73	89,79	88,24	284
BD-obj	60,00	40,00	48,00	30
ID-obj	0,00	0,00	0,00	15
BH-act	76,15	83,84	79,81	99
IH-act	71,21	69,12	70,15	68
BD-act	50,00	37,50	42,86	8
ID-act	0,00	0,00	0,00	4
BH-dis	89,74	92,11	90,91	266
IH-dis	100,00	31,82	48,28	22
BH-func	65,62	63,64	64,62	66
IH-func	31,82	38,89	35,00	18
accuracy			80,89	1.073
macro avg.	59,33	52,77	54,28	1.073
weighted avg.	79,93	80,89	79,93	1.073

Table 3: Overview of results on the test set, broken down per tag type.

corpus. Second, post hoc human judgement provides insight in the number of correctly identified OBJECT spans given the sentence context.

5.1 Predicting defined terms

We use the model trained on SPAR.txt to predict tags for all sentences in the SCOTREG corpus. We then compare whether each of the 128 defined terms is identified at least once by our model. A total of 115 (89,84%) defined terms were found. Table 4 lists the 13 defined terms (10,16%) that were not found. Most of these defined terms exist verbatim in the SCOTREG corpus, but our model splits these spans into multiple parts. However:

- '*average flush*' only occurs as '*average flush volume*' and our model treats '*average*' as a separate FUNCTIONAL span.
- '*High-speed ready in-building physical infrastructure*' never occurs verbatim in the text.

5.2 Post hoc human judgement

We collect all contiguous and discontiguous OBJECT spans that our model predicted on the 13K sentences of the SCOTREG corpus. A total of 16,428 unique potential OBJECT spans are identified. We find that this number decreases slightly, to 15,662, if we remove determiners and lower-case the text. We randomly select 165 out of the 16,5K OBJECT spans, and then one of the sentences in which this object occurs – this sample size provides a 99% confidence level with a 10% margin of error. We exclude objects that match any of the defined terms and exclude sentences that are part of the annotated dataset.

We use Doccano (Nakayama et al., 2018) for annotation. Each of these 165 samples is presented to the annotators as a combination of the OBJECT span and the corresponding sentence context. The task is to annotate whether the predicted OBJECT span is actually an object in the sentence, with a choice between the labels: (1) exact match, (2) partial match, or (3) not an object.

Two domain experts annotated the 165 OBJECT spans, see Table 5. The inter-annotator agreement was found to be Cohen k=0,79. If we take the average of their judgement, this comes down to 116 (70,3%) exact matches, 40 (23,6%) partial matches, and 9 (5,5%) non-objects. Examples of each labelled object and relevant parts of the sentence context include:

- **Exact match**: '*mechanical input air ventilation systems*' in "*Positive input systems - mechanical input air ventilation systems have been* [...]".
- **Exact match**: '*the warning*' in "[...] *the earliest possible warning* [...]" – where '*earliest*' and '*possible*' are modifiers that are not inherently part of the concept '*warning*'.
- **Exact match**: '*wall/roof junctions*' in "[...] *and at wall/roof junctions, wall/floor junctions and* [...]".
- **Partial match**: '*the control equipment*' in "[...] *the control and indicating equipment operates a fire alarm system* [...]" – '*the control and indicating equipment*' should be treated as a single OBJECT span.
- **Partial match**: '*Articles 15 & 16* ' in "[...] *implements the terms of Articles 15 & 16 of Directive 2010/31/EU on* [...]" – should be split into '*Articles 15*' and '*Articles 16*'.
- **Partial match**: '*primary*' in "[...] *educations centres, schools (nursery, primary, secondary, special)* [...]" – should identify the discontiguous part '*school*'.

Undetected defined terms	What we extracted
Alternative exit	Probably split, we find *'alternative'* and *'exit'*
Average flush	Probably split, we find *'flush'* and several related terms, e.g., *'dual flush type'* and *'flush volume'*
Different occupation	Probably split, we find *'land'* and various types of *'occupation'*, e.g., *'single occupation'*, *'multiple occupation'*, *'communal occupation'*
Land in different occupation	See above
Factory (class 1)	Probably split, we find *'factory'*, *'factory building'* and their plurals
Factory (class 2)	See above, we do find *''factory class 2''*
High-speed ready in-building physical infrastructure	We find *'high-speed-ready in-building physical infrastructure'*
Major renovation works	Probably split, we find *'renovation'* and various types of *'works'*, e.g., *'chemical works'*, *'sewage work'* and *'protective works'*
Place of special fire risk	Probably split, we find the discontiguous span *'place'* *'fire risk'*
Public open space	Not found, we find various types of *'space'*, e.g., *'clear space'*, *'outdoor space'* and *'communal spaces'*
Reasonably practicable	Probably split, we find *'practicable'*
Storage building (class 1)	Probably split, we find *'storage building'* and *'storage buildings'*
Storage building (class 2)	See above

Table 4: Overview of the 13 defined terms that were not found in the text by our trained tagger.

	Object		
	Exact match	Partial match	Not an object
Ann. 1	114 (69,1%)	41 (24,8%)	10 (6,1%)
Ann. 2	118 (71,5%)	39 (23,6%)	8 (4,8%)
Avg.	**116 (70,3%)**	**40 (24,2%)**	**9 (5,5%)**

Table 5: Overview of labels by two annotators on 165 OBJECT spans identified in the SCOTREG corpus.

- **Not an object**: *'sleeping'* in "*Rooms intended for sleeping should be* [...]" – should be an ACTION span here.
- **Not an object**: *'land subject'* in "[...] *development may be given approval on land subject to* [...]" – the OBJECT *'land'* is modified by *'subject to'*.
- **Not an object**: *'changes 1'* in "*Schedule 1 - changes to building types 1 and 20.*" – may be the result of overfitting on certain discontiguous patterns.

5.3 Discussion

Despite the small size of SPAR.txt, the trained model discovers a large number (16K) of OBJECT spans in 13K sentences. These spans cover most terms that are explicitly defined in the SCOTREG corpus (89,84%). The defined terms that the model did not identify are expressed in patterns that were never seen during training, although some do not occur verbatim in the texts. A significant proportion (70,3%) of identified OBJECT spans exactly match human judgement. Because annotation is cheap for our task, it is straightforward to create additional gold training samples and improve performance. To this end, partial matches can help identify phenomena that were not seen during training, e.g., *'Articles 15 & 16'* and *'subject to'* as listed above. False positive OBJECT spans provide insight in phenomena that the model currently overfits on, and may potentially help balance future iterations of our dataset. Moreover, the predicted outputs for the SCOTREG corpus are valuable to the creation of a lexicon for ACC.

6 Conclusions

Regulatory documents are an important part of the legal framework, with research on ACC methods focusing on the grand goal of semantic parsing. This study introduces a much simpler parsing task that requires few training examples, with the additional benefit that the collection of a dataset is cheap. We presented the small SPAR.txt dataset and trained a sequence tagger that can process single-word and multi-word spans. We showed that the OBJECT spans identified in the SCOTREG corpus cover most of the existing, limited set of defined terms. Moreover, the model achieves reasonable accuracy when it comes to discovering OBJECT spans, regardless of whether these are discontiguous or not.

The annotation of gold training data for the presented approach is cheap, because the annotation task is simple. But the results can benefit the research on ACC, e.g., the output of our task may support more complicated semantic annotation tasks, IE and IR, as well as the development of a domain-specific lexicon. Future work will focus on clustering the identified spans to develop a semantic lexicon, balancing and growing the dataset, as well as using predicted outputs for IR in support of manual ACC. Finally, we will explore how well the presented approach performs in other domains with similar text characteristics.

Acknowledgements

This research is funded by the IC3 (International Centre for Connected Construction) of Northumbria University. The authors are grateful to Julian Vincent for his thoughts on the annotation process. We would also like to congratulate Dr. Ben Trevett for passing his viva.

References

Yoav Artzi and Luke Zettlemoyer. 2013. Weakly Supervised Learning of Semantic Parsers for Mapping Instructions to Actions. *Transactions of the Association for Computational Linguistics*, 1:49–62.

Timothy Baldwin and Su Nam Kim. 2010. Multiword Expressions. In Nitin Indurkhya and Fred J. Damerau, editors, *Handbook of Natural Language Processing*, second edition, chapter 12, pages 267–292. Chapman and Hall.

Jakob Beetz, Jos Van Leeuwen, and Bauke De Vries. 2009. IfcOWL: A case of transforming EXPRESS schemas into ontologies. *Artificial Intelligence for Engineering Design, Analysis and Manufacturing: AIEDAM*, 23(1):89–101.

Phil Blunsom and Timothy Baldwin. 2006. Multilingual deep lexical acquisition for HPSGs via supertagging. In *COLING/ACL 2006 - EMNLP 2006: 2006 Conference on Empirical Methods in Natural Language Processing, Proceedings of the Conference*, pages 164–171.

Ilias Chalkidis, Manos Fergadiotis, Prodromos Malakasiotis, and Nikolaos Aletras. 2020. LEGAL-BERT: The Muppets straight out of Law School. In *EMNLP 2020 - Conference on Empirical Methods in Natural Language Processing: System Demonstrations, Proceedings*, pages 2898–2904.

David L Chen. 2012. Fast online lexicon learning for grounded language acquisition. In *50th Annual Meeting of the Association for Computational Linguistics, ACL 2012 - Proceedings of the Conference*, volume 1, pages 430–439.

Kenneth Church. 2013. How many multiword expressions do people know? *ACM Transactions on Speech and Language Processing*, 10(2):137–144.

Mathieu Constant, Gülşen Eryiğit, Johanna Monti, Lonneke Van Der Plas, Carlos Ramisch, Michael Rosner, and Amalia Todirascu. 2017. Multiword expression processing: A survey. *Computational Linguistics*, 43(4):837–892.

Matthieu Constant and Anthony Sigogne. 2011. MWU-aware part-of-speech tagging with a CRF model and lexical resources. In *Proceedings of the Workshop on Multiword ...*, June, pages 49–56.

Matthieu Constant, Anthony Sigogne, and Patrick Watrin. 2012. Discriminative strategies to integrate multiword expression recognition and parsing. In *50th Annual Meeting of the Association for Computational Linguistics, ACL 2012 - Proceedings of the Conference*, volume 1, pages 204–212. Association for Computational Linguistics.

Chris Cook. 2017. How legal drafting may be central to fire safety debate - BBC News.

Jacob Devlin, Ming-Wei Chang, Kenton Lee, and Kristina Toutanova. 2018. BERT: Pre-training of Deep Bidirectional Transformers for Language Understanding. In *arXiv preprint arXiv:1810.04805*.

Johannes Dimyadi and Robert Amor. 2013. Automated Building Code Compliance Checking. Where is it at? In *Proceedings of the CIB World Building Congress 2013 and Architectural Management & Integrated Design and Delivery Solutions (AMIDDS)*, 380, pages 172–185.

W. N. Francis and H. Kucera. 1964. A standard corpus of present-day edited American English, for use with digital computers. Technical report, Brown University, Providence.

G Frege. 1996. *Die Grundlagen der Arithmetik. Eine logisch mathematische Untersuchung über den Begriff der Zahl*. Verlage Wilhelm Koebner, Breslau.

Stefan Fuchs. 2021. Natural Language Processing for Building Code Interpretation: Systematic Literature Review Report. Technical Report May, University of Auckland.

Matt Gardner, Joel Grus, Mark Neumann, Oyvind Tafjord, Pradeep Dasigi, Nelson Liu, Matthew Peters, Michael Schmitz, and Luke Zettlemoyer. 2018. AllenNLP: A Deep Semantic Natural Language Processing Platform. *arXiv preprint arXiv:1803.07640*.

Spence Green, Marie Catherine De Marneffe, John Bauer, and Christopher D Manning. 2011. Multiword expression identification with tree substitution grammars: A parsing TOUR DE FORCE with French. In *EMNLP 2011 - Conference on Empirical Methods in Natural Language Processing, Proceedings of the Conference*, pages 725–735.

Jonathan Herzig and Jonathan Berant. 2017. Neural semantic parsing over multiple knowledge-bases. In *ACL 2017 - 55th Annual Meeting of the Association for Computational Linguistics, Proceedings of the Conference (Long Papers)*, volume 2, pages 623–628. Association for Computational Linguistics (ACL).

Eilif Hjelseth and Nick Nisbet. 2011. Capturing Normative Constraints By Use of the Semantic Mark-Up Rase. In *Proceedings of CIB*, March, pages 26–28.

Sepp Hochreiter and Jürgen Schmidhuber. 1997. Long Short-Term Memory. *Neural Computation*, 9(8):1735–1780.

Nora Hollenstein, Nathan Schneider, and Bonnie Webber. 2016. Inconsistency detection in semantic annotation. In *Proceedings of the 10th International Conference on Language Resources and Evaluation, LREC 2016*, pages 3986–3990.

Cheng Zhi Anna Huang, Ashish Vaswani, Jakob Uszkoreit, Noam Shazeer, Ian Simon, Curtis Hawthorne, Andrew M. Dai, Matthew D. Hoffman, Monica Dinculescu, and Douglas Eck. 2019. Music transformer: Generating music with long-term structure. In *7th International Conference on Learning Representations, ICLR 2019*.

Zhiheng Huang, Wei Xu, and Kai Yu. 2015. Bidirectional LSTM-CRF Models for Sequence Tagging. *arXiv preprint arXiv:1508.01991*.

Davies Hywel, Ant Burd, Rachel Smalley, Emma Clancy, Nigel Mason, Stephen Welch, Jeff House, Roger Holdsworth, Craig Renton, Rachel Cooper, Renford Gordon, Lorna Stimson, Graham Cleland, and Susan Johnson. 2020. Final Report of the Expert Group on Structure of Guidance to the Building Regulations. Technical report, Ministry of Housing, Communities & Local Government.

Mandar Joshi, Danqi Chen, Yinhan Liu, Daniel S Weld, Luke Zettlemoyer, and Omer Levy. 2020. SpanBERT: Improving Pre-training by Representing and Predicting Spans. *Transactions of the Association for Computational Linguistics*, 8:64–77.

Tibor Kiss and Jan Strunk. 2006. Unsupervised multilingual sentence boundary detection. *Computational Linguistics*, 32(4):485–525.

Thomas Kollar, Stefanie Tellex, Deb Roy, and Nicholas Roy. 2010. Toward understanding natural language directions. In *5th ACM/IEEE International Conference on Human-Robot Interaction, HRI 2010*, pages 259–266.

John Lafferty, Andrew Mccallum, and Fernando Pereira. 1999. Conditional Random Fields : Probabilistic Models for Segmenting and Labeling Sequence Data Abstract. *Departmental Papers (CIS)*, 2001(June):282–289.

Mirella Lapata and Alex Lascarides. 2003. Detecting Novel Compounds : The Role of Distributional Evidence. *Proceedings of the 11th Conference of the European Chapter for the Association of Computational Linguistics*, pages 235–242.

Sarah B Lawsky. 2017. Formalizing the Code. *SSRN Electronic Journal*, 377(17).

Kaijian Liu and Nora El-Gohary. 2017. Ontology-based semi-supervised conditional random fields for automated information extraction from bridge inspection reports. *Automation in Construction*, 81:313–327.

Christopher D. Manning, Hinrich Schütze, and Gerhard Weikurn. 2002. Foundations of Statistical Natural Language Processing. *SIGMOD Record*, 31(3):37–38.

Seonghyeon Moon, Gitaek Lee, Seokho Chi, and Hyunchul Oh. 2019. Automatic Review of Construction Specifications Using Natural Language Processing. In *Computing in Civil Engineering 2019*, pages 401–407, Reston, VA. American Society of Civil Engineers.

Seonghyeon Moon, Gitaek Lee, Seokho Chi, and Hyunchul Oh. 2021. Automated Construction Specification Review with Named Entity Recognition Using Natural Language Processing. *Journal of Construction Engineering and Management*, 147(1):04020147.

Raymond J Mooney. 2007. Learning for semantic parsing. In *Lecture Notes in Computer Science (including subseries Lecture Notes in Artificial Intelligence and Lecture Notes in Bioinformatics)*, volume 4394 LNCS, pages 311–324. Springer.

Aldrian Obaja Muis and Wei Lu. 2016. Learning to recognize discontiguous entities. In *EMNLP 2016 - Conference on Empirical Methods in Natural Language Processing, Proceedings*, pages 75–84.

Hiroki Nakayama, Takahiro Kubo, Junya Kamura, Yasufumi Taniguchi, and Xu Liang. 2018. doccano: Text Annotation Tool for Human.

R. A. Niemeijer, B. De Vries, and J. Beetz. 2014. Freedom through constraints: User-oriented architectural design. *Advanced Engineering Informatics*, 28(1):28–36.

Joakim Nivre and Jens Nilsson. 2004. Multiword units in syntactic parsing. *Workshop on Methodologies and Evaluation of Multiword Units in Real-World Applications*, pages 39–46.

Pieter Pauwels, Sijie Zhang, and Yong Cheol Lee. 2017. Semantic web technologies in AEC industry: A literature overview. *Automation in Construction*, 73:145–165.

Pavel Pecina and Pavel Schlesinger. 2006. Combining association measures for collocation extraction. In *COLING/ACL 2006*, pages 651–658.

Marcos Pertierra, Sarah Lawsky, Erik Hemberg, and Una May O'Reilly. 2017. Towards formalizing statute law as default logic through automatic semantic parsing. In *CEUR Workshop Proceedings*, volume 2143.

Jim Plume and John Mitchell. 2007. Collaborative design using a shared IFC building model-Learning from experience. *Automation in Construction*, 16(1):28–36.

Soujanya Poria, Basant Agarwal, Alexander Gelbukh, Amir Hussain, and Newton Howard. 2014. Dependency-Based Semantic Parsing for Concept-Level Text Analysis. In *CICLing*, pages 113–127.

Cornelius Preidel and André Borrmann. 2018. BIM-based code compliance checking. In *Building Information Modeling: Technology Foundations and Industry Practice*, pages 367–381. Springer International Publishing.

Dheeraj Rajagopal, Erik Cambria, Daniel Olsher, and Kenneth Kwok. 2013. A graph-based approach to commonsense concept extraction and semantic similarity detection. In *WWW 2013 Companion - Proceedings of the 22nd International Conference on World Wide Web*, pages 565–570.

Carlos Ramisch, Silvio Ricardo Cordeiro, Agata Savary, Veronika Vincze, Verginica Barbu Mititelu, Archna Bhatia, Maja Buljan, Marie Candito, Polona Gantar, Voula Giouli, Tunga Güngör, Abdelati Hawwari, Uxoa Iñurrieta, Jolanta Kovalevskaite, Simon Krek, Timm Lichte, Chaya Liebeskind, Johanna Monti, Carla Parra Escartín, Behrang QasemiZadeh, Renata Ramisch, Nathan Schneider, Ivelina Stoyanova, Ashwini Vaidya, and Abigail Walsh. 2018. Edition 1.1 of the Parseme shared task on automatic identification of verbal multiword expressions. In *LAW-MWE-CxG 2018 - Joint Workshop on Linguistic Annotation, Multiword Expressions and Constructions, Proceedings of the Workshop*, pages 222–240.

Martin Riedl and Chris Biemann. 2015. A single word is not enough: Ranking multiword expressions using distributional semantics. In *Conference Proceedings - EMNLP 2015: Conference on Empirical Methods in Natural Language Processing*, pages 2430–2440.

Ivan A. Sag, Timothy Baldwin, Francis Bond, Ann Copestake, and Dan Flickinger. 2002. Multiword expressions: A pain in the neck for NLP. In *Lecture Notes in Computer Science (including subseries Lecture Notes in Artificial Intelligence and Lecture Notes in Bioinformatics)*, volume 2276, pages 1–15.

Nathan Schneider, Emily Danchik, Chris Dyer, and Noah A Smith. 2014. Discriminative Lexical Semantic Segmentation with Gaps: Running the MWE Gamut. *Transactions of the Association for Computational Linguistics*, 2:193–206.

Scottish Government. 2020. Building Standards Technical handbook 2020: Domestic.

Peter Shaw, Jakob Uszkoreit, and Ashish Vaswani. 2018. Self-attention with relative position representations. In *NAACL HLT 2018 - 2018 Conference of the North American Chapter of the Association for Computational Linguistics: Human Language Technologies - Proceedings of the Conference*, volume 2, pages 464–468.

Jeffrey Mark Siskind. 1996. A computational study of cross-situational techniques for learning word-to-meaning mappings. *Cognition*, 61(1-2 SPEC. ISS.):39–91.

Wawan Solihin, Johannes Dimyadi, and Yong-Cheol Lee. 2019. In Search of Open and Practical Language-Driven BIM-Based Automated Rule Checking Systems. In *Advances in Informatics and Computing in Civil and Construction Engineering*, pages 577–584. Springer International Publishing.

Robert Speer, Catherine Havasi, R Speer, and C Havasi. 2013. ConceptNet 5: A Large Semantic Network for Relational Knowledge. In Iryna Gurevych and Jungi Kim, editors, *The People's Web Meets NLP*, Theory and Applications of Natural Language Processing, chapter 6, pages 161–176. Springer Berlin Heidelberg, Berlin, Heidelberg.

Pontus Stenetorp, Sampo Pyysalo, Goran Topic, Tomoko Ohta, Sophia Ananiadou, and Jun'ichi Tsujii. 2012. BRAT: a Web-based Tool for NLP-Assisted Text Annotation. In *13th Conference of the European Chapter of the ACL*, Figure 1, pages 102–107.

Aline Villavicencio and Marco Idiart. 2019. Discovering multiword expressions.

Adam Wyner, Johan Bos, Valerio Basile, and Paulo Quaresma. 2012. An empirical approach to the semantic representation of laws. In *Frontiers in Artificial Intelligence and Applications*, volume 250, pages 177–180.

Xin Xu and Hubo Cai. 2019. Semantic Frame-Based Information Extraction from Utility Regulatory Documents to Support Compliance Checking. In *Advances in Informatics and Computing in Civil and Construction Engineering*, pages 223–230. Springer International Publishing, Cham.

Luke S Zettlemoyer and Collins Michael. 2005. Learning to map sentences to logical form: Structured classification with probabilistic categorial grammars. In *Proceedings of the 21st Conference on Uncertainty in Artificial Intelligence, UAI 2005*, pages 658–666.

Jiansong Zhang and Nora M. El-Gohary. 2016a. Integrating semantic NLP and logic reasoning into a unified system for fully-automated code checking. *Automation in Construction*, 73:45–57.

Jiansong Zhang and Nora M. El-Gohary. 2016b. Semantic NLP-Based Information Extraction from Construction Regulatory Documents for Automated Compliance Checking. *Journal of Computing in Civil Engineering*, 30(2):04015014.

Ruichuan Zhang and N. El-Gohary. 2019. A machine learning-based method for building code requirement hierarchy extraction. *Proceedings, Annual Conference - Canadian Society for Civil Engineering*, 2019-June:1–10.

Ruichuan Zhang and El-Gohary Nora. 2020. A Machine-Learning Approach for Semantically-Enriched Building-Code Sentence Generation for Automatic Semantic Analysis. In *Construction Research Congress*, pages 1261–1270.

Botao Zhong, Xuejiao Xing, Hanbin Luo, Qirui Zhou, Heng Li, Timothy Rose, and Weili Fang. 2020. Deep learning-based extraction of construction procedural constraints from construction regulations. *Advanced Engineering Informatics*, 43(December 2019):101003.

Peng Zhou and Nora El-Gohary. 2019. Text and Information Analytics for Fully Automated Energy Code Checking. In *Sustainable Civil Infrastructures*, pages 196–208. Springer Science and Business Media B.V.

A Overview of spans and tags for SPAR.txt and SCOTREG predictions

	All	Train	%*	Development	%*	Test	%*	Predicted
Domestic	98	62	63,27	19	19,39	17	17,35	6.313
Non-domestic	102	58	56,86	21	20,59	23	22,55	7.293
								13.606
avg. sent. (token†) length	27,96	28,31		28,05		26,83		26,72
Std. dev	15,31	15,50		14,03		15,92		15,53
Shortest	2	2		4		2		1
Longest	85	85		60		63		199
Span types	3.253	1.985	61,02	633	19,46	635	19,52	216.949
Discourse	1.312	788	60,06	258	19,66	266	20,27	87.957
Object	1.122	695	61,94	224	19,96	203	18,09	74.193
Action	476	294	61,76	82	17,23	100	21,01	31.835
Functional	343	206	60,64	69	20,12	66	19,24	22.964
Nr. discontiguous	193	122	63,21	33	17,10	30	15,54	6,450 Objects 2,007 Actions
avg. span (char) length	7,51	7,49		7,49		7,58		7,14
Discourse	2,56	2,50		2,53		2,77		2,44
Object	12,54	12,41		12,40		13,11		12,40
Action	9,51	9,54		9,87		9,15		8,31
Functional	7,22	7,08		7,29		7,58		6,53
Tag types								
IH-obj	1.551	931	60,03	336	21,66	284	18,31	108.507
BH-dis	1.312	788	60,06	258	19,66	266	20,27	87.957
BH-obj	1.071	659	61,53	219	20,45	193	18,02	74.311
BH-act	472	292	61,86	81	17,16	99	20,97	31.843
BH-func	343	208	60,64	69	20,12	66	19,24	22.964
IH-act	331	205	61,93	58	17,52	68	20,54	19.013
BD-obj	149	94	63,09	25	16,78	30	20,13	6.450
IH-func	136	88	64,71	30	22,06	18	13,24	6.784
ID-obj	134	88	65,67	31	23,13	15	11,19	3.114
IH-dis	45	16	35,56	7	15,56	22	48,89	482
BD-act	34	20	58,82	6	17,65	8	23,53	2.007
ID-act	14	8	57,14	2	14,29	4	28,57	74

Table 6: Overview of sentence and span statistics for SPAR.txt (Gold/Train/Dev/Test), as well as for the predictions (Predictions) over the entire SCOTREG corpus. %* indicates the percentage of all gold data. † Note that BERT tokenization is used here.

B Overview of examples

Sect.	Full sentence	Source	
3.2	**A roof covering or roof light which forms part of an internal ceiling lining should** also follow the guidance to Standard 2.5 Internal linings.	2.8.0 Introduction	Domestic
3.3	**The Building (Scotland) Act 2003 gives Scottish Ministers** the power to make building regulations to:	0.1.1 Introduction	Domestic
	In order to allow unobstructed access to a domestic building for fire and rescue service personnel, **a paved (or equivalent) footpath at least 900mm wide** (see also Section 4 Safety) should be provided to the normal entrances, of a building.	2.12.4 Access for fire and rescue service personnel	Domestic
3.4	Section 6 Energy, indicates that less demanding U-values can be adopted for the **insulation envelope** of certain types of limited life buildings, other than dwellings and residential buildings.	0.6.1 Explanation	Domestic
	In conversions for example, it may be easier to install **self-contained emergency luminaries** than to install a protected circuit to the existing lighting system	2.10.2 Protected circuits	Domestic
3.5	To enable the continued use of existing stocks of building modules and sub-assemblies, subject to fabric insulation meeting the U-values noted in clause 6.C.3, a modifying factor can be applied to increase **the Target Emissions Rating** (TER) for the building.	n_6.C257_i0_s_0	Non-domestic
	This is termed '**offensive fire-fighting**' and is normal practice regardless of whether people are in the building or not.	d_2.14.0_i4_s_1	Domestic
	BS 8000-15: 1990 - Workmanship on building sites	d_0.8.8_i3_#1_s_38	Domestic
	The minimum 3m separation in the diagram below **should be maintained** between each $5m^2$ panel.	d_2.5.7_i5_#1_s_0	Domestic
	The guidance in this clause **takes account of** the audibility levels in adjoining rooms and **the effect of smoke travelling along a ceiling.**	d_2.11.7_i0_s_0	Domestic
	The guidance in this clause **takes account of** the audibility levels in adjoining rooms and the effect of smoke travelling along a ceiling.	d_2.11.7_i0_s_0	Domestic
	CO2 monitoring equipment should be provided in the apartment expected to be **the main or principal bedroom** in a dwelling where infiltrating air rates are less than $15m^3/hr/m^2$ @ 50 Pa.	d_3.14.2_i1_s_0	Domestic
	Non-domestic use within dwellings - accommodation **up to** $50m^2$ used by an occupant of a dwelling in their professional or business capacity should be considered as a part of the dwelling.	d_6.9.1_i3_s_0	Domestic
	In the measurement of height or depth from ground which **is not level** the height or depth shall be taken to be the mean height or depth, except that: for the purpose of types 1, 2, 3, 4, 5, 18 or 19 of schedule 3, and for any other purpose where the difference in level is more than 2.5m the height or depth shall be taken to be the greatest height or depth.	d_0.7.2_i1_#4_s_0	Domestic
	Other pipes should be capped at both ends and at any point of connection, to ensure rats **cannot gain** entry.	n_3.5.5_i1_s_1	Non-domestic
	In order to allow unobstructed access to a domestic building for **fire and rescue service personnel**, a paved (or equivalent) footpath at least **900mm wide** (see also Section 4 Safety) should be provided to the normal entrances, of a building.	d_2.12.4_i1_s_0	Domestic
	The layout of a dwelling, **the size and orientation of the windows**, the thermal mass, level of insulation, airtightness, and ventilation can have a significant affect on the demand for heat.	d_3.13.1_i0_s_0	Domestic
	Standard 7.1 - amendments have been made to guidance with regard to the carbon dioxide (CO2) emissions target within **the Silver and Gold level** of Sustainability labelling in relation to the CO2 emissions target introduced by the 2015 energy standards.	d_7.0.5_i1_#0_s_0	Domestic

Sect.	Full sentence	Source	
	Materials that are susceptible to changes in their properties may be used in building work and will meet the requirements of the regulations if the residual properties, including **the structural properties**:	d_0.8.7_i1_s_0	Domestic
	The collation and dissemination of information relating to **matters of structural concern** is a vital element of achieving safe structures.	d_1.0.1_i2_s_2	Domestic
5.2	Positive input systems - **mechanical input air ventilation systems** have been successfully installed in existing dwellingswith the objective of overcoming problems of surface condensation and mould growth.	3.14.11 Mechanical ventilation and systems	Domestic
	This is to give occupants and staff **the earliest possible warning** of an outbreak of fire and allow time for assisting occupants in an emergency to evacuate the building or for horizontal progressive evacuation initially to an adjacent sub-compartment which leads to a compartment exit.	2.11.5 Hospitals	Non-domestic
	These 'bridges' commonly occur around openings such as lintels, jambs and sills and at **wall/roof junctions**, wall/floor junctions and where internal walls penetrate the outer fabric.	3.15.4 Surface condensation - thermal bridging	Non-domestic
	Normally **the control and indicating equipment** operates a fire alarm system and it may perform other signalling or control functions as well.	2.11.3 Categories of fire detection and fire alarm system	Non-domestic
	This regulation implements the terms of **Articles 15 & 16** of Directive 2010/31/EU on the Energy Performance of Buildings (EPBD).	0.17.1 Explanation	Domestic
	• education centres, **schools (nursery, primary, secondary, special)**	6.9.3 Location of an energy performance certificate	Non-domestic
	Rooms intended for **sleeping** should be separated by a door that will act as a sound barrier and reduce noise transference.	5.2.5 Doors in internal walls	Non-domestic
	Pressure for land development may mean that development may be given planning approval on **land subject** to some risk of flooding.	3.3.0 Introduction	Domestic
	• Schedule 1 - **changes to building types 1** and 20.	0.2.1 Explanation of Regulation 1	Non-domestic

Table 7: Complete overview of the examples used in the paper and their location in SCOTREG. Examples that occur in SPAR.txt have an identifier, such as n_6.C257_i0_s_0. These identifiers are created as follows: domestic (d) or non-domestic (n), the section (6.C2) – in this case concatenated with an integer (57) that is incremented each time a section name is reused, the item index (0 for first item) that indicates which item in the list of this section, and the sentence number (s_0 for first sentence).'#' in the identifier means that the sentence occurs in a list or table, with lists and tables 0-indexed for each section.

Capturing Logical Structure of Visually Structured Documents with Multimodal Transition Parser

Yuta Koreeda[1,2] and Christopher D. Manning[2]
[1]Hitachi America Ltd, Santa Clara, CA, USA
[2]Stanford University, Stanford, CA, USA
{koreeda, manning}@stanford.edu

Abstract

While many NLP pipelines assume raw, clean texts, many texts we encounter in the wild, including a vast majority of legal documents, are not so clean, with many of them being visually structured documents (VSDs) such as PDFs. Conventional preprocessing tools for VSDs mainly focused on word segmentation and coarse layout analysis, whereas fine-grained logical structure analysis (such as identifying paragraph boundaries and their hierarchies) of VSDs is underexplored. To that end, we proposed to formulate the task as prediction of *transition labels* between text fragments that maps the fragments to a tree, and developed a feature-based machine learning system that fuses visual, textual and semantic cues. Our system is easily customizable to different types of VSDs and it significantly outperformed baselines in identifying different structures in VSDs. For example, our system obtained a paragraph boundary detection F1 score of 0.953 which is significantly better than a popular PDF-to-text tool with an F1 score of 0.739.

1 Introduction

Despite recent motivation to utilize NLP for wider range of real world applications, most NLP papers, tasks and pipelines assume raw, clean texts. However, many texts we encounter in the wild, including a vast majority of legal documents (e.g., contracts and legal codes), are not so clean, with many of them being visually structured documents (VSDs) such as PDFs. For example, of 7.3 million text documents found in Panama Papers (which arguably approximates the distribution of data one would see in the wild), approximately 30% were PDFs[1]. Good preprocessing of VSDs is crucial in order to apply recent advances in NLP to real world applications.

Thus far, the most micro and macro extremes of VSD preprocessing have been extensively studied, such as word segmentation and layout analysis (detecting figures, body texts, etc.; Soto and Yoo, 2019; Stahl et al., 2018), respectively. While these two lines of studies allow extracting a sequence of words in the body of a document, neither of them accounts for local, logical structures such as paragraph boundaries and their hierarchies.

These structures convey important information in any domain, but they are particulary important in the legal domain. For example, Figure 1(1) shows raw text extracted from a non-disclosure agreement (NDA) in PDF format. An information extraction (IE) system must be aware of the hierarchical structure to successfully identify target information (e.g., extracting "definition of confidential information" requires understanding of hierarchy as in Figure 1(2)). Furthermore, we must utilize the logical structures to remove debris that has slipped through layout analysis ("Page 1 of 5" in this case) and other structural artifacts (such as semicolons and section numbers) for a generic NLP pipeline to work properly.

Yet, such logical structure analysis is difficult. Even the best PDF-to-text tool with a word-related error rate as low as 1.0% suffers from 17.0% newline detection error (Bast and Korzen, 2017) that is arguably the easiest form of logical structure analysis.

The goal of this study is to develop a fine-grained logical structure analysis system for VSDs. We propose a transition parser-like formulation of logical structure analysis, where we predict a *transition label* between each consecutive pair of text fragments (e.g., two fragments are in a same paragraph, or in different paragraphs of different hierarchies). Based on such formulation, we developed a feature-based machine learning system that fuses multimodal cues: visual (such as indentation and line spacing), textual (such as section num-

[1]Calculated from Obermaier et al. (2016) by regarding their *emails*, *PDFs* and *text documents* as the denominator.

Natural Legal Language Processing Workshop 2021, pages 144–154
November 10, 2021.

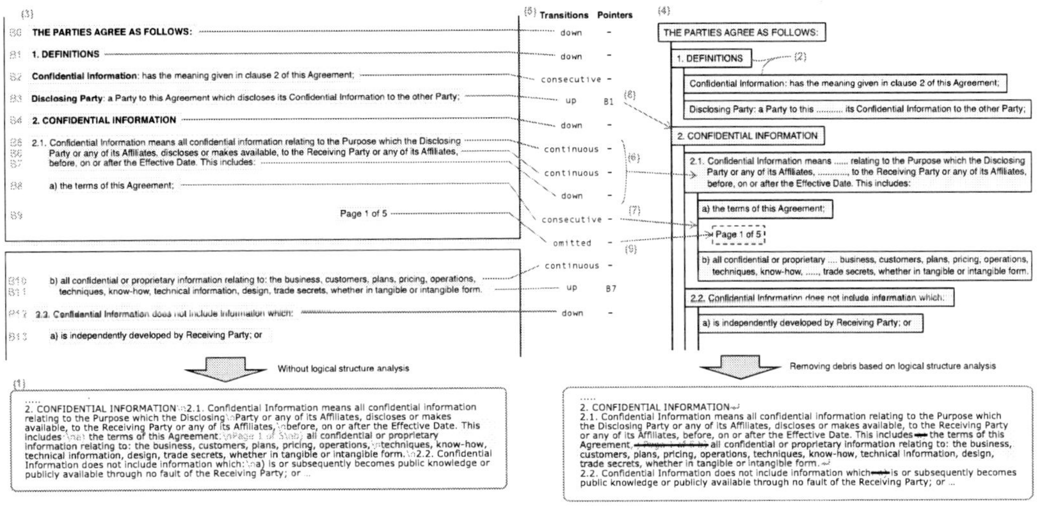

Figure 1: Overview of the logical structure analysis for VSDs and its formulation.

bering and punctuation), and semantic (such as language model coherence) cues. Finally, we show that our system is easily customizable to different types of VSDs and that it significantly outperforms baselines in identifying different structures in VSDs. For example, our system obtained a paragraph boundary detection F1 score of 0.953 that is significantly better than PDFMiner[2], a popular PDF-to-text tool, with an F1 score of 0.739. We open-sourced our system and dataset[3].

2 Problem Setting and Our Formulation

In this study, we concentrate on logical structure analysis of VSDs. The input is a sequence of text blocks (Figure 1(3)) that can be obtained by utilizing existing coarse layout analysis and word-level preprocessing tools. We aim to extract paragraphs and identify their relationships. This is equivalent to creating a tree with each block as a node (Figure 1(4)).

We propose to formulate this tree generation problem as identification of a *transition label* between each consecutive pair of blocks (Figure 1(5)) that defines their relationship in the tree. We define the transition $trans_i$ between i-th block (hereafter b_i) and b_{i+1} as one of the following:

`continuous` b_i and b_{i+1} are continuous in a single paragraph (Figure 1(6)).

`consecutive` b_{i+1} is the start of a new paragraph at the same level as b_i (Figure 1(7)).

`down` b_{i+1} is the start of a new paragraph that is a child (a lower level) of the paragraph that b_i belongs to (Figure 1(6)).

`up` b_{i+1} is the start of a new paragraph that is in a higher level than the paragraph that b_i belongs to (Figure 1(8)).

`omitted` i-th block is debris and omitted (Figure 1(9)). $trans_{i-1}$ is carried over to the relationship betwen b_{i-1} and b_{i+1}.

While `down` is well-defined (because we assume a tree), `up` can be ambiguous as to how many levels we should raise. To that end, we also introduce a *pointer* to each `up` block, which points at b_j whose level b_i belongs to ($ptr_i = b_j$, where $j < i$; Figure 1(8)).

3 Dataset

In this study, we target four types of VSDs in different file formats and languages:

Contract$_{en}^{pdf}$ English NDAs in PDF format.

Law$_{en}^{pdf}$ English executive orders from local authorities.

Contract$_{en}^{txt}$ English NDAs in visually structured plain text format.

Contract$_{ja}^{pdf}$ Japanese NDAs in PDF format.

Examples of each type of VSDs are shown in Figure 2.

For PDFs, we downloaded PDFs from Google.com search result. Since our focus is not on coarse layout analysis or word-level preprocessing, we selected single column documents

[2] https://euske.github.io/pdfminer/

[3] https://github.com/stanfordnlp/pdf-struct

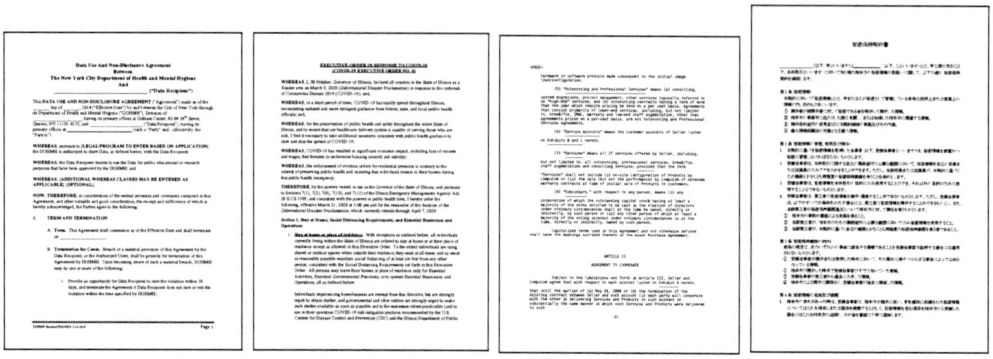

(a) Contract$^{pdf}_{en}$ (b) Law$^{pdf}_{en}$ (c) Contract$^{txt}_{en}$ (d) Contract$^{pdf}_{ja}$

Figure 2: Examples of VSDs in our dataset[4]

and extracted blocks with an existing software. Specifically, we utilized PDFMiner and extracted each `LTTextLine`, which roughly corresponds to each line of text, as a block. We merged multiple `LTTextLines` where `LTTextLines` are vertically overlapping.

For plain texts, we searched documents filed at EDGAR[5]. We simply used each non-blank line of a plain text as a block.

We annotated all documents by hand. We describe more details of the data collection and annotation in Appendix A.1.

The data statistics are given in Table 1. While the number of documents is somewhat limited, we note that each document comes with many text blocks and evaluations were stable. Furthermore, it was enough to reliably show the difference between our system and baselines in our experiments.

	Contract$^{pdf}_{en}$	Law$^{pdf}_{en}$	Contract$^{txt}_{en}$	Contract$^{pdf}_{ja}$
Format	PDF	PDF	Text	PDF
Language	English	English	English	Japanese
#Documents	40	40	22	40
#Text blocks	137.9	165.9	142.0	73.7
Max. depth	3.4	3.9	3.1	3.0
`#continuous`	95.4 (68%)	110.6 (67%)	109.9 (77%)	33.9 (44%)
`#consecutive`	20.3 (17%)	30.8 (20%)	15.3 (12%)	14.9 (20%)
`#up`	8.5 (6%)	7.1 (4%)	4.8 (3%)	11.0 (15%)
`#down`	9.4 (6%)	9.9 (6%)	4.6 (3%)	12.1 (17%)
`#omitted`	4.4 (3%)	7.6 (3%)	7.4 (4%)	1.8 (2%)

A number in the second set of rows indicates an average count over documents. A percentage represents an average ratio of each label.

Table 1: Dataset information

4 Proposed System

4.1 Transition Parser

In this work, we propose to employ handcrafted features and a machine learning-based classifier as the transition parser. This strategy is more suited to our task than utilizing deep learning because (1) we can incorporate visual, textual and semantic cues, and (2) it only requires a small number of training data which is critical in the legal domain where most data is proprietary.

For each block, our parser extracts features from a context of four blocks and performs multi-class classification over the five transition labels. Since `omitted` changes targets of transition, we also omit `omitted` blocks in feature extraction. For $trans_i \neq$ `omitted`, we extract features from $[b_{i-1}, b_i, b_j, b_{j+1}]$ where b_j is the first block after b_i with $trans_j \neq$ `omitted`. For $trans_i =$ `omitted`, we extract features from $[b_{i-1}, b_i, b_{i+1}, b_{i+2}]$. At test time, since we need to know the presence of `omitted` before feature extraction, we run a first pass of predictions to identify blocks with `omitted`, then use that information to dynamically extract features to identify other labels.

Our system can be customized to different types of documents by modifying the features. We have designed a feature set for each document type by visually inspecting the training dataset (Table 2). For Contract$^{txt}_{en}$, we regarded space characters as horizontal spacing and blank lines as vertical spacing, which allowed us to define features that are

[4](a) `http://www.astho.org/Programs/Infectious-Disease/Healthcare-Associated-Infections/Electronic-Health-Records/Toolkit/Data-Use-Agreement-New-York-City/`, (b) `https://www2.illinois.gov/IISNews/21288-Gov._Pritzker_Stay_at_Home_Order.pdf`, (c) `https://www.sec.gov/Archives/edgar/data/86115/0000930661/0000930661-99-001321-index.htm`, and (d) `http://www.septima.co.jp/contracts/27_himitsuhoji.pdf`

[5]`https://www.sec.gov/edgar.shtml`

<table>
<tr><th></th><th></th><th></th><th colspan="3">Document type</th></tr>
<tr><th></th><th>Description</th><th>Blocks</th><th>$\text{Contract}^{pdf}_{en}$ / Law^{pdf}_{en}</th><th>$\text{Contract}^{txt}_{en}$</th><th>$\text{Contract}^{pdf}_{ja}$</th></tr>
<tr><td colspan="6">Visual features</td></tr>
<tr><td>V1</td><td>Indentation (up, down or same)</td><td>1-2, 2-3</td><td>✓</td><td>✓</td><td>✓</td></tr>
<tr><td>V2</td><td>Indentation after erasing numbering</td><td>1-2, 2-3</td><td></td><td>✓</td><td></td></tr>
<tr><td>V3</td><td>Centered</td><td>2, 3</td><td>✓</td><td>✓</td><td>✓</td></tr>
<tr><td>V4</td><td>Line break before right margin*</td><td>1, 2</td><td>✓</td><td>✓</td><td>✓</td></tr>
<tr><td>V5</td><td>Page change</td><td>1-2, 2-3</td><td>✓</td><td></td><td>✓</td></tr>
<tr><td>V6</td><td>Within top 15% of a page</td><td>2</td><td>✓</td><td></td><td>✓</td></tr>
<tr><td>V7</td><td>Within bottom 15% of a page</td><td>2</td><td>✓</td><td></td><td>✓</td></tr>
<tr><td>V8</td><td>Larger line spacing*</td><td>1-2, 2-3</td><td>✓</td><td>✓</td><td>✓</td></tr>
<tr><td>V9</td><td>Justified with spaces in middle</td><td>2, 3</td><td>✓</td><td>✓</td><td>✓</td></tr>
<tr><td>V10</td><td>Similar text in a similar position*</td><td>2</td><td>✓</td><td></td><td>✓</td></tr>
<tr><td>V11</td><td>Emphasis by spaces between characters</td><td>1, 2</td><td></td><td></td><td>✓</td></tr>
<tr><td>V12</td><td>Emphasis by parentheses</td><td>1, 2</td><td></td><td></td><td>✓</td></tr>
<tr><td colspan="6">Textual features</td></tr>
<tr><td>T1</td><td>Numbering transition*</td><td>2</td><td>✓</td><td>✓</td><td>✓</td></tr>
<tr><td>T2</td><td>Punctuated</td><td>1, 2</td><td>✓</td><td>✓</td><td>✓</td></tr>
<tr><td>T3</td><td>List start (<code>/[-;:,]$/</code>)</td><td>1, 2</td><td>✓</td><td>✓</td><td>✓</td></tr>
<tr><td>T4</td><td>List elements (<code>/(;|,|and|or)$/</code>)</td><td>2</td><td>✓</td><td>✓</td><td></td></tr>
<tr><td>T5</td><td>Page number (strict)</td><td>1, 2, 3</td><td>✓</td><td>✓</td><td>✓</td></tr>
<tr><td>T6</td><td>Page number (tolerant)</td><td>1, 2, 3</td><td>✓</td><td>✓</td><td>✓</td></tr>
<tr><td>T7</td><td>Starts with "whereas"</td><td>3</td><td>✓</td><td>✓</td><td></td></tr>
<tr><td>T8</td><td>Starts with "now, therefore"</td><td>3</td><td>✓</td><td>✓</td><td></td></tr>
<tr><td>T9</td><td>Dictionary-like (includes ":" & not V4)</td><td>2, 3</td><td>✓</td><td>✓</td><td></td></tr>
<tr><td>T10</td><td>All capital</td><td>2, 3</td><td>✓</td><td>✓</td><td></td></tr>
<tr><td>T11</td><td>Contiguous blank field (underbars)</td><td>1-2, 2-3</td><td>✓</td><td>✓</td><td>✓</td></tr>
<tr><td>T12</td><td>Horizontal line ("*-=#%_+" only)</td><td>1, 2, 3</td><td></td><td>✓</td><td></td></tr>
<tr><td colspan="6">Semantic features</td></tr>
<tr><td>S1</td><td>Language model coherence*</td><td>1-2-3</td><td>✓</td><td>✓</td><td>✓</td></tr>
</table>

The "Blocks" columns list blocks used to extract features for $trans_2$ (e.g. "1-2, 2-3" means $[b_{i-1}, b_i]$ and $[b_i, b_{i+1}]$ are used to extract two sets of features). Features with a similar intended functionality are assigned the same feature name and implementations may vary for different document types. *: Explained in detail in Section 4.1.

Table 2: List of features for each feature extractor

analogous to those for PDFs.

While readers can reference our open-sourced code for the concrete implementation, we will discuss some of the features that have important implementation details. For a target block b_i:

Numbering transition (T1) A categorical feature that itself is a heuristic transition parser. It identifies a numbering in each block and keeps a memory of the largest numberings by their types (i.e., its alphanumeric type and styling, such as `IV.` and `(a)`). It outputs (1) `continuous` if no numbering is found, (2) `consecutive` if the numbering in b_{i+1} is contiguous to the numbering in b_i, (3) `up` if not consecutive and there is a corresponding number in the memory, and (4) `down` if it is none of above and it is the first number in its numbering type. For example, B0 in Figure 1 is `down` as `1.` is the first numbering type that it sees and "1" will be added to the memory. B1 and B2 are `continuous` as no numbering is found and B3 is `consecutive` as a number "2" is found in the same type as `1.`. B4 is `down` as it contains a new numbering type.

Language model coherence (S1) To determine if b_i should be classified as `omitted`, it utilizes language model to classify whether it is more natural to have b_i or b_{i+1} after b_{i-1}. Specifically, we use GPT-2 (Radford et al., 2019) to calculate language model loss $\ell(i, i-1)$ for b_i given b_{i-1} as a context (i.e., fed into the model but not used in the loss calculation). We then calculate $\ell(i, i-1) - \ell(i+1, i-1)$ as the feature. If it is more coherent to have b_i after b_{i-1}, $\ell(i, i-1)$ will be smaller than $\ell(i+1, i-1)$ and the feature value will be negative. We also utilize $\ell(i+1, i) - \ell(i+1, i-1)$.

Similar text in similar position (V10) Headers and footers tend to appear in similar positions across different pages with similar texts. For example, a contract may have the contract's title on every pages at the same position. This feature is 1 if there exists a block b_j such that blocks' overlapping area is larger than 50% of their bounding box (treating as if they are on the same page), and their edit distance is small[6].

Line break before right margin (V4) A Boolean feature that is 0 if the block spans to the right margin and 1 otherwise (i.e., breaks before the right margin). To distinguish the body and the margin of the document, we

[6] $d(b_i, b_j)/\max(len(b_i), len(b_j)) < 0.1$, where d gives the Levenshtein distance and len gives the length of text.

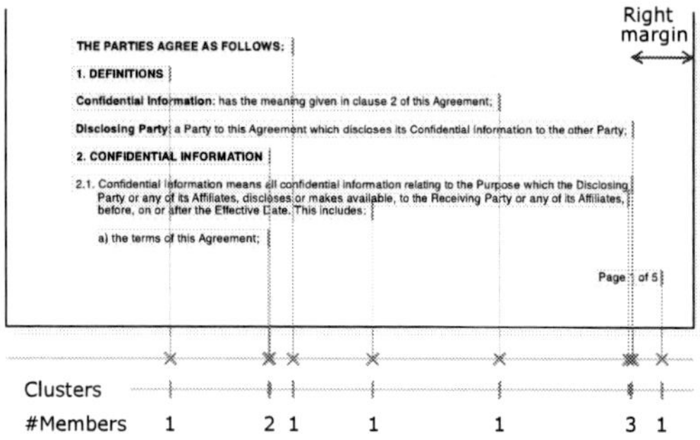

Figure 3: A sketch of how we determine right margin. We apply 1D clustering on the right positions of the blocks and choose the rightmost cluster with at least a user-defined number of members. If we choose to have a minimum of two members, the right margin would be the cluster with three members.

```
class PDFFeatureExtractor(BaseFeatureExtractor):
    def __init__(self, text_boxes):
        bboxes = np.array(
            [tb.bbox for tb in text_boxes])
        page_top = bboxes[:, 3].max()
        page_bottom = bboxes[:, 1].min()
        self.header_thresh = \
            page_top - 0.15 * (page_top - page_bottom)
        ...

    @single_input_feature([1])
    def header_region(self, tb):
        return tb.bbox[3] > self.header_thresh

    @pairwise_feature([(0, 1), (1, 2)])
    def page_change(self, tb1, tb2):
        if tb1 is None or tb2 is None:
            return True
        return tb1.page != tb2.page

    @pointer_feature()
    def pointer_left_aligned(
            self, head_tb, tb1, tb2, tb3):
        return self.left_aligned(tb1)

    ...
```

Figure 4: The Python implmenetation of a feature extractor

apply 1D clustering[7] on the right positions of the blocks and extract the rightmost cluster with minimum members of six per page (to ignore headers/footers) as the right margin (Figure 3). This margin information is used in other features (V3, V6 and V7).

Larger line spacing (V8) A Boolean feature that is 0 if line spacing is *normal* and 1 otherwise. To determine the *normal* line spacing, we apply 1D clustering on line spacings and pick a cluster with the largest number of members.

4.2 Pointer Identification

We also implement the pointer identification with handcrafted features and a machine learning-based classifier. Since a down transition creates a new level that a block can point back to, we extract all pairs of $[b_j, b_i]$ ($b_j \in C_i$) with $trans_i =$ up, $trans_j =$ down and $j < i$. We then extract features from $[b_j, b_i]$ and train a binary classifier to predict $p\,(ptr_i = b_j | b_j, b_i)$. In training, we use ground truth down labels to extract candidates C_i. At test time, we aggregate C_i from predicted transition labels and predict the pointer by $ptr_i = \text{argmax}_{b_j \in C_i}\, p\,(ptr_i = b_j | b_j, b_i)$.

While our pointer points at a block with down (b_j), it is sometimes important to extract features from the first block in the paragraph that b_j belongs to, which we will hereafter refer as $b_{head(j)}$. Using $b_{head(j)}$, we extract the following features from $[b_j, b_i]$:

Consecutive numbering Boolean features on whether a numbering in b_i is contiguous to a numbering in b_j and $b_{head(j)}$, respectively.

Indentation Categorical features on whether indentation gets larger, smaller or stays the same from b_j to b_i and from $b_{head(j)}$ to b_{i+1}, respectively.

Left aligned Binary features on whether b_j, b_{i+1} and $b_{head(j)}$ are left aligned, respectively.

Transition counts We count numbers of blocks $\{b_k\}_{j<k<i}$ with down and with up, respectively. We use these two numbers along with their difference as features. This is based on an intuition that a closer block with down tends to be more important.

Pointer features are also customizable, but we used the same features[8] for all the document types.

While we call our system a "transition parser", we do not employ a stack and instead employ the graph-based parser-like formulation for the pointer identification. We selected this strategy because of the recent success of graph-based parsers (Dozat and Manning, 2017; Zhang et al., 2019).

5 Implementation and Customization

In this section, we briefly describe the implementation of our system that allows easy customization to different types of VSDs. Our system employs modular and customizable design and is implemented in Python. A user may implement a new feature extractor simply by writing a new fea-

[7]We utilized a naïve 1D clustering, where it greedily adds elements from a sorted list to a cluster while the maximum difference of the elements is within a user-defined threshold.

[8]More precisely, the pointer features are implemented slightly different for different document types, such as numbering being modified to Japanese for Contract$^{pdf}_{ja}$, but they are intended to have similar functionalities.

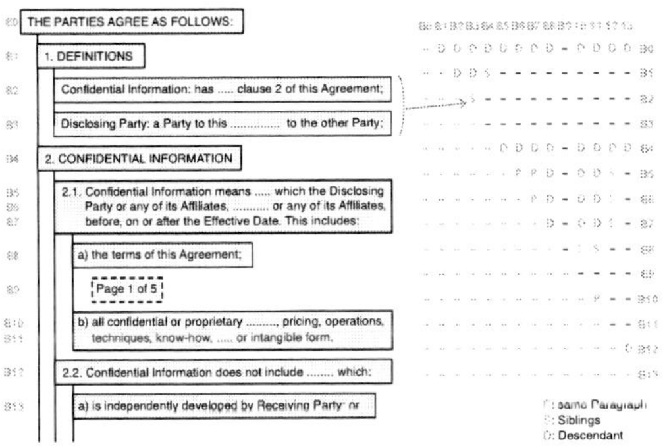

Figure 5: Evaluation from IE perspective. For each of ground truth and predicted trees, we extract a relationship matrix (right) that describes all the pairwise relationships and calculate F1 scores/accuracy by comparing the matrices.

ture extractor class where each feature is implemented as its class function (Figure 4). For example, `@single_input_feature([1])` denotes that the subsequent function should be applied to the second block of each context (thus corresponding to feature V6). Likewise, the features for pointer identification can be implemented by marking a function with `@pointer_feature()`, which takes a candidate block b_j (`tb1`), a target block b_i (`tb2`), the block next to the target block b_{i+1} (`tb3`) and $b_{head(j)}$ (`head_tb`) as an input.

A feature extractor object is instantiated for each document where all feature functions are automatically aggregated to produce the feature vector. A new feature extractor can inherit from an existing feature extractor (e.g., feature extractors for Contract$_{en}^{pdf}$ and Contract$_{ja}^{pdf}$ both inherit from a base PDF feature extractor), which makes it easy to reuse implementations.

6 Experiments

6.1 Evaluation Metrics

While we do report transition prediction accuracy, it is not a true task metric since it is rooted on our formulation of the task. Looking back at our initial motivation in Section 1, we introduce two sets of evaluation metrics.

The first set of metrics is rooted on IE perspective. For IE, it is important to identify ancestor-descendant and sibling relationships because it allows, for example, identifying a subject (in an ancestral block) and its objects (a decendant block and its siblings). Thus, we evaluate F1 scores for identifying pairs of blocks in (1) same paragraph, (2) sibling, and (3) ancestor-descendant relationships, respectively (Figure 5). Note that we do not include cousin blocks in the sibling relationship, because it is not clear whether cousin blocks have any meaningful information in the context of IE.

We use the second set of metrics to evaluate a system's efficacy as a preprocessing tool for more general NLP pipelines. We evaluate paragraph boundary identification metrics since paragraph boundaries can be used to determine appropriate chunks of text to be fed into the NLP pipelines. We also report accuracy for removing debris with `omitted`.

We used five-folds cross validation for the evaluation.

6.2 Baselines

We compared our system against the following baselines:

Numbering baseline (Hatsutori et al., 2017) This baseline detects numberings using a set of regular expressions and identifies dropping in hierarchy when the type of numberings has changed. Adopting Hatsutori et al. (2017) to our problem formulation, our implementation is the same as the feature "numbering transition (T1)."

Visual baseline This baseline relies purely on visual cues; i.e., indentation and line spacing. For each pair of consecutive blocks, this baseline outputs (1) `continuous` when indentation does not change and line spacing is normal (as in feature V8), (2) `consecutive` when indentation does not change and line spacing is larger than normal, (3) `down` when indentation gets larger, and (4) `up` when indentation gets smaller. On `up`, it points back at the closest block with the same indentation.

PDFMiner We use this popular open-source project to detect paragraph boundaries as in Bast and Korzen (2017). PDFMiner relies purely on geometric heuristics to detect paragraph breaks.

6.3 Implementation Details

We used Random Forest (Breiman, 2001) as the transition and pointer classifiers, which is suited for categorical features that occupy the majority of our features. We did not tune hyperparameters of the Random Forest classifier and used default values of scikit-learn (Pedregosa et al., 2011).

For language model coherence feature S1, we

Relationship			Contract$_{en}^{pdf}$			Law$_{en}^{pdf}$			Contract$_{en}^{txt}$			Contract$_{ja}^{pdf}$		
			Visual	Number	Ours	Visual	Number	Ours	Visual	Number	Ours	Visual	Number	Ours
Same paragraph	Micro	P	**0.982**	0.484	0.944	**0.891**	0.219	0.858	**0.993**	0.540	0.983	0.446	0.402	**0.973**
		R	0.683	0.947	**0.951**	0.681	**0.969**	0.957	0.708	0.917	**0.978**	0.552	**0.985**	0.966
		F	0.806	0.641	**0.947**	0.772	0.357	**0.905**	0.826	0.680	**0.980**	0.494	0.571	**0.969**
	Macro	P	**0.980**	0.644	0.955	0.906	0.328	**0.936**	**0.990**	0.595	0.969	0.481	0.478	**0.971**
		R	0.670	**0.966**	0.951	0.634	**0.974**	0.951	0.746	0.934	**0.976**	0.527	**0.985**	0.956
		F	0.782	0.736	**0.948**	0.731	0.452	**0.933**	0.847	0.687	**0.971**	0.450	0.617	**0.955**
Siblings	Micro	P	0.332	0.677	**0.841**	0.430	0.647	**0.849**	0.397	0.780	**0.784**	0.106	0.151	**0.699**
		R	0.323	**0.765**	0.736	0.283	0.504	**0.712**	0.481	**0.763**	0.723	0.506	0.571	**0.691**
		F	0.328	0.718	**0.785**	0.341	0.567	**0.774**	0.435	**0.772**	0.752	0.176	0.238	**0.695**
	Macro	P	0.443	0.678	**0.791**	0.598	0.493	**0.793**	0.482	0.677	**0.814**	0.347	0.237	**0.719**
		R	0.427	0.691	**0.751**	0.417	0.379	**0.696**	0.557	0.603	**0.758**	0.506	0.536	**0.663**
		F	0.337	0.650	**0.748**	0.410	0.385	**0.724**	0.435	0.605	**0.754**	0.292	0.283	**0.671**
Descendants	Micro	P	0.381	0.184	**0.502**	**0.627**	0.132	0.456	0.239	0.190	**0.541**	0.536	0.125	**0.577**
		R	0.123	**0.879**	0.807	0.303	**0.881**	0.858	0.048	**0.888**	0.771	0.340	0.580	**0.826**
		F	0.186	0.304	**0.619**	0.409	0.229	**0.596**	0.080	0.313	**0.635**	0.416	0.205	**0.679**
	Macro	P	0.295	0.242	**0.655**	0.438	0.173	**0.581**	0.193	0.269	**0.639**	0.462	0.122	**0.737**
		R	0.194	**0.848**	0.798	0.314	0.764	**0.837**	0.072	**0.859**	0.735	0.358	0.519	**0.834**
		F	0.203	0.340	**0.641**	0.327	0.230	**0.617**	0.096	0.367	**0.625**	0.372	0.195	**0.739**
Accuracy	Micro		0.772	0.778	**0.914**	0.827	0.685	**0.908**	0.587	0.674	**0.828**	0.618	0.623	**0.940**
	Macro		0.686	0.679	**0.889**	0.732	0.427	**0.840**	0.571	0.580	**0.841**	0.623	0.492	**0.899**
Average F1	Micro		0.440	0.555	**0.784**	0.507	0.384	**0.758**	0.447	0.588	**0.789**	0.362	0.338	**0.781**
	Macro		0.441	0.576	**0.779**	0.489	0.356	**0.758**	0.459	0.553	**0.783**	0.372	0.365	**0.788**

"Micro": Micro-average, "Macro": Macro-average, "P": Precision, "R": Recall, "F": F1 score

Table 3: Results for evaluation on IE perspective

Criteria			Contract$_{en}^{pdf}$				Law$_{en}^{pdf}$				Contract$_{en}^{txt}$			Contract$_{ja}^{pdf}$			
			PDFMiner	Visual	Number	Ours	PDFMiner	Visual	Number	Ours	Visual	Number	Ours	PDFMiner	Visual	Number	Ours
Paragraph boundary	Micro	P	0.672	0.563	0.914	**0.958**	0.546	0.536	0.911	**0.948**	0.465	0.783	**0.955**	0.531	0.603	0.961	**0.970**
		R	0.822	**0.968**	0.700	0.948	0.858	0.916	0.637	**0.948**	**0.989**	0.637	0.945	0.850	0.663	0.627	**0.991**
		F	0.739	0.712	0.793	**0.953**	0.667	0.676	0.750	**0.948**	0.633	0.702	**0.950**	0.653	0.632	0.759	**0.980**
	Macro	P	0.698	0.598	0.921	**0.958**	0.632	0.565	0.866	**0.946**	0.527	0.840	**0.953**	0.585	0.645	0.964	**0.970**
		R	0.798	**0.964**	0.703	0.945	0.874	0.930	0.522	**0.943**	**0.984**	0.633	0.944	0.867	0.653	0.624	**0.988**
		F	0.722	0.729	0.772	**0.947**	0.703	0.692	0.620	**0.940**	0.673	0.693	**0.947**	0.661	0.627	0.745	**0.976**
Block elimination	Micro	P	—	—	—	0.969	—	—	—	0.979	—	—	0.865	—	—	—	1.000
		R	—	—	—	0.897	—	—	—	0.755	—	—	0.914	—	—	—	0.849
		F	—	—	—	0.932	—	—	—	0.852	—	—	0.889	—	—	—	0.919
	Macro	P	—	—	—	0.948	—	—	—	0.929	—	—	0.815	—	—	—	0.929
		R	—	—	—	0.906	—	—	—	0.858	—	—	0.816	—	—	—	0.866
		F	—	—	—	0.913	—	—	—	0.874	—	—	0.800	—	—	—	0.888

"Micro": Micro-average, "Macro": Macro-average, "P": Precision, "R": Recall, "F": F1 score

Table 4: Results for evaluation on preprocessing perspective

used GPT-2 medium[9] for English documents and `japanese-gpt2-medium`[10]) for Japanese documents.

6.4 Results

Structure and preprocessing evaluations are shown on Table 3 and Table 4, respectively. Our system obtained micro-average structure prediction accuracy of 0.914 for Contract$_{en}^{pdf}$, 0.908 for Law$_{en}^{pdf}$, 0.828 for Contract$_{en}^{txt}$ and 0.940 for Contract$_{ja}^{pdf}$, significantly outperforming the best baselines with 0.778, 0.827, 0.674 and 0.623, respectively. Our system performed the best with respect to F1 scores for all but one structure relationships.

The difference was even more significant for paragraph boundary detection. For Contract$_{en}^{pdf}$, our system obtained a micro-average paragraph boundary detection F1 score of 0.953 that is significantly better than PDFMiner with an F1 score of 0.739. PDFMiner performed on par with our visual baseline and generally performed worse than our numbering baseline. This shows the importance of incorporating textual information to preprocess VSDs.

Micro-average transition label prediction accuracies were 0.951 (Contract$_{en}^{pdf}$), 0.938 (Law$_{en}^{pdf}$), 0.955 (Contract$_{en}^{txt}$) and 0.923 (Contract$_{ja}^{pdf}$).

We investigated the importance of each feature with greedy forward selection and greedy backward elimination of the features (Table 5). We can observe that our system makes a balanced use of

[9] `https://huggingface.co/gpt2`

[10] `https://huggingface.co/rinna/japanese-gpt2-medium`

#	Contract$^{pdf}_{en}$ Forward	Contract$^{pdf}_{en}$ Backward	Law$^{pdf}_{en}$ Forward	Law$^{pdf}_{en}$ Backward	Contract$^{txt}_{en}$ Forward	Contract$^{txt}_{en}$ Backward	Contract$^{pdf}_{ja}$ Forward	Contract$^{pdf}_{ja}$ Backward
	All (0.914)	All (0.914)	All (0.908)	All (0.908)	All (0.828)	All (0.828)	All (0.940)	All (0.940)
1	T1, 2 (0.763)	T1, 2 (0.855)	T1, 2 (0.685)	T1, 2 (0.854)	V8, 2-3 (0.333)	T2, 2 (0.820)	T1, 2 (0.596)	T1, 2 (0.934)
2	V10, 2 (0.796)	T10, 3 (0.794)	V8, 2-3 (0.883)	V10, 2 (0.859)	T10, 2 (0.465)	V9, 2 (0.811)	V12, 2 (0.686)	V9, 2 (0.909)
3	T10, 3 (0.818)	T10, 2 (0.794)	V10, 2 (0.893)	T2, 2 (0.836)	T9, 2 (0.716)	T3, 2 (0.805)	V1, 2-3 (0.821)	V8, 2-3 (0.882)
4	T7, 3 (0.853)	V1, 2-3 (0.796)	V8, 1-2 (0.885)	V8, 2-3 (0.800)	T3, 2 (0.727)	V5 (0.785)	T2, 2 (0.813)	S1‡, 2 (0.865)
5	T10, 2 (0.813)	S1‡, 2 (0.808)	V5, 2-3 (0.858)	V1, 2-3 (0.747)	T6, 2 (0.721)	T10, 2 (0.781)	V8, 2-3 (0.887)	T2, 2 (0.856)
6	V1, 2-3 (0.844)	T8, 2-3 (0.801)	T7, 3 (0.881)	V4, 2-3 (0.716)	T4, 2 (0.723)	V8, 2-3 (0.752)	V9, 3 (0.906)	V4, 2 (0.824)
7	V4, 2 (0.868)	T2, 2 (0.774)	V1, 2-3 (0.898)	V9, 2 (0.676)	T2, 2 (0.721)	S1†, 2 (0.749)	T2, 1 (0.913)	V1, 2-3 (0.787)
8	T2, 2 (0.886)	V4, 2-3 (0.692)	V3, 2 (0.904)	S1†, 2 (0.717)	V4, 2 (0.722)	V9, 3 (0.751)	V4, 2-3 (0.926)	V9, 2 (0.799)

Numbers in parentheses show micro-average transition label prediction accuracy. The first line shows the results with all features.
†: $\ell(i, i-1) - \ell(i+1, i-1)$ variant ‡: $\ell(i+1, i) - \ell(i+1, i-1)$ variant.

Table 5: Eight most important features chosen by greedy forward selection and backward elimination.

the visual and textual cues. "Indentation (V1)", "Larger line spacing (V8)" and "numbering hierarchy (T1)", which partially represent the baselines, were ranked high in many cases. At the same time, other features such as "all capital (T10)" and "punctuated (T2)" were also contributing significantly to the accuracy, which made our system much superior to the baselines.

The feature importance revealed that the semantic cue (S1) was no more important than other cues. We suspect that the feature (which compares whether adjacent or non-adjacent block is more likely given a context) had fallen back to mere language model with the context being ignored in some cases, possibly due to GPT-2 not being fine-tuned on the legal domain.

We also conducted a qualitative error analysis. For Contract$^{pdf}_{en}$, we found that our system was performing poorly on documents where they had bold or underlined section titles, followed by paragraphs without any indentation (predicted `continuous` instead of `down`). We believe incorporating typographic features would improve our system as implied by the success of the "all capital (T10)" feature.

For Contract$^{txt}_{en}$, we found that blocks that are all capitals or are all underbars were misclassified as `omitted`. All capital words and underbars are frequently used to denote headers and footers, but they were used as section titles and input fields in these examples. Unlike for Contract$^{pdf}_{en}$, we attribute this problem to lack of training data, as those should have been classified correctly with other features (such as T4 and T8) if the system had seen similar patterns in the training data.

Interestingly, we observed that the system tends to do better in documents that are hierarchically more complex. This may be because hierarchically complex documents tend to incorporate more cues to support humans comprehend the documents.

7 Related Works

As discussed in Section 1, previous works mainly focused on word segmentation and layout analysis, whereas fine-grained logical structure analysis of VSDs is less addressed. Nevertheless, there exist some studies that focus on similar goals.

Abreu et al. (2019) and Ferrés et al. (2018) have tried to deal with logical structure analysis by identifying specific structures in VSDs such as subheadings. However, these studies are too coarse-grained and cannot handle paragraph-level logical structure, thus they are unable to satisfy the need we have discussed in Section 1. FinSBD-3 shared task (Au et al., 2021) is more fine-grained than those works and incorporates extraction of list items. However, its main focus is not on analysis of logical structures; it has only four static levels for list hierarchies and does not consider hierarchies in non-list paragraphs.

Hatsutori et al. (2017) proposed a rule-based system that purely relies on numberings. We compared our system against it in Section 6 and showed that our system, which also incorporates textual and semantic cues, is superior to their method.

Sporleder and Lapata (2004) proposed a paragraph boundary detection method for plain texts that purely relies on textual and semantic cues. While their method is not intended for VSDs, some of their ideas could be incorporated to our work as additional features. We leave use of more advanced semantic cues for a future work.

While the goal is different, our textual features have some similarity to those used in sentence boundary detection (Gillick, 2009). Since our goal is to predict structures as well as boundaries, we employ richer textual and visual features that they do not utilize.

LayoutLM (Xu et al., 2020, 2021) incorporates multimodal self-supervised learning to utilize deep learning for form understanding. While it may alleviate the need for a large training dataset, it is not trivial to adopt the same method for logical structure analysis as text blocks would not fit onto the LayoutLM's context. Furthermore, it is easier to diagnose and to improve our system as it utilizes a combination of hand-crafted features, while deep learning systems tend to be completely black box.

8 Conclusions

We proposed a transition parser-like formulation of the logical structure analysis of VSDs and developed a feature-based machine learning system that fuses visual, textual and semantic cues. Our system significantly outperformed baselines and an existing open-source software on different types of VSDs. The experiment revealed that incorporating both the visual and textual cues is crucial in successfully conducting logical structure analysis of VSDs. As a future work, we will incorporate typographic and more advanced semantic cues.

Acknowledgements

We used computational resource of AI Bridging Cloud Infrastructure (ABCI) provided by the National Institute of Advanced Industrial Science and Technology (AIST) for the experiments.

References

Carla Abreu, Henrique Cardoso, and Eugénio Oliveira. 2019. FinDSE@FinTOC-2019 Shared Task. In *Proceedings of the Second Financial Narrative Processing Workshop*.

Willy Au, Abderrahim Ait-Azzi, and Juyeon Kang. 2021. FinSBD-2021: The 3rd Shared Task on Structure Boundary Detection in Unstructured Text in the Financial Domain. In *Companion Proceedings of the Web Conference 2021*.

Hannah Bast and Claudius Korzen. 2017. A Benchmark and Evaluation for Text Extraction from PDF. In *2017 ACM/IEEE Joint Conference on Digital Libraries*.

Leo Breiman. 2001. Random Forests. *Machine Learning*, 45(1):5–32.

Timothy Dozat and Christopher D. Manning. 2017. Deep Biaffine Attention for Neural Dependency Parsing. In *5th International Conference on Learning Representations*.

Daniel Ferrés, Horacio Saggion, Francesco Ronzano, and Àlex Bravo. 2018. PDFdigest: an Adaptable Layout-Aware PDF-to-XML Textual Content Extractor for Scientific Articles. In *Proceedings of the Eleventh International Conference on Language Resources and Evaluation*.

Dan Gillick. 2009. Sentence Boundary Detection and the Problem with the U.S. In *Proceedings of Human Language Technologies: The 2009 Annual Conference of the North American Chapter of the Association for Computational Linguistics*.

Yoichi Hatsutori, Katsumasa Yoshikawa, and Haruki Imai. 2017. Estimating Legal Document Structure by Considering Style Information and Table of Contents. In *New Frontiers in Artificial Intelligence*, pages 270–283. Springer International Publishing.

Frederik Obermaier, Bastian Obermayer, Vanessa Wormer, and Wolfgang Jaschensky. 2016. About the Panama Papers. *Süddeutsche Zeitung*.

F. Pedregosa, G. Varoquaux, A. Gramfort, V. Michel, B. Thirion, O. Grisel, M. Blondel, P. Prettenhofer, R. Weiss, V. Dubourg, J. Vanderplas, A. Passos, D. Cournapeau, M. Brucher, M. Perrot, and E. Duchesnay. 2011. Scikit-learn: Machine Learning in Python. *Journal of Machine Learning Research*, 12:2825–2830.

Alec Radford, Jeffrey Wu, Rewon Child, David Luan, Dario Amodei, and Ilya Sutskever. 2019. Language Models are Unsupervised Multitask Learners. *OpenAI blog*, 1(8):9.

Carlos Soto and Shinjae Yoo. 2019. Visual Detection with Context for Document Layout Analysis. In *Proceedings of the 2019 Conference on Empirical Methods in Natural Language Processing and the 9th International Joint Conference on Natural Language Processing*.

Caroline Sporleder and Mirella Lapata. 2004. Automatic Paragraph Identification: A Study across Languages and Domains. In *Proceedings of the 2004 Conference on Empirical Methods in Natural Language Processing*.

Christopher Stahl, Steven Young, Drahomira Herrmannova, Robert Patton, and Jack Wells. 2018. DeepPDF: A Deep Learning Approach to Extracting Text from PDFs. In *Proceedings of the Eleventh International Conference on Language Resources and Evaluation*.

The U.S. Securities and Exchange Commission. 2018. *EDGAR® Public Dissemination Service Technical Specification*.

Yang Xu, Yiheng Xu, Tengchao Lv, Lei Cui, Furu Wei, Guoxin Wang, Yijuan Lu, Dinei Florencio, Cha Zhang, Wanxiang Che, Min Zhang, and Lidong Zhou. 2021. LayoutLMv2: Multi-modal pre-training for visually-rich document understanding.

In *Proceedings of the 59th Annual Meeting of the Association for Computational Linguistics and the 11th International Joint Conference on Natural Language Processing*.

Yiheng Xu, Minghao Li, Lei Cui, Shaohan Huang, Furu Wei, and Ming Zhou. 2020. Layoutlm: Pre-training of text and layout for document image understanding. In *Proceedings of the 26th ACM SIGKDD International Conference on Knowledge Discovery & Data Mining*.

Sheng Zhang, Xutai Ma, Kevin Duh, and Benjamin Van Durme. 2019. AMR Parsing as Sequence-to-Graph Transduction. In *Proceedings of the 57th Annual Meeting of the Association for Computational Linguistics*.

A Appendix

A.1 Details of Data Collection and Annotation

In this section, we provide supplemental information regarding the data collection and the annotation discussed in Section 3.

For PDFs, we queried Google search engines and downloaded the PDF files that the search engines returned. We used the following queries and the domains:

Contract$^{pdf}_{en}$ "“non-disclosure” agreement filetype:pdf" on seven domains from countries where English is widely spoken (US “.com”, UK “.co.uk”, Australia “.com.au”, New Zealand “.co.nz”, Singapore “.com.sg”, Canada “.ca”, South Africa “.co.za”).

Law$^{pdf}_{en}$ “site:*.gov “order” filetype:pdf” on “google.com”.

Contract$^{pdf}_{ja}$ "“秘密保持契約書” filetype:pdf" on “google.co.jp”.

For the collection of Contract$^{txt}_{en}$, we first download all the documents filed at EDGAR from 1996 to 2020 in a form of daily archives[11]. We uncompressed each archive and deserialized files using regular expressions by referencing to the EDGAR specifications(The U.S. Securities and Exchange Commission, 2018), which gave us 12,851,835 filings each of which contains multiple documents. We then extracted NDA candidates from the documents by a rule-based filtering. Using meta-data obtained during the deserialization, we extracted documents whose file type starts with “EX” (denotes that it is an exhibit), its file extension is one of “.pdf”, “.PDF”, “.txt”, “.TXT”, “.html”, “.HTML”, “.htm” or “HTM”, and its content is matched by a regular expression “(?<![a-zA-Z;"()]␣*)([Nn]on[-␣][Dd]isclosure)|(NON[-␣]DISCLOSURE)”.

We then randomly selected documents that fulfill following criteria:

- it is an NDA or an executive order,
- it has embedded texts (for PDFs),
- it is a single column document, and
- a similar document is not yet in the dataset.

The last criterion mainly targets contracts from same organizations and executive orders from same authorities. It ensures that we get a wide variety of documents in our dataset.

The datasets were annotated by one of the authors. We did not employ majority vote to improve annotation consistency, because labels can be easily determined by a brief inspection of the document.

[11] https://www.sec.gov/Archives/edgar/Oldloads/

Legal Terminology Extraction with the Termolator

Nhi Pham
New York University
nhi.pham@nyu.edu

Lachlan Pham
New York University
lp2233@nyu.edu

Adam Meyers
New York University
meyers@cs.nyu.edu

Abstract

Domain-specific terminology is ubiquitous in legal documents. Despite potential utility in populating glossaries and ontologies or as arguments in information extraction and document classification tasks, there has been limited work done for legal terminology extraction. This paper describes some work to remedy this omission. In the described research, we make some modifications to the Termolator, a high-performing, open-source terminology extractor which has been tuned to scientific articles. Our changes are designed to improve the Termolator's results when applied to United States Supreme Court decisions. Unaltered and using the recommended settings, the original Termolator provides a list of terminology with a precision of 23% and 25% for the categories of economic activity (development set) and criminal procedures (test set) respectively. These were the most frequently occurring broad issues in Washington University in St. Louis Database corpus, a database of Supreme Court decisions that have been manually classified by topic. Our contribution includes the introduction of several legal domain-specific filtration steps and changes to the web search relevance score; each incrementally improved precision culminating in a combined precision of 63% and 65%. We also evaluated the baseline version of the Termolator on more specific subcategories and on broad issues with fewer cases. Our results show that a narrowed scope as well as smaller document numbers significantly lower the precision. In both cases, the modifications to the Termolator improve precision.

1 Introduction

Automatic terminology extraction systems identify word sequences which are specific to a domain. The basic approach to terminology extraction involves syntactic processing to identify probable candidates. These are subsequently filtered using statistical techniques. What qualifies as key terminology varies depending on the field and intended purpose, resulting in differences in how terminology extraction is approached. This paper seeks to address the lack of terminology extraction approaches in the legal domain.[1] Specifically, we will tune an existing tool to extract terminology from various categories of US Supreme Court opinions.

Supreme Court opinions are public domain and benefit from comprehensive tagging efforts and, as such, previous natural language processing work on Supreme Court case corpora has included automatic classification using word embeddings and neural networks (Undavia et al., 2018). Supreme Court opinions, as compared with more technical legal documents, like contracts or academic papers, are written to justify decisions to a public audience and are thus written in a less constrained form and with more accessible language. Nevertheless, since decisions are made on recurring legal topics, a regular vocabulary of issue-specific terms is likely to emerge. These are precisely the terms that we target and, in doing so, seek to contribute to the classification problem by providing an explicable identifying feature for categories of legal documents. We use Washington University in St. Louis Database of Supreme Court Decisions, manually annotated with broad and narrow categories for our experiments.

This project uses the Termolator (Meyers et al., 2018), a high-performing open-source terminology extractor. The tool requires a foreground consisting of texts in the target topic and a multi-topic background both of which can be customized to need. The benefit of a curated background as opposed to a general corpus used by many other term extractors is that it intuitively allows for the extraction of the key terminology of a specific subdomain.

[1] We claim this to be the first documented application of terminology extraction to the legal domain. We make no claims about other NLP techniques applied to the legal domain.

Natural Legal Language Processing Workshop 2021, pages 155–162
November 10, 2021.

For this paper, by specifying the foreground as a collection of Supreme Court cases in a given foreground topic and the background as opinions in a set of documents about other, varied topics, the terminology extracted are more likely to be specific to that foreground rather than also including general legal terms present in those cases that aren't necessarily representative of the foreground topic. The Termolator also ranks the terms it finds based on a relevance score determined through web search and well-formedness metrics. The Termolator was designed with a focus on science-oriented texts, so in this paper, we make several adjustments to the tool which improve its baseline precision for at least Supreme Court decisions.

2 Previous Work

2.1 Legal Document Classification

There has been some research on legal document classification using a range of methods such as traditional statistical models, neural networks, and state-of-the-art deep learning classifiers. Previous work includes a study on classifying Supreme Court legal opinions using convolutional neural networks (CNNs) and recurrent neural networks (RNNs) (Undavia et al., 2018). The most successful system in the paper was one that combined word2vec with CNNs. Howe et al. (2019) discusses the performance of different machine learning classifiers for Singapore Supreme Court Judgments. The paper compares state-of-the-art natural language processing methods and statistical models applied to legal documents. The authors found that traditional models outperform neural network classifiers on certain metrics, implying that there is still a need to optimize and improve such tools for legal documents.

These papers serve as a motivation for our work because key terminology can be used as an additional feature to improve the training of legal document classifiers. We are considering this as a topic for future research.

2.2 Terminology extraction

Meyers et al. (2018) describes the Termolator, a high-performing terminology extraction system. The tool uses a chunking procedure which favours chunks containing out-of-vocabulary words, nominalizations, technical adjectives, and other specialized word classes. Subsequently, the tool ranks terms via several metrics including: a distributional score and a relevance score. The distributional score favors terms that are more frequent in the foreground documents than the background documents.[2] The relevance score uses the output of a Yahoo websearch (`www.yahoo.com`) and favors terms that occur more frequently in technical documents (articles, dissertations, etc.) than other documents (online stores, social media, wikipedia, etc.). The Termolator has been applied to scientific articles and patents, achieving upwards of 70% precision in identifying key terminology. We experimented with different domain-specific modifications to the Termolator. The baseline results for comparison come from running the original Termolator. We will be using an identical evaluation method as Meyers et al. (2018), randomly selecting 20 terms from each 20% interval in the ranked output, i.e. 20 from the top 20%, 20 from the 21st to 40th percentile and so forth.

3 EXPERIMENTAL SETUP

3.1 Data set

Our data set consists of 8400 US Supreme Court cases downloaded from the Python Textacy package[3] and labelled using the information available on the Washington University in St. Louis Law, The Supreme Court Database[4]. Each document is classified into 14 broad issues in Table 1, which are further categorized into narrow issues, such as search and seizure (under criminal procedure) or antitrust (under economic activity) [5].

Broad Issue	Number of Documents
01 - Criminal Procedure	1924
02 - Civil Rights	1360
03 - First Amendment	658
04 - Due Process	335
05 - Privacy	110
06 - Attorneys	98
07 - Unions	346
08 - Economic Activity	1667
09 - Judicial Power	1149
10 - Federalism	367
11 - Interstate Relation	58
12 - Federal Taxation	304
13 - Miscellaneous	23
14 - Private Law	1

Table 1: Number of documents in each broad issue

Despite a larger number of existing Supreme Court decisions, the data set was limited by what

[2] Similar to the TF-IDF score used in Information Retrieval.

[3] https://github.com/chartbeat-labs/textacy

[4] http://scdb.wustl.edu/

[5] http://scdb.wustl.edu/documentation.php?var=issue

was made available by the Textacy package which consists of the majority of the decisions issued between 1946 to 2016. We also chose to use the entire data set which is slightly larger, but in a similar order of magnitude to data sets used by the Termolator in previous work in order to maximise the Termolator's effectiveness especially given the likelihood of sparser key terminology when compared with scientific documents.

3.2 Method

A script was produced to generate, as needed, two text documents listing the foreground and background for a specified issue number as required by the Termolator. As an initial baseline, the Termolator was run using the recommended settings. The foreground consisted of opinions categorized under the target issue and the background consisted of the remaining opinions.

Our experiments will focus on the most frequent broad and narrow issues. Among the broad issues, the two most frequent ones for which we evaluated the Termolator are:

- **Issue 01** - Criminal Procedure with 1924 court cases
- **Issue 08** - Economic Activity with 1667 court cases

Among the narrow issues, the two most frequent are subtopics of the aforementioned broad issues, respectively:

- **Issue 10050** - Search and Seizure (other than as pertains to vehicles or Crime Control Act), a subtopic of broad issue 01, with 238 court cases
- **Issue 80010** - Antitrust (except in the context of mergers and union antitrust), a subtopic of broad issue 08, with 216 court cases

We focus on whether our extensions to the Termolator generate better results for legal documents while assessing whether the scope of the issue (broad/narrow) and disparities in the numbers of Court cases affect the precision in legal terminology extraction. To further analyze the results, we perform the experiment on the broad issue 05 - Privacy. This broad issue has 110 Court cases, which is of significantly smaller size compared to the issues 01 and 08, but is within the same range as the most frequent narrow issues 10050 and 80010.

In the following subsections, we describe the adjustments in detail. We choose broad issue 08 for our initial experiments as our development set, for purposes of evaluation. Issue 08 has the advantage of being the second highest labelled issue, allowing for a relatively robust foreground from which to extract key terminology. In addition, the topic of economic activity was slightly easier to differentiate key terminology on the basis of relation to the topic i.e. anything relating to a large-scale organization's or a government's finances.

3.3 Baseline and Evaluation

In line with the evaluation procedure of Meyers et al. (2018), a sample of 100 terms were taken from each output, 20 terms were randomly selected from each fifth of the 5000 terms (in rank order) and evaluated as correct or incorrect. A term is considered correct if it:

- has an obvious relationship to the issue area; and
- is not a term that a layperson would understand in a legal context nor could it be frequently used in other court opinions, except in reference to cases within the issue area

We did not consider names of legislation and citations to previous cases as correct terms. We removed these automatically, using a regular expression-based procedure.[6] A selection of output terminology is shown accompanied by its evaluation and justification in Table 2. Some common attributes of incorrect terms are if it:

- includes an incoherent sequence of letters or if it is an acronym (wwsp, cftb)
- is the name of a case or legal act
- is a geographical name (Merrimack River), an organisation name (Trinko) or a person's name (John Brunsman)
- contains any digit (t-2-1)
- is not a noun group (quasi-suspect)

[6]Named entities are sometimes included in terminology detection output and sometimes not. For example, Termeval 2020 (Rigouts Terryn et al., 2020) calculated terminology detection scores both ways. Citations to laws or court decisions have a similar status. Citations, like terminology are characteristic of particular subfields. However, they arguably have a separate status from terms.

Rank	Term	Evaluation	Justification
0	derivative work	✓	related to copyright laws
327	ppg	✗	acronym
1018	engelgau	✗	case name
1070	class certification	✗	not specific to economic activity
1629	atomic energy	✗	general, widely-understood term
1665	licensor	✓	label for economic actor
3070	job freeze	✓	economic phenomenon
3735	quasi-suspect	✗	adjective, general term (note hyphen)
3896	California tax	✗	reference to a specific set of laws
4792	howey test	✓	assesses nature of transactions

Table 2: Selection of key terminology output, evaluation and justification for baseline run on legal issue 08, economic activity.

The evaluation criteria may seem subjective. Some output terms were not obviously associable with the analyzed issue; for example, a layperson could view "flow control" and be able to conjure a logical non-economic definition; however, the term has a specific economic denotation, which given the right context would be considered domain specific. We erred toward labelling these ambiguous terms as valid. An improved evaluation criteria, perhaps created in consultation with a legal expert, could assist in the delineation of key terminology thereby improving inter-annotator agreement.

For the remainder of this section, we describe domain-specific modifications to the Termolator system which improve the Termolator's performance compared to the baseline system.

3.4 Parameter Adjustments

We adjusted the suggested maximum number of terms considered by the Termolator from 30000 to 6000, and number of terms kept from 5000 to 1000. While the suggested parameters were tested successfully on science-oriented topics, we are working with a data set with far fewer key terms. This intuition was confirmed when the baseline output for issue 08 produced a far higher rank-weighted precision ($\sim 35\%$) than overall precision ($\sim 23\%$) indicating that higher-ranked terms were much more frequently identified as correct.

3.5 Case and Legislation Name Filter

Case names and legislation names are essentially named entities. They often contain abbreviations and numbers and are patterned in a way that makes them difficult to process by both standard noun group chunkers, as well as the Termolator's noun group detection component. We used a regular-expression based system to identify these entities and to remove them from the text. This prevents these entities or parts thereof from being considered as terminology candidates by the noun chunker and subsequent stages of the Termolator. As noted in section 3.3, we define terminology to exclude named entities and citations, as these do not serve the same function as the legal terminology we are considering.

There were two separate sets of regular expressions used: one set of patterns to recognize citations to legislation and one set of patterns for citations to previous court cases (case names). Legislation patterns combine keywords and abbreviations (code, act, const. laws, etc.), indicators of subsections (art, article, amendment, etc.), enumerating expressions (Arabic numbers, Roman numbers and consecutive letters) and the section symbol (§) with keywords that are typically part of US legislation references (statute, code, section, etc.). For citatons to court decisions, the two most common patterns are "standard" and "X v Y". Standard case citations are a combination of standard abbreviations for court reporters (cal., reptr., supp., u.s., etc.), additional abbreviations (e.g. for U.S states), punctuation and numbers. For example, "410 U.S. 113 (1973)" is a standard citation (U.S. refers to a court reporter and the numbers refer to years, pages and volumes). The "X v Y" variety of citation is essentially 2 names joined by a **v** indicating "versus". Our regular expressions were quite long and incorporated various lists of key items (e.g. a list of court reporters). The construction of these expressions was guided by information found in the "the Blue Book"(The Harvard Law Review and The University of Pennsylvania Law Review and The Yale Law Journal, 2010), as well as trial and error using a small set of court opinions (e.g. *Roe v Wade*)[7].

We observed that this change had a noticeable effect on the baseline system. The baseline test output included 28 legislation and case names, such as: Nike, Teleflex, Phillipsburg-Easton. These names were likely identified by the baseline system because they are fairly infrequent and are likely to be more highly concentrated in cases related to the legal field to which the legislation or cases pertain: legislation and cases related to economic activity are going to be cited and referred to in cases about economic activity due to the need for similar precedence-related interpretations of laws. This filter is part of the latest version of Termolator.[8]

[7]The actual regular expressions and the system for using them will be part of our Github release of this system.

[8]`https://github.com/AdamMeyers/The_Termolator`

3.6 Digit and Hyphen Filter

Our error analysis of the baseline system suggested that terms containing digits and hyphenated words were incorrect. In contrast, hyphenated terms were given additional weight in the Termolator ranking system owing to the fact that in scientific articles such terms often combine two scientific words composing a singular more specific word (e.g. "X-ray" or "wavelength-variable"). The Supreme Court documents were more likely to use hyphens to combine two common, non-jargon words and the combined word was often an adjective ("Texas-Mexican") or a name ("pre-Jones act"). Additionally, any identified key terminology containing a digit was incoherent out of context ("t-2-1") and likely refers to a section or clause of a cited law or case.

3.7 Customization of Websearch Filter for Legal Documents

As part of its relevance score ranking, the original Termolator incorporates the results of a Yahoo search. Based on the websearch, the Termolator calculates a relevance score between 0 and 1. The relevance score combines the number of hits (on a logarithmic scale) with the percentage of the top 10 hits that are "technical", where it is assumed that a technical hit contains a keyword like "thesis", "article" or "dissertation". A high websearch score indicates that a candidate term is found in many scholarly sources on the Internet. This works well for scientific articles, but not so well for legal documents since it is much easier to find and differentiate scientific texts than legal documents using websearches. Furthermore, websearches often find many documents that would be of little relevance. For example, websearching category-specific terms, like the "foreclosure sale" in the economic activity domain, would often return commercial texts related to that category rather than the legal documents we would need to validate terms.

Therefore, we replaced the Termolator's websearch ranking system with our own program in which we use Harvard's CaseLaw Access Project API [9] as the replacement "search engine". The API is composed of 6,725,065 official, book-published United States state and federal case law ranging from 1658 to 2018. The case law is labelled with pertinent metadata and allows searching by case name, case text and court.

$$\textbf{score} = \frac{log_{10}(all\_count)}{log_{10}(ALL)} \times \frac{log_{10}(SC\_count)}{log_{10}(all\_count)} = \frac{log_{10}(SC\_count)}{log_{10}(ALL)} \simeq \frac{log_{10}(SC\_count)}{7}$$

where **score** $\in [0, 1]$, *SC_count* is the number of Supreme Court cases that the term appears in, *all_count* is the number of all cases, including all state courts, federal courts, and territorial courts, in which the term appears, and *ALL* is simply the size of the API - 6,725,065.

This scoring is parallel to the quantity and quality metrics used in the original Termolator's relevance score. The first part of the product, $\frac{log_{10}(all\_count)}{log_{10}(ALL)}$, essentially reflects the number of times the term appears in the Harvard's CaseLaw data set thereby measuring a term's relevance across the entire database - a 'quantity' metric. And the second part of the product, $\frac{log_{10}(SC\_count)}{log_{10}(all\_count)}$, identifies what fraction of returned court cases are Supreme Court cases thereby measuring a term's relevance among the returned results - a 'quality' metric. This score formula simplifies to approximately $\frac{log_{10}(SC\_count)}{7}$. This formula also ensures the output to be in the range [0,1], guaranteeing compatibility with the Termolator. Given that the input (candidate terminology) and output (score in range $[0, 1]$) are identical in both websearch programs, the Yahoo script was easily replaced by our proposed script.

However, it is important to note that the web relevance scoring function in the Termolator uses the top 10 search results from Yahoo for each term and calculates the proportion of these top 10 which are scientifically relevant. Unlike Yahoo, the Harvard's CaseLaw Access Project API search lacks a ranking algorithm. Without some sorting, the first ten results of a search from the CaseLaw Access Project API are not of greater relevance as compared to the remaining results; additionally, all search results are of the same document type - U.S. cases - as opposed to Yahoo search which considers all kinds of websites and document types. So, in our investigation, we considered a crude measure of quality to be the proportion of results which were Supreme Court documents. However, if there were very few Supreme Court cases relative to the total number of cases containing the search term, the relevance score would be low even though it may simply relate to an issue that is more com-

[9] https://case.law/

monly dealt with in lower federal courts. Instead, an analogous analysis of the top search results from a web search engine but for legal documents could overcome these limitations by taking advantage of the automatic ranking of the search engine, better capturing the intuition that something is key terminology if a high proportion of the top search results link to appropriate sites or documents.

4 RESULTS

Modification	Precision Score
0 - Baseline	23%
1 - Parameter Adjustments	35%
2 - Case/legislation filter	44%
3 - Digits/hyphen filter	31%
4 - Combination of 1, 2, and 3	50%
5 - 4 + Legal Search Customization	63%

Table 3: Precision scores of each modification for broad issue 08 - Economic Activity

We first interpret the result for broad issue 08, our development set. All parameter tuning and calculations of contributions are based on issue 08. We validate these results by testing on additional issues, and demonstrating similar results, at least for other broad issues like broad issue 01.

In the baseline, a precision of 23% was found. After decreasing output size, the various steps of filtration incrementally increased precision. Just excluding terms with both digits or hyphens increased the precision to 31%, with the majority of the incorrect terms being case and legislation names (37 of the 69 labelled incorrect). We found that the removal of hyphenated terms, sometimes at the cost of incorrectly omitting a small number of valid key terminology, was superior to merely decreasing the weight applied to the hyphenated terms. Just excluding references to case names and legislation increased precision to 44%. Combined, these changes improved precision to 50%. This significant increase in precision indicates that that the Termolator is already a good tool at identifying key terminology and that many of the correct terminology is found but the quality of the output is merely diluted by the presence of easily filtered terms. Upon the replacement of the Yahoo websearch relevance score with Harvard's CaseLaw Access Project's API search, alongside the above filtration, precision improved to 63%. A sample evaluation can be seen in table 3. The detailed annotation for all considered issues can be found at: Legal Termolator Annotation Results. The annotators were 2 of the authors (both undergratuate NYU students). Inter-annotator agreement scores varied between 90-95%, largely due to disagreement about whether a layperson would know the meaning of an identified key terminology. [10]

Issue	Category	Baseline Precision	Adjustment Precision
Issue 01 - Criminal Procedure	Broad	25%	65%
Issue 08 - Economic Activity (development set)	Broad	23%	63%
Issue 05 - Privacy	Broad	27%	40%
Issue 10050 - Search and Seizure (Other)	Narrow	19%	30%
Issue 80010 - Antitrust	Narrow	14%	28%

Table 4: Precision Score Summary

In general, our adjusted Termolator is able to produce better results for both broad and narrow categories (see Table 4). Although we tuned our system to the development set (issue 08), the results seem to be the same when tested on the held-out issue 01 data, an issue with similar broadness. We observe the approximately 2.5 times higher precision of 65% compared to the baseline 25% for issue 01. For the narrow issues, the difference between the precision scores of the adjusted Termolator and the baseline for issue 10050 and 80010 is not as high as that of the broad issues, but still marks a 50–100% relative improvement (30% and 28% with adjustments, 19% and 14% baseline). With fewer cases in broad issue 05 in comparison to narrow issues 10050 and 80010, our adjusted Termolator is still able to generate a higher precision of 40% for broad issue 05. These results validate our hypothesis that both the number of cases in an issue and the nature of the issue (broad/narrow) contribute to the change in precision. The fewer cases available to produce a foreground mean there is a smaller range of total key terms and the frequency of any potential term is diminished. The smaller scope of a narrow issue means that fewer outputs would be labelled key terminology as compared to the more encompassing scope of its parent broad issue.

To further investigate the latter hypothesis, we inspected how frequently an output for a narrow issue was labelled incorrect even if it would otherwise have been labelled correct had we been evaluating it for its parent broad issue. For example, the term "exchange commission rate" is not considered key terminology for narrow issue 80010 since there

[10] One of the reviewers was concerned about the expertise of the annotators. By posting these annotations online, we are being transparent.

is no clear association with the topic of antitrust but would have been labelled correct for the corresponding broad issue 08, economic activity. This is another indicator that the broadness of the issue plays a role in the precision score of terminology extraction.

In comparison to the results in Meyers et al. (2018) for scientific documents, the precisions we obtained for broad legal issues with a sufficient number of court cases are somewhat comparable. When run using a 5000 document background and a 500 document foreground on refrigeration patents, the Termolator achieved a 70% precision and when run on a 500 document foreground of semi-conductor patents, the Termolator achieved a 79% precision. The precision increased further when the Termolator was run on larger foregrounds, which is also in line with our adjusted Termolator's results (see Table 4). Beyond the Termolator being developed with a focus on scientific documents and key terminology, the evaluation criteria used in Meyers et al. (2018) could be considered more lenient than our own. The evaluation procedure included terms special to any particular field or subfield, not necessarily the field of the document being annotated. In our investigation, a more analogous evaluation would involve the inclusion of terminology that related not only to the issue area but legal documents in general which would increase the number of terminology identifiable as correct. Additionally, Supreme Court opinions are written with a general audience in mind since they exist to explain the justices' decisions to the public. As such, jargon phrases in need of defining and worthy of classification as key terminology are relatively rarer. This contrasts significantly with the patent and academic article document types which the Termolator was originally designed to analyze and which are far denser with scientific jargon since they are directed at experts in the relevant fields. A more comparable set of legal documents might be contracts whose intended audience is also more specialized or educated. Ultimately, the adjustments to the Termolator certainly improved its precision for the legal field, although it has yet to achieve the same precision as when it was applied to patents by the Termolator's creators. However, this may be attributable to either differences in evaluation methods or irreconcilable differences in data sets.

In addition, it is difficult to measure recall score (or related measures like MAP scores). It is not practical to annotate an entire foreground given that most broad issues currently consist of more than 300 documents and there will be future work on expanding the data set. To understand if we could instead simulate a good measure for recall score, we manually annotated 3 moderate-length documents in the foreground of issue 08 - development set. We observe that more than half of correct terms are only specific to the topic of the document or appear with extremely low frequency in the foreground, and thus not representative enough to be considered "good" terms by the Termolator. In fact, such terms are often ignored since the Termolator models the term importance using some statistical scores, i.e. terms that occur more frequently in the topic-related documents are more important than the off-topic ones. A given case on a highly-specific topic may consist of key terms found nowhere else in the foreground and receive a very low recall score, which would not be a representative sample.

5 Future Work

To build upon the proposed adjustments we made to the Termolator, we aim to extend our data set to a larger size. The current data set contains 8400 Supreme Court cases with a significant variance in the number issue areas. Having a more balanced number of cases in each broad issue could improve our results. A larger set in each category could mean that rarer key terminology is successfully identified, each potentially appearing with greater frequency in the foreground. Similarly, a larger background set could improve results by providing more evidence that given phrases are not foreground-related terms. The difficulty in this lies in the lack of labelled cases; the data set used was manually labelled and likely incredibly labour-intensive demanding a reading thousands of court cases. In tandem, the tasks can be mutually reinforcing, with a higher number of labelled cases, assuming high enough accuracy, allowing for larger data sets for key terminology extraction and, similarly, higher quality terminology can be used for greater accuracy in categorization.

We are simultaneously looking into ways of automatically extending the manual classifications to more data. Towards this end, we are currently working on extensions to the work published in (Undavia et al., 2018). It is possible, that we could obtain better results if we used more data, even if some or all of it were automatically classified. Note that of the approximately 64,000 Supreme Court cases, about half are unusable (really short) and 8400 are annotated. Thus there are about usable 22,000 remaining. However, it is, possible, that other opinions, e.g., circuit court opinions could be used as well.

6 Conclusion

Our adjustments to the Termolator have been shown to improve the precision of the output for Supreme Court cases. These adjustments involved, firstly, the filtering of the most frequently-identified errors followed by a more substantive change to the web-search contribution to the relevance score rankings. We further find that greater precision is achieved when the modified Termolator is applied to broader-scope categories and issues with a greater number of cases. There is significant opportunity to improve and extend upon the investigation of this project to address the relative lack of research in the field of legal terminology extraction.

The modifications to the Termolator described in this paper will be released to the public via Github.

References

Jerrold Soh Tsin Howe, Lim How Khang, and Ian Ernst Chai. 2019. Legal area classification: a comparative study of text classifiers on singapore supreme court judgments. *arXiv preprint arXiv:1904.06470.*

Adam L Meyers, Yifan He, Zachary Glass, John Ortega, Shasha Liao, Angus Grieve-Smith, Ralph Grishman, and Olga Babko-Malaya. 2018. The termolator: terminology recognition based on chunking, statistical and search-based scores. *Frontiers in Research Metrics and Analytics*, 3:19.

Ayla Rigouts Terryn, Veronique Hoste, Patrick Drouin, and Els Lefever. 2020. TermEval 2020: Shared task on automatic term extraction using the annotated corpora for term extraction research (ACTER) dataset. In *Proceedings of the 6th International Workshop on Computational Terminology*, pages 85–94, Marseille, France. European Language Resources Association.

The Harvard Law Review and The University of Pennsylvania Law Review and The Yale Law Journal, editor. 2010. *The bluebook: a uniform system of citation (19th edition.).* Harvard Law Review Association.

Samir Undavia, Adam Meyers, and John E Ortega. 2018. A comparative study of classifying legal documents with neural networks. In *2018 Federated Conference on Computer Science and Information Systems (FedCSIS)*, pages 515–522. IEEE.

Supervised Identification of Participant Slots in Contracts

Dan Simonson
BlackBoiler
Syracuse, NY, USA
dan.simonson@blackboiler.com

Abstract

This paper presents a technique for the identification of participant slots in English language contracts. Taking inspiration from unsupervised slot extraction techniques, the system presented here uses a supervised approach to identify terms used to refer to a genre-specific slot in novel contracts. We evaluate the system in multiple feature configurations to demonstrate that the best performing system in both genres of contracts omits the exact mention form from consideration—even though such mention forms are often the name of the slot under consideration—and is instead based solely on the dependency label and parent; in other words, a more reliable quantification of a party's role in a contract is found in what they do rather than what they are named.

1 Introduction

Contracts create a relationship between two parties, generally centered around some kind of stance object. For example, a non-disclosure agreement (NDA) often features a disclosing party, a receiving party, and some sort of confidential information; similarly, a services agreement may feature a service provider, a service recipient, and some sort of services to be provided. In both types of contracts, the agreement will refer to itself as well.

Contracts contain language that is more repetitive than those typically studied in NLP research (Simonson et al., 2019), but this is not necessarily *consistent* language. A *disclosing party* may be referred to as a "Disclosing Party," "Discloser," "Providing Party," "Company," "Owner," "Client," or any of a limitless set of possible referring expressions, including the actual company name of the *disclosing party*. Further, some of these expressions have no particular relation to either party and may be used ambiguously throughout the corpus–i.e. "Company" may refer to the disclosing party in one contract and the receiving party in another. Thus, while enumeration of such expressions may seem to present a viable heuristic for slot identification in contract language, a more robust technique is required.

We avoid neural network methods for this task for a few reasons. Results from Borchmann et al. (2020) suggest that pre-trained models trained on more general language struggle on the idiosyncrasies of contract language—at least those pre-trained on non-legal data. Further, a resource-intensive slot detection system is not scalable in the desired environment. This is a subprocess of a larger system (Simonson et al., 2020), and thus the footprint in terms of memory and hardware expense need to remain low. We also want to build a system that would provide some transparency into its decisions so users may have an opportunity to customize the system to their needs and preferences. Given that such an understanding of neural network methods remains an on-going research task, a method derived from older techniques promises better opportunities for inspection than techniques that may be more popular.

For this, we look toward more linguistically-informed methods for identifying participant slots in language generally. Schank and Abelson (1977)'s model of script learning from episodic knowledge is a sensible theoretical fit for learning participant slots from contracts. Just as scripts are presumably learned from exposure to repetitive sequences of events, contracts themselves of particular types are also repetitive series of propositions; an individual reading many contracts would readily observe patterns that would generalize into interchangeable participant slots and relationships among them. Chambers and Jurafsky (2008, 2009) present a model for doing exactly that; however, their script learning method is unsupervised, while the sort of slots identified in this work have been prescribed in advance by subject matter experts. Thus, in this model, we turn the techniques pre-

Natural Legal Language Processing Workshop 2021, pages 163–171
November 10, 2021.

sented by Chambers and Jurafsky (2008) on their head to learn participant slots from supervised data.

Section (2) discusses prior work related to contract language and slot identification, particularly how this work exists at the boundary between two threads of thought on slot identification. Section (3) outlines our annotation efforts, their results, and other NLP pre-processing necessary to extract slots. Section (4) describes the mathematical underpinnings of our slot identification technique, and Section (5) enumerates how those mathematical relations are turned into slot selections. Section (6) describes the results of these experiments, and Section (7) goes into more qualitative detail in understanding the causes of the quantitative results.

2 Prior Work

Prior NLP work on contract language is extensive, including summarization (Manor and Li, 2019; Keymanesh et al., 2020) information extraction and understanding (Anish et al., 2019; Borchmann et al., 2020; Agarwal et al., 2021), as well as corpus studies looking at intrinsic properties of contracts (Curtotti and McCreath, 2011; Simonson et al., 2019) or providing new annotations over contract language (Funaki et al., 2020).

We were not able to identify any prior work specifically on participant slots in contracts. Ash et al. (2020) devised a system that identifies the obligations of parties in contracts, leveraging similar features as in this paper but with some key differences. Participants are determined based entirely on their mention form—either overtly, or through a dictionary of synonyms. Mention forms that fall outside of these are ignored, and this technique was not overtly evaluated. As their primary goal was to identify obligations and to look at large volumes of statistics about those obligations within a corpus of employment contracts, the mention form approximation is sensible to make. On the other hand, the goal of the system presented in this paper is to identify mention forms specifically. Since this is part of a user-facing contract review system, ignoring forms that could not be determined in advance would fail to meet the needs of that system; as will be discussed in Section (3.1), such unpredictable mention forms occur frequently.

The theoretical foundation for *slots* comes from Schank and Abelson (1977)'s seminal work on *scripts*—generalizations of events from prior exposure to them. The classic example is that of a "restaurant script"—an understanding of the general series of events and participants involved in visiting a restaurant. While such a conception of knowledge is intuitive, the precise nature of *how* this knowledge should be realized in NLP systems falls into roughly two threads of thought: supervised—where such knowledge is explicitly enumerated—and unsupervised—where such knowledge is inferred from a corpus of text.

While not exactly the same as scripts, some approaches attempt to model *frames* in a supervised manner—that is, rather than inferring them from natural language descriptions in corpora, projects such as *FrameNet* overtly name and describe structured frames and their participant slots (Baker et al., 1998).

However, frames are not scripts or schemas; rather, frames are the building blocks scripts and schemas, which can be thought of as networks of frames with shared participants. Even after years of annotation, the exhaustive enumeration of all frames seems unlikely. In attempting to understand language generally, a system may need to "possess many schema[s], perhaps hundreds of thousands" (Mooney and DeJong, 1985), which motivates an unsupervised approach to extracting such structures. Chambers and Jurafsky (2008) re-ignited interest in related tasks, though most community efforts have centered around performance improvements on or variants of the narrative cloze task (Jans et al., 2012; Pichotta and Mooney, 2014; Mostafazadeh et al., 2016). Other work has continued to focus on the extraction of schemas or scripts as discrete knowledge structures (Chambers and Jurafsky, 2009; Balasubramanian et al., 2013; Simonson and Davis, 2018; Weber et al., 2018).

Latently, in the unsupervised learning of such schemas, participant slots are learned through the identification of sequences of events; in supervised techniques, slots are identified overtly and must be mapped on to text by some means. However, the unique properties of contracts allow us to execute at a hybrid approach. The system described in this paper has mathematical underpinnings that are very similar to those in unsupervised work, particularly Chambers and Jurafsky (2008). However, the overt annotation of a specific genre of contract is much more similar to a frame-based supervised approach, with a subject matter expert deciding in advance what the frame is and what the slots to be labelled are. A specific frame defines each genre of contract, composed of the relationship between the parties specified therein. Table (1) enumerates this explicitly, juxtaposing the terminology used in our own annotation and that used in FrameNet. In an NDA, that frame is FrameNet's *Exchange* while a Services agreement is a *Commercial_transaction.* These differ because FrameNet requires as a core part of a *Commercial_transaction* a *Money* slot which is not often the case in an NDA.

Table 1: Comparison between this paper's analysis of contract genres' slots and their respective FrameNet terminology.

Contract Terminology	FrameNet
NDA	Exchange
receiving party	Exchanger_1
disclosing party	Exchanger_2
confidential information	Themes
Services agreement	Commercial_transaction
service provider	Seller
service receiver	Buyer
services	Goods

3 Data

This section describes two components of our data preparation for slot extraction: the annotation which produced the system's training data (Section 3.1) and and the other NLP pre-processing steps needed to learn and extract participant slots (Section 3.2).

3.1 Annotation

Given the consistency of particular types of contracts, the annotators indicated the mention forms of each of four slots for every document. These were, for NDAs: the *receiving party*, *disclosing party*, *confidential information*, and *agreement*; for Services: *service provider*, *service receiver*, *services*, and *agreement*. Annotators indicated the values for each of these, excluding any determiners. Each defined term had to appear at least twice to be annotated. Ambiguities were noted as well, if they occurred more than once, as some contracts deviate from the defined terms from time-to-time. The annotations are case sensitive; consistent capitalization is important in leveraging the slots.

To train annotators and specify guidelines, the annotators completed two rounds of doubly-annotated documents. After that point, further annotation was completed independently by the trained annotators, according to the guidelines. Kappa scores for different slots were between 0.80 and 1.0, where strict equivalence was the standard. Most disagreements were over the scope of the defined term—e.g. including a determiner in the mention form—rather than the term itself or were due to the omission of an ambiguous mention form.

In total, the annotation team completed 712 NDAs and 214 Services agreements. Figure (1) shows in squarified treemaps the distribution of terms, where area is proportional to the token counts of a given type. Some slots vary more than others, but none are completely invariant. The smallest cells in each treemap are single counts of a particular token type. These are most often proper nouns, generally the name of the company either disclosing information or providing services. If all of these singleton mention forms were grouped as a single type, they would be the second most frequent *disclosing party* type among the NDAs and the most frequent *service provider* type among Services agreements.

3.2 Pre-Processing

For word and sentence tokenization, lemmatization, and dependency parsing, the system uses SpaCy (Honnibal and Johnson, 2015).[1] While SpaCy was not explicitly trained on contract language, for our purposes, the labels are close enough to correct—or at least are consistent enough to derive suitable results. Our observations showed most of its errors being related to either long range dependencies–e.g. relative clauses and coordination between very long VPs–or lexical items unique to contract language–e.g. "warrant" as a verb or "receiving" as part of an NP. The latter case is directly related to our target problem–it was mostly circumvented because cases where "Receiving Party" was capitalized were correctly tagged as proper nouns.

For coreference resolution, the system employs a heuristic technique. Since contract language tends to avoid 3rd person anaphora (Simonson et al., 2019), the system avoids some of the more challenging coreference problems and targets primarily noun phrases headed by common nouns and proper nouns. First, all 1st and 2nd person pronouns are joined into chains unique to each pronoun since their intrinsic deictic properties make them unambiguous. Then the technique builds chains out of all noun phrases that contain the same sequence of lemmas. This sequence is considered the *surface form* of the chain. A noun phrase, in this case, is the regular sequence of part-of-speech tags used in

[1] SpaCy 2.2.3 with en_core_web_sm, version 2.2.5.

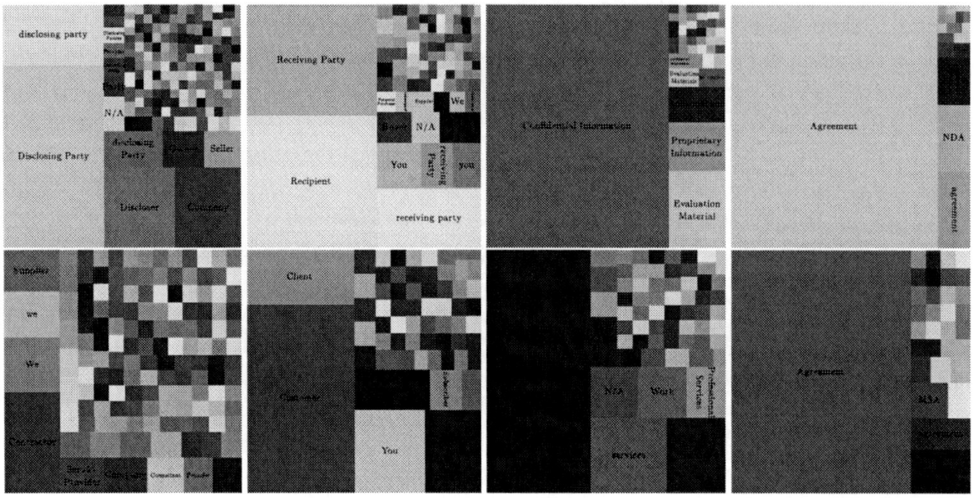

Figure 1: Squarified treemap of the contract slot annotations. The first row are NDA annotations: *disclosing party, receiving party, confidential information, agreement*. The second row are Services annotations: *service provider, service receiver, services, agreement*. Labels are not included on rare items.

Justeson and Katz (1995) but modified to exclude prepositions. A second pass is made where the coreference system checks noun phrases that were not joined with any others into a chain for subsequences of tokens that match the surface form of the chain. In these cases, the markable is joined into the chain.

4 Slot Scoring

To decide which slot a particular chain might represent requires a technique for scoring each chain C with respect to a particular slot type k. This section describes the components of a function S which does exactly that.

Rather than considering all co-referring argument pairs in a chain, as Chambers and Jurafsky (2009) did to assemble schemas, the system considers each link in a chain individually against each possible slot type. Chambers and Jurafsky (2009) were using an unsupervised technique, and thus did not have the extra information of a particular identified slot type; in other words, the slot type was implied by a strong signal between co-referring event arguments. Instead, this system associates the supervised slot class and features derived from each chain link.

During training, each chain is then represented by tuples composed of the slot type k, the mention surface form m, the dependency relation r between the mention and its parent p, which is also represented by its surface form—i.e. $\langle k, m, r, p\rangle$. In the case of a mention's immediate parent being a preposition—in a manner similar to the Stanford typed dependencies' "collapsed dependencies" (de Marneffe et al., 2006)—the relation is derived from the lemma of the preposition (e.g. "prep_in"); the parent is then the parent of the preposition.

For example, from a document where "Recipient" was annotated as *Receiving Party* and "Sensitive Documents" was annotated as *Confidential Information*, "The Recipient shall destroy all copies of the Sensitive Documents" renders three tuples:

- ⟨*RP, Recipient, subj, destroy*⟩,
- ⟨*none, copy, dobj, destroy*⟩, and
- ⟨*DP, Sensitive Documents, prep_of, copy*⟩.

The "none" class retains features to estimate independent probabilities.

Deviating from Chambers and Jurafsky (2008, 2009)'s goals for slot extraction, the system skips the constraint of looking strictly at verbs to extract such relationships. While contracts may tell stories, they are not themselves intended as narrative texts. Rather, it extracts $\langle k, m, r, p\rangle$-tuples for every mention of an entity, regardless of what r is.

In both training and slot identification, the system excludes any chains whose mention form is either "party" or "third party." This is because the meanings of these nouns are often conditioned on determiners and adjuncts with qualities that require more sophisticated handling of the coreference information entailed within them—e.g. "each party" vs "the party." These terms rarely point specifically and unambiguously to one party or the other, and thus do not help to determine the way a slot is referred to in a given text.

From there, the system estimates probabilities as:

$$P(t) = \frac{\text{counts}(t) + \alpha}{\sum_{\tau \in T} \text{counts}(\tau) + \alpha|T|} \quad (1)$$

where $\text{counts}(t)$ is the number of times feature tuple t appeared in the corpus, T is the set of all tuples of features observed for that particular model of the type comparable to that tuple, and α is a constant smoothing parameter.

Permutations of three features determine configurations of the system—in other words, which tuples are counted and included in the set T. This paper refers to each configuration by the feature tuple of the joint probability—e.g. the model that uses the relation r and parent form p features is referred to as the $P(k, r, p)$ model, as it yields the joint probability of a particular class k with the other two features.

Pointwise mutual information (pmi) of a tuple T is defined as:

$$pmi(t) = \log \frac{P(t)}{\prod_{i=0}^{|t|} P(t_i)} \quad (2)$$

The exact contents of T and, consequentially, the probabilities multiplied in the denominator will depend on the specific probability we are using. For example, for the $P(k, r, p)$ model, pmi is realized as:

$$pmi(k, r, p) = \log \frac{P(k, r, p)}{P(k)P(r)P(p)} \quad (3)$$

To prevent rare items from being weighted highly—often a flaw of pointwise mutual information—the system forces PMI to be 0.0 for joint items with counts less than six.

When observing new items in a new document, for a given chain C, the system measures how well it fits with a particular class k using S:

$$S(k, C) = \left(\sum_{f \in C} pmi(\langle k, f_0, ..., f_n \rangle) \right) - |C| \quad (4)$$

where $|C|$ is the length of the chain C. Since the system does not know the class yet, the extracted chains are composed of tuples $\langle m, r, p \rangle$. Thus, S evaluates the pmi of each link of the chain as if it is a member of k. Subtracting the length of the chain—i.e. $-|C|$—acts to penalize longer chains.

5 Slot Selection

A score alone is not enough to decide which chains correlate with which slot. To decide which chains actually represent each slot, the system employs Algorithm (1). This is composed of roughly two parts: a score for every chain as every possible slot and a selection procedure. The first loop scores every chain's association with every class; if a score is 0.0 or less, it is omitted from further consideration. These are sorted from highest score to lowest. The second loop, in the specified reverse score order, assigns chains to particular slots—only if the chain has not yet been assigned to a slot or the slot has not yet been assigned a chain. If a slot has no assignments made to it, it is left blank.

Algorithm 1: Slot selection over a document.

```
Data: coreference chains R extracted from
      a document as a sequence of
      ⟨m, r, p⟩ tuples
Result: assignment of a chain to each slot
scores = [] for slot k ∈ slots do
    for chain C_i ∈ coreference chains R do
        if S(k, C) > 0.0 then
            scores.append(⟨S(k, C), k, i⟩)
scores.sort()
scores.reverse()
slot_selections = {}
for score tuple ⟨s, k, i⟩ in scores do
    if k ∈ slot_selections.keys then
        #skip
    else if i ∈ slot_selections.values then
        #skip
    else
        slot_selections[k] = i
    if slot_selections.keys == slots then
        break
return slot_selections
```

Figure (2) shows an example of Algorithm (1) in practice. The table on the left of Figure (2) represents the full array of scores; these are stored and sorted, resulting in the list of 3-tuples in the center of the figure. The second loop of Algorithm (1) traverses these in order, assigning each chain to

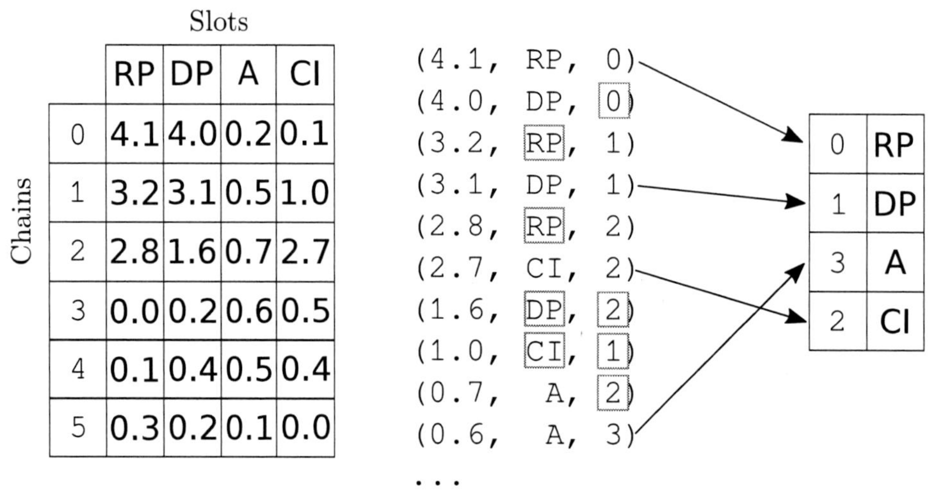

Figure 2: Illustration of an Example of Algorithm (1)

a slot if no constraints interfere. These are illustrated with boxes highlighting cause of interference. For example, the second tuple gives a high score to Chain 0 for the *disclosing party* slot; however, Chain 0 was already selected for *receiving party*, so this tuple is ignored. The next tuple—third from the top—gives a high score to Chain 1 for the *receiving party* slot, but *receiving party* has already been assigned Chain 0, so this tuple is also ignored. Next, the fourth tuple in the sequence assigns a high score for *disclosing party* to Chain 1. Nothing inhibits this, so Chain 1 is assigned to *disclosing party*. This process continues until all slots are assigned for the given document.

To clarify what has happened here, the assignment is of a chain—and specifically, of its surface form—that corresponds with the slot—and its mention form—in the document. Our annotations also correspond with such mention forms, and thus we evaluate based on whether the mention form identified by the system corresponds with the mention form annotated.

6 Results

Evaluation employs a holdout of 19 NDAs and 18 Services agreements against a total of 14 different models—7 for NDAs and 7 for Services—representing different ablations of the features considered.[2] The first ablation predicts class based on only one feature: either the mention $P(k, m)$, dependency relation label $P(k, r)$, or dependency parent $P(k, p)$. The second ablation predicts class based on pairs of features: mention and relation $P(k, m, r)$, mention and parent $P(k, m, p)$, and relation and parent $P(k, r, p)$. The third ablation considers all features jointly, yielding one model $P(k, m, r, p)$.

Table 2: Precision and recall scores for the model ablation study.

Joint prob. in PMI numer.	NDA Prec.	NDA Rec.	Services Prec.	Services Rec.
$P(k, m)$	0.882	0.882	0.639	0.582
$P(k, r)$	0.300	0.039	0.167	0.051
$P(k, p)$	0.691	0.500	0.302	0.241
$P(k, m, p)$	0.900	0.829	0.623	0.544
$P(k, m, r)$	0.855	0.855	0.625	0.570
$P(k, r, p)$	0.947*	0.934*	0.806*	0.734*
$P(k, m, r, p)$	0.901	0.842	0.623	0.544

At the first level of ablation, the mention-only model ($P(k, m)$) performs best on both NDAs and Services agreements. When other features are added to the mentions, however, the mention-

[2] A reviewer pointed out the limitations of this experimental configuration, as the absence of a third dev split lowers the rigorousness of these results. The absence of this further split is, in part, a consequence of the success of the system in production. There have been too few complaints from users about the slot system to justify further improvement.

related models ($P(k, m, p)$ and $P(k, m, r)$) generally decline in performance (NDA recall, Services precision and recall) or experience only small improvement (NDA precision) in performance.

However, when the two features from the first ablation that performed the most poorly are combined, they result in the highest performance over all, across both genres of contract.

7 Analysis

The results in both genres show an interesting trend—when the values are considered independently, mention is the strongest feature in terms of performance. However, this changes in the second level, where mention being excluded and only the dependency-parent pairs of mentions (i.e. $P(k, r, p)$) results in the strongest performance. This outperforms the results in the third ablation, leading to a decline in precision and recall. These trends hold in both the NDA and Services genres of contracts, albeit to different degrees.

The relationship between a candidate chain and the rest of the contract—as embodied through its dependency labels and parent—best embodies the slots, even more than the explicit mention of the label. Though this was somewhat predictable from prior literature, it has not been explicitly tested. It is actually striking that, in a genre of text where the slot itself is so often explicitly named that performance is higher when that explicit naming is omitted, and the decision itself is only directly connected to how a particular entity participates in a contract rather than what it is called.

Among the top performing models, errors were generally concentrated in the terms used to refer to either one of the parties, especially in the NDA results.

Examining the output more closely, mention form's harm to performance can be more readily teased apart. A particularly interesting NDA, "Software Group Inc. NDA" actually expresses a four-part relationship between the State of Minnesota, the State Court Administrator's Office, a contractor, and another company Tyler Technologies. These last three are defined as "Court," "Recipient," and "Tyler" respectively. The agreement seeks to protect, primarily, "Tyler trade secret information," which our annotators marked as the term for *confidential information*, and since it revolves around Tyler's trade secrets, "Tyler" is the *disclosing party*; "Recipient," in this case, is actually the *receiving party*.

Both the $P(k, r, p)$ and $P(k, m, r, p)$ models made errors on this document, but different errors that reveal some of their flaws. The $P(k, m, r, p)$ model missed slots that included "Tyler" in the name, as that explicit mention form was unpredictable in advance. Instead, the model guessed nothing for the *disclosing party* and "information" for *confidential information*. On the other hand, the $P(k, r, p)$ model was able to get both of those slots correct; however, it incorrectly guessed the other defined term "Court" to be the *receiving party*. This is due to a use of "Court" in a very similar manner to "Recipient" and is expressed in relationships very similar to other chains in prior texts labelled *receiving party*. For example, in defining exclusions to the *confidential information*, the contract states (emphasis added):

> "Tyler trade secret information" shall not include (i) any information which was known to or readily ascertainable by proper means by the *Court or Recipient* before being disclosed to the *Court or Recipient* by Tyler; (ii) any information which is or becomes available to the general public without fault or action of the *Court or Recipient...*

The relations expressed here for "Court" are ⟨Court, prep_by, ascertainable⟩, ⟨Court, prep_to, disclosed⟩, and ⟨Court, prep_of, action⟩, all relations indicative of a *receiving party* while "Recipient", in our model, only obtains three instances of ⟨Recipient, conj, Court⟩. A more sophisticated handling of the dependency tree may rectify this—retrieving the proper semantic relationship for "Recipient." Above all, while these are errors, none of them are embarrassing errors; their causes are highly transparent given the design of the model and suggest opportunities for further improvement.

In the Services agreements, the error rate was higher for all models. This may, in part, be due to data sparsity, since far fewer Services agreements were available for annotation. However, there were differences between the slots in each genre. NDAs preferred more generic mention forms—e.g. "Discloser"—while Services agreements usually have at least one company name as one of the parties, so this hurt the $P(k, m, r, p)$ model more than in the NDAs where it labelled at least one slot wrong in all but one evaluation contract (17 of 18) because the mention contained a proper noun. The $P(k, r, p)$ model also made some similar errors, but only in 6 of the 18 contracts. Additionally, Services agreements were more likely to have multiple mention forms for the same slot—for example, the "Apple - Developer Agreement" uses both "you" and "Apple Developer" for *service receiver*. Our algorithm is incapable of determining that both of those chains are part of the same slot—a limitation, but an intentional one, since opening up the possibility for slots to be multiple chains opens up tremendous room for error.

8 Conclusions

This paper demonstrates a technique for identifying participant slots in NDAs and Services agreements. The mention form alone obtains high performance, but performance declines as other features are added. This is likely because the specific mention form makes it harder to capture the highly common phenomenon of referring to a slot by a party name rather than the name of the role. Those features, dependency relation and dependency parent, on their own—excluding mention form—outperform mention form alone. This shows that what a participant does better reflects their role in a contract rather than the specific string used to refer to them.

There are a number of improvements that could be made to future systems. It is possible that a model that considers the disjunction of the mention form and relation-parent pairs could perform even better than those attempted here, which are strictly joint models. This would more tightly conform to Chambers and Jurafsky (2009)'s typed schemas system design. Further annotation of Services agreements would likely result in performance improvements, as well as better traversal of the parse tree, improved parsers for contract language, and architectures that allow for multiple mention form chains to be considered for a single slot to capture ambiguous cases.

Acknowledgements

Special thanks to our annotators Mariam Thomas, Krishna Shah, Jillian Watkins, and Dan Broderick, as well as Jonathan Herr, Viren Shah, and Ryan Mannion for their feedback on this work, as well as the reviewers who strengthened many of the aspects of this work as well as suggested some directions forward.

References

Arvind Agarwal, Laura Chiticariu, Poornima Chozhiyath Raman, Marina Danilevsky, Diman Ghazi, Ankush Gupta, Shanmukha Guttula, Yannis Katsis, Rajasekar Krishnamurthy, Yunyao Li, Shubham Mudgal, Vitobha Munigala, Nicholas Phan, Dhaval Sonawane, Sneha Srinivasan, Sudarshan R. Thitte, Mitesh Vasa, Ramiya Venkatachalam, Vinitha Yaski, and Huaiyu Zhu. 2021. Development of an Enterprise-Grade Contract Understanding System. In *Proceedings of the 2021 Conference of the North American Chapter of the Association for Computational Linguistics: Human Language Technologies: Industry Papers*, pages 222–229, Online. Association for Computational Linguistics.

Preethu Rose Anish, Abhishek Sainani, Nitin Ramrakhiyani, Sachin Pawar, Girish K Palshikar, and Smita Ghaisas. 2019. Towards Disambiguating Contracts for their Successful Execution - A Case from Finance Domain. In *Proceedings of the First Workshop on Financial Technology and Natural Language Processing*, pages 8–13, Macao, China.

Elliott Ash, Jeff Jacobs, Bentley MacLeod, Suresh Naidu, and Dominik Stammbach. 2020. Unsupervised extraction of workplace rights and duties from collective bargaining agreements. In *2020 International Conference on Data Mining Workshops (ICDMW)*, pages 766–774.

Collin F Baker, Charles J Fillmore, and John B Lowe. 1998. The Berkeley Framenet Project. In *Proceedings of the 36th Annual Meeting of the Association for Computational Linguistics and 17th International Conference on Computational Linguistics-Volume 1*, pages 86–90. Association for Computational Linguistics.

Niranjan Balasubramanian, Stephen Solderland, Mausam, and Oren Etzioni. 2013. Generating coherent event schemas at scale. In *Proceedings of the Conference on Empirical Methods in Natural Language Processing (EMNLP)*, pages 1721–1731. Association for Computational Linguistics.

Łukasz Borchmann, Dawid Wisniewski, Andrzej Gretkowski, Izabela Kosmala, Dawid Jurkiewicz, Łukasz Szałkiewicz, Gabriela Pałka, Karol Kaczmarek, Agnieszka Kaliska, and Filip Graliński. 2020. Contract discovery: Dataset and a few-shot semantic retrieval challenge with competitive baselines. In *Findings of the Association for Computational Linguistics: EMNLP 2020*, pages 4254–4268, Online. Association for Computational Linguistics.

Nathanael Chambers and Dan Jurafsky. 2008. Unsupervised learning of narrative event chains. In *Proceedings of the Conference of the Association for Computational Linguistics (ACL)*, pages 789–797. Association for Computational Linguistics.

Nathanael Chambers and Dan Jurafsky. 2009. Unsupervised learning of narrative schemas and their participants. In *Proceedings of the Proceedings of the Joint*

Conference of the 47th Annual Meeting of the Association for Computational Linguistics and the 4th International Joint Conference on Natural Language Processing of the Asian Federation for Natural Language Processing., pages 602–610. Association for Computational Linguistics.

Michael Curtotti and Eric C. McCreath. 2011. A Corpus of Australian Contract Language: Description, Profiling and Analysis. In *Proceedings of the 13th International Conference on Artificial Intelligence and Law*, ICAIL '11, pages 199–208, New York, NY, USA. ACM.

M. de Marneffe, B. MacCartney, and C.D. Manning. 2006. Generating typed dependency parses from phrase structure parses. In *Proceedings of the Language Resources and Evaluation Conference of the European Language Resources Association (LREC)*. Association for Computational Linguistics.

Ruka Funaki, Yusuke Nagata, Kohei Suenaga, and Shinsuke Mori. 2020. A Contract Corpus for Recognizing Rights and Obligations. In *Proceedings of the 12th Language Resources and Evaluation Conference*, pages 2045–2053, Marseille, France. European Language Resources Association.

Matthew Honnibal and Mark Johnson. 2015. An Improved Non-monotonic Transition System for Dependency Parsing. In *Proceedings of the 2015 Conference on Empirical Methods in Natural Language Processing*, pages 1373–1378, Lisbon, Portugal. Association for Computational Linguistics.

B. Jans, S. Bethard, I. Vulić, and M.F. Moens. 2012. Skip n-grams and ranking functions for predicting script events. In *Proceedings of the 13th Conference of the European Chapter of the Association for Computational Linguistics*, pages 336–344. Association for Computational Linguistics.

John Justeson and Slava Katz. 1995. Technical Terminology: Some Linguistic Properties and an Algorithm for Identification in Text. *Natural Language Engineering*, 1:9–.

Moniba Keymanesh, Micha Elsner, and Srinivasan Sarthasarathy. 2020. Toward domain-guided controllable summarization of privacy policies. In *Proceedings of the Natural Legal Language Processing Workshop 2020 co-located with the 26th ACM SIGKDD International Conference on Knowledge Discovery & Data Mining (KDD 2020), Virtual Workshop, August 24, 2020*, volume 2645 of *CEUR Workshop Proceedings*, pages 18–24. CEUR-WS.org.

Laura Manor and Junyi Jessy Li. 2019. Plain English Summarization of Contracts. In *Proceedings of the Natural Legal Language Processing Workshop 2019*, pages 1–11, Minneapolis, Minnesota. Association for Computational Linguistics.

Raymond Mooney and Gerald DeJong. 1985. Learning schemata for natural language processing. In *Proceedings of the 9th International Joint Conference on Artificial Intelligence (IJCAI)*, pages 681–687.

Nasrin Mostafazadeh, Nathanael Chambers, Xiaodong He, Devi Parikh, Dhruv Batra, Lucy Vanderwende, Pushmeet Kohli, and James Allen. 2016. A corpus and evaluation framework for deeper understanding of commonsense stories. *arXiv preprint arXiv:1604.01696*.

Karl Pichotta and Raymond J Mooney. 2014. Statistical script learning with multi-argument events. In *EACL*, volume 14, pages 220–229.

Roger Schank and Robert Abelson. 1977. *Scripts, plans, goals and understanding: An inquiry into human knowledge structures.* Lawrence Erlbaum, New Jersey.

Dan Simonson, Daniel Broderick, and Jonathan Herr. 2019. The Extent of Repetition in Contract Language. In *Proceedings of the Natural Legal Language Processing Workshop 2019*, pages 21–30, Minneapolis, Minnesota. Association for Computational Linguistics.

Dan Simonson and Anthony Davis. 2018. Narrative Schema Stability in News Text. In *Proceedings of COLING 2018*, Santa Fe, NM. Association for Computational Linguistics.

Daniel E. Simonson, Jonathan Herr, Joey T. Avant, Garen P. Riedel, and Daniel P. Broderick. 2020. Systems, Methods, and Computer Program Products for Slot Normalization of Text Data. U.S. Patent and Trademark Office, US10614157.

Noah Weber, Leena Shekhar, Niranjan Balasubramanian, and Nathanael Chambers. 2018. Hierarchical Quantized Representations for Script Generation. In *Proceedings of the 2018 Conference on Empirical Methods in Natural Language Processing*, pages 3783–3792, Brussels, Belgium. Association for Computational Linguistics.

Named Entity Recognition in Historic Legal Text: A Transformer and State Machine Ensemble Method

Fernando Trias*, Hongming Wang, Sylvain Jaume, Stratos Idreos

Harvard University

Abstract

Older legal texts are often scanned and digitized via Optical Character Recognition (OCR), which results in numerous errors. Although spelling and grammar checkers can correct much of the scanned text automatically, Named Entity Recognition (NER) is challenging, making correction of names difficult. To solve this, we developed an ensemble language model using a transformer neural network architecture combined with a finite state machine to extract names from English-language legal text. We use the US-based English language Harvard Caselaw Access Project for training and testing. Then, the extracted names are subjected to heuristic textual analysis to identify errors, make corrections, and quantify the extent of problems. With this system, we are able to extract most names, automatically correct numerous errors and identify potential mistakes that can later be reviewed for manual correction.

1 Introduction

Examining historical legal texts offers insight into the development of legal thinking and the practice of law. In order to facilitate computer processing, older legal texts are typically scanned from paper, microfilm or other physical media and then converted to text using Optical Character Recognition (OCR), which introduces numerous errors. Many of these errors can be corrected automatically using spelling and grammar correcting systems. However, the names of people, places and other proper names cannot be corrected easily, making the study of lawyers, judges and other people unreliable (Hamdi et al., 2020). One use of reliable names is inferring personal biases and connections that may affect outcomes (Clarke, 2018). In order to address this problem, names need to be accurately identified in the text and then corrected and standardized in a process often called Named Entity Disambiguation or NED (Yamada et al., 2016). Nonetheless, extracting accurate names is only part of the solution. In the future, organization names must also be extracted, and the respective roles must be identified.

The process of computationally extracting names from text is more formally called Named Entity Recognition (NER) and has been a difficult problem for many decades (Nadeau and Sekine, 2007). Furthermore, extracting names in legal text provides many domain-specific challenges (Bikel et al., 1999).

This paper describes a two-pronged approach for extracting the names of lawyers arguing cases:

(i) Extract the lawyer names from text using our ensemble model based on a neural network and a state machine.

(ii) Identify and correct transcription errors to uniquely identify lawyers.

Our system for extracting the names of lawyers in legal text uses a transformer-based neural network (Vaswani et al., 2017) feeding a finite state machine. After extraction, the identified names are subjected to several heuristic rules to identify errors, misspelled names and name variations in order to attempt to uniquely identify the lawyers named. When errors cannot be corrected automatically, such as in names with alternative spellings, the extent of the errors is quantified.

In order to develop, train and test this system, we used legal cases from the Harvard Caselaw Access Project (Harvard University, 2018). This project includes the complete text of decisions from United States courts dating back to the 1700s, with over 40 million pages of text spanning over 360 years. In our analysis, we only focused on cases from 1900 to 2010 in jurisdictions that were states as of 1900. Thus, Alaska and Hawaii were not considered. Because states and courts often have different

*Corresponding author. Email: fet535@g.harvard.edu, Harvard University, Cambridge, MA, USA

Natural Legal Language Processing Workshop 2021, pages 172–179
November 10, 2021.

reporting styles that have varied substantially over the years, we segmented most of our analysis by state and then by decade.

2 Related Work

In a typical case text in the United States, lawyers are only identified in the header section on the first page using a relatively standardized format, usually called the "party names". They are rarely mentioned by name in the decision text. A typical party names text would read as follows:

> David P. Sutton, Asst. Corp. Counsel, with whom Charles T. Duncan, Corp. Counsel, Hubert B. Pair, Principal Asst. Corp. Counsel, and Richard W. Barton, Asst. Corp. Counsel, were on the brief, for appellant.

The text is usually a single complex sentence where all principal people, firms and their roles are identified in a mostly standardized and stylized format. Because of the sentence's complexity, the text is sometimes difficult for non-lawyers and automated systems to decipher. The parsing problem is compounded because the style standards and norms vary by location and over time. In addition to containing spelling and transcription errors, words and names are sometimes given as initials, nicknames or abbreviations. All these types of things confound automated systems.

Thus, a solution to the problem can be divided into two parts: (i) extract the names from the text and (ii) standardize the name to identify individuals.

One solution to the the first part of extracting names is documented by Dozier et al. (2010), who describe their work at Westlaw (now part of Thomson Reuters) in 2000 identifying entities in US case law using Bayesian modeling (Dozier and Haschart, 2000). Their process extracts more than just names and involves parsing words in part by using a finite state machine that is specially tailored for each jurisdiction. More recently, Wang et al. (2020) propose a solution based on a neural network architecture that performs well across various domains, including legal text. In addition, Leitner et al. (2019) have developed a very promising system to perform NER in German legal texts that was built and trained on their own dataset (Leitner et al., 2020). This dataset was also used by Bourgonje et al. (2020) in their NER work based on BERT. These approaches apply generically to the entire legal text and are not focused on the grammatically challenging party names text. In any case, lack of a similar dataset for English prevents us from trying these approaches.

Our system differs from previous attempts in that it is an ensemble composed of a transformer-based neural network and a state machine rather than a single architecture. The state machine allows the inclusion of pre-established knowledge of the syntax and style of the named parties text, thereby increasing accuracy. This increased the accuracy by 10% compared with the state-of-the-art transformer-based FLERT model (Schweter and Akbik, 2021).

3 Historical vs. Contemporary Names

Contemporary texts are usually digitally encoded at creation and thus do not suffer from OCR-related errors. In addition, many anachronisms such as the practice of using just initials have been supplanted over time so that currently almost all lawyers use their full name and middle initial. Abbreviations of names, such as "Geo." for "George", have also fallen out of favor. This simplifies the identification of names in contemporary texts.

In addition, contemporary names can be cross referenced with a standardized list of names such as Westlaw, Bloomberg, Martindale-Hubbell and similar directories that contain an almost comprehensive list of lawyers that can be used to uniquely identify individuals in the United States. However, such lists are subject to licensing restrictions and they have limited data for lawyers from the distant past.

Another consideration is that the same name can be used at different times and in different places to refer to different people. Thus, a name is generally only unique for a specific time and place. A related problem is when the same name is used by a parent and child and only differentiated by the use of "Sr.", "Jr.", "II", or similar suffix, if at all. Yet another related problem is the use of an initial instead of a first name. This problem will be discussed in more detail in section 5.2.

4 Model Architecture & Experiments

Our source code is available at `https://harvard-almit.github.io/legal-nlp`. To summarize, we developed a new system that combines a transformer neural network with a finite state machine. In addition we trained an existing architecture with a subset of the Harvard Caselaw Access Project. These two were compared with the benchmark FLERT model.

- FLERT: Pre-trained general-purpose English-language NER model trained on CoNLL03.
- HCL-NER: Architecture based on FLERT but trained on Harvard Caselaw Access Project instead of CoNLL03.
- Ensemble: An ensemble model based on Flair's pre-trained PoS model and a custom state machine.

4.1 FLERT & Transformers

In recent years, numerous neural network models have been developed that can be used to perfrom NER, including Stanford NER, CMU, Flair, ELMo, BERT and many others. When we chose our benchmark to compare with our work, BERT was one candidate because it has been used extensively in a legal context, particularly for text classification by Chalkidis et al. (2020) in LEGAL-BERT. On the other hand, Flair (Akbik et al., 2018) is an easy-to-use Python framework that includes many pre-trained models, and provides more flexibility to extend our work at a later time. In addition to a BERT model, it includes it's own transformer-based model specifically trained for NER, which will serve as our benchmark, and another model for Parts of Speech (POS), which will be used by the ensemble model. Flair's NER model is called FLERT (Schweter and Akbik, 2021) and uses GLoVe (Pennington et al., 2014) global vectors for word embedding along with a Tranformer architecture based on XLM-RoBERTa (Conneau et al., 2020). Although FLERT performs well in ordinary text including the decision text, it does get tripped up by the party names text in the headers of legal decisions that name lawyers. To see why, consider the following example:

> Mr. Thomas A. McHarg, Messrs. Martin, Newcomer & Tinglof, Mr. Victor E. Keyes, attorney general, Mr. Bentley M. McMullin, assistant, Mr. Charles Roach, deputy, for defendant in error.

FLERT will return "Thomas A" and "Charles Roach". It misses McHarg's last name, "Victor E. Keyes" and "Bently M. McMullin". Thus, even though FLERT is tantalizing close, it is not sufficient if it cannot parse this relatively simple example.

Tag	Precision	Recall	F_1
LOC	0.9399	0.9434	0.9416
ORG	0.9014	0.8983	0.8998
PER	0.9600	0.9667	0.9634

Table 1: Validation results for HCL-NER model.

4.2 HCL-NER Model

We hypothesized that one reason that FLERT does not perform well is that it is trained using the CoNLL03 dataset (Tjong Kim Sang and De Meulder, 2003), which consists of Reuters news stories from 1996 to 1997. Because the style of this training text is different from the style of text we aim to parse, we decided to train a new model with an identical architecture to FLERT, but using the Harvard Caselaw dataset instead of CoNLL03. We call this model HCL-NER. Because it duplicates the FLERT architecture, HCL-NER employs a multilingual XLM-RoBERTa (XLM-R) transformer-based model and GLoVe embeddings. The training, test and validation data comprised of 1000 cases selected randomly from the Harvard Caselaw Access Project. Of the 1000 cases, 100 were be reserved for development, 300 for training, 300 for testing and 300 for final validation of the model. These cases were parsed using an early version of the ensemble model described below and then manually reviewed and corrected. Three tags were used for tagging:

- LOC: A location, such as a city or state
- ORG: An organization, company or law firm
- PER: A person

Like FLERT, the model was trained using Stochastic Gradient Descent (SGD) for 150 epochs with the objective of maximizing the F_1 score (Sasaki, 2007). As will be shown later, this model performed slightly better than FLERT but did not perform as well as the ensemble model described below. We suspect that using a larger number of test cases in the future may improve performance.

The results of the HCL-NER model validation for each tag for are summarized in table 1.

Figure 1: Data pipeline for ensemble model

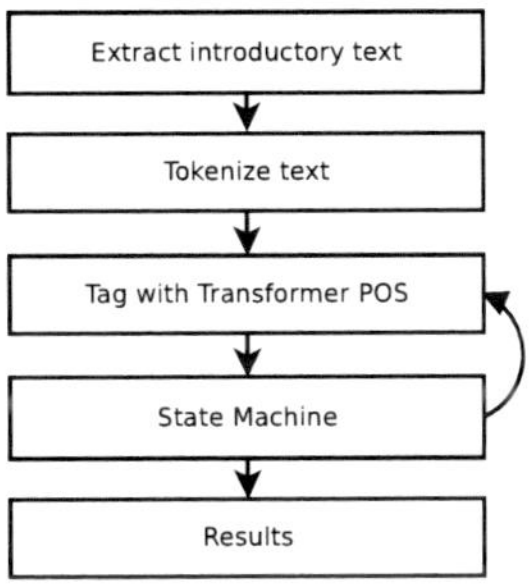

4.3 Ensemble Model

In addition to the HCL-NER model, we created an ensemble model that uses a pre-trained transformer to parse a sentence in order to identify Parts of Speech (PoS). That output is fed to a custom finite state machine that will represent knowledge of the writing style in order to identify the people, firms and roles of the individuals. Figure 1 shows a high level diagram of the ensemble. Although this paper focuses only on the names of people, the framework for identifying the firms and roles is also included, but not tested. This model performed the best of the various models tested.

The ensemble model consists of three distinct stages.

(i) Tokenize the text into distinct symbols and words.

(ii) Tag the tokens with the Part of Speech (PoS).

(iii) Pass the PoS and tokens to the state machine to extract items.

Tokenization is performed using Flair's default tokenizer, which is based on the 'segtok' library. PoS tagging is performed with Flair's standard PoS model, which is based on Long Short-Term Memory (LSTM) for sequence tagging along with a Conditional Random Field (CRF) layer (LSTM-CRF) (Huang et al., 2015). It identifies a number of different parts of speech. Of these, we are interested in:

- NN: Noun, singular or mass; in addition, Flair provides finer grain identification, such as NNP for a proper noun, NNPS for a plural proper noun, etc.
- ',' and '.': Punctuation symbols.
- IN: Preposition or subordinating conjunction.
- CC: Coordinating conjunction.
- Other: Other PoS elements are ignored for now, but they may become useful if the state machine is extended to identify the person's role and other data included in the text.

4.4 State Machine

In it's simplest form, the state machine transitions from one state to another based on the current state, the next token PoS, the token text (in the case of "Mr.'', "Hon.", etc.). However, there are a few cases where transitions will also look ahead several tokens to disambiguate particular esoteric cases. When the state transitions, it returns the text up to the transition marked with the state before the transition. The table 2 summarizes the transitions (including look-ahead exceptions in the notes). In the table, transitions are processed from top to bottom.

4.5 Abbreviations & Nicknames

Listed below are the three types of abbreviations that concern us. Each of these will be handled separately.

- Use of an initial instead of first name
- Abbreviations of words and titles (such as "Asst.", "Atty.", etc.)
- Abbreviations of names (such as "Geo.", "Thos.". etc.)

The simplest of these are the last two: the abbreviations of names, words and titles. These are identified by a period. When encountering a period, the previous word is then looked up in a table of known and typical abbreviations. If it is found, then the period is ignored since it does not mark the end of a sentence and the abbreviation is substituted with the corresponding word or name. Many databases of abbreviations exist for this purpose. In our example implementation, we used the list from Wiktionary (Wikitionary, 2021).

Nicknames are identified similarly to abbreviations. Once a name has been identified, the first name is looked up in a database of known basic nicknames and the formal name is substituted. In our implementation, the list from Northern and Nelson (2011) is used. However, care is required because in some cases, a nickname can be the actual name or can be used to differentiate two people with the same name.

Start State	Token	Condition	New State	Notes
MISC	NN	Match Mr. Hon. etc.	NAME	
MISC	NN	State name?	LOCATION	
MISC	NN	Abbreviation?	NAME	
MISC	NN	Modifier?	MISC	
MISC	NN	Starts with capital?	NAME	
MISC	DT	Starts with capital?	NAME	
NAME	NN	Abbreviation?	NAME	
NAME	‘,’	Look forward for Jr Sr?	NAME	
NAME	‘,’	Corp name?	COMPANY	
NAME	‘,’	City state?	LOCATION	
NAME	‘,’		MISC	End of name
NAME	CC	Is it ‘&’?	FIRM	
NAME	‘.’	Single or double initial?	NAME	
NAME	IN		MISC	End of name
FIRM	NN		FIRM	
FIRM	‘,’		FIRM	
FIRM	CC	Not ‘&’?	MISC	Firms use &
FIRM	Other		MISC	
COMPANY	NN		COMPANY	
COMPANY	Other		MISC	

Table 2: State transitions for ensemble model, one token at a time.

5 Performance Analysis

In this section, we evaluate the performance of our system regarding misspelled names and the use of initials instead of names and finally present a comparison analysis.

5.1 Misspelled Names

For all models, after a name has been extracted, it must be evaluated for possible misspellings due to OCR, transcription or other errors. These accidental misspellings are difficult to distinguish from deliberate alternate spellings. For example,“Clair”, “Claire”, and “Clare” are all possible misspellings of the same name, or they could be deliberate alternate spellings referring to different names. In the past, it was not uncommon for people to use various spellings for the same name depending on local conventions. For this reason, correcting for spelling mistakes in names is tricky and may produce more errors than it fixes if not done carefully. The problem of automatically adjusting misspelled names has been researched since at least the 1920s, beginning with Soundex, a system for encoding words phonetically. Famously, in the 1970s, the New York State Identification and Intelligence System (NYSIIS) (Silbert, 1970) attempted to solve this problem for criminal databases. Snae (2007) summarizes the results of many other name spelling matching systems, including NYSIIS. According to results from that paper, the Double Metaphone algorithm developed by Philips (Philips, 2000) for English seems to perform well in a variety of situations and especially with names.

The Double Metaphone algorithm works by creating a phonetic encoding of a word. To do so, it has a simplified alphabet of 16 consonants plus vowels. The algorithm is a sequence of steps that involve dropping and converting letters until the final encoding is achieved. For example, it begins by dropping duplicates and silent first letters using a few heuristic rules. Thus, for the first step, “written” becomes “riten”. A number of subsequent steps convert letter combinations with similar sounds to the same code. In this way, “sack” becomes “sak” and “enough” becomes “enouf”. Finally, all vowels except the first are removed. Thus “enough” is finally encoded as “enf”. In the example for “Clair”, “Claire” and “Clare” in the paragraph above, all encodings would resolve to “clr” and the algorithm would determine that they are all potentially the same name.

We used the Double Metaphone to match names in the database in order to count the number of potential misspellings and yield an estimate of the

Figure 2: Distribution of worst-case potentially misspelled names over time

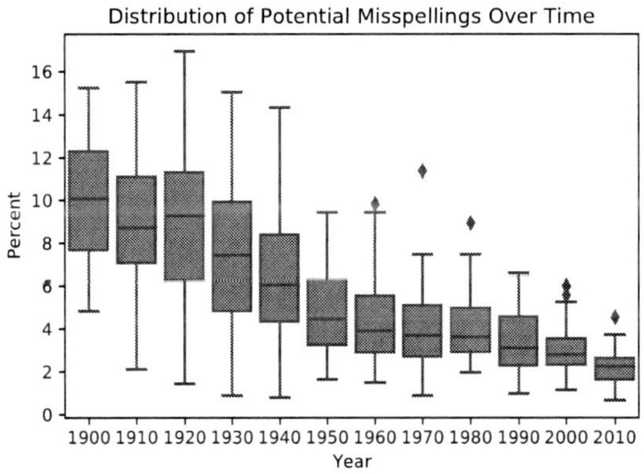

worst-case scenario. For each state and decade, we created a list of all unique names in the dataset. Then we evaluated the Double Metaphone encoding for all names in each list and counted the number of differently spelled names that evaluate to the same encoding, using that number to calculate a percent of total names that are potentially duplicates. The boxplot in Figure 2 shows the distribution of this percent for each state and decade, which shows that the percent of potential misspellings is declining over time. This is expected due to the adoption of entirely digital creation and storage of data and the degradation of older original paper sources that result in more errors for older material.

5.2 Use of Initials Instead of Names

Another difficult problem is resolving the use of an initial as the first name. Although this was very common in some jurisdictions decades ago, the problem is almost non-existent today as shown by Table 3. The table compares the use of initials in 1900 to the use of initials in 2010. Massachusetts, the worst offender in 1900 at 79%, now has approximately only 0.1% use of initials. The highest level of current usage of initials is Kansas at 0.7%.

The problem with initials arises when they are ambiguous and could refer to one or more lawyers. Unfortunately, this problem is impossible to quantify without having a comprehensive list of lawyer names. However, a rough estimate of the extent of the problem can be calculated by looking at the names and seeing if the use of initials could refer to several lawyers whose full names are used elsewhere. In other words, we load up all the names and see if the names with only initials can match full names. Over time, different lawyers could in fact use the same initials as lawyers who practiced before, despite being different people. To mitigate this problem, the data was divided into states and then decades. Thus the comparison was made for every state and every decade. The results for the 10 worst state/decade combinations are shown in table 4.

Table 3: Top 10 states by percent of lawyers using initials in 1900 vs. 2010

	% Names	
State	**1900**	**2010**
Massachusetts	79.0	0.1
Indiana	56.3	0.3
Maine	54.5	0.2
Georgia	48.1	0.4
Kansas	46.0	0.7
Arkansas	45.0	0.7
New Mexico	44.4	0.3
Vermont	44.0	0.3
Arizona	43.5	0.4
Wyoming	43.3	0.2

Table 4: Worst 10 states from 1900 to 2010 for using ambiguous initials shown as a percent of total initials used.

State	**Year**	**Ambg. init.**	**Total**	**% Total**
Oregon	1940	2	1992	0.1
Indiana	1900	8	8763	0.1
Louisiana	1930	5	5612	0.1
Miss.	1940	2	2496	0.1
N. Carolina	1910	3	3882	0.1
Conn.	1900	1	1374	0.1
Oregon	1930	2	2797	0.1
Montana	1940	1	1399	0.1
Utah	1920	1	1542	0.1
Texas	1930	9	14979	0.1

Even though this is not the complete picture, it is possible to estimate that the problem of using an initial for the first name may not be too serious when identifying unique lawyers.

5.3 Comparison

Model performance is compared using 10 random cases from each state, for a total of 490 cases. Each of these texts is reviewed manually to extract the names. First, in order to simplify evaluation and make it more explainable, the accuracy is measured as the percent of the test cases where the

Table 5: Simple accuracy comparison for the various model tested

Method	Errors	Total	Accuracy
FLERT	154	490	68%
HCL-NER	132	490	73%
Ensemble	107	490	78%

Table 6: Confusion matrices for various models tested

Method	TP	FP	FN	Prec.	Rec.
FLERT	622	81	159	0.88	0.80
HCL-NER	661	64	120	0.91	0.84
Ensemble	692	49	89	0.93	0.88

Columns are calculated as: *TP*, True positives; *FP*, False positives; *FN*, False negatives; *Prec.*, Precision: $\frac{TP}{TP+FP}$; *Rec.*, Recall or sensitivity: $\frac{TP}{TP+FN}$

model correctly identified all names. Next, recall and precision are calculated for all test cases. Table 5 summarizes the accuracy results. The ensemble model outperformed both FLERT trained on CoNLL03 and HCL-NER trained on a subset of the Harvard Caselaw Access Project.

Table 6 summarizes the confusion matrices for all test cases, with the following measures:

> *True positives (TP)*: Count of names in the original text correctly identified by the method.
>
> *False positives (FP)*: Count of identified names that were not valid names.
>
> *False negatives (FN)*: Count of names in the original text that were not identified by the method.
>
> *Recall (Rec.) or sensitivity*: True positives divided by all real positives (true positives plus false negatives). This is the portion of actual names that are correctly identified.

Both recall and precision for the ensemble models are improved relative to the FLERT benchmark. Thus, the ensemble model is able to more accurately identify all the names in the text and is also less likely to misidentify names. Although more true positives were identified, the biggest gains were in substantially fewer false negatives and positives. In addition, even though the HCL-NER model was not trained with a large dataset, it also is an improvement over the FLERT model.

6 Conclusion

We propose an ensemble model based on a transformer neural network architecture and a state machine for extracting names from party names in US case law text. The ensemble model improved the accuracy by approximately 10% from the FLERT model. However, once names were extracted, the problem of correcting for errors, misspellings and ambiguities could be fully automated. A number of techniques were discussed that help to quantify the extent of the problem and identify potential data quality issues. Our analysis showed that the number of errors in some jurisdictions could exceed 15% in the decades before 1950, but that this number has been declining significantly over time.

Acknowledgements

We would like to thank the Harvard Caselaw Access Project for providing us with support and access to their database.

References

Alan Akbik, Duncan Blythe, and Roland Vollgraf. 2018. Contextual string embeddings for sequence labeling. In *COLING 2018, 27th international conference on computational linguistics*, pages 1638–1649.

Daniel M Bikel, Richard Schwartz, and Ralph M Weischedel. 1999. An Algorithm that Learns What's in a Name. *Machine Learning*, 34:211–231.

Peter Bourgonje, Anna Breit, Maria Khvalchik, Victor Mireles, Julian Moreno Schneider, Artem Revenko, and Georg Rehm. 2020. Automatic induction of named entity classes from legal text corpora. In *ASLD 2020 – advances in semantics and linked data: Joint workshop proceedings from ISWC 2020. International workshop on artificial intelligence for legal documents (AI4LEGAL-2020), november 2-3, Athens/Virtual, greece*, pages 1–11. CEUR Workshop Proceedings.

Ilias Chalkidis, Manos Fergadiotis, Prodromos Malakasiotis, Nikolaos Aletras, and Ion Androutsopoulos. 2020. LEGAL-BERT: The Muppets straight out of Law School. In *Findings of the Association for Computational Linguistics: EMNLP 2020*, pages 2898–2904, Online. Association for Computational Linguistics.

Jessica A. Clarke. 2018. Explicit Bias. *Northwestern University Law Review*, 113:505.

Alexis Conneau, Kartikay Khandelwal, Naman Goyal, Vishrav Chaudhary, Guillaume Wenzek, Francisco

Guzmán, Edouard Grave, Myle Ott, Luke Zettlemoyer, and Veselin Stoyanov. 2020. Unsupervised Cross-lingual Representation Learning at Scale. In *Proceedings of the 58th Annual Meeting of the Association for Computational Linguistics*, pages 8440–8451, Online. Association for Computational Linguistics.

Christopher Dozier and Robert Haschart. 2000. Automatic Extraction and Linking of Person. *Recherche dInformation Assistee parOrdinateur*, page 18.

Christopher Dozier, Ravikumar Kondadadi, Marc Light, Arun Vachher, Sriharsha Veeramachaneni, and Ramdev Wudali. 2010. Named entity recognition and resolution in legal text. In *Semantic processing of legal texts*, pages 27–43. Springer.

Ahmed Hamdi, Axel Jean-Caurant, Nicolas Sidère, Mickaël Coustaty, and Antoine Doucet. 2020. Assessing and Minimizing the Impact of OCR Quality on Named Entity Recognition. In *Digital Libraries for Open Knowledge*, Lecture Notes in Computer Science, pages 87–101, Cham. Springer International Publishing.

Harvard University. 2018. Caselaw Access Project. Retrieved 4 June 2020 from http://case.law.

Zhiheng Huang, Wei Xu, and Kai Yu. 2015. Bidirectional LSTM-CRF Models for Sequence Tagging. *arXiv:1508.01991 [cs]*. ArXiv: 1508.01991.

Elena Leitner, Georg Rehm, and Julian Moreno-Schneider. 2019. Fine-Grained Named Entity Recognition in Legal Documents. In Maribel Acosta, Philippe Cudré-Mauroux, Maria Maleshkova, Tassilo Pellegrini, Harald Sack, and York Sure-Vetter, editors, *Semantic Systems. The Power of AI and Knowledge Graphs*, volume 11702, pages 272–287. Springer International Publishing, Cham. Series Title: Lecture Notes in Computer Science.

Elena Leitner, Georg Rehm, and Julian Moreno-Schneider. 2020. A Dataset of German Legal Documents for Named Entity Recognition. In *Proceedings of the 12th Language Resources and Evaluation Conference*, pages 4478–4485, Marseille, France. European Language Resources Association.

David Nadeau and Satoshi Sekine. 2007. A Survey of Named Entity Recognition and Classification. *Lingvisticae Investigationes*, 30.

Carlton T Northern and Michael L Nelson. 2011. An unsupervised approach to discovering and disambiguating social media profiles. In *Proceedings of mining data semantics workshop*.

Jeffrey Pennington, Richard Socher, and Christopher Manning. 2014. Glove: Global Vectors for Word Representation. In *Proceedings of the 2014 Conference on Empirical Methods in Natural Language Processing (EMNLP)*, pages 1532–1543, Doha, Qatar. Association for Computational Linguistics.

Lawrence Philips. 2000. The double metaphone search algorithm. *C/C++ Users Journal*, 18(6):38–43.

Yutaka Sasaki. 2007. The truth of the F-measure. *Teach Tutor Mater*.

Stefan Schweter and Alan Akbik. 2021. FLERT: Document-Level Features for Named Entity Recognition. *arXiv:2011.06993 [cs]*. ArXiv: 2011.06993.

Jeffrey M. Silbert. 1970. The World's First Computerized Criminal-Justice Information-Sharing System - The New York State Identification and Intelligence System (NYSIIS). *Criminology*, 8:107.

Chakkrit Snae. 2007. A Comparison and Analysis of Name Matching Algorithms. *World Academy of Science, Engineering and Technology*, 25:6.

Erik F. Tjong Kim Sang and Fien De Meulder. 2003. Introduction to the CoNLL-2003 shared task: language-independent named entity recognition. In *Proceedings of the seventh conference on Natural language learning at HLT-NAACL 2003 - Volume 4*, CONLL '03, pages 142–147, USA. Association for Computational Linguistics.

Ashish Vaswani, Noam Shazeer, Niki Parmar, Jakob Uszkoreit, Llion Jones, Aidan N. Gomez, Lukasz Kaiser, and Illia Polosukhin. 2017. Attention Is All You Need. *Proceedings of the International Conference on Neural Information Processing Systems (NeurIPS)*.

Jing Wang, Mayank Kulkarni, and Daniel Preotiuc-Pietro. 2020. Multi-Domain Named Entity Recognition with Genre-Aware and Agnostic Inference. In *Proceedings of the 58th Annual Meeting of the Association for Computational Linguistics*, pages 8476–8488, Online. Association for Computational Linguistics.

Wikitionary. 2021. Abbreviations for English given names. Retrieved on 30 June 2021 from https://en.wiktionary.org/wiki.

Ikuya Yamada, Hiroyuki Shindo, Hideaki Takeda, and Yoshiyasu Takefuji. 2016. Joint Learning of the Embedding of Words and Entities for Named Entity Disambiguation. *arXiv:1601.01343 [cs]*. ArXiv: 1601.01343.

Summarization of German Court Rulings

Ingo Glaser* and **Sebastian Moser*** and **Florian Matthes**
Technical University of Munich
ingo.glaser@tum.de
sebastian.moser@in.tum.de
matthes@in.tum.de

Abstract

Historically speaking, the German legal language is widely neglected in NLP research, especially in summarization systems, as most of them are based on English newspaper articles. In this paper, we propose the task of automatic summarization of German court rulings. Due to their complexity and length, it is of critical importance that legal practitioners can quickly identify the content of a verdict and thus be able to decide on the relevance for a given legal case. To tackle this problem, we introduce a new dataset consisting of 100k German judgments with short summaries. Our dataset has the highest compression ratio among the most common summarization datasets. German court rulings contain much structural information, so we create a pre-processing pipeline tailored explicitly to the German legal domain. Additionally, we implement multiple extractive as well as abstractive summarization systems and build a wide variety of baseline models. Our best model achieves a ROUGE-1 score of 30.50. Therefore with this work, we are laying the crucial groundwork for further research on German summarization systems.

1 Introduction

Most modern summarization systems are built around a handful of datasets predominantly collected from newspapers. In recent years many researchers saw the need to introduce different datasets to the summarization domain such as ArXiv/PubMed (Cohan et al., 2018), XSum (Narayan et al., 2018), or datasets from the legal domain like BigPatent (Sharma et al., 2019) and BillSum (Kornilova and Eidelman, 2019). As the performance of data-driven systems is highly impacted by the quality and size of the dataset used, we introduce a new dataset for the German legal domain, more specifically a collection of court rulings.

Court rulings are long documents clarifying legal interpretations in a matter of dispute. Due to their complexity and length, it is of critical importance that legal practitioners can quickly identify the content of the verdict and thus decide on the relevance for their legal case.

German court rulings have three basic parts. First, the tenor denotes the explicit decision a judge has made. Second, the main body of a judgment is divided into the facts and the reasoning, explaining why the judge came to their conclusion given the specific preconditions. Third, the rubrum contains meta-information, i.e. previous instances, the most important legal texts referenced, and the guiding principle. The guiding principle shortly summarizes why the specific decision was made and therefore is extremely useful for legal practitioners. This high-level summarization allows them to quickly assess whether the court ruling is important for them or not.

Not all of those pieces of information are found in all verdicts. Especially the guiding principle is only added by the judge or a legal publisher if the judgment contains an important legal decision. A lot of expert knowledge and time is necessary to create this summarization, which is why we want to automate this task. Therefore, with this paper our contributions are the following:

1. A large scale collection of German court rulings for summarization with 100k verdicts
2. A pre-processing pipeline specifically tailored to German court rulings
3. Multiple extractive as well as abstractive summarization models tailored to our dataset

All models described here are implemented in PyTorch. All code for this paper is openly available on GitHub[1].

*Equal contribution

[1]at github.com/sebimo/LegalSum

Natural Legal Language Processing Workshop 2021, pages 180–189
November 10, 2021. ©2021 Association for Computational Linguistics

2 Related Work

The literature differentiates two base approaches to text summarization: (1) extractive and (2) abstractive summarization. In the extractive case, sentences or tokens are copied and extracted from the given text and form a summarization. Contrary, the abstractive summarization system is creating a summary word by word, thus it is not dependent on the words and information used in the verdict. This is why abstractive summarization is often referred to as natural language generation (NLG).

Most commonly, extractive summarization systems use a hierarchical document representation, i.e. words are combined into sentences, sentences are aggregated into documents. Various different architectures with convolutional neural networks (CNN), recurrent neural networks (RNN), and attention mechanisms (Nallapati et al., 2017; Cheng and Lapata, 2016; Jadhav and Rajan, 2018) are used to extract the most important sentences. More recent approaches focus on transformer architectures (Liu and Lapata, 2019; Zhang et al., 2019; Xu et al., 2020; Zhou et al., 2020) and investigate the level of extraction (Xu et al., 2020; Zhou et al., 2020; Jadhav and Rajan, 2018) by selecting words or n-grams instead of whole sentences.

The most common way to tackle abstractive summarization is to use an encoder-decoder structure. Hereby the encoder is aggregating the information from the text and the decoder is a conditional language model producing the words in the summary. Hierarchical document representations are again important and similar modeling approaches are used (Nallapati et al., 2016; Gehrmann et al., 2018; Li et al., 2018; Chopra et al., 2016). In abstractive summarization, there is also a shift towards transformers in recent years (Liu and Lapata, 2019; Dong et al., 2019; Qi et al., 2020; Lewis et al., 2020; Raffel et al., 2020; Zhang et al., 2020).

Many different techniques were found to be useful for summarization. Pointer Networks (Vinyals et al., 2015) allow the selection of words from the input text and are used in extractive (Jadhav and Rajan, 2018) as well as abstractive summarization (See et al., 2017). Some papers use templates or salient sentences in the word generation process (Cao et al., 2018; Bae et al., 2019; Chen and Bansal, 2018). Others try to discourage the system from repeating certain phrases by introducing special loss function such as coverage (See et al., 2017) or novelty (Kryściński et al., 2018).

Especially long documents are challenging and thus multiple approaches try to tackle this problem e.g. by introducing multiple encoders to find a hierarchical representation of the text (Celikyilmaz et al., 2018) or introducing the discourse structure into a hierarchical attention model (Cohan et al., 2018).

3 Dataset

3.1 Dataset acquisition

The dataset consists of verdicts from the Dr. Otto Schmidt publisher and judgments which were scraped from gesetze-bayern.de and justiz.nrw.de. All those verdicts were then automatically translated to a unified JSON format. It contains the meta-information about the verdict: id (unique identifier), date, court, normchain (the most important legal texts referenced), all the referenced norms, the previous instances, mentioned keywords, and verdict title. All the referenced norms are stored with a unique placeholder (__normxyz__), which is used in the text body of the verdict to quickly identify a norm during training. Norms and their placeholder are stored with the verdict and the norm can be reintroduced later on. Additionally, the text segments of the verdict (tenor, facts, reasoning, guiding principle) are stored sentence by sentence, as the sentence segmentation is non-trivial for German legal documents as identified by Glaser et al. (2021). We used their model to automatically segment the verdicts into sentences.

Not every piece of information was directly accessible in the original data formats. For example, the HMTL format of justiz.nrw.de does not contain any annotations regarding referenced norms in the texts, thus it was necessary to extract them. In other cases, the main body of the text was not segmented into facts and reasoning. It was then segmented based on enumeration symbols, headlines, and similar heuristics.

To ensure high data quality, each such processing step was thoroughly tested via unit tests, and the dataset was manually examined by the authors through a graphical user interface. Incorrectly processed verdicts were then corrected. After filtering verdicts that did not have a guiding principle or a text body, we collected a dataset of 100.018 different verdicts with summarizations. Finally, we divided the datasets into a train (80%), validation (10%), and test set (10%).

3.2 Dataset statistics

We collected all data from German court rulings, such that it can be used in other research such as argument mining, prediction of judgments, etc. The oldest verdict is from 1955, the newest from the end of 2020, but the majority of verdicts were issued between 2010 and 2020. 64% of the verdicts are based on at least one previous court ruling, i.e. they might be based on text which is not directly available to us and some details might be omitted or only referenced to. It is possible to infer information about the most common legal areas by looking at the norms from the normchain. The verdicts most commonly deal with civil cases (BGB, ZPO), administrative jurisdiction (VwGO), financial jurisdiction with mostly income tax law (EStG), or social jurisdiction with mostly asylum law (AsylG, AufenthG).

In comparison to other summarization datasets (see Table 1), our dataset contains documents that are on average 3-4 times longer than the most common summarization datasets CNN, Daily Mail, and NYT. It is comparable with the PubMed and ArXic datasets considering the length of the documents but has the highest compression ratio of all datasets listed. The compression ratio is defined as the document length divided by the summary length. Based on this compression ratio, our dataset is comparable to the BigPatent dataset, another legal dataset for the English language. The datasets' average number of 110 sentences is compressed down to on average 2,9 summary sentences.

To denote the overlap between the summary and the text body novelty (See et al., 2017) quantifies the percentage of n-grams from the guiding principle not found in the text. 13.1% of the guiding principles share all their 1-grams with the text body, whereas 20.4% of the summaries have a 5-grams novelty of 100%. This is an indicator that the summaries have some level of abstraction and are not directly copied from the text body. Abstractive or extractive approaches that select words might thus have an advantage on our dataset.

4 Pre-processing

Given the JSON format described above, we build a pre-processing pipeline specifically tailored to the summarization of German verdicts. Sentences from the guiding principle, facts, and reasoning are first split into tokens on spaces and dots. To reduce the overall complexity, each token is then converted to lower case in order to decrease the number of unique tokens. This is mainly to remove possible mixed-cased words at the beginning of sentences as the meaning of a word is in our case clear given its context. Afterwards norm placeholders in the text are replaced with a generic <*norm*> token, numeric tokens with <*num*> and tokens which were anonymized (via "xx", "..", etc.) by <*anon*>, to infer some semantic meaning for them via word embeddings. Then any tokens within parentheses were removed, as in most cases these only contain references to other legal documents. Afterward, all special characters and any enumeration symbols were removed, as German verdicts contain a lot of structural information. Finally, each token is then mapped to a unique identifier.

After all those processing steps, the whole dataset contains around one million unique tokens, thus we only use tokens that appear at least 100 times in the corpus resulting in a total number of tokens around 50.000. Although this vocabulary size seems rather small, it is comparable to other methods (See et al., 2017) and was necessary to reduce the hardware requirements for the neural networks. All tokens which were not selected are replaced by an <*unk*> token in the pre-processed text. Subword-based tokenization would be one option to removing unknown tokens, but we decided against it as only 2.7% of the text is replaced with <*unk*>. We pre-trained GloVe embeddings (Pennington et al., 2014) on those tokens.

5 Method

The basic building blocks of our models, namely CNNs, RNNs, and the attention mechanisms can be defined by their transformations on a sequence of embeddings $X = x_1, \dots, x_N; x_i \in \mathbb{R}^d$. For convenience, given a matrix $M \in \mathbb{R}^{n \times m}$ we define $M_{i,:}$ as the i-th row and $M_{:,j}$ as the j-th column vector. The general structure of both model types can be seen in Figure 1 and will be further explained in the respective subsections.

Formally, a 1-dimensional CNN transforms a sequence $X \in \mathbb{R}^{N \times d}$ into the sequence $Y \in \mathbb{R}^{N \times e}$ by[2]

$$
\begin{aligned}
Y_{i,e_j} &= b_{e_j} \\
&+ \Big(\sum_{k=0}^{d-1} w_{e_j,k} \star X_{:,k}\Big)_i
\end{aligned}
\tag{1}
$$

[2]Definition from pytorch.org

Table 1: Dataset statistics from Cohan et al. (2018) expanded with compression ratio and our dataset. Length denotes the number of tokens. Compression is the percentage of words in the summary compared to the document length. Newsroom and BigPatent statistics taken from Sharma et al. (2019) and XSum from Narayan et al. (2018).

Dataset	#docs	avg. doc length	avg. summary length	compression ratio
CNN	92k	656	43	15.3
Daily Mail	219k	693	52	13.3
NYT	655k	530	38	13.9
PubMed	133k	3016	203	14.9
ArXiv	215k	4938	220	22.4
Newsroom	1212k	751	45	16.7
BigPatent	1341k	3573	117	30.5
XSum	227k	431	23	18.7
Legal	100k	2422	75	32.3

with $\star$ being the cross-correlation operation and b, w learnable weights and hidden state dimensions are d and e.

For the RNN we use a Gated Recurrent Unit (GRU) (Cho et al., 2014) which calculates a new embedding via gates and the previous element in the sequence. We transform a sequence $X \in \mathbb{R}^{N \times d}$ into the sequence $Y \in \mathbb{R}^{N \times e}$ by:

$$\begin{aligned} r_j &= \sigma([W_r X_{t,:}]_j + [U_r Y_{t-1,:}]_j + b_j^r) \\ z_j &= \sigma([W_z X_{t,:}]_j + [U_z Y_{t-1,:}]_j + b_j^z) \\ \hat{h}_j^t &= tanh([W X_{t,:}]_j + [U(r \odot Y_{t-1,:})]_j + b_j^h) \\ Y_{t,j} &= z_j Y_{t-1,:} + (1 - z_j)\hat{h}_j^t \end{aligned} \tag{2}$$

In this case σ is the sigmoid function and $\odot$ the Hadamard product. $W_r, U_r, W_z, U_z, W, U, b$ denote learnable parameters (definition as the PyTorch implementation).

The attention mechanism (Bahdanau et al., 2015) is defined as the weighted sum over the embeddings $x_1, \ldots, x_N \in \mathbb{R}^d$ in the following way:

$$a = \sum_{i=1}^{N} \alpha_i x_i \tag{3}$$

α_i is a weighting for every element in the sequence, and can be calculated by taking the softmax over the attention score $e \in \mathbb{R}^N$, which is calculated for the dot-attention via:

$$e_i = s^T x_i \tag{4}$$

In those formulations $s \in \mathbb{R}^d$ is a learnable parameter and the final attention score is $\alpha = softmax(e)$.

5.1 Extractive

Our extractive summarization system is extracting sentences to create a summarization. Given a verdict $V = (f_1, \ldots, f_n, r_1, \ldots, r_m)$ where f_i denotes a sentence from the facts and r_i denotes a sentences from the reasoning part, we want to find a selection of sentences $S = F \cup R$ with $F \subset \{f_1, \ldots, f_n\}$ and $R \subset \{r_1, \ldots, r_m\}$ which maximizes the ROUGE score compared to the reference summary. For every sentence s_i we want to find a function which tells us whether to include the sentence in the created summary:

$$f(s_i|V, \theta) = \begin{cases} 1, & \text{if } s_i \in S \\ 0, & \text{else} \end{cases} \tag{5}$$

5.1.1 Gold Labels

The decision on labels for the selection process is not straightforward, as in most cases the guiding principle is not directly copied from the body of the verdict. To overcome this mismatch, it is common to greedily select sentences from the text until the ROUGE score between the guiding principle and the selected sentences does not increase anymore (Nallapati et al., 2017). In our case, we went through the verdict and included a sentence, if it increases the ROUGE-2 F1 score of the current selection.

The only problem with this labeling approach is that the resulting summary is way longer than the guiding principle which has on average 75 tokens. With on average 227 tokens the greedy selection is approximately 3 times longer. To combat this issue, we additionally tested a different selection scheme, where we select one sentence from the body of the verdict which has the highest ROUGE-2 F1 score per sentence in the guiding principle. If

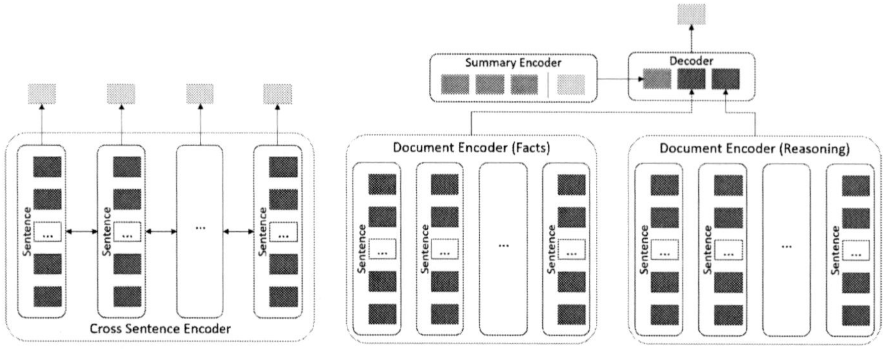

Figure 1: Word embeddings are aggregated to sentence embeddings. For the extractive models (left) information is passed between sentences before classification. In the abstractive case (right) the sentence embeddings are aggregated into document embeddings for facts and reasoning and used in a decoder with the previous words from the summary to predict the current word.

we could not find any overlapping sentences, we used the ROUGE-1 F1 score instead. We then evaluated both labels as an oracle method, to determine what the maximum possible score for each of them would be (see Table 4). There are on average 78 tokens in the one-to-one selection, i.e. lengthwise it is perfectly matching with the reference summary. Surprisingly, the ROUGE scores for the one-to-one selection are higher than the greedy selection. We suspect this is due to the ROUGE-1 criterion in the one-to-one selection. We decided against using ROUGE-1 in the greedy case, as it would further increase the length of the created summary.

5.1.2 Baseline

In addition to the oracle methods, we included other common baselines for the extractive model. One common baseline called lead-3 (Nallapati et al., 2017) simply takes the first 3 sentences of the text as a summary. In our case, we expanded this definition to lead-f-r, which denotes that f sentences are taken from the beginning of the facts and r sentences from the reasoning. Additionally, we also included a random baseline, where we selected 3 random sentences from the whole text. We also tested TextRank (Mihalcea and Tarau, 2004) and LexRank (Erkan and Radev, 2004).

5.1.3 Models

We will now define the models we used for extractive summarization. All following models use the same schema: the token embeddings are processed by multiple Linear layers with ReLU functions in between. Those token hidden states are then used to calculate the sentence embeddings. Linear layers and a Sigmoid function map those to the selection score. The only difference between the models is the way the sentence embeddings are calculated.

We used GloVe (Pennington et al., 2014) to map a word id to a 100-dimensional vector representing its semantics. The sentences are embedded via a CNN, GRU or attention. The CNN model applies multiple 1-dimensional convolutions with ReLU activations in between to the word embeddings. By taking the maximum value over the word embedding dimension, we obtain the sentence embedding. For the RNN model, we pass all the tokens from the sentence into the GRU and then use the embedding of the last word as the sentence embedding. When using attention, the weighted sum is directly used as a sentence embedding.

As the semantics of a sentence are highly dependent on its context, we created cross-sentence layers. The cross-sentence RNN is a bidirectional GRU that passes information around neighboring sentences, the final sentence embedding given by the hidden state of that sentence. The cross-sentence CNN works similarly but uses multiple 1-dimensional Convolutions with ReLUs instead. This way the embedding of a sentence is always dependent on the context of the sentence. We tested the models with and without this cross-sentence information passing.

Each model is trained to optimize the binary cross-entropy loss which is scaled so that the selected sentences gain similar importance to the unimportant sentences. The negative examples are more common, i.e. the training becomes harder without the positive weighting p. The loss for verdict can be formulated in the following way, with V denoting all sentences in the verdict and S denoting the selected summary sentences:

$$L(V,S) = \frac{1}{|V|}(p\sum_{s\in S}\log(f(s|V,\theta)) + \sum_{s\notin S}\log(1-f(s|V,\theta))) \quad (6)$$

We tested all the possible combinations from above. We also fixed the dimensions of each learnable parameter to the embedding size, i.e. during processing each data point has the same dimensionality.

For each training, we choose a random learning rate between 1×10^{-3} and 1×10^{-6} on a log scale, i.e. higher and lower learning rates are equally likely. This was necessary as each model variation needs slightly different learning rates for optimal results and a fixed learning rate would underestimate the performance of a specific model. Each model was trained twice with two different learning rates and we then choose the best model based on the ROUGE-1 F1 score on the validation set. Each model was also tested on the one-to-one and the greedy label selection, i.e. in total, a specific model was trained 4 times. From the two models trained we picked the one with the higher validation set ROUGE-1 performance. Training each model took between 2 and 4 hours.

5.2 Abstractive

The abstractive models produce one word after the other and can be understood as conditional language models which depend on the content of the text and the previously generated words. Given a verdict V we want to approximate the probability distribution over the words w_i in the summary S:

$$P(w_{1,\ldots,n}|V) = \prod_{w_i\in S} P(w_i|w_{1,\ldots,i-1},V) \quad (7)$$

This can be approximated by a neural network, which is trained to predict the current word given the previous words from the summary and the text as features. For abstractive models we did some minor adjustments to the embeddings: we added one <*end*> token to denote that the model wants to end the current sentence.

5.2.1 Models

The abstractive models use the same building blocks as in the extractive case. Instead of passing information between sentences, they are aggregated to one document embedding. We follow the general encoder-decoder structure. The encoder part of the model is calculating embeddings for the two segments in the body of the court ruling and the previously generated words. The sentences from facts and reasoning are embedded using the attention mechanism from above. To create the document embedding, we apply the RNN model over the sentences where the document is represented by the hidden state of the last sentence. We choose this model combination as it gave us the best extractive performance and thus we can assume that it can adequately model the verdict. The previously generated words are used in a GRU and the hidden state for the last word is forwarded through two linear layers followed by ReLUs to create the wanted embedding.

Given an embedding for the generated words, the facts, and reasoning, the decoder will concatenate their representation and then apply three linear layers with ReLU functions in between. The final layer generates a prediction value for each word which is then transformed to the wanted probability by applying a softmax function. We denote this encoder-decoder model as our *Baseline* model.

As a model variation (*Guided*), the attention can be altered to dynamically change its searching behavior. The dot-attention is changed in the following way with $x_{lin}(.)$ denoting one Linear layer which is swapped depending on if the model is currently encoding the facts or the reasoning section, and $p\in\mathbb{R}^d$ denotes the embedding obtained from the previously generated words i.e. $x_{lin}(.)$ maps from $\mathbb{R}^d$ to $\mathbb{R}^{d_1}$:

$$e_i = x_{lin}(p)^T x_i \quad (8)$$

Inspired by the approaches from Cao et al. (2018); Chen and Bansal (2018) and Bae et al. (2019), we further extend the *Guided* model by using extracted sentences as a template for the encoder part of the network. In this model (*Template*), the encoders for the body of the verdict get the embedding from the extracted sentence instead of the embedding from the previously generated words to dynamically alter the aggregation behaviour based on what should be currently generated. The extracted sentence is aggregated via dot-attention.

During training, we generate the summary word for word, i.e. the model is optimized to predict the current word given the previous words from the gold summary. We optimize the log probability of

Method	Greedy			One-to-One		
	ROUGE-1	ROUGE-2	ROUGE-L	ROUGE-1	ROUGE-2	ROUGE-L
Att - x	25.91	8.66	18.07	28.04	10.67	20.21
CNN - x	25.67	8.13	17.90	28.28	10.95	20.64
RNN - x	18.10	2.80	12.08	20.49	4.71	13.72
Att - CNN	23.98	6.62	15.94	18.31	2.98	12.04
Att - RNN	25.07	7.65	17.11	**30.50**	**13.06**	**22.95**
CNN - CNN	18.31	2.98	12.04	29.70	12.30	22.21
CNN - RNN	22.98	5.80	15.15	29.63	12.18	22.02
RNN - CNN	18.20	2.87	12.14	21.17	5.16	14.18
RNN - RNN	22.13	5.96	15.42*	22.05	5.88	15.30*

Table 2: Test performance levels for extractive methods. The methods are written as *sentence - cross-sentence* encoder. We pick the top-3 sentences for each extractive method. ROUGE-L score marked with * is not exact as we needed to remove some verdicts due to recursion errors induced by long generated summaries.

the given word and sum the loss over the whole summary sequence:

$$l(w_i|V,\theta) = \log(f_\theta(w_i)) \tag{9}$$

$$L(w_1,\dots,w_n) = \sum_{w_i \in S} l(w_i|V,\theta) \tag{10}$$

We fixed the learning rate to 5×10^{-3} for the training as each epoch takes multiple hours. As evaluation on an epoch level would be very time-consuming, we instead evaluated the model every 1000 verdicts on 100 verdicts from the validation set. 10 verdicts are batched together for optimization. After the 80th such iteration, we decrease the learning rate by a factor of 0.95 for 20 iterations. We used early stopping with a patience of 30 on the validation loss and training each model took 4-5 days.

For testing, the summarization model is allowed to produce at most 150 tokens or 3 sentences denoted by the <*end*> token. Each summary is then generated word for word, where the model gets the previously generated words as input as well as the text of the verdict. We used the one-to-one extractive labels for *Template*. We use beam search (Rush et al., 2015) with a width of 5 summaries, i.e. in each step, the top-5 summaries based on the joint probability are used for further generation. This heuristic search is stopped if one sentence reaches the ending conditions from above.

As a baseline to the abstractive approaches, we used the Pointer-Generator network from See et al. (2017). We used the same vocabulary size as with the other models, but otherwise, the hyperparameters were not changed.

6 Performance Analysis

To evaluate a given system, we use the ROUGE metric (Lin, 2004) which measures the percentage of n-gram overlap between a gold label summarization $V_{sum} = (w_1,\dots,w_n)$ and a created text $C = (c_1,\dots,c_m)$ with $w_i : i \in \{1,\dots,n\}$ and $c_i : i \in \{1,\dots,m\}$ being the words in the respective texts [3].

In Table 2 we denote the test performance for the extractive methods. In most cases, the model with the greedy target selection performs worse than the one-to-one selection. Models trained on the one-to-one labels might gain a better separation between important and irrelevant sentences and thus we observe a higher summarization score. In our case, a GRU is less desirable for sentence encoding. The models with RNNs as sentence encoders have a maximum ROUGE-1 score of 22.13 percent. As seen in Table 2 our CNN and attention models have a higher level of performance by a wide margin compared to the approaches which use RNNs as sentence encoders. By introducing a cross-sentence layer, the overall performance does increase slightly.

The performance for the abstractive models (Table 3) is worse compared to the extractive models and the baselines. Our current abstractive approaches are not able to adequately model the summarizations. There is a performance increase for the Pointer-Generator model (See et al., 2017), but its summaries are also rather poorly generated. The common problem for all tested abstractive models was that they tend to repeat phrases, thus the quality

[3]Evaluated with the following implementation: `https://github.com/pltrdy/rouge`

Table 3: Test performance for the abstractive models. Baseline and Guided method have converged to a similar language model, but they produce slightly different probability for the words.

Method	ROUGE-1	ROUGE-2	ROUGE-L
Baseline	12.37	0.77	9.96
Guided	12.37	0.77	9.96
Template	10.86	0.65	8.32

Table 4: Test performance for the best models, compared to the baselines. For methods marked with *, we had to exclude some verdicts with long summaries, due to recursion depth of the ROUGE-L calculation.

Method	ROUGE-1	ROUGE-2	ROUGE-L
oracle - One-to-One*	55.12	40.39	51.38
oracle - Greedy*	37.90	26.10	35.16
lead-3-0	11.80	1.52	7.75
lead-0-3	18.44	2.88	12.38
lead-3-3	19.69	3.18	12.42
random	19.95	3.90	13.12
TextRank (Mihalcea and Tarau, 2004)	22.69	5.93	14.95
LexRank (Erkan and Radev, 2004)	24.98	6.87	16.34
Pointer (See et al., 2017)	20.80	5.27	15.98
Ext: Att - RNN	**30.50**	**13.06**	**22.95**
Abs: Baseline	12.37	0.77	9.96

of the summary degrades, which is also reported by other researchers (See et al., 2017). Further research is necessary to investigate whether those low-performance levels are also produced by other abstractive summarization approaches.

Table 4 shows the test performance for all the best models, together with the baselines. Our extractive approach beat all baselines, but we still have room for improvement as seen by the oracle performances. Furthermore, as we can report similar oracle performances to other papers (Xu et al., 2020; Liu and Lapata, 2019), our hypothesis of using summarization techniques for the generation of guiding principles is strengthened.

When comparing the performance numbers with those reported at `nlpprogress.com`, we see the long historic evolution for summarization methods. The legal domain and especially the German language are under-researched in the summarization domain. A lot of work, such as creating appropriate language models is necessary to apply those methods to the German language. With certainty, we can say that there is a necessity to evaluate summarization models on diverse datasets.

7 Conclusion & Future Work

In this paper, we introduced a new dataset for the summarization of German court rulings. We created multiple models specifically tailored to the German legal domain and tested strong baseline models which we want to improve in the future.

Nonetheless, there are still extensions and shortcomings which we want to address in future work. The vocabulary size needs to increase as German is a more morphologically rich language than English. It might be necessary to find more efficient ways to represent and generate compound nouns, the different verb forms, etc. as they drastically increase the size of the necessary vocabulary. Consequently, the model complexity needs to be increased. This does not only include ways to better model the German language but also taking the structure of the verdicts more into account. Court rulings have a more sophisticated structure which we did not entirely utilize in this research paper, i.e. each of the segments is again subdivided into other sub-segments and so on. Embracing this more hierarchical view could make access to information easier and improve the understanding of the source document.

In this research, we laid down the necessary groundwork for further research. In the future, we want to do more qualitative analysis, by letting legal experts evaluate our summarization models. Summarization is far from being solved and in our opinion, it is important to introduce different texts and domains to summarization research.

References

Sanghwan Bae, Taeuk Kim, Jihoon Kim, and Sang-goo Lee. 2019. Summary level training of sentence rewriting for abstractive summarization. In *Proceedings of the 2nd Workshop on New Frontiers in Summarization*, pages 10–20, Hong Kong, China. Association for Computational Linguistics.

Dzmitry Bahdanau, Kyunghyun Cho, and Yoshua Bengio. 2015. Neural machine translation by jointly learning to align and translate. In *International Conference on Learning Representations*.

Ziqiang Cao, Wenjie Li, Sujian Li, and Furu Wei. 2018. Retrieve, rerank and rewrite: Soft template based neural summarization. In *Proceedings of the 56th Annual Meeting of the Association for Computational Linguistics (Volume 1: Long Papers)*, pages 152–161, Melbourne, Australia. Association for Computational Linguistics.

Asli Celikyilmaz, Antoine Bosselut, Xiaodong He, and Yejin Choi. 2018. Deep communicating agents for abstractive summarization. In *Proceedings of the 2018 Conference of the North American Chapter of the Association for Computational Linguistics: Human Language Technologies, Volume 1 (Long Papers)*, pages 1662–1675, New Orleans, Louisiana. Association for Computational Linguistics.

Yen-Chun Chen and Mohit Bansal. 2018. Fast abstractive summarization with reinforce-selected sentence rewriting. In *Proceedings of the 56th Annual Meeting of the Association for Computational Linguistics (Volume 1: Long Papers)*, pages 675–686, Melbourne, Australia. Association for Computational Linguistics.

Jianpeng Cheng and Mirella Lapata. 2016. Neural summarization by extracting sentences and words. In *Proceedings of the 54th Annual Meeting of the Association for Computational Linguistics (Volume 1: Long Papers)*, pages 484–494, Berlin, Germany. Association for Computational Linguistics.

Kyunghyun Cho, Bart van Merriënboer, Caglar Gulcehre, Dzmitry Bahdanau, Fethi Bougares, Holger Schwenk, and Yoshua Bengio. 2014. Learning phrase representations using RNN encoder–decoder for statistical machine translation. In *Proceedings of the 2014 Conference on Empirical Methods in Natural Language Processing (EMNLP)*, pages 1724–1734, Doha, Qatar. Association for Computational Linguistics.

Sumit Chopra, Michael Auli, and Alexander M. Rush. 2016. Abstractive sentence summarization with attentive recurrent neural networks. In *Proceedings of the 2016 Conference of the North American Chapter of the Association for Computational Linguistics: Human Language Technologies*, pages 93–98, San Diego, California. Association for Computational Linguistics.

Arman Cohan, Franck Dernoncourt, Doo Soon Kim, Trung Bui, Seokhwan Kim, Walter Chang, and Nazli Goharian. 2018. A discourse-aware attention model for abstractive summarization of long documents. In *Proceedings of the 2018 Conference of the North American Chapter of the Association for Computational Linguistics: Human Language Technologies, Volume 2 (Short Papers)*, pages 615–621, New Orleans, Louisiana. Association for Computational Linguistics.

Li Dong, Nan Yang, Wenhui Wang, Furu Wei, Xiaodong Liu, Yu Wang, Jianfeng Gao, Ming Zhou, and Hsiao-Wuen Hon. 2019. Unified language model pre-training for natural language understanding and generation. In *33rd Conference on Neural Information Processing Systems (NeurIPS 2019)*.

Günes Erkan and Dragomir R Radev. 2004. Lexrank: Graph-based lexical centrality as salience in text summarization. *Journal of Artificial Intelligence Research - JAIR*, 22:457–479.

Sebastian Gehrmann, Yuntian Deng, and Alexander Rush. 2018. Bottom-up abstractive summarization. In *Proceedings of the 2018 Conference on Empirical Methods in Natural Language Processing*, pages 4098–4109, Brussels, Belgium. Association for Computational Linguistics.

Ingo Glaser, Sebastian Moser, and Florian Matthes. 2021. Sentence boundary detection in german legal documents. In *Proceedings of the 13th International Conference on Agents and Artificial Intelligence - Volume 2: ICAART*, pages 812–821. INSTICC, SciTePress.

Aishwarya Jadhav and Vaibhav Rajan. 2018. Extractive summarization with SWAP-NET: Sentences and words from alternating pointer networks. In *Proceedings of the 56th Annual Meeting of the Association for Computational Linguistics (Volume 1: Long Papers)*, pages 142–151, Melbourne, Australia. Association for Computational Linguistics.

Anastassia Kornilova and Vladimir Eidelman. 2019. BillSum: A corpus for automatic summarization of US legislation. In *Proceedings of the 2nd Workshop on New Frontiers in Summarization*, pages 48–56, Hong Kong, China. Association for Computational Linguistics.

Wojciech Kryściński, Romain Paulus, Caiming Xiong, and Richard Socher. 2018. Improving abstraction in text summarization. In *Proceedings of the 2018 Conference on Empirical Methods in Natural Language Processing*, pages 1808–1817, Brussels, Belgium. Association for Computational Linguistics.

Mike Lewis, Yinhan Liu, Naman Goyal, Marjan Ghazvininejad, Abdelrahman Mohamed, Omer Levy, Veselin Stoyanov, and Luke Zettlemoyer. 2020. BART: Denoising sequence-to-sequence pre-training for natural language generation, translation, and comprehension. In *Proceedings of the 58th Annual Meeting of the Association for Computational*

Linguistics, pages 7871–7880, Online. Association for Computational Linguistics.

Wei Li, Xinyan Xiao, Yajuan Lyu, and Yuanzhuo Wang. 2018. Improving neural abstractive document summarization with structural regularization. In *Proceedings of the 2018 Conference on Empirical Methods in Natural Language Processing*, pages 4078–4087, Brussels, Belgium. Association for Computational Linguistics.

Chin-Yew Lin. 2004. ROUGE: A package for automatic evaluation of summaries. In *Text Summarization Branches Out*, pages 74–81, Barcelona, Spain. Association for Computational Linguistics.

Yang Liu and Mirella Lapata. 2019. Text summarization with pretrained encoders. In *Proceedings of the 2019 Conference on Empirical Methods in Natural Language Processing and the 9th International Joint Conference on Natural Language Processing (EMNLP-IJCNLP)*, pages 3730–3740, Hong Kong, China. Association for Computational Linguistics.

Rada Mihalcea and Paul Tarau. 2004. TextRank: Bringing order into text. In *Proceedings of the 2004 Conference on Empirical Methods in Natural Language Processing*, pages 404–411, Barcelona, Spain. Association for Computational Linguistics.

Ramesh Nallapati, Feifei Zhai, and Bowen Zhou. 2017. Summarunner: A recurrent neural network based sequence model for extractive summarization of documents. In *Proceedings of the Thirty-First AAAI Conference on Artificial Intelligence*, AAAI'17, page 3075–3081. AAAI Press.

Ramesh Nallapati, Bowen Zhou, Cicero dos Santos, Çağlar GuÌ‡lçehre, and Bing Xiang. 2016. Abstractive text summarization using sequence-to-sequence RNNs and beyond. In *Proceedings of The 20th SIGNLL Conference on Computational Natural Language Learning*, pages 280–290, Berlin, Germany. Association for Computational Linguistics.

Shashi Narayan, Shay B. Cohen, and Mirella Lapata. 2018. Don't give me the details, just the summary! topic-aware convolutional neural networks for extreme summarization. In *Proceedings of the 2018 Conference on Empirical Methods in Natural Language Processing*, pages 1797–1807, Brussels, Belgium. Association for Computational Linguistics.

Jeffrey Pennington, Richard Socher, and Christopher D. Manning. 2014. Glove: Global vectors for word representation. In *Empirical Methods in Natural Language Processing (EMNLP)*, pages 1532–1543.

Weizhen Qi, Yu Yan, Yeyun Gong, Dayiheng Liu, Nan Duan, Jiusheng Chen, Ruofei Zhang, and Ming Zhou. 2020. ProphetNet: Predicting future n-gram for sequence-to-SequencePre-training. In *Findings of the Association for Computational Linguistics: EMNLP 2020*, pages 2401–2410, Online. Association for Computational Linguistics.

Colin Raffel, Noam Shazeer, Adam Roberts, Katherine Lee, Sharan Narang, Michael Matena, Yanqi Zhou, Wei Li, and Peter J. Liu. 2020. Exploring the limits of transfer learning with a unified text-to-text transformer. arXiv preprint.

Alexander M. Rush, Sumit Chopra, and Jason Weston. 2015. A neural attention model for abstractive sentence summarization. In *Proceedings of the 2015 Conference on Empirical Methods in Natural Language Processing*, pages 379–389, Lisbon, Portugal. Association for Computational Linguistics.

Abigail See, Peter J. Liu, and Christopher D. Manning. 2017. Get to the point: Summarization with pointer-generator networks. In *Proceedings of the 55th Annual Meeting of the Association for Computational Linguistics (Volume 1: Long Papers)*, pages 1073–1083, Vancouver, Canada. Association for Computational Linguistics.

Eva Sharma, Chen Li, and Lu Wang. 2019. BIGPATENT: A large-scale dataset for abstractive and coherent summarization. In *Proceedings of the 57th Annual Meeting of the Association for Computational Linguistics*, pages 2204–2213, Florence, Italy. Association for Computational Linguistics.

Oriol Vinyals, Meire Fortunato, and Navdeep Jaitly. 2015. Pointer networks. In *Advances in Neural Information Processing Systems*, volume 28. Curran Associates, Inc.

Jiacheng Xu, Zhe Gan, Yu Cheng, and Jingjing Liu. 2020. Discourse-aware neural extractive text summarization. In *Proceedings of the 58th Annual Meeting of the Association for Computational Linguistics*, pages 5021–5031, Online. Association for Computational Linguistics.

Jingqing Zhang, Yao Zhao, Mohammad Saleh, and Peter Liu. 2020. PEGASUS: Pre-training with extracted gap-sentences for abstractive summarization. In *Proceedings of the 37th International Conference on Machine Learning*, volume 119 of *Proceedings of Machine Learning Research*, pages 11328–11339. PMLR.

Xingxing Zhang, Furu Wei, and Ming Zhou. 2019. HIBERT: Document level pre-training of hierarchical bidirectional transformers for document summarization. In *Proceedings of the 57th Annual Meeting of the Association for Computational Linguistics*, pages 5059–5069, Florence, Italy. Association for Computational Linguistics.

Qingyu Zhou, Furu Wei, and Ming Zhou. 2020. At which level should we extract? an empirical analysis on extractive document summarization. In *Proceedings of the 28th International Conference on Computational Linguistics*, pages 5617–5628, Barcelona, Spain (Online). International Committee on Computational Linguistics.

Learning from Limited Labels for Long Legal Dialogue

Jenny Hong
Stanford University
jennyhong@cs.stanford.edu

Derek Chong
Stanford University
derekch@stanford.edu

Christopher D. Manning
Stanford University
manning@cs.stanford.edu

Abstract

We study attempting to achieve high accuracy information extraction of case factors from a challenging dataset of parole hearings, which, compared to other legal NLP datasets, has longer texts, with fewer labels. On this corpus, existing work directly applying pretrained neural models has failed to extract all but a few relatively basic items with little improvement over rule-based extraction. We address two challenges posed by existing work: training on long documents and reasoning over complex speech patterns. We use a similar approach to the two-step open-domain question answering approach by using a Reducer to extract relevant text segments and a Producer to generate both extractive answers and non-extractive classifications. In a context like ours, with limited labeled data, we show that a superior approach for strong performance within limited development time is to use a combination of a rule-based Reducer and a neural Producer. We study four representative tasks from the parole dataset. On all four, we improve extraction from the previous benchmark of 0.41–0.63 to 0.83–0.89 F1.

1 Introduction

In many judicial processes such as legal hearings and criminal trials, decisions are made as a result of lengthy dialogues, in which case factors are discussed in great detail. To study such dialogues, scholars typically invest immense effort to hand label a small number of transcripts with some case factors; the factors are then used in downstream analysis. In most cases, the sheer length of transcribed conversational text all but prohibits any large-scale analysis of the process. Information extraction over dialogues can assist in identifying the underlying factors of a case from transcripts.

The benefits of information extraction are twofold. Automating the extraction of case factors means that a historical legal analysis can now be comprehensive, containing all available transcripts, rather than being limited to the several dozen or hundred transcripts that a single researcher can label by hand. The second advantage is to open the door to *counterdata* applications in law (D'ignazio and Klein, 2020). To date, most machine learning applications in the law have been predictive: given case factors up front, make a prediction of an outcome. In domains where case factors cannot or should not be known prior to the hearing, information extraction can produce case factors *after* a hearing, which enables machine learning to play an alternative role to the role of prediction, the role of oversight (Bell et al., 2021). In our application, information extraction allows the public to audit the parole process, whose case records are otherwise locked away in a filing cabinet.

To be useful for such downstream research, the consensus in legal domain NLP is that information extraction should produce labels that achieve an F1 of at least 0.80 (Hendrycks et al., 2021; Hong et al., 2021). Our corpus, a set of historical California parole hearings, is a particularly difficult application, but also representative of many challenges in criminal law: (1) Parole hearings are longer than documents in existing benchmarks. (2) Existing benchmarks source from written text; parole documents are loosely-structured dialogue. (3) Existing benchmarks contain at least an order of magnitude more labels. (4) Information extraction from formal written documents centers around named entities and relation extraction. By contrast, much of the text in the criminal context serves the purpose of surfacing, discussing, and correcting case factors, which are not necessarily relational. This means parole hearings pose both extractive and abstractive tasks, often across multiple sentences, which is known to be challenging even in more structured settings (Wang et al., 2021).

The scarcity of labels and specificity of the domain suggest that subject matter experts (SMEs)

Natural Legal Language Processing Workshop 2021, pages 190–204
November 10, 2021.

can be helpful. On the parole corpus, weak supervision-based data programming approaches (Ratner et al., 2016; Zheng et al., 2019) achieve F1 scores of only 0.41–0.63 (Hong et al., 2021). We propose an alternative way to involve SMEs, in which we split the problem into two components: a Reducer model which extracts relevant text segments from a hearing, and a Producer model which generates answers from the text segments selected by the Reducer. Our methods effectively achieve extraction at 0.83–0.89 F1.

We show that using an approach with a rule-based Reducer and neural Producer outperforms other commonly-used approaches. Focusing SME effort on developing rules for the Reducer is thus more time-efficient than requiring SMEs to provide additional target labels, whether manually or via data programming. With quality text segments, a neural Producer model can be effectively fine-tuned on just one thousand labels.

2 Related Work

A review of data programming literature suggests that semi-supervised techniques might be a good fit for our problem space. Several existing pipelines combine a limited amount of training data, rule-based systems and neural models to achieve strong results on benchmark datasets (Maheshwari et al., 2020) and in various medical fields (Ling et al., 2019; Smit et al., 2020; Dai et al., 2021). By comparison, weak supervision-based data programming methods tend to focus on bootstrapping in the absence of data (Ratner et al., 2017, 2018), which is a nontrivial performance constraint.

Regardless of supervision strength, an architecture based on rule-based systems may be useful for generating "candidates" as input to downstream neural models; Zhang et al. (2019) explores the time efficiency of manual labeling compared with rule-writing (via regular expressions) for named entity recognition (NER), where results are compared over a bidirectional LSTM-based classifier, finding that in most circumstances, a combination of rule-based and machine-learning classifiers optimizes human time investment.

We therefore adopt the approach of using a rule-based system for candidate generation. One new challenges with our corpus is that parole hearings generally center around one individual, so the candidates for downstream models are not named entities, but more loosely defined segments of the hearing. Compared to NER, there is less prior work exploring rule-based methods for more general retrieval and segmentation.

Our goal of achieving 0.80 F1 in an abstractive format is currently beyond the capabilities of state-of-the-art (SOTA) neural models on comparable tasks, only one of which is in the legal domain.

On Natural Questions (NQ; Kwiatkowski et al., 2019), SOTA models achieve F1 scores of 0.79 and 0.64 on its long and short answer tasks, respectively. However, NQ is purely extractive and averages only 7,300 words per input. On the Doc2EDAG financial statements dataset (Zheng et al., 2019), the Graph-based Interaction model with a Tracker (Xu et al., 2021) surpasses 0.80 F1 when extracting events from documents averaging 912 tokens in length, but this SOTA result drops to 0.76 F1 in the longest quartile. On Open-Domain Question Answering, the SOTA Dense Passage Retrieval (Karpukhin et al., 2020) has an extractive top-5 accuracy of just 0.66. For downstream applications, a model must have a robust top-1 accuracy.

The closest comparable legal dataset is the Contract Understanding Atticus Dataset (CUAD) (Hendrycks et al., 2021). Over CUAD, a SOTA model like RoBERTa (Liu et al., 2019) achieves a lower, and extractive, question answering performance of 0.80 recall at 0.31 precision, representing an F1 score of only 0.45, with documents still averaging one-quarter the length of parole transcripts.

3 Data

We have obtained a corpus of 35,105 parole hearing transcripts, averaging 18,499 words each from 2007–2019.[1] Each hearing is a dialogue, primarily between one or more commissioners and the parole candidate. Most case factors are embellished with history and context, which is important for the procedure of a parole hearing, but challenging for information extraction. Hong et al. (2021) identified eleven fields for information extraction. We study the four fields that the previous study failed to extract with near 0.80 F1: `job_offer` (whether the parole candidate has a job offer upon release), `edu_level` (the candidate's educational level), `risk_assess` (a psychological assessment score), and `last_writeup` (the date of the candidate's last disciplinary writeup in prison).

[1]Transcripts may be requested from the California Department of Corrections and Rehabilitation under the California Public Records Act.

```
COMM: Dr.  [REDACT], R-E-D-A-C-T,
found you to be a moderate risk and
also diagnosed you with anti-social
personality disorder.
```

(a) Example of passage discussing risk_assess, the Comprehensive Risk Assessment score assigned to a parole candidate by a psychologist during an evaluation conducted leading up to the hearing.

```
COMM: When you were going to school,
everything was -- how far did you get in
school?
CAND: Junior high.
COMM: Okay.  Junior high, okay.  And have
you gotten education in prison?
```

(b) Example of passage discussing edu_level, the candidate's level of education. The passage continues for several more conversational turns, in which the commissioner and the candidate discuss various educational programs.

```
COMM: And -- um -- if you are paroled or
-- pardon me -- if you are deported to
[REDACT], what is your plan?
CAND: Well -- um -- I had a couple of
offers from there -- um -- I would
have to -- uh -- check out the -- um
-- [REDACT] center and maybe they could
help me -- you know -- train me to get a
job there and get my life together.
```

(c) Example of passage discussing job_offer, whether the candidate has a job offer upon release.

```
COMM: So when's your last 115?
CAND: Uh, when they had a -- we had a
work -- had a work strike around here.
That was the last 115 I remember.  I
forgot what -- what year it was.
COMM: I'm showing one from maybe January
of 2010 with a mattress.
CAND: Oh, I didn't realize it was a 115.
```

(d) Example of passage discussing last_writeup, the date of the candidate's last disciplinary infraction, or Form 115, in prison.

Figure 1: Example passages of the four features we study. The speaker COMM refers to the presiding commissioner, and the speaker CAND refers to the parole candidate.

Figure 1 shows examples of how these four features arise in dialogue. On average, each annotator takes forty minutes to label a transcript. Only 3% of the dataset is labeled: job_offer, edu_level, and risk_assess each have 1,173 training examples and 106 validation examples, whereas last_writeup has 563 and 48, respectively. The corpus also includes 218 transcripts with labeled spans, i.e. the sentences from which the correct label was determined.

4 Methods

We use a Reducer-Producer paradigm (Figure 2) in the spirit of the Document Retriever-Reader model used in open-domain question answering (ODQA; Chen et al., 2017; Das et al., 2019), with two differences: (1) The Reducer selects one or more relevant passages from within a *single* document (Clark and Gardner, 2017; Krishna et al., 2021), and (2) the Producer model is not necessarily a QA model. We use separate Reducers and Producers for each field. Prior applications of data programming to this corpus used SMEs to write noisy labels for training a neural model; it does not significantly reduce the input text into shorter segments and instead relies on an end-to-end neural approach (Hong et al., 2021). By contrast, our approach uses SMEs to focus on the smaller task of reducing input text and relies on only gold labels, however few, for training the neural model. One subproblem is designed to be tractable for an SME (the Reducer), and the other for a pretrained language model (the Producer).

4.1 Reducer

The SME (1) encodes keywords and patterns into programmatic rules (Zhang et al., 2019), and (2) evaluates the rules against silver-standard metrics. The SME examines any errors and repeats the process until the development subset is covered to >95% recall on silver metrics.

Rules. The SME uses keywords to generate candidate segments and candidate substrings (e.g., for risk assessments, "low" is interesting, but only if it occurs in the proximity of "risk"), sequenced in order of increasing breadth and decreasing precision (Zhang et al., 2019). The framework provides high-level functions that enable SMEs to easily operate on pipelines of candidate segments, filtering in or out, splitting, deoverlapping, and limiting results to create a high-quality reduced output passage.

Evaluation. We reserve the 218 transcripts with labeled spans to serve as a held-out evaluation set. For intermediate SME evaluation and iterations, we use three silver-standard evaluations as a proxy for true Reducer performance: (a) the percentage of results with empty outputs, (b) whether true labels (and common synonyms) appear within reduced passages, and (c) performing interim Producer fine-tuning runs, and evaluating end-to-end performance across a set of hyperparameter sweeps.

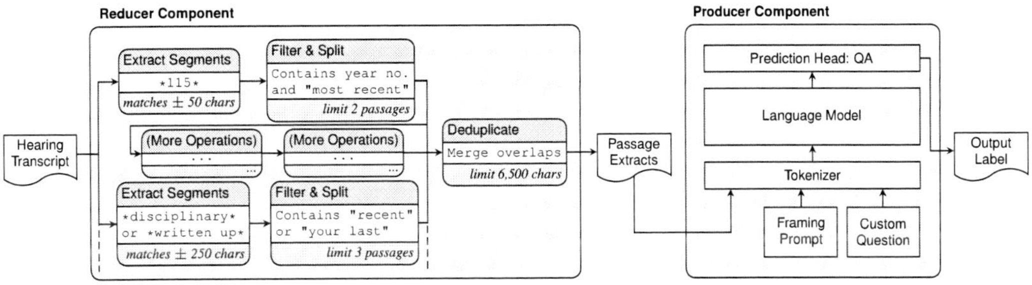

Figure 2: Reducer-Producer architecture sketch for the `last_writeup` field. The Reducer is entirely rule-based, with a few high-level operations over various regular expressions. The Producer is entirely neural and builds on a pretrained language model.

4.2 Producer

We write several simple rule-based Producers to build an understanding of the problem space, and then fine-tune pretrained language models on the passages returned by the Reducer.

Choice of language model. To ensure high training efficacy, we identify the smallest language model that meets the required benchmark in the general case. We evaluate a range of models' capabilities on a small task: For each of the four fields, we identify ten transcripts with particularly challenging dialogue (see Appendix C for examples). We manually extract passages from each transcript and benchmark each language model on its average zero-shot classification accuracy on all 40 passages, across 25 random seeds.

Choice of prediction heads. Fields with a small, fixed set of values are a good fit for a classification head (CLS), such as `edu_level` which is grouped into four categories, and `risk_assess`, for which a psychologist ascribes one of five possible risk levels. Fields with an open-ended set of values may be more suited to the masked language model (MLM) (Hermann et al., 2015; Hill et al., 2016; Chen, 2018; Devlin et al., 2019) or question answering (QA) approach, e.g., `last_writeup` can be any year from 1960–2020.

The MLM and QA heads require a user-defined prompt, which are not always natural for all fields. For example, for `job_offer`, we prompt MLM with token choices, e.g. "*Commissioner: As to whether you have a job offer lined up: You have [one / none].*"). For `last_writeup`, where the correct year exists within each passage, we try various prompts, such as "Your last writeup was in `[MASK]`". We chose prompts with good fine-tuning performance on training data, e.g. for `last_writeup`, we use the prompt "Ignoring chronos and 128s, your most recent 115, RVR (rule violation report) occurred in: `[MASK]`"). QA requires a question formulation, for some fields, we augment QA heads with a prefix sentence containing tokens representing all of the current field's possible classes, a technique used in QA benchmarks such as CoQA (Reddy et al., 2019) and BoolQ (Clark et al., 2019), which enables extractive models to always return values from desired classes.

We tried using a multiple choice reading comprehension (MRC) head (Richardson et al., 2013; Lai et al., 2017; Chen, 2018), which proved to be an an elegant way of grounding the model, with similarities to contrastive learning, and able to generate dynamic classification options, e.g. unlike year classification, MRC choices are *only* the year that appear in the passage. However, MRC requires a full backpropagation across the entire model for each option of every question, which is memory-intensive for passages where over a dozen options might exist per question, and unnecessarily slow even with gradient accumulation. We do not include MRC in our results.

Training details. We use base models from the HuggingFace Transformers library (Wolf et al., 2020), applying standard hyperparameter ranges (Sun et al., 2019) and techniques for training BERT-based models, such as the use of a slanted triangular learning rate. However, we set batch size to 1 and use gradient accumulation to simulate a larger batch size, in order to allow Reducer outputs to be as large as possible (approximately 1,500 tokens for RoBERTA + BigBird Base on a 16GB GPU) without affecting training performance. We ran hyperparameter sweeps for approximately six hours per field on a NVIDIA Tesla V100 GPU.

	Prev F1	Train F1	Val F1	Producer Model	Head
risk_assess	0.53	0.86	**0.83**	Rules	N/A
last_writeup	0.42	0.86	**0.84**	RoB+BB	MLM
edu_level	0.41	0.98	**0.84**	RoB+BB	CLS
job_offer	0.63	0.96	**0.89**	RoB+BB	QA

Table 1: Overall results. Previous best results are from Hong et al. (2021). RoB + BB = RoBERTa + BigBird.

	RL-R	R2-R	BoW-R
`risk_assess`	0.85	0.76	0.88
`last_writeup`	0.87	0.76	0.91
`edu_level`	0.92	0.82	0.95
`job_offer`	0.87	0.72	0.92

Table 2: Evaluating Reducers on labeled spans: Rouge-L and Rouge-2 Recall, Bag-of-Words Recall.

Model Family	Model Variant	Size	Max Len	Benchmark Score
BERT	Base Cased	108M	512	26.7 ± 9.4
	Large Cased	334M	512	33.0 ± 8.0
RoBERTa	Vanilla Base	125M	512	29.8 ± 8.1
	Vanilla Large	355M	512	28.3 ± 8.7
	BigBird Base	**128M**	**4,096**	$\mathbf{30.5 \pm 5.6}$
	BigBird Large	360M	4,096	33.0 ± 6.0
Transfor-mer-XL	Vanilla Base	284M	N/A	32.1 ± 7.6
	XLNet Base	117M	N/A	29.1 ± 5.9
	XLNet Large	361M	N/A	30.2 ± 5.9
GPT	GPT2 Base	124M	2,048	32.2 ± 6.3
	GPT2 Medium	355M	2,048	33.5 ± 5.6
	GPT2 Large	774M	2,048	34.0 ± 7.1
	GPT-Neo 1.3B	1.32B	2,048	34.2 ± 6.3

Table 3: Zero-shot language model performance (average classification accuracy) on a benchmark of complex, challenging passages, over 25 random seeds.

5 Results

Our methods achieve the 0.80 F1 benchmark[2,3] for all four fields, as shown in Table 1. One rule-based Producer achieved an F1 of 0.83 for `risk_assess`, which narrowly outperformed RoBERTa + BigBird model performance of 0.81 F1. However, all other rule-based Producer attempts fell near or below the "Previous F1" mark on their tasks. The `risk_assess` task lends itself to rule-writing, because its values are restricted to combinations of "low," "moderate," and "high", and there are a few phrasings that are commonly used (e.g., "Overall, your risk was low to moderate"). By comparison, neural models may have been confused by the multiple other types of psychological assessments that occur in the text (e.g., PCL-R, HCR-20, LS/CMI), which are all assessed on the same "low," "moderate," and "high" scale.

5.1 Standalone Reducer Performance

Table 2 shows the Reducer's performance on three different measures of recall on the 218 labeled spans. We focus on recall because a Producer can still perform well on a short input even if there are occasional spurious phrases. Also, correct answers are not necessarily unique; labeled spans often point to a single sentence, whereas a fact may be repeated multiple times during the course of a hearing. The Reducer may select *a* correct span, but not the exact sentence selected by the annotator. Recall sidesteps the former issue and slightly mitigates the incorrect penalty imposed by the latter, as similar words may be used in both spans.

The Rouge-L recall ranges from 0.85–0.92: the Reducer frequently finds the exact set of sentences annotated by a human labeler. The Rouge-2 recall is lower, from 0.72–0.82: when the Reducer fails to find the exact sentences, the phrasing of its result is different. However, the bag-of-words recall is still high: 0.88–0.95, which means that the Reducer tends to finds sentences that use almost the same words, if not in the exact same order.

Given the span labeling issue described above, Table 2 is almost certainly an underestimate of Reducer performance. This is supported by other assessments of Reducer performance: end-to-end F1 scores of 0.83–0.89 are effectively a guarantee on the lower bound of Reducer performance, and based on the error analysis in Section 5.4, only a small fraction of errors were due to the Reducer. This implies *significantly* higher true recall scores. This is also in line with our silver-standard Reducer evaluations, which are consistently above 0.95.

5.2 Language Model Benchmarks

Benchmark performance for each language model is provided in Table 3. Figure 3 plots model performance against size and shows power-law scaling characteristics, a known feature of neural language models (Kaplan et al., 2020).

Given the relatively small range in performance between the models in our evaluation set (7.5%

[2]F1 scores are calculated on *exact match* for all prediction heads, instead of the relatively easier bag-of-words metric used in the extractive setting, or precision at 0.80 recall (Hendrycks et al., 2021). This is a more accurate measurement of abstractive performance, which is essential to downstream results.

[3]Related existing work reports F1, but F1 is an imperfect proxy for the impact of errors for downstream analyses. Any application that seeks to use extracted data should perform its own analysis to understand the relative costs of, for example, false positives versus false negatives for a given field.

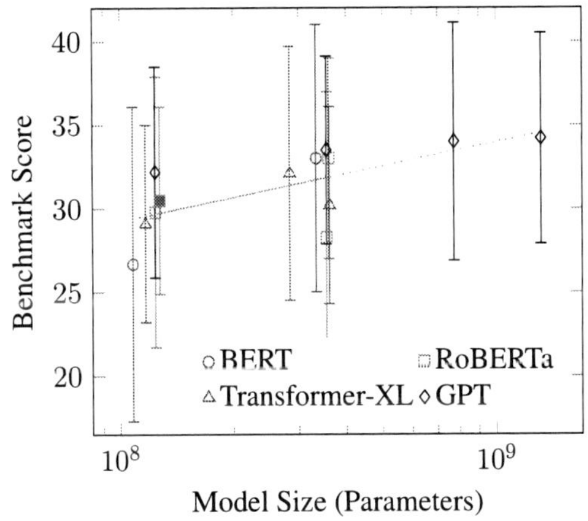

Figure 3: Performance on benchmark from Table 5.2 versus model size.

across all model families and variants), we also run some supplementary tests, finding that (a) models pretrained on question answering datasets performed 10–15% better in this setting, but a comprehensive evaluation was not feasible as QA outputs are extractive and require manual assessment, and (b) large GPT models performed dramatically better in the few-shot setting, with GPT3 performing at 90–100% accuracy on some problems.

We ultimately use RoBERTa + BigBird Base (RoB + BB; Zaheer et al., 2020) as our default model due to its balance of long input length, low computation requirements, and performance. This model supports inputs of up to 4,096 tokens, allowing the Reducer to provide multiple candidate passages without having to split input into multiple model calls and integrate a la Clark and Gardner (2017). It is in the smallest size class of the models tested, facilitating the fine-tuning of large input passages within GPU memory limits. Within its size class, RoB + BB is the second-best performer, performing within 2–3% of models 2–3x its size. Compared to the top performer (GPT2), BERT is known to have better versatility on downstream tasks (Klein and Nabi, 2019) and well-explored fine-tuning characteristics (Sun et al., 2019).

5.3 Prediction Heads

We evaluate the gains from prediction head choice by performing 25 fine-tuning runs for each combination of field and head and reporting the highest validation F1 score achieved for each. To ensure test fairness within a reasonable amount of computation, each run uses a random configuration from

Hyperparameter	Value(s)
Learning Rate	5e-4 to 5e-7
Batch Size (Accumulative)	1, 2, 4, 8, 16
Number of Epochs	6 to 10
LR Warmup Epochs	0.4, 0.6, 0.8, 1.0, 1.2
Dropout	0.1
Adam Optimizer	$\beta_1 = 0.9, \beta_2 = 0.999$

Table 4: Hyperparameter sweep configurations for prediction head selection exercise.

	CLS	MLM	QA
`last_writeup`	0.76	*0.79*	*0.82*
`edu_level`	**0.82**	0.43	0.70
`job_offer`	0.83	0.69	**0.89**

Table 5: The effects of different prediction heads on Validation F1 scores (results in italics are not definitive, as MLM outperforms QA on end-to-end evaluation).

Table 4. F1 scores are recorded at the point where validation loss is at a minimum.

Table 5 shows the performance of each prediction head on each field. `edu_level` and `job_offer` performed comparably to the main runs in Table 1. `last_writeup` performed best under a question answering head during this exercise, but underperformed the masked language model F1 score of 0.84 in Table 1, leaving this result ambiguous. Selecting a suitable prediction head dramatically affects model performance after fine-tuning: suboptimal head choices result in F1 scores of 52-93% of the scores achieved with the best prediction head.

The CLS prediction head performs well across all fields except `last_writeup`, where only 20% of all runs score above 0.25, and most score below 0.10. Classification is not a natural format for this field: in order to classify a passage, the model must learn 50 separate classes, one for each possible year from 1969–2019. CLS performs well when the number of classes is relatively low, especially when the answer is abstractive. However, it tends to fail to understand factual relationships. For example, when used for risk assessment its ratings correlate with the number of times the word "gang" or "murder" occurs in the passage (see Appendix D for more information).

The MLM head has nearly the opposite performance characteristics: it performs best on `last_writeup`, at an average level on `job_offer`, and very poorly on `edu_level`. It is telling that `last_writeup` can be expressed as a sentence with a single masked token (which may hold many values), whereas the classes of the latter are all concepts which do not fit into a single token. The MLM head's F1 scores tend to be several points lower than its accuracy, a symptom of the model occasionally filling the mask with arbitrary freeform values.

The QA heads perform well on `job_offer`, fairly well on `last_writeup`, and at an average level on `edu_level`. The first field is easily expressed as in the form of a yes/no question, and the second field's value is extractable from within the passage as with a regular QA task. However, the third requires the model to parse the passage to locate the answer, classify this into into one of four fixed phrasings, and return this phrasing from the prefix sentence, a task which is somewhat foreign to a question answering-based model.

5.4 Error Analysis

Errors fall into a few clear classes. Approximately 70% of all errors result from what appears to be the model learning spurious associations with co-occurring words. For example, in one conversational turn, a parole candidate describes both his own and the victim's level of education. The Producer incorrectly returns the victim's level of education, which uses the phrase "college courses."

Around 10% of errors result from complex passages (comparable to the examples in Appendix C), which continue to challenge language models. Spoken narrative language can be arbitrarily complex, and grounding in real world knowledge and presuppositions remain hard to encode. In one transcript, the commissioner asks, "Are you working towards a college degree?" which presupposes that the parole candidate completed high school. However, the model classifies this candidate as not having completed high school or a GED, as the transcript does not explicitly mention either. Some passages require numerical abilities which smaller language models tend to find difficult (Dua et al., 2019). Table 3 suggests that a larger language model may improve performance in many cases.

In the remaining 20% of errors, the Reducer failed to find a match for a given transcript or returned an incorrect passage.

Surprisingly, we found that in 15–50% of the total errors returned (varying by field), the model was actually correct, and had identified incorrectly-labeled or ambiguous data. To be conservative, we did not adjust F1 scores upwards and instead excluded the examples from this error analysis.

A detailed breakdown of errors for `edu_level` is provided in Appendix D for illustrative purposes.

6 Discussion

6.1 Combining Rules and Neural Models

Previous approaches to our problem use rule-generated labels to supervise a model. We instead split the problem into two, where the Reducer is entirely rule-based, and the Producer trains only on the few, but high quality, human labels.

Both rule-generated labels and a rule-based Reducer scale with the number of features to extract, but not the complexity of model or dataset. However, given a fixed development time, we find it more valuable for an SME to focus on only the Reducer. In contrast, end-to-end data programming requires rules for the Producer as well, which can be much more challenging to write. On our data, it takes about ten hours for an SME to write Reducer rules for a model that performs at the exceptional recall rates from Table 2. Hong et al. (2021) report the same number of hours per feature for an end-to-end data programming model, which performs much worse overall.

As future work, we hope to investigate whether a well-designed Reducer can improve human performance in creating gold-standard labels, saving time by reducing the need to read through entire transcripts.

6.2 Assessment of Human-in-the-Loop

We find that an hand-written rules can effectively isolate key segments of text in the overwhelming majority of situations.

The tradeoff of incurring the cost of writing rules per each additional feature proved to be very reasonable for our domain. We have few features, and our requirements demand accuracy over speed. In comparison, prior work suggests that for a neural model to achieve accuracy in the same ballpark, the model would require an order of magnitude more spans, which would be a prohibitive cost. In the general case, when applying our architecture, the per-feature cost of SME time should be considered against (a) the potential per-example savings from reducing labeling requirements, and (b) the performance requirements of the problem space.

The Human-in-the-Loop (HITL) approach enables SMEs to exert a positive influence on the quality of both the final model and the dataset. Given a probable baseline label error rate of a few percentage points (Alt et al., 2020; Reiss et al., 2020; Northcutt et al., 2021), as the Reducer's recall increases towards the 0.9 level, many of the mismatches against silver-standard Reducer evaluations and fine-tuning errors will actually be labeling errors. For example, in a case study where we checked `last_writeup` Reducer outputs against a silver-standard evaluation, we found that over 80% of "errors" were actually errors in human labeling. This also provides opportunities for SMEs to apply domain knowledge to more subtle classes of data issues, such as where Reducer rules surface mislabelings caused by labeler confusion.

As such, a unique advantage to HITL over a neural-only model is improving data quality during the training process. Purely neural models are forced to learn from mislabeled data points, which destabilizes benchmarks and damages model performance. (Northcutt et al., 2021) By comparison, we frequently detect label errors prior to fine-tuning, and as errors tend to occur in patches (such as under a particular labeler or a particular time period) we can quickly make corrections or exclude large bad patches from the training dataset. This can significantly increase training performance: excluding a patch of bad labels resulted in a 0.2 F1 improvement in one case. Appendix B elaborates on the data quality improvement process.

6.3 Modular Architecture

The Reducer-Producer architecture is useful for enabling iterative, componentwise development. Components may be improved in isolation as requirements arise, such as improving Reducer coverage or upgrading Producer language models, heads or prompts, and sometimes may be entirely replaced without any impact to their counterparts.

In particular, we hope to leave the door open for a general neural Reducer and Producer, allowing downstream users to perform open-ended querying and exploration of the dataset. This architecture enables future work to continue to use our Producer models, which are already trained. The information bottleneck between its components allows for rigorous measurement of the quality of Reducer output, which enables each component to be trained separately. Additionally, using present models to generate silver-standard data labels may alleviate issues of label scarcity.

7 Conclusion

Our corpus of parole hearings poses the challenge of information extraction with few gold labels: one thousand labels is not enough to locate and identify the answer in a long document. Parole, like many other applications, requires domain-specific knowledge, which raises the question of how best to incorporate the labor of subject matter experts to assist neural models in making optimal use of available labels, in order to achieve high performance on extraction tasks.

We identified two problems with existing work on the parole dataset, which fell short of the 0.80 F1 on many tasks: (1) Text segments remained too long for many SOTA neural models to digest, and contained many spurious signals. (2) Question answering was a useful first approach to handle a wide range of different feature types. However, out-of-the-box, it was rarely the best way to handle each individual feature type.

We present an approach that uses an SME-designed rule-based Reducer to identify relevant text segments, and a neural Producer to generate labels using those text segments.

We argue that it is time-efficient and performant for human SMEs to write mostly keyword-based rules for finding relevant parts of a parole transcript. In a parole transcript, a field of interest might be discussed in practically infinite different ways, but is usually somewhat well-defined by a limited set of words and patterns that are almost always used (for example, "GED", "college courses", "did not graduate" for a parole candidate's level of education). These keywords are relatively easy for a human to identify and write combinations of regular expressions to identify. However, training a neural model to recognize the phrases over the course of 20,000-word documents requires at least an order of magnitude more labels than are available (Hendrycks et al., 2021). Therefore, we focus SME energy on the Reducer, and *only* the Reducer.

For the Producer model, the role of human and machine are reversed. When the text is shortened to a sufficiently succinct context, neural models can be successfully fine-tuned to extract labels at an F1 of 0.80. It is practically impossible for a human to write rules to interpret every possible phrasing of, for example, someone's educational journey. However, pretrained language models excel at producing labels from small, targeted pieces of text. The 1,000 available labels are sufficient for good performance on this task (Zhang et al., 2020). We use a base model that can handle relatively long tokens. We also explore a range of different fine-tuning heads.

Our architecture shows the effectiveness of a modular, two-step approach, where not every module needs to be a neural or machine learning model. Such efforts to involve subject matter experts are especially important in applications that require substantial domain expertise. We hope that this work encourages additional research to better understand other legal processes whose workings are yet opaque to the public.

References

Christoph Alt, Aleksandra Gabryszak, and Leonhard Hennig. 2020. Tacred revisited: A thorough evaluation of the tacred relation extraction task. *arXiv preprint arXiv:2004.14855.*

Kristen Bell, Jenny Hong, Nick McKeown, and Catalin Voss. 2021. The Recon Approach: A new direction for machine learning in criminal law. *Berkeley Technology Law Journal*, 37.

Danqi Chen. 2018. *Neural Reading Comprehension and Beyond.* Ph.D. thesis, Stanford University.

Danqi Chen, Adam Fisch, Jason Weston, and Antoine Bordes. 2017. Reading Wikipedia to answer open-domain questions. In *Proceedings of the 55th Annual Meeting of the Association for Computational Linguistics (Volume 1: Long Papers)*, pages 1870–1879, Vancouver, Canada. Association for Computational Linguistics.

Christopher Clark and Matt Gardner. 2017. Simple and effective multi-paragraph reading comprehension. *arXiv:1710.10723.*

Christopher Clark, Kenton Lee, Ming-Wei Chang, Tom Kwiatkowski, Michael Collins, and Kristina Toutanova. 2019. BoolQ: Exploring the surprising difficulty of natural yes/no questions. In *Proceedings of the 2019 Conference of the North American Chapter of the Association for Computational Linguistics: Human Language Technologies, Volume 1 (Long and Short Papers)*, pages 2924–2936, Minneapolis, Minnesota. Association for Computational Linguistics.

Zhihao Dai, Zhong Li, and Lianghao Han. 2021. Bonebert: A bert-based automated information extraction system of radiology reports for bone fracture detection and diagnosis. In *IDA*, pages 263–274.

Rajarshi Das, Shehzaad Dhuliawala, Manzil Zaheer, and Andrew McCallum. 2019. Multi-step retriever-reader interaction for scalable open-domain question answering. *arXiv preprint arXiv:1905.05733.*

Jacob Devlin, Ming-Wei Chang, Kenton Lee, and Kristina Toutanova. 2019. BERT: Pre-training of deep bidirectional transformers for language understanding. In *Proceedings of the 2019 Conference of the North American Chapter of the Association for Computational Linguistics: Human Language Technologies, Volume 1 (Long and Short Papers)*, pages 4171–4186, Minneapolis, Minnesota. Association for Computational Linguistics.

Catherine D'ignazio and Lauren F Klein. 2020. *Data feminism.* MIT press.

Dheeru Dua, Yizhong Wang, Pradeep Dasigi, Gabriel Stanovsky, Sameer Singh, and Matt Gardner. 2019. Drop: A reading comprehension benchmark requiring discrete reasoning over paragraphs. *arXiv preprint arXiv:1903.00161.*

Dan Hendrycks, Collin Burns, Anya Chen, and Spencer Ball. 2021. CUAD: An expert-annotated NLP dataset for legal contract review. *arXiv preprint arXiv:2103.06268.*

Karl Moritz Hermann, Tomas Kocisky, Edward Grefenstette, Lasse Espeholt, Will Kay, Mustafa Suleyman, and Phil Blunsom. 2015. Teaching machines to read and comprehend. In *NIPS.*

Felix Hill, Antoine Bordes, Sumit Chopra, and Jason Weston. 2016. The goldilocks principle: Reading children's books with explicit memory representations. In *4th International Conference on Learning Representations, ICLR 2016, San Juan, Puerto Rico, May 2-4, 2016, Conference Track Proceedings.*

Jenny Hong, Catalin Voss, and Christopher Manning. 2021. Challenges for information extraction from dialogue in criminal law. In *Proceedings of the 1st Workshop on NLP for Positive Impact*, pages 71–81, Online. Association for Computational Linguistics.

Jared Kaplan, Sam McCandlish, Tom Henighan, Tom B Brown, Benjamin Chess, Rewon Child, Scott Gray, Alec Radford, Jeffrey Wu, and Dario Amodei. 2020. Scaling laws for neural language models. *arXiv preprint arXiv:2001.08361.*

Vladimir Karpukhin, Barlas Oguz, Sewon Min, Patrick Lewis, Ledell Wu, Sergey Edunov, Danqi Chen, and Wen-tau Yih. 2020. Dense passage retrieval for open-domain question answering. In *Proceedings of the 2020 Conference on Empirical Methods in Natural Language Processing (EMNLP)*, pages 6769–6781, Online. Association for Computational Linguistics.

Tassilo Klein and Moin Nabi. 2019. Learning to answer by learning to ask: Getting the best of gpt-2 and bert worlds. *arXiv:1911.02365.*

Kalpesh Krishna, Aurko Roy, and Mohit Iyyer. 2021. Hurdles to progress in long-form question answering. *arXiv:2103.06332.*

Tom Kwiatkowski, Jennimaria Palomaki, Olivia Redfield, Michael Collins, Ankur Parikh, Chris Alberti, Danielle Epstein, Illia Polosukhin, Jacob Devlin, Kenton Lee, et al. 2019. Natural questions: a benchmark for question answering research. *Transactions of the Association for Computational Linguistics*, 7:453–466.

Guokun Lai, Qizhe Xie, Hanxiao Liu, Yiming Yang, and Eduard Hovy. 2017. RACE: Large-scale ReAding comprehension dataset from examinations. In *Proceedings of the 2017 Conference on Empirical Methods in Natural Language Processing*, pages 785–794, Copenhagen, Denmark. Association for Computational Linguistics.

Albee Y Ling, Allison W Kurian, Jennifer L Caswell-Jin, George W Sledge Jr, Nigam H Shah, and Suzanne R Tamang. 2019. A semi-supervised machine learning approach to detecting recurrent metastatic breast cancer cases using linked cancer registry and electronic medical record data. *arXiv preprint arXiv:1901.05958*.

Yinhan Liu, Myle Ott, Naman Goyal, Jingfei Du, Mandar Joshi, Danqi Chen, Omer Levy, Mike Lewis, Luke Zettlemoyer, and Veselin Stoyanov. 2019. Roberta: A robustly optimized bert pretraining approach. *arXiv preprint arXiv:1907.11692*.

Ayush Maheshwari, Oishik Chatterjee, KrishnaTeja Killamsetty, Rishabh Iyer, and Ganesh Ramakrishnan. 2020. Data programming using semi-supervision and subset selection. *arXiv preprint arXiv:2008.09887*.

Curtis G Northcutt, Anish Athalye, and Jonas Mueller. 2021. Pervasive label errors in test sets destabilize machine learning benchmarks. *arXiv preprint arXiv:2103.14749*.

Alex Ratner, Braden Hancock, Jared Dunnmon, Roger Goldman, and Christopher Ré. 2018. Snorkel metal: Weak supervision for multi-task learning. In *Proceedings of the Second Workshop on Data Management for End-To-End Machine Learning*, pages 1–4.

Alexander Ratner, Stephen H Bach, Henry Ehrenberg, Jason Fries, Sen Wu, and Christopher Ré. 2017. Snorkel: Rapid training data creation with weak supervision. *Proceedings of the VLDB Endowment. International Conference on Very Large Data Bases*, 11(3):269–282.

Alexander Ratner, Christopher De Sa, Sen Wu, Daniel Selsam, and Christopher Ré. 2016. Data programming: Creating large training sets, quickly. *Advances in Neural Information Processing Systems*, 29:3567.

Siva Reddy, Danqi Chen, and Christopher D Manning. 2019. CoQA: A conversational question answering challenge. *Transactions of the Association for Computational Linguistics*, 7:249–266.

Frederick Reiss, Hong Xu, Bryan Cutler, Karthik Muthuraman, and Zachary Eichenberger. 2020. Identifying incorrect labels in the conll-2003 corpus. In *Proceedings of the 24th Conference on Computational Natural Language Learning*, pages 215–226.

Matthew Richardson, Christopher J.C. Burges, and Erin Renshaw. 2013. MCTest: A challenge dataset for the open-domain machine comprehension of text. In *Proceedings of the 2013 Conference on Empirical Methods in Natural Language Processing*, pages 193–203, Seattle, Washington, USA. Association for Computational Linguistics.

Akshay Smit, Saahil Jain, Pranav Rajpurkar, Anuj Pareek, Andrew Y Ng, and Matthew P Lungren. 2020. Chexbert: combining automatic labelers and expert annotations for accurate radiology report labeling using bert. *arXiv preprint arXiv:2004.09167*.

Chi Sun, Xipeng Qiu, Yige Xu, and Xuanjing Huang. 2019. How to fine-tune bert for text classification? In *China National Conference on Chinese Computational Linguistics*, pages 194–206. Springer.

Peng Wang, Zhenkai Deng, and Ruilong Cui. 2021. Tdjee: A document-level joint model for financial event extraction. *Electronics*, 10(7):824.

Thomas Wolf, Lysandre Debut, Victor Sanh, Julien Chaumond, Clement Delangue, Anthony Moi, Pierric Cistac, Tim Rault, Rémi Louf, Morgan Funtowicz, Joe Davison, Sam Shleifer, Patrick von Platen, Clara Ma, Yacine Jernite, Julien Plu, Canwen Xu, Teven Le Scao, Sylvain Gugger, Mariama Drame, Quentin Lhoest, and Alexander M. Rush. 2020. Transformers: State-of-the-art natural language processing. In *Proceedings of the 2020 Conference on Empirical Methods in Natural Language Processing: System Demonstrations*, pages 38–45, Online. Association for Computational Linguistics.

Runxin Xu, Tianyu Liu, Lei Li, and Baobao Chang. 2021. Document-level event extraction via heterogeneous graph-based interaction model with a tracker. In *Proceedings of the 59th Annual Meeting of the Association for Computational Linguistics and the 11th International Joint Conference on Natural Language Processing (Volume 1: Long Papers)*, pages 3533–3546, Online. Association for Computational Linguistics.

Manzil Zaheer, Guru Guruganesh, Kumar Avinava Dubey, Joshua Ainslie, Chris Alberti, Santiago Ontanon, Philip Pham, Anirudh Ravula, Qifan Wang, Li Yang, and Amr Ahmed. 2020. Big bird: Transformers for longer sequences. In *Advances in Neural Information Processing Systems*, volume 33, pages 17283–17297. Curran Associates, Inc.

Jingqing Zhang, Yao Zhao, Mohammad Saleh, and Peter Liu. 2020. Pegasus: Pre-training with extracted gap-sentences for abstractive summarization. In *International Conference on Machine Learning*, pages 11328–11339. PMLR.

Shanshan Zhang, Lihong He, Eduard Dragut, and Slobodan Vucetic. 2019. How to invest my time: Lessons from human-in-the-loop entity extraction. In *Proceedings of the 25th ACM SIGKDD International Conference on Knowledge Discovery & Data Mining*, pages 2305–2313.

Shun Zheng, Wei Cao, Wei Xu, and Jiang Bian. 2019. Doc2EDAG: An end-to-end document-level framework for Chinese financial event extraction. In *Proceedings of the 2019 Conference on Empirical Methods in Natural Language Processing and the 9th International Joint Conference on Natural Language Processing (EMNLP-IJCNLP)*, pages 337–346, Hong Kong, China. Association for Computational Linguistics.

A Reducer Operations and Rules

SMEs write Reducers for each field by composing pipelines of high-level operations, as described in Table 6. Operations run on an input transcript or a list of text segments, and emit matches which are compiled into a final output passage.

Operation	Parameter	Description
Extract Segments		Extracts a list of segments from a raw transcript which match one or more regular expressions (regexes).
	Input	Transcript text with any preprocessing.
	Regex	Accepts a list of regexes and searches the transcript separately for each item, returning matches in the same left-to-right order they are found.
	Limit	Length of segment returned around each match.
Filter & Split		Filters a list of segments against two lists of regexes, to return two lists of matching and non-matching segments.
	Regex	Accepts a "filter in" regex list which segments must match, and a "filter out" regex list which segments must not match.
Emit Matches		Saves segments from a given list to a specified list for future compilation.
	Limit	Length of segment to store around each match, and maximum segments to store.
Deduplicate		Ensures a list of segments is free of duplicate or overlapping text ranges. Merges segments with partial overlaps.
Compile Passage		Merges a list of segments into a single text passage.
	Separator	String inserted between each segment.
	Limit	Trims passage to a maximum length.

Table 6: Overview of Reducer operations.

To illustrate these operations in use, the pipeline for `job_offer` is provided in Table 7.

#	Param.	Value(s)
01	**Extract Segments**	
	Input	Transcript (lowercase)
	Regex	`job offer`
	Limit	1,000 chars centered on each match
02	**Filter & Split**	
	Input	Operation 01
	Regex	`letter`
03	**Emit Matches**	
	Input	Operation 02: Matches only
	Limit	2 segments
	Effect	*Emits 2x1,000-char segments which mention "job offer" in proximity to "letter".*
04	**Emit Matches**	
	Input	Operation 02: Non-matches only
	Limit	2 segments, 500 chars centered on each match
	Effect	*Emits 2x500-char segments which mention "job offer" but not "letter".*
		(Continued overleaf)
05	**Extract Segments**	
	Input	Transcript (lowercase)
	Regexes	`jobs? ([\w,]+ ){2,10}offer OR offer\w+ ([\w,]+ ){2,10}job`
	Limit	500 chars centered on each match
06	**Emit Matches**	
	Input	Operation 05
	Limit	2 segments
	Effect	*Emits 2x500-char segments in which "job" and "offer" are within ten words of each other.*
07	**Extract Segments**	
	Input	Transcript (lowercase)
	Regex	`(?:find\w+|locat\w+|get\w+) (\w+ ){0,5}(?:work |employment|job(?! offer))`
	Limit	1,000 chars centered on each match
08	**Emit Matches**	
	Input	Operation 07
	Limit	2 segments
	Effect	*Emits 2x1,000-char segments in which a verb and a noun about job hunting are within five words of each other.*
09	**Extract Segments**	
	Input	Transcript (lowercase)
	Regex	`(?:job(?! offer)|employ|hire|work)`
	Limit	1,000 chars centered on each match
10	**Filter & Split**	
	Input	Operation 09
	Regexes	`letter AND offer`
11	**Emit Matches**	
	Input	Operation 10: Matches only
	Limit	2 segments
	Effect	*Emits 2x1,000-char segments which contain a word about employment in proximity to both "offer" or "letter".*
12	**Filter & Split**	
	Input	Operation 10: Non-matches only
	Regex	`letter`
13	**Emit Matches**	
	Input	Operation 12: Matches only
	Limit	2 segments
	Effect	*Emits 2x1,000-char segments which contain a word about employment in proximity to only "letter".*
14	**Emit Matches**	
	Input	Operation 12: Non-matches only
	Limit	5 segments
	Effect	*Catch-all: Emits 5x1,000-char segments which contain a word about employment.*
15	**Deduplicate**	
	Input	All emitted segments
16	**Compile Passage**	
	Input	Operation 15
	Separator	`[SEP]`
	Limit	First 6,500 characters

Table 7: Reducer pipeline for `job_offer`.

B Improving Data Quality using Silver-Standard Evaluations

Mismatches on silver-standard Reducer evaluations were often a product of real label errors: the datasets examined in Northcutt et al. (2021) had a 3.4% error rate on average, which is a similar order of magnitude to label errors encountered in our dataset when performing detailed manual verification.

The parole dataset includes records that span over more than a decade, and labeling has occurred in several waves over the years. As such, the semantic meanings of labels includes subtle shifts and inconsistencies. For example, a blank label might mean any one of the following:

- the annotator was uncertain,
- the transcript is unclear,
- the transcript is clear but the situation itself is ambiguous,
- "none" is a reasonable answer in this situation (such as `last_writeup` for a candidate with zero writeups),
- the feature was not applicable in this situation (such as `job_offer` for a candidate who is not working age); or
- the feature was simply not fully annotated.

To address these issues, we: (a) write code to correct issues where this is possible, (b) drop entire sections of low-quality train labels where patterns of errors exist, (c) hand-correct validation labels and keep track of all manual corrections, and (d) write small data transforms to simplify the job of the Producer (e.g., fixing common spelling and transcription errors).

C Sample Challenging Passages

Table 8 provides examples of the complex, challenging passages selected to benchmark language models in section 5.2, trimmed for brevity and redacted as per the conventions described within Figure 1.

D Supplemental Error Analysis: `edu_level`

This section provides a detailed breakdown of the error analysis for a single field and data split (`edu_level`, Validation), in order to illustrate typical patterns of errors encountered in our fine-tuned models.

This field was fine-tuned with a classification (CLS) prediction head, and correctly classified 89/106 of its labeled examples. Its 17 incorrectly-classified examples are examined in Table 9. The four possible values this field may hold are:

- NA: Did not finish high school
- HS: Completed high school or GED
- SC: Some college classes
- GC: Graduated from college

Field	Passages
risk_assess	**COMM**: With respect to violence risk assessment conclusions [...] the doctor uses a number of measurements. One is the PCL, which is the psychopathy checklist, and states that, "Overall score placed Mr. [REDACT] in the moderate range of psychopathy. [...]" Historically, on the HCR checklist, HCR20, the doctor writes, "[...] he has risk factors that place him in the low moderate risk range for future violence [...] The inmate's overall LS/CMI score indicates that he is in the medium category." And then the doctor goes on to discuss the historical domain and concludes, "[...] the inmate presents a moderate risk for future violence. [...] In the clinical or more current and dynamic domain of risk assessment [...] the inmate presents a moderate risk of future violence. As for the management of future risk domain [...] the inmate presents as a low risk of future violence. Overall then, risk assessment estimates suggests that the inmate poses a low moderate likelihood to become involved in a violent offense if released to the free community."
edu_level	**COMM**: Okay. So, and at the last hearing, it was discussed and I don't want to get - Well, that's parole plans. We're not going to talk about that right now. But, so you've taken a number of courses. It looks like in 2013, 2014, General Studies. Are you working towards a college degree? **CAND**: No. We're not able to take a college degree where I'm at. **COMM**: You say you've taken World War II, Europe Civilization, Ecology. Are these television courses or - **CAND**: They're videotapes, CDs.
job_offer	**COMM**: Do you have any job offers if you were to get a parole date? **CAND**: Uh, I used to be a mechanic before in, uh, [REDACT], my not in a company, but uh, in uh, a little shop with my friends. **COMM**: Do you have any job offers as a plumber? **CAND**: Yes. No, no, no, no, no, no. Not as a plumber. But, uh, I got, uh, as a mechanic I got offer with my cousin. **COMM**: Okay. Yeah. But he's in the United States, right? **CAND**: No, he's in [REDACT].
last_writeup	**COMM**: You've had 19 115s, starting in 1996, and most of these have been covered in prior hearings but, sort of running through them, couple in 1996, two in 1997, four in 1998, two in 1999, three in 2001, 2002, 2004, 2005, there was a pair. And then 2008, disobeying a direct order was your final 115. What was the 2005, knowingly providing a false claim?

Table 8: Examples of complex, challenging passages.

#	Source	Type	Label	Pred.	Error Details
1	Dataset	Ambiguous situation	HS	NA	Self-reported overseas high school completion (no records)
2	Dataset	Ambiguous situation	SC	HS	Vocational courses but taken at a college
3	Dataset	Mislabeling	HS	SC	Transcript explicitly discusses college courses taken
4	Reducer	Reducer pattern miss	NA	HS	Did not capture key sentence: *"I loved school. You know, I played the cello, you know, was ahead in school. I was graduating. I needed one credit to graduate from high school."*
5	Producer	Spurious associations	NA	HS	Two discussions about GED
6	Producer	Spurious associations	SC	HS	Confirms receipt of GED twice plus vocational training, just one brief mention of a college course
7	Producer	Spurious associations	NA	HS	Cluster of words: "school", "high school", "GED"
8	Producer	Spurious associations	SC	HS	Three mentions of graduating high school, one brief mention of college courses
9	Producer	Spurious associations	SC	GC	Candidate discusses the future receipt of an Associate's degree, later uses word "degree"
10	Producer	Spurious associations	NA	HS	Mentions "school" twice, "grade" three times
11	Producer	Spurious associations	SC	HS	Confirms receipt of GED twice, vocational training, two mentions of college courses
12	Producer	Spurious associations	SC	HS	Confirms receipt of GED twice, vocational training, mentions two colleges but not classes, units or degrees
13	Producer	Spurious associations	NA	HS	Mentions "school" three times, "college" twice
14	Producer	Spurious associations	GC	SC	Candidate confirms he has been doing college courses and is close to qualifying for an AA degree, but later notes he already has one degree
15	Producer	Spurious associations	SC	HS	Cluster of discussion around hgh school diploma, GED (four mentions) and reading scores
16	Producer	Spurious associations	SC	HS	Four separate mentions of having receiving GED, one small mention of college courses
17	Producer	Complex phrasing	NA	HS	Description is challenging to interpret: *"I started ditching school and hanging out when I was in high school. I think part of the reason for that was because we never had anything at home, everything was always, seemed like we're always struggling for everything, you know. Our electric bill, I didn't want to keep living like that, so I left, I left when I was 13 years old."*

Table 9: Example-level error assessments: `edu_level`.

Automating Claim Construction in Patent Applications: The CMUmine Dataset

Ozan K. Tonguz **Yiwei Qin** **Yimeng Gu** **Hyun (Hannah) Moon**
Department of Electrical and Computer Engineering
Carnegie Mellon University
Pittsburgh, PA 15213-3890, USA
{tonguz, yiweiq, yimengg}@andrew.cmu.edu, hyunm@alumni.cmu.edu

Abstract

Intellectual Property (IP) in the form of issued patents is a critical and very desirable element of innovation in high-tech. In this position paper, we explore the possibility of automating the legal task of Claim Construction in patent applications via Natural Language Processing (NLP) and Machine Learning (ML). To this end, we first create a large dataset known as CMUmine™and then demonstrate that, using NLP and ML techniques the Claim Construction in patent applications, a crucial legal task currently performed by IP attorneys, can be automated. To the best of our knowledge, this is the first public patent application dataset. Our results look very promising in automating the patent application process.

1 Introduction

In the USA, European Union (EU), and Asia, most of the high-tech industries (semiconductors, wireless, Internet, Telecommunications, Robotics, Sensors, etc.) are characterized by the innovations they introduce and the inventions they make in a specific area of technology and these innovations are considered to be the intellectual property (IP) of these companies, a very important asset for any high-tech company. To protect their IP, high-tech companies file for patent applications to make it official that they own that specific idea and invention that could involve a new system or apparatus, new method, and new algorithms and/or software.

In general, filing patents that describe new inventions is a lengthy, cumbersome, and very costly process since most high-tech companies have to hire law firms, litigation attorneys who specialize in IP, and technical professionals called patent "agents", or "patent engineers" for writing and filing such patent applications. After an inventor prepares a well-written document describing his/her invention, she/he submits this document to an IP attorney who takes this document that is known as "Invention Disclosure" and prepares a patent application that can be submitted in the US to the United States Patent and Trademark Office (USPTO).

The main sections of a patent comprise the following sections:

1) Title and Inventors
2) Abstract
3) Introduction (background of the invention and "prior art")
4) Invention Summary
5) Description of the invention including figures (also known as "specifications")
6) Claims (independent claims and dependent claims)

A key observation we make is that, if the Invention Disclosure is well prepared by the inventor, then the main contribution of the IP attorney to the patent application is to formulate the claims of the specific invention. In legal terms, this task is known as "Claim Construction". An IP attorney will not typically change the other parts of an invention (e.g., the specifications section of the invention); instead, he will formulate the main claims of the invention in the form of:

(i) Independent Claims
(ii) Dependent Claims

and then append these claims to the end of the invention disclosure for the official submission of the patent application to the USPTO. Typically, patents in information technology have 3 Independent Claims and 5 or 6 dependent claims per independent claim that do depend on each of the 3 independent claims, thus resulting in a total of 20 or more claims in a patent application. In general, the independent claims concern the following aspects of an invention:

1) System or apparatus claim
2) Method claim
3) Software claim

Natural Legal Language Processing Workshop 2021, pages 205–209
November 10, 2021.

2 Problem Statement

In this position paper, we explore the possibility of replacing the "human agents" with an automated solution (i.e., "the machine") in patent application process. In other words, we investigate whether the construction of the independent and dependent claims prepared by an IP attorney can be automated by using AI, Natural Language Processing (NLP), and Machine Learning (ML). The key observation behind this is the underlying pattern in preparing the claims in a patent application: the IP attorney gets a well written Invention Disclosure from an inventor and, based on that and a brief conversation with the inventor, prepares the claims of a patent application. Can this process be automated? Our results suggest that the use of NLP and ML can indeed automate "Claim Construction" tasks and, therefore, the patent application process. As a proof-of-concept, among all the claims constructed by IP attorneys, this paper focuses on generating the First Independent Claim. The approach we pursue in this paper is to formulate the problem as a text summarization problem [El-Kassas et al., 2021].

3 Related Work

Text summarization aims to briefly summarize the key information of any longer input text. Text summarization techniques using NLP has been successfully applied to various fields, including news [Grusky et al., 2018] [Fabbri et al., 2019], scientific papers [Lu, 2011] [Clement et al., 2019] and patents [Grusky et al., 2020]. Specifically, in [Grusky et al., 2020], the author models the text summarization task as follows: a granted patent's description is the input text, and its summary is regarded as the gold-standard summary. Our task is similar to other text summarization tasks, i.e., summarizing the First Independent Claim from a longer Invention Disclosure. Therefore, a viable approach that might work is to model our task as a text summarization task.

4 Data Collection and Dataset Construction

To meet our goal, we started by collecting a large dataset consisting of 300K patent applications, known as Carnegie Mellon University Machine Interpreted Natural-Language Engineering (**CMUmine™**). Using this very large data set, dubbed **CMUmine™**, of 317,356 previous US patent applications, we create a training set, a validation data set, and a test set that comprise 253,976, 31,736, and 31, 644 data points (i.e., previous patent applications), respectively. This is the first public and largest patent application dataset to the best of our knowledge. BigPatent [Grusky et al., 2020] is a well-known large text summarization dataset in patent domain, but it does not include patent claims and cannot be used for claim construction.

4.1 Description

Our dataset consists of issued patent applications collected from USPTO Bulk Data Storage System (BDSS) Version 1.1.0 [1]. Specifically, our raw data comes from the *Patent Application Full Text Data (No Images) (MAR 15, 2021 - PRESENT)* in the link above. We only used the patent applications issued in 2005 and 2006 to construct our dataset. Based on a detailed literature review on popular text summarization dataset's size, we decided to collect roughly 300,000 data points. Initially, we began to process data from the year 2002 and found that from the year 2002 to year 2004 datasets have non-standardized data structures. When we processed the year 2005 data set, it had a suitable structure for processing the data. It also met our expectations on the amount of data needed to train models after accumulating two years of data in a row. Therefore, we decided to use the year 2005 to 2006 data envisioning that the same arguments can be applied for data collected in recent years as well. Our data set can be found at this link[2].

4.2 Data Processing

The raw data on USPTO BDSS is in the format of XML, e.g., *ipa150903.xml*. Each xml file contains all the patent applications issued during that week of a certain year.

Considering the fact that patent applications are organized in different ways, to reduce the variation in size of summary and First Independent Claim and build a more representative dataset, we applied filter conditions to remove outliers. We only kept patent applications whose Invention Summary and First Independent Claim's length are within the percentile [10%,90%], that is [150,1500] words for

[1] `https://bulkdata.uspto.gov/`

[2] `https://drive.google.com/drive/u/0/folders/1J4sAcM_21G39VuZT1jv6RqLTEM_UngWS`

Invention Summary and [35, 300] words for First Independent Claim.

4.3 Dataset Structure

Our dataset consists of training set, validation set, and test set with a ratio of 8:1:1. Under train/validation/test folder, there are 6 subfolders: 1) abstract; 2) background; 3) summary; 4) detailed description; 5) first independent claim; and 6) claims. Under each sub-folder, every single file is named in the format of `{patent application No.}_{sub-folder name}`. All the files only contain text data. It was observed that not every US patent application contains a detailed description section. If a patent application does not have a detailed description section, we do not include it in the detailed description sub-folder. Around 2/3 (two thirds) of patent applications in our dataset have detailed description part.

4.4 Dataset Analysis

To have good insights into the features of our dataset, we use several automatic metrics to quantify its important features (e.g., average length, extractivity, compression, novel words).

Compression ratio [Grusky et al., 2020]: ratio between source document and output length. Compression ratio is measured by

$$CMP(S, O) = \frac{S}{O}, \tag{1}$$

where |S| and |O| denote the length of the source document and output sequence, respectively.

Coverage [Grusky et al., 2020]: measures the percentage of words in the output sequence that are part of an extractive fragment in the source document. Coverage is measured by

$$Coverage(S, O) = \frac{1}{O} \sum_{f \in F(S,O)} |f|, \tag{2}$$

where F (S, O) is the set of shared sequences of tokens in source S and output sequence O.

Density [Grusky et al., 2020]: measures the average length of the extractive fragment. Density is measured by

$$Density(S, O) = \frac{1}{|O|} \sum_{f \in F(S,O)} |f|^2. \tag{3}$$

Copy Length [Chen et al., 2020]: measures the average length of segments in output sequence copied from source document.

Novelty n-gram ratio [Narayan et al., 2018]: the proportion of segments in the output sequence that haven't appeared in source documents. The segments can be instantiated as n-grams.

As mentioned before, our dataset includes different parts of an invention disclosure document. Since the useful information to generate claims are scattered to different sections of this document, it is important to evaluate the features of different parts to decide which part is the best to use as the input sequence for our model to generate claims. For simplicity, we do not consider the combination of two parts and the detailed description part, whose length exceeds the capacity of both Recurrent Neural Networks (RNN) based model and Transformer [Vaswani et al., 2017] based model. We evaluate the dataset characteristics using Abstract, Introduction, or Invention Summary as source document and First Independent Claims as the output. The dataset evaluation result is shown in Table 1.

From Table 1, we observe that the summary part has the highest extractive rate, which is reflected in the highest density, coverage, copy length and lowest novelty words ratio. This means the summary part is the most informative part for generating claims, so we use the summary part as the model input in our work.

5 Approach

As described in Section 2, we formulate our problem as a text summarization task, so we use popular summarization systems: Pointer Generator (PG)[See et al., 2017] and PEGASUS [Zhang et al., 2019]. We used the training data set to train our model, the validation data set to fine-tune our model in terms of hyper parameters and then evaluated the performance of our model in generating the First Independent Claim (FIN) on the test set. The results obtained are compared with the "Gold Standard" that represent the versions of the same FIN constructed by humans (i.e., IP attorneys). The obtained machine-generated results are compared in terms of ROUGE-1, ROUGE-2, and ROUGE-L [Lin, 2004] scores based on the statistical distributions of the results obtained, i.e., the probability density functions (pdf's) of the results.

6 Results

6.1 Evaluation of the generated first claim

Table 2 reports F1 scores of ROUGE-1 (R1), ROUGE-2 (R2), ROUGE-L (RL) for all models.

	Summary	Abstract	Background
Mean Source Length	615.5	123.2	726.6
Mean Output Length	123.8	123.8	123.8
Compression Ratio	4.97	0.995	5.87
Novelty1-gram/2-gram	0.20/0.38	0.36/0.58	0.53/0.85
Density	20.18	9.22	1.58
Coverage	0.86	0.73	0.65
Copy Length	9.01	4.41	1.55

Table 1: Intrinsic Characteristics of patent applications in the CMUmine dataset

	R1	R2	RL
Pointer Generator	65.51	52.95	59.25
PEGASUS	75.97	64.47	70.54

Table 2: Average F1 scores of the first independent claim generated with the test set for Rouge-1, Rouge-2, and Rouge-L.

It can be observed from Table 2 that the performance of self-attention approach is distinctively higher than the Pointer Generator approach. PEGASUS works very well on our dataset with average ROUGE scores achieving 60-70%, which is a very high score for the abstractive summarization task in NLP. The state-of-the-art ROUGE score for popular text summarization datasets are among 30-60% [Zhang et al., 2019]. This attests to the fact that using NLP techniques, it is possible to accurately generate the FIN that is arguably the most important claim among all the claims in a patent application.

Figure 1 shows the probability distributions of the resulting rouge scores when one uses the Pegasus approach on our test set of 31,644 data points.

Based on the obtained probability distributions (i.e., probability density functions) shown in Figure 1, and the expected value (mean) of these distributions, one can observe that our chosen model performs very well on the dataset.

7 Discussion

While the results reported look very promising, our current experiments have the following limitations: 1) We used abstractive summarization to generate the first independent claim which limits the input length. This might be solved by using a combination of extractive summarization, like heuristics, and abstractive summarization; 2) Our results show that our generated claim is mainly a summary of what the inventor writes. However, the claims generated should also establish the novelty of the invention by looking at other patents and/or published papers in the public domain for similar inventions in the same space, instead of only focusing on one single patent application, which requires incorporating external knowledge; 3) Using ROUGE score as the evaluation metric, which focuses on the syntax similarities between the generated claims and the gold standards, might not be sufficient to evaluate the quality of the generated claims. Other aspects, such as semantic similarity, factuality, etc. need to be considered as well. We plan to address these problems in future work.

8 Conclusion

Our results suggest that claim construction and the patent application process can be largely automated in the future with the help of AI, natural language processing, and machine learning. This will have far-reaching consequences such as:

- democratizing the landscape for innovation and inventions, thus enabling small businesses, underrepresented groups, and individual inventors (in addition to big companies) to file for patents in a much more cost-effective manner to own IP;
- expediting the submission and issuing of patent applications dramatically (from 3 or 4 years to less than 1 year), thus making the IP litigation process much more efficient;
- facilitating disruptive changes in the IP litigation process by AI where the machine will be able to do some, if not most, of the legal tasks currently performed by humans.

We hope that our results will stimulate further research into using AI, Natural Language Processing, and Machine Learning for automating the patent application process.

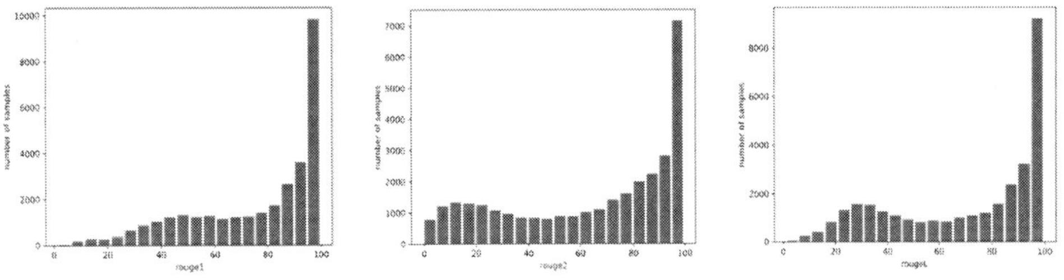

Figure 1: Probability Distribution of F1 scores for ROUGE-1, ROUGE-2, and ROUGE-L.

References

Yiran Chen, Pengfei Liu, Ming Zhong, Zi-Yi Dou, Danqing Wang, Xipeng Qiu, and Xuanjing Huang. Cdevalsumm: An empirical study of cross-dataset evaluation for neural summarization systems, 2020.

Colin B. Clement, Matthew Bierbaum, Kevin P. O'Keeffe, and Alexander A. Alemi. On the use of arxiv as a dataset. *CoRR*, abs/1905.00075, 2019. URL `http://arxiv.org/abs/1905.00075`.

Wafaa S El-Kassas, Cherif R Salama, Ahmed A Rafea, and Hoda K Mohamed. Automatic text summarization: A comprehensive survey. *Expert Systems with Applications*, 165:113679, 2021.

Alexander Fabbri, Irene Li, Tianwei She, Suyi Li, and Dragomir Radev. Multi-news: A large-scale multi-document summarization dataset and abstractive hierarchical model. In *Proceedings of the 57th Annual Meeting of the Association for Computational Linguistics*, pages 1074–1084, Florence, Italy, July 2019. Association for Computational Linguistics.

Max Grusky, Mor Naaman, and Yoav Artzi. Newsroom: A dataset of 1.3 million summaries with diverse extractive strategies. In *Proceedings of the 2018 Conference of the North American Chapter of the Association for Computational Linguistics: Human Language Technologies, Volume 1 (Long Papers)*, pages 708–719, New Orleans, Louisiana, June 2018. Association for Computational Linguistics.

Max Grusky, Mor Naaman, and Yoav Artzi. Newsroom: A dataset of 1.3 million summaries with diverse extractive strategies, 2020.

Chin-Yew Lin. Rouge: A package for automatic evaluation of summaries. In *Text summarization branches out*, pages 74–81, 2004.

Zhiyong Lu. PubMed and beyond: a survey of web tools for searching biomedical literature. *Database*, 2011, 01 2011. ISSN 1758-0463. doi: 10.1093/database/baq036. URL `https://doi.org/10.1093/database/baq036`. baq036.

Shashi Narayan, Shay B. Cohen, and Mirella Lapata. Don't give me the details, just the summary! topic-aware convolutional neural networks for extreme summarization, 2018.

Abigail See, Peter J. Liu, and Christopher D. Manning. Get to the point: Summarization with pointer-generator networks, 2017.

Ashish Vaswani, Noam Shazeer, Niki Parmar, Jakob Uszkoreit, Llion Jones, Aidan N Gomez, Ł ukasz Kaiser, and Illia Polosukhin. Attention is all you need. In I. Guyon, U. V. Luxburg, S. Bengio, H. Wallach, R. Fergus, S. Vishwanathan, and R. Garnett, editors, *Advances in Neural Information Processing Systems*, volume 30. Curran Associates, Inc., 2017.

Jingqing Zhang, Yao Zhao, Mohammad Saleh, and Peter J. Liu. PEGASUS: pre-training with extracted gap-sentences for abstractive summarization. *CoRR*, abs/1912.08777, 2019.

Effectively Leveraging BERT for Legal Document Classification

Nut Limsopatham
Microsoft Corporation
Redmond, WA
nut.limsopatham@microsoft.com

Abstract

Bidirectional Encoder Representations from Transformers (BERT) has achieved state-of-the-art performances on several text classification tasks, such as GLUE and sentiment analysis. Recent work in the legal domain started to use BERT on tasks, such as legal judgement prediction and violation prediction. A common practise in using BERT is to fine-tune a pre-trained model on a target task and truncate the input texts to the size of the BERT input (e.g. at most 512 tokens). However, due to the unique characteristics of legal documents, it is not clear how to effectively adapt BERT in the legal domain. In this work, we investigate how to deal with long documents, and how is the importance of pre-training on documents from the same domain as the target task. We conduct experiments on the two recent datasets: ECHR Violation Dataset and the Overruling Task Dataset, which are multi-label and binary classification tasks, respectively. Importantly, on average the number of tokens in a document from the ECHR Violation Dataset is more than 1,600. While the documents in the Overruling Task Dataset are shorter (the maximum number of tokens is 204). We thoroughly compare several techniques for adapting BERT on long documents and compare different models pre-trained on the legal and other domains. Our experimental results show that we need to explicitly adapt BERT to handle long documents, as the truncation leads to less effective performance. We also found that pre-training on the documents that are similar to the target task would result in more effective performance on several scenario.

1 Introduction

Recent advances in deep learning contribute to effective performances of several natural language processing (NLP) tasks on legal text documents, such as, violation prediction (Chalkidis et al., 2020), overruling prediction (Zheng et al., 2021), legal judgement prediction (Chalkidis et al., 2019), legal information extraction (Chalkidis et al., 2018), and court opinion generation (Ye et al., 2018).

Bidirectional Encoder Representations from Transformers (BERT) (Devlin et al., 2019) has gained attentions from the NLP community due to its effectiveness on several NLP tasks (Chalkidis et al., 2019, 2020; Zheng et al., 2021). Importantly, the effectiveness of BERT is mainly due to the transfer learning ability that leverages semantic and syntactic knowledge from pre-training on a large non-labeled corpus (Devlin et al., 2019; Chalkidis et al., 2020; Zheng et al., 2021). However, Chalkidis et al. (2019) reported that BERT could not effectively handle long documents in the European Court of Human Rights (ECHR) dataset. In addition, pre-training BERT is costly. We need access to a special type of machines to pre-train BERT on a large corpora (Devlin et al., 2019; Liu et al., 2019; Zheng et al., 2021).

In this work, we investigate how to effectively adapt BERT to handle long documents, and how importance of pre-training on in-domain documents. Specifically, we will focus on two legal document prediction tasks, including ECHR Violation Dataset (Chalkidis et al., 2021) and Overruling Task Dataset (Zheng et al., 2021). The ECHR Violation Dataset provides a multi-label classification task. Given a list of facts described in free-texts, the task is to identify which articles of the European Convention were violated. The Overruling Task is a binary classification task to predict whether a legal statement will be later overruled by the same or higher ranking court (Zheng et al., 2021). We will discuss more about the two tasks in Section 4.2.

The main contributions of this paper are three-fold:

1. We investigate how to effectively adapt BERT to deal with long documents (i.e. documents containing more than 512 tokens).
2. We analyse the impacts of pre-training on different types of documents, especially in-

Natural Legal Language Processing Workshop 2021, pages 210–216
November 10, 2021. ©2021 Association for Computational Linguistics

domain documents, on the performance of a fine-tuned BERT model.

3. We thoroughly evaluate the approaches to adapt BERT on long documents and pre-trained models to identify best practises for using BERT in legal document classification tasks.

The remainder of the paper is organised as follows. Section 2 further discusses related work and positions our work in the literature. Section 3 describes the two research questions we aim to answer in this paper and how we will find the answers. Sections 4 and 5 discuss our experimental setup and results. Section 6 provides more insight from the experimental results and answers the two research questions. Finally, we provide concluding remarks in Section 7.

2 Related Work

Legal documents, such as EU & UK legislation, European Court of Human Rights (ECHR) cases, Case Holdings On Legal Decisions (CaseHOLD) are normally written in a descriptive language in a non-structured text format and have unique characteristics that are different from those of other domains. In order to advance Legal NLP research, several tasks and datasets have been developed, including violation prediction on the ECHR dataset (Chalkidis et al., 2020), court overruling (Zheng et al., 2021), legal docket classification (Nallapati and Manning, 2008) and court view generation (Ye et al., 2018). In this work, we focus on text classification, which is a main research area of legal NLP.

Bidirectional Encoder Representations from Transformers (BERT) is a language representation model that is optimized during pre-training by self-training using a masked language model prediction and a next sentence prediction as a joint training objective (Devlin et al., 2019). As shown in Figure 1, BERT model architecture is built upon a multi-layer bidirectional Transformer encoder of Vaswani et al. (2017), where the number of input tokens is limited to 512. Pre-training BERT enables effective transfer learning from a large dataset before fine-tuning the model on a specific task (Devlin et al., 2019; Vaswani et al., 2017). Importantly, Devlin et al. (2019) used this transfer learning method to achieve the state-of-the-art performance on several NLP datasets, such as GLUE (Wang et al., 2018), SQuAD (Rajpurkar et al., 2016), Concept Normalisation (Limsopatham and Collier, 2015, 2016) and Novel Named Entity Recognition (Derczynski et al., 2017). In particular, when fine-tuning BERT, we normally add a classification layer (either SoftMax or Sigmoid) on the C (or CLS) representation in BERT output layer, in order to compute the prediction probabilities as in Figure 1. In the legal domain, Zheng et al. (2021) found that pre-training BERT on legal documents before fine-tuning on particular tasks lead to a better performance than pre-training BERT on general documents. However, Chalkidis et al. (2019) found that BERT did not perform well on the violation prediction task due to the length of the documents that are mostly longer than 512 tokens. They dealt with the long legal documents by using a hierarchical BERT technique (Chalkidis et al., 2019). Difference from the previous work, we investigate the effectiveness of variances of pre-trained BERT-based models and compare several methods to handle the long legal documents in legal text classification.

Several attempts (Beltagy et al., 2020; Zaheer et al., 2020; Pappagari et al., 2019) have been made to enable BERT-like models to work on documents with more than 512 tokens. For example, Beltagy et al. (2020) and Zaheer et al. (2020) used several different attention-mechanism techniques, such as global attentions and sliding window attentions to enable learning on a longer number of tokens. Pappagari et al. (2019) investigated different approaches to apply BERT on sequence chunks of texts in a document before aggregating the features using techniques, such as max pooling and mean pooling. In this work, we adapt these techniques to learn how to effectively use BERT on long legal documents.

3 Research Questions

This section discusses research questions we aim to answer in this paper.

RQ1 For legal text classification, does pre-training on the in-domain documents lead to a more effective performance than pre-training on general documents?

To answer the first research question, we compare the performance of variances of BERT-based models that are pre-trained on general documents or different types of legal documents. Examples of the models are BERT (Devlin et al., 2019) and LEGAL-BERT (Chalkidis et al., 2020). The complete list of models will be described in Section 4.3.

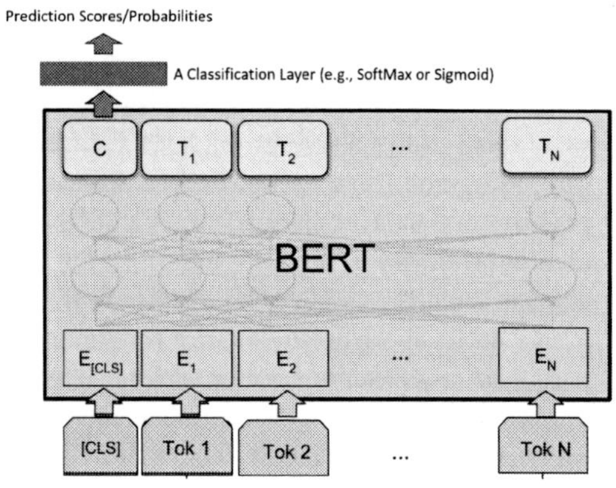

Figure 1: An example of fine-tuning BERT model on a classification task.

We fine-tune the models on the violation prediction and court overruling prediction tasks. We provide detailed information about the tasks in Section 4.2.

RQ2 How to adapt BERT-based models to effectively deal with long documents in legal text classification?

For RQ2, we discuss the performances of several BERT variances (including truncating long documents from the front or from the back), as well as hierarchical BERT models (Pappagari et al., 2019) that learn to combine output vectors of BERT using different strategies, such as, max pooling (Krizhevsky et al., 2012), and mean pooling (Krizhevsky et al., 2012) before applying a classification layer.

4 Experimental Setup

In Section 3, we have discussed the two main research questions to be investigated in this paper. In this section, we discuss the hyper-parameters of our models in Section 4.1. Then, we provide the details of the two legal text classification datasets (Section 4.2) and the variances of the BERT models (Section 4.3) used in the experiments.

4.1 Hyper-parameters

We use the transformers library[1] to develop and train BERT models in our experiments. For all experiments, we fine-tune the models using AdamW optimizer (Loshchilov and Hutter, 2017), learning rate of 5e-5 and a linear learning-rate scheduler. We used a batch size of 16 and fine-tune the models on individual tasks for 5 epochs[2].

4.2 Datasets

4.2.1 ECHR Violation (Multi-Label) Dataset

The dataset contains 11k cases from the European Convention of Human Rights public database (Chalkidis et al., 2021). Each case contains a list of paragraphs representing facts in the case. The task is to predict which of the human right articles of the Convention are violated (if any) in a given case. The number of target labels are 40 ECHR articles (Chalkidis et al., 2021).

Table 1 provides statistical information of the ECHR Violation (Multi-Label) dataset. In particular, the dataset is separated into 3 folds: training, development and testing with the number of data points (cases) of 9,000, 1,000 and 1,000, respectively. On average, the number of tokens within a case is between 1,619 - 1,926, which are more than 512 tokens supported by BERT.

This is a multi-label classification task where we follow Chalkidis et al. (2021) and evaluate the classification performance in terms of micro-F1 score.

4.2.2 Overruling Task Dataset

This dataset is composes of 2,400 data-points, which are legal statements that are either overruled or not overruled by the same or the higher ranked court (Sulea et al., 2017; Zheng et al., 2021).

We show the statistics of the Overruling Task Dataset in Table 2. The average and the maximum number of tokens within a statement (i.e. case) is 21.94 and 204, respectively. Therefore, the BERT model should directly support this dataset without any alteration.

Follow Zheng et al. (2021), the task is modeled as a binary classification, where we conduct a 10 folds cross-validation on the dataset. Finally, we report the average of the F1-score across the 10 folds with a standard deviation value (Zheng et al., 2021).

4.3 Model Variances

Next, we discuss the variances of adapting **Model*, which is a pre-trained BERT-based model from Table 3, to deal with long documents in the experiments. The used methods are as follows:

[1]https://huggingface.co/transformers/

[2]Our preliminary results showed that 5 epochs resulted in most effective performances for most of the used models.

Fold	# Cases	Max # Words	Min # Words	Avg. # Words	Max # Labels	Min # Labels	Avg. # Labels
Training	9,000	35,426	69	1619.24	10	0	1.8
Development	1,000	14,493	84	1,784.03	7	0	1.7
Testing	1,000	15,919	101	1,925.73	6	1	1.7

Table 1: Statistics: ECHR Violation (Multi-Label).

# Cases	2,400
Max # Words	204
Min # Words	1
Avg. # Words	21.94
Ratio of Negative:Positive Labels	1:1.03

Table 2: Statistics: Overruling Task Dataset.

- **RR-*Model*** – Remove tokens in the rear of the input texts if the length is more than 512 and fine-tune the model on each classification task (similar to vanilla BERT (Devlin et al., 2019)).
- **RF-*Model*** – Remove tokens in the front of the input texts if the length is more than 512 and fine-tune the model on each classification task.
- **MeanPool-*Model*** – Apply the model on every chunk of n tokens before using a mean function to average the features from the same dimensions of the output vector representations of the chunks. Then, use a classification layer for each classification task. In this work, we set $n = 200$.
- **MaxPool-*Model*** – Apply the model on every chunk of n tokens before using a max function to select features from each dimension, based on the highest scores among the same dimensions of the output vector representations of the chunks, as a final vector representation. Then, use a classification layer for each classification task.

In addition, we include other two baselines that use different attention techniques, in order to cope with document longer than 512 tokens:

- **BigBird** – Fine-tuning the BigBird from Zaheer et al. (2020), which was pre-trained using English language corpora, such as BookCorpus and English portion of the CommonCrawl News, on each classification task. BigBird is a variance of BERT that uses several attention techniques, such as, random attention, window attention and global attention, so that it can deal with documents longer than 512 tokens.
- **LongFormer** – Fine-tuning the LongFormer from Beltagy et al. (2020), which was pre-trained using BookCorpus and English Wikipedia, on each classification task. LongFormer is a variance of BERT that uses several attention techniques, such as, sliding window attention, dilated sliding window, and global attention, so that it can handle documents longer than 512 tokens.

5 Experimental Results

In this section, we compare the variances of BERT-based models on the ECHR Violation Dataset (Section 5.1) and Overruling Task Dataset (Section 5.2), respectively.

5.1 ECHR Violation Dataset

Table 4 reports the performances in terms of Micro-F1 score on different approaches to deal with long legal documents.

First, when comparing the performance of different BERT pre-trained models, we found that **-ECHR-Legal-BERT* outperformed the other pre-trained models across all of the methods used for adapting BERT to deal with long documents. This finding supported that pre-training BERT on the documents that are more similar to the task would lead to a better performance. Please note that **-ECHR-Legal-BERT* was pre-training using documents from the ECHR Violation Dataset, as mentioned in Table 3. Moreover, we observed that **-RoBERTa* performs comparably to **-Harvard-Law-BERT*. This provides an insight that if the in-domain documents (or documents similar to the task) are limited, pre-training the model on a large corpus could also lead to an effective performance.

Next, as shown in Table 4, when comparing the performance of *RR-** and *RF-** in Table 4, we found that the micro F-1 scores of *RR-** (e.g. 0.6466 for BERT) is worse than those of the corresponding *RF-** (e.g. 0.6803 for BERT). This shows

BERT	The BERT (bert-base-uncased) from Devlin et al. (2019), which were pre-trained using BookCorpus and English Wikipedia.
ECHR-Legal-BERT	The BERT (bert-base-uncased) from Chalkidis et al. (2020), which were pre-trained using legal documents including the ECHR dataset.
Harvard-Law-BERT	The BERT (bert-base-uncased) from Zheng et al. (2021), which were pre-trained using the entire Harvard Law case corpus.
RoBERTa	The RoBERTa (roberta-base) from Liu et al. (2019), which were pre-trained using English language corpora, such as BookCorpus and English portion of the CommonCrawl News. RoBERTa is a variance of BERT which trains only to optimize the dymamic masking language model.

Table 3: Pre-trained BERT-based Models used in the experiment.

Approach	Micro F-1
RR-BERT	0.6466
RR-ECHR-Legal-BERT	0.6699
RR-Harvard-Law-BERT	0.6590
RR-RoBERTa	0.6656
RF-BERT	0.6803
RF-ECHR-Legal-BERT	0.7090
RF-Harvard-Law-BERT	0.6896
RF-RoBERTa	0.6925
MeanPool-BERT	0.7075
MeanPool-ECHR-Legal-BERT	0.7196
MeanPool-Harvard-Law-BERT	0.7009
MeanPool-RoBERTa	0.6949
MaxPool-BERT	0.7110
MaxPool-ECHR-Legal-BERT	**0.7213**
MaxPool-Harvard-Law-BERT	0.7010
MaxPool-RoBERTa	0.7000
BigBird	**0.7308**
LongFormer	0.7238

Table 4: Comparing the performances on ECHR Violation Dataset.

that for this ECHR Violation Dataset, the back sections of the cases are more important than the front sections. Importantly, removing texts at the back of the input as suggested by Devlin et al. (2019) could lead to a poor performance. In addition, the best approach, *MaxPool-ECHR-Legal-BERT*, achieved 0.7213 Micro F-1 score, which was significantly better than any of the *RR-** and *RF-**, supported that truncation worsened the classification performance.

Finally, we observed that *BigBird* and *LongFormer* (Micro-F1 score 0.7308 and 0.7238, respectively) outperformed the other baselines that adapted BERT to deal with longer documents. This supported that BigBird and LongFormer that were explicitly designed to with long documents using different variances of attention techniques could lead to a better performance than aggregating results from applying BERT on multiple chunks of text.

5.2 Overruling Task Dataset

In this section, we discuss the performances on the Overruling Task Dataset. As discussed in Section 4.2.2, the lengths of the documents in this dataset are shorter than 512 tokens. Therefore, we can directly use BERT without any changes.

Table 5 reported the performance in terms of F-1 score averaged across 10 folds cross-validation, along with the standard deviation (STD). From Table 5, we observed that *Harvard-Law-BERT* and *ECHR-Legal-BERT* achieved the best and the 2nd best performances (0.9756 and 0.9725, respectively). This supported the impacts of pre-training on the in-domain documents. Meanwhile, *RoBERTa* achieved the 3 rank (0.9683 F-1 score) demonstrated that if no in-domain documents available, pre-training on a large corpus could also be effective. These results are inline with the findings in Section 5.1.

On the other hand, BigBird and LongFormer (0.9570 and 0.9569, respectively) performed a marginally worse than the other approaches. This could be due to the fact that BigBird and LongFormer are explicitly modelled to deal with long documents. Specifically, for shorter documents al-

Approach	Mean F1 ± STD
BERT	0.9656 ± 0.010
ECHR-Legal-BERT	0.9725 ± 0.005
Harvard-Law-BERT	**0.9756** ±0.010
RoBERTa	0.9683 ± 0.010
BigBird	0.9570 ± 0.010
LongFormer	0.9569 ± 0.009

Table 5: Comparing the performances, in terms of F1-score, of different BERT pre-trainings on the Overruling Task Dataset.

lowing multi-head attentions to freely attend to any tokens would lead to a more effective performance than restricting them to be on particular sliding windows or specific areas (e.g. global attentions or randomized attentions).

6 Discussions

In this section, we provide further discussions on the experimental results from Section 5, in order to answer the research questions posed in Section 3.

RQ1 For legal text classification, does pre-training on the in-domain documents lead to a more effective performance than pre-training on general documents?

Yes, based on the experiments on both datasets, the model pre-trained on documents in the legal domain (*ECHR-Legal-BERT* and *Harvard-Law-BERT*) achieved the highest performance as shown in Tables 4 and 5, respectively. In addition, as discussed in Sections 5.1 and 5.2, *RoBERTa* achieved competitive performances on both datasets supported that pre-training on a large dataset could be a good option, if in-domain data cannot be obtained.

RQ2 How to adapt BERT-based models to effectively deal with long documents in legal text classification?

From the performances of *RR-* and *RF-*, in Section 5.1, we found that truncating long documents (on either ends) lessened the classification performance due to the lost of data. From the experimental result reported in Table 4, BigBird and Longformer (even though not pre-trained on in-domain documents) outperformed other approaches that adapted BERT to deal with long documents. This highlighted the importance of explicitly handling long documents during designing the model architecture. Next, both *MaxPool-** and *MeanPool-** achieved F-1 performances that are markedly better than the other approaches. Therefore, it is the most desirable to use BigBird or Longformer that were explicitly designed to deal with long legal documents. An alternative method but less effective is to apply BERT on chunks of n tokens before using appropriate function (e.g. max or mean) to aggregate the vector representation across all the chunks before applying a classification layer, as described in Section 4.3.

7 Conclusions

We have discussed the challenges of using BERT for text classification in the legal domains, and posed two research questions regarding the pre-train documents and how to cope with long documents. To answer the research questions, we conducted the experiments on the ECHR Violation Dataset and the Overruling Task Dataset. Our experimental result showed that the models pre-trained on the domain similar to the task enhanced the performance. In addition, the experiments on ECHR Violation Dataset supported that truncating or discarding parts of a document resulted in a poor performance. Importantly, BigBird and Longformer, which explicitly handled long documents using different attention techniques, achieved the best performance on long legal document classification. Alternatively, applying BERT on chunks of texts before aggregating the vector representation across all of the chunks using an appropriate function (e.g. max or mean) could achieve a reasonable result.

References

Iz Beltagy, Matthew E Peters, and Arman Cohan. 2020. Longformer: The long-document transformer. *arXiv preprint arXiv:2004.05150*.

Ilias Chalkidis, Ion Androutsopoulos, and Nikolaos Aletras. 2019. Neural legal judgment prediction in english. In *Proceedings of the 57th Annual Meeting of the Association for Computational Linguistics*, pages 4317–4323.

Ilias Chalkidis, Ion Androutsopoulos, and Achilleas Michos. 2018. Obligation and prohibition extraction using hierarchical rnns. *arXiv preprint arXiv:1805.03871*.

Ilias Chalkidis, Manos Fergadiotis, Prodromos Malakasiotis, Nikolaos Aletras, and Ion Androutsopoulos.

2020. Legal-bert:"preparing the muppets for court'". In *Proceedings of the 2020 Conference on Empirical Methods in Natural Language Processing: Findings*, pages 2898–2904.

Ilias Chalkidis, Manos Fergadiotis, Dimitrios Tsarapatsanis, Nikolaos Aletras, Ion Androutsopoulos, and Prodromos Malakasiotis. 2021. Paragraph-level rationale extraction through regularization: A case study on european court of human rights cases. In *Proceedings of the Annual Conference of the North American Chapter of the Association for Computational Linguistics*, Mexico City, Mexico. Association for Computational Linguistics.

Leon Derczynski, Eric Nichols, Marieke van Erp, and Nut Limsopatham. 2017. Results of the wnut2017 shared task on novel and emerging entity recognition. In *Proceedings of the 3rd Workshop on Noisy User-generated Text*, pages 140–147.

Jacob Devlin, Ming-Wei Chang, Kenton Lee, and Kristina Toutanova. 2019. Bert: Pre-training of deep bidirectional transformers for language understanding. pages 4171–4186.

Alex Krizhevsky, Ilya Sutskever, and Geoffrey E Hinton. 2012. Imagenet classification with deep convolutional neural networks. *Advances in neural information processing systems*, 25:1097–1105.

Nut Limsopatham and Nigel Collier. 2015. Adapting phrase-based machine translation to normalise medical terms in social media messages. In *Proceedings of the 2015 Conference on Empirical Methods in Natural Language Processing*, pages 1675–1680.

Nut Limsopatham and Nigel Collier. 2016. Normalising medical concepts in social media texts by learning semantic representation. In *Proceedings of the 54th Annual Meeting of the Association for Computational Linguistics (Volume 1: Long Papers)*, pages 1014–1023.

Yinhan Liu, Myle Ott, Naman Goyal, Jingfei Du, Mandar Joshi, Danqi Chen, Omer Levy, Mike Lewis, Luke Zettlemoyer, and Veselin Stoyanov. 2019. Roberta: A robustly optimized bert pretraining approach. *arXiv preprint arXiv:1907.11692*.

Ilya Loshchilov and Frank Hutter. 2017. Decoupled weight decay regularization. *arXiv preprint arXiv:1711.05101*.

Ramesh Nallapati and Christopher D Manning. 2008. Legal docket classification: Where machine learning stumbles. In *Proceedings of the 2008 Conference on Empirical Methods in Natural Language Processing*, pages 438–446.

Raghavendra Pappagari, Piotr Zelasko, Jesús Villalba, Yishay Carmiel, and Najim Dehak. 2019. Hierarchical transformers for long document classification. In *2019 IEEE Automatic Speech Recognition and Understanding Workshop (ASRU)*, pages 838–844. IEEE.

Pranav Rajpurkar, Jian Zhang, Konstantin Lopyrev, and Percy Liang. 2016. Squad: 100,000+ questions for machine comprehension of text. In *Proceedings of the 2016 Conference on Empirical Methods in Natural Language Processing*, pages 2383–2392.

Octavia-Maria Sulea, Marcos Zampieri, Shervin Malmasi, Mihaela Vela, Liviu P Dinu, and Josef Van Genabith. 2017. Exploring the use of text classification in the legal domain. *arXiv preprint arXiv:1710.09306*.

Ashish Vaswani, Noam Shazeer, Niki Parmar, Jakob Uszkoreit, Llion Jones, Aidan N Gomez, Łukasz Kaiser, and Illia Polosukhin. 2017. Attention is all you need. In *Advances in neural information processing systems*, pages 5998–6008.

Alex Wang, Amanpreet Singh, Julian Michael, Felix Hill, Omer Levy, and Samuel R Bowman. 2018. Glue: A multi-task benchmark and analysis platform for natural language understanding. In *International Conference on Learning Representations*.

Hai Ye, Xin Jiang, Zhunchen Luo, and Wenhan Chao. 2018. Interpretable charge predictions for criminal cases: Learning to generate court views from fact descriptions. In *Proceedings of the 2018 Conference of the North American Chapter of the Association for Computational Linguistics: Human Language Technologies, Volume 1 (Long Papers)*, pages 1854–1864.

Manzil Zaheer, Guru Guruganesh, Kumar Avinava Dubey, Joshua Ainslie, Chris Alberti, Santiago Ontanon, Philip Pham, Anirudh Ravula, Qifan Wang, Li Yang, et al. 2020. Big bird: Transformers for longer sequences. In *NeurIPS*.

Lucia Zheng, Neel Guha, Brandon R Anderson, Peter Henderson, and Daniel E Ho. 2021. When does pretraining help? assessing self-supervised learning for law and the casehold dataset of 53,000+ legal holdings. In *Proceedings of the Eighteenth International Conference on Artificial Intelligence and Law*, pages 159–168.

Semi-automatic Triage of Requests for Free Legal Assistance

Meladel Mistica[♦♥] **Jey Han Lau**[♦]
Brayden Merrifield[♣] **Kate Fazio**[♣] **Timothy Baldwin**[♦]
[♦] Computing and Information Systems, The University of Melbourne
[♥] School of Languages and Cultures, The University of Queensland
[♣] Innovation and Engagement, Justice Connect
{m.mistica, jeyhan.lau}@unimelb.edu.au, tb@ldwin.net
{brayden.merrifield, kate.fazio}@justiceconnect.org.au

Abstract

Free legal assistance is critically under-resourced, and many of those who seek legal help have their needs unmet. A major bottleneck in the provision of free legal assistance to those most in need is the determination of the precise nature of the legal problem. This paper describes a collaboration with a major provider of free legal assistance, and the deployment of natural language processing models to assign area-of-law categories to real-world requests for legal assistance. In particular, we focus on an investigation of models to generate efficiencies in the triage process, but also the risks associated with naive use of model predictions, including fairness across different user demographics.

1 Introduction

The number of Australians with unmet legal needs is estimated to be over 4 million people per year and growing (out of a total population of around 25 million): each year approximately 8.5 million Australians will have a legal problem and only around 4.5 million will access any assistance (Coumarelos et al., 2012; The Department of Justice and Regulation, 2012) — an indication that free legal assistance services are critically under-resourced. A bottleneck for free legal assistance providers is the determination of what (if any) specific legal needs the individual has. We investigate the viability of semi-automating this step by building a model that suggests how to categorise lay descriptions of problems/incidents into legal areas. It is critical that we develop models which will perform equally well for users of all backgrounds, generalise well from small amounts of curated data, and potentially dynamically interact with the help-seeker to clarify the nature of the case. However, in this preliminary work, our aim is to develop initial models as a means to ascertain what biases manifest in our given data, and to have a workable model upon which we can make incremental measurable improvements.

Text classification of any real-world data can be a challenge for many reasons. In the case of legal text classification, the classes themselves or the legal categorisation of a possible case, can vary from organisation to organisation, and also from court to court; there is no universally agreed-upon set of areas of law neatly defined into a taxonomy (Goncalves and Quaresma, 2005; Sulea et al., 2017a; Soh et al., 2019; Tuggener et al., 2020). Furthermore, a case can span multiple areas of law — for example, a FAMILY LAW matter could also fall under the umbrella of GUARDIANSHIP AND ADMINISTRATION, or a CHARITIES LAW issue may also have aspects regarding EMPLOYEES AND VOLUNTEERS. In addition to the issues surrounding the inherent fuzziness of legal categories, the descriptions of legal issues themselves exhibit a range of language styles: those who seek free legal help are not versed in the legal domain, and may have varying linguistic styles, reflecting their social, cultural, and educational background.

We report on an ongoing collaboration between Justice Connect, a public benevolent institution, as defined by the Australian government,[1] that aims to ameliorate social inequalities through legal assistance and community engagement, and Melbourne University whose aim is to alleviate the help-seeker intake bottleneck. In Section 2, we outline the importance of accessible legal assistance to those most in need, and the barriers to be overcome in providing this service to the community. Section 3 details the data collection and corpus creation process. We designed and developed an annotation platform exclusively for volunteer lawyers to annotate online requests for help from the public through the Justice Connect intake portal. Our experiments and results are outlined in Section 4

[1] https://www.acnc.gov.au/charity/232d6dcbcaa1550da90f825fe6fab643#history

Natural Legal Language Processing Workshop 2021, pages 217–227
November 10, 2021.

and 5, which describe the initial fine-tuned BERT classifiers (Devlin et al., 2019) on the small curated help-seeker data informally describing issues in their own words on matters they believe require legal assistance. As a starting point, we wanted to leverage the patterns of language usage encoded in BERT given our relatively small data set. The main risk is that while robust results can be achieved by fine-tuning over relatively little labelled data in this manner, the data used in developing the pre-trained models can lead to these models implicitly capturing a variety of biases about the world (Bender et al., 2021). In Section 6, we reveal how these biases manifest for our given data set, not only in terms of which areas of law the models can, or cannot, reliably predict, but also which demographic groups the model has inherent difficulty in representing. Finally, in Section 8, we discuss how we can overcome these biases for future iterations of the model while keeping in mind the protection and privacy of the help-seekers who are most vulnerable.

2 Background

Unresolved legal problems have been shown to lead to significant life impacts at high levels of frequency, including financial strain (29%), stress-related illness (20%), physical ill health (19%), relationship breakdown (10%), and having to move home (5%) (Coumarelos et al., 2012).

Even when a person is eligible for free legal assistance, there are various ecosystem-level barriers that increase the difficulty of finding and engaging with a legal service. One such barrier is the disconnection between a person who has recognised that their problem may have a legal dimension but does not yet know the technical terminology around their issue, and a legal service that can assist that person with the problem they have. This barrier is exacerbated in online settings, as people search via search engines and directories for legal services without the right search terms and technical language required to successfully reach relevant services.

In a follow-up survey by Justice Connect, many applicants, in requesting help online, self-identify this issue: e.g. "[there are] too many seperate courts and unclear what laws do what (sic)", "it's complex and i am not an expert!" and "[I'm unsure of the category] because of the family relationship together with financial issue".

Legal services also experience this issue as a bottleneck in their processes, where significant resources are required to assist applicants to determine the nature of the problem that they have (especially difficult given that many users of such services have little or no formal experience with the legal system), whether it is legal in nature, and what specific legal services should be provided. Lack of knowledge and capability often results in "failing to identify a legal problem, consulting non-legal advisers instead of legal experts, or taking no action to resolve the problem" (The Department of Justice and Regulation, 2016, p120).

Legal area classification (Goncalves and Quaresma, 2005; Sulea et al., 2017a,b; Soh et al., 2019; Tuggener et al., 2020) can potentially help to alleviate this bottleneck, in providing semi-automatic legal triaging of user-supplied textual descriptions of the issue.

3 Data Set Development

The corpus upon which the data set is derived comes from requests for help via the Justice Connect web-based intake tool.[2] After a series of eligibility questions, the help-seeker is asked to provide more information about the issue that has brought them to the Justice Connect portal.

The description entered by the help-seeker is manually de-identified for names, dates, locations, and any other sensitive information in preparation for annotation. This is then presented to an annotator via an interface which was developed by Justice Connect in consultation with Melbourne University. Based on the description, the annotator selects one or more areas of law that they deem appropriate from the 33 options (including NOT A LEGAL ISSUE) shown in Table 1. The annotation task is a two stage process: first the areas of law are chosen including specifying certainty levels which reflect how well the text supports the area of law they have chosen, as shown in Figure 1. In the second stage, the annotators are asked to highlight the relevant passages that support their decision to label the document as belonging to a particular legal area.[3]

The annotations were collected over a period

[2]For the privacy and protection of the help seekers, we are not able to share the intake took data of real-world examples. Although the data has been anonymised, the risk too high given the sensitivity of the material and its recency.

[3]We do not use the span-level information from Step 2 in this work, but the highlighting of passages can be seen in Figure 3 in the Appendix.

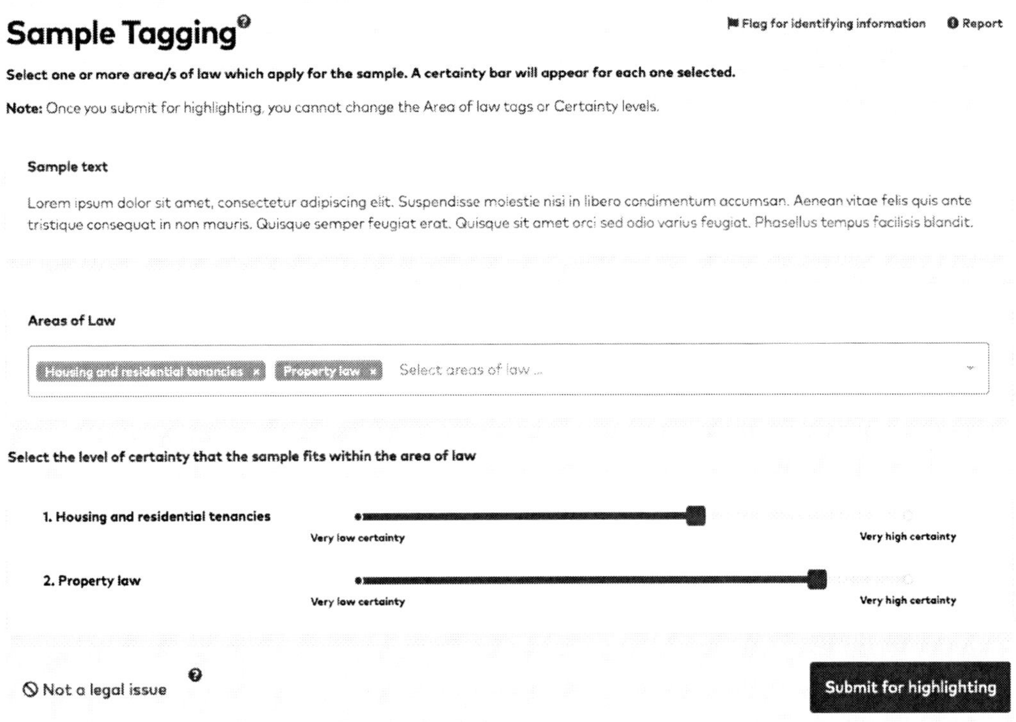

Figure 1: Step 1: Choosing the areas of law and certainty levels

of five and half months,[4] and are based on 4,062 unique descriptions. Each text sample was annotated by up to 7 different lawyers, noting that a single sample could be annotated as falling under multiple areas of law, making our task a multi-label classification problem.

Our annotators are lawyers from firms that were approached based on their level of engagement with Justice Connect. A number of firms had previously shown interest in pilot and project opportunities through Justice Connect's subscription model. Annotators were self-elected, or chosen by each firm's pro bono coordinators. They were asked to disclose how many years they had been practicing in total. Of these firms, there were 231 lawyers – all admitted to practice law in Australia – who were signed up for the annotation task. In addition, there were 12 Justice Connect-based lawyers who self-elected to participate as annotators, taking the total number of lawyers to 243 over 9 firms throughout Australia.

We derive three different labellings of the data from these annotations:

Majority-vote: majority-vote labels for each text sample based on a per-class majority vote over the annotators. That is, in order for a label to apply it must have been assigned by at least half of the annotators.

Confidence-weighted: the weighted mean of the 'certainty' or 'confidence' score for each label, as self-assessed by the annotator on a scale of 1–100 (according to the placement of a slider), by averaging over the confidence scores for all annotators who assigned a given label.

Annotator-weighted: the proportion of annotators who assigned a given area of law to the instance, divided by the number of annotators (constrained to be at least 3).

As an illustration of how confidence- and annotator-weighting work, one text sample (Entry ID 3085) had 3 annotators: the first annotator labelled it with the tags Litigation and dispute resolution and Employees and volunteers, giving a score of 42% and 100%, respectively; the second annotator applied the same labels but rated them both 100; and the third annotator tagged this excerpt with Employees and volunteers and Personal safety with confidence ratings 79 and 67, re-

[4]From 16 November 2020 to 30 April 2021

AREA OF LAW	M/C	A
BANKING & FINANCE	137	96
BUILDING & CONSTRUCTION	229	61
CHARITIES LAW	40	32
CONSUMER LAW	145	107
CORPORATE & COMMERCIAL LAW	82	53
CRIMINAL LAW	458	375
ELDER LAW	45	29
EMPLOYEES & VOLUNTEERS	725	559
ENVIRONMENT	9	7
FAMILY LAW	442	375
FINES & INFRINGEMENTS	115	89
FUNDRAISING LAW	1	1
GUARDIANSHIP & ADMINISTRATION	82	61
HEALTH	129	94
HOUSING & RESIDENTIAL TENANCIES	577	468
IT	2	1
INQUIRIES	62	4
INSURANCE	62	39
INTELLECTUAL PROPERTY	21	20
LITIGATION & DISPUTE RESOLUTION	1258	732
MIGRATION	121	95
NATIVE TITLE	1	1
NEIGHBOURHOOD DISPUTES	55	42
NOT A LEGAL ISSUE	259	195
PERSONAL SAFETY	190	168
PLANNING & LOCAL GOVERNMENT	62	50
PRIVACY	43	34
PROPERTY LAW	182	131
PUBLIC & ADMINISTRATIVE LAW	249	165
TAX	37	26
TORTS & COMPENSATION	226	180
TRUSTS/EQUITY	22	14
WILLS, ESTATES & PROBATE	90	63

Table 1: Areas of Law, and the number of text samples belonging to each in the majority-vote (M), confidence-weighted (C), and annotator-weighted (A) data sets.

spectively. Under confidence-weighting, therefore, the overall weight for LITIGATION AND DISPUTE RESOLUTION is (42/100 + 100/100)/2 = 0.71, whereas for annotator-weighting, the score is 2/3 = 0.67.

One difference between the annotator-weighted labelling as compared to the confidence-weighted or majority-vote labelling is that it has fewer instances: the annotator-weighted data set has 3,154 instances while the other two have 4,062. This is because of the constraint that at least 3 annotators tag the text for annotator-weighting.

Table 1 shows the number of instances categorised under each area of law for the majority-vote (and confidence-weighted) data set and the annotator-weighted data set, noting that multiple areas of law can apply to the one text sample.

4 Experiments

We performed fine-tuning experiments using BERT, with early stopping based on the validation loss. In addition, we experimented with various values for the dropout rate during training, with the final value being set to 0.001. The batch size was set to 32 and the number of epochs was set to 50. All experiments are based on 20-fold cross-validation, and were run 10 times and averaged, with each run having the data split into 20 folds randomly. The non-testing portion of each fold was split into 90/10 for training/validation. For experiments over the confidence-weighted and annotator-weighted data sets, we train over the given label representation, but evaluate on the majority-vote data. We do this because the majority-vote labelled data is our approximation of a manually curated gold-standard data set, also for direct model comparability.

Given that the number of labels is quite large (33 areas of law, including NOT A LEGAL ISSUE), we wanted to see if grouping the tags into small thematic groups would increase accuracy. We experimented with 2 grouping structures: (1) "legal", based on legal specialisations; and (2) "theme", based on topics or themes that may be shared between the areas of law. These groupings were agreed upon by trained lawyers at Justice Connect, where the first group was determined by answering the question, *In general, if a lawyer specialises in area X, do they often specialise in area Y too?*, and for the latter, *What areas of law have common narratives or topics shared between them, when people describe issues pertaining to these areas of law?*

We include three baselines to gauge how difficult the task is:

1. "random": choose 0 to 7 labels at random (based on uniform sampling, without replacement) for each instance, noting that there were between 0 and 7 areas of law for each instance in the majority-vote data set[5]
2. "shuffle": select N labels at random, where N is the number of assigned labels to the instance in either the majority-vote or annotator-weighted data set (recognising that this information would not be available for a genuinely "unseen" instance)
3. "majority": label using the most popular area(s) of law (ranked by how many instances they have been assigned in the training data).

[5]Note that in the case of 0 areas of law, NOT A LEGAL ISSUE is assigned, and in the case of >0 areas of law, they are drawn from the remainder of the labels.

For the majority-vote data set, on average 1.5 labels are applied to each text sample, and therefore the first version of majority, we assign the 2 most popular areas of law. The annotator-weighted data set has an average of 1.3 labels per instance, so for the second version of majority, we assign the single highest-occurring label.

5 Results

Table 2 shows the micro-averaged precision, recall, and f1-score for the BERT models trained over the three data sets (majority-vote, confidence-weighted, and annotator-weighted) but evaluated over majority-vote for direct comparability. For the baselines, the two numbers in each cell indicate the results obtained based on majority-vote vs. annotator-weighted.

The results show that while the confidence-weighted-trained system outperforms the other systems with respect to precision, recall is low and misses out on correctly classifying instances well over half the time. Although, when it does label instances, it gets them correct 83.8% of the time. The annotator-weighted-trained model obtains the highest recall, and also obtains the best trade-off between precision and recall, as reflected in the best f1-score. All models perform well above all three baselines, for all of precision, recall, and f1-score.

For all 3 BERT models, recall is rather low. In the original experiments, if the model predicted a given label with a probability ≥50%, we output it as a prediction, but it is also possible to adjust the probability threshold to a value other than 50% (with higher values expected to lead to higher precision and lower recall, and lower values expected to lead to higher recall and lower precision). In a follow-up experiment, we learned a threshold per label (area of law) based on the training data. While these experiments, shown in Table 3 generally led to improvements in recall, it degraded precision substantially, with the net effect of an overall drop in f1-score. As such, in the remainder of our experiments, we maintain a fixed threshold of 0.50.

In the previous experiments, the validation data was the same type as the training data (e.g. for 'annotator-weighted', the training and validation data were both labelled with the annotator-weighted approach), but final evaluation was based on the majority-vote labelling. This means that for the models trained on 'annotator-weighted' and 'confidence-weighted', we optimise hyperparameters on the basis of one labelling strategy, and perform our final evaluation based on a separate labelling strategy ('majority-vote'). In the next experiment, we seek to rectify this mismatch by also validating on 'majority-vote' data.

The results in Table 4 show a slight boost in recall in both cases, but overall validating on majority-vote data has relatively little impact.

Table 5 shows the results of the groupings experiment, in which we both label and evaluate all instances based on the coarser-grained 'theme' (groupings of the areas of law by topic) or 'legal' (groupings according to legal specialisation) label set,[6] using majority-vote labelling. Overall, recall improves slightly with grouped labels, in comparison to the original results over the fine-grained label set. However, precision does not improve, meaning it is difficult to justify employing the 'theme' (or the 'legal') system over the 'annotator-weighted' system, because the loss in the granularity of distinctions between the specific areas of law does not justify the small gain in recall.

Summarising the findings of these experiments, the best of the models is trained on 'annotator-weighted' labels, without modifying the probability threshold or majority-vote data validation. It is this model that we experiment with in the remainder of the paper, in terms of scoping out its viability for live deployment in semi-automatically triaging of incoming requests for legal assistance.

6 Analysis

As shown in Table 1, not all areas of law are distributed equally. For example, there are far more instances tagged as EMPLOYEES AND VOLUNTEERS than PRIVACY. It would be natural to expect that the predictive performance over PRIVACY would be lower, given the sparsity of labelled instances in the training data.

Table 6 shows the breakdown of precision, recall, and f1-score (along with the raw count of true negatives, false positives, false negatives, and true positives) for each label. There were no classes where the number of false positives was greater than the number of true positives, resulting in relatively high precision scores. Recall, on the other hand, is rather low, meaning that the model is conservative in its predictions. However, a more conservative low re-

[6]See Figure 2 in Appendix for details.

	SYSTEM	p	r	f
Baselines	shuffle	.059/.065	.059/.065	.059/.065
	random	.041/.046	.074/.075	.052/.057
	majority	.232/.244	.168/.322	.195/.278
BERT	majority-vote	0.770	0.545	0.638
	confidence-weighted	**0.838**	0.460	0.594
	annotator-weighted	0.781	**0.588**	**0.671**

Table 2: Results for the three baselines, and BERT trained on the three data sets (majority-vote, confidence-weighted, and annotator-weighted); evaluation in each case is against the majority-vote test set.

SYSTEM	p	r	f
majority-vote	0.565	0.555	0.560
confidence-weighted	0.622	0.521	0.567
annotator-weighted	0.743	0.569	0.645

Table 3: Results for dynamic probability thresholding of the BERT models

SYSTEM	p	r	f
confidence-weighted	0.839	0.462	0.596
annotator-weighted	0.772	0.608	0.680

Table 4: Using majority-vote data for validation

call, high precision, system provides greater utility than a high recall, low precision, system because we are able to trust the predictions from the system in assigning lawyers with speciality in different areas of law. That is, we want to be confident that a pro bono lawyer who is assigned to a client is suitably credentialled to provide assistance relevant to the specifics of the request, noting that they will quickly pick up on any aspects of the case which they are not qualified to deal with (i.e. areas of law the classifier has missed) and be able to potentially bring in extra expertise without extra overhead. That is, the cost of a lawyer getting up to speed with a particular case is very much higher than the cost of that lawyer identifying extra dimensions of legal expertise that need to be brought on board, such that precision is more important than recall.

To assist in the interpretation of the model after deployment, we further categorised the areas of law according to 4 tiers, as shown in Table 6. The determining of these tiers is roughly guided by the f0.5-score ($\beta = 0.5$) of each area of law, shown in the column *f0.5*. In constructing the tiers, we place

SYSTEM	p	r	f
theme	0.776	0.629	0.695
legal	0.777	0.612	0.684

Table 5: Groups by themes legal specialisation

a greater importance on precision rather than recall. Tier III and IV classes, with an f0.5-score of < 0.55, are those that are least 'trustworthy' if the system was to emit them as a prediction. Even though some classes have a precision of 1.000 (e.g. INTELLECTUAL PROPERTY and TRUSTS/EQUITY), are still be treated as lower-tier classes for a number of reasons — these classes have far fewer instances and therefore the ability of the model to learn features for these classes is comparatively degraded (and the high precision is perhaps more luck than a reproducible trend). This is reflected in the very poor results in the recall and thus overall f1-score of these classes. The classes in Tiers I and II have higher precision and an f0.5 that range between 0.55 and 0.925. For the areas of law in these tiers with a higher precision, we expect that when a model predicts a text sample as one of these classes, that we can be fairly confident of that prediction.

7 Fairness

From the metadata provided by Justice Connect, we analyse 6 sub-groups of help-seeker:

1. Seniors (SEN) = 102 instances;
2. Aboriginal/Torres Strait Islanders (ATS) = 54 instances;
3. public housing tenants (PUB) = 91 instances;
4. those who do not identify as heterosexual or cisgender (LGB) = 104 instances;
5. those who are homeless or as risk of becoming homeless (HOM) = 175; and

Area of Law	p	r	f1	f0.5	TN	FP	FN	TP
TIER I								
Migration	0.959	0.737	0.833	0.904	3056	3	25	70
Insurance	0.941	0.410	0.571	0.747	3114	1	23	16
Employees and volunteers	0.931	0.896	0.913	0.924	2558	37	58	501
Fines and infringements	0.922	0.528	0.671	0.802	3061	4	42	47
Wills, estates and probate	0.919	0.540	0.680	0.806	3088	3	29	34
Building and construction	0.891	0.672	0.766	0.836	3088	5	20	41
Housing and residential tenancies	0.897	0.835	0.884	0.865	2641	45	77	391
Family law	0.828	0.760	0.793	0.813	2720	59	90	285
TIER II								
Planning and local government	0.864	0.380	0.528	0.689	3101	3	31	19
Consumer law	0.758	0.467	0.578	0.674	3031	16	57	50
Not a legal issue	0.745	0.554	0.635	0.697	2922	37	87	108
Criminal law	0.721	0.592	0.650	0.691	2693	86	153	222
Litigation and dispute resolution	0.709	0.552	0.621	0.671	2256	166	328	404
Neighbourhood disputes	0.737	0.333	0.459	0.593	3107	5	28	14
Guardianship and administration	0.719	0.377	0.495	0.609	3084	9	38	23
TIER III								
Charities Law	0.875	0.219	0.350	0.547	3121	1	25	7
Tax	0.857	0.231	0.364	0.556	3127	1	20	6
Elder Law	0.750	0.103	0.182	0.332	3124	1	26	3
Property law	0.682	0.443	0.537	0.616	2996	27	73	58
Torts and compensation	0.650	0.372	0.473	0.565	2938	36	113	67
Health	0.625	0.372	0.467	0.550	3039	21	59	35
Personal safety	0.575	0.387	0.463	0.524	2938	48	103	65
Corporate and commercial law	0.562	0.340	0.424	0.497	3087	14	35	18
Banking and finance	0.512	0.427	0.466	0.492	3019	39	55	41
TIER IV								
Intellectual Property	1.000	0.150	0.261	0.469	3134	0	17	3
Trusts/equity	1.000	0.071	0.133	0.279	3140	0	13	1
Privacy	0.500	0.059	0.105	0.200	3118	2	32	2
Public and administrative law	0.519	0.339	0.410	0.469	2937	52	109	56
Fundraising law	0.000	0.000	0.000	0.000	3153	0	1	0
IT	0.000	0.000	0.000	0.000	3153	0	1	0
Inquiries	0.000	0.000	0.000	0.000	3150	0	4	0
Environment	0.000	0.000	0.000	0.000	3147	0	7	0
Native title	0.000	0.000	0.000	0.000	3153	0	1	0

Table 6: Breakdown of the performance for the 'annotator-weighted' system per class, as well as the TN (true negative), FP (false positive), FN (false negative), and TP (true positive) counts.

6. those who disclosed their household income as being less than \$50K group (LOW) = 1,686 instances.

Of these, the SEN group fared the worst with an overall f1-score of 0.540, as shown in Table 7. This table shows that the ATS and SEN groups fared below the average and the worst for SEN.

Aboriginal and Torres Strait Islanders make up 1.7% of the total data, and make up a comparable percentage of FAMILY LAW cases (1.8%) and CRIMINAL LAW cases (1.9%), however at a far lower performance than the average when compared to data for all demographics. For example CRIMINAL LAW cases have p = 0.571, r = 0.571, and f1 = 0.571 (vs.

Self-Identified	p	r	f
Aboriginal and Torres Strait Islander ATS	**0.723**	**0.573**	**0.638**
Public housing tenants PUB	0.793	0.635	0.706
LGBTQI LGB	0.794	0.612	0.693
Homeless (or at risk) HOM	0.801	0.591	0.681
Low income LOW	0.796	0.610	0.691
Seniors SEN	**0.714**	**0.439**	**0.543**
All Data	0.781	0.588	0.671

Table 7: Results for self-identified groups in the data

p = 0.721, r = 0.592, and f = 0.650 when evaluating over all the data). For Litigations and dispute resolutions, the largest overall class, the performance for ATS was p = 0.333, r = 0.600, and f = 0.429 (vs. p = 0.709, r = 0.552, and f1 = 0.621 when evaluating over all the data). However only 0.7% of documents in this class were submitted by those who identified as ATS.

The number of submitted requests by seniors (SEN: those who identify as being over 65 years of age) are almost double the number of Aboriginal and Torres Strait Islanders, making up slightly over 3% of the total number of samples in the data (3.2% of the data used in the annotator-weighted system). Our initial hypothesis for the poor performance of the SEN data was that perhaps they made enquiries in certain areas of law that inherently had low performance. For example, if most of the seniors' enquiries fell in the Tier III and IV categories, then this would help explain the overall poorer performance of the SEN group. However, our analysis showed otherwise: the vast majority of classes with at least 5 instances from the SEN group are Tier I or Tier II, and yet for the majority of these, the relative performance is below the overall performance for that class, as seen in Table 8. This table shows the breakdown of the areas of law for SEN where the number of true instances is at least 5.

Many of the enquiries by seniors fall in Tier I and II categories, which make up the best-performing classes in general. Even though the SEN group only makes up around 3% of the total number of instances, they do however make up almost 21% of all enquires regarding Elder Law, over 6% of all Banking and finance, almost 6% of Consumer law, and 10% of Planning and local government. While Property law and Planning and local government perform well in comparison to the overall results for these classes, the other classes within Tier I and II categories underperform. In particular, Employees and volunteers and Family law are overall top-performing classes as shown in Table 6, yet perform poorly for the SEN group, obtaining an f1-score of 0.571 and 0.545, respectively. Furthermore, in instances where precision is high for a class, recall often pulls down the f1-score for the SEN group.[7] This points to the model being systematically biased against this particular demographic, pointing to the need for explicit model debiasing.

8 Conclusion

The findings of our paper presents a preliminary exploration of the application of NLP for social good. The results of this paper shows the importance of building fairer models. One approach as a future avenue in this endeavour is by incorporating adversarial learning (Li et al., 2018) or null space projection (Ravfogel et al., 2020) to learn representations that are invariant to subgroups, so as to limit the model from learning undesirable correlations between the legal categories and sub-group features. The challenge though, is that subgroup information is not always available in the data, particularly in the Justice Connect intake tool to request help where all demographic information is volunteered and not mandatory. This means that possibly identifying *proxy attributes* (e.g. postcode and education level as a potential means to identify income status) or areas of law that are highly associated with certain sub-groups (e.g. Migration issues may be likely submitted by persons whose main language is not English, and Elder Law issues may likely be submitted by seniors). In addition to the subgroups already presented in this study, in our next iteration

[7]This is the case for areas of law such as Neighbourhood disputes and Consumer law, which can be seen in Table 8 (in the Appendix).

Area of Law	p	r	f	Tier
Employees and volunteers	0.500	0.667	0.571	Tier I
Family law	0.600	0.500	0.545	Tier I
Housing and residential tenancies	0.750	0.462	0.571	Tier I
Litigation and dispute resolution	0.556	0.652	0.600	Tier II
Not a legal issue	0.667	0.750	0.706	Tier II
Criminal law	0.714	0.500	0.588	Tier II
Neighbourhood disputes	1.000	0.500	0.667	Tier II
Planning and local government	1.000	0.600	0.750	Tier II
Banking and finance	0.400	0.333	0.364	Tier III
Consumer law	1.000	0.167	0.286	Tier II
Elder Law	0.000	0.000	0.000	Tier III
Torts and compensation	0.000	0.000	0.000	Tier III
Property law	1.000	0.700	0.824	Tier III

Table 8: Breakdown of areas of law for SEN for where number of true instances ≥ 5

we will expand our set of the subgroups to include people who identify as CALD (culturally and linguistically diverse), those who identify as having a disability, as well as information on education levels.

References

Emily M Bender, Timnit Gebru, Angelina McMillan-Major, and Shmargaret Shmitchell. 2021. On the dangers of stochastic parrots: Can language models be too big? In *Proceedings of the 2021 ACM Conference on Fairness, Accountability, and Transparency*, pages 610–623.

Christine Coumarelos, Deborah Macourt, Julie People, Hugh M. McDonald, Zhigang Wei, Reiny Iriana, and Stephanie Ramsey. 2012. Legal Australia-wide survey (LAW survey): Legal need in Australia. Law and Justice Foundation of NSW.

Jacob Devlin, Ming-Wei Chang, Kenton Lee, and Kristina Toutanova. 2019. BERT: Pre-training of deep bidirectional transformers for language understanding. In *Proceedings of the 2019 Conference of the North American Chapter of the Association for Computational Linguistics: Human Language Technologies, Volume 1 (Long and Short Papers)*, pages 4171–4186, Minneapolis, Minnesota. Association for Computational Linguistics.

Teresa Goncalves and Paulo Quaresma. 2005. Evaluating preprocessing techniques in a text classification problem. In *Proceedings of the Conference of the Brazilian Computer Society*.

Yitong Li, Timothy Baldwin, and Trevor Cohn. 2018. Towards robust and privacy-preserving text representations. In *Proceedings of the 56th Annual Meeting of the Association for Computational Linguistics (Volume 2: Short Papers)*, pages 25–30, Melbourne, Australia.

Shauli Ravfogel, Yanai Elazar, Hila Gonen, Michael Twiton, and Yoav Goldberg. 2020. Null it out: Guarding protected attributes by iterative nullspace projection. In *Proceedings of the 58th Annual Meeting of the Association for Computational Linguistics*, pages 7237–7256, Online.

Jerrold Soh, How Khang Lim, and Ian Ernst Chai. 2019. Legal area classification: A comparative study of text classifiers on Singapore Supreme Court judgments. In *Proceedings of the Natural Legal Language Processing Workshop 2019*, pages 67–77, Minneapolis, Minnesota. Association for Computational Linguistics.

Octavia-Maria Sulea, Marcos Zampieri, Shervin Malmasi, Mihaela Vela, Liviu P. Dinu, and Josef van Genabith. 2017a. Exploring the use of text classification in the legal domain.

Octavia-Maria Sulea, Marcos Zampieri, Mihaela Vela, and Josef van Genabith. 2017b. Predicting the law area and decisions of french supreme court cases.

The Department of Justice and Regulation. 2012. Access to justice review. Victorian Government Report.

The Department of Justice and Regulation. 2016. Access to justice review. Victorian Government Report.

Don Tuggener, Pius von Däniken, Thomas Peetz, and Mark Cieliebak. 2020. LEDGAR: A large-scale multi-label corpus for text classification of legal provisions in contracts. In *Proceedings of the 12th Language Resources and Evaluation Conference*, pages 1235–1241, Marseille, France. European Language Resources Association.

Appendix

Group by Similar Theme/Topic

- Group 0 - not a legal issue
  - NOT A LEGAL ISSUE
- Group 1 – protecting personal interests
  - INTELLECTUAL PROPERTY
  - PRIVACY
  - CONSUMER LAW
  - EMPLOYEES AND VOLUNTEERS
- Group 2 – common law elements
  - TRUSTS/EQUITY
  - TORTS AND COMPENSATION
- Group 3 – relating to insurance
  - INSURANCE
  - BUILDING AND CONSTRUCTION
- Group 4 - litigation
  - LITIGATION AND DISPUTE RESOLUTION
- Group 5 – organisations/corporations
  - CORPORATE AND COMMERCIAL LAW
  - BANKING AND FINANCE
  - TAX
  - CHARITIES LAW
  - FUNDRAISING LAW
  - IT
- Group 6 – land and housing
  - PROPERTY LAW
  - HOUSING AND RESIDENTIAL TENANCIES
  - NATIVE TITLE
  - NEIGHBOURHOOD DISPUTES
- Group 7 – family or personal affairs
  - FAMILY LAW
  - GUARDIANSHIP AND ADMINISTRATION
  - WILLS
  - HEALTH
  - ELDER LAW
- Group 8 – relating to government
  - PUBLIC AND ADMINISTRATIVE LAW
  - PLANNING AND LOCAL GOVERNMENT
  - ENVIRONMENT
  - MIGRATION
  - INQUIRIES
- Group 9 – relating to crimes
  - FINES AND INFRINGEMENTS
  - PERSONAL SAFETY
  - CRIMINAL LAW

Group by Legal Expertise

- Group 0 - not a legal issue
  - NOT A LEGAL ISSUE
- Group 1 – corporate
  - CORPORATE AND COMMERCIAL LAW
  - BANKING AND FINANCE
  - TAX
  - CHARITIES LAW
  - FUNDRAISING LAW
- Group 2 – IP and technology
  - IT
  - PRIVACY
  - INTELLECTUAL PROPERTY
- Group 3 – property/real estate
  - PROPERTY LAW
  - HOUSING AND RESIDENTIAL TENANCIES
  - NEIGHBOURHOOD DISPUTES
- Group 4 – family law
  - FAMILY LAW
  - GUARDIANSHIP AND ADMINISTRATION
  - ELDER LAW
- Group 5 – wills and estates
  - WILLS
  - TRUSTS/EQUITY
- Group 6 – government
  - PUBLIC AND ADMINISTRATIVE LAW
  - INQUIRIES
  - MIGRATION
- Group 7 – planning and environment
  - NATIVE TITLE
  - PLANNING AND LOCAL GOVERNMENT
  - ENVIRONMENT
- Group 8 – criminal
  - CRIMINAL LAW
  - FINES AND INFRINGEMENTS
  - PERSONAL SAFETY
- Group 9 – personal injury/compensation
  - TORTS AND COMPENSATION
  - CONSUMER LAW
  - HEALTH
- Group 10: – EMPLOYEES AND VOLUNTEERS
- Group 11: – INSURANCE
- Group 12: – BUILDING AND CONSTRUCTION
- Group 13: – LITIGATION&DISPUTE RESOLUTION

Figure 2: Groupings by theme/topic and legal specialisations

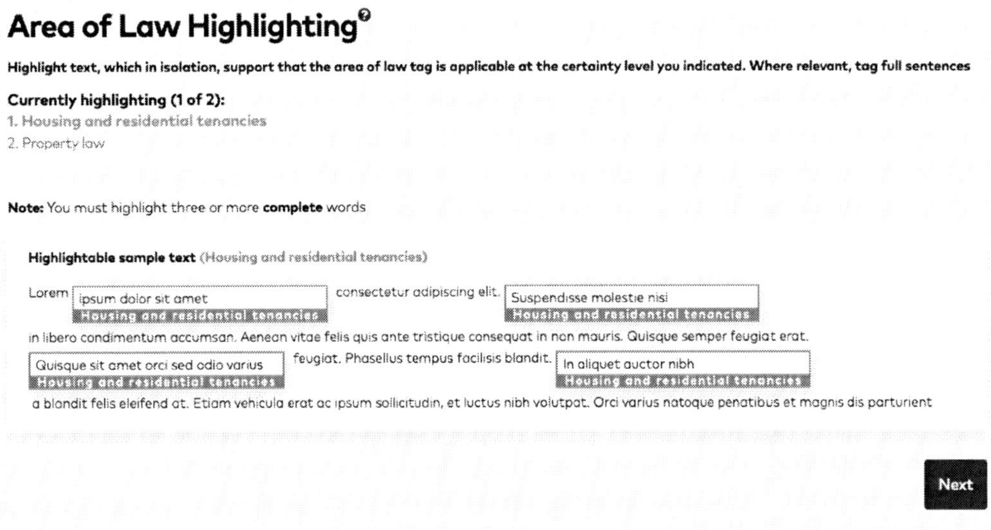

Figure 3: Step 2: Highlighting supporting text for the areas of law chosen

Automatic Resolution of Domain Name Disputes

Wayan Oger Vihikan[♦] **Meladel Mistica**[♥]
Inbar Levy[♣] **Andrew F. Christie**[♣] **Timothy Baldwin**[♦]
[♦] Computing and Information Systems, The University of Melbourne
[♥] School of Languages and Cultures, The University of Queensland
[♣] Melbourne Law School, The University of Melbourne
wvihikan@student.unimelb.edu.au, m.mistica@uq.edu.au
{a.christie, inbar.levy}@unimelb.edu.au, tb@ldwin.net

Abstract

We introduce the new task of domain name dispute resolution (DNDR), that predicts the outcome of a process for resolving disputes about legal entitlement to a domain name. The ICANN UDRP establishes a mandatory arbitration process for a dispute between a trademark owner and a domain name registrant pertaining to a generic Top-Level Domain (gTLD) name (one ending in .COM, .ORG, .NET, etc). The nature of the problem leads to a very skewed data set, which stems from being able to register a domain name with extreme ease, very little expense, and no need to prove an entitlement to it. In this paper, we describe the task and associated data set. We also present benchmarking results based on a range of models, which show that simple baselines are in general difficult to beat due to the skewed data distribution, but in the specific case of the respondent having submitted a response, a fine-tuned BERT model offers considerable improvements over a majority-class model.

1 Introduction

Domain name abuse, or cybersquatting, is the act of registering and using a domain name in bad faith. Examples of such behaviour include registering a generic Top-Level Domain (gTLD) name (i.e. one ending in .COM, .ORG, .NET, etc) that incorporates another's trademark, with the intent to on-sell it to the trademark owner; to dupe the public into erroneously assuming that the owner of the domain name is the trademark owner; or to interfere with the trademark owner's business, to name a few. A victim of cybersquatting has a means to remedy the situation. In 1999, the agency responsible for the internet's naming system, the Internet Corporation for Assigned Names and Numbers (ICANN), introduced a fast and low-cost mandatory arbitration system as an alternative to the slow and expensive litigation of cybersquatting disputes — the Uniform Domain Name Dispute Resolution Policy (UDRP).[1] Since its establishment, approximately 80,000 complaints have been resolved through the process (Christie, 2020).

UDRP cases, over 90% of which are in English, are decided by an arbitration panel comprising either one or three experienced trademark lawyers. The typical arbitrator's fee of USD 1,000 is small relative to the time expended and the usual hourly rate for legal services of this type. The performance of the task is, in effect, cross-subsidized by the arbitrator's day job. We introduce this task as a means to assist the service providers and arbitrators by automatically pre-assessing complaints. The ultimate aim is to identify those complaints whose characteristics are predictive of success. Doing so has the potential to aid in the optimal allocation of finite resources — in this case, the time and expertise of the arbitrator — because such cases should be relatively easier for the arbitrator to decide. By identifying the easier cases, service providers and arbitrators can direct more resources towards the remainder of complaints, with the result that the cases most in need of resources are given a greater share of time. That should improve the quality of decision-making, benefiting all stakeholders in the domain name system.

The distribution of outcomes under the UDRP is highly skewed. Of the complaints that proceed to a panel determination, 87% succeed. However, the distribution of cases is also highly skewed by whether or not a response to the complaint is filed. In the arbitration process, the domain name registrant has the right to file a rebuttal (a "response") to the complainant's claim. For nearly three-quarters of all complaints, no response is filed, in which case the complaint almost always (94% of the time) succeeds. Where a response is filed, however, the success rate is only 66% (Christie, 2014). It follows that cases where a response is filed are of particular

[1] https://www.icann.org/resources/pages/policy-2012-02-25-en

Natural Legal Language Processing Workshop 2021, pages 228–238
November 10, 2021. ©2021 Association for Computational Linguistics

interest to the task.

While we are by no means the first to propose the task of legal judgment prediction (Aletras et al., 2016; Zhong et al., 2018a; Chalkidis et al., 2019; Zhong et al., 2020), previous work has focused almost exclusively on criminal or human rights cases, which we argue have sensitivities and ethical dimensions that are yet to be fully quantified (Leins et al., 2020; Tsarapatsanis and Aletras, 2021). Part of our intention with this paper is to introduce a "lower-stakes" task/data set in terms of its direct and indirect implications for individuals and civil liberties, which is far from "solved" in terms of current NLP capabilities.

In the introduction of this new task, we outline in Section 2 the process of how a complaint is dealt with once it is submitted to an ICANN-accredited service provider, and how a decision on the complaint is reached by the arbitrator appointed to decide it. In this study, we ultimately aim to ascertain if providing predicted outcomes to the arbitrators will assist them in the dispute resolution process — not as a means to make the decision for them, but as a way to pre-sort the difficult cases from the straightforward ones. In Section 3, we describe how we develop our corpus for the DNDR data set, and Section 4 details how we prepare this data for our experiments as well as the set-up of the fine-tuning experiments. Given that the data set is highly skewed towards one class, we expect that the reporting of the overall binary task to not impressively exceed a majority-class baseline. However, the results from the important partitioning of the data between cases with and without responses in Section 5 shows that this task has the potential to aid arbitrators in performing their duties. In Section 6, we discuss how we foresee AI to be of use in legal processes and assisting legal professionals in their decision-making, and why it's important to define best practice when it comes to employing artificial intelligence to assist in the legal domain.

2 Background

A domain name dispute commences when a trademark owner ("complainant") files a complaint with an ICANN-accredited service provider, seeking a remedy against a domain name registrant ("respondent"). Of the six bodies accredited by ICANN as UDRP service providers,[2] the largest by far is the World Intellectual Property Organisation (WIPO). Over 52,000 cases — more than one half all UDRP disputes — have been filed with WIPO (Christie, 2020). Its case-load is growing, with filings in 2020 topping 4,000.[3]

To obtain a remedy, the complainant must show that four conditions are satisfied: (1) the complainant owns a trademark; (2) the domain name is identical or confusingly similar to that trademark; (3) the respondent has no rights or legitimate interests in the domain name; and (4) the respondent registered and has used the domain name in bad faith. The dominant service provider, WIPO, has a pro forma Model Complaint form. As a result, complaints filed with WIPO are highly standardized in terms of structure and form.

Upon the filing of a complaint, WIPO checks it for compliance with administrative requirements, obtains certain information about the domain name and the registrant of it, then notifies the complaint to the respondent. The respondent has 20 business days in which to file a response. Once the deadline for filing a response has passed, WIPO appoints a panel and supplies it with the case file — essentially, the complaint and any response. The panel has 14 days in which to decide the case and to write a decision justifying its outcome, which are both publicly disclosed (Christie, 2014).

A panel decision will generally come to one of two outcomes: either the complaint succeeds, or the complaint fails (is "denied"). In a small number of cases, where the parties settle the dispute after commencement but prior to a decision being rendered, the panel will "terminate" the complaint. Where the complaint succeeds, the panel will order one of two remedies, based on the desires of the complainant: either cancellation of the domain name, or transfer of the domain name to the complainant. The registrar of the domain name will give effect to the order (i.e. either cancel or transfer the domain name) unless the respondent challenges the decision by filing a court case in the appropriate jurisdiction (Christie, 2002), something which almost never happens. Thus, in practice, the panel's decision is final and binding. Ideally the task would be undertaken on the complaint and any response that was filed. Unfortunately, however, neither of those documents are published. Instead we use the panelist's decision, which is publicly

[2]For the list of accredited service providers, see `https://www.icann.org/resources/pages/providers-6d-2012-02-25-en`

[3]For full statistics, see `https://www.wipo.int/amc/en/domains/statistics/outcome.jsp`

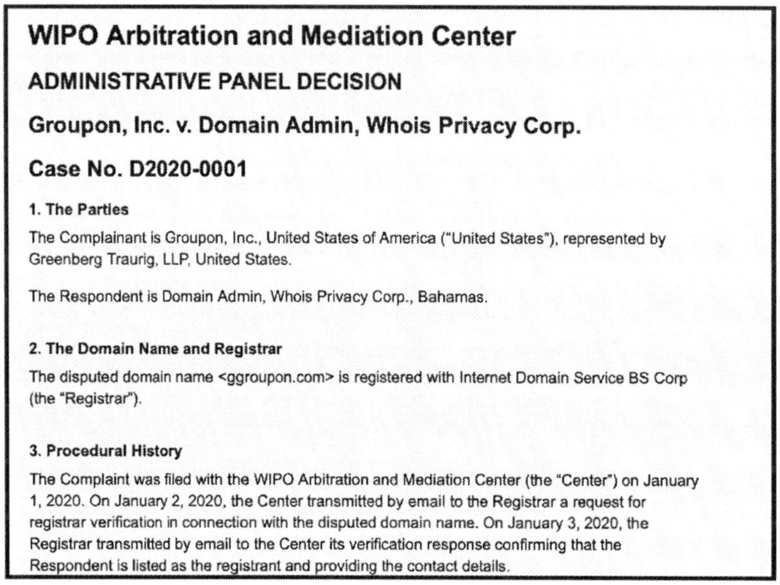

WIPO Arbitration and Mediation Center

ADMINISTRATIVE PANEL DECISION

Groupon, Inc. v. Domain Admin, Whois Privacy Corp.

Case No. D2020-0001

1. The Parties

The Complainant is Groupon, Inc., United States of America ("United States"), represented by Greenberg Traurig, LLP, United States.

The Respondent is Domain Admin, Whois Privacy Corp., Bahamas.

2. The Domain Name and Registrar

The disputed domain name <ggroupon.com> is registered with Internet Domain Service BS Corp (the "Registrar").

3. Procedural History

The Complaint was filed with the WIPO Arbitration and Mediation Center (the "Center") on January 1, 2020. On January 2, 2020, the Center transmitted by email to the Registrar a request for registrar verification in connection with the disputed domain name. On January 3, 2020, the Registrar transmitted by email to the Center its verification response confirming that the Respondent is listed as the registrant and providing the contact details.

Figure 1: Excerpt from a panel decision document showing the first sections, from `https://www.wipo.int/amc/en/domains/search/text.jsp?case=D2020-0001`.

available. WIPO decisions are highly standardized in structure and form. They typically contain seven sections, with the following headings: (1) "The Parties"; (2) "The Domain Name and Registrar"; (3) "Procedural History"; (4) "Factual Background"; (5) "Parties' Contentions"; (6) "Discussion and Findings"; and (7) "Decision". Sections (4) and (5) are the panel's summaries of the facts, and the arguments about the legal import of those facts, respectively, that are contained in the complaint and response. They are, therefore, a proxy for the information that is contained in the complaint and response, which are not publicly available.

3 Corpus Creation

The corpus was derived by the scraping the text from the published decision of each gTLD domain name case[4] for the years 2000 to mid-2020. Figure 1 shows the first sections of a sample decision. Each section of the decision is extracted and stored in JSON format, as shown in Figure 2, with the text of each section labeled according to its heading.

For the period between January 2000 and August 2020, we extracted over 33k decisions in total. We found WIPO decisions in a number of languages, including Swedish, Spanish, French, and Chinese. However, the number of non-English cases were too few (a little less than 3k), and therefore we opted to create an English-only corpus for our initial release of the data set. After filtering on the English documents using saffsd/langid library (Lui and Baldwin, 2012), we arrived at a distribution of decision outcomes shown in Table 1.

For this preliminary work, we decided to only keep the outcome labels that had enough instances to be able to reasonably train a model, which is why we only kept the top 3 labels: TRANSFER, COMPLAINT DENIED, and CANCELLATION (which account for over 99% of the data), as shown in Table 2.

The purpose of the task is to predict the outcome of the case based on the complainant's grievance and the respondent's counter to it. As detailed in Section 2, the grievance in the form in which it was filed with the service provider (the complaint) is *not* published. This is also the case for the respondent's counter to the grievance (the response). However, the contents of both the complaint and the response are summarized by the panel in the sections on "Factual Background" and "Parties' Contentions". We retain those sections, as a proxy for the facts alleged by complainant and the respondent, and for their legal arguments pertaining to those facts.

We also retain the three preceding sections of the decision. The first two of these are "The Parties" and "The Domain Name and Registrar", in

[4]`https://www.wipo.int/amc/en/domains/decisionsx/index.html`

```
{
    "case-0": {
        "status": "transfer",
        "url": "https://www.wipo.int/amc/en/domains/search/text.jsp?case=D2020-0001",
        "no": "D2020-0001",
        "complainant": "Groupon, Inc.",
        "respondent": "Domain Admin, Whois Privacy Corp.",
        "title": "",
        "text": {
            "section-3": {
                "h3": "3. Procedural History",
                "p": [
                    "The Complaint was filed with the WIPO Arbitration and Mediation Center...
                ],
                "a": []
            },
            "section-4": {
                "h3": "4. Factual Background",
                "p": [
                    "The Complainant is a major player in local commerce that offers consumers a...
                ],
                "a": []
            },
            "section-5": {
                "h3": "5. Parties' Contentions",
                "p": [],
                "a": []
            },
            "section-6": {
                "h4": "A. Complainant",
                "p": [
                    "The Complainant contends that the disputed domain name is confusingly similar to...
                ],
                "a": []
            },
            "section-7": {
                "h4": "B. Respondent",
                "p": [
                    "The Respondent did not reply to the Complainant's contentions."
                ],
                "a": []
            }
        }
    }
}
```


Figure 2: The panel decision document in json format showing the sections of the data from Figure 1.

which the complainant, the respondent, the domain name, and the registrar are named. The third is the "Procedural History", in which is recorded the dates on which the complaint and response were filed, the date on which the panel was appointed, and the name of the panelist(s).

The final two sections of the decision are "Discussion and Findings", in which the panel analyzes whether or not the complainant has proven its claim; and "Decision", in which the outcome is formally recorded. We remove those sections, as they contain the outcome of the case, which is the very thing the task is seeking to predict.

In total there were 33,841 cases at the time of scraping. However, not all of them could be collected. There are four cases that are not available, and 67 cases cannot be scraped due to inconsistencies in the HTML tags. On top of that, there are 2,757 non-English cases. So, after the filtering, 31,013 cases remained. We filtered the data further by selecting cases that have both Procedural History and Discussion and Findings sections. Moreover, we only chose cases that have transfer, complaint denied, and cancellation decision. In the end we obtained 30,311 cases. This data set only contains Procedural History, Factual Background, and Parties' Contentions sections from each cases. The vocabulary size of the data set is roughly 245K unique tokens. The data set is split into training, development, and testing set. Their length on average is 1,131, 940, and 939 words respectively. However, these numbers are reduced after performing text processing before training the model.

We provide a Data Statement (Bender and Friedman, 2018) for the data set in the Appendix.

4 Experiments

We conducted a series of experiments on our new data set. We developed 2 RNN models, 3 BERT models, as well as 2 non-neural models. Given that the data set is highly imbalanced, we also provide a majority-class baseline.

TRANSFER	29,565
COMPLAINT DENIED	3,397
CANCELLATION	530
TRANSFER, DENIED IN PART	110
COMPLAINT DENIED WITH DISSENTING OPINION	71
TRANSFER WITH DISSENTING OPINION	65
COMPLAINT DENIED, TRANSFER IN PART	32
TERMINATED BY PANEL (ORDER PUBLISHED)	11
COMPLAINT DENIED WITH DISSENTING AND CONCURRING OPINION	5
TRANSFER WITH CONCURRING OPINION	5
CANCELLATION, TRANSFER IN PART	4
TRANSFER, DENIED IN PART WITH DISSENTING OPINION	4
CANCELLATION, DENIED IN PART	3
COMPLAINT DENIED, TRANSFER IN PART WITH DISSENTING OPINION	2

Table 1: Document count per decision category after filtering for English documents.

TRANSFER	26,865
COMPLAINT DENIED	2,970
CANCELLATION	476

Table 2: The three largest categories after removing cases with HTML issues and further clean-up

	Label	Train	Dev	Test
1	ACCEPT	21,645	2,848	2,848
0	DENY	2,604	183	183

Table 3: WIPO data set: division of training, development and testing data for cases that accept or deny the complainant's claims.

4.1 Data Preparation

Of three labels in our data set, TRANSFER and CANCELLATION largely amount to the same result of the case for the complainant being upheld, while COMPLAINT DENIED is a rejection of the complainant's claims. As such, we merge the first two classes into ACCEPT to define a binary classification task.

Table 3 shows the number of instances per class based on an 80/10/10 split of the data into training/development/testing partitions, determined chronologically to reflect the reality of applying the model to future data (with the training instances being the earliest data, followed by the development, and finally the test data).

Each case is represented as a JSON file with seven fields: (1) the (binary) outcome decision; (2) the URL of the original case description; (3) the WIPO case number; (4) the name of the complainant; (5) the name of the respondent; (6) the title of the case; and (7) the textual content of the case, structured based on headings and section boundaries. All of the data described as well as the code is available for download.[5]

4.2 Method

We first developed two RNN-based models: (1) BiGRU (a bidirectional GRU: Cho et al. (2014)); and (2) BiLSTM (a bidirectional LSTM: Hochreiter and Schmidhuber (1997)). For both of these models we use GLoVE pretrained word vectors (Pennington et al., 2014), derived from 42 billion tokens of Common Crawl[6] with 300-dimension vectors.[7] For both models the pretrained GLoVE embeddings are not updated in the training phase (i.e. they are set to 'untrainable').

The BiGRU and BiLSTM models are built using the layers module in Tensorflow's Keras API, with the pretrained embeddings being passed through a SpatialDropout layer with value 0.2, followed by either an LSTM or GRU layer with 128 units and 0.2 dropout. It is then followed by the second (reverse-direction) layer but with 64 units, a 0.2 dropout layer, and finally a dense layer that has 3 units as output, with softmax activation. The loss is calculated using categorical cross-entropy,

[5]Data: `https://people.eng.unimelb.edu.au/tbaldwin/resources/wipo/`; Code: `https://github.com/vihikan/automatic-resolution-of-domain-name-disputes`

[6]`https://commoncrawl.org`

[7]`https://nlp.stanford.edu/projects/glove/`

trained using the Adam optimizer (Kingma and Ba, 2017) with a learning rate of 0.001. We iterate through 20 epochs with a batch size of 64.

We next train 3 variants of BERT (Devlin et al., 2019): (1) OOBERT (out-of-the-box BERT); (2) FTBERT (fine-tuned BERT); and (3) LEGAL-BERT, a BERT model pre-trained on legal documents (Chalkidis et al., 2020) which we fine-tune over our data. The difference between OOBERT and FTBERT is that we additionally pre-train FTBERT over the non-test data using the masked language model objective. By default, the BERT base model has 12 transformer layers, and in this experiment, we freeze the first eight layers, in addition to the embeddings layer. The classification layer has 64 units followed by a dropout layer with value of 0.2, and an output layer with 3 units. The loss is once again calculated using cross-entropy loss with the Adam optimizer and a learning rate of 1e-5.

The BERT models are trained for 20 epochs. To save on training time, an early stopping algorithm is implemented by monitoring the macro-averaged F1 score with a patience of 3 and minimum delta of 0.0001.

To counter the effects of randomization, we perform all experiments with the RNN and BERT models 5 times with different random seeds, and average over the runs.

As non-neural baselines, we train a logistic regression (LOGREG) and linear-kernel SVM (SVM) model over TFIDF-weighted feature vectors.

In terms of document representation, for BIGRU and BILSTM we truncate the document to the first 5,000 tokens, for the BERT models we truncate to the first 512 tokens, and for LOGREG and SVM we represent the full document as a (TF-IDF weighted) bag of words without truncation.

4.3 Evaluation

We evaluate based on accuracy, macro-averaged precision, recall and f1-score. In addition to the overall results, we also break down results across cases that have a response and those that do not.

Although the "Procedural History" section of the decision states in plain language whether or not a response was filed, there is no convenient machine-readable category that discretely labels a case as having a response or not, and this information needs to be extracted from the decision. In the "Parties' Contentions" section, the panelist generally states whether or not the respondent exercised their right to respond. For example, the panelist can report that *The Respondent did not reply to the Complainant's contentions.* Other examples of a negative response are *The Respondent, having been duly notified of the Complaint and of these proceedings, did not reply to the Complainant's contentions or take any part in these proceedings* and *The Respondent expressed his willingness to transfer the disputed domain name to the Complainant, but the parties were not able to reach a settlement. The Respondent did not reply to the Complainant's contentions substantively.* The variation in these examples show that automatically detecting a non-response isn't entirely straightforward.

In determining whether a substantive response was made to the complaint for the purpose of partitioning cases based on whether there was a response or not, we develop the following set of heuristics for the "Parties' Contentions" section, where 'RESPONSE = 1' means there was a response, and 'RESPONSE = 0' means there was not.

- IF the "Respondent" section is empty
  - THEN, RESPONSE = 0
- IF the "Respondent" section is non-empty
  - IF text includes *did not*, *has not*, or *no response*
    - IF the text length is ≤ 100 words
      - THEN, RESPONSE = 0
    - OTHERWISE, RESPONSE = 1
  - OTHERWISE, RESPONSE = 1

We set the threshold of 100 words because if there was any prose in the respondent's section of the report that was less than 100 words, it usually only indicated that the respondent did not reply in any substantive way. Employing the above heuristics, we found that of the 3,031 instances in the test set, 441 had responses and 2,590 did not.

5 Results

Table 4 reports the accuracy (ACC), and macro-average precision (P), recall (R) and f1-score (F).

As can be seen, the Majority-class baseline is high due to natural skew in the data set.

In terms of accuracy, all systems exceed the majority-class baseline, with little difference between the best-performing BERT models and the

Model	Acc	Macro-average		
		P	R	F
Majority	0.940	0.470	0.500	0.484
LogReg	0.959	**0.888**	0.710	0.769
SVM	0.960	0.869	0.733	0.783
BiGRU	0.953	0.815	0.731	0.763
BiLSTM	0.951	0.800	0.725	0.755
ooBERT	0.956	0.833	0.732	0.769
FTBERT	0.960	0.837	**0.792**	**0.813**
LegalBERT	**0.961**	0.848	0.773	0.805

Table 4: Overall results for DNDR

traditional machine learning models (LogReg and SVM). However, LegalBERT slightly improves over the other models in terms of raw accuracy. For the macro-average precision, recall, and f1-score, all systems far exceed the baseline, with the overall best-performing model being FTBERT with an f1-score of 0.813 ($\sigma = 0.009$), primarily due to the high recall of 0.792. LegalBERT is a close second with an f1-score of 0.805 ($\sigma = 0.010$).

Of all the models, LogReg performs best in terms of precision with 0.888, but unfortunately its low recall of 0.710 diminishes its overall performance. The RNN models (BiGRU and BiLSTM) perform the worst of the trained models, in terms of accuracy, precision, and f1-score, and are omitted for the remainder of the paper.

Although all systems outperform the majority-class baseline, it is difficult to ascertain the benefit of these systems in terms of real-world utility, and their ability to indeed assist a panelist in their task. If they do not perform substantially above the majority-class baseline, then our systems are not better the simple (and, in practical terms, useless) majority-class baseline heuristic of labeling every case as TRANSFER.

We know from previous analyses that cases in which no response is filed will almost always succeed, as it is almost certain that such cases are straightforward instances of illegitimate cybersquatting. Conversely, where the complaint is not clear-cut, there is more incentive for a respondent to contest it. Thus, we expect that it is only the more difficult cases that have had responses filed.

Table 5 shows the breakdown of the results split into the two cases of with a response vs. without a response. Looking first at the 'No Response' column, in terms of accuracy all systems are on par with the majority-class baseline. However, LogReg far exceeds all the other methods in terms of macro-averaged precision, recall, and f1-score. While this result may at first glance seem surprising, it is important to bear in mind that LogReg and SVM have a representation of the entire document, where the BERT models only capture the first 512 tokens. As such, there is a tradeoff between the expressiveness of the model (higher for the BERT models) and how holistic the document representation is (better for LogReg and SVM), which we see play out in these results.

Looking next to the 'Response' column of Table 5, we see that the trained models generally perform well above baseline, with all trained models other than ooBERT far exceeding the majority class baseline, and FTBERT and LegalBERT achieving almost identical precision, recall, and f-score. It is interesting to observe that LegalBERT has no advantage over FTBERT in this setting, that is extensive pre-trained over legal texts of different types prior to pre-training over the WIPO data, is almost identical to simply pre-training over the WIPO data.

6 Related Work and Discussion

This is the first work to propose predicting judgments of IP cases, in the low-stakes (but technically challenging, as evidenced by the empirical results) setting of World Intellectual Property Organisation domain name resolution cases. While the legal context for this research and resulting data set are novel, we are in no way the first to propose judgment prediction as a task for Legal NLP (Kort, 1957; Lawlor, 1963; Aletras et al., 2016; Zhong et al., 2018a; Chalkidis et al., 2019; Zhong et al., 2020, inter alia). Perhaps the most popular judgment-related data set is the Chinese AI and Law challenge data set ("CAIL 2018"), where the task is to predict which of 202 charges the accused is guilty of as a multi-label classification task, based on more than 2.6m criminal cases published by the Supreme People's Court of China in Mandarin Chinese (Xiao et al., 2018). The original competition attracted over 200 submitting teams (Zhong et al., 2018b), and included two other tasks: (1) law articles: identify criminal law articles that are cited as being relevant to a given case; and (2) sentencing: predict the jail sentence, in months, for the guilty party. The data set has since been used

Model	Response				No Response			
	Acc	P	R	F	Acc	P	R	F
Majority	0.692	0.346	0.500	0.409	0.982	0.491	0.500	0.495
LogReg	0.828	**0.827**	0.753	0.775	0.982	**0.888**	**0.710**	**0.769**
SVM	0.828	0.820	0.759	0.779	0.982	0.759	0.584	0.625
ooBert	0.692	0.770	0.738	0.750	0.982	0.769	0.586	0.628
ftBert	0.831	0.808	**0.806**	**0.803**	0.982	0.763	0.598	0.642
LegalBert	**0.834**	0.808	0.798	0.802	0.982	0.753	0.573	0.611

Table 5: Breakdown of results based on response vs. no response

widely as a benchmark data set for reasoning and legal NLP (Yang et al., 2019; Li et al., 2019; Xu et al., 2020; Zhong et al., 2020).

For English, the most popular data set is perhaps that of Chalkidis et al. (2019) based on over 11k European Court of Human Rights ("ECtHR") cases, in the form of two tasks: (1) a binary classification task: does the case violate any of the 66 articles and protocols of the ECtHR; and (2) a multi-label classification task: which, if any, of the 66 articles and protocols does a given case violate.[8] Other data sets include a French data set of 126k cases from the French Supreme Court (Şulea et al., 2017), an English data set of 5k cases from the UK Court of Appeal (Strickson and De La Iglesia, 2020), an English data set of 28k cases from the Supreme Court of the United States (Katz et al., 2017), and a German data set of around 6k tax law appeal cases from the German Fiscal Courts (Waltl et al., 2017).

While the majority of this work has focused solely on the task of predicting the case judgment, Chalkidis et al. (2019) equally focus on using the trained models to analyze the fairness of judicial decisions, and more generally as an analytic tool for enhancing understanding of how judicial decisions are made.

Methodologically speaking, much of the past work has approached judgment prediction using off-the-shelf topic classification methods (e.g. using TF-IDF-weighted bag-of-words document representations with a linear-kernel SVM or naive Bayes model, similar to our LogReg and SVM), although recently the data sets of Xiao et al. (2018) and Chalkidis et al. (2019) have equally been used as benchmark data sets to evaluate longer-context pre-trained LMs over (based on the fact that the average document length tends to be much longer than the standard 512 token limitation of conventional BERT models).

As alluded to in the introduction, Leins et al. (2020) recently questioned the appropriateness of data sets such as Xiao et al. (2018), on the grounds of issues such as there being only superficial anonymisation of the data (leading to risk of the model learning demographic biases based on names and place mentions), privacy concerns (e.g. LMs fine-tuned on the data would potentially generate outputs containing sensitive information regarding defendants mentioned in the data), the data set being developed without engagement with the relevant legal authorities, and the appropriateness of the criminal domain for the deployment of automatic decision-making tools, given the high personal stakes for defendants. While noting some of the counter-examples to these concerns of Tsarapatsanis and Aletras (2021) and the need for further debate regarding the ethics of the applications of legal NLP, we return to our earlier claim that legal areas such as domain name disputes are a more appropriate short-term application domain for judgment prediction, in the sense that there are very few personal sensitivities which would have implications on the later life of the individuals represented in the data.

WIPO documents are relatively consistent in formatting and content between cases, similarly to the ECtHR documents, e.g., which follow a rigid format. The WIPO documents are generally more consistent than other legal cases, in which there is a significant issue for NLP techniques, as discussed by Higgins et al. (2020).

7 Conclusion

We have introduced a new large-scale data set for legal judgment prediction, derived from domain

[8]There is also a third task of case importance regression, on a scale of 1–4, where no explicit judgment prediction is made.

name dispute cases from the World Intellectual Property Organisation where a complainant has applied for a domain name to be transferred or cancelled on the grounds of trademark infringement. The data set is released with a data statement as defined by Bender and Friedman (2018) in the Appendix.

In the context of binary classification of the complaint being accepted or denied, we provided results for a number of benchmark NLP methods. In terms of macro-averaged f-score (to counter the effects of class imbalance), we showed that BERT with fine-tuning performed the best, including over the subset of cases where a response has been submitted. However, we equally showed that there is considerable room for improvement in the results, and plenty of room for further work on this task.

In terms of future work, we aim to further build on the models presented in this paper, and test their utility as decision support models. Our initial design was to simply experiment with the threshold of the model's output as a means to trade off precision for recall, and rely on the probability score as a proxy for model confidence and a measure of reliability. However, pretrained models such as BERT and LEGALBERT can suffer from severe miscalibration due to over-parameterisation. (Desai and Durrett, 2020; Kong et al., 2020).

As a first step, we aim to perform model calibration experiments to address the over-confidence issues commonly seen in these fine-tuned models. Further to this step, we will validate the accuracy of these calibrated models by revisiting the errors made by the system and verifying the original judgments by the panelists with a fresh set of legal eyes.

References

Nikolaos Aletras, Dimitrios Tsarapatsanis, Daniel Preoţiuc-Pietro, and Vasileios Lampos. 2016. Predicting judicial decisions of the European Court of Human Rights: A natural language processing perspective. *PeerJ Computer Science*, 2:e93.

Emily M. Bender and Batya Friedman. 2018. Data statements for natural language processing: Toward mitigating system bias and enabling better science. *Transactions of the Association for Computational Linguistics*, 6:587–604.

Ilias Chalkidis, Ion Androutsopoulos, and Nikolaos Aletras. 2019. Neural legal judgment prediction in English. In *Proceedings of the 57th Annual Meeting of the Association for Computational Linguistics*, pages 4317–4323, Florence, Italy. Association for Computational Linguistics.

Ilias Chalkidis, Manos Fergadiotis, Prodromos Malakasiotis, Nikolaos Aletras, and Ion Androutsopoulos. 2020. LEGAL-BERT: The muppets straight out of law school. In *Findings of the Association for Computational Linguistics: EMNLP 2020*, pages 2898–2904, Online. Association for Computational Linguistics.

Kyunghyun Cho, Bart van Merriënboer, Dzmitry Bahdanau, and Yoshua Bengio. 2014. On the properties of neural machine translation: Encoder–decoder approaches. In *Proceedings of the Eighth Workshop on Syntax, Semantics and Structure in Statistical Translation (SSST-8)*.

Andrew F. Christie. 2002. The ICANN domain-name dispute resolution system as a model for resolving other intellectual property disputes on the internet. *Journal of World Intellectual Property*, 5(1).

Andrew F. Christie. 2014. Online dispute resolution — the phenomenon of the UDRP. In Paul Torremans, editor, *Research Handbook on Cross-Border Enforcement of Intellectual Property*, chapter 16. Edward Elgar, Cheltenham, UK.

Andrew F. Christie. 2020. WIPO and IP Dispute Resolution. In Sam Ricketson, editor, *The Elgar Companion to the World Intellectual Property Organization*, chapter 14. Edward Elgar, Cheltenham, UK.

Shrey Desai and Greg Durrett. 2020. Calibration of pre-trained transformers. In *Proceedings of the 2020 Conference on Empirical Methods in Natural Language Processing (EMNLP)*, pages 295–302, Online. Association for Computational Linguistics.

Jacob Devlin, Ming-Wei Chang, Kenton Lee, and Kristina Toutanova. 2019. BERT: Pre-training of deep bidirectional transformers for language understanding. In *Proceedings of the 2019 Conference of the North American Chapter of the Association for Computational Linguistics: Human Language Technologies, Volume 1 (Long and Short Papers)*, pages 4171–4186.

Andrew Higgins, Inbar Levy, and Thibaut Lienart. 2020. The bright but modest potential of algorithms in the courtroom. In Rabeea Assy and Andrew Higgins, editors, *Principles, Procedure, and Justice: Essays in honour of Adrian Zuckerman*, pages 113–132. Oxford University Press.

Sepp Hochreiter and Jürgen Schmidhuber. 1997. Long short-term memory. *Neural Computation*, 9(8):1735–1780.

Daniel Martin Katz, Michael J Bommarito, and Josh Blackman. 2017. A general approach for predicting the behavior of the Supreme Court of the United States. *PloS one*, 12(4):e0174698.

Diederik P. Kingma and Jimmy Ba. 2017. Adam: A method for stochastic optimization. arXiv cs.LG 1412.6980.

Lingkai Kong, Haoming Jiang, Yuchen Zhuang, Jie Lyu, Tuo Zhao, and Chao Zhang. 2020. Calibrated language model fine-tuning for in- and out-of-distribution data. In *Proceedings of the 2020 Conference on Empirical Methods in Natural Language Processing (EMNLP)*, pages 1326–1340, Online. Association for Computational Linguistics.

Fred Kort. 1957. Predicting supreme court decisions mathematically: A quantitative analysis of the "right to counsel" cases. *American Political Science Review*, 51(1):1–12.

Reed C Lawlor. 1963. What computers can do: Analysis and prediction of judicial decisions. *American Bar Association Journal*, pages 337–344.

Kobi Leins, Jey Han Lau, and Timothy Baldwin. 2020. Give me convenience and give her death: Who should decide what uses of NLP are appropriate, and on what basis? In *Proceedings of the 58th Annual Meeting of the Association for Computational Linguistics*, pages 2908–2913, Online. Association for Computational Linguistics.

Shang Li, Hongli Zhang, Lin Ye, Xiaoding Guo, and Binxing Fang. 2019. Mann: A multichannel attentive neural network for legal judgment prediction. *IEEE Access*, 7:151144–151155.

Marco Lui and Timothy Baldwin. 2012. langid.py: An off-the-shelf language identification tool. In *Proceedings of the ACL 2012 System Demonstrations*, pages 25–30, Jeju Island, Korea. Association for Computational Linguistics.

Jeffrey Pennington, Richard Socher, and Christopher Manning. 2014. GloVe: Global vectors for word representation. In *Proceedings of the 2014 Conference on Empirical Methods in Natural Language Processing (EMNLP)*, pages 1532–1543, Doha, Qatar. Association for Computational Linguistics.

Benjamin Strickson and Beatriz De La Iglesia. 2020. Legal judgement prediction for UK courts. In *Proceedings of the 2020 The 3rd International Conference on Information Science and System*, pages 204–209.

Octavia-Maria Şulea, Marcos Zampieri, Mihaela Vela, and Josef van Genabith. 2017. Predicting the law area and decisions of French Supreme Court cases. In *Proceedings of the International Conference Recent Advances in Natural Language Processing, RANLP 2017*, pages 716–722.

Dimitrios Tsarapatsanis and Nikolaos Aletras. 2021. On the ethical limits of natural language processing on legal text. In *Findings of the Association for Computational Linguistics: ACL-IJCNLP 2021*, pages 3590–3599, Online.

Bernhard Waltl, Georg Bonczek, Elena Scepankova, Jörg Landthaler, and Florian Matthes. 2017. Predicting the outcome of appeal decisions in Germany's tax law. In *International Conference on Electronic Participation*, pages 89–99.

Chaojun Xiao, Haoxi Zhong, Zhipeng Guo, Cunchao Tu, Zhiyuan Liu, Maosong Sun, Yansong Feng, Xianpei Han, Zhen Hu, Heng Wang, and Jianfeng Xu. 2018. CAIL2018: A large-scale legal dataset for judgment prediction. *arXiv preprint arXiv:1807.02478*.

Nuo Xu, Pinghui Wang, Long Chen, Li Pan, Xiaoyan Wang, and Junzhou Zhao. 2020. Distinguish confusing law articles for legal judgment prediction. In *Proceedings of the 58th Annual Meeting of the Association for Computational Linguistics*, pages 3086–3095.

Wenmian Yang, Weijia Jia, Xiaojie Zhou, and Yutao Luo. 2019. Legal judgment prediction via multi-perspective bi-feedback network. In *Proceedings of the Twenty-Eighth International Joint Conference on Artificial Intelligence, IJCAI 2019*, pages 4085–4091. ijcai.org.

Haoxi Zhong, Zhipeng Guo, Cunchao Tu, Chaojun Xiao, Zhiyuan Liu, and Maosong Sun. 2018a. Legal judgment prediction via topological learning. In *Proceedings of the 2018 Conference on Empirical Methods in Natural Language Processing*, pages 3540–3549, Brussels, Belgium. Association for Computational Linguistics.

Haoxi Zhong, Yuzhong Wang, Cunchao Tu, Tianyang Zhang, Zhiyuan Liu, and Maosong Sun. 2020. Iteratively questioning and answering for interpretable legal judgment prediction. In *Proceedings of the AAAI Conference on Artificial Intelligence*, pages 1250–1257.

Haoxi Zhong, Chaojun Xiao, Zhipeng Guo, Cunchao Tu, Zhiyuan Liu, Maosong Sun, Yansong Feng, Xianpei Han, Zhen Hu, Heng Wang, and Jianfeng Xu. 2018b. Overview of CAIL2018: Legal judgment prediction competition. *ArXiv*, abs/1810.05851.

A Appendix — Data Statement

A.1 Curation Rationale

Goal: This data set was created with the goal of building models to automatically categorize domain name disputes pertaining to generic Top-Level Domains (gTLDs, i.e. domain names ending in .com, .org, .net, etc), in close collaboration with lawyers (who are also co-creators of the data set), including a panelist who has processed a large number of cases through WIPO.

Background: Domain name disputes can be lodged with an ICANN-accredited service provider, such as the World Intellectual Property Organisation (WIPO) for arbitration. The 'complainant' lodges a complaint, and the 'respondent' can in turn file a response. A panel then decides on the case and writes up a justification of their decision. These reports are publicly disclosed, and form the basis of this data set.

A.2 Language Variety

BCP47: en

Background: The data set was derived from WIPO panelists' written reports as part of the arbitration process in settling domain name disputes. These are formal written reports by 1 or 3 panelists and follow a highly structured format (expected set of headings). The collection of reports are written in a variety of languages, however a vast majority (over 90%) are written in English. This collection only includes English reports.

Further Information: The variety of English cannot be further specified because panelists can be from various countries/regions.

A.3 Demographic Information

Age: Unknown

Gender: Unknown

Race/Ethnicity: Unknown

Native Language: Unknown

Socioeconomic Status: All registered or practising lawyers

Number of different speakers represented: Unknown

Further Information: The current list of panelists can be found here: `https://www.wipo.int/amc/en/domains/panel/panelists.jsp`

A.4 Annotation Information

Age: N/A

Gender: N/A

Race/Ethnicity: N/A

Native Language: N/A

Socioeconomic Status: N/A

Number of different speakers represented: N/A

Further Information: The 'annotation' was derived from the categories published on WIPO's decision page: `https://www.wipo.int/amc/en/domains/decisionsx/index.html`. These categories were binarized for the purposes of the domain name dispute resolution (DNDR) described in this paper.

A.5 Text Characteristics

Modality: Written text in a report format

A.6 Other Information

Original Format/Encoding: HTML

Method of Collection: The text was scraped from the WIPO site from custom-built tools using bs4 (BeautifulSoup).

A.7 Provenance Appendix

Provenance: All text derived from `https://www.wipo.int/amc/en/domains/decisionsx/index.html`

Date: Collection dates from January 2000 to August 2020.

Association for Computational Linguistics
209 N. Eighth Street
Stroudsburg, Pennsylvania 18360

ISBN 978-1-7138-9167-3